THE S
SU
GROUP DIRECTORY

Twenty-Second Edition
2007

A guide to self-help and other support groups in New Jersey with national organizations, model and online groups.

Edited by

Anita M. Broderick and Wendy Rodenbaugh

New Jersey Self-Help Group Clearinghouse

Saint Clare's Health System
100 East Hanover Ave., Suite 202
Cedar Knolls, NJ 07927-2020

1-800-367-6274 or 973-326-6789
Fax: 973-326-9467
Website: www.selfhelpgroups.org

* In Memory *

This Directory is dedicated to the memories of Gary Deterding and Alan Lunt, two extraordinary individuals, who passed away over the last year.

For over seventeen years, Gary Deterding was a beloved member and facilitator of New Beginnings, a support group for persons experiencing mental illness, which became a chapter of DBSA. Throughout the years, Gary was a compassionate role model, guide and friend to all of the other group members. His strength, encouragement and wisdom were shared with all. For all who were lucky enough to know him, Gary's compassion, energy, vision and passion will be sorely missed.

With great insight, intelligence and a keen eye on recovery, Alan Lunt presented several unique Clearinghouse workshops (one was on spirituality, another on journaling) which were both well received and enjoyed by the attendees. One was even presented at a McDonald's because no one had the key to the original meeting site. Alan just rolled with the flow and delivered a wonderful workshop amid the Egg McMuffin sandwiches! Alan spent much of his time writing and developing his ideas on recovery. As he once wrote "I require the freedom and self-determination to proceed under my own power, to succeed or fail through my own efforts, to have my dreams and visions meet the risk and uncertainty of daily life. This is RECOVERY."

Throughout the years, both Gary and Alan were great supporters and friends to self-help groups and the Clearinghouse. We will truly miss them and feel blessed to have known Gary and Alan.

ISBN 1-930683-07-3
Twenty-Second Edition
May 2007

ACKNOWLEDGEMENTS

We are grateful to the **Division of Mental Health Services, NJ Department of Human Services** for their initial and continued funding and support that makes the Clearinghouse services possible. We appreciate too, the efforts of the many dedicated **support group representatives** whose volunteer time and energy make this directory possible.

We wish to express our deep appreciation to all of our wonderful and hardworking **volunteers** who have contributed their time and energy in helping callers and extending the services of the Clearinghouse. Our heartfelt thanks go to:

Donna Ammiano
Deanna Baum
Barbara Blumenfeld
Diane Clarke
Pat de la Fuente
Leah Dorman
Lois Fallat
Mary Ellen Kerin
Howard Lerner
Pete Lodato
Baiba Ozols
Pauravi Patel
Loretta Rankin
Paul Riddleberger
Harry Salle
Janet Stone
Sekhar Subramani
Berit Wenner

To the rest of our Clearinghouse staff:

Jeanne Rohach Thank you for all your encouragement, assistance and humor – you lift our spirits and lighten our work load each day.

Barbara White Thank you for your ongoing support throughout the year and especially your "helpful hints" during the directory publishing process. Your patient teaching is greatly appreciated.

Ed Madara Thank you for sharing your compassion, dedication and knowledge – truly an inspiration for us all.

In addition, special thanks to **Kelly Lozito** for her assistance in designing our 2007 Edition cover.

TABLE OF CONTENTS

FAMILY/PARENTING

HEALTH

Need help finding a specific group? Give us a call – we're here to help!
Call 1-800-367-6274

ABOUT THE CLEARINGHOUSE

Our N.J. Self-Help Group Clearinghouse was established in 1981 to promote the awareness, utilization, development and understanding of mutual aid self-help groups. Sponsored by Saint Clare's Health System and funded primarily by state government, the Clearinghouse provides information and referral, consultation services, and training primarily to help people find and form self-help groups.

The Clearinghouse maintains a database of information on over 4,500 groups within the state and over 1,100 national organizations, one-of-a-kind group models and online groups. Easy access to this information is assured through our toll-free phone lines.

An important component of our work is the development of new groups as needs arise. For example, if a caller inquires about a support group for any situation,and our computer search yields nothing in the caller's area, we often invite the caller to consider joining with others to start a group. If they are interested, we can advise them on how they can develop a group, and include them in our database. Subsequent callers would then be referred to this contact person if they were interested in helping them to start that type of a group.

The Clearinghouse also sponsors training conferences and free workshops on starting groups, facilitation skills, publicity, group maintenance and other issues of interest to group leaders.

Other services provided by the Clearinghouse include speaking engagements, a variety of guides and hand-outs on specific and general issues related to group development, research projects, facilitation workshops, speakers' bureau and a website on the Internet. We also work with the media to increase public awareness of self-help groups and their value.

Various volunteer and student opportunities exist at the Clearinghouse. We offer a variety of rewarding volunteer positions, as well as opportunities for internships and applied research that supports self-help groups. Call us for details.

"Never doubt that a small group of thoughtful, committed citizens can change the world; indeed, it's the only thing that ever does." – Margaret Mead

HOW TO USE THIS DIRECTORY

For an overview of the variety of groups available, review the **Table of Contents**, which is a categorization of self-help groups according to the general problem or concern addressed. To find a mutual aid self-help group for a particular concern, turn to the **Index** at the end of the directory. The index will refer you to pages in the directory where listings of groups dealing with your concern may be found.

Within each category, listings are arranged in a geographical order, with statewide groups shown first, local groups next (in alphabetical order by county), and finally national organizations, model and online groups.

In some categories, there are additional resources at the end of the listing. Note that: **Statewide** listings include New Jersey groups that cover all or a large portion of the state; **local groups** can either be autonomous groups or chapters of national organizations; **National groups** have chapters in several states and provide assistance to persons interested in starting local chapters; **national networks** usually don't have face-to-face meetings but link members together for mutual support; **Model** one-of-a-kind groups usually have just one or two local groups but are willing to help others start similar groups in their areas; and **online groups** and resources are included to supplement areas where few face-to-face support groups have been identified.

Each group listing includes the group name, a brief description of the group, meeting and contact information. If there are no dues or fees listed, it means that the group is free of charge, although many groups will "pass the hat" for contributions for refreshments, literature and other group expenses. All of the groups listed are non-profit. If you use a wheelchair, please be sure to call the group first to make sure that the meeting site is wheelchair accessible.

Remember, when calling a group, please show your consideration for others. Many of the phone numbers given are home numbers, so several tries may be necessary, and contact persons may shift periodically from one member to another. With few exceptions, contact numbers are not hotlines (see separate helpline listings beginning on page 645). We request that you not call group contacts too early in the morning or too late at night. In our listings, we have tried to indicate whether the phone numbers are best reached during the day or evening.

If you leave a message on an answering machine, speak very clearly and slowly, and include your area code. Sometimes contact people are unable to return calls because they cannot understand the messages left. Also, please be thoughtful of the type of message you leave for the contact person (either on an answering machine or with another person), especially when it concerns sensitive issues. Leave discreet messages—you never know if the person answering the phone or listening to the messages on the answering machine knows that the contact person is a member of a certain group. These days, you'll probably be checking out the website of the national group that we give you. But if you do write to a national or local group, it's good to enclose a self-addressed stamped envelope to help defer the expenses and make it easier for the group to respond quickly.

When you cannot find an appropriate group, or a group you wanted has disbanded, please call the Clearinghouse to see if there have been any additional groups identified since the directory was printed, or if there are any groups in the process of forming. Also, ask yourself if you or someone you know would be interested in joining with others to form a self-help group. If so, please call us to find out how we can help you.

Don't use this directory after one year has gone by! Much of the information changes in that time. After a year, consider the directory to be out-of-date and ready for the recycling bin. If this directory is replacing an older edition, we request that you take this opportunity now to recycle your older directory. Consider passing the old directory on to a student or colleague to help educate them to the wide variety of groups available. Do tell them they need to call the Clearinghouse for the most current groups and contacts. We are continually updating information on meetings, group contact persons and location changes. We also identify new groups that are added to our database. Please call us for the most up-to-date information on groups.

PLEASE NOTE: The Clearinghouse has made every effort to include as many different support groups as possible. However, the Clearinghouse reserves the right to include or exclude any names, groups or telephone contacts at its absolute discretion. Inclusion of an organization does not signify approval, nor does omission of any organization signify disapproval. A few groups may have escaped our attention. The use of any materials contained herein is entirely the responsibility of the reader. The Clearinghouse further disclaims any and all liability for any use or non-use of the information herein. There are no warranties implied or expressed in any of the information provided. The information provided is based upon that which is supplied by the groups themselves. The Clearinghouse is not responsible for printing, insertion, or deletion errors.

Finally, understand that the quality of individual groups will differ, sometimes even among those with the same name. Phone and visit the group to see if it is *for you*. The ultimate evaluation and very survival of any self-help group is determined by those who attend it and decide whether or not to continue as contributing members.

WHAT IS A SELF-HELP GROUP?

Most of the self-help groups listed on the following pages can better be described as mutual aid groups because they derive their energy from members helping one another. Among the various organizations that deal with stressful life situations, we look for those that provide opportunities for mutual help. In addition, three other characteristics constitute a self-help group: the group is composed of peers, i.e. people who share a similar experience or situation; the group is primarily run by and for its members who have a sense of ownership of the group; and the group is voluntary and non-profit in that there are no fees for services, although the group may charge dues or request donations.

While the focus of our Clearinghouse is on the development of self-help groups that are run by members themselves, we include in our listings some support groups that are run by professionals (identified in their listing as "professionally-run"). While professionally-run support groups are not self-help groups, we include them in the directory if the meetings are free or have a nominal charge, the professional does not receive a fee from members for facilitating the group, and the purpose of the group is mutual support among peers.

Please understand that there are other types of self-help organizations that do indeed provide mutual aid and support. They include civic, ethnic, fraternal, housing, cultural, political, church and neighborhood groups — some of which spring up naturally without even a name or with little structure beyond mutual help discussions. However, groups in any one of these categories could, by their nature and sheer numbers, warrant a separate directory of their own and are therefore not included here.

"As a kid I learned that my brother and I could walk forever on a railroad track and never fall off – if we just reached across the track and held each other's hand." -- Steve Potter

HOW SELF-HELP GROUPS HELP

Have you ever noticed that when you have a problem it helps to talk with someone who has had a similar problem? Simply finding others who have "been there" and realizing that "you are not alone" can in itself be a great relief. Providing this opportunity for needed peer support is one way mutual aid self-help groups help.

With time, some self-help groups resemble an extended family, providing a caring community that is often available 24 hours a day without forms, fees or appointments. Yet the groups also emphasize self-reliance, as each member assumes responsibility for helping him or herself.

Within such groups, people who share similar problems and needs gather to help one another cope with the problems they face. The problem may be a disability, a chronic illness, loss of a loved one, an addiction or any one of hundreds of other difficult life situations. Social support can make it easier to cope with a stressful situation, and this alleviation of stress can be directly related to the prevention of further illness and distress.

Another important way that self-help groups help is the way in which members, not only receive help from their peers, but can also provide help to others. Helping someone else deal with a problem that you also experience builds self-confidence and reinforces the use of coping strategies that have worked for you and others. Those who have been able to cope with a particular problem can serve as valuable role models for those who are just beginning to reach out for encouragement and practical information.

Self-help groups are not meant to replace needed professional services, although they supplement and sometimes prevent the need for them. Many groups tap professionals as advisors, guest speakers, consultants, trainers and referral resources. When pooling their personal experiences, coping skills and insights, group members will often come to recognize the specific agencies and therapists who best meet their needs. For literature and research study references on additional ways that self-help groups help, contact the Clearinghouse.

"We make a living by what we get.
We make a life by what we give."
-- Henry Bucher

CHOOSING A SUPPORT GROUP

Whether you are a professional considering groups for your clients, or a person simply looking for a helpful group for yourself, you may wonder if a support group is right for you. Let's examine the choices from those two perspectives.

Professional Considerations

For caring professionals who realize that they cannot be all things to their clients, support groups are welcome community resources that supplement professional assistance, and in so doing, can help prevent professional burnout. Groups also provide support at times when professional offices are closed, whether it is the actual meetings or the phone support often available between meetings. Since the groups provide the unique support of "others who have been there," they can be especially helpful for clients who feel alone and isolated with the stressful situation they face. Groups provide a variety of other benefits: acceptance, positive role models, normalization, coping skills, practical information, education, community, sometimes a "program to work" as in 12-step groups, advocacy and even "helper therapy" - the ability to help others in the group.

In providing a referral, a professional can point out the potential value of a group. In actually making the referral, it's helpful to suggest to the client that they check out the support group to "see if it is for you." If the client has Internet access, and if the local group is part of a national one, suggest they check out the national website to learn more about the group. It's often helpful to have the brochures of particular groups that are most often referred to, since the group's brochure explains what the group offers and takes away the fear of the unknown. Ideally these brochures should be available in the waiting area, too.

For the Person Seeking a Group

When looking for a support group, first identify the source of your stress (e.g., the specific illness, addiction, loss, etc.) and any special situation (being a caregiver, parent or friend of the person with the problem). In addition to a group's problem focus, there are many other differences in the types of groups available. Some support groups are member-run, while others have professional facilitators; some have a very narrow focus while others are very broad; some are based upon either spiritual or religious beliefs, while many are not; some are very structured while others have little structure at all; some focus on emotional support, education or advocacy, while others are more social. These differences may be important to you, so the more you learn about a group, the better you will be able to choose the right group for you.

Learn About a Group Before Attending a Meeting The best information about a group comes from the group itself. Most groups have a phone contact person who will answer any questions you have about the group before you attend a meeting. Also, most groups have a national website, brochure and other literature that describes their group's purpose and activities.

Questions You Might Ask In addition to finding out the meeting time and place, there are other questions you may want to ask before attending. You might ask about the people in the group: do they understand what you are going through because they have had similar experiences? How many usually attend the meeting (more people means more interest and energy, but less time for each member to share concerns)? What is the ratio of men to women, or the age range of the members (if it makes a difference to you)? You might inquire about any meeting formats and any costs associated with joining the group.

The First Meeting You Attend Once you decide to attend a meeting, there are many aspects of the group you can learn about first hand. One of the first impressions you'll get about the group will be how welcome you feel. Do people welcome you and introduce themselves to you? Do they sit near you, smile at you and in general make you feel like they are glad you're there? How much mutual help occurs within the group? Do people really help each other, or is it one or two people giving advice to everyone else? If the group is led by a professional, why is he or she leading the group, and what kind of leadership style does he or she exert?

If the members lead the group, how is leadership decided upon? Is it rotated, shared among group members, or limited to just one or two people? What other roles are assumed by group members? How many people help to run the group? Again, a good match between your needs and the group is what you're seeking.

Another observation you can make has to do with general group tone. Does it seem like the group is helpful to its members? Do people seem glad to see each other? Is there positive energy? Humor? Honesty? Do people listen to each other? Do they show concern, respect, understanding and acceptance?

Sometimes you will find a group that's perfect for you on the first try. Other times you may have to try several types of groups or a different meeting of the same group before you've found the best match. The bottom line is whether you feel the group meets your needs. Finally, after you have chosen and benefited from a self-help group, please consider staying for a while to "give back" and help others. Self-help groups depend upon such volunteer efforts. Your volunteer efforts will not only help others, but will most probably benefit you in terms of your own physical and mental well-being.

HOW THE CLEARINGHOUSE HELPS PEOPLE START GROUPS

Remember, if there is no group for you (or your client, if you are a professional), consider joining with others to start one – call the Clearinghouse for free help.

Our Clearinghouse provides a variety of services — a vital one being the assistance given to people interested in starting groups. Whether you are a lay person or a supportive professional who recognizes the need for a group, we can help. Some callers contact the Clearinghouse already committed to the idea of starting a group. Other callers, when there is no local group available for their problem, respond affirmatively to the question, "Would you be interested in joining with others to start a group?" and are put in touch with a Clearinghouse group development consultant.

Assistance is available to help people develop self-help groups for a wide variety of life situations and transitions, medical or emotional problems, addictions—just about any issue which affects a person's daily life.

Literature: The Clearinghouse has a wide range of printed materials related to self-help which are available to people starting groups, including:

- General how-to's which explain the basic steps in getting a group started; from finding co-founders, to structuring a group meeting.
- Group development materials from specific groups explaining how to start that type of group.
- Many other related materials, such as how to write a press release or group maintenance strategies.

Networking With Other Groups: One way beginning groups can "learn the ropes" is by learning how others have done it. The Clearinghouse staff can put you in touch with representatives of similar groups. You can call or visit a local group to ask how they got their group started: what they do to find members, what they do in their meetings, what problems they encounter in their groups and how they solve those problems. Contact with a nationally organized group can provide group development information, newsletters, pamphlets and brochures, and many other kinds of information and services. You can contact and learn from others who "have been there." Having a support network of such people can be very helpful for both the short and long run. This continuing dialogue models the support and concern that a self-help group provides its members.

Our Referrals to Persons Interested in Starting Groups: The Clearinghouse can list you as a person interested in starting a group on its database so that we can refer any callers interested in helping you. This is just one of the ways you may find others who are similarly interested in working with you to help create a new group in your area.

Training Workshops: The Clearinghouse offers periodic workshops on issues related to self-help which may be useful to those beginning groups, as well as to leaders of existing groups. The Clearinghouse also periodically co-sponsors special interest conferences with self-help groups and other organizations.

Phone Help: Once a person has decided to start a group and begins to work with a Clearinghouse consultant, this relationship usually continues until the group has started. On-going phone contact is available to discuss issues or problems that come up while the person is starting the group, such as: what kind of meeting place would be suitable and ways to locate such a space; how to enlist others to help you start the group; or how to do outreach for membership. Sometimes the consultant can suggest ways to locate speakers or provide more specific printed materials for a particular problem or need. Sometimes it's simply a question of providing support and encouragement when things seem overwhelming and discouraging; at other times, the satisfaction of sharing a success.

Clearinghouse Relationship to Those Starting Groups: In the interest of maintaining the best climate possible for the development of an independent, member-run mutual aid self-help group, the Clearinghouse primarily provides telephone assistance and resource materials. Clearinghouse consultants are available to offer advice, suggestions and guidelines on the development of your group, but you are under no obligation to follow through on those suggestions. We provide neither implied nor actual sponsorship or co-sponsorship of any group developed.

"I am only one, but I still am one.
I cannot do everything, but I still can do something.
And because I cannot do everything, I will not refuse to do the
something that I can do." -- Helen Keller

IDEAS AND SUGGESTIONS FOR STARTING A MUTUAL AID SELF-HELP GROUP

Self-help groups offer people who face a common problem the opportunity to meet with others and share their experiences, knowledge, strengths and hopes. Run by and for their members, self-help groups can better be described as "mutual help" groups. Hundreds of these groups are started each week across the nation by ordinary people with a little bit of courage, a fair sense of commitment, and a good amount of caring. The following guidelines are based on our experience at the Clearinghouse helping hundreds of individuals to start groups. While there is no one recipe for developing a group (different national groups offer different model approaches), here is an overview of the basic steps and strategies. Call us for additional ideas and specific how-to's.

Don't Re-invent the Wheel: If you are interested in starting a group around a particular concern or problem, find out what groups already exist for it. Call our Clearinghouse to confirm that there are no existing local groups that may address your issue. Check first in this Directory for any national self-help groups that address your concern. Visit their websites. Contact and ask them for what help and "how-to" starter packet information they can provide, and which of their groups might be closest to you. You can also speak to a Clearinghouse group consultant and ask for their help. In addition to free consultation, literature and contacts, the consultant can also list your interest on our computer to network you with any callers interested in helping you. We can provide you with suggestions as to which local organizations and professionals may be able to help.

Think "Mutual-Help" From the Start: Find a few others who share your interest in starting (not simply joining) a self-help group. Starting a group should not be on one person's shoulders alone. So, put out flyers or letters that specifically cite your interest in hearing from those who would be interested in "joining with others to help start" such a group. Include your first name and phone number. Make copies and post them at places you feel most appropriate, e.g., library, community center or post office. Mail copies to key people whom you think would know others like yourself. Post it on any online message boards that deal with the issue or your local community message boards. When, hopefully, you receive calls, discuss with the caller what their interests are, share your vision of what you would like to see the group do, and finally ask if they would be willing to work with you for a specific period of time to try to get the group off the ground. Discuss sharing the workload. Delegate responsibilities, such as: greeting people at the door and introducing new members; bringing refreshments; making coffee; or co-chairing the meeting, etc.

Once a couple of people have said yes, you have a "core group" or "steering committee" - and you won't have to do it alone. It's much easier to start a group if the work is shared. But most importantly, if several people are involved in the initial work at that first meeting (refreshments, publicity, name tags, greeting new people, etc.), you will model for newcomers what your self-help group is all about - not one person doing it all, but the volunteer efforts and the active participation of all the members.

Find a Suitable Meeting Place and Time: Try to obtain free meeting space at a local church, synagogue, library, community center, hospital or social service agency. If you anticipate a small group and feel comfortable with the idea, you could even consider initial meetings in members' homes. Would evening or day meetings be better for members? Many prefer weeknights. It is also easier for people to remember the meeting date if it's a fixed day of the week or month, like the second Thursday of the month, etc.

Publicize and Run Your First Public Meeting: Reaching potential members is never easy. Depending upon the problem area, consider where potential members go. Would they be seen by particular doctors or agencies? Contacting physicians, clergy or other professionals can be one approach to try. Posting flyers in post offices, community centers, hospitals and libraries is another. Free announcements in the community calendar sections of local newspapers can be especially fruitful. Consider simply calling the paper and asking to speak with an editor to suggest an article on the group and the issue. Editors are often grateful for the idea. The first meeting should be arranged so that there will be ample time for you to describe your interest and work, while allowing others the opportunity to share their feelings and concerns. Do those attending agree that such a group is needed? Will they attend another meeting, helping out as needed? What needs do they have in common that the group could address? Based on group consensus, you can make plans for your next meeting.

If your group intends to have guest speakers, another idea for a first meeting is to arrange for a good speaker and topic that can be publicized well in advance. But be sure to build in time for people to discuss the speaker's points in light of their own experiences, i.e., after questions and answers with the speaker, have a discussion group or (if a large turnout) break into smaller discussion groups. Then come together as a full group and present the idea of continuing discussions as an ongoing self-help group.

Identify and Respond to the Felt Needs of Your Members: If your group is new and doesn't follow a set program for helping members help one another, always remember to plan your groups' activities and goals based upon the expressed needs of your members. Share your vision. At the very first meeting, go "round-robin" permitting each member an opportunity to say what they would like to see the group do. Then discuss these needs and come to a consensus as to which needs you will address first. Don't make the mistake of thinking that you know the members' needs without ever asking them.

Remember to regularly ask your new members about their needs, and what they think the group might do to meet those needs. Similarly, be sure to avoid the pitfall of the core group members possibly becoming a clique. The welcoming of new people into the group is a process that continues well beyond welcoming them at the door.

Future Meeting: Considerations for future meetings may be the following:

- *Define the purpose (mission) of the group in no more than two sentences.* Is it clear? You may want to add it to any flyer or brochure that you develop for the group. Some groups also include any guidelines that they have for their meetings right on their flyer or brochure.

- *Membership.* Who can attend meetings and who cannot? Do you want regular membership limited to those with the problem and an associate membership for spouses and family?

- *Meeting format.* What choice or combination of discussion time, education, business meeting, service planning, socializing, etc. best suits your group? What guidelines might you use to assure that discussions be non-judgmental, confidential and informative? Topics can be selected or guest speakers invited. A good discussion group size may be about 7 to 15. As your meeting grows larger, consider breaking down into smaller groups for discussion.

- *Ongoing use of professionals.* Consider using professionals as speakers, advisors, sources of needed space or services, educators, helpful gatekeepers, advocates, possible trainers, researchers, consultants to your group or simply as sources of continued referrals. All you have to do is ask them.

- *Help between meetings.* Many groups encourage the exchange of telephone numbers or a telephone list to provide members with help over the phone when it is needed between meetings. Older groups have a buddy system that pairs newcomers with veteran members.

- *Projects.* Begin with small projects, e.g. developing a flyer, obtaining newspaper coverage by calling editors, beginning a newsletter, etc. Rejoice and pat yourselves on the back when you succeed with these first projects. Then, if the group desires, work your way up to more difficult tasks and projects, e.g. planning a conference, advocating the introduction of specific legislation, developing a visitation program, etc.

- *Sharing responsibilities and nurturing new leaders.* You will want to look for all the different, additional roles that people can play in helping other members and making the group work, e.g., group librarian, arranging for speakers, greeter of new members, group liaison with an agency, etc. In asking for volunteers, it's easier to first ask the group what specific tasks they think would be helpful. If you haven't yet experienced it, you'll come to know the special "helper's high" satisfaction of helping others. Don't be selfish. Remember to let your members feel the fine satisfaction of helping others in the group. By sharing responsibilities you help create opportunities for others to become key members and leaders in the group.

- *Lastly, expect your group to experience regular "ups and downs"* in terms of attendance and enthusiasm. It's natural and to be expected. You may want to consider joining or forming a coalition or state association of leaders from the same or similar types of self-help groups, for your own periodic mutual support and for sharing program ideas and successes.

The Self-Help Group Clearinghouse publishes a directory of support groups *annually*. Information, contacts, locations, chapters and facilitators are always changing. New groups are added and disbanded groups removed. Therefore, we advise you not to depend solely upon entries in this directory past one full year of its publication. At, or before that time, please call us to inquire about the newest directory edition. At any time you may also call our helpline through which we distribute the most up-to-date information on support groups and hotlines.

Self-Help Group Clearinghouse Helpline

1-800-367-6274

A B U S E

CHILD ABUSE (PHYSICAL / EMOTIONAL)

(see also sexual abuse, toll-free helplines)

STATEWIDE

Parents Anonymous *(BILINGUAL) Professionally-run.* Self-help for parents who are under stress and who want to improve their relationships with their children. Groups meet weekly and are facilitated by a volunteer professional. Many groups provide childcare. Groups meet in most counties throughout the state with some bilingual groups available. Online parent support group available. Write: Parents Anonymous, 127 Route 206, Suite 10, Hamilton, NJ 08610. Call 1-800-843-5437 (stressline) or 609-585-7666 (office). *Website:* http://www.pa-of-nj.org *E-mail:* panjstress@aol.com

ATLANTIC

Parents Anonymous *Professionally-run.* Self-help for parents who are under stress and who want to improve their relationships with their children. Meets Tues., 5-7pm, Interstate Reality Management, 925 Caspean Ave., Atlantic City. Before attending call Charles Peterson 609-348-4563 or Parents Anonymous 1-800-843-5437.

BERGEN

H.O.P.E.S. (Healing Ourselves Physically, Emotionally and Spiritually) *Professionally-run.* Self-help for adult survivors of any form of child abuse. Meets Thurs. and Fri., 6:30-8pm, St. Mark's Episcopal Church, 118 Chadwick Rd., Teaneck. Call Sara 201-357-4490, Anne 201-287-0527 or Parents Anonymous 1-800-843-5437. *Website:* http://www.pa-of-nj.org

Parents Anonymous *Professionally-run.* Self-help for parents who are under stress and who want to improve their relationships with their children. Call Parents Anonymous 1-800-843-5437. Meets Thurs., 7-8:30pm, Teaneck High School, 100 Elizabeth St., Room 203, Teaneck. Call Stacy Wendell 201-503-9378.

BURLINGTON

H.O.P.E.S. (Healing Ourselves Physically, Emotionally and Spiritually) *Professionally-run.* Self-help for adult survivors of any form of child abuse. Meets

Tues., 7-9pm, Family Service Center, 770 Woodlane Rd., Suite 23, Mt. Holly. Call Charles Robinson 609-387-2915 (day) or Parents Anonymous 1-800-843-5437. *Website:* http://www.pa-of-nj.org

Parents Anonymous *Professionally-run.* Self-help for parents who are under stress and who want to improve their relationships with their children. Call Parents Anonymous 1-800-843-5437.

Lumberton Meets Tues., 7-9pm, Family Support Organization, 774 Eayrestown Rd. Call Russ H. 609-265-8838 (day) or Terry 609-265-8838.

Mt. Holly Meets Thurs., 7-9pm, Family Service Center, Suite 23, 770 Woodlane Rd.

Willingboro Meets Tues., 7:30-9pm, New Life Deliverance, 2 Salem Rd. and Levitt Parkway. Call Pastor Rose Sparrow Melton 609-871-8798.

CAMDEN

Parents Anonymous *Professionally-run.* Self-help for parents who are under stress and who want to improve their relationships with their children. Call Parents Anonymous 1-800-843-5437.

Camden Meets Wed., 8:30-10am, Camden OEO, 538 Broadway. Before attending call Deborah James 856-963-0501.

Gloucester City Meets Wed., 6:30-8:30pm, Camden County Health Center, 700 Monmouth and Railroad Ave. Before attending call Elsie Lobell 856-456-0473, 856-663-0028 or 856-456-0810.

Merchantville Meets Thurs., 6:30-8:30pm, Family Support Organization, 23 West Park Ave., Suites 103-104. Before attending call Susan Doherty Funke 856-662-2600.

Sicklerville Meets Wed., 6-7:30pm, St. James Christian Church, 516 Church Rd. Before attending call Lelia Brittingham 856-524-4924.

ESSEX

Parents Anonymous *Professionally-run.* Self-help for parents who are under stress and who want to improve their relationships with their children. Call Parents Anonymous 1-800-843-5437.

East Orange Meets Thurs., 10am-11:30am, East Orange Child Development Center, 42 Chestnut St. Call Janet Lester 973-676-1110.

East Orange *(Grandparents Group)* Meets Thurs., noon-2pm, East Orange Child Development Center, 42 Chestnut St.. Before attending call Ms. Rutledge 973-676-1110.

Irvington Meets Wed., 9-11am, Grove St. Elementary School, 602 Grove St. Before attending call Donna 973-399-6949.
Newark Childcare available. Meets Thurs., 1-2:30pm, Choices Inc., 169 Roseville Ave. Before attending call Juanita 973-481-1889 (day).

HUDSON

Parents Anonymous *Professionally-run.* Self-help for parents who are under stress and who want to improve their relationships with their children. Meets Wed., 6-7:30pm, HCCAP, 880 Bergen Ave., Room 302, Jersey City. Before attending call Jenissa or Peter 201-789-5588 or Parents Anonymous 1-800-843-5437.

MERCER

Parents Anonymous *(Parents of Teens) Professionally-run.* Self-help for parents of teenagers who are under stress and who want to improve their relationships with their children. Meets Wed., 6-8pm, Parents Anonymous Office, 127 Rt. 206 South, Suite 10, Hamilton. Before attending call Orysia 609-585-7666 or Parents Anonymous 1-800-843-5437.

MIDDLESEX

Parents Anonymous *Professionally-run.* Self-help for parents who are under stress and who want to improve their relationships with their children. Call Parents Anonymous 1-800-843-5437.
Middlesex Meets Wed., 7-8:30pm, Middlesex Free Public Library, 1300 Mountain Ave., Room B. Call Cheri Easterlin 732-648-7514 .
New Brunswick Childcare available. Meets Thurs., 11:30am-1pm, Ebenezer Baptist Church Center, 112 Lee Ave. Call Lauren 732-448-1159.
Woodbury Meets Thurs., 6:30-8:30pm, Woodbury Child Development Center, 36 Carpenter St. Call Donna Backus 609-458-7901.

MONMOUTH

Parents Anonymous *Professionally-run.* Self-help for parents who are under stress and who want to improve their relationships with their children. Call Parents Anonymous 1-800-843-5437.
Freehold Meets Tues., 10am-noon, Monmouth County Human Services Bldg., 3000 Kozloski Rd., First Floor. Ask about childcare. Before attending call Jackie 732-901-0522.

Keansburg *(KEANSBURG RESIDENTS ONLY)* Meets Wed., 9-11am, Bolger Middle School, 100 Palmer Place. Before attending call Jeff 732-787-2007 ext. 2554.

MORRIS

H.O.P.E.S. (Healing Ourselves Physically, Emotionally and Spiritually) *Professionally-run.* Self-help for adult survivors of any form of child abuse. Meets Wed., 7:30-9:30pm, First Presbyterian Church, 35 Church St., Rockaway. Before attending call Janice Taitel 973-586-8979 or Parents Anonymous 1-800-843-5437. *Website:* http://www.pa-of-nj.org

SALEM

Parents Anonymous *Professionally-run.* Self-help for parents who are under stress and who want to improve their relationships with their children. Child care available. Meets Wed., 6-8pm, Inter-Agency Council, 98 Market St., Salem. Before attending call Cora 856-935-7510 ext. 8319 or Parents Anonymous 1-800-843-5437.

SUSSEX

Parents Anonymous *Professionally-run.* Self-help for parents who are under stress and who want to improve their relationships with their children. Childcare available. Call Parents Anonymous 1-800-843-5437.

Hopatcong Meets Thurs., 7-8pm, Center for Prevention and Counseling, Hopatcong Middle School, David Rd. Call Heidi Savioli 973-383-4787.

Newton Meets Tues., 10am-12 noon, Christ Episcopal Church, 62 Main St. Call Jane Lupo 973-383-4787.

UNION

Parents Anonymous *Professionally-run.* Self-help for parents who are under stress and who want to improve their relationships with their children. Call 1-800-843-5437.

Cranford Child care and transportation provided. Meets Wed., 10am-noon, Cranford United Methodist Church, Walnut and Lincoln Ave. Before attending call Joan 908-276-5894 (eve).

Plainfield Meets 1st and 3rd Wed., 7-8:30pm, 518 Watchung Ave. Call Christine 908-868-8447.

Plainfield Meets Wed., 10am-noon, United Church of Christ, 220 West 7th St. Call Agnes McLean 908-731-4272.

Union Meets Thurs., 7-9pm, Union Hospital, 1000 Galloping Hill Rd. Call Chris Rasmussen 908-789-7625.

Westfield Meets 2nd and 4th Wed., 6:30-8:30pm, Family Support Organization, 137 Elmer St. Call Rosalie Kennedy 908-789-7625.

NATIONAL

Adult Survivors of Child Abuse *International. 11 affiliated groups. Founded 1991.* Mutual support for adult survivors of physical, sexual, and/or emotional child abuse or neglect. Encourages victims to become survivors, then thrivers. Online support group meetings, monthly newsletter, group starter manual and general information. Offers assistance in starting groups. Write: Survivors, P.O. Box 14477, San Francisco, CA 94114-0038. Call 415-928-4576. *Website:* http://www.ascasupport.org *E-mail:* ascaoutreach@yahoo.com

Parents Anonymous, Inc. *National. Founded 1969.* Country's oldest child abuse prevention organization. Opportunity for parents to learn new skills, transform their attitudes and behaviors and create lasting changes in their lives. Group meetings offer structured children's programs. Helps to develop new community groups by providing training, technical assistance, materials and networking. Write: Parents Anonymous, Inc., 675 W. Foothill Blvd., Suite 220, Claremont, CA 91711-3475. Call 909-621-6184. *Website:* http://www.parentsanonymous.org *E-mail:* parentsanonymous@parentsanonymous.org

Shaken Baby Alliance *National. Founded 1998.* Promotes public awareness and education, victim and family support. Offers networking, victim advocacy and literature. Dues $30-50/yr. Provides assistance in starting groups. Provides case consultation services to professionals involved in diagnosing, investigating and prosecuting physical child abuse. Online listserv. Write: Shaken Baby Alliance, 4516 Boat Club Rd., Suite 114, Fort Worth, TX 76135. Call 1-877-636-3727 or 817-882-8686; Fax: 817-882-8687. *Website:* http://www.shakenbaby.com *E-mail:* info@shakenbaby.com

ONLINE

Abused Survivors *Online. 510 members. Founded 1998.* Support group that offers an outstretched hand to adult survivors of abuse (physical, verbal, emotional, or sexual). Open only to survivors. *Website:* http://health.groups.yahoo.com/group/AbusedSurvivors/

End Verbal Abuse *Online. 1570 members. Founded 2000.* Informational, anti-abuse email support group for those who are dedicated to overcoming obstacles in leaving a verbal abuser in a healthy and safe manner, resolving abusive behavior, protecting children from abuse or recovery after leaving an abuser. *Website:* http://health.groups.yahoo.com/group/End_Verbal_Abuse

Take Root *Online. Founded 2000.* Peer support for adults (age 18+) who were abducted as a child by a parent or family member. Offers literature, information, referrals, newsletter, peer support and advocacy. Write: Take Root, P.O. Box 930, Kalama, WA 98625. Call 1-800-766-8674. *Website:* http://www.takeroot.org *E-mail:* liss@takeroot.org

SEXUAL ABUSE / INCEST / RAPE

(see also child abuse, toll-free helplines)

STATEWIDE

12 Steps To Healing With a Christian Emphasis 12-Step. Mutual support for adult and youth survivors of sexual assault. The group meets for 12 weeks and each week a different step is reviewed. Meeting location varies throughout Northern New Jersey. For information call Erin 973-398-2862 or 973-919-0703 (cell). *E-mail:* thadnerin@optonline.net

SNAP (Survivors Network of those Abused by Priests) (*5 groups throughout NJ)* Support for men and women who were sexually abused by any clergy person (priest, brother, nun, deacon, teacher, etc.) Extensive phone network, newsletter, advocacy, conferences, information and referrals. Monthly organizational and planning meetings. Call 201-715-6510 or 732-632-7687. *E-mail:* pat.serrano@verizon.net or mecrawf@comcast.net

BERGEN

H.O.P.E.S. (Healing Ourselves Physically, Emotionally and Spiritually) *Professionally-run.* Self-help for adult survivors of any form of child abuse. Meets Thurs. and Fri., 6:30-8pm, St. Mark's Episcopal Church, 118 Chadwick Rd., Teaneck. Call Sara Accordino 201-357-4490 (day), Anne 201-287-0527 or Parents Anonymous 1-800-843-5437. *Website:* http://www.pa-of-nj.org

Men's Survivor Group *Professionally-run.* Mutual support for male survivors of child sexual abuse. Group runs for 12-16 sessions 2-3 times/yr. Meets Mon., YWCA of Bergen County, Rape Crisis Center, Hackensack. Before attending call Christine 201-487-2227 (24 hr. hotline); TDD: 201-487-0916. *Website:* http://www.bergencountyrapecrisis.org *E-mail:* bcrcc@aol.com

SNAP (Survivors Network of those Abused by Priests) Support for men and women who were sexually abused by any clergy person (priest, brother, nun, deacon, teacher, etc.) Survivors and immediate family only. For meeting information contact Kevin Kingree. Call 908-630-9235 or Sean O'Neill 845-365-1927. *E-mail:* kkingree@alertmarketing.com

Support for Significant Others *Professionally-run.* Mutual support for families, friends and significant others of sexual abuse survivors to understand about sexual victimization and learn how to be supportive. Also available to parents of a child who was molested. Meets for 12 week sessions twice/yr., YWCA, 75 Essex St., Suite 108, Hackensack. Before attending call 201-487-2227. *Website:* http://www.ywcabergencounty.org

Survivors of Rape *Professionally-run.* Support for adult female survivors of sexual assault. Meets Thurs., YWCA, 75 Essex St., Suite 108, Hackensack. Before attending call 201-487-2227 (24 hr); TTY: 201-487-0916. *Website:* http:www.bergencountyrapecrisis.org *E-mail:* bcrcc@aol.com

BURLINGTON

H.O.P.E.S. (Healing Ourselves Physically, Emotionally and Spiritually) *Professionally-run.* Self-help for adult survivors of any form of child abuse. Meets Tues., 7-9pm, Family Service Center, 770 Woodlane Rd., Suite 23, Mt. Holly. Call Parents Anonymous 1-800-843-5437 or Charles Robinson 609-387-2915 (day). *Website:* http://www.pa-of-nj.org

SNAP (Survivors Network of those Abused by Priests) South NJ Support for men and women who were sexually abused by any clergy person (priest, brother, nun, deacon, teacher, etc.) Survivors and immediate family only. Meetings throughout Burlington and Camden counties. Call Barbara 609-636-0226.

CAMDEN

Healing Hearts Ministry *Professionally-run.* Christian-based confidential support group for individuals who have been mishandled or sexually abused. Education, rap sessions, guest speakers and phone help. Meets 2nd and 4th Fri., 7-8pm,

Bethany Baptist Church, 10 Foster Ave., Annex Building, Gibbsboro. Call Charlene Ransom 856-782-6755 (day). *Website:* http://www.abundantharvest.com *E-mail:* healinghearts@abundantharvest.com

SNAP (Survivors Network of those Abused by Priests) South NJ Support for men and women who were sexually abused by any clergy person (priest, brother, nun, deacon, teacher, etc.) Survivors and immediate family only. Meetings throughout Burlington and Camden counties. Call Barbara 609-636-0226.

Survivors of Incest Anonymous 12-Step. Program for men and women, 18 yrs. or older, who have been victims of child sexual abuse, are not abusing any child and want to be survivors. Literature and newsletter. Meets Sat., 9:30-11am, The Starting Point, 215 Highland Ave., Suite C, Westmont. Call Natalie 856-858-5630 (eve) or Helen 856-768-1925 (day).

HUNTERDON

Women's Crisis Services *Professionally-run.* Support for victims of domestic violence and sexual assault. Also provides shelters and other services. Meetings vary, Women's Crisis Center, 47 E. Main St., Flemington. Call 908-788-7666 (day) or hotline 1-888-988-4033 (24 hr); TTY: 1-866-954-0100. *Website:* http://www.womenscrisisservices.org *E-mail:* agencyinfo@womenscrisisservices.org

HUDSON

Women's Project Groups *Professionally-run.* Education, support, workshops and groups to help women on subjects such as self-esteem, domestic violence, employment and stress management. Meets various days and times, Christ Hospital, 176 Palisade Ave., Jersey City. Call Michele Bernstein 201-795-8375 ext. 8416 (day).

MERCER

SASS (Sexual Abuse Survivor Support) *Professionally-run.* Mutual support, education and coping skills for female rape survivors ages 13-26. Rap sessions. Meets Thurs., 7:30-9pm, HiTOPS, 21 Wiggins St., Princeton. Before attending call Elizabeth Walters 609-683-0179 ext. 18 (day). *E-mail:* elizabeth@hitops.org

MIDDLESEX

Adult Survivors of Sexual Assault *Professionally-run.* Provides a safe, confidential environment for female survivors to share and receive support. Rap sessions. Group runs for 19 weeks, twice a year in Edison. Pre-registration required. Call Michelle Montalto 1-877-665-7273 (day).

Male Survivors of Sexual Abuse/Assault *Professionally-run.* Provides a safe, confidential environment for male survivors of sexual abuse or assault to learn to cope with the effects of the abuse. Rap sessions. Runs for 10 weeks, 3 times a year, Edison. Call Jeanne Manchin 1-877-665-7273 (day).

Women in Conflict Support Group Mutual support for women who have experienced sexual assault and/or domestic abuse. Goal is to help individuals gain control over their lives and move from being a victim to a survivor. Meets bimonthly, Robert Wood Johnson University Hospital, One Robert Wood Johnson Place, New Brunswick. Before attending call 732-418-8110 (day).

MONMOUTH

Women Survivors of Sexual Abuse / Incest *Professionally-run.* To aid in the empowerment of women who have been sexually victimized. Helps deal with the isolation, shame and powerlessness that can result. Members encouraged to be in therapy and must not be actively abusing substances. Meets Mon., 6-9pm, Freehold Community Counseling Service, 30 Jackson Mill Rd., Freehold. Call Patricia Ervin 732-409-6260.

MORRIS

Adult Survivors Group *(BILINGUAL) (WOMEN ONLY) Professionally-run.* Mutual support for female survivors of sexual abuse. Helps survivors process their feelings and understand the pain. Education, guest speakers, rap sessions. Groups meet for 12 consecutive weeks in Denville. Call Sonia Reyes 973-216-6432.

H.O.P.E.S. (Healing Ourselves Physically, Emotionally and Spiritually) *Professionally-run.* Self-help for adult survivors of any form of child abuse. Meets Wed., 7:30-9:30pm, First Presbyterian Church, 35 Church St., Rockaway. Before attending call Janice Taitel 973-586-8979 or Parents Anonymous 1-800-843-5437. *Website:* http://www.pa-of-nj.org

SNAP (Survivors Network of those Abused by Priests) North NJ Support for men and women who were sexually abused by any clergy person (priest, brother, nun, deacon, teacher, etc.) Survivors and immediate family only. Meets 1st and 3rd Thurs., 7-9pm, Pax Christi Center, St. Joseph's Church, West Main St, Mendham. Call Kevin 908-630-9235. *E-mail:* kkingree@alertmarketing.com

OCEAN

Survivors of Incest Anonymous 12-step program for women (18+) who want to recover from having been sexually abused. Literature. Meets Thurs., 7-8:30pm, United Church of Christ, 1681 Ridgeway Rd., (Route 571), Toms River. Call Cathy 732-363-3839 (eve).

PASSAIC

Passaic County Women's Center *(BILINGUAL) Professionally-run.* Support groups for survivors of domestic violence and/or sexual assault. Discussions include coping skills, legal issues and parenting skills. Groups meet weekly in Paterson. Call Sophie Robinson 973-881-0725 (day) or hotline 973-881-1450 (24 hr).

SNAP (Survivors Network of those Abused by Priests) Latino *(SPANISH/ENGLISH)* Support for men and women who were sexually abused by any clergy person (priest, brother, nun, deacon, teacher, etc.) Survivors and immediate family only. Meets 1st Sun. 6-8pm, 169 Union Blvd., Totowa, NJ. Call 973-766-5214. *E-mail:* snaplatino@aol.com

SALEM

Survivors of Childhood Sexual Abuse *Professionally-run.* Support, education and information for survivors of childhood sexual abuse, and their families. Opportunity to share with other survivors. Groups offered periodically based on needs and run for 6-8 weeks. For information call 856-935-6655 (24 hr); TTY: 856-935-7118.

SOMERSET

Survivors of Sexual Violence *Professionally-run.* Supportive and confidential group for adult female survivors of sexual assault and abuse. Provides a therapeutic environment to aid in the healing of sexual trauma. Rap sessions and literature. Meets for 10 week sessions several times a year, Women's Health and Counseling Center, Somerville. Pre-registration required. Call Chrisula 908-526-2335 ext. 130

(day). *Website:* http://www.womenandhealth.org *E-mail:* ctasiopoulos@womenandhealth.org

SUSSEX

Sexual Trauma Resource Center *Professionally-run.* Support groups for female and male survivors of sexual assault, sexual abuse and incest. Meetings vary, Newton. Call 973-300-5609 or 973-875-1211 (24 hr hotline); TTY: 973-875-1211. *E-mail:* strc@nac.net

SNAP (Survivors Network of those Abused by Priests) Northwest NJ Support for men and women who were sexually abused by any clergy person (priest, brother, nun, deacon, teacher, etc.) Survivors and immediate family only. Serves Sussex and Warren Counties. Contact Nora through e-mail for group information. *E-mail:* nconnors01@earthlink.net

WARREN

SNAP (Survivors Network of those Abused by Priests) Northwest NJ * Support for men and women who were sexually abused by any clergy person (priest, brother, nun, deacon, teacher, etc.) Survivors and immediate family only. Serves Sussex and Warren Counties. Contact Nora through e-mail for group information. *E-mail:* nconnors01@earthlink.net

NATIONAL

Adult Survivors of Child Abuse *International. 11 affiliated groups. Founded 1991.* Mutual support for adult survivors of physical, sexual, and/or emotional child abuse or neglect. Encourages victims to become survivors, then thrivers. Online support group meetings, monthly newsletter, group starter manual and general information. Offers assistance in starting groups. Write: Adult Survivors, P.O. Box 14477, San Francisco, CA 94114-0038. Call 415-928-4576. *Website:* http://www.ascasupport.org *E-mail:* ascaoutreach@yahoo.com

Healing Alliance, The *Resource. Founded 1991.* Information for recovery and healing for survivors of sexual abuse, specializing in clergy sexual abuse. Offers workshops to organizations and the public on healing and prevention. Write: The Healing Alliance, P.O. Box 429, Pewee Valley, KY 40056. Call 502-241-5544; Fax: 502-241-0031. *Website:* http://www.healingall.org *E-mail:* info@healingall.org

Incest Resources, Inc. *Resource. Support groups in Boston, MA area. Founded 1980.* Provides educational and resource materials for female and male survivors of childhood sexual abuse, and the professionals who work with them. International listing of survivor self-help groups, manual for starting survivor self-help group and many other resources. For complete information send self-addressed envelope with two 1st class stamps. Write: Incest Resources, Inc., 46 Pleasant St., Cambridge, MA 02139. (NO CALLS PLEASE) *Website:* http://www.incestresourcesinc.org./

Incest Survivors Anonymous (I.S.A.) *International. Founded 1980.* Uses 12-step/12-traditions, principles and tools of recovery. Fellowship of men, women and teens who meet to share their experience, strength and hope so that they may recover from their incest experiences and break free to freedom and a new peace of mind. Offers several packets of information, pen pals, I.S.A. Email Family Letter and cassettes. Not open to initiators, pedophiles, or satanists. Provides assistance in starting I.S.A. groups. When writing send a self-addressed stamped envelope (2 stamps). Write: I.S.A., P.O. Box 17245, Long Beach, CA 90807-7245. Call 562-428-5599. *Website:* http://www.lafn.org/medical/isa *E-mail:* isa@lafn.org

Male Survivor: National Organization Against Male Sexual Victimization *National. Founded 1995.* Information and referrals for male survivors of sexual assault and the professionals working with them. Conference every two years. Referrals to local resources. Newsletter. Periodic regional retreats offered. Online bulletin board and chat room. Write: NOMSV, PMB 103, 5505 Connecticut Ave., NW, Washington, DC 20015-2601. Call 1-800-738-4181. *Website:* http://www.malesurvivor.org

Molesters Anonymous *Model. Founded 1985.* Provides support with anonymity and confidentiality for men who molest children. Use of "thought stoppage" technique and buddy system. Groups are initiated by a professional but become member-run. Group development manual $9.95. Write: Jerry Goffman, PhD, 1040 S. Mt. Vernon Ave., G-306, Colton, CA 92324. Call Dr. Jerry Goffman 951-312-1041. *E-mail:* jerrygoffman@hotmail.com

S.A.R.A. (Sexual Assault Recovery Anonymous) Society *National. 20 groups. Founded 1983.* Education and self-help for adults and teens who were sexually abused as children. Group development guidelines and assistance provided for starting groups. Literature for recovery and prevention available. Newsletter. Dues $10/yr. Write: SARA Society, P.O. Box 16, Surrey, BC V3T 4W4 Canada. Call 604-584-2626; Fax: 604-584-2636. *Website:* http://www.sarasociety.ca *E-mail:* sarasociety@telus.net

SESAME (Stop Educator Sexual Abuse, Misconduct and Exploitation) *National network. Founded 1993.* Support network for victims, their families, academia and professionals who have been impacted by, or work with cases of sexual abuse, sexual exploitation or harassment by teachers or other school staff. Aims to raise public awareness by providing information and referrals, e-mail/phone support, literature, advocacy, newsletter. Write: SESAME, Inc., P.O. Box 94601, Las Vegas 89193-4601. Call 702-371-1290. *Website:* http://www.sesamenet.org *E-mail:* Babe4justice@aol.com

SNAP (Survivors Network of those Abused by Priests) *International. 50+ affiliated groups. Founded 1989.* Support for men and women who were sexually abused by any clergy person (priest, brother, nun, deacon, teacher, etc.) Extensive phone network, newsletter, advocacy, conferences, information and referrals. Information on finding support groups. Dues $25 (optional). Write: SNAP, P.O. Box 6416, Chicago, IL 60680. Call 312-409-2720. *Website:* http://www.snapnetwork.org *E-mail:* SNAPBlaine@hotmail.com

Survivor Connections, Inc. *National network. Founded 1993.* Grassroots activist organization for non-offending survivors of sexual assault by family, ritual, youth leaders, counselors, doctors, clergy, etc. Online newsletter, referrals. Website coordinators for "To Tell The Truth" events run by other organizations, groups or individuals. Maintains confidential database of reported perpetrators. Write: Survivor Connections, Inc., c/o Frank Fitzpatrick, 52 Lyndon Rd., Cranston, RI 02905. Call 401-941-2548; *Website:* http://www.members.cox.net/totellthetruth or http://www.members.cox.net/survivorconnections *E-mail:* survivorconnections@cox.net

Survivors of Incest Anonymous *International. 300 groups. Founded 1982.* 12-step program for men and women, 18 yrs. or older, who have been victims of child sexual abuse, are not abusing any child and want to be survivors. Newsletter $15/yr, literature $30/13 pieces. Offers assistance in starting groups, volunteer information, referral line and speakers bureau. Send self-addressed stamped envelope when writing (include a donation if possible). Write: SIA, P.O. Box 190, Benson, MD 21018-9998. Call 410-893-3322. *Website:* http://www.siawso.org *E-mail:* feedback@siawso.org

ONLINE

Abused Survivors *Online. 510 members. Founded 1998.* Support group that offers an outstretched hand to adult survivors of abuse (physical, verbal, emotional, or sexual). Open only to survivors. *Website:* http://health.groups.yahoo.com/group/abusedsurvivors/

Positive Partners of Survivors *Online.* Support for anyone who has a loved one who was sexually abused. Offers mutual support and understanding. Provides chat room, e-group, and message board. *Website:* http://groups.yahoo.com/group/positivepartnersofsurvivors/ *E-mail:* hrtfelt32@aol.com or simonshek@idirect.com

Stigma, Inc. *Online.* For individuals conceived by rape or incest. Also offers support to women who became pregnant by assault or are raising rape or incest conceived children. In addition, a community forum for supportive visitors to discuss issues. Email support lists, chat room, optional contacts to obtain general support and information. Write: Stigma, Inc., P.O. Box 109, Bonner Springs, KS 66012. *Website:* http://www.stigmatized.org

SPOUSE ABUSE / DOMESTIC VIOLENCE

(see also toll-free helplines)

ATLANTIC

Atlantic County Women's Center Mutual support and education for persons affected by spouse abuse. Goal is to end domestic violence through legal advocacy, information, and group support. Also has "Alternatives to Violence" program for men for a slight fee. For information call Atlantic County Women's Center 1-800-286-4184 or 609-646-6767 (for men's program). *Website:* http://www.acwc.org

BURLINGTON

Providence House *Professionally-run.* Support, education and counseling for victims who are, or have been, in abusive situations. Childrens counseling services. Call 1-877-871-7551.

CAMDEN

Domestic Violence Women's Support Group Support group for female victims and survivors of domestic violence. Group focuses on solutions that help end the abuse and increase education. Rap sessions, literature, phone help, buddy system and guest speakers. Meets Wed., Gloucester Township. For information call Michele Walsh 609-386-2220 (day).

Women's Domestic Violence Support Group *(BILINGUAL) Professionally-run.* Mutual support for female victims/survivors of domestic violence. Educational series and advocacy. Meets Tues., Collingswood; and Wed., Camden. For meeting information call Maida Vilches 856-963-5668 ext. 11 (day). *Website:* http://www.ccwomenscenter.org

CAPE MAY

CARA Buddy System *Professionally-run.* Confidential support for battered women to discuss problems and share resources. Rap sessions, guest speakers, phone help, and literature. Meets Wed., 7:30pm, CARA, Cape May Court House. Before attending call Juanita Battle 609-522-6489 (day) or CARA 1-877-294-2272 (day); TTY: 609-463-0818.

M.E.N.D. (Men Exploring New Directions) *Professionally-run.* To help men learn other ways of coping with anger and stop violence in families. Rap sessions, phone help, literature. Meets Thurs., 7-9pm, Burdette Tomlin Memorial Hospital, Cape May Court House. Register before attending. Call 609-522-6489 (day) or 1-877-294-2272; TTY: 609-463-0818.

CUMBERLAND

ACT (Abuse Ceases Today) *Professionally-run.* Mutual support for men to help deal with their anger. Educational series, rap sessions, literature. Meets Tues., 6-8pm, location confidential. For meeting information call 856-691-3713 (day); TTY: 856-691-6024.

ESSEX

Babyland Family Services, Inc. *Professionally-run.* support for women who have been in abusive relationships. Aim is to educate, liberate, and empower domestic violence victims and survivors. Shelter and hotline. Pre-requisite requirements. Also offers a men's PEACE group ($2 fee). Meets at various locations in Essex County. Call 973-484-4446 (24 hr). *Website:* http://www.babyland.org

HUNTERDON

Women's Crisis Services *Professionally-run.* Support group and services for victims of domestic violence and sexual assault. Also serves children who are witnesses of domestic violence. Offers a men's program for a fee. Meetings vary, Women's Crisis Services, 47 E. Main St., Flemington. Call 908-788-7666 (day) or hotline 1-888-988-4033 (24 hr); TTY: 1-866-954-0100. *Website:* http://www.womenscrisisservices.org *E-mail:* agencyinfo@womenscrisisservices.org

MIDDLESEX

Manavi Support Group *(SOUTH ASIAN)* Mutual support for any South Asian woman (Indian, Pakistan, Bangladeshi, Nepali, Sri Lankan) who has experienced spousal or partner abuse. Advocacy, guest speakers and literature. Child care available. Meets 2nd and 4th Sat., 1:30-3:30pm, New Brunswick. Call Aisha 732-435-1414 (day). *Website:* http://www.manavi.org *E-mail:* manavi@manavi.org

Women Aware, Inc. *(BILINGUAL) Professionally-run.* Support groups, education, and advocacy for battered women. Information on emergency shelter and other services. Call 732-249-4504 (Voice/TTY) (24 hr); legal advocacy 732-937-9525 (day). *Website:* http://www.womenaware.net *E-mail:* womenaware@aol.com

Women in Conflict Support Group Mutual support for women, primarily ages 20-50, who have been sexually assaulted. Goal is to help individuals gain control over their lives and move from being a victim to a survivor. Meets bimonthly, Robert Wood Johnson University Hospital, One Robert Wood Johnson Place, New Brunswick. Before attending call 732-418-8110 (day).

MONMOUTH

Amanda's Easel Art Therapy Program *Professionally-run.* Art therapy support groups for children and non-offending adults directly affected by domestic violence. Meets various times and locations. Call Cindi Westendorf 732-787-6503 for directions and meeting times.

MORRIS

Jersey Battered Women's Service, Inc. *Professionally-run.* Provides support groups and a safe home for victims or survivors of domestic violence and/or abusive relationships. Children's program available. Legal advocacy. Call 1-877-722-8733 (helpline); TDD: 973-285-9095 (24 hr). Also Jersey Center for Non-Violence offers services to assist batterers in stopping abuse and in developing alternative behaviors. Call 973-539-7801. *Website:* http://www.jbws.org *E-mail:* info@jbws.org

Can't find an appropriate group in your area? The Clearinghouse helps people start groups. Give us a call at 1-800-367-6274.

PASSAIC

Domestic Violence/Parenting Support Group *Professionally-run.* Provides emotional support and networking for women who are, or who have been, in domestic violent situations. Educational series, social group, advocacy and guest speakers. Also offers parenting classes. Meets Thurs., 6-8pm, Senior Citizen Center, 330A Passaic St., Passaic. Call Miriam Torres 973-365-5740 (day) or Tom Fischetti 973-365-5741 (day). *Website:* http://www.passaicalliance.org *E-mail:* prevention@passaicalliance.org

Passaic County Women's Center *(BILINGUAL) Professionally-run.* Support groups for survivors of domestic violence and/or sexual assault. Discussions include coping skills, legal issues and parenting skills. Various groups meet weekly in Paterson. Call Tracy Francese or Evelyn Murphy 973-881-0725 (day) or Hotline 973-881-1450 (24 hr).

SALEM

Female Victims and Survivors of Family Violence *Professionally-run.* Support, education and information for women to share with other victims. Meets bi-weekly in a confidential location in Salem County. Also men's batterers program. Call 856-935-6655 (24 hr); TTY/TDD: 856-935-7118.

SUSSEX

Domestic Abuse Services, Inc. Mutual support for survivors of domestic violence and abuse. Meets in Newton. Call 973-579-2386 or 973-875-1211 (24 hr hotline); TTY: 973-875-6369 (24 hr). *Website:* http://www.dasi.org *E-mail:* dasi@nac.net

UNION

Project Protect *Professionally-run.* Provides support to victims of domestic violence. Also educational programs for men who are violent, abusive or over-controlling. Fee for men's group. Meetings vary in Elizabeth. Call 908-355-1995 (day).

WARREN

Women's Domestic Violence Support Groups *Professionally-run.* Provides a supportive and confidential environment to help women victims of domestic violence work towards healing. Need prior screening to attend. Educational series.

Meets Mon. in the Phillipsburg and Belvidere areas. For meeting information call 908-453-4181; TTY: 908-453-2553. *Website:* http://www.darccwc.org

NATIONAL

Batterers Anonymous *National. Founded 1980.* Self-help program for men who wish to control their anger and eliminate their abusive behavior toward women. Buddy system. Group development manual ($9.95). Write: B.A., Attn. Dr. Jerry Goffman, 1040 S. Mt. Vernon Ave., G-306, Colton, CA 92324. Call Dr. Jerry Goffman 951-312-1041 (leave message and return address). *E-mail:* jerrygoffman@hotmail.com

Pathways To Peace *International. 11 groups. Founded 1998.* Self-help group program for anger management. Offers peer support education, workbook ($19.95), and assists with starting groups. Write: Pathways To Peace, P.O. Box 259, Cassadaga, NY 14718. Call 1-800-775-4212 or 716-595-3886 (voice/fax). *Website:* http://www.pathwaystopeaceinc.com/index.htm#1 *E-mail:*transfrm@netsync.net

ONLINE

Abused Guys *Online.* Provides support for male victims of domestic violence. Offers online chat room and message forum. Must join the group to post. *Website:* http://groups.yahoo.com/group/abusedguys *E-mail:* abusedguy@yahoo.com

Battered Husbands Support *Online. Founded 1998.* Support for men who have been, or who are currently being, battered by a female or male partner. Offers message boards, chat room and useful links. *Website:* http://health.groups.yahoo.com/ group/batteredhusbandssupport

End Verbal Abuse *Online. 1570 members. Founded 2000.* Informational, anti-abuse email support group for those who are dedicated to overcoming obstacles to leaving a verbal abuser in a healthy and safe manner, resolving abusive behavior, protecting children from abuse, or recovery after leaving an abuser. *Website:* http://health.groups.yahoo.com/ group/End_Verbal_Abuse

Woman's Emotional Abuse Support *Online. Founded 1999.* Offers mutual support and understanding for victims of verbal abuse. Provides message boards, chat room, links and e-mail group. *Website:* http://groups.yahoo.com/ group/womansemotionalabusesupport/

ADDICTIONS / DEPENDENCIES

ALCOHOL ABUSE

(see also toll-free helplines)

STATEWIDE

Al-Anon's Adult Children 12-Step. Fellowship offering comfort, hope and friendship through shared experiences for adult children of alcoholics. Weekly meetings available throughout New Jersey. Write: Al-Anon's Adult Children, 73 S. Fullerton Ave., 2nd Floor, Montclair, NJ 07042. For local meeting information call Al-Anon Information Service North New Jersey 973-744-8686 (day) or South New Jersey 856-547-0855 (day). *Website:* http://www.northjerseyal-anon.org

Al-Anon Family Groups 12-Step. Fellowship of families and friends of alcoholics. Offers comfort, hope and friendship through shared experiences. Includes groups for parents, children and adult children, gays, men and women. Some groups offer babysitting services. Weekly meetings throughout New Jersey.

North Jersey Information Service *(MULTILINGUAL)* (Covers Bergen, Essex, Hudson, Hunterdon, Middlesex, Monmouth, Morris, Passaic, Somerset, Sussex, Union and Warren counties) Call Al-Anon Information Service 973-744-8686 (day). Write: Al-Anon Family Groups, 73 S. Fullerton Ave., Montclair, NJ 07042. *Website:* http://www.northjerseyal-anon.org

South Jersey Intergroup (Covers Atlantic, Burlington, Camden, Cape May, Cumberland, Gloucester, Mercer, Ocean and Salem counties) Write: Al-Anon Family Groups, South Jersey Information Service, 116 White Horse Pike, Haddon Heights, NJ 08035. Call Al-Anon Information Service 856-547-0855 (10am-3pm); Fax: 856-547-7111.

Alcoholics Anonymous *(BILINGUAL)* 12-Step. Fellowship of men and women who share their experiences, strengths and hopes to help each other recover from alcoholism. Groups meet weekly throughout New Jersey.

Cape/Atlantic Intergroup (Covers Atlantic and Cape May counties) Write: A.A., 32 Blackhorse Pike, P.O. Box 905, Pleasantville, NJ 08232. Call 609-641-8855; Spanish-speaking 609-344-0202. *Website:* http://www.capeatlanticintergroup.org

Central Jersey Intergroup (Covers Mercer County and parts of Ocean, Monmouth, Middlesex, Somerset and Hunterdon counties) Write: A.A. Central Jersey Intergroup, P.O. Box 4096, Trenton, NJ 08610. Call 609-656-8900 (24 hr.); Spanish-speaking call 973-824-0555. *Website:* http://www.centraljerseyintergroup.org

North Jersey Intergroup (Covers Bergen, Essex, Hudson, Hunterdon, Middlesex, Monmouth, Morris, Ocean, Passaic, Somerset, Sussex, Union and Warren counties) Write: A.A., 2400 Morris Ave., Union, NJ 07083. Call 1-800-245-1377 or 908-687-8566 (24 hr.); Spanish speaking 973-824-0555 *Website:* http://www.nnjaa.org
South Jersey Intergroup (Covers Burlington, Camden, Cumberland, Gloucester and Salem counties) Write: A.A., P.O. Box 2514, Cherry Hill, NJ 08034. Call 856-486-4444 (24 hr.); Spanish-speaking 973-824-0555. *Website:* http://www.aasj.org

Families Anonymous 12-Step. Program for relatives and friends concerned about the use of drugs, alcohol or related behavioral problems. Meetings throughout NJ. Call 1-800-736-9805 or 732-291-1467.

Lawyers Concerned for Lawyers Statewide network of independent, self-help groups that support attorneys, judges and law students in recovery from alcoholism and drug dependence. Based on the 12-steps but not affiliated with A.A., and is not meant to be a substitute for participation in A.A. or other fellowships. The NJ Lawyers Assistance Program performs an "intergroup function" for LCL. All services free and confidential. Write: NJLAP, NJ Law Center, One Constitution Square, New Brunswick, NJ 08901-1520. Call 1-800-246-5527 (day) or 732-937-7549 (day). For information about women's group, call Denise 732-937-7541. *Website:* http://www.njlap.org *E-mail:* njlap@aol.com

Nurse Recovery Group *Professionally-run.* Mutual support and information for nurses who are recovering from addictions. Sharing of professional concerns and encouragement. Meets in most counties. Write: Peer Assistance Project, 1479 Pennington Rd., Trenton, NJ 08618. Call 1-800-662-0108 (day).

Professional Assistance Program of New Jersey *Professionally-run.* For physicians and other licensed professionals suffering from alcohol, chemical dependency, psychiatric or physical disabilities. Local groups are independently member-run and strictly confidential. Some are A.A. affiliated. Write: Professional Assistance Program of NJ, 742 Alexander Rd., Princeton, NJ 08540. Call Linda Pleva, Executive Assistant - Administrator 609-919-1660 (day). *E-mail:* Linda.Pleva@papnj.org

Signs of Sobriety *Professionally-run.* Provides alcoholism and drug addiction services to persons who are deaf or hard-of-hearing. Makes referrals to deaf and sign interpretered 12-step groups throughout NJ (alcohol or drug addiction, gambling, families of alcoholics, etc) Offers prevention awareness, education classes, Sober Camp annual summer retreat, and Sober/Deaf activities for deaf or hard of hearing individuals in recovery. Newsletter. Write: SOS, 100 Scotch Rd., 2nd Floor, Ewing, NJ 08628. Call TTY: 1-800-332-7677; Voice: 609-882-7677 (day); Fax: 609-882-6808. *Website:* http://www.signsofsobriety.org *E-mail:* info@signsofsobriety.org

ATLANTIC

Addictions Victorious of South Jersey, Inc. 12-Step. Christ-centered support group for men and women who, in their struggle with substance abuse and emotional problems, come together that they may solve their problems and help others as well. Guest speakers, rap sessions, phone help, literature and newsletter. Optional donation. *Website:* http://www.addvicinc.org

> **Egg Harbor City** Meets Thurs., 7:30pm, Christ's Wesleyan Church, 800 Philadelphia Ave. Call Mark 609-457-3260 or 609-965-8056 and Church 609-965-5835.
>
> **Mays Landing** Meets Tues., 7:30pm, Light of the World Church, 111 Route 50. Call Bob 609-457-0186 or Pastor George Sanders 609-517-3776.

Al-Anon Family Groups 12-Step. Fellowship of families and friends of alcoholics. Offers comfort, hope and friendship through shared experiences. Includes groups for children and adult children. Call Al-Anon Information Services 856-547-0855 (10am-3pm) or 973-744-8686 (day).

Alcoholics Anonymous *(BILINGUAL)* 12-Step. Fellowship of men and women who share their experience, strength and hope with each other that they may solve their common problem and help others to recover from alcoholism. Young people's groups also available. Call 609-641-8855. *Website:* http://www.capeatlanticintergroup.org

Dual Recovery Anonymous *Professionally-run.* 12-Step. Mutual support for alcoholics and drug abusers with psychiatric disorders. Meets Thurs., 1:30-2:30pm, C.O.D.I. Building, 901 Atlantic Ave., Egg Harbor City. Call Suzanne 609-965-6871 (day).

Family Support Group Mutual support for parents and families of persons diagnosed with both a mental illness and alcohol addiction. Sharing of emotional and practical coping skills. Guest speakers. Meets 2nd Thurs., 10am and 4th Thurs., 4:30pm, Mental Health Association, 1127 North New Rd., Absecon. Call Christine Gromadzyn, MSW 609-272-1700 (day).

Lawyers Concerned for Lawyers Self-help group that supports recovery from alcoholism and drug dependence for attorneys, judges, law students and others in the legal system. Based on the 12-step program adapted from A.A. All inquiries are confidential. Meets Wed., 5:30pm, 1555 Zion Rd., Suite 201, Northfield. Call John 609-641-2266 (day) or NJ Lawyers Assistance Program 1-800-246-5527. *Website:* http://www.njlap.org *E-mail:* info@njlap.com

Nurse Recovery Group *Professionally-run.* Mutual support and information for nurses who are recovering from addictions. Sharing of professional concerns and encouragement. Meets in Pomona. Call 1-800-662-0108 (day).

BERGEN

Al-Anon Family Groups 12-Step. Fellowship of families and friends of alcoholics. Offers comfort, hope and friendship through shared experiences. Includes groups for children and adult children. Call Al-Anon Information Services 973-744-8686 (day).

Al-Anon's Adult Children 12-Step. Fellowship offering comfort, hope and friendship through shared experiences for adult children of alcoholics. Call Al-Anon Information Services 973-744-8686 (day).

Fort Lee Meets Sat., 10:30am, First Reformed Church, 2420 Lemoine Ave.

Maywood Meets Thurs., 7:30pm, Lutheran Redeemer Church, 471 Maywood Ave.

Alateen 12-Step. Fellowship of young persons (age 10+) whose lives have been affected by someone else's drinking. An active adult member of Al-Anon serves as a sponsor. Meets Tues., 7:30pm, St. Mark's Episcopal Church, 118 Chadwick Rd., Teaneck. Call Al-Anon Information Services 973-744-8686 (day). *Website:* http://www.nj-al-anon.org

Alcoholics Anonymous *(BILINGUAL)* 12-Step. Fellowship of men and women who share their experience, strength and hope with each other that they may solve their common problem and help others to recover from alcoholism. Young people's groups also available. Call 1-800-245-1377 or 908-687-8566 (24 hr.); Spanish-speaking 973-824-0555. *Website:* http://www.nnjaa.org

CARE (Christians, Addictions, Recovery and Education) 12-Step. Support ministry for substance abusers and their families to help find sobriety, solace and a way to a comfortable non-judgmental Christian walk. Meets Mon., 7:30pm, Church of the Nazarene, 285 E. Midland Ave., Paramus. Call 201-262-3323 (9:30am-4pm). *Website:* http://www.maranathanj.org

Families Anonymous 12-Step. For relatives and friends concerned about the use of drugs, alcohol or related behavioral problems.

Englewood Meets Fri., 7:30pm, Englewood Hospital, Learning Center, Main Floor, 350 Engle St. Call Jesse 201-944-0256.

Mahwah Meets Wed., 7:30-8:30pm, Church of the Immaculate Conception, 900 Darlington Ave. Call Richard or Barbara 201-327-0748. *Website:* http://www.familiesanonymous.org *E-mail:* famahwah@verizon.net

Tenafly Meets Tues., 7:30pm, Trinity Lutheran Church, Basement, 430 Knickerbocker Rd. Call Judy or Gene 201-262-7758 (day) or Jesse 201-944-0256.

JACS (Jewish Alcoholics, Chemically Dependent Persons and Significant Others) Follows 12-step program. Mutual support for all Jews in recovery and their family members. Meets 2nd and 4th Wed., 7:30pm, Jewish Family Service of Bergen County, 1485 Teaneck Rd., Teaneck. Call 201-837-9090 (day).

Nurse Recovery Group *Professionally-run.* Mutual support and information for nurses who are recovering from addictions. Sharing of professional concerns and encouragement. Meets in Teaneck. Call 1-800-662-0108 (day).

Parent Support Group - New Jersey, Inc. *Professionally-run.* Confidential support group for parents of chemically dependent children (ages 13-40+). Meets Mon., 6:30pm, Behavioral Health Center, Room E222, Bergen Pines Hospital, Paramus. Call Karol Sullivan or Adrienne Mellana 1-800-561-4299 or 973-736-3344 (day). *Website:* http://www.psgnjhomestead.com

Psychiatrically Recovering Alcoholics 12-Step. Mutual support for psychiatrically recovering alcoholics who suffer from emotional and mental disorders to share experience, strength and hope while recovering from alcoholism and psychiatric disorders. Meets Tues., 7-8pm, Bethany Presbyterian Church, Palisade Ave. and William St., Englewood. Call Ed 201-541-8452.

Seniors Count *Professionally-run.* 12-Step. Support for persons (age 60+) who are recovering from substance abuse or co-dependency. Meets Fri., 1:30-3pm, Presbyterian Church, 150 East Palisades Ave., 2nd Floor, Englewood. Call Anne Wennhold 201-569-6667. *Website:* http://www.vanostinstitute.org *E-mail:* vanost@msn.com

Women For Sobriety Self-help designed specifically to help women with addictions achieve sobriety. Helps develop self-esteem and coping skills. Donation $2. Meets Tues., noon-1pm and Thurs., 7-8:30pm (new members 6:45pm), YWCA, 112 Oak St., Ridgewood. Call 201-487-2224 (day) or Nina Wegener, LCSW 201-612-0511 (day).

BURLINGTON

Addictions Victorious of South Jersey, Inc. 12-Step. Christ-centered support group for men and women who, in their struggle with substance abuse and emotional problems, come together that they may solve their problems and help others as well. Guest speakers, rap sessions, phone help, literature and newsletter. Optional donation. *Website:* http://www.addvicinc.org

Burlington Meets Tues., 7pm, Burlington Center Mall Ministries, Route 541. Call Scott or Lisa 609-953-1380.

Lumberton Meets Thurs., 7pm, Lighthouse Tabernacle, 716 Main St. Call Harry or Ronnie 609-267-2657.

Al-Anon Family Groups 12-Step. Fellowship of families and friends of alcoholics. Offers comfort, hope and friendship through shared experiences. Includes groups for children and adult children. Call Al-Anon Information Services 856-547-0855 (10am-3pm) or 973-744-8686 (day).

Alcoholics Anonymous 12-Step. Fellowship of men and women who share their experience, strength and hope with each other that they may solve their common problem and help others to recover from alcoholism. Young people's groups also available. Call 856-486-4444 (24 hr.); Spanish-speaking 973-824-0555. *Website:* http://www.aasj.org

Double Trouble Mutual support for persons with a substance abuse problem who are also taking medication for psychiatric problems. Meets Sun., Mon. and Wed., 8:30pm, Hampton Hospital, 650 Rancocas Rd., Cafeteria, Westampton. Call Pam Sachs 609-267-7000 (day).

Families Who Are Hurting Mutual support and encouragement for families who are hurting due to an addiction of a loved one, loss of a spouse or for those caring for a loved one with dementia. Meets 1st Sat., 6pm, Rose of Sharon Lutheran Church, Route 528, Jacobstown. Call Bill Millet 609-758-2746.

Nurse Recovery Group *Professionally-run.* Mutual support and information for nurses who are recovering from addictions. Sharing of professional concerns and encouragement. Meets in Moorestown. Call 1-800-662-0108 (day).

Overcomers 12-Step. Christian-focused recovery group for anyone suffering from any type of addiction, dependency or compulsive disorder. Meets Thurs., 7:30-9pm, Fellowship Alliance Chapel, 199 Church Rd., Medford. Call 609-953-7333 (day).

Rap Room Parent-to-Parent Coalition *Professionally-run.* Support and education for parents of teens and young adult children dealing with substance/alcohol addictions. Mutual sharing, advocacy, guest speakers, crisis intervention and referral. Meets 1st Tues., 7-9pm, Greentree Executive Campus, 1003A Lincoln Drive West, Marlton. Call Louise 856-983-3328. *Website:* http://www.raproom.org

CAMDEN

Addictions Victorious of South Jersey, Inc. 12-Step. Christ-centered support group for men and women who, in their struggle with substance abuse and emotional problems, come together that they may solve their problems and help others as well. Guest speakers, rap sessions, phone help, literature and newsletter. Optional donation. *Website:* http://www.addvicinc.org

Barrington Meets Mon., 7pm, Grace Bible Church, 887 Clements Bridge Rd. Call Ginny 856-232-0207.

Camden Meets Tues., 6pm, Fellowship House, 1722 S. Broadway. Call Lucy 856-964-4545.

Lindenwold Meets Mon., 7pm, Garden Lake Bible Church, 63 First Ave. Call Pastor Dave 856-783-3802 or 856-357-4194.

Sicklerville Meets Fri., 6pm, Christ Care Unit Missionary Baptist Church, Sicklerville and Grimes Rd. Call Quinton and Pricilla 856-262-1833 or Murphy 856-875-1145.

Somerdale Meets Thurs., 8pm, Park Avenue Community Church, 431 Hilltop Ave. Call Colleen 856-435-0309. *Website:* http://www.addvicinc.org

Al-Anon Family Groups 12-Step. Fellowship of families and friends of alcoholics. Offers comfort, hope and friendship through shared experiences. Includes groups for children and adult children. Call Al-Anon Information Services 856-547-0855 (10am-3pm) or 973-744-8686 (day).

Alateen 12-Step. Fellowship of young persons (ages 9-18) whose lives have been affected by someone else's drinking. An active adult member of Al-Anon serves as a sponsor. Meets Sun., 8:15pm, St. Peter Celestine School, 420 Kings Highway, Cherry Hill. Call Al-Anon Information Services 856-547-0855 (day).

Alateen 12-Step. Fellowship of young persons whose lives have been affected by someone else's drinking. An active adult member of Al-Anon serves as a sponsor. Meets Wed., 8-9pm, JFK Hospital, Chapel Ave. and Cooper Landing Rd., 5th Floor, Conference Room C, Cherry Hill. Call Al-Anon Information Services 856-547-0855 (day).

Alcoholics Anonymous *(BILINGUAL)* 12-Step. Fellowship of men and women who share their experience, strength and hope with each other that they may solve their common problem and help others to recover from alcoholism. Young people's groups also available. Call 856-486-4444 (24 hr.); Spanish-speaking call 973-824-0555. *Website:* http://www.aasj.org

Camden County Parent-to-Parent Mutual support for parents of children of any age who have alcohol or drug-related problems. Guest speakers, literature and phone help. Meets 2nd & 4th Tues., 6:30-8:30pm, Bellmawr Library, 35 E. Browning Rd., Bellmawr. Call Kathleen Dobbs 856-968-2301 (day).

Dual Recovery Anonymous Mutual support for alcoholics/addicts who are taking medication for psychiatric problems. Meets Wed., 6-7pm, MICA Club, 498 Marlboro Ave., Cherry Hill. Call 856-662-0955 (voice/TDD) (day).

Lawyers Concerned for Lawyers Self-help group that supports recovery from alcoholism and drug dependence for attorneys, judges, law students and others in the legal system. Based on the 12-step program adapted from AA. All inquiries are confidential. Meets 1st and 3rd Wed., 6pm, Steininger Center, Board Room, 19 E. Ormond Ave., Cherry Hill. Call John 609-261-3841 (day) or NJ Lawyers Assistance Program 1-800-246-5527. *Website:* http://www.njlap.org *E-mail:* info@njlap.com

Nurse Recovery Group *Professionally-run.* Mutual support and information for nurses who are recovering from addictions. Sharing of professional concerns and encouragement. Meets in Haddonfield. Call 1-800-662-0108 (day).

Victoria sobre Addicciones *(SPANISH)* 12-Step. Group for both Christian and non-Christian men and women who, in their struggle with substance abuse and emotional problems, come together that they may solve their problems and help others as well. Guest speakers, rap sessions, phone help, literature and newsletter. Optional donation. Meets Tues., 6pm, Fellowship House, 1722 S. Broadway, Camden. Call Lucy 856-964-4545. *Website:* http://www.addvicinc.org

CAPE MAY

Addictions Victorious of South Jersey, Inc. 12-Step. Christ-centered support group for men and women who, in their struggle with substance abuse and emotional problems, come together that they may solve their problems and help others as well. Guest speakers, rap sessions, phone help, literature and newsletter. Optional donation. Meets Mon., 7pm, Seashore Community Church of Nazarene, 446 Seashore Rd., Cape May. Call Phil 609-408-1191, Marty 609-827-1517 or Church 609-886-6196. *Website:* http://www.addvicinc.org

Al-Anon's Adult Children 12-Step. Fellowship offering comfort, hope and friendship through shared experiences for adult children of alcoholics. Meets Wed., 7pm, Burdette Tomlin Hospital, Stone Harbor Blvd. and Route 9, Cape May Court House. Call Al-Anon 973-744-8686 (day).

Al-Anon Family Groups 12-Step. Fellowship of families and friends of alcoholics. Offers comfort, hope and friendship through shared experiences. Includes groups for children and adult children. Call Al-Anon Information Services 856-547-0855 (10am-3pm) or 973-744-8686 (day).

Alateen 12-Step. Fellowship of young persons whose lives have been affected by someone else's drinking. An active adult member of Al-Anon serves as a sponsor. Meets Thurs., 8pm, Church of the Resurrection, 200 W. Tuckahoe Rd., Marmora. Call Al-Anon Information Services 856-547-0855 (day).

Alcoholics Anonymous 12-Step. Fellowship of men and women who share their experience, strength and hope with each other that they may solve their common problem and help others to recover from alcoholism. Young people's groups also available. Call 609-641-8855. *Website:* http://www.capeatlanticinterrgroup.org

CUMBERLAND

Al-Anon Family Groups 12-Step. Fellowship of families and friends of alcoholics. Offers comfort, hope and friendship through shared experiences. Includes groups for children and adult children. Call Al-Anon Information Services 856-547-0855 (10am-3pm) or 973-744-8686 (day).

Alateen 12-Step. Fellowship of young persons (ages 12-18) whose lives have been affected by someone else's drinking. An active adult member of Al-Anon serves as a sponsor. Meets Thurs., 8-9pm, First Presbyterian Church (basement), 119 N. Second St., Millville. Call Al-Anon Information Services 856-547-0855 (day).

Alcoholics Anonymous *(BILINGUAL)* 12-Step. Fellowship of men and women who share their experience, strength and hope with each other that they may solve their common problem and help others to recover from alcoholism. Young people's groups also available. Call 856-486-4444 (24 hr.); Spanish-speaking 973-824-0555. *Website:* http://www.aasj.org

Double Trouble in Recovery 12-Step. Assists consumers who suffer a severe and persistent mental illness to work on their recovery from addiction to substances. Meets Tues., 1-3pm, Special Needs Adult Partial Care Program, Cumberland County Guidance Center, 2038 Carmel Rd., Millville. Call Mary or Lorraine 856-825-6810.

Overcomer's Outreach *(Shiloh Faith Meeting)* Christian 12-Step. Fellowship to overcome any type of addiction or compulsive behavior, anxiety, depression or loneliness using God's word as a basis for recovery. Discussion, Bible study, prayer and phone help. Meets Thurs., 7-8pm, Shiloh 7th Day Baptist Church, East Ave., Shiloh. Call Rev. Chrowiger 856-455-0488 (day) or Frank B. Mulford 856-451-8698 (day). *E-mail:* ahfarm@hotmail.com

ESSEX

Al-Anon's Adult Children 12-Step. Fellowship offering comfort, hope and friendship through shared experiences for adult children of alcoholics. Meets Tues., 8pm, First Presbyterian Church, 10 Fairview Ave., Verona. Call Al-Anon Information Services 973-744-8686.

Al-Anon Family Groups 12-Step. Fellowship of families and friends of alcoholics. Offers comfort, hope and friendship through shared experiences. Includes groups for children and adult children. Call Al-Anon Information Services 973-744-8686 (day).

Alcoholics Anonymous *(BILINGUAL)* 12-Step. Fellowship of men and women who share their experience, strength and hope with each other that they may solve their common problem and help others to recover from alcoholism. Young people's groups also available. Call 1-800-245-1377 or 908-687-8566 (24 hr.); Spanish speaking 973-824-0555. *Website:* http://www.nnjaa.org

BASA/Brothers and Sisters of Siblings *Professionally-run.* Confidential support group for siblings with a chemically dependent sibling. Meets 2nd and 4th Wed., 7pm, St. Cloud Presbyterian Church, Old Indian Rd. and Ridgeway Ave., West Orange. Call Karol Sullivan or Adrienne Mellana 973-736-3344 (day) or 1-800-561-3299. *Website:* http://www.psgnjhomestead.com *E-mail:* psgnj1@aol.com

Double Trouble Support for persons in dual recovery from a mental illness and a substance or alcohol addiction. Meets Mon., 5-6pm, Where Peaceful Waters Flow, 47 Cleveland St., Orange. Call Richard 973-677-7700 (day).

Families Anonymous 12-Step. Support for families and friends concerned about the use of drugs or related behavioral problems. Sharing of experiences, strengths and hopes. Dues $1. Meets Wed., 7:30pm, First Episcopal Church of the Holy Spirit, 36 Gould St., Verona. Call Jim 973-338-6952 or Roxy 973-667-1067 (day).

Lawyers Concerned for Lawyers Self-help group that supports recovery from alcoholism and drug dependence for attorneys, judges, law students and others in the legal system. Based on the 12-step program adapted from A.A. All inquiries are confidential. Meets Tues., 7:30pm, United Way Bldg., Room 60 S. Fullerton Ave., 211 A, Montclair. Call Kenneth 973-429-5588 (day), 973-509-6062 (eve) or NJLAP 1-800-246-5527. *Website:* http://www.njlap.org *E-mail:* info@njlap.com

Parents Support Group - New Jersey Inc. *Professionally-run.* Confidential support group for parents of a chemically dependent child (ages 13-40+). Meets Wed., 6pm and Thurs., 6:30pm, St. Cloud Presbyterian Church, Old Indian Rd. and Ridgeway Ave., West Orange. Call Karol Sullivan 973-736-3344 (9am-3pm) or 1-800-561-4299 (24. hr hotline).

Reformers Anonymous Faith-based group to help people find freedom from addictions: alcohol, debt, drugs, eating disorders, gambling, internet, sex/love addiction, smoking, etc. Literature, newsletter and phone help. Meets Fri., 7-9pm, First Baptist Church, 257 Bloomfield Ave., Caldwell. Call Pastor Eli Miranda 201-724-9208 (day) or church 973-226-1004 (day).

GLOUCESTER

Addictions Victorious of South Jersey, Inc. 12-Step. Christ-centered support group for men and women who in their struggle with substance abuse and emotional problems come together that they may solve their problems and help others as well. Guest speakers, rap sessions, phone help, literature and newsletter. Optional donation. *Website:* http://www.addvicinc.org

Glassboro Meets Tues., 7pm, Olivet Wesleyan Church, 711 Heston Rd. Call Chip 856-881-8241.

Pitman Meets Mon. and Thurs., 7:30pm, The Rock Church, 205 Esplanade Ave. Call Laura 856-582-2277.

Al-Anon Family Groups 12-Step. Fellowship of families and friends of alcoholics. Offers comfort, hope and friendship through shared experiences. Includes groups for children and adult children. Call Al-Anon Information Services 856-547-0855 (10am-3pm) or 973-744-8686 (day).

Alcoholics Anonymous *(BILINGUAL)* 12-Step. Fellowship of men and women who share their experience, strength and hope with each other that they may solve their common problem and help others to recover from alcoholism. Young people's groups also available. Call 856-486-4444 (24 hr.); Spanish-speaking 973-824-0555. *Website:* http://www.aasj.org

Gloucester County Parent To Parent Coalition *Professionally-run.* Confidential meetings and focus on providing parents with support, information, resources, and referrals for dealing with substance abuse and related problems. Guest speakers, educational series, literature. Meets 2nd and 4th Mon., 7:30-9:30pm, Washington Township Municipal Building, 523 Egg Harbor Rd., Meeting Room C, Washington Township. Call 856-589-6446 (day).

"Teens Only" Recovery Group *Professionally-run.* Support for teens (ages 13-20) in recovery from drugs and alcohol. Meets Thurs., 7-8:30pm, Washington Township Municipal Building, 523 Egg Harbor Rd., Washington Township. Call Donna Rullo 856-589-6446 (day). *E-mail*: wtfcs@twp.wasington.nj.us

HUDSON

Al-Anon Family Groups 12-Step. Fellowship of families and friends of alcoholics. Offers comfort, hope and friendship through shared experiences. Includes groups for children and adult children. Call Al-Anon Information Services 973-744-8686 (day).

Alcoholics Anonymous *(BILINGUAL)* 12-Step. Fellowship of men and women who share their experience, strength and hope with each other that they may solve their common problem and help others to recover from alcoholism. Young people's groups also available. Call 1-800-245-1377 or 908-687-8566 (24 hr.); Spanish-speaking 973-824-0555. *Website:* http://www.nnjaa.org

HUNTERDON

Al-Anon Family Groups 12-Step. Fellowship of families and friends of alcoholics. Offers comfort, hope and friendship through shared experiences. Includes groups for children and adult children. Call Al-Anon Information Services 973-744-8686 (day).

Alcoholics Anonymous *(BILINGUAL)* 12-Step. Fellowship of men and women who share their experience, strength and hope with each other that they may solve their common problem and help others to recover from alcoholism. Young people's groups also available. Call 1-800-245-1377 or 908-687-8566 (24 hr.); Spanish-speaking 973-824-0555. *Website:* http://www.nnjaa.org

Nurse Recovery Group *Professionally-run.* Mutual support and information for nurses who are recovering from addictions. Sharing of professional concerns and encouragement. Meets in Flemington. Call 1-800-662-0108 (day).

Overcomers In Christ Recovery program that deals with every aspect of addiction and dysfunction (spiritual, physical, mental, emotional and social). Uses Overcomers goals which are Christ-centered. Resources, information and referrals. Guest speakers, literature and phone help. Meets Fri., 7:30-9pm, Church of the Nazarene, 80 Beaver Ave., Annandale. Call Mary & Ed Powers 908-638-6166 (day/eve) or Patti Willsey 908-238-0358 (day/eve).

MERCER

Al-Anon's Adult Children 12-Step. Fellowship offering comfort, hope and friendship through shared experiences for adult children of alcoholics. Meets Thurs., 7:30pm, Unitarian Church, Cherry Hill Rd. and Route 206, Princeton. Call Al-Anon Information Services 973-744-8686 (day).

Al-Anon Family Groups 12-Step. Fellowship of families and friends of alcoholics. Offers comfort, hope and friendship through shared experiences. Includes groups for children and adult children. Call Al-Anon Information Services 856-547-0855 (10am-3pm) or 973-744-8686 (day).

Alateen 12-Step. Fellowship of young persons whose lives have been affected by someone else's drinking. An active adult member of Al-Anon serves as a sponsor. Call Al-Anon Information Services 856-547-0855 (day).

Hamilton Township Meets Tues., 8pm, St. Mark's Lutheran Church, 351 White Horse Pike.

Hightstown Meets Wed., 8-9pm, St. Anthony's Church School, Route 33 and Maxwell Ave.

Alcoholics Anonymous 12-Step. Fellowship of men and women who share their experience, strength and hope with each other that they may solve their common problem and help others to recover from alcoholism. Young people's groups also available. Call 609-656-8900 (24 hr.); Spanish-speaking 973-824-0555. *Website:* http://www.centraljerseyintergroup.org

Families Anonymous 12-Step. Program for families, especially parents of those with substance abuse or other disruptive behavioral problems. Meets Mon., 7:30pm, St. Lawrence Rehab Center, 2381 Lawrenceville Rd., Route 206 S., Lawrenceville. Call Joan 609-883-1403. *Website:* http://www.familiesanonymous.org *E-mail:* joan@brra.com

Nurse Recovery Group *Professionally-run.* Mutual support and information for nurses who are recovering from addictions. Sharing of professional concerns and encouragement. Meets in Trenton. Call 1-800-662-0108 (day).

Princeton ACOA (Adult Children Of Alcoholics) 12-Step. Fellowship for adult children from alcoholic or dysfunctional families. Optional meeting donation $1. Meets Thurs., 7:30-9pm, Unitarian Church of Princeton, 50 Cherry Hill Rd., Princeton. Call Audrey 609-716-8063.

Together We Can 12-Step. Fellowship of men and women who share their experience, strength and hope with each other that they may solve their common problem of alcoholism and/or overeating. Meets Mon. and Thurs., 7pm, Trinity Church, 33 Mercer St., Princeton. Call Janet 609-273-6955.

MIDDLESEX

Al-Anon Adult Children 12-Step. Fellowship offering comfort, hope and friendship through shared experiences for adult children of alcoholics. Meets Fri., 8pm, St. Luke's Episcopal Church, 17 Oak Ave. and Route 27, Metuchen. Call Al-Anon Information Services 973-744-8686 (day).

Al-Anon Family Groups 12-Step. Fellowship of families and friends of alcoholics. Offers comfort, hope and friendship through shared experiences. Includes groups for children and adult children. Call Al-Anon Information Service 973-744-8686 (day).

Alateen 12-Step. Fellowship of young persons (ages 12-19) whose lives have been affected by someone else's drinking. An active adult member of Al-Anon serves as a sponsor. Meets Fri., 8pm, St. Joseph's Parish Center, 80 High St., Carteret. Call Al-Anon Information Services 973-744-8686.

Alcoholics Anonymous 12-Step. Fellowship of men and women who share their experience, strength and hope with each other that they may solve their common problem and help others to recover from alcoholism. Young people's groups also available. Call 1-800-245-1377 or 908-687-8566 (24 hr.); Spanish-speaking 973-824-0555. *Website:* http://www.nnjaa.org

Double Trouble Mutual support for alcoholics or drug addicts who are taking medication for psychiatric problems. Optional donation. Meets Thurs. 7:30pm, UMDNJ - The Club, 189 New St., Room B, New Brunswick. Call Tim 732-235-6116 (day).

Double Trouble Meeting 12-Step. Support to those who are recovering from both a mental illness and substance abuse. Guest speakers. Meets Mon., 7-8pm, Oak Tree Presbyterian Church, 445 Plainfield Rd., Edison. Call Michelle Gorman 732-321-0191 (day). *E-mail:* mgorman@voa-gny.org

Lawyers Concerned for Lawyers *(WOMEN ONLY)* Self-help group that supports recovery from alcoholism and drug dependence for attorneys, judges, law students and others in the legal system. Based on the 12-step program adapted from A.A. All inquiries are confidential. Meets one Sat. per month, New Brunswick. Call Denise at NJLAP 732-937-7541 or 1-800-246-5527 (day). *Website:* http://www.njlap.org *E-mail:* denise@njlap.org

Nurse Recovery Group *Professionally-run.* Mutual support and information for nurses who are recovering from addictions. Sharing of professional concerns and encouragement. Meets in Woodbridge. Call 1-800-662-0108 (day).

Overcomer's Outreach Christian 12-Step. Fellowship to overcome any type of addiction or compulsive behavior, anxiety, depression or loneliness using God's word as a basis of recovery. Discussion, Bible study, prayer and phone help. Meets

Thurs., 7-8:30pm, Metuchen Assembly of God, 130 Whitman St., Metuchen. Call Janet 732-388-2856 (eve) or Pat 732-321-6896.

Parent Support Group - New Jersey, Inc. Confidential support group for parents of chemically dependent children (ages 13-40+). Meets Thurs., 7pm, St. Peter's Episcopal Church, 505 Main St., Spotswood. Call Karol Sullivan or Adrienne Mellana 1-800-561-4299 or 973-736-3344 (day). *Website:* http://www.psgnjhomestead.com *E-mail:* psgnj1@aol.com

SMART Recovery (Self-Management And Recovery Training) *Professionally-run.* Self-help group for individuals wanting to gain their independence from addictive behaviors (drugs, including alcohol and nicotine and other compulsive behaviors including gambling, eating disorders). SMART is an abstinence program based on cognitive-behavioral education and principles, especially those of rational-emotive behavior therapy. Meets Mon., 6-7:30pm, Rutgers University, Busch Campus, Psychology Building, Room A224, Piscataway. Call Tom Morgan 732-445-0902. *Website:* http://www.smartrecovery.org

MONMOUTH

Al-Anon Adult Children 12-Step. Fellowship offering comfort, hope and friendship through shared experiences for adult children of alcoholics. Meets Sun., 7:30pm, First Baptist Church, 86 Maple Ave., Red Bank. Call Al-Anon Information Services 973-744-8686 (day).

Al-Anon Family Groups 12-Step. Fellowship of families and friends of alcoholics. Offers comfort, hope and friendship through shared experiences. Includes groups for children and adult children. Call Al-Anon Information Services 973-744-8686 (day).

Alcoholics Anonymous *(BILINGUAL)* 12-Step. Fellowship of men and women who share their experience, strength and hope with each other that they may solve their common problem and help others to recover from alcoholism. Young people's groups also available. Call 1-800-245-1377 or 908-687-8566 (24 hr.); Spanish-speaking 973-824-0555. *Website:* http://www.centraljerseyintergroup.org

Double Trouble Dual Recovery 12-Step. Support for those who have an emotional/psychiatric illness and are alcohol/chemically addicted. Meets Mon. and Thurs., 10:15-11am, Park Place Program, 1011 Bond St., Asbury Park. Call Mark

732-869-2781 (day) or Mike Rafter 732-869-2765 (day). *E-mail:* msullivan@meridianhealth.com

Dual Recovery Mutual support for alcoholics or drug abusers who are taking medication for psychiatric problems. Transportation available. Meets Tues., 7pm, Freehold Self-Help Center, 17 Bannard St., Freehold. Call Vernetta 732-502-4614 or George 732-502-5848 (day).

Dual Recovery Anonymous Mutual support for alcoholics/addicts who are taking medication for psychiatric problems. Meets Tues. and Fri., 10:30-11:30am, CPC/Aberdeen Counseling Center, 1088 Highway 34, Aberdeen. Call Mark 732-290-1700 ext. 5307 (day).

Families Anonymous 12-Step. Fellowship of families and friends concerned about the use of drugs, alcohol and/or related behavioral problems. *Website:* http://www.familiesanonymous.org

Holmdel Meets Mon., 7:30pm, Bayshore Community Hospital, 723 N. Beers St. Call Mary Lou 732-583-2238 (eve) or Nancy 732-264-5948 (6-8pm).

Leonardo Meets Mon., 7:30pm, Middletown Township Complex, Leonardville Rd. Call 732-291-1467 (eve).

Ocean Grove Meets Mon., 7:30pm, St. Paul's United Methodist Church, 80 Embury Ave. Call Diana 732-988-3903.

Red Bank Meets Thurs., 7:30-9pm, United Methodist Church, 247 Broad St. Call 732-462-7707. *E-mail:* higley@optonline.net

Mission Possible *(WOMEN ONLY) Professionally-run.* 12-Step. Christ-centered support group for women dealing with alcohol and substance abuse issues. Families and friends welcome. Phone help. Meets 2nd and 4th Tues., 7:30-9pm, Family Life Center, 4041 Squankum Rd., Room 6, Allenwood. Call Minister Donna Ridge 732-938-4353 ext. 230.

Nurse Recovery Group *Professionally-run.* Mutual support and information for nurses who are recovering from addictions. Sharing of professional concerns and encouragement. Meets in Red Bank and Neptune. Call 1-800-662-0108 (day).

Parent Support Group - New Jersey, Inc. Confidential support group for parents of chemically dependent children (ages 13-40+). Meets Tues., 7pm, Church of the Nativity, 180 Ridge Rd., Fair Haven. Call Karol Sullivan or Adrienne Mellana 1-800-561-4299 or 973-736-3344 (day). *Website:* http://www.psgnjhomestead.com *E-mail:* psgnj1@aol.com

MORRIS

A.A. for MICA Patients Alcoholics Anonymous meeting for persons who also have a mental illness. Meets Fri., 7:30pm, New Views, Greystone Park Hospital, Main Building, 1st Floor, North Tier, Morris Plains. Call Tom Wicks 973-292-4015 (9am-4pm). *E-mail:* newviews@nac.net

Al-Anon's Adult Children 12-Step. Fellowship offering comfort, hope and friendship through shared experiences for adult children of alcoholics. Call Al-Anon Information Services 973-744-8686 (day). *Website:* http://www.al-anon.org

Dover Meets Tues., 7pm, First Memorial Presbyterian Church, 51 W. Blackwell St.

Parsippany Meets Sat., 7:30pm, Presbyterian Church, 1675 Route 46 East.

Stirling Meets Fri., 8:15pm, First Presbyterian Church, 158 Central Ave.

Al-Anon Family Groups 12-Step. Fellowship of families and friends of alcoholics. Offers comfort, hope and friendship through shared experiences. Includes groups for children and adult children. Call Al-Anon Information Services 973-744-8686 (day).

Alateen 12-Step. Fellowship of young persons (ages 13-19) whose lives have been affected by someone else's drinking. An active adult member of Al-Anon serves as a sponsor. Meets Tues., 7:30pm, St. David's Episcopal Church, Kinnelon Rd., Kinnelon. Call Al-Anon Information Services 973-744-8686 (day).

Alcohol and Drug Family Education *Professionally-run.* Support for families facing the chemical dependency of a family member. Deals with co-dependency issues. Meets Thurs., 6:30-8pm, Morristown Memorial Hospital, Outpatient Behavioral Health, Morristown. Pre-registration required. Call 1-888-247-1400.

Alcoholics Anonymous *(BILINGUAL)* 12-Step. Fellowship of men and women who share their experience, strength and hope with each other that they may solve their common problem and help others to recover from alcoholism. Young people's groups also available. Call 1-800-245-1377 or 908-687-8566 (24 hr.); Spanish-speaking 973-824-0555. *Website:* http://www.nnjaa.org

Calix Society Mutual support to promote the spiritual development of Catholic alcoholics. Members of other faiths welcome. Mass followed by group discussion.

Meets last Sat., 10am, St. Lawrence Center (rear of church parking lot), Chester. Call Thomas Gibbons 908-876-4343 (day/eve).

Dual Recovery Anonymous Mutual support for alcoholics or drug addicts with psychiatric disorders.

> **Boonton** Meets Tues., noon-1pm, MICA Group Room and Fri., noon-1pm, IOP Group Room; and Sun., noon-1pm, Executive Dining Room, Saint Clare's Hospital. Call Nikki R. 973-664-0596.
>
> **Denville** Meets Wed., noon-1pm, St. Clares Behavioral Health Center, 50 Morris Ave., Auditorium. Call Jacqueline Felczak 973-316-1867.

Families Anonymous 12-Step. Mutual support for parents, relatives and friends of persons with drug or alcohol problems. Peer-counseling. Meets Tues., 7:30-9pm, First Presbyterian Church, 35 Church St., Rockaway. Call 973-586-2440 (eve).

Lawyers Concerned for Lawyers Self-help group that supports recovery from alcoholism and drug dependence for attorneys, judges, law students and others in the legal system. Based on the 12-step program adapted from A.A. All inquiries are confidential. Meets Wed., 7:30pm, Center for Behavioral Health, 95 Mt. Kemble Ave., Morristown. Call Albert 973-538-0280 (day/eve) or NJ Lawyers Assistance Program 1-800-246-5527. *Website:* http://www.njlap.org *E-mail:* njlap@aol.com

Nurse Recovery Group *Professionally-run.* Mutual support and information for nurses who are recovering from addictions. Sharing of professional concerns and encouragement. Meets in Boonton. Call 1-800-662-0108 (day).

Psychiatrically Recovering 12-Step. Mutual support for psychiatrically recovering people who wish to refrain from using alcohol or drugs, abusing food or any other compulsive behavior. Call Richie S. 973-865-4851 (day/eve).

> **Cedar Knolls** Meets Mon. and Thurs., 10am, Saint Clare's Behavioral Health Center, 100 East Hanover Ave., 1st Floor.
>
> **Denville** Meets Mon., 1pm, Saint Clare's Behavioral Health Center, 50 Morris Ave., Room B-1.
>
> **Pompton Plains** Meets Fri., 11am, New Bridge Services Inc, 640 Newark-Pompton Turnpike.

OCEAN

Adult Children of Alcoholics Self-help group for adult children of alcoholics or dysfunctional families. Follows the 12-step program adapted from AA. Meets Tues., 7:45-9pm, Toms River Church of Christ, 1126 Hooper Ave., Toms River. Call Stephanie 732-573-1535 (answering machine).

Al-Anon's Adult Children 12-Step. Fellowship offering comfort, hope and friendship through shared experiences for adult children of alcoholics. Meets Sun., 7pm, Ocean Medical Center, Jack Martin Blvd., Second Floor Conference Room, Brick. Call Al-Anon Information Services 973-744-8686 (day).

Al-Anon Family Groups 12-Step. Fellowship of families and friends of alcoholics. Offers comfort, hope and friendship through shared experiences. Includes groups for children and adult children. Call Al-Anon Information Services 856-547-0855 (10am-3pm).

Alateen 12-Step. Fellowship of young persons (age 7+) whose lives have been affected by someone else's drinking. An active adult member of Al-Anon serves as a sponsor. Meets Sat., 11am, Brick Hospital, Jack Martin Blvd., Brick. Call Al-Anon Information Services 856-547-0855.

Alcoholics Anonymous *(BILINGUAL)* 12-Step. Fellowship of men and women who share their experience, strength and hope with each other that they may solve their common problem and help others to recover from alcoholism. Young people's groups also available. Call 1-800-245-1377 or 908-687-8566 (24 hr.). For Long Beach Island/Southern Ocean City call 609-494-5130; Spanish-speaking 973-824-0555. *Website:* http://www.aasj.org

Checkpoint Support to help overcome dependencies and addictions through accountability, encouragement and spiritual development. Meets Thurs., 7-8:30pm, Shore Vineyard Church, 320 Compass Ave., Beachwood. Call 732-244-3888 (day).

Double Trouble Mutual support for persons with a substance abuse problem who are also taking medication for psychiatric problems.

> Bayville Meets Mon., 6-7pm, Ocean Mental Health Services, 160 Route 9. Call Matt Mantone 732-349-5550 ext. 139 (day).
>
> Bayville Meets Fri., 7:30-8:30pm, Ocean Mental Health Services, Route 9. Call Bill Bradley, Meg Stenson or JoAnn Bonnett 732-905-1132 (day).

Double Trouble in Recovery Support and encouragement for those who are chemically addicted and also in recovery from a psychiatric illness. Meets Wed., 7:30-8:30pm, Brighter Days Center, S & F Plaza, 2008 Route 37 East, Suite 6, Toms River. Call Tina Riccelli 732-270-6061 (day).

Families Anonymous 12-Step. For relatives and friends concerned about the use of drugs or related behavioral problems. Meets Tues., 7:30pm, St. Andrews United

Methodist Church, 1528 Church Rd., Toms River. Call 732-864-0548. *E-mail:* FamAnonTR@Comcast.net

Lawyers Concerned for Lawyers Self-help group that supports recovery from alcoholism and drug dependence for attorneys, judges, law students and others in the legal system. Based on the 12-step program adapted from A.A. All inquiries are confidential. Meets Tues., 7:15pm, St. Mary's By The Sea, 804 Bay Ave., Meeting Room, Point Pleasant. Call Fred 732-785-6314 (pager number; day) or NJ Lawyers Assistance Program 1-800-246-5527. *Website:* http://www.njlap.org *E-mail:* info@njlap.com

Overcomers In Christ Recovery program that deals with every aspect of addiction and dysfunction (spiritual, physical, mental, emotional and social). Uses Overcomers goals which are Christ-centered. Resources, information and referrals. Literature. Meets Mon., 7pm, America's Keswick, 601 Route 530, Whiting. Separate groups for men and women. For women's group call Diane Hunt 732-350-1187 ext. 47. For men's group call Pastor Mike 732-350-1187 ext. 39. *Website:* http://www.americaskeswick.org

Parent Support Group - New Jersey, Inc. Confidential support group for parents of chemically dependent children (ages 13-40+). Meets Mon., 7pm, Presbyterian Church of Toms River, 1070 Hooper Ave., Toms River. Call Karol Sullivan or Adrienne Mellana 1-800-561-4299 or 973-736-3344 (day). *Website:* http://www.psgnjhomestead.com *E-mail:* psgnj1@aol.com

Parents Group, Inc., The Mutual support and referrals for parents in crisis from their teenage and adult children's chemical/alcohol abuse. Works with, and outreaches to, community resources for prevention, awareness and intervention. Meets Tues., 7-9pm, Toms River. Call Mary and Michael Holland 732-929-4443 (day/eve). *E-mail:* starfishpg@comcast.net

PASSAIC

Al-Anon Family Groups 12-Step. Fellowship of families and friends of alcoholics. Offers comfort, hope and friendship through shared experiences. Includes groups for children and adult children. Call Al-Anon Information Services 973-744-8686 (day).

Al-Anon's Adult Children 12-Step. Fellowship offering comfort, hope and friendship through shared experiences for adult children of alcoholics. Meets Tues.,

8pm, (beginners 7pm), Preakness Reformed Church, 131 Church Lane, Wayne. Call Al-Anon Information Services 973-744-8686 (day).

Alcoholics Anonymous *(BILINGUAL)* 12-Step. Fellowship of men and women who share their experience, strength and hope with each other that they may solve their common problem and help others to recover from alcoholism. Young people's groups also available. Call 1-800-245-1377 or 908-687-8566 (24 hr.); Spanish-speaking call 973-824-0555. *Website:* http://www.nnjaa.org

Nurse Recovery Group *Professionally-run.* Mutual support and information for nurses who are recovering from addictions. Sharing of professional concerns and encouragement. Meets in Passaic. Call 1-800-662-0108 (day).

Parent Support Group - New Jersey, Inc. *Professionally-run.* Confidential support group for parents of chemically dependent children (ages 13-40+). Meets Mon., 6:30pm, St. Joseph's Hospital, 224 Hamburg Turnpike, 6th Floor, Room 6B, Wayne. Call Karol Sullivan or Adrienne Mellana 1-800-561-4299 or 973-736-3344 (day). *Website:* http://www.psgnjhomestead.com *E-mail:* psgnj1@aol.com

Psychiatrically Recovering 12-Step. Mutual support for psychiatrically recovering people who wish to refrain from using alcohol or drugs, abusing food or any compulsive behavior. Meets Fri., 9:45am, New Bridge Visions, 22 Riverview Dr., Wayne. Call Richie S. 973-865-4851 (day/eve).

SALEM

Al-Anon Family Groups 12-Step. Fellowship of families and friends of alcoholics. Offers comfort, hope and friendship through shared experiences. Includes groups for children and adult children. Call Al-Anon Information Services 856-547-0855 (10am-3pm).

Alcoholics Anonymous *(BILINGUAL)* 12-Step. Fellowship of men and women who share their experience, strength and hope with each other that they may solve their common problem and help others to recover from alcoholism. Young people's groups also available. Call 856-486-4444 (24 hr.); Spanish-speaking 973-824-0555. *Website:* http://www.aasj.org

SOMERSET

Al-Anon Family Groups 12-Step. Fellowship of families and friends of alcoholics. Offers comfort, hope and friendship through shared experiences. Includes groups for children and adult children. Call Al-Anon Information Services 973-744-8686 (day).

Alateen 12-Step. Fellowship of young persons (ages 8-18) whose lives have been affected by someone else's drinking. An active adult member of Al-Anon serves as a sponsor. Meets Fri., 8:30pm, Somerset Hospital, Rehill Ave., Somerville. Call Al-Anon Information Services 973-744-8686 (day).

Alcoholics Anonymous *(BILINGUAL)* 12-Step. Fellowship of men and women who share their experience, strength and hope with each other that they may solve their common problem and help others to recover from alcoholism. Young people's groups also available. Call 1-800-245-1377 or 908-687-8566 (24 hr.); Spanish-speaking 973-824-0555. *Website:* http://www.nnjaa.org

Bright Futures for Kids *Professionally-run.* Provides support, education and counseling for children (ages 4-12) who are affected by a family member's alcohol and/or drug addiction. Children learn how to express their feelings, coping skills, a sense of responsibility and the ability to resist peer pressure. Meets Sun., 11am-1pm, Carrier Clinic, Atkinson Amphitheater, Classroom 3, 252 Route 601, Belle Mead. Call Community Relations Dept. 908-281-1513.

Lawyers Concerned for Lawyers Self-help group that supports recovery from alcoholism and drug dependence for attorneys, judges, law students and others in the legal system. Based on the 12-step program adapted from A.A. All inquires are confidential. Meets Tues., 6pm, 70 Grove St., Somerville. Call NJ Lawyers Assistance Program 1-800-246-5527. *Website:* http://www.njlap.org *E-mail:* njlap@aol.com

Nurse Recovery Group *Professionally-run.* Mutual support and information for nurses who are recovering from addictions. Sharing of professional concerns and encouragement. Meets in Belle Mead. Call 1-800-662-0108 (day).

Parent Support Group - New Jersey, Inc. Confidential support group for parents of chemically dependent children (ages 13-40+). Meets Mon., 7pm, Carrier Foundation, Admissions Building, Belle Mead. Call Karol Sullivan or Adrienne Mellana 1-800-561-4299 or 973-736-3344 (day). *Website:* http://www.psgnjhomestead.com *E-mail:* psgnj1@aol.com

Psychiatrically Recovering 12-Step. Mutual support for psychiatrically recovering people who wish to refrain from using alcohol or drugs, abusing food or any other compulsive behavior. Meets Thurs., 7:30pm, Richard Hall Community Mental Health Center, 500 N. Bridge St., Room 121, Bridgewater. Call Richie S. 973-865-4851 (day/eve).

Weekend Co-dependency Program *Professionally-run.* Support and education for families and friends of alcohol/drug abusers or those dealing with persons with any addiction problems. Educational lectures, discussion groups and parents group. Meets Sat. and Sun., 9:30am-3pm, Carrier Clinic, Atkinson Amphitheater, 252 Route 601, Belle Mead. Call 908-281-1513 (day) or 908-281-1000 (eve/weekend). *Website:* http://www.carrier.org

SUSSEX

Al-Anon Family Groups 12-Step. Fellowship of families and friends of alcoholics. Offers comfort, hope and friendship through shared experiences. Includes groups for children and adult children. Call Al-Anon Information Services 973-744-8686 (day).

Al-Anon's Adult Children 12-Step. Fellowship offering comfort, hope and friendship through shared experiences for adult children of alcoholics. Meets Wed., 8pm, Holy Counselor Lutheran Church, Sandhill Rd., Vernon. Call Al-Anon Information Services 973-744-8686 (day).

Alateen 12 Step. Fellowship of young persons (age 13+) whose lives have been affected by someone else's drinking. An active adult member of Al-Anon serves as a sponsor. Meets Mon., 7:30pm, Westside United Methodist Church, 16 Maxim Dr., Hopatcong. Call Al-Anon Information Services 973-744-8686 (day).

Alcoholics Anonymous *(BILINGUAL)* 12-Step. Fellowship of men and women who share their experience, strength and hope with each other that they may solve their common problem and help others to recover from alcoholism. Young people's groups also available. Call 1-800-245-1377 or 908-687-8566 (24 hr.); Spanish-speaking 973-824-0555. *Website:* http://www.nnjaa.org

Double Trouble in Recovery 12-Step. Support and encouragement for those who are chemically addicted and are also in recovery from a psychiatric illness. Call Pat Devlin 973-383-8770 or Joe Shane 973-534-3449. *E-mail:* PatriciaDevlin@yahoo.com or JBWShane@nac.net

Newton Meets Wed., 5pm, Center for Prevention, 2nd floor classroom, 61 Spring St.

Newton Meets Sat., 10:30am, Sussex House at Newton Memorial Hospital, 175 High St.

Newton Meets Fri., 3:30pm, (only if weather is pleasant - into the Fall), within the Gazebo near Park Place, at County Common, Park Place and Main St.

Lawyers Concerned for Lawyers Self-help group that supports recovery from alcoholism and drug dependence for attorneys, judges, law students and others in the legal system. Based on the 12-step program adapted from A.A. All inquiries are confidential. Meets Sat., 9am, Newton. Call Mary Jean 973-729-1847 or NJ-LAP 1-800-246-5527. *Website:* http://www.njlap.org

UNION

Al-Anon Family Groups 12-Step. Fellowship of families and friends of alcoholics. Offers comfort, hope and friendship through shared experiences. Includes groups for children and adult children. Call Al-Anon Information Services 973-744-8686 (day).

Alcohol and Drug Family Education *Professionally-run.* Support for families facing the chemical dependency of a family member. Deals with co-dependency issues. Meets Tues., 6:30-8pm, 46 Beauvoir Ave., Summit. Call 908-522-4800 (day).

Alcoholics Anonymous *(BILINGUAL)* 12-Step. Fellowship of men and women who share their experience, strength and hope with each other that they may solve their common problem and help others to recover from alcoholism. Young people's groups also available. Call 1-800-245-1377 or 908-687-8566 (24 hr.); Spanish-speaking 973-824-0555. *Website:* http://www.nnjaa.org

Families of Addiction *Professionally-run.* Mutual support for families of persons with an alcohol or drug addiction. Meets Tues., 6:30-8pm, Overlook Hospital, 46-48 Beauvoir Ave., Summit. Before attending call Rosemary Walsh 908-522-4878.

Nurse Recovery Group *Professionally-run.* Mutual support and information for nurses who are recovering from addictions. Sharing of professional concerns and encouragement. Meets in Berkeley Heights. Call 1-800-662-0108 (day).

Overcomer's Outreach Christian 12-Step. Fellowship to overcome any type of addiction or compulsive behavior, anxiety, depression or loneliness using God's word as a basis of recovery. Discussion, Bible study, prayer and phone help. Call Carmen 908-245-2788.

> **Cranford** Meets Mon., 7pm, Harvest Training Center at Calvary Tabernacle, 69 Myrtle St.
>
> **Elizabeth** Meets Thurs., 7:30pm, Union Baptist Church, 1088 E. Grand St.
>
> **Elizabeth** Meets Tues., 7:30pm, Mount Teman AME Church, 160 Madison Ave.

Parent Support Group - New Jersey, Inc. *Professionally-run.* Confidential support group for parents of chemically dependent children (ages 13-40+). Meets Tues., 6:30pm, Central Presbyterian Church, 70 Maple Ave., Library Room, Summit. Call Karol Sullivan or Adrienne Mellana 1-800-561-4299 or 973-736-3344 (day). *Website:* http://wwwpsgnjhomestead.com *E-mail:* psgn1@aol.com

Psychiatrically Recovering 12-Step. Mutual support for psychiatrically recovering people who wish to refrain from using alcohol or drugs, abusing food or any other compulsive behavior. Meets Tues., 9:30am, Occupational Center of Union County, New Building, 291 Cox St., Activity Room, Roselle. Call Richie S. 973-865-4851 (day/eve).

WARREN

Al-Anon Family Groups 12-Step. Fellowship of families and friends of alcoholics. Offers comfort, hope and friendship through shared experiences. Includes groups for children and adult children. Call Al-Anon Information Services 973-744-8686 (day).

Alcoholics Anonymous *(BILINGUAL)* 12-Step. Fellowship of men and women who share their experience, strength and hope with each other that they may solve their common problem and help others to recover from alcoholism. Young people's groups also available. Call 1-800-245-1377 or 908-687-8566 (24 hr.); Spanish-speaking 973-824-0555. *Website:* http://www.nnjaa.org

Dual Recovery Anonymous Mutual support for alcoholics or drug addicts who are taking medication for psychiatric problems. Dues $2/month. Meets Tues., 7-8pm and Sat., 3-4pm, Better Future Self-Help Center, 21 West Washington Ave., Washington. Call Fonda 908-835-1180.

NATIONAL

Adult Children of Alcoholics World Services Organization, Inc. *International. 1500+ meetings. Founded 1977.* 12-Step. Program of recovery for individuals who were raised in an alcoholic or otherwise dysfunctional household. Group development guidelines, newsletter and literature. Send a self-addressed stamped envelope when writing. Write: ACA, P.O. Box 3216, Torrance, CA 90510-3216. Call 310-534-1815 (directs you to website or postal address for request). *Website:* http://adultchildren.org *E-mail:* info@adultchildren.org

Al-Anon Family Groups, Inc. World Services Headquarters *(MULTILINGUAL) International. 23,972 groups. Founded 1951.* 12-Step. Fellowship of men, women, adult children and children whose lives have been affected by the compulsive drinking of a family member or friend. Opportunity for personal recovery and growth. Guidelines for starting groups. Literature is available in over 34 languages. Write: Al-Anon Family Groups, Inc., 1600 Corporate Landing Parkway, Virginia Beach, VA 23454-5617. Call 757-563-1600; for meeting information call 1-888-425-2666 (Mon.-Fri., 8am-6pm EST) (English/French/Spanish); Fax: 757-563-1655. *Website:* http://www.al-anon.org *E-mail:* wso@al-anon.org

Alateen *(MULTILINGUAL) International. 1770 groups. Founded 1957.* 12-Step. Fellowship of young persons whose lives have been affected by someone else's drinking. An active adult member of Al-Anon who is certified as eligible to serve the area as a sponsor for each group. Group development guidelines and newsletter. Literature is available in over 30 languages. Write: Alateen, c/o Al-Anon Family Group Headquarters Inc., 1600 Corporate Landing Parkway, Virginia Beach, VA 23454-5617. Call 757-563-1600; for meeting information call 1-888-425-2666 (Mon.-Fri., 8am-6pm EST) (English/French/Spanish); Fax: 757-536-1655. *Website:* http://www.al-anon.alateen.org *E-mail:* wso@al-anon.org

Alcoholics Anonymous World Services, Inc. . *(MULTILINGUAL) International. 106,000 groups worldwide. Founded 1935.* 12-Step. Fellowship of women and men who have found a solution to their drinking problem. The only requirement for membership is a desire to stop drinking. Supported by voluntary contributions of its members and groups. A.A. neither seeks nor accepts outside funding. Members observe personal anonymity at the public level, thus emphasizing A.A. principles rather than personalities. For more information check your local phone directory. Write: General Service Office, P.O. Box 459, Grand Central Station, New York, NY 10163. Call 212-870-3400; Fax: 212-870-3003. *Website:* http://www.aa.org

Alcoholics Victorious *International. 150 affiliated groups. Founded 1948.* 12-Step. Christian-oriented group for those recovering from alcohol or chemical dependency. Information and referrals, literature, phone support, conferences, support group meetings and newsletter. Assistance in starting groups. How-to materials. Write: Alcoholics Victorious, c/o Association of Gospel Rescue Missions, 1045 Swift Ave., North Kansas City, MO 64116-4127. Call 1-800-624-5156 or 816-471-8020; Fax: 816-471-3718. *Website:* http://www.alcoholicsvictorious.org *E-mail:* info@alcoholicsvictorious.org

Anesthetists in Recovery *National network. Founded 1984. 150 member network of recovering nurse anesthetists.* Provides phone support, information and referrals to groups and treatment. Write: AIR, c/o Art, 8233 Brookside Rd., Elkins Park, PA 19027. Call 215-635-0183 or 215-872-6821. *Website:* http://health.groups.yahoo.com/group/airforsobriety *E-mail:* a.to.z@comcast.net

Calix Society *International. 20 chapters. Founded 1947.* Fellowship of Catholic alcoholics maintaining their sobriety through Alcoholics Anonymous. Concerned with total abstinence, spiritual development and sanctification of the whole personality of each member. Bimonthly newsletter. Assistance in chapter development. Write: Calix Society, 2555 Hazelwood Ave., St. Paul, MN 55109. Call 651-773-3117 (Voice/Fax) or 1-800-398-0524 (Voice/Fax). *Website:* http://www.calixsociety.org *E-mail:* calix@usfamily.net

Chemically Dependent Anonymous *National. 65 affiliated groups. Founded 1980.* Purpose is to carry the message of recovery to the chemically dependent person. For those with a desire to abstain from drugs or alcohol. Information, referrals, phone support and conferences. Group development guidelines. Write: Chemically Dependent Anonymous, P.O. Box 813, Annapolis, MD 21401. Call 1-888-232-4673. *Website:* http://www.cdaweb.org

Double Trouble in Recovery, Inc. *National. 250+ affiliated groups. Founded 1989.* Fellowship of men and women who share their experience, strength, and hope with each other so that they may solve their common problems and help others to recover from their particular addiction(s) and mental disorders. For persons dually-diagnosed with an addiction as well as a mental disorder. Literature, information, referrals and conferences. D.T.R. Basic Guide Book. Assistance in starting new groups. Write: DTR, Inc., P.O. Box 245055, Brooklyn, NY 11224. Call 718-373-2684. *Website:* http://www.doubletroubleinrecovery.org *E-mail:* HV613@aol.com

Dual Disorders Anonymous *National. 25 chapters. Founded 1982.* 12-step. Fellowship of men and women who come together to help those members who suffer from both a mental disorder and alcoholism and/or drug addiction. Group development guidelines. Write: Dual Disorders Anonymous, P.O. Box 681264, Schaumburg, IL 60168-1264. Call Chuck 847-577-1853. *Website:* http://www.msnusers.com/dualdisordersanonymous

Dual Recovery Anonymous *International. Chapters worldwide. Founded 1989.* A self-help program for individuals who experience a dual disorder of chemical dependency and a psychiatric or emotional illness. Based on the principles of the 12-steps and the personal experiences of individuals in dual recovery. Literature, newsletter and assistance in starting local groups. Write: DRA, P.O. Box 8107, Prairie Village, KS 66208. Call 1-877-883-2332. *Website:* http://www.draonline.org

Families Anonymous *International. 500+ groups. Founded 1971.* 12-Step. Fellowship for relatives and friends of persons with drug, alcohol or behavioral problems. Members learn to achieve their own serenity in spite of the turmoil which surrounds them. Besides many booklets, pamphlets and bookmarks, publications include daily thought book, "Today A Better Way" and a bi-monthly newsletter "The Twelve-Step Rag." Offers group development guidelines. Write: FA, P.O. Box 3475, Culver City, CA 90231-3475. Call 1-800-736-9805; Fax: 310-815-9682. *Website:* http://www.FamiliesAnonymous.org *E-mail:* famanon@FamiliesAnonymous.org

Free N One Recovery *National. 55 affiliated groups. Founded 1985.* Group teaches people to be free mentally and spiritually, as well as free of drugs and alcohol. Family support groups available. Information and referrals, phone support, literature and conferences. Assistance in starting local chapters. Write: Free N One Recovery, 5838 S. Overhill Dr., Los Angeles, CA, 90043. Call 323-295-0009; Fax 310-764-5439. *Website:* http://www.freenone.org *E-mail:* freenone@msn.com

I.C.A.P. Intercongregational Addictions Program *International. Founded 1979.* Network of recovering alcoholic women in religious orders. Helps Roman Catholic women who are or have been members of religious orders and are alcoholic or chemically dependent, compulsive eaters, compulsive gamblers, etc. Information, referrals, assistance in meeting other members, phone support, conferences and e-newsletters. Write: ICAP, 7777 Lake St., Suite 115, River Forest, IL 60305-1734. Call 708-488-9770; Fax: 708-488-9774. *Website:* http://www.2icap.org *E-mail:* lclose1@core.com

International Doctors in Alcoholics Anonymous *International network. 6000 members. 175 affiliated groups. Founded 1949.* Opportunity for doctoral level health care professionals to discuss common problems and find common solutions to drug and alcohol problems. Annual meetings (1st week Aug.), phone support, newsletter, information and referrals. Mutual help meetings at conferences of other organizations. Write: IDDAA, c/o Gordon L. Hyde, MD, Exec. Director, 3311 Brookhill Circle, Lexington, KY 40502. Call 859-277-9379 (day). *Website:* http://www.idaa.org

International Lawyers in Alcoholics Anonymous *International. 40+ affiliated groups. Founded 1975.* Serves as a clearinghouse for support groups for lawyers who are recovering alcoholics or have other chemical dependencies. Newsletter, annual conventions and group development guidelines. Write: ILAA, c/o Eli Gauna, 14123 Victory Blvd., Van Nuys, CA 91401. Call 818-785-6541 (day); Fax: 818-785-3887. *Website:* http://www.ilaa.org

International Ministers & Pastors in Recovery *International. Founded 1988.* Mutual support for pastors and ministers recovering from addictions and actively participating in a 12-step recovery program. Provides phone network, information and referrals. Assistance in starting local groups. Write: Int'l. Ministers & Pastors in Recovery, P.O. Box 219, Augusta, MO 63332. *E-mail:* Fresh12st@aol.com

International Nurses Anonymous *International. Founded 1988.* Support and advocacy network for nurses who are involved in a 12-step recovery program. Membership is open to any RN, LPN (or LVN), nursing student or former nurse who considers themselves to be members of a 12-step group - including but not limited to: AA, NA, OA, Ala-non, Nar-anon, ACOA, CODA, etc. Newsletter and one-to-one networking. Plans for International Conference for 2008. Call Kathy 704-992-0678. *Website:* http://intnursesanon.org

JACS (Jewish Alcoholics, Chemically Dependent Persons and Significant Others) *International. Founded 1980.* For alcoholic and chemically dependent Jews, families, friends, associates and the community. Networking, community outreach, retreats, newsletter, literature, spiritual events and speakers bureau. Write: JACS, 120 W. 57th St., New York, NY 10019. Call 212-397-4197 (day); Fax: 212-399-3525. *Website:* http://www.jacsweb.org *E-mail:* jacs@jacsweb.org

LifeRing Secular Recovery *International. Founded 1999.* Secular community of persons who are building lives free of dependency on alcohol and other drugs. Group activities are not associated with religion or spirituality. Members practice complete abstinence from alcohol and other addicting drugs. Peer support, literature, information, referrals and advocacy activities. Guidelines available for starting similar groups. Large online e-mail support group and several smaller special interest groups (women, weight loss, stop smoking, etc). Online chats, forum. Publishes sobriety literature. Write: LifeRing Secular Recovery, 1440 Broadway, Suite 312, Oakland, CA 94612-2041. Call 1-800-811-4142 or 510-763-0779. *Website:* http://www.unhooked.com *E-mail:* service@lifering.org

Moderation Management *International. 20 groups. Founded 1993.* Behavioral change program and support network for people concerned about their drinking and who desire to make positive lifestyle changes. Empowers individuals to accept personal responsibility for choosing and maintaining their own path, whether moderation or abstinence. Promotes early self-recognition of risky drinking behavior when moderation is a more easily achievable goal. Online meetings, chatroom topic meetings and listserv. Write: Moderation Management Network, Inc., 22 West 27th St., New York, NY. Call 212-871-0974. *Website:* http://moderation.org *E-mail:* mm@moderation.org

Overcomers In Christ *International. Founded 1987.* Recovery program that deals with every aspect of addiction and dysfunction (spiritual, physical, mental, emotional and social). Uses Overcomers Goals which are Christ-centered. Literature, resources, information and referrals. Assistance in starting new groups. Write: Overcomers In Christ, P.O. Box 34460, Omaha, NE 68134-04604. Call 402-573-0966; Fax: 402-573-0960. *Website:* http://www.OvercomersInChrist.org *E-mail:* OIC@OvercomersInChrist.org

Overcomers Outreach, Inc. *International. 700 affiliated groups. Founded 1985.* 12-Step. Christ-centered support group for persons with any compulsive behaviors, as well as their families and friends. Uses the 12-steps of A.A. and applies them to the Scriptures. Uses Jesus Christ as "higher power." Supplements involvement in other 12-step groups. Newsletter, group development guidelines and conferences. Write: Overcomers Outreach, P.O. Box 922950, Sylmar, CA 91392-2950. Call 1-800-310-3001. *Website:* http://www.overcomersoutreach.org *E-mail:* info@overcomersoutreach.org

Psychologists Helping Psychologists *National network. Founded 1980.* For doctoral-level psychologists or students who've had a personal experience with alcohol or drugs. Aim is to support each other in recovery and help others to recover. Regional/national get-togethers and newsletter. Write: Psychologists Helping Psychologists, 3484 S. Utah St., Arlington, VA 22206-1921. Call Ann Stone 703-243-4470; Fax: 703-243-7125. *E-mail:* AnnS@Erols.com

Recoveries Anonymous *International. 50 chapters.* Spiritual recovery group for anyone seeking a solution for any kind of addiction, problem or behavior. Family and friends welcome. "How To Begin..." guides and "Start A Group" kit can be downloaded free from the website. Write: RA, P.O. Box 1212, East Northport, NY 11731. *Website:* http://www.r-a.org *E-mail:* raus@r-a.org

Secular Organizations for Sobriety (Save Ourselves) *International. 20,000 members. Founded 1986.* Mutual help for alcoholics and addicts who want to acknowledge their addiction and maintain sobriety as a separate issue from religion or spirituality. Newsletter. Guidelines and assistance available for starting groups. Real-time online chats and e-groups available. Write: S.O.S., 4773 Hollywood Blvd., Hollywood, CA 90027. Call 323-666-4295; Fax: 323-666-4271. *Website:* http://www.cfiwest.org/sos *E-mail:* sos@cfiwest.org

SMART Recovery (r) (Self-Management And Recovery Training) *National. 225+ affiliated groups. Founded 1994.* Network of self-help groups for individuals wanting to gain their independence from addictive and compulsive behaviors. SMART Recovery is an abstinence program based on cognitive-behavioral principles, especially those of rational-emotive behavior therapy. Newsletter, information, referrals, literature and assistance in starting local groups. Write: SMART Recovery, 7537 Mentor Ave., Suite 306, Mentor, OH 44060. Call 1-866-951-5357 or 440-951-5357 (day); Fax: 440-951-5358. *Website:* http://www.smartrecovery.org *E-mail:* info@smartrecovery.org

Social Workers Helping Social Workers *National network. Founded 1980.* Supports recovery from alcohol or other chemical dependence, either their own or that of a significant other, among social workers (BSW/MSW) or MSW matriculating students. Social workers with other addictions are welcome to attend meetings. Newsletter, annual conferences, some regional retreats/meetings, continuing education, daily e-mail digest and group development guidelines. Write: SWHSW, c/o Betty Check, 5228 S. Kenwood Ave., Chicago, IL 60615. Call 773-493-6940 (confidential voice mail). *Website:* http://www.socialworkershelping.org *E-mail:* SWHSWIL@aol.com

Veterinarians in Recovery *National network. Founded 1990.* Support network for veterinarians in recovery from alcoholism and addiction. Provides information and referrals, phone support and newsletter. Online e-mail listserv. Maintains database of members for support. Al-Anon members and recovering veterinarian staff welcome at meetings. Many VIR members also are members of International

Doctors in A.A., and meet during their annual conference. Write: VIR, c/o Jeff H., 180 County Rd. 741, Clanton, AL 35046. Call 205-335-4222. *E-mail:* jeffhalldvm@charter.net

Women For Sobriety *International. 150 groups. Founded 1976.* Program designed specifically to help the woman alcoholic achieve sobriety. Addresses need to overcome depressed feelings and guilt. Monthly newsletter, information and referrals, phone support, group meetings, conferences and group development guidelines. Write: Women for Sobriety, P.O. Box 618, Quakertown, PA 18951-0618. Call 215-536-8026; Fax: 215-538-9026. *Website:* http://www.womenforsobriety.org *E-mail:* NewLife@nni.com

ONLINE

Conduct Disorders Parent Message Board *Online.* Support for parents living with a child with one of the many behavior disorders including: attention deficit hyperactivity disorder, oppositional defiance disorder, conduct disorder, depression and substance abuse. Parents with children of all ages welcome. *Website:* http://www.conductdisorders.com

CO-DEPENDENCY / DYSFUNCTIONAL FAMILIES

BERGEN

Co-DA (Co-Dependents Anonymous) 12-Step. Fellowship for persons who have an inability to maintain functional relationships. For those who have a desire for healthy, fulfilling relationships with themselves and others. Donation $1-2. Meets Wed., 8-9:30pm, Lutheran Church of Redeemer, 471 Maywood Ave., Maywood. Call Dorothy 973-546-9322.

Seniors Count 12-Step. Support for persons (age 60+) who are recovering from substance abuse or co-dependency. Meets Fri., 1:30-3pm, Van Ost Institute For Family Living, Presbyterian Church, 150 East Palisades Ave., 2nd Floor, Englewood. Call Anne Wennhold 201-569-6667. *Website:* http://www.vanostinstitute.org *E-mail:* vanost@msn.com

"To bear other people's afflictions, everyone has courage and enough to spare."
-- Ben Franklin

CAMDEN

Co-DA (Co-Dependents Anonymous) 12-Step. Fellowship for persons who have an inability to maintain functional relationships. For those who want to learn to develop healthy, fulfilling relationships with others and themselves. Meets Fri., 7:30pm, The Starting Point, 215 Highland Ave., Suite C, Westmont. Call 856-854-3155 (day). *Website:* http://www.startingpoint.org *E-mail:* info@startingpoint.org

CUMBERLAND

Co-D.A. (Co-Dependents Anonymous) 12-Step. Fellowship for people unable to maintain functional relationships. For those with a desire to help in learning to maintain healthy, fulfilling relationships with others and themselves. Meets 2nd Mon., 7:30-8:30pm, 7 Bridgeton Ave., Bridgeton. Call Christianna 856-453-0888.

HUNTERDON

Overcomers In Christ Recovery program that deals with every aspect of addiction and dysfunction (spiritual, physical, mental, emotional and social). Uses Overcomers goals which are Christ-centered. Resources, information and referrals. Guest speakers, literature and phone help. Meets Fri., 7:30-9pm, Church of the Nazarene, 80 Beaver Ave., Annandale. Call Mary & Ed Powers 908-638-6166 (day/eve) or Patti Willsey 908-238-0358 (day/eve).

MERCER

Princeton ACOA 12-Step. Fellowship for adult children from alcoholic and dysfunctional families. Optional meeting donation $1/wk. Meets Thurs., 7:30-9pm, Unitarian Church of Princeton, 50 Cherry Hill Rd., Princeton. Call Audrey 609-716-8063.

MONMOUTH

Co-DA (Co-Dependents Anonymous) 12-Step. Fellowship for persons unable to maintain functional relationships. For those with a desire for healthy, fulfilling relationships with others and themselves.

Middletown Meets Tues., 8-9pm, King of Kings Lutheran Church, Room 10/Library, Harmony Rd. Call Bill 732-721-8616 (eve).

Wayside *(Sunday Night Wayside)* Phone help. Meets Sun., 7-8pm, St. Anselm Church, 1028 Wayside Rd. Call Betsy 732-542-9050 (eve).

OCEAN

Adult Children of Alcoholics 12-Step. Self-help group for adult children of alcoholics or dysfunctional families. Meets Tues., 7:45-9pm, Toms River Church of Christ, 1126 Hooper Ave., Toms River. Call Stephanie 732-573-1535 (answering machine).

Overcomers In Christ Recovery program that deals with every aspect of addiction and dysfunction (spiritual, physical, mental, emotional and social). Uses Overcomers goals which are Christ-centered. Literature, resources, information and referrals. Meets Mon., 7pm, America's Keswick, 601 Route 530, Whiting. Separate groups for men and women. Women's group call Diane Hunt 732-350-1187 ext. 47. Men's group call Pastor Mike 732-350-1187 ext. 39. *Website:* http://www.americaskeswick.org

SOMERSET

Co-DA (Co-Dependents Anonymous) 12-Step. For persons unable to maintain functional relationships. For those with a desire for healthy, fulfilling relationships with others and themselves. Meets Sat., 9-10:30am and Mon., 7-8:15pm, United Methodist Church, Church St., Kingston. Call 609-921-6812 (day).

Weekend Co-dependency Program *Professionally-run.* Support and education for families and friends of alcohol/drug abusers or those dealing with persons with any addiction problems. Educational lectures, discussion groups and parents group. Meets Sat. and Sun., 9:30am-3pm, Carrier Clinic, Atkinson Amphitheater, 252 Route 601, Belle Mead. Call 908-281-1513 (day) or 908-281-1000 (eve/weekend). *Website:* http://www.carrier.org

UNION

Co-D.A. (Co-Dependents Anonymous) 12-Step. Fellowship of men and women whose common purpose is to develop healthy relationships. For those who have a desire to build and maintain fulfilling relationships with themselves and others. Meets Tues., 7:30-9pm, All Saints Episcopal Church, 559 Park Ave., Scotch Plains. Call Joe F. 908-272-1926 (before 10pm).

NATIONAL

Co-Dependents Anonymous *International. Founded 1986.* 12-Step. Self-help program of recovery from co-dependence. Members share experience, strength and hope in an effort to find freedom and peace in relationships with themselves and others. Library of literature and audio tapes. Guidelines on starting a similar group available. Newsletter and listing of local support groups online. Write: CoDA, P.O. Box 33577, Phoenix, AZ 85067-3577. For local support groups call 602-277-7991. *Website:* http://www.coda.org *E-mail:* outreach@coda.org

Overcomers In Christ *International. Founded 1987.* Recovery program that deals with every aspect of addiction and dysfunction (spiritual, physical, mental, emotional and social). Uses Overcomers Goals which are Christ-centered. Resources, literature, information and referrals. Assistance in starting new groups. Write: Overcomers In Christ, P.O. Box 34460, Omaha, NE 68134-04604. Call 402-573-0966; Fax: 402-573-0960. *Website:* http://www.OvercomersInChrist.org *E-mail:* OIC@OvercomersInChrist.org

Overcomers Outreach, Inc. *International. 700 affiliated groups. Founded 1985.* 12-Step. Christ-centered support group for persons with any compulsive behavior, as well as their families and friends. Uses the 12-steps of A.A. and applies them to the Scriptures. Uses Jesus Christ as "higher power." Supplements involvement in other 12-step groups. Newsletter, group development guidelines and conferences. Write: Overcomers Outreach, P.O. Box 922950, Sylmar, CA 91392-2950. Call 1-800-310-3001. *Website:* http://www.overcomersoutreach.org *E-mail:* info@overcomersoutreach.org

Recoveries Anonymous *International. 50 chapters.* Spiritual recovery group for anyone seeking a solution for any kind of addiction, problem or behavior. Family and friends welcome. "How To Begin" guide and "Start A Group" kit can be downloaded free from the website. Write: RA, P.O. Box 1212, East Northport, NY 11731. *Website:* http://www.r-a.org *E-mail:* raus@r-a.org

We can also refer callers to over 100 individuals who are seeking others to help start new support groups throughout NJ. Give us a call to find out more.

1-800-367-6274

DEBT / OVERSPENDING

(see also toll-free helplines)

BERGEN

Debtor's Anonymous 12-Step. Program for those who wish to stop incurring debt. Meets Fri., 7:30-9pm, St. Paul's Lutheran Church, Church St. and Longfellow Rd., Teaneck. Call 908-580-8200 or 1-877-717-3328. *Website:* http://www.njpada.org

BURLINGTON

Debtor's Anonymous 12-Step. Program for those who wish to stop incurring debt. Meets Thurs., 7:30pm, Second Baptist Church, 319 Mill Rd., Room 4, Second Floor, Moorestown. Call Judy P. 856-482-6892 or 1-877-717-3328. *Website:* http://www.njpada.org

Overcomers 12-Step. Christian-focused recovery group for anyone suffering from any type of addiction, dependency or compulsive disorder. Meets Thurs., 7:30-9pm, Fellowship Alliance Chapel, 199 Church Rd., Medford. Call 609-953-7333 (day).

CUMBERLAND

Overcomer's Outreach *(Shiloh Faith Meeting)* Christian 12-Step. Fellowship to overcome any type of addiction or compulsive behavior, anxiety, depression or loneliness using God's word as a basis of recovery. Discussion, Bible study, prayer and phone help. Meets Thurs., 7-8pm, Shiloh Seventh Day Baptist Church, East Ave., Shiloh. Call Rev. Chrowiger 856-455-0488 (day) or Frank B. Mulford 856-451-8698 (day). *E-mail:* ahfarm@hotmail.com

ESSEX

Debtors Anonymous 12-Step. Program for those who wish to stop incurring debt. Meets Mon., 8pm, (beginners 7:30pm), Watchung Presbyterian Church, 375 Watchung Ave., (GSP exit 151), Bloomfield. Call Jane 973-667-2404 (day), Jeanette 973-509-9236 (eve) or 1-877-717-3328. *Website:* http://www.njpada.org

Reformers Anonymous Faith-based group to help people find freedom from addictions: alcohol, debt, drugs, eating disorders, gambling, internet, sex/love addiction, smoking, etc. Literature, newsletter and phone help. Meets Fri., 7-9pm,

First Baptist Church, 257 Bloomfield Ave., Caldwell. Call Pastor Eli Miranda 201-724-9208 (day) or church 973-226-1004 (day).

MIDDLESEX

Debtors Anonymous 12-step. For people to share experiences and common problem of incurring debt. Our goal is to stay solvent and help other compulsive debtors achieve solvency. Meets Sun., 7pm, (beginners 6:30pm), St. Luke's Episcopal Church, Oak St. and Route 27 North, Metuchen. Call 1-877-717-3328. *Website:* http://www.njpada.org

Overcomer's Outreach Christian 12-Step. Fellowship to overcome any type of addiction or compulsive behavior, anxiety, depression and loneliness using God's word as a basis of recovery. Discussion, Bible study, prayer and phone help. Meets Thurs., 7-8:30pm, Metuchen Assembly of God, 130 Whitman St., Metuchen. Call Janet 732-388-2856 (eve) or Pat 732-321-6896.

MORRIS

Debtors Anonymous 12-Step. Program for those who wish to stop incurring debt. Meets Wed., 8pm, Saint Clare's Hospital, Powerville Rd., Boonton. Call 1-877-717-3328. *Website:* http://www.njpada.org

SMART Recovery (Self-Management And Recovery Training) Self-help group for individuals wanting to gain their independence from addictive behaviors (drugs, including alcohol and nicotine and other compulsive behaviors including gambling, eating disorders). SMART is an abstinence program based on cognitive-behavioral education and principles, especially those of rational-emotive behavior therapy. Meets Thurs., 7-8:30pm, 152 Speedwell Ave., Morristown. Call Rich 973-983-8755. *Website:* http://www.smartrecovery.org

SOMERSET

Debtors Anonymous 12-Step. Program for those who wish to stop incurring debt. Meets Tues., 7pm beginners, 7:30-8:30pm, Presbyterian Church of Basking Ridge, East Oak St., Basking Ridge. Call Diana D. 908-647-7659 (eve) or 1-877-717-3328. *Website:* http://www.njpada.org

UNION

Overcomer's Outreach Christian 12-Step. Fellowship to overcome any type of addiction or compulsive behavior, anxiety, depression or loneliness using God's word as a basis of recovery. Discussion, Bible study, prayer and phone help. Call Carmen 908-245-2788.

Cranford Meets Mon., 7pm, Harvest Training Center at Calvary Tabernacle, 69 Myrtle St.

Elizabeth Meets Tues., 7:30pm, Mount Teman AME Church, 160 Madison Ave.

Elizabeth Meets Thurs., 7:30pm, Union Baptist Church, 1088 E. Grand St.

NATIONAL

Debtors Anonymous *International. 520 groups. Founded 1976.* 12-Step. Fellowship that provides mutual help in recovering from compulsive indebtedness. Primary purpose of members is to stay solvent and help other compulsive debtors achieve solvency. Newsletter and phone support network. Offers online support and listings of local meetings. Write: DAGSB, P.O. Box 920888, Needham, MA 02492-0009. Call 781-453-2743; Fax: 781-453-2745. *Website:* http://www.debtorsanonymous.org *E-mail:* new@debtorsanonymous.org

I.C.A.P. (Intercongregational Addictions Program) *International. Founded 1979.* Network of recovering alcoholic women in religious orders. Helps Roman Catholic women who are or have been members of religious orders and are alcoholic, or chemically dependent, compulsive eaters, compulsive gamblers, etc. Information, referrals, assistance in meeting other members, phone support, conferences and e-newsletters. Write: ICAP, 7777 Lake St., Suite 115, River Forest, IL 60305-1734. Call 708-488-9770; Fax: 708-488-9774. *Website:* http://www.2icap.org *E-mail:* lclose1@core.com

Overcomers In Christ *International. Founded 1987.* Recovery program that deals with every aspect of addiction and dysfunction (spiritual, physical, mental, emotional and social). Uses Overcomers Goals which are Christ-centered. Literature, resources, information and referrals. Assistance in starting new groups. Write: Overcomers In Christ, P.O. Box 34460, Omaha, NE 68134-04604. Call 402-573-0966; Fax: 402-573-0960. *Website:* http://www.OvercomersInChrist.org *E-mail:* OIC@OvercomersInChrist.org

Overcomers Outreach, Inc. *International. 700 affiliated groups. Founded 1985.* 12-Step. Christ-centered support group for persons with any compulsive behaviors, as well as their families and friends. Uses the 12-steps of A.A. and applies them to the Scriptures. Uses Jesus Christ as "higher power." Supplements involvement in other 12-step groups. Newsletter, group development guidelines and conferences. Write: Overcomers Outreach, P.O. Box 922950, Sylmar, CA 91392-2950. Call 1-800-310-3001. *Website:* http://www.overcomersoutreach.org *E-mail:* info@overcomersoutreach.org

Recoveries Anonymous *International. 50 chapters.* Spiritual recovery group for anyone seeking a solution for any kind of addiction, problem or behavior. Family and friends welcome. "How To Begin…" guides and "Start A Group" kit can be downloaded free from the website. Write: RA, P.O. Box 1212, East Northport, NY 11731. *Website:* http://www.r-a.org *E-mail:* raus@r-a.org

Spenders Anonymous *National.* Support for those who have problems spending compulsively using the 12-step approach. Script for running a meeting is at their website. Call 651-649-4573. *Website:* http://www.spenders.org

ONLINE

Shopping Addicts Support *Online.* For people who are, or think they may be, addicted to shopping to help and support each other. For anyone who has a problem and is trying to overcome it. *Website:* http://health.groups.yahoo.com/group/shopping_addicts

DRUG ABUSE

(see also toll-free helplines)

STATEWIDE

Cocaine Anonymous 12-Step. Fellowship of men and women who share their experience, strengths and hopes that they may solve their common problem and help others to recover from addiction. Call Dominick 732-360-2999 (day) or 212-262-2463 (recording). *Website:* http://www.ca-ny.org

Families Anonymous 12-Step. Program for relatives and friends concerned about the use of drugs, alcohol or related behavioral problems. Meetings throughout NJ. Call 732-291-1467.

Lawyers Concerned for Lawyers Statewide network of independent, self-help groups that support attorneys, judges, law students and others in the legal system in recovery from alcoholism and drug dependence. Based on the 12-steps but not affiliated with A.A. Not meant to be a substitute for participation in A.A. or other fellowships. The NJ Lawyers Assistance Program performs an "intergroup function" for LCL. All services free and confidential. Write: NJLAP, NJ Law Center, One Constitution Square, New Brunswick, NJ 08901-1520. Call 1-800-246-5527 (day) or 732-937-7549 (day). *Website:* http://www.LawyersAssistance.org *E-mail:* njlap@aol.com

Nar-Anon Family Group/Narateen Provides help for family members and friends of drug abusers by offering comfort, hope and friendship through shared experiences. Meeting locations throughout New Jersey. For information call Nar-Anon Answering Service 1-800-484-7385 (security code 4257) (day/eve) or 609-587-7215. *Website:* http://www.naranonofnj.org

Narcotics Anonymous *(BILINGUAL)* 12-Step. Fellowship of men and women seeking recovery from drug addiction. The only requirement for membership is the desire to stop using drugs. Meeting locations statewide, including several bilingual groups. Write: Central and South Jersey Regional Service Conference, P.O. Box 4257, Trenton, NJ 08610; North New Jersey Regional Service Conference, P.O. Box 8229, Newark, NJ 07102. Call 1-800-992-0401 or 732-933-0462. *Website:* http://www.nanj.org

Nurse Recovery Group *Professionally-run.* Mutual support and information for nurses who are recovering from addictions. Sharing of professional concerns and encouragement. Meets in Atlantic, Bergen, Burlington, Camden, Hunterdon, Mercer, Middlesex, Monmouth, Morris, Passaic, Somerset and Union counties. Write: Peer Assistance Project, 1479 Pennington Rd., Trenton, NJ 08618. Call 800-662-0108 (day).

Professional Assistance Program of New Jersey *Professionally-run.* For physicians and other licensed professionals suffering from alcohol, chemical dependency, psychiatric or physical disabilities. Local groups are independently member-run and strictly confidential. Some are A.A. affiliated. Write: Professional Assistance Program of NJ, 742 Alexander Rd., Princeton, NJ 08540. Call Linda Pleva, Executive Assistant - Administrator 609-919-1660 (day). *E-mail:* Linda.Pleva@papnj.org

Signs of Sobriety *Professionally-run.* Provides alcoholism and drug addiction services to persons who are deaf or hard-of-hearing. Makes referrals to deaf and sign interpretered 12-step groups throughout NJ (alcohol or drug addiction, gambling, families of alcoholics, etc). Offers prevention awareness, education classes, SoberCamp-annual summer retreat and Sober/Deaf activities for deaf or hard of hearing individuals in recovery. Newsletter. Write: SOS, 100 Scotch Rd., 2nd Floor, Ewing, NJ 08628. Call TTY: 1-800-332-7677; Voice: 609-882-7677 (day); Fax: 609-882-6808. *Website:* http://www.signsofsobriety.org *E-mail:* info@signsofsobriety.org

ATLANTIC

Addictions Victorious of South Jersey, Inc. 12-Step. Christ-centered support group for men and women who in their struggle with substance abuse and emotional problems come together that they may solve their problems and help others as well. Guest speakers, rap sessions, phone help, literature and newsletter. Optional donation. *Website:* http://www.addvicinc.org

Egg Harbor City Meets Thurs., 7:30pm, Christ's Wesleyan Church, 800 Philadelphia Ave. Call Mark 609-457-3260 or 609-965-8056 and Church 609-965-5835.

Mays Landing Meets Tues., 7:30pm, Light of the World Church, 111 Route 50. Call Bob 609-457-0186 or Pastor George Sanders 609-517-3776.

Dual Recovery Anonymous *Professionally-run.* 12-Step. Mutual support for alcoholics or drug abusers with psychiatric disorders. Meets Thurs., 1:30-2:30pm, C.O.D.I. Building, 901 Atlantic Ave., Egg Harbor City. Call Suzanne 609-965-6871 (day).

Lawyers Concerned for Lawyers Self-help group that supports recovery from alcoholism and drug dependence for attorneys, judges, law students and others in the legal system. Based on the 12-step program adapted from A.A. All inquiries are confidential. Meets Wed., 5:30pm, 1555 Zion Rd., Suite 201, Northfield. Call John 609-641-2266 (day) or NJ Lawyers Assistance Program 1-800-246-5527. *Website:* http://www.njlap.org *E-mail:* njlap@aol.com

Nar-Anon Family Group Provides help for family members and friends of drug abusers by offering comfort, hope and friendship through shared experiences. Meeting locations throughout New Jersey. For information call Nar-Anon Answering Service 1-800-484-7385 (security code 4257) (day/eve) or 609-587-7215. *Website:* http://www.naranonofnj.org

Narcotics Anonymous 12-Step. Fellowship of men and women seeking recovery from drug addiction. The only requirement for membership is the desire to stop using drugs. Call 1-800-992-0401 or 732-933-0462. *Website:* http://www.nanj.org

Nurse Recovery Group *Professionally-run.* Mutual support and information for nurses who are recovering from addictions. Sharing of professional concerns and encouragement. Meets in Pomona. Call 1-800-662-0108 (day).

BERGEN

CARE (Christians, Addictions, Recovery and Education) 12-Step. Support ministry for substance abusers and their families to help our brothers and sisters find sobriety, solace and a way to a comfortable non-judgmental Christian walk. Meets Mon., 7:30pm, Church of the Nazarene, 285 East Midland Ave., Paramus. Call 201-262-3323 (9:30am-4pm). *Website:* http://www.maranathanj.org

Double Jeopardy Peer Support Group *Professionally-run.* Emotional support and information for men and women who have HIV/HCV and substance abuse issues. Meets Thurs., 6:30-8pm, Buddies of New Jersey, 149 Hudson St., Hackensack. Call Susan 201-489-2900 (10am-6pm).

Families Anonymous 12-Step. For relatives and friends concerned about the use of drugs or related behavioral problems. *Website:* http://www.familiesanonymous.org

Englewood Meets Fri., 7:30pm, Englewood Hospital, Learning Center, Main Floor, 350 Engle St. Call Jesse 201-944-0256.

Mahwah Meets Wed., 7:30-8:30pm, Church of the Immaculate Conception, 900 Darlington Ave. Call Richard or Barbara 201-327-0748. *E-mail:* famahwah@verizon.net

Tenafly Meets Tues., 7:30pm, Trinity Lutheran Church, 430 Knickerbocker Rd. Call Judy or Gene 201-262-7758 (day) or Jesse 201-944-0256.

JACS (Jewish Alcoholics, Chemically Dependent Persons and Significant Others) Follows 12-step program. Mutual support for all Jews in recovery and their family members. Meets 2nd and 4th Wed., 7:30pm, Jewish Family Service of Bergen County, 1485 Teaneck Rd., Teaneck. Call 201-837-9090 (day).

Nar-Anon Family Group 12-Step. Provides help for family members and friends of drug abusers by offering comfort, hope and friendship through shared experiences. Call Nar-Anon Answering Service 1-800-484-7385 (security code 4257) (day/eve) or 609-587-7215. *Website:* http://www.naranonofnj.org

Narcotics Anonymous 12-Step. Fellowship of men and women seeking recovery from drug addiction. The only requirement for membership is the desire to stop using drugs. Call 1-800-992-0401 or 732-933-0462. *Website:* http://www.nanj.org

Nurse Recovery Group *Professionally-run.* Mutual support and information for nurses who are recovering from addictions. Sharing of professional concerns and encouragement. Meets in Teaneck. Call 1-800-662-0108 (day).

Parent Support Group - New Jersey, Inc. *Professionally-run.* Confidential support group for parents of chemically dependent children (ages 13-40+). Meets Mon., 6:30pm, Behavioral Health Center, Room E 222, Bergen Pines Hospital, Paramus. Call Karol Sullivan or Adrienne Mellana 1-800-561-4299 or 973-736-3344 (day). *Website:* http://www.psgnjhomestead.com

Psychiatrically Recovering Alcoholics 12-Step. Mutual support for psychiatrically recovering alcoholics who suffer from emotional and mental disorders to share experience, strength and hope while recovering from alcoholism and psychiatric disorders. Meets Tues., 7-8pm, Bethany Presbyterian Church, Palisade Ave. and William St., Englewood. Call Ed 201-541-8452 (day/eve).

Seniors Count *Professionally-run.* 12-Step. Support for persons (age 60+) recovering from substance abuse or co-dependency. Meets Fri., 1:30-3pm, Presbyterian Church, 150 East Palisades Ave., 2nd Floor, Englewood. Call Anne Wennhold 201-569-6667. *Website:* http://www.vanostinstitute.org *E-mail:* vanost@msn.com

Women For Sobriety Self-help designed specifically to help women with addictions achieve sobriety. Helps develop self-esteem and coping skills. Donation $2. Meets Tues., noon-1pm and Thurs., 7-8:30pm, (new members 6:45pm), YWCA, 112 Oak St., Ridgewood. Call 201-487-2224 (day) or Nina Wegener 201-612-0511, LCSW (day).

BURLINGTON

Addictions Victorious of South Jersey, Inc. 12-Step. Christ-centered support group for men and women who, in their struggle with substance abuse and emotional problems, come together that they may solve their problems and help others as well. Guest speakers, rap sessions, phone help, literature and newsletter. Optional donation. *Website:* http://www.addvicinc.org

Burlington Meets Tues., 7pm, Burlington Center Mall Ministries, Route 541. Call Scott or Lisa 609-953-1380.

Lumberton Meets Thurs., 7pm, Lighthouse Tabernacle, 716 Main St. Call Harry or Ronnie 609-267-2657.

Double Trouble Mutual support for persons with a substance abuse problem who are also taking medication for psychiatric problems. Meets Sun., Mon., and Wed., 8:30pm, Hampton Hospital, 650 Rancocas Rd., Cafeteria, Westampton. Call Pam Sachs 609-267-7000 (day).

Families Who Are Hurting Mutual support and encouragement for families who are hurting due to an addiction of a loved one, loss of a spouse or for those caring for a loved one with dementia. Meets 1st Sat., 6pm, Rose of Sharon Lutheran Church, Route 528, Jacobstown. Call Bill Millet 609-758-2746.

Nar-Anon Family Group 12-Step. Help for families and friends of drug abusers by offering comfort, hope and friendship through shared experiences. For meeting information call Nar-Anon Answering Service 1-800-484-7385 (security code 4257) or 609-587-7215. *Website:* http://www.naranonofnj.org

Narcotics Anonymous 12-Step. Fellowship of men and women seeking recovery from drug addiction. The only requirement for membership is the desire to stop using drugs. Several meeting locations throughout the county. For meeting information call 1-800-992-0401 or 732-933-0462. *Website:* http://www.nanj.org

Nurse Recovery Group *Professionally-run.* Mutual support and information for nurses who are recovering from addictions. Sharing of professional concerns and encouragement. Meets in Moorestown. Call 1-800-662-0108 (day).

Overcomers 12-Step. Christian-focused recovery group for anyone suffering from any type of addiction, dependency or compulsive disorder. Meets Thurs., 7:30-9pm, Fellowship Alliance Chapel, 199 Church Rd., Medford. Call 609-953-7333 (day).

Rap Room Parent-to-Parent Coalition *Professionally-run.* Support and education for parents of teens and young adult children dealing with substance/alcohol addictions. Mutual sharing, advocacy, guest speakers, crisis intervention and referrals. Meets 1st Tues., 7-9pm, Greentree Executive Campus,

1003A Lincoln Drive West, Marlton. Call Louise 856-983-3328. *Website:* http://www.raproom.org

CAMDEN

Addictions Victorious of South Jersey, Inc. 12-Step. Christ-centered support group for men and women who in their struggle with substance abuse and emotional problems come together that they may solve their problems and help others as well. Guest speakers, rap sessions, phone help, literature and newsletter. Optional donation. *Website:* http://www.addvicinc.org

Barrington Meets Mon., 7pm, Grace Bible Church, 887 Clements Bridge Rd. Call Ginny 856-232-0207.

Camden Meets Tues., 6pm, Fellowship House, 1722 South Broadway. Call Lucy 856-964-4545.

Lindenwold Meets Mon., 7pm, Garden Lake Bible Church, 63 First Ave. Call Pastor Dave 856-783-3802 or 856-357-4194.

Sicklerville Meets Fri, 6pm, Christ Care Unit Missionary Baptist Church, Sicklerville Rd. Call Quinton and Pricilla 856-262-1833 or Murphy 856-875-1145.

Somerdale Meets Thurs., 8pm, Park Avenue Community Church, 431 Hilltop Ave. Call Colleen 856-435-0309.

Camden County Parent-to-Parent Mutual support for parents of children (any age) who have alcohol or drug related problems. Guest speakers, literature and phone help. Meets 2nd and 4th Tues., 6:30-8:30pm, Bellmawr Library, 35 E. Browning Rd., Bellmawr. Call Kathleen Dobbs 856-968-2301 (day).

Dual Recovery Anonymous (DRA) 12-Step. Mutual support for alcoholics/addicts who are taking medication for psychiatric problems. Meets Wed., 6-7pm, MICA Club, 498 Marlboro Ave., Cherry Hill. Call 856-662-0955.

Lawyers Concerned for Lawyers (LCL) Self-help group that supports recovery from alcoholism and drug dependence for attorneys, judges, law students and others in the legal system. Based on the 12-step program adapted from A.A. All inquiries are confidential. Meets 1st and 3rd Wed., 6pm, Steininger Center, Board Room, 19 East Ormond Ave., Cherry Hill. Call John 609-261-3841 (day) or NJ Lawyers Assistance Program 1-800-246-5527. *Website:* http://www.njlap.org *E-mail:* njlap@aol.com

Nar-Anon Family Group 12-Step. Provides help for family members and friends of drug abusers by offering comfort, hope and friendship through shared experiences. Call Nar-Anon Answering Service 1-800-484-7385 (security code 4257) (day/eve) or 609-587-7215. *Website:* http://www.naranonofnj.org

Narcotics Anonymous 12-Step. Fellowship of men and women seeking recovery from drug addiction. The only requirement for membership is the desire to stop using drugs. Call 1-800-992-0401 or 732-933-0462. *Website:* http://www.nanj.org

Nurse Recovery Group *Professionally-run.* Mutual support and information for nurses who are recovering from addictions. Sharing of professional concerns and encouragement. Meets in Haddonfield. Call 1-800-662-0108 (day).

Victoria sobre Addicciones *(SPANISH)* 12-Step. Christ-centered support group for men and women who, in their struggle with substance abuse and emotional problems, come together that they may solve their problems and help others as well. Guest speakers, rap sessions, phone help, literature and newsletter. Optional donation. Meets Tues., 6pm, Fellowship House, 1722 S. Broadway, Camden. Call Lucy 856-964-4545. *Website:* http://www.addvicinc.org

CAPE MAY

Addictions Victorious of South Jersey, Inc. 12-Step. Christ-centered support group for men and women who in their struggle with substance abuse and emotional problems come together that they may solve their problems and help others as well. Guest speakers, rap sessions, phone help, literature and newsletter. Optional donation. Meets Mon., 7pm, Seashore Community Church of Nazarene, 446 Seashore Rd., Cape May. Call Phil 609-408-1191, Marty 609-827-1517 or Church 609-886-6196. *Website:* http://www.addvicinc.org

Cocaine Anonymous 12-Step. Fellowship of men and women who share their experience, strengths and hopes that they may solve their common problem and help others to recover from addiction. Rap sessions, guest speakers and literature. Meets Sun., 7-8pm, McKeon Hall, 1224 Bayshore Rd. and Washington Ave., Villas. Call Stuart 609-807-0129 (eve).

Nar-Anon Family Group 12-Step. Provides help for family members and friends of drug abusers by offering comfort, hope and friendship through shared experiences. Call Nar-Anon Answering Service 1-800-484-7385 (security code 4257) (day/eve) or 609-587-7215. *Website:* http://www.naranonofnj.org

Narcotics Anonymous 12-Step. Fellowship of men and women seeking recovery from drug addiction. The only requirement for membership is the desire to stop using drugs. Call 1-800-992-0401 or 732-933-0462. *Website:* http://www.nanj.org

CUMBERLAND

Double Trouble in Recovery 12-Step. Assists consumers who suffer a severe and persistent mental illness to work on their recovery from addiction to substances. Meets Tues., 1-3pm, Special Needs Adult Partial Care Program, Cumberland County Guidance Center, 2038 Carmel Rd., Millville. Call Mary or Lorraine 856-825-6810.

Nar-Anon Family Group 12-Step. Provides help for family members and friends of drug abusers by offering comfort, hope and friendship through shared experiences. Call Nar-Anon Answering Service 1-800-484-7385 (security code 4257) (day/eve) or 609-587-7215. *Website:* http://www.naranonofnj.org

Narcotics Anonymous 12-Step. Fellowship of men and women seeking recovery from drug addiction. The only requirement for membership is the desire to stop using drugs. Call 1-800-992-0401 or 732-933-0462. *Website:* http://www.nanj.org

Overcomer's Outreach *(Shiloh Faith Meeting)* Christian 12-Step. Fellowship to overcome any type of addiction or compulsive behavior, anxiety, depression or loneliness using God's word as a basis of recovery. Discussion, Bible study, prayer and phone help. Meets Thurs., 7-8pm, Shiloh Seventh Day Baptist Church, East Ave., Shiloh. Call Rev. Chrowiger 856-455-0488 (day) or Frank B. Mulford 856-451-8698 (day).E-mail: ahfarm@hotmail.com

ESSEX

BASA/Brothers and Sisters of Siblings *Professionally-run.* Confidential support group for siblings with a chemically dependent sibling. Meets 2nd and 4th Wed., 7pm, St. Cloud Presbyterian Church, Old Indian Rd. and Ridgeway Ave., West Orange. Call Karol Sullivan or Adrienne Mellana 973-736-3344 (day) or 1-800-561-3299. *Website:* http://www.psgnjhomestead.com *E-mail:* psgnj1@aol.com

Double Trouble *Professionally-run.* Support for HIV+ persons who are also substance abusers. Meets Wed., noon-2pm, North Jersey Community Research Initiative, 393 Central Ave., 2nd Floor, Newark. Call 973-483-3444. *Website:* http://www.njcri.org

Families Anonymous 12-Step. Support for families and friends concerned about the use of drugs or related behavioral problems. Sharing of experiences, strengths and hopes. Meets Wed., 7:30pm, First Episcopal Church of the Holy Spirit, 36 Gould St., Verona. Call Jim 973-338-6952 or Roxy 973-667-1067 (day).

Lawyers Concerned for Lawyers (LCL) Self-help group that supports recovery from alcoholism and drug dependence for attorneys, judges, law students and others in the legal system. Based on the 12-step program adapted from A.A. All inquiries are confidential. Meets Tues., 7:30pm, United Way Bldg., Room 211A, 60 S. Fullerton Ave., Montclair. Call Kenneth 973-429-5588 (day) or 973-509-6062 (eve) or NJLAP 1-800-246-5527. *Website:* http://www.njlap.org *E-mail:* njlap@aol.com

Nar-Anon Family Group 12-Step. Provides help for family members and friends of drug abusers by offering comfort, hope and friendship through shared experiences. Call Nar-Anon Answering Service 1-800-484-7385 (security code 4257) (day/eve) or 609-587-7215. *Website:* http://www.naranonofnj.org

Narcotics Anonymous 12-Step. Fellowship of men and women seeking recovery from drug addiction. The only requirement for membership is the desire to stop using drugs. Call 1-800-992-0401 or 732-933-0462. *Website:* http://www.nanj.org

Parents Support Group - New Jersey Inc. *Professionally-run.* Confidential support group for parents of a chemically dependent child (ages 13-40+). Meets Wed., 6pm, and Thurs., 6:30pm, St. Cloud Presbyterian Church, Old Indian Rd. and Ridgeway Ave., West Orange. Call Karol Sullivan 973-736-3344 (9am-3pm) or 1-800-561-4299 (24 hr. hotline).

Reformers Anonymous Faith-based group to help people find freedom from addictions: alcohol, debt, drugs, eating disorders, gambling, internet, sex/love addiction, smoking, etc. Literature, newsletter and phone help. Meets Fri., 7-9pm, First Baptist Church, 257 Bloomfield Ave., Caldwell. Call Pastor Eli Miranda 201-724-9208 (day) or church 973-226-1004 (day).

GLOUCESTER

Addictions Victorious of South Jersey, Inc. 12-Step. Christ-centered support group for men and women who in their struggle with substance abuse and emotional problems come together that they may solve their problems and help others as well. Guest speakers, rap sessions, phone help, literature and newsletter. Optional donation. *Website:* http://www.addvicinc.org

Glassboro Meets Tues., 7pm, Olivet Wesleyan Church, 711 Heston Rd. Call Chip 856-881-8241.
Pitman Meets Mon. and Thurs., 7:30pm, The Rock Church, 205 Esplanade Ave. Call Laura 856-582-2277.

Gloucester County Parent To Parent Coalition *(WASHINGTON RESIDENTS ONLY) Professionally-run.* Confidential meetings and focus on providing parents with support, information, resources, and referrals for dealing with substance abuse and related problems. Guest speakers, educational series and literature. Meets 2nd and 4th Mon., 7:30-9:30pm, Washington Township Municipal Building, 523 Egg Harbor Rd., Meeting Room C, Washington Township. Call 856-589-6446 (day).

Nar-Anon Family Group 12-Step. Provides help for family members and friends of drug abusers by offering comfort, hope and friendship through shared experiences. Call Nar-Anon Answering Service 1-800-484-7385 (security code 4257) (day/eve) or 609-587-7215. *Website:* http://www.naranonofnj.org

Narcotics Anonymous 12-Step. Fellowship of men and women seeking recovery from drug addiction. The only requirement for membership is the desire to stop using drugs. Call 1-800-992-0401 or 732-933-0462. *Website:* http://www.nanj.org

Parent Support Group *(WASHINGTON TOWNSHIP RESIDENTS ONLY)* Parent-to-parent support group for parents and concerned adults who have children in alcohol/drug recovery or are currently abusing substances. Meets 2nd and 4th Mon., 7:30pm, Washington Township Municipal Building, Meeting Room C, Washington Township. Call 856-589-6446.

"Teens Only" Recovery Group *Professionally-run.* Support for teens (ages 13-20) in recovery from drugs and alcohol. Meets Thurs., 7-8:30pm, Washington Township Municipal Building, 523 Egg Harbor Rd., Washington Township. Call Donna Rullo 856-589-6446 (day). Website: wtfcs@twp.washington.nj.us

HUDSON

Nar-Anon Family Group 12-Step. Provides help for family members and friends of drug abusers by offering comfort, hope and friendship through shared experiences. Call Nar-Anon Answering Service 1-800-484-7385 (security code 4257) (day/eve) or 609-587-7215. *Website:* http://www.naranonofnj.org

Narcotics Anonymous 12-Step. Fellowship of men and women seeking recovery from drug addiction. The only requirement for membership is the desire to stop using drugs. Call 1-800-992-0401 or 732-933-0462. *Website:* http://www.nanj.org

HUNTERDON

Nar-Anon Family Group 12-Step. Provides help for family members and friends of drug abusers by offering comfort, hope and friendship through shared experiences. Call Nar-Anon Answering Service 1-800-484-7385 (security code 4257) (day/eve) or 609-587-7215. *Website:* http://www.naranonofnj.org

Narcotics Anonymous 12-Step. Fellowship of men and women seeking recovery from drug addiction. The only requirement for membership is the desire to stop using drugs. Call 732-933-0462. *Website:* http://www.nanj.org

Nurse Recovery Group *Professionally-run.* Mutual support and information for nurses who are recovering from addictions. Sharing of professional concerns and encouragement. Meets in Flemington. Call 1-800-662-0108 (day).

Overcomers In Christ Recovery program that deals with every aspect of addiction and dysfunction (spiritual, physical, mental, emotional and social). Uses Overcomers goals which are Christ-centered. Resources, information and referrals. Guest speakers, literature and phone help. Meets Fri., 7:30-9pm, Church of the Nazarene, 80 Beaver Ave., Annandale. Call Mary & Ed Powers 908-638-6166 (day/eve) or Patti Willsey 908-238-0358 (day/eve).

MERCER

Families Anonymous 12-Step. Program for families, especially parents of those with substance abuse or other disruptive, behavioral problems. Meets Mon., 7:30pm, St. Lawrence Rehabilitation Center, 2381 Lawrenceville Rd. (Route 206 S.), Lawrenceville. Call Joan 609-883-1403 (eve). *Website:* familiesanonymous.org *E-mail:* joan@brra.com

Nar-Anon Family Group 12-Step. Provides help for family members and friends of drug abusers by offering comfort, hope and friendship through shared experiences. Call Nar-Anon Answering Service 1-800-484-7385 (security code 4257) (day/eve) or 609-587-7215. *Website:* http://www.naranonofnj.org

Narcotics Anonymous 12-Step. Fellowship of men and women seeking recovery from drug addiction. The only requirement for membership is the desire to stop using drugs. Call 1-800-992-0401 or 732-933-0462. *Website:* http://www.nanj.org

Nurse Recovery Group *Professionally-run.* Mutual support and information for nurses who are recovering from addictions. Sharing of professional concerns and encouragement. Meets in Trenton. Call 1-800-662-0108 (day).

MIDDLESEX

Double Trouble Mutual support for alcoholics or drug addicts who are taking medication for psychiatric problems. Optional donation. Meets Thurs., 7:30pm, UMDNJ - The Club, 189 New St., Room B, New Brunswick. Call Tim 732-235-6900 (day).

Double Trouble Meeting 12-Step. Support for those who are recovering from both a mental illness and substance abuse. Guest speakers. Meets Mon., 7-8pm, Oak Tree Presbyterian Church, 445 Plainfield Rd., Edison. Call Michelle Gorman 732-321-0191 (day). *E-mail:* mgorman@voa-gny.org

Lawyers Concerned for Lawyers (LCL) Self-help group that supports recovery from alcoholism and drug dependence for attorneys, judges, law students and others in the legal system. Based on the 12-step program adapted from A.A. All inquiries are confidential. Meets one Sat. per month (by invitation only), New Brunswick. Call Denise at NJLAP 732-937-7541 or 1-800-246-5527 (day). *Website:* http://www.njlap.org *E-mail:* denise@njlap.org

Nar-Anon Family Group 12-Step. Provides help for family members and friends of drug abusers by offering comfort, hope and friendship through shared experiences. Call Nar-Anon Answering Service 1-800-484-7385 (security code 4257) (day/eve) or 609-587-7215. *Website:* http://www.naranonofnj.org

Narcotics Anonymous 12-Step. Fellowship of men and women seeking recovery from drug addiction. The only requirement for membership is the desire to stop using drugs. Call 1-800-992-0401 or 732-933-0462. *Website:* http://www.nanj.org

Nurse Recovery Group *Professionally-run.* Mutual support and information for nurses who are recovering from addictions. Sharing of professional concerns and encouragement. Meets in Woodbridge. Call 1-800-662-0108 (day).

Overcomer's Outreach Christian 12-Step. Fellowship to overcome any type of addiction or compulsive behavior, anxiety, depression and loneliness using God's word as a basis of recovery. Discussion, Bible study, prayer and phone help. Meets Thurs., 7-8:30pm, Metuchen Assembly of God, 130 Whitman St., Metuchen. Call Janet 732-388-2856 (eve) or Pat 732-321-6896.

Parent Support Group - New Jersey, Inc. Confidential support group for parents of chemically dependent children (ages 13-40+). Meets Thurs., 7pm, St. Peter's Episcopal Church, 505 Main St., Spotswood. Call Linda Leck, Karol Sullivan, or Adrienne Mellana 1-800-561-4299 or 973-736-3344 (day). *Website:* http://www.psgnjhomestead.com *E-mail:* psgnj1@aol.com

SMART Recovery (Self-Management And Recovery Training) *Professionally-run.* Self-help group for individuals wanting to gain their independence from addictive behaviors (drugs, including alcohol and nicotine, and other compulsive behaviors i.e. gambling, eating disorders). SMART is an abstinence program based on cognitive-behavioral education and principles, especially those of rational-emotive behavior therapy. Meets Mon., 6-7:30pm, Rutgers University, Busch Campus, Psychology Building, Room A224, Piscataway. Call Tom Morgan 732-445-0902. *Website:* http://www.smartrecovery.org

MONMOUTH

Cocaine Anonymous 12-Step. Fellowship of men and women who share their experience, strengths and hopes that they may solve their common problem and help others to recover from addiction. Meets Fri., 8:30-9:30pm, Clubhouse, 32 Throckmorton St., Freehold. Call Phil W. 732-580-1588 (day).

Double Trouble Dual Recovery 12-Step. Support for those who have an emotional/psychiatric illness and are alcohol/chemically addicted. Meets Mon. and Thurs., 10:15-11am, Park Place Program, 1011 Bond St., Asbury Park. Call Mark 732-869-2781 (day) or Mike Rafter 732-869-2765 (day). *E-mail:* msullivan@meridianhealth.com

Dual Recovery Mutual support for alcoholics or drug abusers who are taking medication for psychiatric problems. Transportation available. Meets Tues., 7pm, Freehold Self-Help Center, 17 Bannard St., Freehold. Call Vernetta 732-502-4614 or George 732-502-5848 (day).

Dual Recovery Anonymous 12-Step. Professionally co-facilitated. Mutual support for any person recovering from mental illness and substance abuse. Meets Tues.

and Fri., 10:30-11:30am, CPC/Aberdeen Counseling Center, 1088 Highway 34, Aberdeen. Call Mark 732-290-1700 ext. 5307 (day).

Families Anonymous 12-Step. Fellowship of families and friends concerned about the use of drugs, alcohol and/or related behavioral problems.

Holmdel Meets Mon., 7:30pm, Bayshore Community Hospital, 723 North Beers St. Call Mary Lou 732-583-2238 (eve) or Nancy 732-264-5948 (6-8pm).

Leonardo Meets Mon., 7:30pm, Middletown Township Complex, Leonardville Rd. Call 732-291-1467 (eve).

Ocean Grove Meets Mon., 7:30pm, St. Paul's United Methodist Church, 80 Embury Ave. Call Diana 732-988-3903.

Red Bank Meets Thurs., 7:30-9pm, United Methodist Church, 247 Broad St. Call 732-462-7707 (day). *E-mail:* higley@optonline.net

Mission Possible *(WOMEN ONLY) Professionally-run.* 12-Step. Christ-centered support group for women dealing with alcohol and substance abuse issues. Families and friends welcome. Phone help. Meets 2nd and 4th Tues., 7:30-9pm, Family Life Center, 4041 Squankum Rd., Room 6, Allenwood. Call Minister Donna Ridge 732-938-4353 ext. 230.

Nar-Anon Family Group Provides help for family members and friends of drug abusers by offering comfort, hope and friendship through shared experiences. Meeting locations throughout New Jersey. For information call Nar-Anon Answering Service 1-800-484-7385 (security code 4257) (day/eve) or 609-587-7215. *Website:* http://www.naranonofnj.org

Narcotics Anonymous 12-Step. Fellowship of men and women seeking recovery from drug addiction. The only requirement for membership is the desire to stop using drugs. Call 1-800-992-0401 or 732-933-0462. *Website:* http://www.nanj.org

Nurse Recovery Group *Professionally-run.* Mutual support and information for nurses who are recovering from addictions. Sharing of professional concerns and encouragement. Meets in Red Bank and Neptune. Call 1-800-662-0108 (day).

Parent Support Group - New Jersey, Inc. Confidential support group for parents of chemically dependent children (ages 13-40+). Meets Tues., 7pm, Church of the Nativity, 180 Ridge Rd., Fair Haven. Call Karol Sullivan or Adrienne Mellana 1-800-561-4299 or 973-736-3344 (day). *Website:* http://www.psgnjhomestead.com *E-mail:* psgnj1@aol.com

T.M.E.W. (The Most Excellent Way) Christian alternative to chemical dependency. Principles of recovery are based upon God's words. Open to anyone desiring freedom from addictive and compulsive behavior. For local meeting information call Frank 732-741-0048, Mike C. 917-304-9074, Frank C. 732-842-4749 or Jack C. 732-741-7807. *Website:* www.mostexcellentway.com

MORRIS

Alcohol and Drug Family Education *Professionally-run.* Support for families facing the chemical dependency of a family member. Deals with co-dependency issues. Meets Thurs., 6:30-8pm, Morristown Memorial Hospital, Outpatient Behavioral Health, Morristown. Pre-registration required. Call 1-888-247-1400.

Dual Recovery Anonymous Mutual support for alcoholics or drug addicts with psychiatric disorders.

Boonton Meets Tues., noon-1pm, MICA Group Room; Fri., noon-1pm, IOP Room and Sun., noon-1pm, Executive Dining Room, Saint Clares Hospital. Call Nikki R. 973-664-0596.

Denville Meets Wed., noon-1pm, St. Clare's Behavioral Health Center, 50 Morris Ave., Auditorium. Call Jacqueline Felczak 973-316-1867.

Families Anonymous 12-Step. Mutual support for parents, relatives and friends of persons with drug or alcohol problems. Peer-counseling. Meets Tues., 7:30-9pm, First Presbyterian Church, 35 Church St., Rockaway. Call 973-586-2440 (eve).

Lawyers Concerned for Lawyers (LCL) Self-help group that supports recovery from alcoholism and drug dependence for attorneys, judges, law students and others in the legal system. Based on the 12-step program adapted from A.A. All inquiries are confidential. Meets Wed., 7:30pm, Center for Behavioral Health, 95 Mt. Kemble Ave., Morristown. Call Albert 973-538-0280 (day/eve) or NJ Lawyers Assistance Program 1-800-246-5527. *Website:* http://www.njlap.org *E-mail:* njlap@aol.com

Nar-Anon Family Group 12-Step. Provides help for family members and friends of drug abusers by offering comfort, hope and friendship through shared experiences. Call Nar-Anon Answering Service 1-800-484-7385 (security code 4257) (day/eve) or 609-587-7215. *Website:* http://www.naranonofnj.org

Narcotics Anonymous 12-Step. Fellowship of men and women seeking recovery from drug addiction. The only requirement for membership is the desire to stop using drugs. Call 1-800-992-0401 or 732-933-0462. *Website:* http://www.nanj.org

Narcotics Anonymous for MICA Patients Narcotics Anonymous meeting for those who also have a mental illness. Meets Thurs., 7:30pm, New Views, Greystone Park Hospital, Main Building, 1st Floor, North Tier, Morris Plains. Call Tom Wicks 973-292-4015 (9-4pm). *E-mail:* newviews@nac.net

Nurse Recovery Group *Professionally-run.* Mutual support and information for nurses who are recovering from addictions. Sharing of professional concerns and encouragement. Meets in Boonton. Call 1-800-662-0108 (day).

Psychiatrically Recovering 12-Step. Mutual support for psychiatrically recovering people who wish to refrain from using alcohol or drugs, abusing food or any other compulsive behavior. Call Richie S. 973-865-4851 (day/eve).

Cedar Knolls Meets Mon. and Thurs., 10am, Saint Clare's Behavioral Health Center, 100 East Hanover Ave., Group Room, First Floor.

Denville Meets Mon., 1pm, Saint Clare's Behavioral Health Center, 50 Morris Ave., Room B-1.

Pompton Plains Meets Fri., 11am, New Bridge, 640 Newark-Pompton Turnpike.

SMART Recovery (Self-Management And Recovery Training) Self-help group for individuals wanting to gain their independence from addictive behaviors (drugs, including alcohol and nicotine and other compulsive behaviors i.e. gambling, eating disorders). SMART is an abstinence program based on cognitive-behavioral education and principles, especially those of rational-emotive behavior therapy. Meets Thurs., 7-8:30pm, 152 Speedwell Ave., Morristown. Call Rich 973-983-8755. *Website:* http://www.smartrecovery.org

OCEAN

Checkpoint Support to help overcome dependencies and addictions through accountability, encouragement and spiritual development. Meets Thurs., 7-8:30pm, Shore Vineyard Church, 320 Compass Ave., Beachwood. Call 732-244-3888 (day).

Double Trouble 12 Step. Fellowship offering mutual support for persons with a substance abuse problem who are also taking medication for psychiatric problems.

Bayville Meets Mon., 6-7pm, Ocean Mental Health Services, 160 Route 9. Call Matt Mantone 732-349-5550 ext. 139 (day).

Bayville Meets Fri., 7:30-8:30pm, Ocean Mental Health Services, 160 Route 9. Call Bill Bradley, Meg Stenson or JoAnn Bonnett 732-905-1132 (day).

Double Trouble in Recovery Support and encouragement for those who are chemically addicted and also in recovery from a psychiatric illness. Meets Wed., 7:30-8:30pm, Brighter Days Center, S & F Plaza, 2008 Route 37 East, Suite 6, Toms River. Call Tina Riccelli 732-270-6061 (day).

Families Anonymous 12-Step. For relatives and friends concerned about the use of drugs or related behavioral problems. Meets Tues., 7:30pm, St. Andrews United Methodist Church, 1528 Church Rd., Toms River. Call 732-864-0548. *E-mail:* FamAnonTR@Comcast.net

Lawyers Concerned for Lawyers (LCL) Self-help group that supports recovery from alcoholism and drug dependence for attorneys, judges, law students and others in the legal system. Based on the 12-step program adapted from A.A. All inquiries are confidential. Meets Tues., 7:15pm, St. Mary's By The Sea, 804 Bay Ave., Meeting Room, Point Pleasant. Call Fred 732-785-6314 (pager number; day) or NJ Lawyers Assistance Program 1-800-246-5527. *Website:* http://www.njlap.org *E-mail:* njlap@aol.com

Nar-Anon Family Group 12-Step. Provides help for family members and friends of drug abusers by offering comfort, hope and friendship through shared experiences. Call Nar-Anon Answering Service 1-800-484-7385 (security code 4257) (day/eve) or 609-587-7215. *Website:* http://www.naranonofnj.org

Narcotics Anonymous 12-Step. Fellowship of men and women seeking recovery from drug addiction. The only requirement for membership is the desire to stop using drugs. Call 1-800-992-0401 or 732-933-0462. *Website:* http://www.nanj.org

Overcomers In Christ Recovery program that deals with every aspect of addiction and dysfunction (spiritual, physical, mental, emotional and social). Uses Overcomers goals which are Christ-centered. Literature, resources, information and referrals. Meets Mon., 7pm, America's Keswick, 601 Route 530, Whiting. Separate group for men and women. For women's group call Diane Hunt 732-350-1187 ext. 47. For men's group call Pastor Mike 732-350-1187 ext. 39. *Website:* http://www.americaskeswick.org

Parent Support Group - New Jersey, Inc. Confidential support group for parents of chemically dependent children (ages 13-40+). Meets Mon., 7pm, Presbyterian Church of Toms River, 1070 Hooper Ave., Toms River. Call Karol Sullivan or Adrienne Mellana 1-800-561-4299 or 973-736-3344 (day). *Website:* http://www.psgnjhomestead.com *E-mail:* psgnj1@aol.com

Parents Group, Inc., The Mutual support and referrals for parents in crisis due to their teenage or adult children's chemical/alcohol addiction. Works with, and outreaches to, community resources for prevention, awareness and intervention. Meets Tues., 7-9pm, Toms River. Call Mary and Michael Holland 732-929-4443. *E-mail:* starfishpg@aol.com

PASSAIC

Nar-Anon Family Group 12-Step. Provides help for family members and friends of drug abusers by offering comfort, hope and friendship through shared experiences. Call Nar-Anon Answering Service 1-800-484-7385 (security code 4257) (day/eve) or 609-587-7215. *Website:* http://www.naranonofnj.org

Narcotics Anonymous 12-Step. Fellowship of men and women seeking recovery from drug addiction. The only requirement for membership is the desire to stop using drugs. Call 1-800-992-0401 or 732-933-0462. *Website:* http://www.nanj.org

Nurse Recovery Group *Professionally-run.* Mutual support and information for nurses who are recovering from addictions. Sharing of professional concerns and encouragement. Meets in Passaic. Call 1-800-662-0108 (day).

Parent Support Group - New Jersey, Inc. Confidential support group for parents of chemically dependent children (ages 13-40+). Meets Mon., 6:30pm, St. Joseph's Hospital, 6th Floor, Room 6B, 224 Hamburg Turnpike, Wayne. Call Karol Sullivan or Adrienne Mellana 1-800-561-4299 or 973-736-3344 (day). *Website:* http://www.psgnjhomestead.com *E-mail:* psgnj1@aol.com

Psychiatrically Recovering 12-Step. Mutual support for psychiatrically recovering people who wish to refrain from using alcohol or drugs, abusing food, or any other compulsive behavior. Meets Fri., 9:45am, New Bridge: Visions, 22 Riverview Dr., Wayne. Call Richie S. 973-865-4851 (day/eve).

SALEM

Nar-Anon Family Group 12-Step. Provides help for family members and friends of drug abusers by offering comfort, hope and friendship through shared experiences. Call Nar-Anon Answering Service 1-800-484-7385 (security code 4257) (day/eve) or 609-587-7215. *Website:* http://www.naranonofnj.org

Narcotics Anonymous 12-Step. Fellowship of men and women seeking recovery from drug addiction. The only requirement for membership is the desire to stop using drugs. Call 1-800-992-0401 or 732-933-0462. *Website:* http://www.nanj.org

SOMERSET

Bright Futures for Kids *Professionally-run.* Provides support, education and counseling for children (ages 4-12) who are affected by a family member's alcohol and/or drug addiction in learning how to express their feelings, coping skills, a sense of responsibility and the ability to resist peer pressure. Meets Sun., 11am-1pm, Carrier Clinic, Atkinson Amphitheater, Classroom 3, 252 Route 601, Belle Mead. Call Community Relations 908-281-1513.

Lawyers Concerned for Lawyers (LCL) Self-help group that supports recovery from alcoholism and drug dependence for attorneys, judges, law students and others in the legal system. Based on the 12-step program adapted from A.A. All inquires are confidential. Meets Tues., 6pm, 70 Grove St., Somerville. Call NJ Lawyers Assistance Program 1-800-246-5527. *Website:* http://www.njlap.org *E-mail:* njlap@aol.com

Nar-Anon Family Group 12-Step. Provides help for family members and friends of drug abusers by offering comfort, hope and friendship through shared experiences. Call Nar-Anon Answering Service 1-800-484-7385 (security code 4257) (day/eve) or 609-587-7215. *Website:* http://www.naranonofnj.org

Narcotics Anonymous 12-Step. Fellowship of men and women seeking recovery from drug addiction. The only requirement for membership is the desire to stop using drugs. Call 1-800-992-0401 or 732-933-0462. *Website:* http://www.nanj.org

Nurse Recovery Group *Professionally-run.* Mutual support and information for nurses who are recovering from addictions. Sharing of professional concerns and encouragement. Meets in Belle Mead. Call 1-800-662-0108 (day).

Parent Support Group - New Jersey, Inc. *Professionally-run.* Confidential support for parents of chemically dependent children (ages 13-40+). Meets Mon., 7pm, Carrier Foundation, Admissions Building, Belle Mead. Call Karol Sullivan or Adrienne Mellana 1-800-561-4299 or 973-736-3344 (day). *Website:* http://www.psgnjhomestead.com *E-mail:* psgnj1@aol.com

Psychiatrically Recovering 12-Step. Mutual support for psychiatrically recovering people who wish to refrain from using alcohol or drugs, abusing food or any other compulsive behavior. Meets Thurs., 7:30pm, Richard Hall Community Mental Health Center, 500 North Bridge St., Room 121, Bridgewater. Call Richie S. 973-865-4851 (day/eve).

Weekend Co-dependency Program *Professionally-run.* Support and education for families and friends of alcohol/drug abusers or those dealing with persons with addiction problems. Educational lectures, discussion group, and parents group. Meets Sat. and Sun., 9:30am-3pm, Atkinson Amphitheater, Carrier Clinic, 252 Route 601, Belle Mead. Call 908-281-1513 (day) or 908-281-1000 (eve/weekend). *Website:* http://www.carrier.org

SUSSEX

Double Trouble in Recovery 12-Step. Support and encouragement for those who have are chemically addicted and also have a psychiatric illness. For information call Pat Devlin 973-383-8770 or Joe Shane 973-534-3449. *E-mail:* PatriciaDevlin@yahoo.com or JBWShane@nac.net

Newton Meets Wed., 5pm, Center for Prevention, 2nd floor classroom, 61 Spring St.

Newton Meets Fri., 3:30pm, (only if weather is pleasant - into the Fall), within the Gazebo near Park Place, at County Common, Park Place and Main St.

Newton Meets Sat., 10:30am, Sussex House at Newton Memorial Hospital, 175 High St.

Lawyers Concerned for Lawyers (LCL) Self-help group that supports recovery from alcoholism and drug dependence for attorneys, judges, law students and others in the legal system. Based on the 12-step program adapted from A.A. All inquiries are confidential. Meets Sat., 9am, Newton. Call Mary Jean 973-729-1847 or NJ-LAP 1-800-246-5527. *Website:* http://www.njlap.org

Nar-Anon Family Group 12-Step. Provides help for family members and friends of drug abusers by offering comfort, hope and friendship through shared experiences. Call Nar-Anon Answering Service 1-800-484-7385 (security code 4257) (day/eve) or 609-587-7215. *Website:* http://www.naranonofnj.org

Narcotics Anonymous 12-Step. Fellowship of men and women seeking recovery from drug addiction. The only requirement for membership is the desire to stop using drugs. Several meeting locations throughout the county. For meeting information call 1-800-992-0401 or 732-933-0462. *Website:* http://www.nanj.org

UNION

Alcohol and Drug Family Education *Professionally-run.* Support for families facing the chemical dependency of a family member. Deals with co-dependency issues. Meets Tues., 6:30-8pm, 46 Beauvoir Avenue, Summit. Call 908-522-4800 (day).

Families of Addiction *Professionally-run.* Mutual support for families of persons with an alcohol or drug addiction. Meets Wed., 6:30-8pm, Overlook Hospital, 46-48 Beauvoir Ave, Summit. Before attending call Rosemary Walsh 908-522-4800.

Nar-Anon Family Group 12-Step. Provides help for family members and friends of drug abusers by offering comfort, hope, and friendship through shared experiences. Call Nar-Anon Answering Service 1-800-484-7385 (security code 4257) (day/eve) or 609-587-7215. *Website:* http://www.naranonofnj.org

Narcotics Anonymous 12-Step. Fellowship of men and women seeking recovery from drug addiction. The only requirement for membership is the desire to stop using drugs. Call 1-800-992-0401 or 732-933-0462. *Website:* http://www.nanj.org

Nurse Recovery Group *Professionally-run.* Mutual support and information for nurses who are recovering from addictions. Sharing of professional concerns and encouragement. Meets in Berkeley Heights. Call 1-800-662-0108 (day).

Overcomer's Outreach Christian 12-Step. Fellowship to overcome any type of addiction or compulsive behavior, anxiety, depression or loneliness using God's word as a basis of recovery. Discussion, Bible study, prayer and phone help. Call Carmen 908-245-2788.

> **Cranford** Meets Mon., 7pm, Harvest Training Center at Calvary Tabernacle, 69 Myrtle St.
>
> **Elizabeth** Meets Tues., 7:30pm, Mount Teman AME Church, 160 Madison Ave.

Parent Support Group - New Jersey, Inc. Confidential support group for parents of chemically dependent children (ages 13-40+). Meets Tues., 6:30pm, Central Presbyterian Church, 70 Maple Ave., Library Room, Summit. Call Karol Sullivan or Adrienne Mellana 1-800-561-4299 or 973-736-3344 (day). *Website:* http://www.psgnjhomestead.com *E-mail:* psgnj1@aol.com

Psychiatrically Recovering 12-Step. Mutual support for psychiatrically recovering people who wish to refrain from using alcohol or drugs, abusing food or any other compulsive behavior. Meets Tues., 9:30am, Occupational Center of Union County, New Building, 291 Cox St., Activity Room, Roselle. Call Richie S. 973-865-4851 (day/eve).

WARREN

Dual Recovery Anonymous (DRA) Mutual support for alcoholics or drug addicts who are taking medication for psychiatric problems. Dues $2/month. Meets Tues., 7-8pm and Sat., 3-4pm, Better Future Self-Help Center, 21 West Washington Ave., Washington. Call Fonda 908-835-1180.

Nar-Anon Family Group 12-Step. Provides help for family members and friends of drug abusers by offering comfort, hope and friendship through shared experiences. Call Nar-Anon Answering Service 1-800-484-7385 (security code 4257) (day/eve) or 609-587-7215. *Website:* http://www.naranonofnj.org

Narcotics Anonymous 12-Step. Fellowship of men and women seeking recovery from drug addiction. The only requirement for membership is the desire to stop using drugs. Call 1-800-992-0401 or 732-933-0462. *Website:* http://www.nanj.org

NATIONAL

Alcoholics Victorious *International. 150 affiliated groups. Founded 1948.* 12-Step. Christian-oriented group for those recovering from alcohol or chemical dependency. Information and referrals, literature, phone support, conferences, support group meetings and newsletter. Assistance in starting groups. How-to materials. Write: Alcoholics Victorious, c/o Association of Gospel Rescue Missions, 1045 Swift St., Kansas City, MO 64116-4127. Call 1-800-624-5156 or 816-471-8020; Fax: 816-471-3718. *Website:* http://alcoholicsvictorious.org *E-mail:* info@alcoholicsvictorious.org

Anesthetists in Recovery *National network. Founded 1984. 150+ member network of recovering nurse anesthetists.* Provides phone support, information and referrals to groups and treatment. Write: AIR, c/o Art, 8233 Brookside Rd., Elkins Park, PA 19027. Call 215-635-0183 or 215-872-6821; Fax: 215-829-8757. *Website:* http://health.groups.yahooo.com/group/airforsobriety/ *E-mail:* a.to.z@comcast.net

Chemically Dependent Anonymous *National. 65 affiliated groups. Founded 1980.* Purpose is to carry the message of recovery to the chemically dependent person. For those with a desire to abstain from drugs/alcohol. Information and referrals, phone support, conferences. and group development guidelines. Write: Chemically Dependent Anonymous, P.O. Box 813, Annapolis, MD 21401. Call 1-888-232-4673. *Website:* http://www.cdaweb.org

Co-Anon Family Groups *International. 28 groups. Founded 1985.* 12-Step. Program for families and friends of cocaine, crack and other drug addicts, whether they are actively using or not. Online e-mail and face-to-face meetings. Provides assistance in starting new groups. Write: Co-Anon Family Groups, P.O. Box 12722, Tucson, AZ 85732-2722. Call 1-800-898-9985 or 520-513-5028. *Website:* http://www.co-anon.org *E-mail:* info@co-anon.org

Cocaine Anonymous, Inc. *International. 2,500 chapters. Founded 1982.* 12-Step. Fellowship of men and women who share their experience, strength, and hope that they may solve their common problem and help others to recover from addiction. Quarterly newsletter. Group starter kit available. Write: Cocaine Anonymous, 3740 Overland Ave., Suite C, Los Angeles, CA 90034-6337. For local chapters call 1-800-347-8998 (24 hr.) or 310-559-5833 (business office); Fax: 310-559-2554. *Website:* http://ca.org *E-mail:* cawso@ca.org

Crystal Meth Anonymous 12-Step. Fellowship for those in recovery from addiction to crystal meth. Open to families and friends. Information on starting a group available. Meetings list available on website. Write: CMA, 8205 Santa Monica Blvd., PMB 1-114, West Hollywood, CA 90046-5977. Call 213-488-4455. *Website:* http://www.crystalmeth.org

Double Trouble in Recovery, Inc. *National. 800+ affiliated groups. Founded 1989.* Fellowship of men and women who share their experience, strength and hope with each other so that they may solve their common problems and help others to recover from their particular addiction(s) and mental disorders. For persons dually-diagnosed with an addiction as well as a mental disorder. Literature, conferences, information and referrals. D.T.R. Basic Guide Book. Assistance in starting new groups. Write: DTR, Inc., P.O. Box 245055, Brooklyn, NY 11224. Call 718-373-2684. *Website:* http://www.doubletroubleinrecovery.org *E-mail:* HV613@aol.com

Dual Disorders Anonymous *National. 25 chapters. Founded 1982.* 12-Step. Fellowship of men and women who come together to help those members who suffer from both a mental disorder and alcoholism and/or drug addiction. Group development guidelines. Write: Dual Disorders Anonymous, P.O. Box 681264, Schaumburg, IL 60168-1264. Call Chuck 847-577-1853. *Website:* http://msnusers.com/dualdisordersanonymous

Dual Recovery Anonymous *International. Chapters worldwide. Founded 1989.* A self-help program for individuals who experience a dual disorder of chemical dependency and a psychiatric or emotional illness. Based on the principles of the 12-steps and the personal experiences of individuals in dual recovery. Literature, newsletter, assistance in starting local groups. Write: DRA, P.O. Box 8107, Prairie Village, KS 66208. Call 1-877-883-2332. *Website:* http://www.draonline.org

Families Anonymous *International. 500+ groups. Founded 1971.* 12-Step. Fellowship for relatives and friends of persons with drug, alcohol or behavioral problems. Members learn to achieve their own serenity in spite of the turmoil which surrounds them. Besides many booklets, pamphlets, bookmarks, publications include daily thought book, "Today A Better Way" and a bimonthly newsletter "The Twelve-Step Rag." Offers group development guidelines. Write: FA, P.O. Box 3475, Culver City, CA 90231-3475. Call 1-800-736-9805; Fax: 310-815-9682. *Website:* http://www.FamiliesAnonymous.org *E-mail:* famanon@FamiliesAnonymous.org

Free N One Recovery *National. 55 affiliated groups. Founded 1985.* Group teaches people to be free mentally and spiritually, as well as free of drugs and alcohol. Family support groups available. Information and referrals, phone support, literature and conferences. Assistance in starting local chapters. Write: Free N One Recovery, 5838 S. Overhill Dr., Los Angeles, CA 90043. Call 323-395-0009; Fax: 310-764-5439. *Website:* http://www.freenone.org *E-mail:* freenone@msn.com

I.C.A.P. (Intercongregational Addictions Program) *International. Founded 1979.* Network of recovering alcoholic women in religious orders. Helps Roman Catholic women who are or have been members of religious orders and are alcoholic or chemically dependent, compulsive eaters, compulsive gamblers, etc. Information, referrals, assistance in meeting other members, phone support, conferences and e-newsletters. Write: ICAP, 7777 Lake St., Suite 115, River Forest, IL 60305-1734. Call 708-488-9770; Fax: 708-488-9774. *Website:* http://www.2icap.org *E-mail:* lclose1@core.com

International Doctors in Alcoholics Anonymous *International network. 6000 members. 175 affiliated groups. Founded 1949.* Opportunity for doctoral level health care professionals to discuss common problems and find common solutions to drug and alcohol problems. Annual meetings (1st week Aug.), phone support, newsletter, information and referrals. Mutual help meetings at conferences of other organizations. Write: IDAA, c/o Gordon L. Hyde, MD, Exec. Director, 3311 Brookhill Circle, Lexington, KY 40502. Call 859-277-9379 (day). *Website:* http://www.idaa.org

International Lawyers in Alcoholics Anonymous *International. 40+ affiliated groups. Founded 1975.* Serves as a clearinghouse for support groups for lawyers who are recovering alcoholics or have other chemical dependencies. Newsletter, annual conventions. Group development guidelines. Write: ILAA, c/o Eli Gauna, 14123 Victory Blvd., Van Nuys, CA 91401. Call 818-785-6541; Fax: 818-785-3887. *Website:* http://www.ilaa.org

International Nurses Anonymous *International. Founded 1988.* Support and advocacy network for nurses who are involved in a 12-step recovery program. Membership is open to any RN, LPN (or LVN), nursing student or former nurse who considers themselves to be members of a 12-step group - including but not limited to: AA, NA, OA, Ala-non, Nar-anon, ACOA, CODA, etc. Newsletter and one-to-one networking. Plans for International Conference for 2008. Call Kathy 704-992-0678. *Website:* http://intnursesanon.org

J.A.C.S. (Jewish Alcoholics, Chemically Dependent Persons and Significant Others) *International. Founded 1980.* For alcoholic and chemically dependent Jews, families, friends, associates and the community. Networking, community outreach, retreats, newsletter, literature, spiritual events and speakers bureau. Write: JACS, 120 W. 57th St., New York, NY 10019. Call 212-397-4197 (day); Fax: 212-399-3525. *Website:* http://www.jacsweb.org *E-mail:* jacs@jacsweb.org

LifeRing Secular Recovery *International. Founded 1999.* Secular community of persons who are building lives free of dependency on alcohol and other drugs. Group activities are not associated with religion or spirituality. Members practice complete abstinence from alcohol and other addicting drugs. Peer support, literature, information, referrals and advocacy activities. Guidelines available for starting similar groups. Large online email support group and several smaller special interest groups (women, weight loss, stop smoking, etc). Online chats, forum. Publishes sobriety literature. Write: LifeRing Secular Recovery, 1440 Broadway, Suite 312, Oakland, CA 94612-2041. Call 1-800-811-4142 or 510-763-0779. *Website:* http://www.unhooked.com *E-mail:* service@lifering.org

Marijuana Anonymous World Services *International. 50+ groups. Founded 1989.* 12-Step. Fellowship of men and women who desire to stay clean of marijuana. Literature and starter packets. Various online meetings. Write: M.A., P.O. Box 2912, Van Nuys, CA 91404. Call 1-800-766-6779 (recorded message). *Website:* http://www.marijuana-anonymous.org *E-mail:* office@marijuana-anonymous.org

Methadone Anonymous Support *International. 400+ affiliated groups. Founded 1991.* Self-help group for and led by, current and former methadone maintenance treatment patients. Open to anyone interested in recovery from chemical dependency. Literature, conferences, support group meetings and online chat rooms (methadone users, detox, chronic pain, buprenorphine/suboxone treatment, caregivers, methadone pregnancy info, etc). Assistance in starting local groups. *Website:* http://www.methadonesupport.org *E-mail:* carol@methadonesupport.org

Nar-Anon World Service Organization *International. 1,600 groups. Founded 1967.* 12-Step. Group offering self-help recovery to families and friends of addicts. Members share their experience, hope and strength with each other. Packet of information for starting new groups. Nar-Ateen and Nar-Atot programs available. Write: Nar-Anon Family World Service Organization, 22527 Crenshaw Blvd., Suite 200B, Torrance, CA 90505. Call 1-800-477-6291 or 310-534-8188; Fax: 310-534-8688. *Website:* http://www.nar-anon.org *E-mail:* naranonwso@hotmail.com

Narcotics Anonymous *International. 40,000+ meetings per week in 120 countries. Founded 1953.* 12-Step. Worldwide organization whose primary purpose is to help any individual stop using drugs. No dues, fees, or registration. The only requirement for membership is the desire to stop using drugs. Information is available in several languages, on audio tape, CD and in Braille. Write: NAWS, P.O. Box 9999, Van Nuys, CA 91409. Call 818-773-9999; Fax: 818-700-0700. *Website:* http://www.na.org *E-mail:* fsmail@na.org

National Family Partnership (formerly Parents for Drug-Free Youth) *National. 58 affiliates. Founded 1980.* Drug prevention, education, information and networking for parents to address drug prevention. Legislative advocacy on federal level and information resource for state and local efforts. Annual Red Ribbon Campaign, resource center, drug prevention and anti-tobacco resource. Write: National Family Partnership, 2490 Coral Way, Suite 501, Miami, FL 33145. Call 1-800-705-8997; Fax: 305-856-4815. *Website:* http://www.nfp.org *E-mail:* ireyes@informedfamilies.org

Overcomers In Christ *International. Founded 1987.* Recovery program that deals with every aspect of addiction and dysfunction (spiritual, physical, mental, emotional and social). Uses Overcomers goals which are Christ-centered. Resources, literature, information and referrals. Assistance in starting new groups. Write: Overcomers In Christ, P.O. Box 34460, Omaha, NE 68134-04604. Call 402-573-0966; Fax: 402-573-0960. *Website:* http://www.OvercomersInChrist.org *E-mail:* OIC@OvercomersInChrist.org

Overcomers Outreach, Inc. *International. 700 affiliated groups. Founded 1985.* 12-Step. Christ-centered support group for persons with any compulsive behaviors, as well as their families and friends. Uses the 12-steps of A.A. and applies them to the Scriptures. Uses Jesus Christ as "higher power." Supplements involvement in other 12-step groups. Newsletter, group development guidelines, conferences. Write: Overcomers Outreach, P.O. Box 922950, Sylmar, CA 91392-2950. Call 1-800-310-3001. *Website:* http://www.overcomersoutreach.org *E-mail:* info@overcomersoutreach.org

Pills Anonymous *Model. 2 groups in New York City.* Self-help, self-supporting, anonymous 12-step program, based on A.A., for those who want to help themselves and others recover from chemical addiction. Groups meets in New York City. Call 212-874-0700. *Website:* http://www.geocities.com/panonjh/ *E-mail:* panonjh@yahoo.com

Prescriptions Anonymous *National. Founded 1998.* Non-profit organization helping those affected by prescription or over-the-counter addictions with co-occurring illnesses. Prescription Anonymous 12-step meetings offer members and families group support, phone consultations and informational literature. Assistance in starting new group meetings. Write: Prescriptions Anonymous, Inc., P.O. Box 10534, Gaithersburg, MD 20898-0534. Call 301-641-6533. *Website:* http://www.prescriptionanonymous.org *E-mail:* Cindy@prescriptionanonymous.org

Psychologists Helping Psychologists *National network. Founded 1980.* For doctoral-level psychologists or students who've had a personal experience with alcohol or drugs. Aim is to support each other in recovery and help others to recover. Tries to educate psychology community. Regional/national get-togethers and newsletter. Write: Psychologists Helping Psychologists, 3484 S. Utah St., Arlington, VA 22206-1921. Call Ann Stone 703-243-4470; Fax: 703-243-7125. *E-mail:* AnnS@Erols.com

Recoveries Anonymous *International. 50 chapters.* Spiritual recovery group for anyone seeking a solution for any kind of addiction, problem or behavior. Family and friends welcome. "How To Begin..." guides and "Start A Group" kit can be downloaded free from the website. Write: RA, P.O. Box 1212, East Northport, NY 11731. *Website:* http://www.r-a.org *E-mail:* raus@r-a.org

Secular Organizations for Sobriety (Save Ourselves) *International. 20,000 members. Founded 1986.* Mutual help for alcoholics and addicts who want to acknowledge their addiction and maintain sobriety as a separate issue from religion or spirituality. Newsletter. Guidelines and assistance available for starting groups. Write: S.O.S., 4773 Hollywood Blvd., Hollywood, CA 90027. Call 323-664-4295; Fax: 323-664-4271. *Website:* http://www.cfiwest.org/sos/ *E-mail:* sos@cfiwest.org

SMART Recovery Self-Help Network (Self-Management And Recovery Training) *National. 275 affiliated groups. Founded 1994.* Network of self-help groups for individuals wanting to gain their independence from addictive and compulsive behaviors. SMART Recovery is an abstinence program based on cognitive behavioral principles, especially those of rational-emotive behavior therapy. Newsletter, information, referrals, literature and assistance in starting local groups. Write: SMART Recovery, 7537 Mentor Ave., Suite 306, Mentor, OH 44060. Call 866-951-5357; Fax: 440-951-5358. *Website:* http://www.smartrecovery.org *E-mail:* info@smartrecovery.org

Social Workers Helping Social Workers *National network. Founded 1980.* Supports recovery from alcohol or other chemical dependence, either their own or that of a significant other, among social workers (BSW/MSSW) or MSW matriculating students. Social workers with other addictions are welcome to attend meetings. Newsletter, annual conferences, some regional retreats/meetings, continuing education, daily e-mail digest and group development guidelines. Write: SWHSW, c/o Betty Check, 5228 S. Kenwood Ave., Chicago, IL 60615-4006. Call Betty Check, LCSW 773-493-6940 (confidential voice mail); *Website:* http://www.socialworkershelping.org *E-mail:* SWHSWIL@aol.com

Veterinarians in Recovery *National network. Founded 1990.* Support network for veterinarians in recovery from alcoholism and addiction. Provides information and referrals, phone support and newsletter. Online e-mail listserv. Maintains database of members for support. Al-Anon members and recovering veterinarian staff welcome at meetings. Many VIR members also are members of International Doctors in A.A., and meet during their annual conference. Write: VIR, c/o Jeff H., 180 County Rd. 741, Clanton, AL 35046. Call 205-335-4222. *E-mail:* jeffhalldvm@charter.net

ONLINE

Conduct Disorders Parent Message Board *Online. 6592 members. Founded 1995.* Support for parents living with a child with one of the many behavior disorders including: attention deficit hyperactivity disorder, oppositional defiance disorder, conduct disorder, depression and substance abuse. Parents with children of all ages welcome. *Website:* http://www.conductdisorders.com

GAMBLING

(see also toll-free helplines)

STATEWIDE

Gam-Anon *North/Central NJ* 12-Step. Fellowship of family members and friends of compulsive gamblers. Follows the 12-step program adapted from A.A. Various meeting locations throughout New Jersey. Write: Gam-Anon, P.O. Box 177, Lodi, NJ 07644. Call 973-815-0988.

Gamblers Anonymous *New Jersey Intergroup* Fellowship of men and women who share their experiences, strengths and hopes with each other in order to recover from their common problem of compulsive gambling. Various meeting locations throughout New Jersey. Write: G.A., P.O. Box 283, Kearny, NJ 07032. Call NJ Intergroup 1-877-994-2465 (24 hr). *Website:* http://www.ga4nj.com

Signs of Sobriety *Professionally-run.* Provides alcoholism and drug addiction services to persons who are deaf or hard-of-hearing. Makes referrals to deaf and sign interpretered 12-step groups throughout NJ (alcohol or drug addiction, gambling, families of alcoholics and general 12-step meetings). Provides prevention and education classes. Offers SoberCamp-annual summer retreat and Sober/Deaf activities for deaf and hard of hearing individuals in recovery. Newsletter. Write: SOS, 100 Scotch Rd., 2nd Floor, Ewing, NJ 08628. Call TTY: 1-800-332-7677; Voice: 609-882-7677 (day); Fax: 609-882-6808. *Website:* http://www.signsofsobriety.org *E-mail:* info@signsofsobriety.org

ATLANTIC

Gam-Anon 12-Step. Fellowship of family members and friends of compulsive gamblers. Follows 12-step program adapted from A.A. Meets Thurs., 8-10pm, Our Lady of Sorrows Church, Wabash Ave. and Poplar Ave., Linwood. Call 609-266-3933.

Gamblers Anonymous 12-Step. Fellowship of men and women who share experiences, strengths and hopes with each other to recover from compulsive gambling. Call NJ Intergroup 1-877-994-2465 (24 hr). *Website:* http://www.ga4nj.com

Absecon Meets Mon., 7-9pm and Fri, 10am-noon, St. Elizabeth Anne Seaton Church, Rectory, 591 New Jersey Ave.

Brigantine Meets Sat., 10am-noon, Community Presbyterian Church, 1501 Brigantine Ave. and 15th St.

Linwood Meets Thurs., 8-10pm, Our Lady of Sorrow Church, Wabash Ave. and Poplar Ave.

Margate Meets Sun., 10:30am-noon, Margate Library, 8100 Atlantic Ave.

BERGEN

Gam-Anon 12-Step. Fellowship of family members and friends of compulsive gamblers. Call Gam-Anon Hotline 973-815-0988.

Fair Lawn Meets Tues., 7pm and Fri., 8pm, Episcopal Church of Atonement, 1-36 30th St. and Rosalie Ave.

Paramus Meets Tues., 8pm, Bergen Regional Medical Center, 230 East Ridgewood Ave.

Gamblers Anonymous 12-Step. Fellowship of men and women who share experiences, strengths and hopes with each other to recover from compulsive gambling. Call NJ Intergroup 1-877-994-2465 (24 hr). *Website:* http://www.ga4nj.com

Carlstadt Meets Wed., 7:30-9:45pm, First Presbyterian Church, 457 Division Ave.

Fair Lawn Meets Wed. and Fri., 8-10pm, Episcopal Church of Atonement, 1-36 30th St.

Hasbrouck Heights Meets Sat., 10-11:30am, St. John the Divine Episcopal Church, Terrace Ave. and Jefferson Ave.

Westwood Meets Sun., 8-9:45pm, United Methodist Church, 105 Fairview Ave.

BURLINGTON

Gam-Anon 12-Step. Fellowship of family members and friends of compulsive gamblers. Meets Sun., 5pm, Hampton Behavioral Health Center, 650 Rancocas Rd., Westampton Township. Call 609-267-7000.

Gamblers Anonymous 12-Step. Fellowship of men and women who share experiences, strengths and hopes with each other to recover from compulsive gambling. Call NJ Intergroup 1-877-994-2465 (24 hr). *Website:* http://www.ga4nj.com

> **Moorestown** Meets Mon., 8-9:30pm, Trinity Church, Main St.
>
> **Rancocas** Meets Sun., 5:30pm and Wed., 7:30-9pm, Hampton Hospital, 650 Rancocas Rd.

Overcomers 12-Step. Christian-focused recovery group for anyone suffering from any type of addiction, dependency or compulsive disorder. Rap sessions, guest speakers and literature. Meets Thurs., 7:30-9pm, Fellowship Alliance Chapel, 199 Church Rd., Medford. Call 609-953-7333 (day).

CAPE MAY

Gamblers Anonymous 12-Step. Fellowship of men and women who share experiences, strengths and hopes with each other to recover from compulsive gambling. Meets Sun., 7-8pm, Holy Trinity Episcopal Church, 2998 Bay Ave., Ocean City. Call NJ Intergroup 1-877-994-2465 (24 hr). *Website:* http://www.ga4nj.com

CUMBERLAND

Overcomer's Outreach *(Shiloh Faith Meeting)* Christian 12-Step. Fellowship to overcome any type of addiction or compulsive behavior, anxiety, depression or loneliness using God's word as a basis of recovery. Discussion, Bible study, prayer and phone help. Meets Thurs., 7-8pm, Shiloh Seventh Day Baptist Church, East Ave., Shiloh. Call Rev. Chrowiger 856-455-0488 (day) or Frank B. Mulford 856-451-8698 (day). *E-mail:* ahfarm@hotmail.com

ESSEX

Gam-Anon 12-Step. Fellowship of family members and friends of compulsive gamblers. Call Gam-Anon Hotline 973-815-0988.

> **Bloomfield** Meets Tues., 8:30-10:30pm, Bethany United Presbyterian Church, 293 West Passaic St.
>
> **Nutley** Meets Mon., 8pm and Fri., 8:30pm, St. Paul's Congregational Church, 10 St. Paul's Pl.

Gamblers Anonymous 12-Step. Fellowship of men and women who share experiences, strengths and hopes with each other to recover from compulsive gambling. Call NJ Intergroup 1-877-994-2465 (24 hr). *Website:* http://www.ga4nj.com

Bloomfield Meets Tues. and Thurs., 8:30-10:30pm, Bethany United Presbyterian Church, Basement Level, 293 W. Passaic Ave.

Nutley Meets Mon., 8-10pm and Fri., 8:30-10:30pm, St. Paul's Congregational Church (side entrance), 1st Floor, 10 St. Paul's Place.

West Orange Meets Tues., 8-10pm, St. Cloud Presbyterian Church, Lower Level, 5 Ridgeway Ave.

Reformers Anonymous Faith-based group to help people find freedom from addictions: alcohol, debt, drugs, eating disorders, gambling, internet, sex/love addiction, smoking, etc. Literature, newsletter and phone help. Meets Fri., 7-9pm, First Baptist Church, 257 Bloomfield Ave., Caldwell. Call Pastor Eli Miranda 201-724-9208 (day) or church 973-226-1004 (day).

GLOUCESTER

Gamblers Anonymous 12-Step. Fellowship of men and women who share experiences, strengths and hopes with each other to recover from compulsive gambling. Call NJ Intergroup 1-877-994-2465 (24 hr). *Website:* http://www.ga4nj.com

Blackwood Meets Fri., 8-10pm, Blackwood Methodist Church, 35 East Church St.

Woodbury Meets Tues., 7-8:30pm, St. Stephen's Lutheran Church, 230 North Evergreen Ave.

HUDSON

Gamblers Anonymous 12-Step. Fellowship of men and women who share their experiences, strengths and hopes with each other to recover from compulsive gambling. Meets Wed., 8-9:30pm, Old Bergen Church, 1 Highland Ave., Rear Entrance, Jersey City. Call NJ Intergroup 1-877-994-2465 (24 hr). *Website:* http://www.ga4nj.com

MERCER

Gamblers Anonymous 12-Step. Fellowship of men and women who share experiences, strengths and hopes with each other to recover from compulsive gambling. Meets Tues., 8:30-10pm, University Office Plaza, 3635 Quakerbridge Rd., Suite 7, Hamilton. Call NJ Intergroup 1-877-994-2465 (24 hr). *Website:* http://www.ga4nj.com

MIDDLESEX

Gam-Anon 12-Step. Fellowship of family members and friends of compulsive gamblers. Call Gam-Anon Hotline 973-815-0988.

Metuchen Meets Tues., 7pm, St. Luke's Episcopal Church, 17 Oak St.

Parlin Meets Wed. and Thurs., 8pm, Messiah Lutheran Church, 3091 Bordentown Ave.

Gamblers Anonymous 12-Step. Fellowship of men and women who share experiences, strengths and hopes with each other to recover from compulsive gambling. Call NJ Intergroup 1-877-994-2465 (24 hr). *Website:* http://www.ga4nj.com

Edison Meets Sat., 10-11:30am, Oak Tree Presbyterian Church, 455 Plainfield Rd.

Metuchen *(Young Gamblers)* Meets Tues., 7-9pm, St. Luke's Episcopal Church, 17 Oak St.

Overcomer's Outreach Christian 12-Step. Fellowship to overcome any type of addiction or compulsive behavior, anxiety, depression and loneliness using God's word as a basis of recovery. Discussion, Bible study, prayer and phone help. Meets Thurs., 7-8:30pm, Metuchen Assembly of God, Rose and Whitman St., Metuchen. Call Janet 732-388-2856 (eve) or Pat 732-321-6896.

SMART Recovery (Self-Management and Recovery Training) *Professionally-run.* Self-help group for individuals wanting to gain their independence from addictive behaviors (drugs, including alcohol and nicotine, and other compulsive behaviors i.e. gambling, eating disorders). SMART is an abstinence program based on cognitive-behavioral education and principles, especially those of rational-emotive behavior therapy. Meets Mon., 6-7:30pm, Rutgers University, Busch Campus, Psychology Building, Room A224, Piscataway. Call Tom Morgan 732-445-0902. *Website:* http://www.smartrecovery.org

MONMOUTH

Gamblers Anonymous 12-Step. Fellowship of men and women who share experiences, strengths and hopes with each other to recover from compulsive gambling. Call NJ Intergroup 1-877-994-2465 (24 hr). *Website:* http://www.ga4nj.com

Colts Neck Meets Tues., 8-9:30pm and Sun. 6:30-8pm, St. Mary's Church, Spiritual Center Building, Route 34 and Phalanx Rd.

<u>Freehold</u> Meets Fri., 8-9:30pm, Hope Lutheran Church, 211 Elton-Adelphia Rd.
<u>Ocean Township</u> Meets Mon., 8-9:30pm, Church of St. Anselm, 1028 Wayside Rd.

MORRIS

Gam-Anon 12-Step. Fellowship of family members and friends of compulsive gamblers. Meets Tues., 8-10pm, Saint Clare's Behavioral Health Center, Powerville Rd., Boonton. Call Gam-Anon Hotline 973-815-0988.

Gamblers Anonymous 12-Step. Fellowship of men and women who share experiences, strengths and hopes with each other to recover from compulsive gambling. Meets Tues., 8-9:45pm, Saint Clare's Behavioral Health Center, Powerville Rd., Boonton. Call NJ Intergroup 1-877-994-2465 (24 hr). *Website:* http://www.ga4nj.com

SMART Recovery (Self-Management And Recovery Training) Self-help group for individuals wanting to gain their independence from addictive behaviors (drugs, including alcohol and nicotine, and other compulsive behaviors including gambling, eating disorders). SMART is an abstinence program based on cognitive-behavioral education and principles, especially those of rational-emotive behavior therapy. Meets Thurs., 7-8:30pm, Beginnings, 65 Spring St., Morristown. Call Rich 973-983-8755. *Website:* http://www.smartrecovery.org

OCEAN

Checkpoint Support to help overcome dependencies and addictions through accountability, encouragement and spiritual development. Meets Thurs., 7-8:30pm, Shore Vineyard Church, 320 Compass Ave., Beachwood. Call 732-244-3888 (day).

Gam-Anon 12-Step. Fellowship of family members and friends of compulsive gamblers. Meets Thurs., 7-9pm and Sat., 9:30-11:30am, Presbyterian Church of Toms River, 1070 Hooper Ave., Toms River. Call Gam-Anon Hotline 973-815-0988.

Gamblers Anonymous 12-Step. (Open Meeting) Fellowship of men and women who share experiences, strengths and hopes with each other to recover from compulsive gambling. Call NJ Intergroup 1-877-994-2465 (24 hr). *Website:* http://www.ga4nj.com

Pt. Pleasant Spouses, family members and significant others welcome. Meets Wed., 7:30-9:30pm, Central United Methodist Church, 729 Arnold Ave.

Toms River Meets Thurs., 7-9pm and Sat. 9:30-11:30am, Presbyterian Church of Toms River, 1070 Hooper Ave.

Toms River Meets Fri., 7:30-9pm, Holy Cross Lutheran Church, 1500 Hooper Ave.

SOMERSET

Gam-Anon 12-Step. Fellowship of family members and friends of compulsive gamblers. Meets Thurs., 7-8:30pm, Lyons Veterans Administration Medical Center, Building # 143, Lyons. Call Gam-Anon Hotline 973-815-0988.

Gamblers Anonymous 12-Step. Fellowship of men and women who share their experience, strengths and hopes with each other in order to recover from their common problem of compulsive gambling. Call NJ Intergroup 1-877-994-2465 (24 hr). *Website:* http://www.ga4nj.com

Basking Ridge Meets Sat., 10-11am, Church of Saint James Parish Community Center, 184 South Finley Ave., Room 4.

Lyons Meets Thurs., 7-9:30pm, Lyons Veterans Administration Medical Center, Bldg. # 143, Multi-Purpose Room, 151 Knollcroft Rd.

SUSSEX

Gamblers Anonymous 12-Step. Fellowship of men and women who share their experiences, strengths and hopes with each other in order to recover from their common problem of compulsive gambling. Meets Mon., 7-8:30pm, Sparta United Methodist Church, 71 Sparta Ave., Sparta. Call NJ Intergroup 1-877-994-2465 (24 hr) or church 973-729-7773 (day).

UNION

Gam-Anon 12-Step. Fellowship of family members and friends of compulsive gamblers. Meets Mon., 7:45-10pm, Temple Israel of Union, 2372 Morris Ave., Union. Call Gam-Anon Hotline 973-815-0988.

Gamblers Anonymous 12-Step. Fellowship of men and women who share experiences, strengths and hopes with each other to recover from compulsive gambling. Call NJ Intergroup 1-877-994-2465 (24 hr). *Website:* http://www.ga4nj.com

Union Meets Sun., 7-9pm, Union Methodist Church, Berwyn St. and Overlook Terrace.

Union Meets Mon., 7:45-10pm; Wed., 1-2pm and Sun., 8-9:30pm, Temple Israel of Union, 2378 Morris Ave.

Overcomer's Outreach Christian 12-Step. Fellowship to overcome any type of addiction or compulsive behavior, anxiety, depression or loneliness using God's word as a basis of recovery. Discussion, Bible study, prayer and phone help. Call Carmen 908-245-2788.

Cranford Meets Mon., 7pm, Harvest Training Center at Calvary Tabernacle, 69 Myrtle St.

Elizabeth Meets Tues., 7:30pm, Mount Teman AME Church, 160 Madison Ave.

Elizabeth Meets Thurs., 7:30pm, Union Baptist Church, 1088 E. Grand St.

NATIONAL

Bettors Anonymous *Model. 5 groups in Massachusetts. Founded 1990.* 12-Step. Fellowship who share their experience, hope and strength with each other in order to help themselves and others recover from compulsive gambling. The only requirement for membership is a desire to stop gambling. Literature, phone help, information and referrals. Meetings in Massachusetts. Provides assistance in starting local groups. Write: Bettors Anonymous, P.O. Box 304, Wilmington, MA 01887. Call 978-988-1777 or 781-662-5199. *Website:* http://www.bettorsanonymous.org

Gam-Anon Family Groups *International. 325 groups. Founded 1960.* 12-Step. Fellowship for men and women who are husbands, wives, relatives or friends of compulsive gamblers, who have been affected by the gambling problem. Purpose is to learn acceptance and understanding of the gambling illness, to use the program to rebuild lives', and give assistance to those who suffer. A few groups have Gam-a-teen groups for children of gamblers. Write: Gam-Anon, P.O. Box 157, Whitestone, NY 11357. Call 718-352-1671 (Tues. and Thurs., 9am-5pm); Fax: 718-746-2571. *Website:* http://www.gam-anon.org

Gamblers Anonymous *International. Approximately 2400 chapters. Founded 1957.* 12-Step. Fellowship of men and women who share experiences, strengths and hope with each other to recover from compulsive gambling. Monthly bulletin for members. Offers assistance in starting new groups. Write: G.A., P.O. Box 17173, Los Angeles, CA 90017. Call 213-386-8789; Fax: 213-386-0030. *Website:* http://www.gamblersanonymous.org *E-mail:* isomain@gamblersanonymous.org

I.C.A.P. (Intercongregational Addictions Program) *International. Founded 1979.* Network of recovering alcoholic women in religious orders. Helps Roman Catholic women who are or have been members of religious orders and are alcoholic or chemically dependent, compulsive eaters, compulsive gamblers, etc. Information, referrals, assistance in meeting other members, phone support, conferences and e-newsletters. Write: ICAP, 7777 Lake Street, Suite 115, River Forest, IL 60305-1734. Call 708-488-9770; Fax: 708-488-9774. *Website:* http://www.2icap.org *E-mail:* lclose1@core.com

Overcomers In Christ *International. Founded 1987.* Recovery program that deals with every aspect of addiction and dysfunction (spiritual, physical, mental, emotional and social). Uses Overcomers Goals which are Christ-centered. Literature, resources, information and referrals. Assistance in starting new groups. Write: Overcomers In Christ, P.O. Box 34460, Omaha, NE 68134-04604. Call 402-573-0966; Fax: 402-573-0960. *Website:* http://www.OvercomersInChrist.org *E-mail:* OIC@OvercomersInChrist.org

Overcomers Outreach, Inc. *International. 700 affiliated groups. Founded 1985.* 12-Step. Christ-centered support group for persons with any compulsive behaviors, as well as their their families and friends. Uses the 12-steps of A.A. and applies them to the Scriptures. Uses Jesus Christ as "higher power." Supplements involvement in other 12-step groups. Newsletter, group development guidelines and conferences. Write: Overcomers Outreach, P.O. Box 922950, Sylmar, CA 91392-2950. Call 1-800-310-3001; *Website:* http://www.overcomersoutreach.org *E-mail:* info@overcomersoutreach.org

Recoveries Anonymous *International. 50 chapters.* Spiritual recovery group for anyone seeking a solution for any kind of addiction, problem or behavior. Family and friends welcome. “How To Begin…” guides and “Start A Group” kit can be downloaded free from the website. Write: RA, P.O. Box 1212, East Northport, NY 11731. *Website:* http://www.r-a.org *E-mail:* raus@r-a.org

SEX / LOVE ADDICTION

STATEWIDE

New Jersey/Delaware Valley Sexaholics Anonymous Intergroup Mutual support for those who want to stop their sexually self-destructive thinking and behavior to become sexually sober. Several meeting locations throughout NJ. Call 1-800-739-2465 or 732-886-2142. *Website:* http://www.sa.org

S.L.A.A. (Sex and Love Addicts Anonymous) 12-Step. Fellowship for those who desire to stop living out a pattern of sex and love addiction, compulsive sexual behavior or emotional attachment. Meets in several locations throughout New Jersey. Write: Greater Delaware Valley Intergroup, The Augustine Fellowship (SLAA), P.O. Box 7437, Philadelphia, PA 19101. Call the Delaware Valley Intergroup 215-731-9760; Inspirational Line 215-574-2120 (day). *Website:* http://www.slaadvi.org *E-mail:* slaadvi@critpath.org

BERGEN

S-Anon 12-Step. Offers support for family members and the loved ones of those who are sexually addicted. Literature, phone help, and newsletter. Donation $2. Meets Tues., 7:30-8:30pm, First Presbyterian Church, 64 Passaic St., Hackensack. Call Renee 551-206-9019.

Sexaholics Anonymous Mutual support for those who want to stop their sexually self-destructive thinking and behavior to become sexually sober. For meeting information call Tom A. 908-351-3870, NJ Intergroup 1-800-739-2465 or 732-886-2142. *Website:* http://www.orgsites.com/nj/sa

> **Teaneck** Meets Tues. and Fri., 7am, St. Anatasias Church, 1095 Teaneck Rd.
>
> **Wyckoff** Meets Sun., 4:30pm, Bethany Church, 568 Wellington Dr., Cornerstone Room.

S.L.A.A. (Sex and Love Addictions Anonymous) 12-Step. Fellowship for those who desire to stop living out a pattern of sex and love addiction, compulsive sexual behavior or emotional attachment. Meets Tues., 8pm, United Methodist Church, 201 Degraw Ave., Teaneck. Call Delaware Valley Intergroup 215-731-9760.

Need help finding a specific group? Give us a call – we're here to help!
Call 1-800-367-6274

BURLINGTON

S-Anon 12-Step. Offers support for family members and the loved ones of those who are sexually addicted. Literature. Meets Mon., 7:30-8:30pm, Prince of Peace Lutheran Church, 61 Route 70 East, Marlton. Call 856-751-3545 (day).

S-Anon Couples Group 12-Step. Offers support for couples dealing with a sexual addiction. Meets 3rd Sat., 7:30pm, Prince of Peace Church, 61 Route 70 East, Marlton. Call 856-751-3545 (day).

CAMDEN

Sexaholics Anonymous Mutual support for those who want to stop their sexually self-destructive thinking and behavior to become sexually sober. For information call Tom A. 908-351-3870, NJ Intergroup 1-800-739-2465 or 732-886-2142. *Website:* http://www.orgsites.com/nj/sa

Cherry Hill Meets Thurs., 7pm, Kennedy Memorial Hospital, 2201 Chapel Ave. West.

Stratford Meets Wed., 7pm, Kennedy Gerontology Center.

Westmont Meets Sat., 8am, Starting Point Inc., 215 Highland Ave.

S.L.A.A. (Sex and Love Addicts Anonymous) 12-Step. Fellowship for those who desire to stop living out a pattern of sex and love addiction, compulsive sexual behavior or emotional attachment. Call Delaware Valley Intergroup 215-731-9760.

Cherry Hill Meets Sun., 7pm, Tues., 7:30pm and Sat., 7pm, Kennedy Memorial Hospital, 2201 Chapel Ave. West.

Gibbsboro Meets Mon., 7:30pm, St. Andrew the Apostle Church, Gibbsboro-Kresson Rd. Call Michael 856-983-5953.

Stratford Meets Fri., 8pm, St. Luke's Church, 55 Warwick Rd. Call Greg 215-219-7533.

CAPE MAY

S.L.A.A. (Sex and Love Addictions Anonymous) 12-Step. Fellowship for those who desire to stop living out a pattern of sex and love addiction, compulsive sexual behavior or emotional attachment. Meets Mon., 7pm, Trinity United Methodist Church, 20 North Route 9, Marmora. Call Delaware Valley Intergroup 215-731-9760.

ESSEX

Reformers Anonymous Faith-based group to help people find freedom from addictions: alcohol, debt, drugs, eating disorders, gambling, internet, sex/love addiction, smoking, etc. Literature, newsletter and phone help. Meets Fri., 7-9pm, First Baptist Church, 257 Bloomfield Ave., Caldwell. Call Pastor Eli Miranda 201-724-9208 (day) or church 973-226-1004 (day).

Sexaholics Anonymous Mutual support for those who want to stop their sexually self-destructive thinking and behavior to become sexually sober. Meets Thurs., 8pm, (Tues., 8pm, July/Aug.), Unitarian Church, 67 Church St., Montclair. For meeting information call Tom A. 908-351-3870, NJ Intergroup 1-800-739-2465 or 732-886-2142. *Website:* http://www.orgsites.com/nj/sa

S.L.A.A. (Sex and Love Addictions Anonymous) 12-Step. Fellowship for women who desire to stop living out a pattern of sex and love addiction, compulsive sexual behavior or emotional attachment. Call Delaware Valley Intergroup 215-731-9760.

> **Montclair** Meets Mon., 7:30pm First United Methodist Church, 24 North Fullerton St., Chapel Room, 1st Floor.
>
> **Montclair** Meets Fri., 8:30pm, St. Luke's Church, South Fullerton St. & Union St. Call George 973-481-5267.

HUDSON

Hoboken S.A.A. (Serenity Acceptance Affirmation) 12-Step. Support group for anyone concerned about their own addictive or compulsive sexual behavior. Meets Sun., 7-8:30pm, Hoboken Evangelical Free Church, 833 Clinton St., Hoboken. Call Dave 201-459-8858. *Website:* http://www.saa-recovery.org

Sexaholics Anonymous Mutual support for those who want to stop their sexually self-destructive thinking and behavior to become sexually sober. Meets Tues., 7:30pm, Mt. Carmel Guild Catholic Services, 249 Virginia Ave., Jersey City. For information call Tom A. 908-351-3870, NJ Intergroup 1-800-739-2465 or 732-886-2142. *Website:* http://www.orgsites.com/nj/sa

MERCER

S.L.A.A. (Sex and Love Addicts Anonymous) 12-Step. Fellowship for those who desire to stop living out a pattern of sex and love addiction, compulsive sexual behavior or emotional attachment. Call Delaware Valley Intergroup 215-731-9760.

Ewing Meets Sun., 7pm, Trinity United Methodist Church, 1985 Pennington Rd. Call Brian 609-538-8118 (day).
Trenton Meets Tues., 7pm, Saint Michael's Episcopal Church, 140 N. Warren St.

MIDDLESEX

Sexaholics Anonymous Mutual support for those who want to stop their sexually self-destructive thinking and behavior to become sexually sober. Meets Sun., 5pm and Wed., 7:30pm, St. Luke's Episcopal Church, Oak Ave., Metuchen. For meeting information call Tom A. 908-351-3870, NJ Intergroup 1-800-739-2465 or 732-886-2142. *Website:* http://www.orgsites.com/nj/sa

MONMOUTH

S-Anon Offers support for family members and the loved ones of those who are sexually addicted. Meets Mon., 7:30pm, The United Methodist Church, Broad St., Red Bank. Before attending call Lisa 732-610-6400.

Sexaholics Anonymous Mutual support for those who want to stop their sexually self-destructive thinking and behavior to become sexually sober. For meeting information call Tom A. 908-351-3870, NJ Intergroup 1-800-739-2465 or 732-886-2142. *Website:* http://www.orgsites.com/nj/sa
Neptune Meets Mon., 7:30pm, St. Leo's Church, Hurley's Lane, Lincroft. Meets Fri., 7:30pm, Jersey Shore Medical Center, Route 33 West.
Red Bank Meets Sun., 8:30am, Riverview Medical Center, Blazedale Bldg., 5th Floor Auditorium, Riverview Plaza.
Red Bank Meets Wed., noon, 1st Baptist Church, 84 Maple Ave.

MORRIS

S-Anon For family members and loved ones of those who are sexually addicted. Donation $2/mtg. Meets Mon., 8-9pm, St. John's Episcopal Church, 11 S. Bergen St., Dover. Call Barbara S. 973-659-0901.

Sexaholics Anonymous Mutual support for those who want to stop their sexually self-destructive thinking and behavior to become sexually sober. Call Tom A. 908-351-3870 (day), NJ Intergroup 1-800-739-2465 or 732-886-2142. *Website:* http://www.orgsites.com/nj/sa
Dover Meets Mon., 8pm, St. John's Episcopal Church, 11 S. Bergen St.

<u>**Morris Plains**</u> Meets Tues., noon; Thurs., noon; and Fri., noon, St. Paul's Episcopal Church, Hillview Ave. and Mountain Way.

S.L.A.A. (Sex and Love Addictions Anonymous) 12-Step. Fellowship for those who desire to stop living out a pattern of sex and love addiction, compulsive sexual behavior or emotional attachment. Meets Tues., 7:30pm, Morristown Memorial Hospital, 100 Madison Ave., Franklin Wing, Room F571, Morristown. Call Lee 908-876-4081 or Delaware Valley Intergroup 215-731-9760.

OCEAN

Sexaholics Anonymous Mutual support for those who want to stop their sexually self-destructive thinking and behavior to become sexually sober. For meeting information call Tom A. 908-351-3870, NJ Intergroup 1-800-739-2465 or 732-886-2142. *Website:* http://www.orgsites.com/nj/sa

<u>**Beachwood**</u> Meets Tues., 8pm, St. Paul Lutheran Church, 130 Cable Ave.

<u>**Toms River**</u> Meets Sat., 9:30am, Presbyterian Church of Toms River, 1070 Hooper Ave.

PASSAIC

Sexaholics Anonymous Mutual support for those who want to stop their sexually self-destructive thinking and behavior to become sexually sober. Meets Mon., 7:30pm and Sat., 7:30am, United Methodist Church, 139 Church St., Little Falls. For information call Tom A. 908-351-3870, NJ Intergroup 1-800-739-2465 or 732-886-2142. *Website:* http://www.orgsites.com/nj/sa

SOMERSET

Freedom Group 12-Step. Christ-based support group for men wanting freedom from being sexually driven. Confidential. Rap sessions, phone help, literature and guest speakers. Call Millington Baptist Church 908-647-0594 ask for "Freedom Group" or Paul 908-705-3265.

Sexaholics Anonymous Mutual support for those who want to stop their sexually self-destructive thinking and behavior to become sexually sober. Meets Tues., 7pm and Thurs., 7pm, Wilson Memorial Union Church, Hillcrest Rd., Watchung. Call Tom A. 908-351-3870 (day), NJ Intergroup 1-800-739-2465 or 732-886-2142. *Website:* http://www.orgsites.com/nj/sa

S.L.A.A. (Sex and Love Addicts Anonymous) 12-Step. Fellowship for those who desire to stop living out a pattern of sex and love addiction, compulsive sexual behavior or emotional attachment. Call Delaware Valley Intergroup 215-731-9760.

> **Bound Brook** Meets Sun. and Thurs., 8pm, Bound Brook Presbyterian Church, 409 Mountain Ave. and E. Union Ave. Call Steve 908-413-2470.
>
> **Kingston** *(MEN ONLY)* Meets Mon., 5:30pm, Kingston United Methodist Church, Church St.
>
> **Kingston** Meets Thurs., 6pm, Kingston United Methodist Church, Church St.

UNION

Sexaholics Anonymous Mutual support for those who want to stop their sexually self-destructive thinking and behavior to become sexually sober. For meeting information call Tom A. 908-351-3870, NJ Intergroup 1-800-739-2465 or 732-886-2142. *Website:* http://www.orgsites.com/nj/sa

> **Cranford** Meets Mon. and Wed., 7:15am; Mon.-Fri., noon; Fri., 8pm; Sat., 7:30pm and Sun., 1:30pm, Cranford United Methodist Church, 201 Lincoln Ave.
>
> **Elizabeth** Meets Sat., noon, St. Mary's of the Assumption, Race St.
>
> **Elizabeth** *(WOMEN ONLY)* Meets Thurs., 7pm, St. Paul's Evangelical Lutheran Church, 81 Galloping Hill Rd.

NATIONAL

Augustine Fellowship, Sex and Love Addicts Anonymous *International. 1234 affiliated groups. Founded 1976.* 12-Step. Fellowship based on A.A. for those who desire to stop living out a pattern of sex and love addiction, obsessive/compulsive sexual behavior or emotional attachment. Newsletter, journal, information and referrals, conferences and phone support. Write: Augustine Fellowship, 1550 NE Loop 410, Suite 118, San Antonio, TX, 78209. Call 210-828-7900; Fax: 781-255-9190. *Website:* http://www.slaafws.org *E-mail:* slaafws@slaafws.org

COSA (Codependents Of Sex Addicts) *International. 50+ affiliated groups. Founded 1980.* A Self-help program of recovery using the 12 steps adapted from A.A. and Al-Anon, for those involved in relationships with people who have compulsive sexual behavior. Assistance in starting new groups. Newsletter ($24). Write: COSA NSO, Inc., P.O. Box 14537, Minneapolis, MN 55414. Call 763-537-6904 (answering service - leave message). *Website:* http://www.cosa-recovery.org *E-mail:* info@cosa-recovery.org

Overcomers In Christ *International. Founded 1987.* Recovery program that deals with every aspect of addiction and dysfunction (spiritual, physical, mental, emotional and social). Uses Overcomers goals which are Christ-centered. Literature, resources, information and referrals. Assistance in starting new groups. Write: Overcomers In Christ, P.O. Box 34460, Omaha, NE 68134-04604. Call 402-573-0966; Fax: 402-573-0960. *Website:* http://www.OvercomersInChrist.org *E-mail:* OIC@OvercomersInChrist.org

Overcomers Outreach, Inc. *International. 700 affiliated groups. Founded 1985.* 12-Step. Christ-centered support group for persons with any compulsive behaviors, as well as their families and friends. Uses the 12-steps of A.A. and applies them to the Scriptures. Uses Jesus Christ as "higher power." Supplements involvement in other 12-step groups. Newsletter, group development guidelines and conferences. Write: Overcomers Outreach, P.O. Box 922950, Sylmar, CA 91392-2950. Call 1-800-310-3001. *Website:* http://www.overcomersoutreach.org *E-mail:* info@overcomersoutreach.org

Recoveries Anonymous *International. 50 chapters.* Spiritual recovery group for anyone seeking a solution for any kind of addiction, problem or behavior. Family and friends welcome. "How To Begin..." guides and "Start A Group" kit can be downloaded free from the website. Write: RA, P.O. Box 1212, East Northport, NY 11731. *Website:* http://www.r-a.org *E-mail:* raus@r-a.org

S-Anon *International. 280 affiliated groups. Founded 1984.* 12-Step. Support group for persons who have a friend or family member with a sexual addiction. Assistance available for starting groups. Conferences. and quarterly newsletter ($14). Write: S-Anon, P.O. Box 111242, Nashville, TN 37222. Call 1-800-210-8141. *Website:* http://www.sanon.org *E-mail:* sanon@sanon.org

Sex Addicts Anonymous *International. 736 groups. Founded 1977.* 12-Step. Fellowship of men and women who share their experience, strength and hope with each other so they may overcome their sexual addiction or dependency. Open to all who share a desire to stop compulsive sexual dependency. Bimonthly newsletter. Write: ISO of SAA, P.O. Box 70949, Houston, TX 77270. Call 713-869-4902 or 1-800-477-8191. *Website:* http://www.saa-recovery.org *E-mail:* iinfo@saa-recovery.org

Sexaholics Anonymous *International. 700 chapters. Founded 1979.* Program of recovery for those who want to stop sexually self-destructive thinking and behavior. Mutual support to achieve and maintain sexual sobriety. Phone network, quarterly newsletter, literature and books. Guidelines to help start a similar group.

Write: S.A., P.O. Box 3565, Brentwood, TN 37024-3565. Call 615-370-6062 or 1-866-424-8777; Fax: 615-370-0882. *Website:*http://www.sa.org *E-mail:* saico@sa.org

Sexual Compulsives Anonymous *International. 118+ groups. Founded 1982. (BILINGUAL)* Fellowship of men and women who share their experience, strength and hope that they may solve their common problem and help others to recover from sexual compulsion. Based on the 12-step model of recovery. Newsletter, information and referrals, phone support, conferences. Guidelines for starting similar groups. Write: SCA, P.O. Box 1585, Old Chelsea Station, New York, NY 10011. Call 1-800-977-4325. *Website:* http://www.sca-recovery.org *E-mail:* info@sca-recovery.org

Sexual Recovery Anonymous *International. 32 affiliated groups. Founded 1990.* 12-Step. Fellowship of men and women who share their experience, strength and hope with each other that they may solve their common problem and help others to recover. For those with a desire to stop compulsive sexual behavior. Online referrals, literature and support also available. Write: SRA, P.O. Box 1296, Redondo Beach, CA 90278. Call 212-340-4650 (recorded information); 323-850-8565 (Los Angeles area) or 604-290-9382 (BC, Canada). *Website:* http://www.sexualrecovery.org *E-mail:* info@sexualrecovery.org

SMOKING / NICOTINE

(see also toll-free helpline)

STATEWIDE

Nicotine Anonymous 12-Step. Self-help program of recovery for people who want to help themselves and others recover from nicotine addiction and live free of nicotine in all forms. For meeting information call Bill C. 201-947-3305. *Website:* http://www.nicotine-anonymous.org

ONLINE

New Jersey Quitnet *Online.* Provides access to peer support groups where one can learn from others who are quitting and get advice from those who have successfully quit. Once registered, members get a Quitting Guide to help them develop their individually tailored plan for quitting. *Website:* http://www.nj.quitnet.com

ATLANTIC

Nicotine Anonymous 12-Step. Mutual support for persons wishing to stop smoking and their use of nicotine.

Atlantic City Meets Tues., 10:30am, St. James AME Church, 101 N. New York Ave. Call Alberta J. 609-652-2883.

Galloway Meets Tues., 7:45pm, St. Mark's All Saints Episcopal Church, 429 S. Pitney Rd. Call Lori D. 609-652-2883.

Somers Point Meets Mon., 7pm, Shore Memorial Hospital, Shore Rd., Conference Center. Call Alice A. 609-748-0747.

BERGEN

Nicotine Anonymous 12-Step. Mutual support for persons wishing to stop smoking and their use of nicotine. Call Bill C. 201-947-3305.

Paramus Meets Wed., 7pm, Valley Hospital, 15 Essex Rd.

Teaneck Meets Sat., 7pm, St. Mark's Episcopal Church, 118 Chadwick Rd.

BURLINGTON

Nicotine Anonymous 12-Step. Mutual support for persons wishing to stop smoking and their use of nicotine. Meets Tues., 6pm, Divine Word Missionaries, Gym, 2nd Floor, 101 Park St., Bordentown. Call Tom D. 609-298-1866.

CAMDEN

Nicotine Anonymous 12-Step. Fellowship of men and women who want to achieve and maintain a nicotine-free life.

Cherry Hill Meets Mon., 7pm, Kennedy Hospital, 5th Floor, Chapel Ave. Call Ellie G. 856-354-0887.

Westmont Meets Wed., 6pm, Starting Point, 215 Highland Ave. Call Carol L. 856-354-0431.

CAPE MAY

Nicotine Anonymous 12-Step. Fellowship of men and women who want to achieve and maintain a nicotine-free life. Call Joseph P. 609-729-9145.

Wildwood Meets Wed., 7pm, The Cape Self-Help, 4410 Pacific Ave.

Wildwood Meets Sat., 3:30-4:30pm, The Hut, 113 West Oak Ave.

ESSEX

Reformers Anonymous Faith-based group to help people find freedom from addictions: alcohol, debt, drugs, eating disorders, gambling, internet, sex/love addiction, smoking, etc. Literature, newsletter and phone help. Meets Fri., 7-9pm, First Baptist Church, 257 Bloomfield Ave., Caldwell. Call Pastor Eli Miranda 201-724-9208 (day) or church 973-226-1004 (day).

MERCER

Nicotine Anonymous 12-Step. Fellowship of men and women who want to achieve and maintain a nicotine-free life. Meets Fri., 7pm, Hamilton Hospital Library near Gift Shop, Whitehorse and Klockner Rd., Hamilton. Call Josephine J. 609-890-9176.

MIDDLESEX

Nicotine Anonymous 12-Step. Fellowship of men and women who want to achieve and maintain a nicotine-free life.

> **Edison** Meets Tues., 7:30-8:30pm, Mortgage Money Mart, Tano Mall, 1st Bldg., 1st Floor, 1199 Amboy Ave. Call Frank N. 732-548-9423 (day).
>
> **Metuchen** Meets Mon., 7:30pm, Centenary United Methodist Church, Room 20, 200 Hillside Ave. Call Frank N. 732-548-9423 (day).
>
> **New Brunswick** Meets Thurs., 5pm, Tobacco Dependence Clinic, 317 George Rd. Call Lori D. 609-404-4644.

SMART Recovery (Self-Management and Recovery Training) *Professionally-run.* Self-help group for individuals wanting to gain their independence from addictive behaviors (drugs, including alcohol and nicotine and other compulsive behaviors i.e. gambling, eating disorders). SMART is an abstinence program based on cognitive-behavioral education and principles, especially those of rational-emotive behavior therapy. Meets Mon., 6-7:30pm, Rutgers University, Busch Campus, Psychology Building, Room A224, Piscataway. Call Tom Morgan 732-445-0902. *Website:* http://www.smartrecovery.org

MONMOUTH

Smoke Free Support Group *Professionally-run.* Offers support and education for those who are thinking about quitting, recently quit or are struggling to quit smoking. Meets 4th Tues., (except June, July, Aug.), 7-9pm, Monmouth Medical

Center, 300 Second Ave., Long Branch. Pre-registration required. Before attending call 732-923-6990 (day).

MORRIS

Nicotine Anonymous 12-Step. Fellowship of men and women who want to achieve and maintain a nicotine-free life. Meets Thurs., 6:30pm, Saint Clare's Behavioral Health Center, Powerville Rd., Boonton. Call Toni D. 973-283-9324.

SMART Recovery (Self-Management And Recovery Training) Self-help group for individuals wanting to gain their independence from addictive behaviors (drugs, including alcohol and nicotine, and other compulsive behaviors including gambling, eating disorders). SMART is an abstinence program based on cognitive-behavioral education and principles, especially those of rational-emotive behavior therapy. Meets Thurs., 7-8:30pm, Beginnings, 65 Spring St., Morristown. Call Rich 973-983-8755. *Website:* http://www.smartrecovery.org

PASSAIC

Nicotine Anonymous 12-Step. Fellowship of men and women who want to achieve and maintain a nicotine-free life. Meets Tues., 9pm, Eva's Recovery Center, 393 Main St., Paterson. Call Samuel B. 973-851-7469.

NATIONAL

Nicotine Anonymous World Services *International. 500+ groups. Founded 1985.* 12-Step. Program for people who want to recover from nicotine addiction and live free of nicotine in all forms. Welcomes all, including persons using cessation programs and nicotine withdrawal aids. Write: NAWS, 419 Main St. PMB #370, Huntington Beach, CA 92648. Call 1-877-879-6422 or 415-750-0328. *Website:* http://www.nicotine-anonymous.org

Recoveries Anonymous *International. 50 chapters.* Spiritual recovery group for anyone seeking a solution for any kind of addiction, problem or behavior. Family and friends welcome. “How To Begin…” guides and “Start A Group” kit can be downloaded free from the website. Write: RA, P.O. Box 1212, East Northport, NY 11731. *Website:* http://www.r-a.org *E-mail:* raus@r-a.org

B E R E A V E M E N T

BEREAVEMENT (GENERAL)

STATEWIDE

COPS (Concerns Of Police Surviving, Inc.) *(Garden State Chapter)* Peer support for families and co-workers of police officers who have died in the line of duty. Mutual sharing, phone help, rap sessions and social events. For information call 609-625-1024. *Website*: http://www.gardenstatecops.com *E-mail:* gssnjcops@gardenstatecops.com

Iraq/Afghanistan War Family Bereavement Groups *Professionally-run.* Veteran centers in New Jersey have support groups and related services for families of military killed in the war. Meetings vary. Write: Ann Talmage, Newark Vet Center, 2 Broad St., Suite 703, Bloomfield, NJ 07003. For information contact the nearest center: Newark (Essex) 973-748-0980; Jersey City (Hudson) 201-748-4467; Trenton (Mercer) 609-989-2260; Ventnor (Atlantic) 609-487-8387. *Website:* http://www.va.gov/rcs *E-mail:* ann.talmage@med.va.gov

National Donor Family Council *(Serves NY and NJ)* Mutual support for families who donated the organs/tissues of a loved one who died. Provides free literature, educational programs, email groups and local resources. Quarterly newsletter, pen pals and advocacy efforts. Write: National Donor Family Council, 30 E. 33rd St., 3rd Floor, New York, NY 10016. Call 212-889-2210 or 1-800-622-9010; Fax: 212-689-9261. *Website:* http://www.donorfamily.org *E-mail:* donorfamily@kidney.org

Rainbows, Inc. *Professionally-run.* Time-limited support groups for children and teens (ages 4-17) who are grieving a loss due to death, divorce, abandonment or other life-altering experience. Groups meet for a specific number of sessions and are held periodically. Some programs have concurrent groups for the parents. Helps implement programs throughout the state in schools, churches and social service agencies. *Website:* http://www.rainbowsnj.org *E-mail:* info@rainbowsnj.org

> **Central New Jersey** (Covers Burlington, Mercer, Monmouth and Ocean counties) Write: Marilyn Schipp, Trenton Diocese, Family Life Office, P.O. Box 5147, Trenton, NJ 08638-0147. For any upcoming group sessions planned call Marilyn Schipp 609-406-7400 ext. 5557 (day).
>
> **Northern New Jersey** (Covers Bergen, Essex, Hudson, Hunterdon, Middlesex, Morris, Passaic, Somerset, Sussex, Union and Warren

counties) Write: Rainbows, Inc., NJ State Chapter, 55 Woodland Ave., Summit, NJ 07901. For any upcoming group sessions planned call Alice Forsyth 908-608-0888 (day).

Southern New Jersey (Covers Atlantic, Camden, Cape May, Cumberland, Gloucester and Salem counties) Write: Sister Pat McGrenra, Gesu School, 1700 West Thompson St., Philadelphia, PA 19121. For any upcoming group sessions planned call Sister Pat McGrenra 215-763-3660 ext. 204 (day).

ATLANTIC

Coping With Loss *Professionally-run.* Mutual support and education for persons grieving the death of a loved one. Group runs for 6 week sessions, 4 times per year. Meeting location varies throughout Atlantic County. Call 609-272-2424 (day).

Grief Support Mutual support and encouragement for persons who are grieving the loss of a loved one. Group meets for 8 weeks twice per year. Meets Tues., 7pm, Saint Joseph's Church, Somers Point. For information call Shirlee 609-629-0248 or Nancy 609-926-7766.

BERGEN

Bereavement Support Group Mutual support for adults who have suffered the loss of a loved one due to cancer. Newsletter. Meets Thurs., 6:30-8:30pm, Gilda's Club Northern NJ, 575 Main St., Hackensack. Call 201-457-1670 (day).

Bereavement Support Group *Professionally-run.* Mutual support and education for persons who have suffered the loss of a loved one. Literature. Groups run for 6-8 week sessions, 3 times per year, Hospice at Bergen Community Health Care, 400 Old Hook Rd., Conference Room, 2nd Floor, Westwood. Call Elizabeth Steel, Frances Castello, or Wendy Megerman 201-358-2900 (day).

Bereavement Support Group *Professionally-run.* Mutual support and education for persons experiencing the grief and loss of a loved one. Groups run for approximately 8 sessions, are offered periodically throughout the year. Meets at Englewood Hospital Medical Center, Home Health and Hospice Services, 75 Demarest Ave., Englewood. Pre-registration is required. Call Nicholas J. Biancola Jr. 201-541-2677 (day) or 201-894-3333 (day/eve).

Bereavement Support Group *Professionally-run.* Offers support to help persons grieve for a loved one. Groups run for approximately 6 weeks, two times per year. Meets at Holy Name Hospital Home Care, 718 Teaneck Rd., Teaneck. Call 201-833-3740 ext. 2766 (day).

Bereavement Support Group *Professionally-run.* Support and comfort for those grieving the loss of a loved one. Meets for 8 week sessions, several times a year, Wallington Presbyterian Church, Paterson St. and Bond St., Wallington. For meeting information call Rev. Peter Carey 973-779-2640.

Bereavement Support Group *Professionally-run.* Support for newly bereaved (2 years or less) who are experiencing normal grief. Meetings vary, Urban Plaza Building, 25 E. Salem St., 3rd Floor, Hackensack. Pre-registration required. Call 201-342-7766 (day).

Color of Grief, The *Professionally-fun.* Provides support and education to children (ages 12-17) who have experienced the loss of a parent due to cancer. Parent group meets concurrently. Rap sessions and literature. Meetings vary, Cancer Care, 141 Dayton St., Suite 204, Ridgewood. Call Susan Barrett, MSW, LSW 201-301-6811 (day).

Healing Hope Support with a spiritual emphasis on helping those who suffer catastrophic loss including death, divorce, serious illness, etc. Meets 1st and 3rd Tues., 7:30-9pm, Cornerstone Christian Church, 495 Wyckoff Ave., Wyckoff. Call Kris 201-847-8107 (eve).

Journeys Bereavement Group for Children Offers emotional support and education for children ages 3-17 who are suffering with grief or life-threatening illness. Meets in Paramus. Before attending call Mary Maguire Reddy 201-291-6243.

New Start Bereavement Groups Offers emotional support and education for grief and its impact on the bereaved. Meetings vary, Dorothy Kraft Building, 15 Essex Rd., Paramus. Before attending call Mary Maguire Reddy 201-291-6243.

Pathways Bereavement Support Group *Professionally-run.* Support group with educational components for people in a more advanced stage of bereavement, (loss 4 or more months ago). Group runs for 8 sessions various times per year. Meets at Valley Hospice, 15 Essex Rd., Paramus. Pre-registration required. Call Mary Maguire Reddy 201-291-6243.

Rainbows Peer Support Group *Professionally-run.* Peer support for children, (age 4 - teens), who have experienced a family loss because of death, separation, divorce or abandonment. Goals are to provide peer support, furnish an understanding of the grief experience, assist in building a stronger sense of self-esteem and teach appropriate coping mechanisms. Parents' group meets concurrently. Meets Tues., (Sept.-Dec.) and Wed., (Jan.-Apr.), Ridgewood YMCA, 112 Oak St., Ridgewood. Registration required. Call Kathy Meding 201-444-5600 ext. 332 (day). For any other new group sessions planned, call the regional representative, Alice Forsyth 908-608-0888 (day). *E-mail:* kmeding@ridgewoodym.org

Safe Space Support for bereaved high school teens who have lost a loved one through death. Education, mutual sharing and literature. Meets for 8 week sessions, Creative Living Center, 37E Allendale Ave., Allendale. Call Dan Bottorff 201-327-2424 ext. 253 or Penny Gadzini ext 254. *Website:* http://www.creativelivingresource.org

Separated, Divorced and Bereaved Catholics Referrals to groups for emotional/spiritual support and social activities for separated, divorced, bereaved men and women. Groups are sponsored by various parishes throughout the county and are open to people of any faith. Call Family Life Ministries, Archdiocese of Newark 973-497-4327.

VITAS Innovative Hospice Care *Professionally-run.* Forum for sharing one's grief experience, giving and receiving support, learning about the grief process and promoting healing. Meets for 8 weeks, 4-5 times/yr., Norwood. Call Carley Anne Tsaglos 973-885-0912 (day).

BURLINGTON

Bereavement Support Group Mutual support for those suffering the loss a loved one. Various meeting locations and times. See group listings and contacts online at: *http://*www.dioceseoftrenton.org/church/consolation.asp (scroll down to "Support Groups for Bereavement") or call Office of Family Life, Trenton Diocese 609-406-7400 ext. 5557 (day).

Bereavement Support Group for Friends and Family *Professionally-run.* Support for friends and family grieving the death of a loved one to help cope with the loss. Meets 3rd Wed., (except July/Aug.), 7-8:30pm, Dougherty's Funeral Home, 2200 Trenton Rd., Levittown, PA. Call Deborah Gawthrop 215-624-8190 (day).

Big Hurts, Little Tears *Professionally-run.* Support group for 3-5 year-olds who have been affected by a loss. Meetings vary, Samaritan Hospice, Marlton. Pre-registration required. Before attending call The Samaritan Center for Grief Support 1-800-596-8550.

Daughters Without Mothers *Professionally-run.* Support group for women who are grieving the loss of a mother. Education, discussions and an opportunity to share stories. Meetings vary, Samaritan Hospice, Marlton. Pre-registration required. Before attending call The Samaritan Center for Grief Support 1-800-596-8550.

Grief For The Loss Of A Pet *Professionally-run.* Support group for persons coping with the loss of a animal companion. Meetings vary, Samaritan Hospice, Marlton. Pre-registration required. Before attending call The Samaritan Center for Grief 1-800-596-8550.

Helping Hand Grief Support Group Christian-based support for persons bereaving the loss of a loved one (including death of a child, loss to homicide or suicide) through education, encouragement, counseling and understanding. Families welcome. Meets 1st and 3rd Mon., 7-9pm, for 10 week sessions, Fellowship Alliance Chapel, (Log house in back of church), 199 Church Rd., Medford. Call Wanda and George Stein 609-953-7333 ext. 309 (day/eve).

Just the Guys *Professionally-run.* Mutual support for adult men grieving the loss of a family member or friend. Meetings vary, Samaritan Hospice, Marlton. Pre-registration required. Before attending call The Samaritan Center for Grief Support 856-596-8550.

SIGH (Sharing In Grief and Hope) *Professionally-run.* Mutual support for anyone who has experienced the death of a loved one. Meets various days and locations. Pre-registration required. Before attending call The Samaritan Center for Grief Support 1-800-596-8550.

VITAS Hospice – Living With Loss *Professionally-run.* Forum for sharing one's grief experience, giving and receiving support, learning about the grief process and promoting healing. Meets for 6 weeks, 4 times/yr., Dennison-McGee Funeral Home, 869 Beverly Rd., Burlington. Call James K. Chrysler 856-778-0222 (day).

CAMDEN

Bereavement Support Group Support and comfort for newly bereaved adults grieving the loss of a loved one within the past year. Families welcome. Phone help and literature. Runs for 8 week sessions, 2 times per year in various locations and times. Call Bereavement Coordinator 856-414-1155 (day).

Breath of Life Bereavement Support Group *Professionally-run.* Mutual support for anyone grieving the loss of a loved one. Education, rap sessions, guest speakers and phone help. Meets monthly, 7-8pm, Bethany Baptist Church, 1115 Gibbsboro Rd., Lindenwald. Call Charlene Ransom 856-782-9540 (day) or Niki Brown 856-782-6749 (day). *Website:* http://www.abundantharvest.com *E-mail:* revnbrown@verizon.net

Counseling Network for Loss and Transition Grief Groups *Professionally-run.* Provides emotional and educational support for persons grieving the loss of a loved one. Offers various groups, both time-limited and on-going, for general bereavement, loss of spouse, and a group for young widows. Meeting time and location varies in Philadelphia, PA area. For information call Debbie Gawthrop 215-624-8190 (day). *E-mail:* dgawthropcnlt@cs.com

Grief Management of St. Rose of Lima Mutual support for anyone grieving the loss of a significant person in their life due to death, separation or divorce. Families welcome. Meets Thurs., (for 12 week sessions), 7:30-9:30pm, St. Rose of Lima, 300 Kings Highway, Parish Lounge, Haddon Heights. Before attending call Sister Eucharista Johnson 856-310-1770. *Website:* http://www.strosenj.com

St. Agnes Grief Support Ministry Mutual support for anyone who is grieving the loss of a loved one. Literature and phone help. Meets for 8 weeks, 3 times per year, St. Agnes Church, 701 Little Gloucester Rd., Conference Room Rectory, Blackwood. Before attending call Pat Reilly 856-228-7906 (eve.).

VITAS Hospice – Living With Loss *Professionally-run.* Forum for sharing one's grief experience, giving and receiving support, learning about the grief process and promoting healing. Meets for 6 weeks, 4 times/yr., Kennedy Hospital – Stratford, 18 E. Laurel Rd., 3rd Floor Conference Room, Stratford. Call James K. Chrysler 856-778-0222 (day).

"One of the hardest things in life is having words in your heart that you can't utter." -- James Earl Jones

ESSEX

Adult Bereavement Group *Professionally-run.* Offers mutual support for adults bereaving the death of a loved one. Newly bereaved group meets twice per month for eight weeks. Also offers an ongoing group for persons who have already attended a professionally-run bereavement group or had professional counseling. Meets 1st and 3rd Mon., 6-7pm, Hospice of NJ, 400 Broadacres Dr., 4th Floor, Bloomfield. For information call Michael Teague 973-893-0818 ext. 213 or Jason Coveleski 973-893-0818 ext. 206.

Adult Bereavement Support Group *Professionally-run.* Mutual support for any adult who has experienced a significant loss. Meets for 6 week sessions, (Spring/Fall), St. Barnabas Hospice and Pallative Care Center, 187 Millburn Ave., Millburn. Call Judith Zucker, LCSW 973-322-4817 (day).

Daughter's Bereavement Mutual support for adult women who have experienced the loss of their mother. Meets for 6 week sessions, St. Barnabas Hospice and Pallative Care Center, 95 Old Short Hills Rd., West Orange. For meeting information call Judith Zucker, LCSW 973-322-4817 (day).

Family Bereavement Group *Professionally-run.* Group for those who lost spouses with young children (ages 5-18) at home. Separate groups for children run concurrently. Meets 6:30-8pm, Saint Barnabas Corporate Building, 95 Old Short Hills Rd., West Orange. For meeting day call Judith Zucker, LCSW 973-322-4817 (day).

Growing Through Loss Bereavement Group *Professionally-run.* Offers a caring and supportive environment for persons grieving the loss of a loved one. Meets for 6-8 weeks twice a year, (Spring/Fall), St. Barnabas Medical Center, Old Short Hills Rd., Livingston. Registration required. Call Pastoral Care 973-322-5015 (day). Fax: 973-322-2410.

Our Lady of The Lake Bethany Support Group *Professionally-run.* Provides mutual support for persons affected by the loss of a loved one. Offers mutual sharing, education, literature and guest speakers. Meets twice a month, 7:30-9pm, Our Lady of The Lake Church, 32 Lakeside Ave., Rectory, Verona. For meeting information call JoAnn 973-585-7278 (eve).

Rainbows, Inc. *Professionally-run.* Peer support for children and adolescents (kindergarten - eighth grade) who are grieving a loss due to death, divorce, abandonment or other life altering situation. For any other new group sessions planned, call the regional representative Alice Forsyth 908-608-0888 (day).

<u>**Livingston**</u> Meets Mon., 5:30-6:30pm, Linda and Rudy Slucker Center for Women, 513 West Mt. Pleasant Ave. Call 973-994-4994 (day). *Website:* http://www.centerforwomennj.org *E-mail:* centerforwomen@jwessex.org

<u>**Verona**</u> Meets Mon., (Spring/Fall), 7 week sessions, First Presbyterian Church, 10 Fairview Ave. Call Barbara 973-857-0626 (day).

Separated, Divorced and Bereaved Catholics Referrals to groups for emotional/spiritual support and social activities for separated, divorced or bereaved men and women. Groups are sponsored by various churches throughout the county and are open to people of any faith. For information call Family Life Ministry, Newark Diocese 973-497-4327.

Survivors of Murdered Children *Professionally-run.* Mutual support and understanding for families and friends who have lost a loved one to murder. Guest speakers, advocacy, speakers' bureau, social and buddy system. Meets 2nd Fri., 6:30pm, ECHOES - The Grief Center, 116 Main St., Orange. Call Beverly Henderson 973-675-1199.

Teen Bereavement Support Group *Professionally-run.* Support for teens, age 12-18, bereaving the loss of a loved one. Meets for 6 week sessions, St. Barnabas Hospice and Pallative Care Center, 187 Millburn Ave., Millburn. Call Judith Zucker, LCSW 973-322-4817 (day).

GLOUCESTER

Center for People in Transition *Professionally-run.* Assists displaced homemakers to become emotionally and economically self-sufficient through life skills training, career decision making, education or vocational training and supportive services. Evening divorce and bereavement support groups for men and women. Call 856-415-2222 (day). *E-mail:* peopleintransition@gccnj.edu

J.O.Y. Bereavement Support Group *Professionally-run.* Mutual support for men and women grieving the loss of a loved one. Guest speakers, educational series, phone help and literature. Meets 3rd Wed., 7-9pm, Gloucester County Library, Bridgeton Pike, (Route 45), Mullica Hill. Call Joyce 856-223-1803 (day).

HUDSON

Bereavement Support *Professionally-run.* Support for anyone grieving the loss of a loved one. Meets Thurs., 6:30pm, Christ Hospital, Palisades Ave., Chapel, Jersey City. Before attending call Pastoral Care Dept. 201-795-8397.

Hudson Hospice Bereavement Group *Professionally-run.* Provides a supportive environment for those grieving the recent death of someone close. The overall goal of the group is to help people move toward the reconciliation of grief. Meets 1st and 2nd Wed., in Bayonne. For meeting information call Hospice 201-433-6225 (day). *E-mail:* OLS9395@comcast.net

Hudson Hospice Children's Bereavement Support Group *Professionally-run.* Program to help grieving families. Children (ages 4-17) attend a weekly art therapy group while the parents participate in a companion parent group. Groups meet for 10 week sessions in Bayonne. Call Sharon or Sister Alice McCoy 201-433-6225 (day). *E-mail:* ols9395@comcast.net

Rainbows, Inc. *Professionally-run.* Peer support for children and adolescents (kindergarten - eighth grade) who are grieving a loss due to death, divorce or abandonment. Parent group meets concurrently. Meets Thurs., 7-8pm, (Oct.-Dec.), St. Anne's School, Parish Center, Jersey City. Call Sister Alberta 201-656-2490 (day) or 201-963-0998 (eve). For any other new group sessions planned, call the regional representative, Alice Forsyth 908-608-0888 (day). *Website:* http://www.stanncsjc.com

Separated, Divorced and Bereaved Catholics Referrals to groups for emotional/spiritual support and social activities for separated, divorced or bereaved men and women. Groups are sponsored by various churches throughout the county, and are open to people of any faith. For information call Family Life Ministry, Newark Diocese 973-497-4327.

HUNTERDON

Bereavement Support Group Mutual support for persons who have experienced the death of a loved one. Sessions run for 6-8 weeks, 2 times per year. Meets various locations throughout the county. For meeting information call Family Life Office 732-562-1990 ext. 1624.

Grieving and Growing Through Loss *Professionally-run.* Mutual support for persons going through the grief process. Meets 2nd and 4th Thurs., 7-8:30pm, Hunterdon Hospice Office, Hunterdon Regional Community Health Care, 5 Bartles Corner Rd., Flemington. Call 908-788-6600 (day).

MERCER

Bereavement Support Group Mutual support for those suffering the loss of a loved one. Various meeting locations and times. See group listings at: http://www.dioceseoftrenton.org/church/consolation.asp (scroll down to "Support Groups for Bereavement") or call Office of Family Life, Trenton Diocese 609-406-7400 ext. 5557 (day).

Bereavement Support Group *Professionally-run.* Mutual support for individuals whose loss has occurred at least 2 or more months ago. Meets 2nd and 4th Tues., 5-6:30pm, Cancer Institute of NJ at Hamilton, 2575 Klockner Rd., Hamilton. Before attending call Elsje Reiss, MSW, LCSW 609-584-2818 (day).

Caring and Sharing *Professionally-run.* Mutual support for anyone suffering the loss of a loved one. Meets 1st Wed., 7-9pm, Saul Colonial Home, 3795 Nottingham Way, Hamilton Square. Call Mary Lou Pizzullo 609-587-7072 (day). *Website:* http://www.saulfuneralhomes.com *E-mail:* mlpizzullo@saulfuneralhomes.com

Coping with Bereavement *Professionally-run.* Support for those who have lost a family member or friend. Meets 3rd Mon., 1-2:30pm, Princeton Senior Resource Center, Suzanne Patterson Building, (behind Borough Hall), 45 Stockton St., Princeton. Call Joann Laveman, LCSW or Cheryl Regis 609-497-4900 (day).

SIGH (Sharing In Grief and Hope) *Professionally-run.* Mutual support for any person who has experienced the death of a loved one. Meeting days vary, Hamilton Township. Pre-registration required. Before attending call The Samaritan Center for Grief Support 1-800-596-8550.

MIDDLESEX

Journey Through Grief Bereavement Support Group A non-denominational support group for the recently bereaved. Phone help. Meets 2nd Mon., 7:30-9pm, Queenship of Mary Church, Dey Rd. and Scudders Mill Rd., Plainsboro. Call Lorrie Quinlan 732-821-8447 (day).

St. James Bereavement Support Group On-going emotional support for those who have lost a loved one through death. Meets in Woodbridge. Call Sister Marie Pierson 732-634-0500 ext. 14 (day). *E-mail:* sistermarie@stjamesonline.org

MONMOUTH

Art Therapy for Bereaved Children *Professionally-run.* Bereavement program for children who have lost a loved one. Uses art therapy to help children address their feelings. Meets periodically for 7 week sessions, Riverview Medical Center, 1 Riverview Plaza, Red Bank. Call 732-530-2382.

Bereavement Support Group Mutual support for those suffering the loss of a loved one. Various meeting locations and times. See group listings at: http://www.dioceseoftrenton.org/church/consolation.asp (scroll down to "Support Groups for Bereavement") or call Office of Family Life, Trenton Diocese 609-406-7400 ext. 5557 (day).

Bereavement Support Group *Professionally-run.* Mutual support for the loss of a spouse and adult children bereaving the death of a parent. Meets for 6 weeks, several times per year, Riverview Medical Center, Cancer Center, 1 Riverview Plaza, Red Bank. Call Sister Vida O'Leary 732-530-2382.

Bereavement Support Group *Professionally-run.* Mutual support for adults dealing with the death of a loved one. Meets 2nd and 4th Tues., 7:30pm, Bayshore Community Hospital, TCU Activity Room, 727 N. Beers St., (main lobby to 2 East Floor), Holmdel. Call Chaplain Anna Esposito 732-739-5888 (day).

HUGS (Help Us Grieve Someone) Confidential non-denominational bereavement group where those who have lost loved ones can share their feelings with others who truly understand what they are going through. Literature. Meets twice a month, 7:30pm, Old Tennent Presbyterian Church, 452 Tennent Rd., Old Scott's Hall, Tennent. For information call Rose Olson 732-845-9475 (day/eve). *Website:* http://www.hugsonline.net

Living With Loss *Professionally-run.* Mutual support for persons who have experienced the loss of a loved one. Meets Mon., 11:30am-1pm, Centra State Medical Center, Route 537, Freehold. Call Bunny Salomon 732-617-2221 (day/eve).

Mourning After, The *Professionally-run.* Support for people who are grieving the loss of a loved one. Group uses a wide range of interactive and creative interventions to assist in the grieving process. Meets Fri., 11:30am-1pm, Center Playhouse, 35 South St., (downtown) Freehold. Call Bernice Garfield or Bob Szita 732-577-1076 (day/eve). *Website:* http://www.actionartz.com *E-mail:* griefcounseling@actionartz.com

Saint Rose Bereavement Support Group *Professionally-run.* Support for those who are experiencing grief due to the death of a loved one. Offers support to members while working through the changes in their lives by sharing their stories in a faith community. Guest speakers, phone help, literature, prayer and music. Meets 1st and 3rd Thurs., 7:30-8:30pm, (June/Aug. meetings are held only on 1st Thurs.), St. Rose Rectory, 603 7th Ave., Belmar. Call Deacon Normand or Marie Bailey 732-774-0515 (day/eve) or Rosemarie Reilly 732-681-4745 (day/eve).

MORRIS

Adult Bereavement Support Group *Professionally-run.* Support for bereaved adults who have lost a loved one due to cancer or other long-term illness. Runs for 8-week sessions, St. Clare's Hospital, Pocono Rd., Denville. For information call Brandy Johnson, MSW, 973-625-6176 (day). *E-mail:* bjohnson@saintclares.org

Children's Bereavement Group *Professionally-run.* Provides support to children (age 6-13) who have experienced a recent loss due to cancer. Runs for 8 week sessions. For information call Brandy Johnson, MSW 973-625-6176 (day). *E-mail:* BJohnson@saintclares.org

Compassionate Care Hospice Support Group *Professionally-run.* Support for anyone grieving the loss of a loved one. Rap sessions. Meets Thurs., 7-8:30pm, Compassionate Care Hospice, 140 Littleton Rd., Suite 200, Parsippany. Call Lisa Morrow 973-402-4712 (day).

Living Through Grief *Professionally-run.* Mutual support for persons who have recently experienced the death of a loved one. Group runs for 8 week, various times per year. Meets various times and locations. Call Atlantic Hospice 973-379-8440.

Pet Loss Support Group *Professionally-run.* Helps individuals cope with the loss or impending loss of their companion animal to work through feelings of grief and mourning. Under 18 welcome. Meets 1st and 3rd Tues., 7:30pm, St. Hubert's Giralda, Woodland Ave., Madison. For information call 973-377-7094 (day).

Rainbows and Prism Peer support for children and adolescents (kindergarten - eighth grade) who are grieving the loss of a parent due to death or divorce. Parent group meets concurrently. Meets Tues., 7:15-8pm Sept.-Jan.), Our Lady of Magnificent, 2 Miller Rd., Kinnelon. Call Claudette Meehan 973-492-9406 (eve) or Peggy Tana 973-838-7265. For any upcoming group sessions planned call Alice Forsyth 908-608-0888 (day).

Rainbows, Inc. *Professionally-run.* Peer support for children and adolescents (kindergarten - eighth grade) who are grieving a loss due to death, divorce or abandonment. Group runs for 14 weeks in winter and 7 weeks in summer. Meets Tues., 7-7:45pm, St. Francis Residential Community, 122 Diamond Spring Rd., Denville. Before attending call Diane 973-627-2134 (day/eve). For any other new group sessions planned, call the regional representative, Alice Forsyth 908-608-0888 (day).

Separation, Divorce, and Bereavement Support Group Emotional and spiritual support for men and women in all stages of separation, divorce, bereavement and other emotional pain. Phone help, pen pals and buddy system. Meets Thurs., 6:30pm, Morris County Library, 30 E. Hanover Ave., Whippany. Call Laura 973-581-1636 (day/eve) or Eric 201-247-6582 (day/eve).

OCEAN

Bereavement for Adults Mutual support for adults bereaving the loss of a loved one. Educational series, rap sessions and guest speakers. Meetings vary, Hospice of NJ-Toms River, 40 Bey Lea Rd., Toms River. For meeting information call Jeremy Lees 732-818-3460 (day).

Bereavement Support Group Mutual support for those suffering the loss a loved one. Various meeting locations and times. See group listings at: http://www.dioceseoftrenton.org/church/consolation.asp (scroll down to "Support Groups for Bereavement") or call Office of Family Life, Trenton Diocese 609-406-7400 ext. 5557 (day).

"Who then can so softly bind up the wound of another as he who has felt the same wound himself." -- *Thomas Jefferson*

Better Bereavement Support for anyone bereaving the loss of a loved one. Meets 1st and 3rd Tues., 7:30-9pm, (schedule varies June/Aug.), Ocean Medical Center, 425 Jack Martin Blvd., Brick. Pre-registration required. Call 1-800-560-9990 (day).

Grief Share Support, education and sharing for persons grieving the loss of someone close to them. Families welcome. Meets Wed., 7:30-8:30pm, Shore Vineyard Church, Compass Ave. and Spring St., Beachwood. Call Jackie 732-244-3888 (day).

Journey Through Grief *Professionally-run.* Support for men and women of all ages to work through the normal stages of grief with education and group support. Focuses on situations which frequently occur after the loss of a loved one. Meets at St. Francis Center, 4700 Long Beach Blvd., Brant Beach. Before attending call 609-494-1554 (day).

Kids Bereavement Support Group *Professionally-run.* Support for children (age 7-14) who are bereaving the loss of a parent, grandparent, sibling or friend. Rap sessions. Meets 1st Thurs., 5:30-6:30pm, Center for Kids and Family, 591 Lakehurst Rd., Toms River. Call 732-505-5437 (day).

Recently Bereaved Support Group *Professionally-run.* Support for anyone bereaving the recent loss of a loved one. Meets Mon., 10am, Jewish Family and Children's Services, 301 Madison Ave., Lakewood. Call Rita Sason or Carol Powell 732-363-8010 (Mon-Thurs). *E-mail:* jfcs@ocjf.org

PASSAIC

Lighted Path, The *Professionally-run.* Mutual support for persons who have suffered the loss of a loved one. Meets for 6 week sessions, 2-3 times a year, Pathways Counseling Center, 16 Pompton Ave., Pompton Lakes. Call Peg Buczek 973-835-6337 (day).

Passaic Valley Hospice Bereavement Support Group *Professionally-run.* Offers mutual support and education for anyone who has experienced the death of a loved one. Sharing of feelings and experiences in a safe supportive environment. Literature and guest speakers. Meets for 6 week sessions, 4 times per year, Passaic Valley Hospice, 783 Riverview Dr., Totowa. Call Al Jousset, Hospice Chaplain 973-785-7406 (day).

SALEM

Bereavement Support Group *Professionally-run.* Mutual support to help facilitate an individual's grief process within a safe and confidential environment. Under 18 welcome. Group runs for 8 week sessions, Mon., 7-8:30pm, Memorial Hospital of Salem County, 310 Salem-Woodstown Rd., Salem. Call Rev. Walt Kellen 856-678-8500 ext. 315 (day).

SOMERSET

Bereavement Support Group *Professionally-run.* Support for individuals who have experienced the death of a loved one from cancer. Share thoughts, feelings and information. Meets Mon., 6-7:30pm, The Wellness Community of Central New Jersey, 3 Crossroads Dr., Bedminster. Pre-registration required. Before attending call Ellen Levine, LCSW 908-658-5400 (day).

Grief Support Group Support for those grieving the loss of a loved one. Meets one Sun. a month, 11:45-1pm, Lamington Presbyterian Church, Bedminster. For meeting information call Barbara Pereyra 908-832-0168. *E-mail:* bpereyra@delbarton.org

JANUS Bereavement Group *Professionally-run.* Support and education for anyone who has experienced a loss through death, separation/divorce, retirement, loss of a job, health or relocation. Helps individuals accept and adjust to the loss. Meets 2nd Tues., 7:30-9pm, in Bridgewater and Branchburg. Call Barbara Ronca, LCSW 908-218-9062 (Mon.-Fri., 9am-3pm).

VNA of Somerset Hills Bereavement Support Group *Professionally-run.* Mutual support for family and friends bereaving the loss of a loved one. Meets 2nd and 4th Tues., 11am-12:30pm, Somerset Medical Center, 110 Rehill Ave., Somerville. Call Mary Lou Daley, LCSW 908-766-0180 (day). *E-mail:* mldaley@visitingnurse.org

SUSSEX

Bereavement Support Group Support for anyone who has suffered a loss. Rap sessions, phone help and literature. Meets 2nd and 4th Wed., 7-8:30pm, Office of Dr. Dennis Fielding, 17 Route 23 North, Hamburg. Call Linda Patete 973-827-8518 (eve). *E-mail:* ljpatete@yahoo.com

Bereavement Support Group Support for those grieving the loss of a loved one. Families and friends welcome. Guest speakers, education and literature. Meets for 2 sessions, 2 times year, Blessed Kateri Tekakwitha Roman Catholic Church, Sparta. Call Laura 973-726-8978 (eve) or Janice 973-729-9348 (eve).

Coping with Loss Support for those grieving the loss of a loved one through death. Phone help, literature, rap sessions and mutual sharing. Meets 4th Tues., 10-11:30am, United Methodist Church, West Ann St., Milford, PA. Call Lorri Opitz 973-383-0115 or Diana Sebzda 908-852-8730.

Coping with Loss Support Group *Professionally-run.* Provides a safe and supportive environment for those who have lost a loved one where they can share experiences and feelings. Meets 2nd Mon., 7-8:30pm, Karen Ann Quinlan Hospice, 99 Sparta Ave., Newton. Call Diana Sebzda 973-383-0115 or 1-800-882-1117. *E-mail:* bereavement@karenannquinlanhospice.org

Project Self-Sufficiency *Professionally-run.* Support for single parents, teen parents, displaced homemakers and low-income families. Offers peer support groups for single parents and teen parents, loss recovery groups for children, parenting skills training and support, family activities, physical and emotional health educational seminars and more in conjunction with comprehensive job training and educational services designed to promote self-sufficiency. Meetings vary. Call Deborah Berry-Toon 973-383-5129 (day). *E-mail:* PSS@garden.net

UNION

Bereavement Support Group *Professionally-run.* Support for families and friends who have lost a loved one to cancer. Meets every other Mon., 5:30-6:30pm, Overlook Hospital, 99 Beauvoir Ave., Conference Room 1, Summit. Before attending call Kristen Scarlett, LPC, NCC 908-522-5255 (day).

Bereavement Support Groups *Professionally-run.* Mutual support for persons grieving the loss of a loved one. Series of 5 week meetings with separate groups for spouses and other family members. Meets various times, United Methodist Church, 1441 Springfield Ave., New Providence. Call Bereavement Coordinator 973-379-8440 (day).

Can't find an appropriate group in your area? The Clearinghouse helps people start groups. Give us a call at 1-800-367-6274

Center For Hope Hospice Bereavement Support Group *Professionally-run.* Separate support groups for adults, teens and children (age 5+) who have experienced the death of a loved one. Donations accepted. Groups meet various times, Center for Hope Hospice, Acadia House, 175 Glenside Ave., Scotch Plains. Call Center for Hope Hospice 908-654-3711 (day). *Website:* http://www.centerforhope.com *E-mail:* ddandrilli@centerforhope.com

Homicide Survivors *Professionally-run.* Provides support to family members and friends of homicide victims. Rap sessions, guest speakers. Meets 3rd Mon., (except July/Aug.), 7:15-9pm, Robert Wood Johnson Hospital, Rahway. Call Elaine O'Neal 908-527-4596 (day).

Lazarus Ministry *Professionally-run.* Support group for adults experiencing the loss of a loved one or friend through death. Meetings vary, 7:30pm, 321 South Broad St., Elizabeth. Call Sister Elaine Maguire 908-352-5154 (day).

Separated, Divorced and Bereaved Catholics Referrals to groups for emotional/spiritual support and social activities for separated, divorced, or bereaved men and women. Groups are sponsored by various churches throughout the county and are open to people of any faith. Call Family Life Ministry, Newark Diocese 973-497-4327.

WARREN

Grief Recovery Program *Professionally-run.* Provides comfort, support, and healing to persons (age 18+) who have suffered the loss of a loved one. Groups run for 4 weeks, (April and October), 7-9pm, Hackettstown Regional Medical Center, 651 Willow Grove St., Hackettstown. Call Carl Bannister 908-850-7757 (day).

Grief Support Group *Professionally-run.* Provides support for those coping with the loss of a partner, child, parent, or friend. Dues $20 (literature, refreshments, handouts, etc.) per 6 week session. Meets 3 times per year, Warren Hospital, Chapel, 185 Roseberry St., Phillipsburg. Call 908-859-6700 ext. 2048 (day).

NATIONAL

ACCESS (AirCraft Casualty Emotional Support Services) *National network. Founded 1996.* Matches persons who have lost a loved one in an aircraft related tragedy to volunteers who previously experienced a similar loss. Goal is to help fill the void that occurs when the emergency and disaster relief organizations disband, the initial shock subsides and the natural grieving process intensifies. Offers guidelines to help start a similar group. Persons communicate through e-mail or by phone. Online newsletter. Write: ACCESS, 1202 Lexington Ave., #335, New York, NY, 10028. Call 1-877-227-6435. *Website:* http://www.accesshelp.org *E-mail:* info@accesshelp.org

COPS (Concerns Of Police Survivors, Inc.) *National. 50 chapters. Founded 1984.* Provides resources for the surviving families of law enforcement officers killed in the line of duty according to Federal criteria. Also offers law enforcement training. Quarterly newsletter, departmental guidelines and peer support. Provides annual National Police Survivors' Conference each May during National Police Week. Special hands-on programs for survivors. Summer camp for children (ages 6-14) and their parent/guardian, parents' retreats, spouses get-aways. Outward Bound experiences for young adults (ages 15-20), siblings retreat, adult children's and in-laws retreat. Write: COPS, P.O. Box 3199, 3096 South State Highway 5, Camdenton, MO 65020. Call 573-346-4911; Fax: 573-346-1414. *Website:* http://www.nationalcops.org *E-mail:* cops@nationalcops.org

GriefShare *National. 3200 affiliated groups. Founded 1998.* Network of Christian support groups to assist those grieving the loss of a loved one. Groups show videos and have group discussions. Information and referrals, literature, and help in starting groups. Write: GriefShare, P.O. Box 1739, Wake Forest, NC 27588. Call 1-800-395-5755 or 919-562-2112; Fax: 919-562-2114. *Website:* http://www.griefshare.org *E-mail:* info@griefshare.org

National Donor Family Council *National. Founded 1992.* Mutual support for families who donated the organs/tissues of a loved one who died. Provides free literature, educational programs, email groups and local resources. Quarterly newsletter, pen pals and advocacy efforts. Write: National Donor Family Council, 30 E. 33rd St., 3rd Floor, New York, NY 10016. Call 212-889-2210 or 1-800-622-9010; Fax: 212-689-9261. *Website:* http://www.donorfamily.org *E-mail:* donorfamily@kidney.org

National Fallen Firefighters Foundation Survivors Support Network *National network. Founded 1992.* Provides emotional support to spouses, families and friends of firefighters who have died in the line of duty. Members are matched with survivors of similar experiences to help them cope during the difficult months following the death. Write: National Fallen Firefighters Foundation, P.O. Drawer 498, Emmitsburg, MD 21727. Call 301-447-1365; Fax: 301-447-1645. *Website:* http://www.firehero.org *E-mail:* firehero@firehero.org

National Organization of Parents Of Murdered Children *National. Over 235 chapters in US, Canada, Costa Rica. Founded 1978.* Nationwide self help support organization for the family and friends of those who have died by violence. Newsletter published 3 times a year. Court accompaniment also provided by many chapters. Parole Block Program and Second Opinion Service also available. Offers assistance in starting local chapters. Write: POMC, 100 E. 8th St., B-41, Cincinnati, OH 45202. Call 1-888-818-7662 or 513-721-5683 (office); Fax: 513-345-4489. *Website:* http://www.pomc.com *E-mail:* NatlPOMC@aol.com

RAINBOWS *International. 8600 affiliated groups. Founded 1983.* Establishes peer support groups in churches, schools, or social agencies for children and adults who are grieving a death, divorce or other painful transition in their family. Groups are led by trained adults. Online newsletter, information and referrals. Write: RAINBOWS, 2100 Golf Rd., Suite 370, Rolling Meadows, IL 60008-4231. Call 1-800-266-3206 or 847-952-1770; Fax: 847-952-1774. *Website:* http://www.rainbows.org *E-mail:* info@rainbows.org

TAPS (Tragedy Assistance Program for Survivors) *National network.* Provides support for persons who have lost a loved one while serving in the armed forces (Army, Air Force, Navy, Marine Corps, National Guard, Reserves, Service Academies, Coast Guard and contractors serving beside the military). Offers networking, crisis information, problem solving assistance and liaison with military agencies. Also TAPS youth programs. Annual seminar. Write: TAPS, 1621 Connecticut Ave., NW, Suite 300, Washington, DC 20009. Call 1-800-959-8277 or 202-588-8277; Fax: 202-588-0784. *Website:* http://www.taps.org *E-mail:* info@taps.org

Twinless Twin Support Group *International network. 12 regional directors. Founded 1986.* Mutual support for twins and other multiples who have lost their twin or multiple(s). Information, phone support, local meetings, annual conference. Parents of infant/child age survivor twins welcome. Publishes "Twinless Times." Dues $50/yr. Write: Twinless Twin Support Group, P.O. Box 980481, Ypsilanti, MI 48198. Call 1-888-205-8962. *Website:* http://www.twinlesstwins.org *E-mail:* contact@twinlesstwins.org

"If someone listens, or stretches out a hand, or whispers a word of encouragement, or attempts to understand a lonely person, extraordinary things begin to happen." -- Loretta Girzartis

Wings of Light, Inc. *National. 3 support networks. Founded 1995.* Support and information network for individuals whose lives have been touched by aviation accidents. Separate networks for airplane accident survivors, families and friends of persons killed in airplane accidents and persons involved in rescue, recovery and investigation of crashes. Information and referrals, phone support. Write: Wings of Light, Inc., PMB 448, 16845 N. 29th Ave., Suite 1, Phoenix, AZ 85053. Call 623-516-1115. *Website:* http://www.wingsoflight.org

ONLINE

Adult Sibling Grief *Online.* Support for those who have suffered the devastating loss of an adult sibling. Chat rooms, message board and resources. *Website:* http://www.adultsiblinggrief.com

Autoerotic Asphyxiation Support *Online. Founded 1999.* Supportive message board for family and friends of those who have died by autoerotic asphyxiation. *Website:* http://groups.yahoo.com/group/autoeroticasphyxiationsupport and http://www.silentvictims.org

Delta Society *Online.* Maintains a list of pet bereavement support groups, pet loss resource persons, counselors and hotlines. Call 425-679-5500; Fax: 425-679-5539. *Website:* http://www.deltasociety.org *E-mail:* info@deltasociety.org

Drowning Support Network *Online. Founded 2002.* Offers support for people who have lost loved ones in drownings or other water accidents, especially those in which no remains were found or in which the recovery process has been lengthy or difficult. *Website:* http://health.groups.yahoo.com/group/drowningsupportnetwork/

GROWW (Grief Recovery Online - Widows and Widowers) *Online.* Support groups for widowed and other persons bereaving the loss of a loved one. Offers a large variety of chat rooms, run by volunteers, dealing with specific issues (loss of someone to drugs, a child, sibling, parent, loss due to long term illness, sudden death, violent losses, gays and lesbians, men and many more). Write: GROWW, 11877 Douglas Rd., #102 - PMB 101, Alpharetta, GA 30005. *Website:* http://www.groww.org

Pet Loss Grief Support Website *Online. (MULTILINGUAL)* Moderated board that offers support and understanding for persons grieving the loss of their pet or who have a pet who is ill. Provides personal support and thoughtful advice. Also offers "Monday Pet Loss Candle Ceremony," a chat room, tribute pages and other resources. *Website:* http://www.petloss.com

DEATH OF A CHILD / FETAL LOSS

(see also bereavement, suicide, crime)

ATLANTIC

Compassionate Friends Support for parents, grandparents and siblings bereaving the death of a child. Meets 2nd Wed., 7:30-9pm, Grace Lutheran Church, Shore Rd. and Dawes Ave., Somers Point. Call Patty Semprevivo 609-296-1298 (day) or Compassionate Friends 1-877-969-0010. *Website:* http://www.compassionatefriends.org *E-mail:* tcfnj@comcast.net

BERGEN

Compassionate Friends Support for parents grieving the death of a child. Grandparents and siblings are welcomed. Speakers' bureau. Meets 4th Tues., 7:30-9:30pm, (beginners 7:15pm), Christian Healthcare Center, Mountain Ave., Wyckoff. Call Compassionate Friends 201-567-0089 (day/eve). *Website:* http://www.compassionatefriends.org

Healing Hearts *Professionally-run.* Self-help support for parents who have lost children to congenital heart defects. Mutual sharing, phone help and literature. Meets 4th Thurs., 7:30-10pm, Don Imus Pediatric Center, Hackensack Medical Center, 30 Prospect Ave., Hackensack. Call Scott and Diane Hosmer 201-641-4580 (eve) or Scott 973-575-4550 ext. 2516 (day) or 201-414-3715.

Parents Who Have Lost A Child Support Group Mutual support, education and spirituality for parents who have lost a child. Meets 3rd Mon., 7:30pm, St. Peter the Apostle Church, 445 Fifth Ave., Rectory Basement, River Edge. Call Mary Davis 201-261-5400 (day) or 201-265-3688 (eve).

Perinatal Bereavement - Healing Hearts *Professionally-run.* Provides support for parents who have experienced a miscarriage, ectopic pregnancy, stillbirth or infant death to help with the grieving process. Meets 3rd Thurs., 7:30-9pm, Valley Hospital, 233 N. Van Dien Ave., Conference Center, Room # 2, Ridgewood. Before attending call Trudy Heerema, LCSW 201-447-8539 (day).

Perinatal Bereavement Support Group *Professionally-run.* For parents and significant others who have experienced the loss of a pregnancy or infant death. Meets 3rd Wed., 7:30pm, Englewood Hospital, Englewood. Call Sue Dziemian 201-384-8258 (day/eve).

Pregnancy and Newborn Loss Support Group *Professionally-run.* An opportunity for parents who have experienced the loss of an infant, miscarriage, or stillbirth to share their experiences with other parents. Provides information and resources for parents, families and friends on perinatal grief. Guest speakers. Meets 1st Tues., 7:30-9pm, Holy Name Hospital, 718 Teaneck Rd., Teaneck. Call Perinatal Bereavement Hotline 201-833-3058 (day).

SIDS/Infant Loss Support Group *(BILINGUAL) Professionally-run.* Support for parents who have lost a child to a sudden infant death. Families welcome. Meets 2nd Thurs., 7-8:30pm, Hackensack University Medical Center, Hackensack. Before attending call 1-800-545-7437.

Turning Point A Women's Resource Center *Professionally-run.* Confidential post-abortion support group using God's word as a basis for inner healing. Group meets for 8-12 weeks as needed in Bergenfield. Call Bev Frutchey 973-584-8884 (day/eve) or Turning Point 201-501-8876. *E-mail:* Frutchey1@Juno.com

BURLINGTON

Bereaved Parents *Professionally-run.* Support for parents bereaving the loss of a child. Meetings vary, Samaritan Hospice, Marlton. Pre-registration required. Before attending call The Samaritan Center for Grief Support 1-800-596-8550. *Website:* http://www.samaritanhospice.org

Grief Recovery After Substance Passing (GRASP) Support for parents who have suffered the death of a child due to substance abuse. Provides opportunity for parents to share their grief and experiences without shame or recrimination. Meets 3rd Tues., 7pm, Rap Room, 1003 Lincoln Dr. West, (off Route 73), Suite A, Marlton. Call 856-983-3328 (day).

Helping Hand Grief Support Group Christian-based support for someone bereaving the loss of a loved one (including death of a child, loss to homicide or suicide) through education, encouragement, counseling and understanding. Families welcome. Meets 1st and 3rd Mon., 7-9pm, for 10 week sessions, Fellowship Alliance Chapel, (Log house in back of church), 199 Church Rd., Medford. Call Wanda and George Stein 609-953-7333 ext. 309 (day/eve).

SIDS/Infant Loss Support Group *(BILINGUAL) Professionally-run.* Support for parents who have lost a child to a sudden infant death. Families welcome. Meets 1st Thurs., 7-8:30pm, West Jersey Hospital, Marlton. Before attending call 1-800-545-7437.

CAMDEN

Compassionate Friends Support for parents bereaving the death of a child. Grandparents and relatives welcome. Rap sessions and newsletter. Meets 3rd Fri., 8-9:30pm, Senior Center, Oak and Oakland Ave., Audubon. Call Lynne 856-401-8967 or Compassionate Friends 1-877-969-0010. *Website:* http://www.compassionatefriends.org

SIDS/Infant Loss Support Group Support for parents who have lost a child to a sudden infant death. Meeting days and time varies, West Jersey Hospital, Voorhees. Before attending call 1-800-545-7437.

UNITE Grief Support *Professionally-run.* Mutual support for parents who have experienced the loss of a child, either during pregnancy, at birth or up to the first year of life. Discussion of experiences and feelings in an atmosphere of support and respect. Meets 1st and 3rd Mon., 7-9pm, Virtua at Voorhees, Barry Brown Health Education Center, 106 Carnie Blvd., Voorhees. Call 1-888-847-8823.

CUMBERLAND

Helping Hands *Professionally-run.* Provides emotional support for parents who have lost a child to miscarriage, stillbirth or infant death. Open to grandparents as well. Meets 2nd Mon., 7pm, South Jersey Health Care, Vineland. Before attending call Judy Ford, RN BSN 856-507-2768 (day).

ESSEX

Compassionate Friends Offers friendship and understanding for parents bereaving the death of a child. Meets in Nutley area. For meeting information call Rose Rappapert 973-239-1711 (day) or Pat Gerges 973-535-9022 (eve). *Website:* http://www.compassionatefriends.org

HOPE (Helping Other Parents Endure) Mutual support, education and spirituality for parents who have lost a child. Meets 1st Wed., 7:30-9:30pm, (July and August meets 7pm), St. Thomas the Apostle, 60 Byrd Ave., Parish Center, Bloomfield. Call Mary Margaret or Bob Corriston 201-288-6886 (eve), 1-877-633-2629 ext. 5442 (day) or Ann and Jack Muller 201-358-8752. *E-mail:* bmmc917@optonline.net or mulleraj@optonline.net

Parents of Murdered Sons and Daughters Support and advocacy for mothers and families of murdered children. Rap sessions and guest speakers. Meets 3rd Sun., East Orange General Hospital, 300 Central Ave., East Orange. Before attending call Christine Johnson 973-399-5029.

Perinatal Bereavement Group *Professionally-run.* Mutual support for parents who have experienced a miscarriage, infant death or stillbirth. Meets 1st Wed., 7:30pm, St. Barnabas Medical Center, Livingston. Call Dorothy Kurzweil, LCSW 973-322-5745 (day) or Social Services 973-322-5855 (day).

SIDS/Infant Loss Support Group *(BILINGUAL) Professionally-run.* Support for parents who have lost a child to a sudden infant death. Families welcome. Meets 3rd Wed., 10am-noon, University Hospital, Campus, Newark. Before attending call 1-800-545-7437.

Survivors of Murdered Children *Professionally-run.* Mutual support and understanding for families and friends who have lost a loved one to murder. Guest speakers, advocacy, speakers' bureau, social and buddy system. Meets 2nd Fri., 6:30pm, ECHOES - The Grief Center, 116 Main St., Orange. Call Beverly Henderson 973-675-1199.

GLOUCESTER

Bereaved Parents *Professionally-run.* Support for parents to help deal with the long-term grief of the loss of a child. Meetings vary, Woodbury. For starting dates and times call The Samaratian Center for Grief Support 1-800-596-8550.

Grief Group for Parents Support for parents grieving the loss of a child to drugs. Rap sessions and buddy system. Meets 1st and 3rd Wed., Washington Township Municipal Building, 523 Egg Harbor Rd., Meeting Room C, Sewell. Call Donna Rullo 856-589-6446 (day).

HOPING (Helping Other Parents In Normal Grief) *Professionally-run.* Support for parents who have experienced miscarriage, stillbirth, ectopic pregnancy or newborn death. Meets 4 times per year, Underwood Memorial Hospital, 509 N. Broad St., Woodbury. Before attending call 856-845-0100 ext. 2749 (day).

"Very few burdens are heavy if everyone lifts." -- Sy Wise

HUNTERDON

Compassionate Friends Support for parents bereaving the death of a child. Group discussions, lectures, literature and phone help. Meets monthly in High Bridge. For meeting information call Jay and Roselee Persinko 908-638-8717 (eve/weekends) or Compassionate Friends 1-877-969-0010. *Website:* http://www.compassionatefriends.org *E-mail:* compassionatefriends-hunterdon@earthlink.net

Parents of Murdered Children Support for parents who have survived murder or homicide to come together and share their experiences and pain. Meets 3rd Thurs., 7-9pm, Family Support Organization, 4 Minneakoning Rd., 2nd Floor, Flemington. Call 732-227-1023. E-mail: stanley184@patmedia.net

MERCER

Compassionate Friends Mutual support for parents, grandparents or adult siblings bereaving the death of a child. Guest speakers, newsletter and phone help. Meets 1st Mon., 7:30-9pm, Robert Wood Johnson University Hospital at Hamilton, One Hamilton Health Place, Human Resources, Building #2, Hamilton. Call Chaplain Jeff Pierfy 609-631-6980 (day). *Website:* http://www.compassionatefriends.org *E-mail:* jpierfy@rwjuhh.edu

Time for Healing *Professionally-run.* A confidential support group for parents who have ended a pregnancy after abnormal prenatal test results. Adult family members welcome. Phone help available. Meets one Sun. per month, Capital Health System, 446 Bellevue Ave., Trenton. Before attending call Carolee Watkins 609-394-4072 ext. 2 (day).

MIDDLESEX

Compassionate Friends - Central Jersey Chapter Mutual support for parents, grandparents or siblings grieving the death of a child. Phone help, guest speakers, rap sessions, literature and newsletter. Meets 2nd Sun., 2-4pm, St. Peter's Episcopal Church, 505 Main St., Parish Hall, Spotswood. Call Dick Quaintance 732-548-1419 (eve), Kathy Dopart 732-549-3807 (eve), or Compassionate Friends 1-877-969-0010. *Website:* http://www.compassionatefriends.org

Parent-to-Parent SIDS Support Group *Professionally-run.* Support for parents who have lost a child to a sudden infant death. Meets 1st Tues., noon-2pm, UMDNJ, Clinical Academic Building, New Brunswick. Before attending call 1-800-545-7437.

SHARE *Professionally-run.* Provides support for parents, their families and friends who have experienced miscarriage, stillbirth or neonatal death. Offers phone help and literature. Meets 2nd Thurs., 7-9pm, St. Peter's University Hospital, 254 Easton Ave., New Brunswick. Call Dawn Brady 732-745-8600 ext. 5214 (day).

MONMOUTH

C.H.I.L.D. (Caring Help In Lost Dreams) *Professionally-run.* Bereavement group for parents and surviving siblings who have lost a child of any age. Offers emotional support to help cope with the unnatural loss of a deeply loved child. Meets 1st Thurs., 7:30-9pm, CentraState Medical Center, Route 537, Freehold. Call Bunny Salomon 732-617-2221.

S.H.A.R.E. *Professionally-run.* For parents grieving the loss of an infant through miscarriage, ectopic pregnancy, stillbirth or death of a newborn. Newsletter, phone help, guest speakers and literature. Meets 2nd Tues., 7:30-9:30pm, Riverview Medical Center, 1 River Plaza, Booker Conference Room, Red Bank. Call Pam Rossano 732-530-2315 (day), Kathy De Fazio 732-450-2871 or 1-800-560-9990 (day).

MORRIS

Compassionate Friends Mutual support for parents, grandparents and siblings bereaving the death of a child. Newsletter. Call 973-270-7908. *Website:* http://www.compassionatefriends.org *E-mail:* tcf_nj@yahoo.com

> **Chatham** Meets 3rd Sun., 7:00-9:30pm, (2nd Sun., June and Dec.), Chatham Township Presbyterian Church, 240 Southern Blvd.
>
> **Parsippany** Meets 2nd Thurs., 7:30-10pm, St. Christopher's Church, 1050 Littleton Rd., Room 101.

M.I.D.S. (Miscarriage, Infant Death, Stillbirth) Mutual support and information for bereaved parents who have experienced stillbirth, miscarriage, infant death or ectopic pregnancy. Meets 2nd Wed., 8pm, Parsippany. Call Janet Tischler 973-884-1016. *Website:* http://www.MIDSinc.org *E-mail:* MIDS1982@yahoo.com

RTS Perinatal Bereavement Services *Professionally-run.* For families who have experienced the loss of a baby through miscarriage, ectopic pregnancy, stillbirth or newborn death. Meets 3rd Wed., 7:30-9pm, Morristown Memorial Hospital, Patient Education Center, Morristown. Call Labor and Delivery 973-971-5748 (day/eve).

SHARE - Pregnancy and Infant Loss Support Group *Professionally-run.* Mutual support for parents who have lost a baby through neonatal death, miscarriage, ectopic pregnancy, or stillbirth. Pen pals, monthly meetings, guest speakers, lending library and phone help available. Meets 3rd Tues., 7:30-9pm, 28 Drake Rd., Mendham. To confirm meeting date call Lucy 973-543-2495 (day). *Website:* http://www.shareatlanta.org *E-mail:* SHARENONJ@msn.com

Turning Point A Women's Resource Center *Professionally-run.* Confidential post-abortion support group using God's word as a basis for inner healing. Group meets for 8-12 weeks as needed in Ledgewood. Call Bev Frutchey 973-584-8884 (day/eve) or Turning Point 201-501-8876. *E-mail:* Frutchey1@Juno.com

OCEAN

Compassionate Friends Mutual self-help support for parents and siblings grieving the death of a child. Includes parents of stillbirth or fetal death. Monthly newsletter, occasional speakers, library. Meets 1st Tues., 7:30pm, Children's Memorial Garden, Winding River Park, Toms River. Call Compassionate Friends 732-244-6439 (day/eve). *Website:* http://www.oceantcf.com *E-mail:* oceantcf@yahoo.com

SOMERSET

Compassionate Friends Provides mutual support for parents bereaving the death of a child. Rap sessions, guest speakers, newsletter. Meets 4th Sun., 7:30pm, Temple Sholom, Bridgewater. Call Dossie Weissbein 908-725-7736 (day/eve), Marilyn and Fred Mountjoy 908-722-6199 (day/eve) or Compassionate Friends 1-877-969-0010. *Website:* http://www.freewebs.com/cfbridgewater *E-mail:* cfbridgewater@patmedia.net

Parents of Murdered Children Support for parents who have survived murder or homicide to come together and share their experiences and pain. Meets 1st Mon., 7-9pm, Somerset Baptist Church, 9 Pershing Ave., Somerset. Call 732-227-1023. E-mail: stanley184@patmedia.net

UNION

F.A.T.E. (Feelings After Termination Experience) *Professionally-run.* Support for couples or individuals who have terminated a pregnancy due to fetal abnormalities. Meets bi-monthly, Overlook Hospital, Summit. Call Gisela Rodriguez 973-972-3302 (day). *E-mail:* rodriggi@umdnj.edu

Parents of Murdered Children Support for parents who have survived murder or homicide to come together and share their experiences and pain. Meets 2nd Tues., 7-9pm, First Baptist Church, 100 High St., Cranford. Call 732-227-1023. *E-mail:* stanley184@patmedia.net

NATIONAL

AGAST *International. Founded 1989.* Dedicated to assisting grandparents in the death of a grandchild. Offers support, literature and bimonthly newsletter. Also provides online message board, contact information and newsletter. Write: AGAST, 12200 E. State Route 69, Lot 382, Dewey, AZ 86327. Call 1-888-774-7437. *Website:* http://www.agast.org *E-mail:* reachout@agast.org

Alive Alone, Inc. *National network. Founded 1988.* Self-help network of parents who have lost an only child or all of their children. Provides education and publications to promote communication and healing, to assist in resolving grief and to develop means to reinvest lives for a positive future. Bimonthly newsletter. Write: Alive Alone, c/o Kay Bevington, 1112 Champaign Dr., Van Wert, OH 45891. *Website:* http://www.alivealone.org *E-mail:* alivalon@bright.net

AMEND (Aiding Mothers and Fathers Experiencing Neonatal Death) *National network. Founded 1974.* Offers support and encouragement to parents having a normal grief reaction to the loss of their baby. Provides one-to-one peer counseling with trained volunteers. Write: AMEND, 4324 Berrywick Terrace, St. Louis, MO 63128. Call 314-487-7582. *Website:* http://www.amendgroup.com E-mail martha@amendgroup.com

Bereaved Parents of the USA *National. 80+ affiliated groups. Founded 1995.* Designed to aid and support bereaved parents and their families who are struggling to survive their grief after the death of a child. Information and referrals, newsletter, phone support, conferences, support group meetings. Assistance and guidelines in starting groups. Write: Bereaved Parents of the USA, P.O. Box 95, Park Forest, IL 60466. Call 708-748-7866. *Website:* http://www.bereavedparentsusa.org

CLIMB, Inc. (Center for Loss In Multiple Birth) *International network. Founded 1987.* Support by and for parents who have experienced the death of one or more of their twins or higher multiples during pregnancy, birth, in infancy or childhood. Newsletter, information on specialized topics, pen pals, phone support. Write: CLIMB, P.O. Box 91377, Anchorage AK 99509 Call 907-222-5321. *Website:* http://www.climb-support.org *E-mail:* climb@pobox.alaska.net

Compassionate Friends, The *National. 600 chapters. Founded 1969.* Offers mutual support, friendship and understanding to families following the death of a child of any age. Provides information on the grieving process, referrals to local chapter meetings and publishes quarterly magazine ($20/yr). Also has a sibling network. Write: The Compassionate Friends, P.O. Box 3696, Oak Brook, IL 60522-3696. Call 1-877-969-0010; Fax: 630-990-0246. *Website:* http://www.compassionatefriends.org *E-mail:* nationaloffice@compassionatefriends.org

First Candle/SIDS Alliance *(BILINGUAL) National. 50 chapters. Founded 1987.* Provides education, advocacy, research and support for families of babies who have died from SIDS (sudden infant death syndrome), stillbirth and miscarriages. Bilingual grief counselors available 24 hrs. Newsletter, conferences, chapter development guidelines. Write: First Candle/SIDS Alliance, 1314 Bedford Ave., Suite 210, Baltimore, MD 21208. Call 1-800-221-7437 or 410-653-8226; Fax: 410-653-8709. *Website:* http://www.firstcandle.org *E-mail:* info@firstcandle.org

GRASP (Grief Recovery After Substance Passing) *Model. 1 group in California. Founded 2002.* Support and advocacy group for parents who have suffered the death of a child due to substance abuse. Provides opportunity for parents to share their grief and experiences without shame or recrimination. Provides information and suggestions for those wanting to start a similar group elsewhere. Write: GRASP, c/o Patricia Wittberger, 62 Holly Ribbons Circle, Bluffton, SC 29909. Call 843-705-2217. *Website:* http://www.grasphelp.com *E-mail:* mom@jennysjourney.org

M.I.S.S. Foundation, The *International. 20 affiliated groups. Founded 1995.* Offers emergency and on-going support for families suffering from the loss a child. Provides information, referrals, phone support, newsletter, pen pals, literature, advocacy and online chat room support. Information on local group development. Local support group listings online. Write: M.I.S.S., P.O. Box 5333, Peoria, AZ 85385-5333. Call 623-979-1000; Fax: 623-979-1001. *Website:* http://www.missfoundation.org *E-mail:* joanne@missfoundation.org

National Organization of Parents of Murdered Children *National. Over 230 chapters in the U.S., Canada, and Costa Rica. Founded 1978.* Nationwide self-help support organization for families and friends of those who have died by violence. Newsletter 3 times a year. Court accompaniment also provided by many chapters. Parole Block Program and Second Opinion Service also available. Offers assistance in starting local chapters. Write: NOPMC, 100 E. 8th St., B-41, Cincinnati, OH 45202. Call 1-888-818-7662 or 513-721-5683 (office); Fax: 513-345-4489. *Website:* http://www.pomc.com *E-mail:* NatlPOMC@aol.com

SHARE: Pregnancy and Infant Loss Support, Inc. *National. 100 chapters. Founded 1977.* Mutual support for bereaved parents and families whose lives have been touched by the tragic death of a baby through early pregnancy loss, stillbirth or in the first few months of life. Provides support toward positive resolution of grief experienced at the time of or following the death of a baby. Information, education and resources on the needs and rights of bereaved parents and siblings. Provides newsletter, pen pals, information re: professionals and pastoral care. Chapter development guidelines. Online message board and weekly chat rooms. Write: National SHARE Office, St. Joseph Health Center, 300 First Capital Dr., St. Charles, MO 63301. Call 1-800-821-6819 or 636-947-6164; Fax: 636-947-7486. *Website:* http://www.nationalshareoffice.com *E-mail:* share@nationalshareoffice.com

UNITE, Inc. *National. 12 groups. Founded 1975.* Support for parents grieving a miscarriage, stillbirth or infant death. Also provides support for parents through subsequent pregnancies. Group meetings, phone help, newsletter, lending libraries, annual conference. Offers guidelines for starting and facilitating a group. Grief counselor training programs. Professionals in advisory roles. Write: UNITE, Inc., c/o Jeanes Hospital, 7600 Central Ave., Philadelphia, PA 19111-2499. Online referrals to local support group meetings and times. Call 1-888-488-6483 (tape). *Website:* http://www.unitegriefsupport.org *E-mail:* administrator@unitegriefsupport.org

ONLINE

A Heartbreaking Choice *Online.* Resource for parents who have had to terminate a wanted pregnancy due to prenatal news such as birth defects or risk to the well-being of the mother. Listserv email list, discussion forum and grandparents forum. *Website:* http://www.aheartbreakingchoice.com

Angels of Addiction *Online. Founded 2005.* Mutual support for bereaved parents who have lost a child of any age to drug overdose/use. Message board. *Website:* http://health.groups.yahoo.com/ group/angelsofaddiction/

MyMolarPregnancy.com *Online. Founded 2001.* Information, links, references and a number of interactive web features for women who have had a molar pregnancy. Support group, message board and chatroom. *Website:* http://www.mymolarpregnancy.com

Parent Soup Message Board *Online.* Offers a large variety of message boards which deal with parenting issues including infertility, pregnancy, parenting challenges, parents of disabled, pregnancy loss, newborn babies, toddlers, equipment, adoption, family issues, etc. *Website:* http://www.parentsoup.com/boards

Triplet Connection, The *Online. Founded 1983.* Online forum of parents who have lost one or more children in multiple births. Information on selection reduction. Write: The Triplet Connection, P.O. Box 429, Spring City, UT 84662. Call 435-851-1105, Fax 435-462-7466. *Website:* http://www.tripletconnection.org *E-mail:* tc@tripletconnection.org

SUICIDE SURVIVORS

(see also bereavement, death of a child, widows)

ATLANTIC

Heartbreak to Healing Mutual support and understanding for persons who have lost a loved one to suicide. Group meets last Tues., 7:30pm, Grace Lutheran Church, Somers Point. For information call Dolores Thomas 609-345-3230.

BERGEN

Survivors After Suicide *Professionally-run.* Provides support for family members and friends of people who died by suicide. Open to all. Meets 1st and 3rd Wed., 7:15-8:45pm, Vantage Health System, 2 Park Ave., Dumont. Call 201-385-4400 (day) or Lynne Nierenberg 201-837-6321 (day/eve).

BURLINGTON

Helping Hand Grief Support Group Christian-based support for someone bereaving the loss of a loved one (including death of a child, loss to homicide, or suicide) through education, encouragement, counseling and understanding. Families welcome. Meets 1st and 3rd Mon., 7-9pm, for 10 week sessions, Fellowship Alliance Chapel, (Log house in back of church), 199 Church Rd., Medford. Call Wanda and George Stein 609-953-7333 ext. 309 (day/eve).

Living Through Suicide *Professionally-run.* Christian-based support for those who have lost a loved one to suicide. Meets 4th Mon., 7-9pm, Fellowship Alliance Chapel, (Log house in back of church), 199 Church Rd., Medford. Call Wanda Stein 609-953-7333 ext. 309.

Sharing Suicide's Sorrows *Professionally-run.* Support for family and friends grieving a death from suicide. Meetings vary, The Center for Grief Support, 5 Eves Dr., Suite 180, Marlton. Call 1-800-596-8550.

CAMDEN

Friends and Families of Suicide For those who have lost a loved one to suicide. Meets 2nd Tues., 7:45pm, Our Lady of Grace Church, 35 North White Horse Pike, Somerdale. Call Barbara 856-307-0331 or Gail 856-858-7044. *E-mail:* survivingsuicidenj@yahoo.com

MERCER

Surviving After Suicide *Professionally-run.* For those who have lost a loved one to suicide. Meets 2nd Wed., 7:30pm, Robert Wood Johnson University Hospital, 1 Hamilton Health Place, Hamilton. Call Peggy Farrell 732-462-5267 or Jeff Pierfy 609-631-6980.

MIDDLESEX

Surviving After Suicide *Professionally-run.* Group for survivors after the suicide of a family member or friend. Meets 3rd Mon., 7:30-9:30pm, University of Medicine and Dentistry of NJ, University Behavioral Health Care, 671 Hoes Lane, Piscataway. Call Peggy Farrell 732-462-5267. *E-mail:* farrmarg@aol.com

MONMOUTH

Surviving After Suicide *Professionally-run.* Group for survivors after the suicide of a family member or friend. Meets 2nd Tues., 7:30-9:30pm, Bayshore Memorial Hospital, Conference Room A, 717 N. Beers St., Holmdell. Call Peggy Farrell 732-462-5267. *E-mail:* farrmarg@aol.com

MORRIS

Survivors of Suicide Mutual support and discussion for people who have had someone close to them commit suicide. Meets 2nd and 4th Wed., 7:30-9pm, Grace Episcopal Church, Madison. Call Jane Cole 973-786-5178 (day/eve).

OCEAN

Survivors After Suicide For those who have lost a loved one to suicide. Meets 2nd Thurs., 7:30pm, St. Francis Center, Long Beach Blvd., Brant Beach. Call Jo and Roger 609-361-7608.

Survivors of Suicide Mutual support for those who have lost a loved one to suicide. Meets 3rd Tues., 7-9pm, Kimball Medical Center, Center for Healthy Living, 198 Prospect St., Lakewood. Call Jim Romer 732-886-4475 (day). *E-mail:* jromer@sbhcs.com

Survivors of Suicide Support Group Grief support and understanding for those who have lost a loved one to suicide. Meets 2nd Wed., 7:30-9:30pm, St. Dominic's Church, 250 Old Squaw Rd., Brick. Call Dave Thelen 732-899-8483 (eve).

NATIONAL

American Association of Suicidology *Resource. 350 affiliated groups.* Referrals to local support groups for survivors of suicide nationwide. Directory of groups ($15). Newsletter, pamphlets, brochures, etc., available for a fee. Book available on starting self-help groups ($30). Write: American Association of Suicidology, 5221 Wisconsin Ave., NW, Second Floor, Washington, DC 20015. Call 202-237-2280; Fax: 202-237-2282; *Website:* http://www.suicidology.org *E-mail:* info@suicidology.org

American Foundation for Suicide Prevention *Resource. Founded 1987.* Provides state-by-state directory of survivor support groups for families and friends who have lost someone to suicide. Training programs available to start similar groups. Write: American Foundation For Suicide Prevention, 120 Wall St., 22nd Floor, New York, NY 10005. Call 1-888-333-2377 or 212-363-3500 ext. 10; Fax: 212-363-6237. *Website:* http://www.afsp.org *E-mail:*inquiry@afsp.org

Heartbeat *International. 35 chapters. Founded 1980.* Mutual support for those who have lost a loved one through suicide. Information, referrals, phone support and chapter development guidelines on-line. Speakers on suicide bereavement.

Write: Heartbeat, 2015 Devon St., Colorado Springs, CO 80909. Call 719-596-2575. *Website:* http://www.heartbeatsurvivorsaftersuicide.org *E-mail:* archlj@msn.com

Suicide Anonymous *Model. 2 groups in Tennessee. Founded 1996.* 12-Step. Fellowship of men and women who share their experience, strength and hope with each other in order to solve their common problem of suicidal ideation and behavior. Provides a safe environment for people to share their struggles with suicide, to prevent suicides and develop strategies for support and healing from the devastating effects of suicidal preoccupation and behavior. Networking, literature, advocacy. Assistance in starting new groups. Write: Suicide Anonymous, 5158 Stage Rd., Suite 120, Memphis, TN, 38134. Call 901-383-1924; Fax: 901-763-1876. *Website:* http://www.suicideanonymous.org *E-mail:* info@suicideanonymous.org

ONLINE

Friends And Family Of Suicide *Online. Founded 1998.* Provides online support to survivors of suicide. Offers moderated e-mail mailing list. *Website:* http://www.friendsandfamiliesofsuicide.com Direct sign up address: http://health.groups.yahoo.com/groups/FFofSuicides *E-mail:* arlynsmom@cs.com

Parents of Suicide *Online. Founded 1998.* Support for parents whose sons and daughters have died due to suicide. Annual retreat. Offers private chat room, e-mail discussion group, listserv. *Website:* http://www.parentsofsuicide.com Direct sign up address: http://health.groups.yahoo.com/group/parentsofsuicides *E-mail:* arlynsmom@cs.com

WIDOWS / WIDOWERS

(see also bereavement, suicide, single parenting)

STATEWIDE

Catholic Divorce Ministry The Ministry of the North American Conference of Separated and Divorced Catholics Ministry serving individuals experiencing separation, divorce or death of a spouse. Offers leadership training conferences, resources materials and social activities. Referrals to self-help groups statewide. Call Charlie Rauh 201-986-9676. *Website:* http://www.nacsdc.org (click into Region 3)

BERGEN

Partners Bereavement Support Group *Professionally-run.* Support for spouses/partners bereaving the loss of a loved one to cancer in the past year. Group meets for 8 week sessions, various days, Cancer Care, 141 Dayton St., Ridgewood. For information call 201-444-6630 (day). *Website:* http://www.cancercare.org *E-mail:* njinfo@cancercare.org

Separated, Divorced and Bereaved Catholics Referrals to groups for emotional/spiritual support and social activities for separated, divorced or bereaved men and women. Groups are sponsored by various churches throughout the county and are open to people of any faith. For information call Family Life Ministry, Newark Diocese 973-497-4327.

BURLINGTON

Bereavement Support Group for Widows and Widowers *Professionally-run.* Provides mutual support for widows and widowers. Meets 3rd Wed., (except July/Aug.), 7-8:30pm, and 2nd and 4th Wed., 1:30-2:45pm, Dougherty's Funeral Home, 2200 Trenton Rd., Levittown, PA. Call Deborah Gawthrop 215-624-8190 (day).

Early Endings *Professionally-run.* Support for young widow and widowers. Mutual support for persons who have lost a spouse or companion early in their lives. Meetings vary, Samaritan Hospice, Marlton. Pre-registration required. Before attending call The Samaritan Center for Grief Support 1-800-596-8550. *Website:* http://www.samaritanhospice.org

Families Who Are Hurting Mutual support and encouragement for families who are hurting due to an addiction of a loved one, loss of a spouse or for those caring for a loved one with dementia. Meets 1st Sat., 6pm, Rose of Sharon Lutheran Church, Route 528, Jacobstown. Call Bill Millet 609-758-2746.

Grieving the Love of Your Life *Professionally-run.* Support for anyone, age 50 and over, grieving the loss of a spouse or a partner. Meeting days and locations vary. Pre-registration required. Before attending call The Samaritan Center for Grief Support 1-800-596-8550. *Website:* http://www.samaritanhospice.org

H.O.P.E. (Helping Other People Evolve, Inc.) Support and information for recently (up to 2 yrs) widowed men and women of all ages. Group runs for 10 week sessions, 4 times per year. Meets in various locations. Registration fee $20. Call H.O.P.E. 1-888-920-2201 (Mon., Wed., Fri., 10am-1pm). *E-mail:* hopesnj@juno.com

Widows and Widowers Support Support for anyone feeling the loss of their spouse. Meets 1st Sat., 7pm, Lourdes Medical Center of Burlington County Hospital, 218A Sunset Rd., Willingboro. Before attending call Helen Tellerin 609-871-0783.

CAMDEN

Counseling Network for Loss and Transition Grief Groups *Professionally-run.* Provides emotional and educational support for persons grieving the loss of a loved one. Offer various groups, both time-limited and on-going, for general bereavement, loss of spouse and a group for young widows. Meeting time and location varies in Philadelphia, PA area. For information call Debbie Gawthrop 215-624-8190 (day).

Early Endings *Professionally-run.* Support for young widow and widowers. Mutual support for persons who have lost a spouse or companion early in their lives. Meetings vary. Pre-registration required. Before attending call The Samaritan Center for Grief Support 1-800-596-8550. *Website:* http://www.samaritanhospice.org

H.O.P.E. (Helping Other People Evolve, Inc.) Helps the recently widowed to cope with their loss and to move forward to become self-reliant persons. Group runs for 10 week sessions, 4 times per year. Meets in various locations. Registration fee $20. Call H.O.P.E. 1-888-920-2201 (Mon., Wed., Fri., 10am-1pm). *E-mail:* hopesnj@juno.com

To Live Again Support and encouragement for widows and widowers (age 45+). Newly widowed meets Tues., 7pm, Queen of Heaven Church, Cherry Hill. General group meets 2nd Mon., 7:30pm, St. Peter's Celestine School, Cafeteria, Cherry Hill. Dues $15/yr. Call Rita 856-779-9438 (day) or Stanley 856-662-6754 (eve).

We can also refer callers to over 100 individuals who are seeking others to help start new support groups throughout NJ. Give us a call for more information.
1-800-367-6274

CAPE MAY

H.O.P.E. (Helping Other People Evolve, Inc.) Support and information for recently (up to 2 yrs.) widowed men and women of all ages. Group runs for 10 week sessions, 4 times per year. Meets in various locations. Registration fee $20. Call H.O.P.E. 1-888-920-2201 (Mon., Wed., Fri., 10am-1pm). *E-mail:* hopesnj@juno.com

CUMBERLAND

H.O.P.E. (Helping Other People Evolve, Inc.) Helps the recently widowed to cope with their loss, move forward and become self-reliant. Group runs for 10 week sessions, 4 times per year. Registration fee $20. For meeting information call H.O.P.E. 1-888-920-2201 (Mon., Wed., Fri., 10am-1pm). *E-mail:* hopesnj@juno.com

ESSEX

Family Bereavement Group *Professionally-run.* Group for spouses who lost spouses with young children (ages 5-18) at home. Separate groups for children run concurrently. Meets 6:30-8pm, Saint Barnabas Corporate Building, 95 Old Short Hills Rd., West Orange. For meeting day call Judith Zucker, LCSW 973-322-4817 (day).

Separated, Divorced and Bereaved Catholics Referrals to groups for emotional and spiritual support for separated, divorced or bereaved men and women. Groups are sponsored by various churches throughout the county and are open to people of any faith. For information call Family Life Ministry, Newark Diocese 973-497-4327.

Widows Moving On For widows that have dealt with the bereavement phase and now want to meet other widows to talk about getting on with their lives. Groups start periodically and run for 6 weeks. Registration fee $45. Meets 7:30-9pm, Linda and Rudy Slucker NCJW Center for Women, 513 West Mt. Pleasant Ave., Livingston. Call Center for Women 973-994-4994 (day). *Website:* http://www.centerforwomennj.org *E-mail:* centerforwomen@ncjwessex.org

Widows Support Groups Mutual support for widows of all ages. Groups start periodically and run for 6 weeks. Registration fee $45. Meets at Linda and Rudy Slucker NCJW Center for Women, Livingston. Call Project GRO 973-994-4994.

Website: http://www.centerforwomennj.org *E-mail:* centerforwomen@ncjwessex.org

Young Widows Moving On For young widows that have dealt with the bereavement phase and now want to meet other widows to talk about getting on with their lives. Groups start periodically and run for 6 weeks. Registration fee $45. Linda and Rudy Slucker NCJW Center for Women, 513 West Mt. Pleasant Ave., Livingston. Call Center for Women 973-994-4994 (day). *Website:* http://www.centerforwomennj.org *E-mail:* centerforwomen@ncjwessex.org

Young Widows Support Group Mutual support for widows in their 40's and younger. Groups start periodically and run for 6 weeks. Registration fee $45. Meets at Linda and Rudy Slucker NCJW Center for Women, Livingston. Call Project GRO 973-994-4994. *Website:* http:www.centerforwomennj.org *E-mail:* centerforwomen@ncjwessex.org

GLOUCESTER

Early Endings *Professionally-run.* Support for young widows and widowers. Mutual support for people who have experienced the death of a spouse or companion early in their lives. Meetings vary. Pre-registration required. Before attending call The Samaritan Center for Grief Support 1-800-596-8550. *Website:* http://www.samaritanhospice.org

H.O.P.E. (Helping Other People Evolve, Inc.) Helps the recently widowed to cope with their loss, move forward and become self-reliant. Group runs for 10 week sessions, 4 times per year. Registration fee $20. Meets in Mantua. Call H.O.P.E. 1-888-920-2201 (Mon., Wed., Fri., 10am-1pm). *E-mail:* hopesnj@juno.com

HUDSON

Separated, Divorced and Bereaved Catholics Referrals to groups for emotional/spiritual support for separated, divorced or bereaved men and women. Groups are sponsored by various churches throughout the county and are open to people of any faith. Call Family Life Ministry, Newark Diocese 973-497-4327.

HUNTERDON

Catholic Widows and Widowers Mutual support for widowed persons of any faith. Groups for the recently bereaved as well as for those further along. Various meeting locations and times. Call Family Life Office 732-562-1990 ext. 1624 (day).

MERCER

Early Endings *Professionally-run.* Support for young widow and widowers. Mutual support for people who have experienced the death of a spouse or companion early in their lives. Meetings vary. Call 856-596-8550.

H.O.P.E. (Helping Other People Evolve, Inc.) Support and information for recently (up to 2 yrs) widowed men and women of all ages. Group runs for 10 week sessions, 4 times per year. Meets in various locations. Registration fee $20. Call H.O.P.E. 1-888-920-2201 (Mon., Wed., Fri., 10am-1pm). *E-mail:* hopesnj@juno.com

Starting Over *Professionally-run.* Support for widows and widowers under the age of 50 or those with dependent children. Meets 1st and 3rd Tues., 7-9pm, Saul Colonial Home, 3795 Nottingham Way, Hamilton Square. Before attending call Mary Lou Pizzullo or Deborah Myslinski 609-587-7072 (day). *Website:* http://www.saulfuneralhomes.com *E-mail:* mlpizzullo@saulfuneralhomes.com

MIDDLESEX

Catholic Widows and Widowers Mutual support for widowed persons of any faith. Groups for the recently bereaved as well as for those further along. Various meeting locations and times. For information call the Family Life Office, Metuchen Diocese 732-562-1990 ext. 1624 (day).

Spousal Bereavement Group *Professionally-run.* Helps persons who have lost their spouse within the last two years to understand the grieving process and share feelings, while adjusting to new roles. Young widows/widowers (under age 55), meets 2nd and 4th Tues., 7-8:15pm and widows/widowers (55 and over), meets 3rd Tues., 7-8:30pm, JFK Medical Center, 65 James St., Edison. Pre-registration required. Before attending call 732-321-7769 (day).

St. Thomas WOW'S (Widows Or Widowers) Mutual support for widows and widowers. Open to persons of any faith. Rap sessions, education, social and guest speakers. Annual dues $8 per year, $1 per meeting. Meets 1st Tues., (except July/Aug.), 7pm, St. Thomas the Apostle Church, One St. Thomas Plaza, Pastoral Center, Old Bridge. Call Deacon John J. Fitzsimmons 732-251-4000 (day) or Irene Sutton 732-251-1458 (eve).

MONMOUTH

Bereavement Support Group *Professionally-run.* Mutual support for the loss of a spouse and adult children bereaving the death of a parent. Meets for 6 weeks, several times per year, Riverview Medical Center, Cancer Center, 1 Riverview Plaza, Red Bank. Call Sister Vida O'Leary 732-530-2382. *E-mail:* Reegroup@aol.com

Growing Through Loss *Professionally-run.* Mutual bereavement support for "younger" widows and widowers (ages 30-60, plus or minus). Non-sectarian. Opportunity to share thoughts. Meets 1st and 3rd Mon., 7:30-9pm, (once a month Jan., Feb., Mar.), Temple Shaari Emeth, 400 Craig Rd., Manalapan. For meeting information call Temple Shaari Emeth 732-462-7744 or Bunny Soloman 732-617-2221 (day/eve).

Separated / Divorced / Widows and Widowers Support Group Support for persons who have lost their spouse due to separation, divorce or death (past bereavement stage) to help members get on with their lives. Not for crisis situations. Not intended as a social group. Meets Tues., 7:30pm, St. Veronica's Rectory Cellar, Route 9 North, Howell. Call Ree 732-431-0446 or Cookie 732-577-6964 (day). *Website:* http://www.divorceheadquarters.com

Spouse Bereavement Group *Professionally-run.* Mutual support for persons bereaving the death of a spouse. Meets for 6 weeks, several times per year, Riverview Medical Center, 1 Riverview Plaza, Red Bank. Before attending call 732-530-2382.

Women's Support Group Helps women who are displaced homemakers facing the loss of their primary source of income due to separation, divorce, disability, or death of spouse. Issues addressed include self-sufficiency, career development, assertiveness, self-esteem, divorce, separation, widowhood and other related topics. Groups are set-up as needed in Asbury Park, Long Branch, West Keansburg, and Lincroft. Call Robin Vogel 732-495-4496 (day) or Mary Ann O'Brien 732-229-8675.

MORRIS

Begin Again Mutual support for widows or widowers bereaving the death of a spouse. Rap sessions, phone help and guest speakers. Meets 2nd and 4th Fri., 6-8:45pm, Convent at St. Peter's Church, 189 Baldwin Road, Parsippany. Call Lucille 973-334-7924 (day).

Circle of Life Offers support for anyone feeling the loss of their spouse. Dues $30/yr. Meets 2nd Sun., 6pm, First Church of Hanover, Mt. Pleasant Ave. and Hanover Rd., Parish House, East Hanover. Call Jan 973-884-8989. *E-mail:* njcircle@yahoo.com

Living with Loss of Spouse Mutual support for those who have lost a spouse and have completed a professionally-led bereavement group or had professional counseling. Rap sessions and phone help. Meets 2nd and 4th Wed., 7-8:30pm, St. Clare's Hospital, 25 Pocono Rd., Urban 1, Conference Room, Denville. Call John Evans 973-895-3444. *E-mail:* jevans66@optonline.net

Widow/Widower Support Group *Professionally-run.* Opportunity for widows and widowers to share experiences and feelings with other newly bereaved who are living through similar circumstances. Rap sessions. Meets 4th Tues., 1-2:30pm, Chilton Memorial Hospital, 97 West Parkway, Pompton Plains. Call Joan Beloff 973-831-5167 (day).

Widowed Early Support and social group for widows and widowers who have lost their spouse before the age of 65. Must be past the bereavement stage. Guest speakers, social activities, newsletter. Annual membership $25/yr. Meetings vary, 7pm, Resurrection Parish, Community Room, Randolph. Call Chris Ippolito 973-398-9068.

Widows and Widowers Support Group *Professionally-run.* Provides support, education and mutual sharing for widows and widowers. Literature. Meets 4 times year, for 8 week sessions, Morristown Memorial Hospital, 100 Madison Ave., Morristown. Before attending call Michelle 973-971-4767 (day), Zsuzsa 973-971-5402 (day) or Chris Anderson 973-971-7911 (day).

OCEAN

Community Medical Center Bereavement Support Group *Professionally-run.* For adults who have experienced the recent loss of a spouse. Meets Mon., 10-11:30am, Community Medical Center, Hooper Ave., Toms River. Pre-registration required. Before attending call Bereavement Coordinator 732-818-6826 (day).

Young Widows' Support Group Provides support and information for young women, (ages 20-55), who have lost their husband. Meets monthly, Church of St. Luke, 1674 Old Freehold Rd., Toms River. For meeting information call church 732-286-2222.

PASSAIC

Widow/Widower Support Group *Professionally-run.* Support and sharing of experiences for newly widowed persons. Meets 2-3 times year, for 6 week sessions, Pathways Counseling Center, 16 Pompton Avenue, Pompton Lakes. Registration required. Call Peg Buczek 973-835-6337 (day).

Widows/Widowers Support Group Mutual support for all widowed persons. Provides guest speakers, group discussions, phone help, peer-counseling, visitation and refreshments. Newly bereaved persons meet 2nd and 4th Wed., 7:30pm, persons past bereavement stage meet 2nd and 4th Mon., 7:30pm, St. Philip the Apostle Church, Valley Rd., Clifton. Call John Cerullo 973-472-4494 (day/eve).

SOMERSET

Catholic Widows and Widowers Mutual support for widowed persons of any faith. Groups for the recently bereaved as well as for those further along. Various meeting locations and times. Call Family Life Office, Metuchen Diocese 732-562-1990 ext. 1624 (day).

JANUS Bereavement Group *Professionally-run.* Support and education for anyone who has experienced a loss through death, separation/divorce, retirement, loss of a job, health or relocation. Helps individuals accept and adjust to the loss. Meets 2nd Tues., 7:30-9pm, in Bridgewater and Branchburg. Call Barbara Ronca, LCSW 908-218-9062 (Mon.-Fri., 9am-3pm).

Single Senior Women Support for women (age 60+) who are divorced, separated or widowed. Meets 2nd and 4th Thurs., 10am-noon, Office on Aging, 92 East Main St., 1st Floor, Conference Room, Somerville. Call Erin 908-704-6339 (day).

UNION

Bereavement Support Groups *Professionally-run.* Mutual support for persons grieving the loss of a loved one. Series of 5 weekly meetings with separate groups for spouses and other family members. Meets various times, United Methodist Church, 1441 Springfield Ave., New Providence. Call Bereavement Coordinator 973-379-8440 (day).

Hospice Bereavement Support Group *Professionally-run.* Mutual support for persons bereaving the death of spouse. Rap sessions, literature, guest speakers. Group runs for 8 weeks (Spring/Fall). Meets Wed., 1:30-3pm, Robert Wood

Johnson University Hospital at Rahway, 865 Stone St., Rahway. For information call Shannon Wiese 732-499-6169 (day). *E-mail:* swiese@rwjuhr.com

Separated, Divorced and Bereaved Catholics Referrals to groups for emotional and spiritual support for separated, divorced or bereaved men and women. Groups are sponsored by various churches throughout the county and are open to people of any faith. Call Family Life Ministry 973-497-4327.

WARREN

Catholic Widows and Widowers Mutual support for widowed persons of any faith. Groups for the recently bereaved as well as for those further along. Various meeting locations and times. Call the Family Life Office, Metuchen 732-562-1990 ext. 1624 (day).

NATIONAL

Beginning Experience, The *International. 112 teams. Founded 1974.* Support programs for divorced, widowed and separated adults and their children enabling them to work through the grief of a lost marriage. Write: The Beginning Experience, c/o International Ministry Center, 1657 Commerce Dr., South Bend, IN 46628. Call 574-283-2079 or 1-866-610-8877; Fax: 574-283-0287. *Website:* http://www.beginningexperience.org *E-mail:* jan@beginningexperience.org

COPS (Concerns Of Police Survivors, Inc.) *National. 48 chapters. Founded 1984.* Provides resources for the surviving families of law enforcement officers killed in the line of duty according to Federal criteria. Also offers law enforcement training. Quarterly newsletter, departmental guidelines, peer support. Provides annual National Police Survivors' Conference each May during National Police Week. Special hands-on programs for survivors. Summer camp for children (ages 6-14) and their parent/guardian. Parents' retreats, spouse get-away, Outward Bound experiences for young adults (ages 15-20), siblings retreat, adult children's and in-laws retreats. Write: COPS, P.O. Box 3199, 3096 South State Highway 5, Camdenton, MO 65020. Call 573-346-4911; Fax: 573-346-1414. *Website:* http://www.nationalcops.org *E-mail:* cops@nationalcops.org

North American Conference of Separated and Divorced Catholics *International.* 3000+ groups. *Founded 1974.* Religious, educational and emotional aspects of separation, divorce, remarriage and widowhood are addressed through self-help groups, conferences and training programs. Families of all faiths are welcome. Group development guidelines. Newsletter. Membership dues start at

$35 (includes newsletter, discounts, and resources). Write: NACSDC, P.O. Box 10, Hancock, MI 49930. Call 906-482-0494; Fax: 906-482-7470. *Website:* http://www.nacsdc.org *E-mail:* office@nacsdc.org

Society of Military Widows *National. 24 chapters. Founded 1968.* Support and assistance for widows/widowers of members of all U.S. uniformed services. Helps people in coping with adjustment to life on their own. Promotes public awareness. Bimonthly magazine/journal. Dues $12. Chapter development guidelines. Online listing on local chapters. Write: Society of Military Widows, 5535 Hempstead Way, Springfield, VA 22151. Call 253-750-1342 or 1-800-842-3451 press 5. *Website:* http://www.militarywidows.org *E-mail:* hgrant@naus.org

ONLINE

GROWW (Grief Recovery Online - Widows and Widowers) *Online.* Support groups for widowed and other persons bereaving the loss of a loved one. Offers a large variety of chat rooms run by volunteers, dealing with specific issues (loss of someone to drugs, a child, sibling, parent, loss due to long-term illness, sudden death, violent losses, gays and lesbians, men and many more). Write: GROWW, 11877 Douglas Rd., # 102-PMB 101, Alpharetta, GA 30005. *Website:* http://www.groww.org

Young Widow - Chapter Two *Online.* Mutual support group for young widows and widowers, who share experiences, and strengths through its message board. Also provides a listing of local face-to-face groups, links to other related online e-mail discussion groups and websites for the young widowed persons. *Website:* http://www.youngwidow.org

SERENITY PRAYER

GOD GRANT ME THE SERENITY
TO ACCEPT THE THINGS I CANNOT CHANGE,
THE COURAGE TO CHANGE THOSE THINGS I CAN
AND THE WISDOM TO KNOW THE DIFFERENCE.

D I S A B I L I T I E S

AMPUTATION / LIMB DIFFERENCES

(see also general disabilities and specific disorder)

BERGEN

Kessler Leg Amputee Support Group Provides mutual support for both trans-tibial (below knee) and trans-femoral (above knee) amputees. Families welcome. Rap sessions, guest speakers, literature and buddy system. Meets 3rd Thurs., 6-7:30pm, Kessler Institute, 300 Market St., Saddle Brook. Call Cynthia Macaluso 201-368-6087 (day).

BURLINGTON

Amputee Support Group Offers mutual support for physical, emotional and social issues for patients and their families dealing with an amputation. Rap sessions and guest speakers. Meets 3rd Wed., 7-8:30pm, Marlton Rehab Hospital, 92 Brick Rd., Marlton. Call Andrea Varone 856-988-8778 ext. 2030.

ESSEX

S.H.A.G. (Self-Help Amputee Group) Mutual support for amputees and their families (under 18 welcome). Phone support. Dues $10/yr. Meets 1st Sat., 10am, Kessler Institute, West Orange. Call Ann Silvestrini 973-748-8785 (day/eve).

OCEAN

James F. Gorman Amputee Support Group of NJ Mutual support, encouragement and education for amputees, families, friends, caregivers or anyone who has involvement with an amputee. Rap sessions, guest speakers, literature, social, phone help and buddy system. Dues $5. Meets 1st Wed., noon-1:30pm, Health South Rehabilitation Hospital of Toms River, 14 Hospital Dr., Toms River. Call ~~Larry 732-255-5480 (day/eve) or John 609-494-3107. *E-mail:* lszczepan@aol.com~~ SCOTT 609 971 0006

NATIONAL

American Amputee Foundation, Inc. *National. Founded 1975.* Self-help and educational information, referrals and peer support for amputees. Hospital visitation and counseling. Group development guidelines, national resource directory for patients, families and caregivers. Write: American Amputee Foundation, P.O. Box 250218, Little Rock, AR 72225. Call 501-666-2523 (day); Fax: 501-666-8367. *Website:* http://www.americanamputee.org

Amputee Coalition of America *National. 240 affiliated groups.* Mission is to reach out to people with limb loss and to empower them through education, support and advocacy. Maintains the National Limb Loss Information Center which is a comprehensive source of information for people living with limb differences. Offers referrals to ACA certified peer visitors. Publishes information packet on starting a support group and two magazines "inMotion" and "First Step: A Guide for Adapting to Limb Loss". Write: Amputee Coalition of America, 900 East Hill Ave, Suite 285, Knoxville, TN 37915. Call 1-888-267-5669; Fax: 865-525-7917. *Website:* http://www.amputee-coalition.org *Email:* acainfo@amputee-coalition.org

National Amputation Foundation, Inc. *National. Founded 1919.* Offers support, referrals and information to all amputees. "Amp to Amp" program links individuals with others with similar amputations. Newsletter, information and referrals. Dues $25/yr. Donated medical equipment given to any person in need. Items must be picked up at the office. Write: National Amputation Foundation, 40 Church St., Malverne, NY 11565. Call 516-887-3600; Fax: 516-887-3667. *Website:* http://www.nationalamputation.org *E-mail:* amps76@aol.com

ONLINE

I-CAN (International Child Amputee Network) *Online. 350 members. Founded 1995.* Mailing list for parents of children with either acquired or congenital limb loss. Opportunity to share experiences with other parents and mentors who grew up as amputees. *Website:* http://www/child-amputee.net *Listserv:* I-CAN@listserv.icors.org *E-mail:* jbaughn@child-amputee.net

LimbDifferences.org *Online. Founded 1981.* A comprehensive resource for families and friends of children with limb differences. Establishes contact with other families of children with limb differences through its forum. *Website:* http://www.limbdifferences.org

Need help finding a specific group? Give us a call – we're here to help!
Call 1-800-367-6274

AUTISM / ASPERGER SYNDROME

(see also parents of the disabled)

STATEWIDE

ASPEN (Asperger Syndrome Education Network) Information and support for parents of children with Asperger syndrome, pervasive developmental disorder and high functioning autism. Discussion groups, guest speakers and statewide workshops. Dues $25/yr. Write: ASPEN, 9 Aspen Circle, Edison, NJ 08820. Call Lori Shery 732-321-0880 (9am-2pm). *Website:* http://www.aspennj.org *E-mail:* info@aspennj.org

COSAC (Center for Outreach and Services for the Autism Community) *(BILINGUAL)* Helps families, individuals, teachers and agencies concerned about the welfare and treatment of children and adults with autism. Pen pals for siblings, guest speakers, information, referral, advocacy assistance, newsletter and workshops. Support groups statewide. Write: COSAC, 1450 Parkside Ave., Suite 22, Ewing, NJ 08638. Call 1-800-428-8476 (day) or 609-883-8100 ext. 28. *Website:* http://www.njcosac.org *E-mail:* information@njcosac.org

ONLINE

Autism_Parents_and_Pros_NJ *Online. 129 members. Founded 2004.* New Jersey support group for family members and professionals in the world of autism to connect and share support and information about experiences. *Website:* http://health.groups.yahoo.com/group/Autism_Parents_and_Pros_NJ/

ATLANTIC

ASPEN - Atlantic/Cape May Counties (Asperger Syndrome Parents Education Network) Information and support for parents of children with Asperger syndrome/PDD-NOS, and high functioning autism. Discussion groups and guest speakers. Usually meets 3rd Wed., 7-8:30pm, Atlantic County Library, 40 Farragant Ave., Mays Landing. Before attending call Florence Castro 609-625-2142. *Website:* http://www.aspenacms.southjersey.com *E-mail:* aspenacmc@yahoo.com

FACES (Families for Autistic Children Education and Support Group) Discusses topics important to families touched by autism. Guest speakers, workshops, play groups and social opportunities. Meets 4th Thurs., 5pm, South Jersey Children's Museum, Shore Mall, Egg Harbor Township. Call Trish

609-625-1697 or FACES 609-412-3750. *Website:* http://www.facesautismsupport.org *E-mail:* Trish@facesautismsupport.org *Online chatroom:* http://health.groups.yahoo.com/facesautism

BERGEN

ASPEN (Asperger Syndrome Parents Education Network) Provides resource information, education, caring, sharing and understanding to parents of children with Asperger syndrome. Phone help, literature, newsletter. Dues $25/yr. Meets 2nd Mon., Good Shepherd Lutheran Church, 233 South Highwood Ave., Glen Rock. Call 201-391-0758. *Website:* http://www.aspennj.org

ASPEN Support for individuals with Asperger syndrome/PDD-NOS and high functioning autism. Families and friends welcome. Discussion groups and guest speakers. Meets 3rd Wed., 7:30-9pm, West Bergen Mental Healthcare, 120 Chestnut St., Ridgewood. Call Mary 201-825-3286. *Website:* http://www.aspennj.org

COSAC (Center for Outreach and Services for the Autism Community) Mutual support for parents of children with autism. Families welcome. Guest speakers, literature and phone help. Meets 1st Fri., 8-10pm, Mt. Carmel Church, Passaic St., Ridgewood. Call Gary 201-503-9476. *Website:* http://www.njcosac.nj

BURLINGTON

P.A.C.T (Chapter of Autism Society of America) Support and sharing of information by parents of autistic children. Outside activities with siblings and families. Newsletter. Meets 2nd Tues., (Sept.-May), 7:30-9pm, Christ Presbyterian Church, Main St., Marlton. Call 856-722-8518 (day). *Website:* http://www.solvingthepuzzle.com

CAMDEN

GRASP (Global and Regional Asperger Syndrome Partnership) Support network for adults diagnosed with high functioning autism or Asperger syndrome. Meets 2nd Sat., 2-4pm, Easttown Library, 720 First Ave., Berwyn, PA. Call Robert 610-993-8096. *Website:* http://health.groups.yahoo.com/group/GRASP_Philadelphia_PA/

CAPE MAY

FACES (Families for Autistic Children Education and Support Group) Discusses topics important to families touched by autism. Guest speakers, workshops, play groups and social opportunities. Free childcare provided (call first). Meets 1st Mon., 6:30pm, Ocean Acadamy, Crest Haven Ave., Cape May Court House. Call Linda Kelly 609-465-0086 or FACES 609-412-3750. *Website:* http://www.facesautismsupport.org *E-mail:* facesgroup@comcast.net *Online chatroom:* http://health.groups.yahoo.com/facesautism

CUMBERLAND

FACES (Families for Autistic Children Education and Support Group) Discusses topics important to families touched by autism. Guest speakers, workshops, play groups and social opportunities. Meets Wed., various times, 223 E. Main St., (corner of 3rd and Rt. 49), Millville. Call Deanne O'Donnell 856-765-0077. *Website:* http://www.facesautismsupport.org

ESSEX

ADD Action Group Information about alternative solutions for attention deficit disorder, learning disabilities, hyperactivity, dyslexia and autism. Educational series, guest speakers, literature, phone help. Usually meets 3rd Thurs. 7-8:45pm, Millburn Public Library, 200 Glen Ave., Millburn. Pre-registration required. Before attending call Lynne Berke 973-731-2189 (day/eve). *E-mail:* LTBerke@aol.com

ASPEN (Asperger Syndrome Parents Education Network) Support for parents and families of children whose lives are affected by Asperger syndrome/PDD-NOS and high functioning autism. Guest speakers and literature. Dues $25/yr. Meets 3rd Mon., 7:30-9:30pm, JCC of Metrowest, 760 Northfield Ave., West Orange. Call Anita 973-669-5757 (day). *Website:* http://www.aspennj.org

COSAC (Center for Outreach and Services for the Autism Community) Mutual support for parents of children with autism. Families welcome. Guest speakers, literature and phone help. Meets 1st Mon., 7-9pm, Temple/Congregation Beth Ahm, 56 Grove Ave., Verona. Call Michele Havens 201-486-5607 (day/eve). *Website:* http://www.njcosac.org *E-mail:* mhavens523@aol.com

GLOUCESTER

ASPEN (Asperger Syndrome Parents Education Network) Information and support for parents of children with Asperger syndrome, PPD-NOS and high functioning autism. Discussion groups and guest speakers. Dues $25/yr. Meets 2nd Wed., 7-9pm, Gloucester County Library, 389 Wolfert Station Rd., Mullica Hill. Call Beth 609-320-2542 (day). *E-mail:* aspen_sj@yahoo.com

HUDSON

COSAC (Center for Outreach and Services for the Autism Community) Mutual support for parents of children with autism. Families welcome. Guest speakers, literature and phone help. *Website:* http://www.njcosac.org

> **Bayonne** Meets 1st Wed., 7pm, Jewish Community Center, 1050 Kennedy Blvd. Call 609-883-8100 ext. 45 (day).
>
> **Union City** *(SPANISH SPEAKING)* Meets 1st Thurs., 7-9pm, St. Augustine's Church, 3900 New York Ave. Call Susana 201-864-7262.

HUNTERDON

ASPEN (Asperger Syndrome Education Network) *(Hunterdon County Adult Issues)* Young adult group for persons 18 and up who have Asperger syndrome, high functioning autism or PDD. Discussion, social and guest speakers. Meets 3rd Sun., Health Quest, 310 Highway 31 North, Flemington. Call Matt and Carolyn 908-236-6153 (day). *Website:* http://www.aspergerfriends.com

COSAC (Center for Outreach and Services for the Autism Community) Mutual support for parents of children with autism. Families welcome. Meets 2nd Mon., JW Tumbles, 186 Center St., Clinton. Call Marybeth Ruchlin 908-730-7002 (day) or 908-387-1383 (eve). *Website:* http://www.njcosac.org

Sharing and Caring of Bucks County Information and support for parents of children with autism, Asperger syndrome, mental retardation and related disorders. Discussion groups, guest speakers, sib-shop sibling support group, social and recreational activities. Meets 2nd Thurs., (except Jul/Aug), 7-9pm, St. Vincent DePaul Church, Education Building, Hatboro Rd., Richboro, PA. Call Holly 215-321-3202 (Mon.-Fri., 10am-6pm).

"Everyday courage has few witnesses. But yours is no less noble because no drum beats for you, and no crowds shout your name." –Robert Louis Stevenson

MERCER

ASPEN (Asperger Syndrome Parents Education Network) *(Central NJ Chapter)* Information and support for parents of children with Asperger syndrome/PDD-NOS and high functioning autism. Discussion groups and guest speakers. Dues $25/yr. Meetings vary, 7-9pm, West Windsor Library, Princeton Junction. Call Beth 609-275-5922 (day). *Website:* http://www.aspennj.org *E-mail:* Blondedawg@aol.com

COSAC (Center for Outreach and Services for the Autism Community) Mutual support for parents of children with autism. Families welcome. Meets 3rd Fri., 7-9pm, Mercer County Community College, Room SC 108, Hamilton. Call Kelly 609-584-8825 (eve). *Website:* http://www.njcosac.org

MIDDLESEX

ASPEN (Asperger Syndrome Parents Education Network) Information and support for parents of children with Asperger syndrome, PDD-NOS and high functioning autism. Discussion groups and guest speakers. Dues $25/yr. Meets monthly, Wed., 7:30-9:30pm, Community Campus-JCC, 1775 Oak Tree Rd., Edison. Call Lori Shery 732-321-0880 (day). *Website:* http://www.aspennj.org *E-mail:* info@aspennj.org

COSAC (Center for Outreach and Services for the Autism Community) Mutual support for parents of children with autism. Families welcome. Meets 1st Thurs., 7-9pm, Raritan Valley Academy, Stelton Rd., Piscataway. Call Steve 732-390-1796. *Website:* http://njcosac.org

MONMOUTH

ASPEN - Adult Issues Support for families of adults with high functioning autism and Asperger syndrome. Offers socialization opportunities, advocacy, literature, rap sessions, phone help, mutual sharing and education. Dues $25/yr. Meets Mon., 7-8:30pm, Monmouth County Library Headquarters, 125 Symmes Dr., Manalapan. Call Mary Laresch 609-409-1007.

ASPEN (Asperger Syndrome Education Network) Information and support for parents of children with Asperger syndrome/PDD-NOS and high functioning autism. Discussion groups and guest speakers. Meets 3rd Wed., 7-9pm, Monmouth County Library, Headquarters, Symmes Dr., Manalapan. Call Ann Hiller 732-446-7610 (day). *Website:* http://www.aspennj.org *E-mail:* ann0912@aol.com

MORRIS

ASPEN (Asperger Syndrome Parents Education Network) For parents and families of children with Asperger syndrome, high functioning autism and other pervasive developmental disorders to provide support, education, advocacy and sharing of resources. Guest speakers, literature. Dues $25/yr. Meets last Wed., 7:30-9:30pm, Saint Clare's Hospital, Conference Room D, 400 West Blackwell St., Dover. Call Janice 973-541-0178. *Website:* http://www.aspennj.org *E-mail:* janmlem1@hotmail.com

OCEAN

ASPEN (Asperger Syndrome Parents Education Network) Support for parents and families of children whose lives are affected by Asperger syndrome/PDD-NOS. Guest speakers. Dues $25/yr. Meetings vary, Temple Beth Shalom, Whitty and Old Freehold Rd., Toms River. Before attending call Eileen 732-473-9630 (day). *Website:* http://www.aspennj.org *E-mail:* aspenoc@comcast.net

FACES (Families for Autistic Children Education and Support Group) Discusses topics important to families touched by autism. Guest speakers, workshops, play groups and social opportunities. Childcare provided free of charge (must call first). Meets last Fri., 6:30pm, Southern Ocean County Hospital Resource Center at Ocean Club, 700 Route 9 South, Manahawkin. Call Jackie and Ed Seeger 609-294-0443 or FACES 609-412-3750. *Website:* http://www.facesautismsupport.org *E-mail:* facesgroup@comcast.net *Online chatroom*: http://health.groups.yahoo.com/facesautism

PASSAIC

Autism/Asperger Support Group Support and education for parents of children with autism and Asperger syndrome. Rap sessions, buddy system, newsletter and phone help. Meets last Wed., 7-9pm, Hillcrest Community Center, 1810 Macopin Rd., Room 25, West Milford. Call Julie Rikon 973-728-0999 or Angela Abdul 973-728-0999 (day). *Website:* http://www.ascfamily.org *E-mail:* ascfamily@hotmail.com

"Information is pretty thin stuff, unless mixed with experience."
-- Clarence Day, 1921

SALEM

Salem County Autism Support Group Mutual support and education for anyone concerned about the treatment of children and adults with autism. Guest speakers, literature and newsletter. Meets 2nd Wed., 7-9pm, Small Wonders Pre-School, 3 Ferry Rd., Pennsville. Call Nancy Gayle 856-678-5741 (day) or 856-678-4534 (eve).

SOMERSET

ASPEN (Asperger Syndrome Parents Education Network) Provides resource information, education, caring, sharing and understanding to parents of children with Asperger syndrome. Open to any interested person. Phone help, literature, newsletter. Meets 2nd Thurs., 7:30pm, (Sept.-May), Hillsborough Presbyterian Church, Route 206 South and Homestead Rd., Hillsborough. Call Inez 908-904-1610 (before 9pm). *Website:* http://www.aspennj.org *E-mail:* dgutman@patmedia.net

UNION

COSAC (Center for Outreach and Services for the Autism Community) Mutual support for parents of children with autism. Families welcome. Meets 4th Tues., (except July and Dec.), 7:30-9:30pm, Children's Specialized Hospital, New Providence Rd., Mountainside. Before attending call Deb 908-233-8510 (before 8pm). *Website:* http://www.njcosac.org

WARREN

COSAC (Center for Outreach and Services for the Autism Community) Mutual support for parents of children with autism. Families welcome. Guest speakers, literature and phone help. Meets 4th Mon., 7:30-9pm, Hackettstown Hospital, Willow Grove St., Hackettstown. Call Jodi 973-663-2505 (day). *Website:* http://www.njcosac.nj

NATIONAL

Autism Network for Hearing and Visually Impaired Persons *International network. Founded 1992.* Provides communication, education, research and advocacy for persons with autism combined with a hearing or visual disability, their families and professionals. Sharing of educational materials, phone help, support groups, referrals and conferences. Write: Autism Network for Hearing and

Visually Impaired Persons, 7510 Ocean Front Ave., Virginia Beach, VA 23451. Call 757-428-9036 *E-mail:* d.bartel@cox.net

Autism Network International *International. Founded 1992.* Organization run by and for autistic people. Provides peer support and tips for coping and problem-solving. Information and referrals. Advocacy, education, retreats/conferences. Online listserv. Write: ANI, P.O. Box 35448, Syracuse, NY 13235-5448. Call 315-476-2462 (long-distance calls will be returned collect). *Website:* http://www.ani.ac *E-mail:* jisincla@mailbox.syr.edu

Autism Society of America *National. 200+ chapters. Founded 1965.* Organization of parents, professionals and citizens working together via education, advocacy, research for children and adults on the autism spectrum. Magazine, searchable database and annual conference. Write: ASA, 7910 Woodmont Ave., Suite 300, Bethesda, MD 20814. Call 301-657-0881, 1-800-328-8476 (information and referral only), Fax: 301-657-0869. *Website:* http://www.autism-society.org/ *E-mail:* info@autism-society.org

GRASP-The Global and Regional Asperger Syndrome Partnership *National. 13 chapters. Founded 2003.* Support network for adults with a diagnosis on the autism spectrum with high functioning autism, Asperger syndrome or pervasive developmental disorder. Newsletter, literature, advocacy, information and referrals and assistance in starting local chapters. Also has an Orthodox Jewish Network for the Tri-State area in New York along with a teen group. Write: GRASP, 135 E. 15th St., New York, NY, 10003. Call 646-242-4003; Fax: 212-529-9996. *Website:* http://www.grasp.org *E-mail:* info@grasp.org

ONLINE

Families of Adults Afflicted with Asperger's Syndrome *Online.* Offers support to the family members of adult individuals with Asperger's syndrome. Bulletin board, e-mail list and resources. *Website:* http://www.faaas.org

OASIS (Online Asperger Syndrome Information and Support) *Online.* Interactive webpage providing information and support for Asperger syndrome and related disorders. Includes research papers, descriptions, local, national and international support groups. Message boards and chat rooms, family contributions, research projects, links to evaluators and other AS pages and online resources. Forums for families affected by Asperger syndrome and the professionals working with them. *Website:* http://www.aspergersyndrome.org *Messageboard:* http://forums.delphiforums.com/aspergeroasis *E-mail:* bkirby@udel.edu

BLIND / VISUALLY IMPAIRED

(see also specific disorder, toll-free helplines)

STATEWIDE

American Council of the Blind of Central New Jersey Consumer organization for visually impaired persons age 16+. Information, referrals, advocacy, special events and fundraising. Meets 5 times per year, Sat., central NJ. Dues $10/yr. Write: ACBC-NJ, 66 Fox Rd., Apt. 7B, Edison, NJ 08817. Call David M. Zulli 732-985-3175 ext. 5. *E-mail:* dmzulli1@optonline.net

DOROT/University Without Walls Telephone Support Teleconference support groups for persons age 59+ who are coping with vision loss, caregiving, aging issues, etc. There is a $10 registration fee and $15 tuition per support group. Scholarships are available. Write: DOROT, 171 W. 85th St., NY, NY 10024. For more information call DOROT 1-877-819-9147. *Website:* http://www.dorotusa.org

National Federation of the Blind of New Jersey Advocacy, self-help, education and support for blind persons, their families and friends. Under 18 welcome. Visitation, phone help, guest speakers. Annual state conference. Quarterly newsletter, "Sounding Board" available in print and cassette. Dues $5/yr. Write: NFBNJ, 254 Spruce St., Bloomfield, NJ 07003. Call Joe Ruffalo 973-743-0075 (9am-5pm). *Website:* http://www.nfb.org *E-mail:* nfbnj@yahoo.com

New Jersey Association of the Deaf-Blind, Inc. Purpose of group is to meet the needs of the deaf-blind, deaf, blind, or communication impaired and their families in NJ. Provides advocacy, case management, education, information and referrals. Residential, community, support, employment, family support and training services available. Write: NJADB, Inc., 24 K Worlds Fair Dr., Somerset, NJ 08873. Call 732-805-1912 (voice/TTY).

Parents of Blind Children - NJ Support, information, training and advocacy for parents of blind and visually impaired children. Technology demonstration site, newsletter, seminars. Dues $10/yr. Write: POBC, 23 Alexander Ave., Madison, NJ 07940. Call Carol Castellano 973-377-0976 (day). *Website:* http://www.blindchildren.org *E-mail:* blindchildren@verizon.net

ATLANTIC

VIP Flyers Mutual support for individuals who are blind or visually impaired. Families welcome. Rap sessions, guest speakers, literature, phone help, buddy system and speakers' bureau. Meets 4th Tues., 11am-1pm, John D. Young Blind Center, 100 Crestview Ave., Absecon. Call Ann Burns 609-677-1199 (Tues., Wed., Thurs.). *E-mail:* annburns@lionsblindcenter.org

BERGEN

Adjustment to Vision Loss Support Support for persons dealing with vision loss to exchange helpful information, offer and obtain emotional support while learning practical solutions for dealing with vision loss.

> **Teaneck** Meets 3rd Fri., 10:30am-12:30pm, St. Luke's Church, 118 Chadwick Rd. Call Dorothy Barrow 201-837-5197 (after 3pm).
>
> **Westwood** Meets 4th Mon., 1-3pm, Pascack Valley Hospital, 250 Old Hook Rd. Call Paul Ingram 201-666-0833.

Focus on Eyes Support Group for the Visually-Impaired Mutual support for blind and visually impaired persons. Meets 1st Tues., (except July/Aug.), 10am-noon, Fair Lawn Municipal Building, Fair Lawn Ave., Fair Lawn. Call Marion 201-797-6937 or Helen Markowitz 201-797-8839.

BURLINGTON

Choices Support Group Mutual support for blind and visually impaired persons, their families and friends. Rap sessions, phone help, guest speakers, literature, buddy system and speakers' bureau. Meets 4th Tues., 10am-1pm, Resources for Independent Living, Inc., 310 High St., Clubhouse (rear of building), Burlington City. Call Joe Zesski 609-747-7745 or 609-747-1875 (TTY). *E-mail:* info@rilnj.org

CAMDEN

National Federation of the Blind of New Jersey Mutual support, information and advocacy for blind persons, their families and friends. Under 18 welcome. Visitation, phone help, guest speakers. Dues $1.50/month. Meets 3rd Sat., 10am-noon, Kennedy Memorial Hospital, 5th Floor, Conference Room A, Cherry Hill. Call Linda Deberardinis 856-764-7014 or Edward Godfrey 856-848-6372 (eve).

PILOTS (People Interested in Lending Others Their Support) Offers mutual support, education and social group for blind and visually-impaired persons (ages 35-65). Meets 2nd Fri., 11:30am-2pm, (except Nov., meets 3rd Fri.) R-Mac's Restaurant, 427 West Crystal Lake Ave., Haddon Township. Call Annemarie Del Sordo 856-629-7219 (eve) or Linda Deberardinis 856-764-7014.

ESSEX

Foresighters *(WEST ORANGE RESIDENTS ONLY)* Support for blind and visually impaired persons. Meets 4th Thurs., 1-3pm, West Orange. Call Helen Gromann 973-731-4650 (day).

National Federation of the Blind of New Jersey Mutual support, information and advocacy for blind persons, their families and friends. Dues $5/yr. Meets 3rd Sat., 10am-noon, Beth Israel Hospital, 201 Lyons Ave., Newark. Call Sumara 732-255-0920 (day).

S.C.I.L.S. (Senior Community Independent Living Services) Support for seniors (age 55+) who are visually impaired/blind. Family and friends are welcome. Offers rap sessions, social group, literature, educational materials, mutual sharing and guest speakers. Transportation provided. Meets 3rd Wed., 1:30-2:45pm, (except June, July, Aug.), Bloomfield Civic Center, Bloomfield. Call Lauri Matera 201-656-6001 ext. 152.

GLOUCESTER

SHADES, INC. Mutual aid self-help for blind and visually impaired persons. Emotional support, sharing of experiences, guest speakers and information. Meets 4th Thurs., 11am-2pm, Gloucester County Library, Route 45, Mullica Hill. Call Kathryn 856-589-5438.

HUDSON

S.C.I.L.S. (Senior Community Independent Living Services) *(BILINGUAL)* Support for interpersonal sharing, support and personal growth for blind and visually impaired persons (age 55+). Several small informal groups meet in various locations. Spanish-speaking group available. Call 201-656-6001 (day).

HUNTERDON

Hunterdon Eye Openers Support for persons dealing with vision loss to exchange helpful information, offer and obtain emotional support while learning practical solutions for dealing with vision loss. Meets 1st Thurs., 11:30am, Senior Services, Building # 3, Gauntt Pl., Flemington. Call Barbara 908-638-4452.

MERCER

Adjustment to Vision Loss Support Support for persons dealing with vision loss to exchange helpful information, offer and obtain emotional support while learning practical solutions for dealing with vision loss. Dues $10/yr. Meets 3rd Thurs., 7:30-9:30pm, 1985 Pennington Rd., Ewing. Call Ottilie Lucas 609-882-2446. *E-mail:* ottilie@verizon.net

National Federation of the Blind Support and advocacy for the blind community. Family and friends are welcome to attend. Dues $10/yr. Meets 3rd Sat., 10am-noon, Lawrence Library, 2751 Brunswick Pike, Lawrenceville. Call Mary Jo 609-588-2145 (day) or 609-888-5459 (eve). *Website:* nfbnj@yahoo.com

MIDDLESEX

Adjustment to Vision Loss Support Support for persons dealing with vision loss to exchange helpful information, offer and obtain emotional support while learning practical solutions for dealing with vision loss.

Metuchen Meets 4th Thurs., 7-9pm, (Mar.-Oct.), Metuchen Public Library, (rear entrance), 480 Middlesex Ave. Call Phyllis Boeddinghaus 732-548-1391.

Monroe Township Meets 3rd Thurs., 10:30am-noon, Monroe Twp. Senior Center, 1 Municipal Plaza. Call Judy Kalman 732-521-6111.

Monroe Township Meetings vary, Monroe Village. Call Ted Alter 732-521-6418. *E-mail:* talter@phsnet.org

Perth Amboy Dues $10/yr. Meets 3rd Mon., 7-9pm, Grace Lutheran Church, 600 New Brunswick Ave. Call Kelly Leary 732-388-1322. *E-mail:* kaklleary@aol.com

Eye Openers Of Central New Jersey Mutual aid self-help for blind and visually impaired persons. Emotional support, sharing of experience and information. Meets 1st Thurs., 7:15-9:15pm, at local restaurants. Call Bernard Zuckerman 732-494-0753 (day/eve).

MONMOUTH

Middletown Area Visually Challenged Group Support for persons dealing with vision loss to exchange helpful information, offer and obtain emotional support while learning practical solutions for dealing with vision loss. Meets 2nd Tues., 11am-noon, N.J.B.C.A., Camp Happiness, 18 Burlington Ave., Leonardo. Call Charles Blood 732-671-9371.

V.I.P. (Visually Impaired Persons) Support Group *(NEPTUNE RESIDENTS ONLY)* Mutual support and information for blind and visually impaired persons (age 60+). Educational series, advocacy, rap sessions, guest speakers, phone help. Meets last Wed., 10-11:30am, Neptune Senior Center, 1825 Corlies Ave., Neptune. Call Ellen 732-988-8855 (day).

MORRIS

North Jersey Retinitis Pigmentosa Support Group Mutual support for persons with retinitis pigmentosa, macular degeneration, Usher's syndrome or related disorders and their families. Provides education, referrals, phone help, rap sessions and guest speakers. Meetings vary, 1:30-4pm, Morristown. Before attending call Jean and Don Perlman 973-584-6471 (day/eve), Susan Strechay 973-267-2419 (eve) or Glorie Isakower 609-409-7985 (Usher's syndrome).

V.I.P. (Visually Impaired Persons) Mutual aid self-help for blind and visually impaired persons. Emotional support, sharing of experiences and information. Meets 2nd Wed., (except July/Aug.), 11am-1:30pm, Diamond Spring Lodge, 230 Diamond Spring Rd., Denville. Call Mary Ann Speenburgh 973-884-0039.

OCEAN

Adjustment to Vision Loss Support Support for persons dealing with vision loss to exchange helpful information, offer and obtain emotional support while learning practical solutions for dealing with vision loss. Meets 2nd Tues., 11am-noon, Leisure Village East, 1015 B Aberdeen Dr., Lakewood. Call Betty Gumanow 732-920-1522.

Eye Openers Of Point Pleasant/Brick Mutual aid self-help for blind and visually impaired persons. Emotional support, sharing of experiences and information.

Pt. Pleasant Beach Meets 4th Tues., 10am-noon, Pt. Pleasant Presbyterian Church, Education Annex, Bay and Forman Aves. Call George 732-892-5117.

Toms River Meets 3rd Tues., 12:30-2:30pm, Dover Township Municipal Bldg., Washington St. Call Jim Fox 732-244-7057 (day). *E-mail:* Jim2447057@comcast.net

Low Vision Support Group Support for persons afflicted with low vision, their families and friends. Guest speakers, mutual sharing, and educational programs. Meets 1st Wed., 1pm, Ocean Club, 700 Route 9 South, Stafford Township. Call Betty 609-978-3559.

UNION

Self-Help Group for the Visually-Impaired Provides mutual support and education for those that are blind or visually-impaired. Meets 1st Thurs., noon-2pm, (except July/Aug.), Senior Citizen Center, Bonnel Court, Union. Call Agnes 908-790-9336 (eve).

NATIONAL

American Council of the Blind *National. 70 affiliates. Founded 1961.* Aims to improve the well-being of all blind and visually impaired people and their families through education, support and advocacy. National conference, information and referrals, phone support, state and special interest affiliates (e.g. guide dog users, blind lawyers, teachers and students), magazine published ten times per year (available in Braille, half speed cassette, large print, CD-ROM and online or via e-mail). Scholarships. Online job bank. Chapter development guidelines. Write: American Council of the Blind, 1155 15th St. NW, #1004, Washington, DC 20005. Call 1-800-424-8666 or 202-467-5081; Fax: 202-467-5085. *Website:* http://www.acb.org *E-mail:* info@acb.org

Aniridia Foundation International *International. Founded 2002.* Offers support, data studies, research and education to the public, medical community and members. Offers information, referrals, literature, newsletter, phone support, pen pals and conferences. Online e-mail support and chat rooms. Write: USA Aniridia Network, 1138 North Germantown Pkwy, Suite 101, PMB # 109, Cordova, TN 38016 Call 901-752-8835. *Website:* http://www.aniridia.net *E-mail:* info@aniridia.net

Association for Macular Diseases, Inc. *National. Local support groups. Founded 1978.* Support for persons suffering from macular diseases and their families. Distributes information on vision equipment. Supports national eye bank donor projects devoted solely to macular disease research. Quarterly newsletter, phone support network, participates in seminars, group development guidelines. Dues $20/year. Write: Association for Macular Diseases, 210 E. 64th St., New York, NY 10021. Call 212-605-3719 (eve); Fax: 212-605-3795. *Website:* http://www.macula.org

Autism Network for Hearing and Visually Impaired Persons *International network. Founded 1992.* Provides communication, education, research and advocacy for persons with autism combined with a hearing or visual disability, their families and professionals. Sharing of educational materials, phone help, support groups, referrals and conferences. Write: Autism Network for Hearing and

Visually Impaired Persons, 7510 Ocean Front Ave., Virginia Beach, VA 23451. Call 757-428-9036; Fax: 757-428-0019.

Blinded Veterans Association *National. 54 regional groups. Founded 1945.* Information, support and outreach to blinded veterans including those who were blinded in combat and those suffering from age-related macular degeneration and other eye diseases. Help in obtaining prosthetic devices and accessing the latest technological advances to assist the blind. Information on benefits and rehabilitation programs. Quarterly newsletter. Regional meetings. Write: BVA, 477 H St., NW, Washington, DC 20001. Call 202-371-8880 or 1-800-669-7079; Fax: 202-371-8258. *Website:* http://www.bva.org *E-mail:* bva@bva.org

Council of Citizens with Low Vision International *International. Founded 1979.* Encourages low vision people to make full use of vision through use of equipment, technology and services. Education and advocacy. Newsletter, information and referrals, group development guidelines, scholarships and conferences. Write: CCLVI, 1155 15th St. NW, Suite 1004, Washington, DC 20005. Call 1-800-733-2258. *Website:* http://www.cclvi.org

Foundation Fighting Blindness, Inc., The *National. Founded 1971.* Offers information and referral services for affected individuals and their families, as well as doctors and eye care professionals. Provides comprehensive information kits on retinitis pigmentosa, macular degeneration and Usher syndrome. Newsletter presents articles on coping, research updates and Foundation news. Supports research into the causes, treatments, preventive methods and cures for the entire spectrum of retinal degenerative diseases. National conferences. Annual fees $25. Write: Foundation Fighting Blindness Inc., 11435 Cronhill Dr., Owings Mill, MD 21117-2220. Call 1-800-683-5555 or 410-568-0150 (Mon.-Fri., 9am-4pm); 1-800-683-5551 (TDD) or 410-363-7139; Fax: 410-363-2393. *Website:* http://www.FightBlindness.org *E-mail:* info@blindness.org

Lighthouse International *Resource.* Mission is to overcome vision impairment for people of all ages through rehabilitation services, education, research and advocacy. Free literature on eye diseases (macular degeneration, glaucoma, cataracts, diabetes and more) and various resource lists (reading options, adaptive computer technology, financial aid, etc.) Provides contact information for support groups, low vision services, rehabilitation agencies, state agencies and advocacy groups. Write: Lighthouse International, 111 East 59th St., New York, NY 10022. Call 1-800-829-0500 or 212-821-9200; Fax: 212-821-9705; TDD: 212-821-9713. *Website:* http://www.lighthouse.org *E-mail:* info@lighthouse.org

MAB Community Services *National. 34 groups. Founded 1903.* Support network for persons coping with sight loss. Sponsors support groups for elders and mixed ages. Outreach services, phone support, community volunteers, Braille transcriptions, recording studio, large print literature, cassettes and newsletter. Assistive devices for a fee. Write: MAB Community Services, 313 Pleasant St., Watertown, MA, 02472. Call 617-926-4232 or 1-800-852-3029 (MA only); Fax: 617-926-1412. *Website:* http://www.mabcommunity.org *E-mail:* fweisse@mabcommunity.org

National Association for Parents of Children with Visual Impairments *National. 21 groups. Founded 1980.* Outreach and support for parents of children with visual impairments. Promotes formation of local parent support groups. Increases public awareness. Quarterly newsletter. Dues $25/family. Group development guidelines. Write: NAPVI, Inc., P.O. Box 317, Watertown, MA 02471-0317. Call 1-800-562-6265; Fax: 617-972-7444. *Website:* http://www.napvi.org *E-mail:* napvi@perkins.org

National Association for Visually Handicapped *(MULTILINGUAL) National. Founded 1954.* Support for visually impaired seniors. Newsletter, phone support, information and referrals. Bi-monthly support group for visually impaired seniors. Guide to starting groups for elders losing sight. Free large print loan library by mail and optical library. Large print informational materials available in English, some in Russian, Spanish and Chinese. Write: NAVH, c/o C. Gomez, 22 West 21st St., 6th Floor, New York, NY 10010. Call 212-889-3141 or 1-888-205-5951; Fax: 212-727-2931. *Website:* http://www.navh.org *E-mail:* navh@navh.org

National Federation of the Blind *National. 52 affiliates. Founded 1940.* Serves as both an advocacy and a public information vehicle. Contacts newly blind persons to help with adjustment. Provides information on services and applicable laws. Student scholarships. Assists blind persons who are victims of discrimination. Literature, monthly meetings and magazine. Assistance in starting new groups. Write: National Federation of the Blind, 1800 Johnson St., Baltimore, MD 21230-4998. Call 410-659-9314; Fax: 410-685-5653. *Website:* http://www.nfb.org *E-mail:* communityrelations@nfb.org

National Keratoconus Foundation *National network. 5 groups. Founded 1986.* Provides information and support to persons with keratoconus, an eye condition where the cornea progressively thins causing a cone-like bulge. Newsletter, phone support, information and referrals. Online support group. Encourages research into cause and treatment. Write: NKCF, 8733 Beverly Blvd., Suite 201, Los Angeles, CA 90048. Call 1-800-521-2524; Fax: 310-623-1837. *Website:* http://www.nkcf.org *E-mail:* info@nkcf.org

National Organization of Parents of Blind Children *National. 25 chapters. Founded 1983.* Serves as both an advocacy and public information vehicle. Provides information on services available. Offers positive philosophy and insights into blindness and practical guidance in raising a blind child. Magazine ("Future Reflections"), parent seminars, free parents' information packet, meetings, conventions. Dues $8. Write: NOPBC, Attn: Barbara Cheadle, National Federation of the Blind, 1800 Johnson St., Baltimore, MD 21230. Call 410-659-9314 ext. 2360; Fax 410-685-5653. *Website:* http://www.nfb.org/nopbc *E-mail:* bcheadle@nfb.org

Vision Northwest *Regional model. 42 groups. Founded 1983.* Mission is to reach out with compassion, encouragement and understanding to those coping with vision loss, their families and friends. Helps persons with vision loss to become more independent through a network of peer support groups and individual peer counseling. Information and referral, membership newsletter, community newsletter. Loan-lending optical aids network. Write: Vision Northwest, 9225 SW Hall Blvd., Suite G, Tigard, OR 97223. Call 503-684-8389; Fax: 503-684-9359. *Website:* http://www.visionnw.com *E-mail:* info@visionnw.com

ONLINE

Aniridia Network *Online. Founded 1998.* International network that aims to bring people with aniridia (missing one or both irises) together for support. Provides practical information. Offers chat room and e-group. Write: Aniridia Network, 109 Gavin Way, Colchester Essex, CO4 9FR UK. *Website:* http://www.aniridia.org *E-mail:* hannah@aniridia.org

Duane's Retraction Syndrome *Online. Members 1061. Founded 1999.* A place for those affected by Duane's retraction syndrome (an eye mobility disorder) to share experiences and information with others. *Website:* http://health.groups.yahoo.com/group/duanes/

Leber's Congenital Amaurosis eGroup *Online.* Provides a listserv for persons who are interested in sharing, support and information relating to this genetic disorder. *Website:* http://groups.yahoo.com/group/LCA

Can't find an appropriate group in your area? The Clearinghouse helps people start groups. Give us a call at 1-800-367-6274

BRAIN INJURY / COMA

(see also general disabilities, specific disorder, toll-free helplines)

STATEWIDE

Brain Injury Association of NJ Provides information, education, outreach, prevention, advocacy and support services to all persons affected by brain injury. Write: Brain Injury Association of NJ, 1090 King George Post Rd., #708, Edison, NJ 08837. Call 732-738-1002 (day) or 1-800-669-4323 (day); Fax: 732-738-1132 *Website:* http://www.bianj.org *E-mail:* info@bianj.org

ATLANTIC

Brain Injury Association of NJ *Professionally-run.* Emotional support and education for persons with brain injuries, their families and friends. Meets 2nd Thurs., 7pm, Bacharach Institute for Rehabilitation, 61 W. Jimmie Leeds Rd., Pomona. Call Nutan Ravani 856-589-5797 (day) or Helpline 1-800-669-4323.

BERGEN

Brain Injury Support Group Emotional support and education for persons with brain injuries, their families and friends. Meets 3rd Mon., 6:30pm, Pascack Valley Hospital, Conference Rooms 1 and 2, Old Hook Rd., Westwood. Call Joe 201-666-2015.

BURLINGTON

Brain Injury Association of NJ *Professionally-run.* Emotional support and education for persons with brain injuries and their families. Meets 2nd and 4th Wed., 7pm, Marlton Rehabilitation Hospital, 92 Brick Rd., Marlton. Call Lisa Cohen 856-988-8700 ext. 2046 (day) or Helpline 1-800-669-4323.

CAMDEN

Brain Injury Association of NJ *Professionally-run.* Emotional support and education for persons with brain injuries and their families. Meets 3rd Mon. (except July/Aug.), 7-9pm, Rehabilitation Services, 425 Kings Highway, Haddonfield. Call Katie Kelly 856-616-8299 ext. 240 or Helpline 1-800-669-4323.

CUMBERLAND

Brain Injury Association of NJ *Professionally-run.* Emotional support and education for persons with brain injuries and their families. Meets 1st Tues., 7pm, Rehabilitation Hospital of South Jersey, 1237 West Sherman Ave., Vineland. Call Dr. Chris Wolf 856-696-7100 ext. 224.

ESSEX

Brain Injury Association of NJ *(BILINGUAL) Professionally-run.* Emotional support and education for persons with brain injuries, their families and friends. Meets 2nd Tues., 6:30pm, Kessler Institute for Rehabilitation, West Orange. Call Betty Collins 973-731-3600 (English) or Dr. Juan Arango 973-324-3558 (Spanish).

GLOUCESTER

Brain Injury Association of NJ *Professionally-run.* Emotional support and education for person with head injuries and their families. Meets 4th Mon., 6:30pm, Moss Rehab/Drucker Brain Injury Center, 135 South Broad Ave., Meets 4th Mon., 6:30pm, Moss Rehab/Drucker Brain Injury Center, 135 South Broad Ave., Woodbury. Call Cynthia Abbott-Gaffney 856-853-9900 ext. 102.

Brain Injury Support Group. Mutual support, friendship, networking and social activities for individuals who have sustained a brain injury. Meets Wed., 7-9:30pm, Apostles' Lutheran Church, 4401 Black Horse Pike, Turnersville. Call Teresa May 856-629-8487 or the church 856-629-4228.

HUNTERDON

Brain Injury Support Group Support group for people who have brain injury due to AVM's, aneurysm, blunt head trauma, tumors, stroke and all other brain injury conditions. Families welcome. Guest speakers and literature. Meets 2nd Thurs., 7-9pm, Hunterdon Medical Center, 2100 Wescott Dr., Flemington. Call Gwen Bartlett-Palmer 908-638-5194.

MERCER

Brain Injury Association of NJ *Professionally-run.* Emotional support and education for persons with brain injuries, their families and friends. Meets 1st Wed., 6:30pm, St. Lawrence Rehab Hospital, Room 117, 2381 Lawrenceville Rd.,

Lawrenceville. Call David Searles 609-896-9500 ext. 2303 or Helpline 1-800-669-4323.

MIDDLESEX

Brain Injury Association of NJ *Professionally-run.* Emotional support and education for persons with head injuries and their families. Meets 2nd Tues., 6pm, Johnson Rehab Institute, Center for Head Injuries, 2048 Oak Tree Rd., Edison. Call Carolyn Weil 732-906-2640 ext. 42230 (day).

Brain Trauma Survivors Mutual support and advocacy for spouses and families of brain trauma survivors. Meets twice monthly on Fri., 7-8:30pm, Saint James Church, Emmaus House, 2nd Floor, 174 Grove St., Woodbridge. For date of next meeting call Kathleen 908-353-6922.

COPSA Spouse Support Group Mutual support and understanding for spouses of persons with any type of memory loss (Alzheimer's, Parkinson's, vascular disease, stroke, head injury, dementia, etc.). Meets 1st and 3rd Mon., 9:30-11am, UBHC, 671 Hoes Lane, Piscataway. Call Mary Catherine Lundquist 732-235-2858 (day).

TBI Support Group Mutual support sharing of concerns and frustrations for persons with traumatic brain injuries. Families welcome. Meets 1st Tues., 10am, Edison Library, Meeting Room, 777 Grove St., Edison. Call Kathleen Orsetti 732-738-4388 (day); 732-738-9644 (TDD). *Website:* http://www.adacil.org *E-mail:* peersupport@adacil.org

MONMOUTH

Brain Injury Association of NJ *Professionally-run.* Emotional support and education for persons with head injuries and their families. Meets 1st Tues., 7pm, Dorbrook Park Recreation Area, Route 537, Colts Neck. Call 732-738-1002.

MORRIS

Adults with Brain Injury *Professionally-run.*Mutual support for adults (age 16+) with acquired brain injury and their families. Opportunity for patients with similar experiences to exchange information, coping skills and understanding. Meets 1st Tues., 6pm, Kessler Institute for Rehabiliation/Welkind Facility, 201 Pleasant Hill Rd., Chester. Call Rachel Jacobowitz 973-252-2612.

OCEAN

Brain Injury Association of NJ *Professionally-run.* Emotional support and education for persons with head injuries, their families and friends. Meets 3rd Tues., 6pm, Community Medical Center, 99 Highway 37 West, Toms River. Call Vicki Hardy 732-557-8000 ext. 10226 or Pam Lightfoot 732-557-8000 ext. 11547.

PASSAIC

Brain Injury Association Family Support Group *Professionally-run.* Support for family members and caregivers of neurologically impaired people (brain injury, aneurysm, stroke, etc). Sharing sessions, guest speakers, literature. Meets 2nd Wed., 6:30pm, Rehab Specialists, 401 Haledon Ave., Haledon. Call Renee Carandang 973-427-2600 ext. 17 (family contact).

Voices that Count Encouragement, emotional support and socializing for head injured adults. Meets 2nd Wed., 6:30pm, Rehab Specialists, 401 Haledon Ave., Haledon. Before attending call Lori Netter 973-427-2600 ext. 19.

SOMERSET

Somerset/Hunterdon County Brain Injury Support Group *Professionally-run.* Emotional support for persons with illnesses and injuries affecting the brain, their families and friends. Information, socialization, educational series and guest speakers. Meets 3rd Thurs., 6:30pm, Neurobehavioral Institute of NJ, 626 N. Thompson St., Raritan. Call Mary Liz McNamara 908-725-8877 (day).

SUSSEX

Brain Injury Association of NJ *Professionally-run.* Emotional support and education for persons with brain injuries, their families and friends. Meets 2nd Wed., 8pm, Redeemer Lutheran Church, 37 Newton-Sparta Rd., Newton. Call Angel McLaughlin 732-627-9890 ext. 202 or Helpline 1-800-669-4323.

NATIONAL

Brain Injury Association, Inc. *National. 42 state associations. 600 affiliated groups. Founded 1980.* Advocacy organization providing services to persons with brain injuries, their families and professionals. Increases public awareness through state associations, support groups, information and resource network, seminars, conferences, literature and prevention programs. Guidelines for starting similar groups. Write: Brain Injury Association, 8201 Greensboro Dr., Suite 611, McLean, VA 22102. Call 1-800-444-6443 (National Brain Injury Information Center) or 703-761-0750; Fax: 703-761-0755. *Website:* http://www.biausa.org *E-mail:* braininjuryinfo@biausa.org

Coma Recovery Association *National network. Founded 1980.* Support and advocacy for families of coma and traumatic brain injury survivors. Provides information, referrals and support group for family members and survivors. Quarterly newsletter and yearly conferences for families, brain injury professionals and survivors. Write: Coma Recovery Association, 8399 Republic Airport, Suite 106, Farmingdale, NY 11735. Call 631-756-1826; Fax 631-756-1827. *Website:* http://www.comarecovery.org *E-mail:* inquiry@comarecovery.org

ONLINE

Brain Injury Information, The NETwork (TBINET) *Online.* Various support group email lists for brain injury, stroke and other "medical" related issues. Has lists for caregivers, family and friends. *Website:* http://www.tbinet.org

BRAIN TRUST, The Healing Exchange *Online. Founded 1993.* Mission is to create an exchange of information and support among people affected by brain tumors and related conditions including patient-survivors, families, caregivers and health professionals. Online support groups cover a large range of brain tumors, acquired injuries and other special interests. Write: T.H.E. BRAIN TRUST, 186 Hampshire St., Cambridge, MA 02139-1320. Call 617-876-2002 or 1-877-252-8480; Fax: 617-876-2332. *Website:* http://www.braintrust.org *E-mail:* info@braintrust.org

BURN SURVIVORS

(see also facial disfigurement)

ESSEX

Burn Peer Support Group Education and support for burn patients and their families. Visitations, phone help. Meets monthly, St. Barnabas Medical Center, Old Short Hills Rd., Livingston. Call Susan Fischer 973-322-5276 (day).

NATIONAL

Burns United Support Groups *National. 2 affiliated groups. Founded 1986.* Mutual support for children and adults. who have survived being burned, no matter how major or minor the burn. Also for the family and friends of the survivor.

Outreach visitation, newsletter, pen pals, phone support, assistance in starting groups. Write: Burns United Support Groups, c/o Donna Schneck, P.O. Box 36416, Detroit, MI 48236. Call 313-881-5577 or 313-717-7277.

Phoenix Society for Burn Survivors, Inc., The *International. Founded 1977.* Mission is to uplift and inspire anyone affected by burns through peer support, collaboration, education and advocacy. Services include support services referrals and quarterly newsletter "Burn Support News." SOAR Peer Support Program, annual World Burn Congress, family services, online chat sessions, toll-free information and referral line, advocacy and educational programs. Write: The Phoenix Society, 1835 RW Berends Dr. SW, Grand Rapids, MI 49519. Call 1-800-888-2876 or 616-458-2773; Fax: 616-458-2831. *Website:* http://www.phoenix-society.org *E-mail:* info@phoenix-society.org

ONLINE

Burn Survivors Online *Online.* Information and support for burn survivors and their families throughout the world. Burn survivor profiles, burn statistics, peer support scheduled chats, outreach to newly burned patients and families. List of books, articles, question and answer forum. *Website:* http://www.burnsurvivorsonline.com

CEREBRAL PALSY

(see also general disabilities, parents of disabled, toll-free helplines)

STATEWIDE

Cerebral Palsy of New Jersey Provides services statewide to advance the independence of children and adults with all types of disabilities. Programs include advocacy, employment services, family support, respite, assistive technology, substance abuse prevention, information and referral, personal assistance services and a technology lending center. Write: CP of New Jersey, 354 South Broad St., Trenton, NJ 08608. Call 609-392-4004 or 1-888-322-1918; 609-392-7044 (TDD). *Website:* http://www.cpofnj.org *E-mail:* info@cpofnj.org

NATIONAL

United Cerebral Palsy Associations, Inc. *National. 140 affiliates. Founded 1949.* Supports local affiliates that run programs for individuals with cerebral palsy and other disabilities. Local programs include support groups for parents and adults with cerebral palsy. Information and referral, advocacy, research reports, information packets. Write: UCP, 1660 L St., NW, Suite 700, Washington, DC 20036-5603. Call 1-800-872-5827; Fax: 202-776-0414. *Website:* http://www.ucp.org

ONLINE

Cerebral Palsy Network *Online. 1,366 members. Founded 2000.* Aim is to make a difference in the lives of individuals with cerebral palsy and their loved ones. *Website:* http://groups.yahoo.com/group/cerebralpalsynetwork/ *E-mail:* cerebralpalsynetwork@yahoogroups.com

DEAF / HEARING IMPAIRED / TINNITUS / MENIERE'S DISEASE

(see also vestibular, toll-free helplines)

STATEWIDE

ALDA (Association of Late-Deafened Adults) - Garden State Support, education and advocacy on behalf of all people with hearing loss, especially the post-lingually deafened. Accessible education workshops, guest speakers, advocacy, social events. Yearly dues: $15/individual; $20/family. Free newsletter on request. Meets at East Brunswick Library. All education meetings provide sign language interpreters and CART captioning. Call Elinore Bullock 908-832-5083 (Cap-Tel). *Website:* http://www.alda-gs.org *E-mail:* elinorebullock7@earthlink.net

ALDA-NJ (Association of Late Deafened Adults) Informal social group for persons who became deaf later in life, whose first language is spoken English and who now rely on visual clues or various aids to understand the spoken word. Meets in private homes. Write: Elinore Bullock, 3 Tamarack Farm Lane, Califon, NJ 07830-3415. Call 908-832-5083 (CapTel) or 908-832-5082 (voice). *E-mail:* elinorebullock7earthlink.net

New Jersey Association of the Deaf-Blind, Inc. Purpose of group is to meet the needs of the deaf-blind, deaf, blind or communication impaired and their families in NJ. Provides advocacy, case management, education, information and referrals. Residential, community, family, employment support and training services. Write: NJ Association of Deaf-Blind, Inc., 24 K Worlds Fair Drive, Somerset, NJ 08873. Call 732-805-1912 (voice/TTY).

Signs of Sobriety Provides alcoholism and drug addiction services to persons who are deaf or hard-of-hearing. Makes referrals to deaf and sign interpretered 12-step programs. Provides prevention and education classes. Offers S.T.E.P.S. Program, a weekly peer support group for recovering individuals. Sponsors sober/deaf activities. Newsletter. Write: SOS, 100 Scotch Rd., # 2, Ewing, NJ 08628-2507. Call TTY: 1-800-332-7677; Voice: 609-852-7677 (day); Fax: 609-882-6808. *Website:* http://www.signsofsobriety.org *E-mail:* info@signsofsobriety.org

BERGEN

HLA (Hearing Loss Association of America) *(Bergen County Chapter)* Mutual support and information for people who are hard-of-hearing. Guest speakers. Dues $10/yr. Meets 2nd Wed., (Dec., Mar., June, Sept.), 1:30-3pm, Classic Residence, 655 Pomander Walk, Teaneck. Call Arlene Romoff 201-995-9594 (voice/TTY).

CAMDEN

South Jersey Tinnitus Support Group Information and support for tinnitus sufferers and family members. Meets 1st Thurs., (except July/Aug.), 7:30pm, Virtua Hospital, Barry Brown Education Building, Voorhees. Call Linda Beach 856-346-0200, [redacted], Mary Ann Halladay 609-429-5055 ext. 25 or TDD: 856-346-0623 (day). *Website:* http://www.pro-oto.com *E-mail:* linda.beach@gmail.com

MERCER

Tinnitus Association of New Jersey Mutual support for person afflicted with tinnitus, their families and friends. Rap sessions, guest speakers, coping skills, literature, newsletter. Meets 1st Sat., 10-11:30am, First Presbyterian Church, Ewing. Call Dhyan Cassie 856-983-8981 (day).

MIDDLESEX

HLA (Hearing Loss Association of America) *(Middlesex County Chapter)* Mutual support and information for people who are hard-of-hearing. Rap sessions, guest speakers. Dues $10/yr includes monthly newsletter. Meets 3rd Tues., (except July and Aug.), 7:30-9pm, First Baptist Church of South Plainfield, 201 Hamilton Blvd., South Plainfield. Call Marie Nordling 732-721-4183. *E-mail:* mcnord@yahoo.com

New Jersey CODA - (Children Of Deaf Adults) Provides mutual support for hearing adult children (age 18+) of deaf parents. Also open to deaf parents with children under 18. Promotes family awareness and individual growth in hearing children of deaf parents. Speakers' bureau, discussion sessions and phone assistance. Call Mariann Linfante Jacobson 732-548-2571. *E-mail:* jac2003@prodigy.net

MONMOUTH

HLA (Hearing Loss Association of America) *(Monmouth/Ocean Chapter)* Mutual support and information for people who cannot hear well. Guest speakers, rap sessions and literature. Families welcome. Meets 1st Sun., 1:30-4pm, (Oct.-June), Allaire Senior Center, Wall Circle Park, 1983 Route 34 South, Wall Township. Call Joleen Marsillo 732-657-1561. *E-mail:* jrmars813@yahoo.com

MORRIS

Deaf Senior Citizens of Northwest Jersey *(SIGN LANGUAGE)* Support for deaf senior citizens, non-seniors and interpreter students. Provides mutual sharing social, lecture series and discusses health issues associated with being deaf. Group conducted in American Sign Language. Meets 1st Fri., 1-4pm, St. Peter's Episcopal Church, Parish Hall, Boulevard, Mountain Lakes. Call Lila Taylor 973-361-6032 (TDD) or Beverly 973-361-5666. *Website:* http://www.dawninc.org

PASSAIC

DIAL, Inc. Center for Independent Living Provides people with disabilities with information and referral, peer counseling, advocacy and independent living skills program. Deaf and hard-of-hearing outreach services. Dues $15/yr./individual, $25/yr./family. Meets last Tues., 6:30-9:30pm, Clifton Center for Seniors and Citizens with Disabilities, Clifton. Call 973-470-8090 (day); TTY: 973-470-2521. *Website:* http://www.dial-cil.org *E-mail:* info@dial-cil.org

NATIONAL

Alexander Graham Bell Association for Deaf and Hard of Hearing Parent Section *International. Founded 1958.* Network of parents whose members promote advocating independence through listening and talking. Concerned with early diagnosis and auditory, language and speech training for children who are deaf or hard-of-hearing. Works to preserve parents' and children's rights by advocating auditory-oral and auditory-verbal education. Serves as clearinghouse to dispense information and exchange ideas. Write: AG Bell - Parents Section, 3417 Volta Pl., NW, Suite 310, Washington, DC 20007. Call 202-337-5220; TTY: 202-337-5221; Fax: 202-337-8314. *Website:* http://www.agbell.org *E-mail:* info@agbell.org

American Society for Deaf Children *National. 120 affiliates. Founded 1967.* Information and support for parents and families with children who are deaf or hard-of-hearing. Quarterly magazine, biennial conventions, information and referral. Guidelines for starting similar groups. Dues $40/yr. Write: American Society for Deaf Children, 3820 Hartzdale Dr., Camp Hill, PA, 17011. Call Parent hotline: 1-800-942-2732, 1-866-895-4206 or 717-909-5577 (voice/TTY); Fax: 717-909-5599. *Website:* http://www.deafchildren.org *E-mail:* asdc1@aol.com

American Tinnitus Association *National. 50 groups. Founded 1971.* Information, education, advocacy and support for persons affected by tinnitus. Funds research. Dues $35/yr includes quarterly magazine. Write: American Tinnitus Association, P.O. Box 5, Portland, OR 97207. Call 1-800-634-8978 or 503-248-9985. *Website:* http://www.ata.org *E-mail:* tinnitus@ata.org

Autism Network for Hearing and Visually Impaired Persons *International network. Founded 1992.* Provides communication, education, research and advocacy for persons with autism combined with a hearing or visual disability, their families and professionals. Sharing of educational materials, phone help, support groups, referrals and conferences. Write: Autism Network for Hearing and Visually Impaired Persons, 7510 Ocean Front Ave., Virginia Beach, VA 23451. Call 757-428-9036; Fax: 757-428-0019.

CODA (Children Of Deaf Adults) *International. 12 affiliated groups. Founded 1983.* Provides mutual support for hearing children of deaf parents. Promotes family awareness and individual growth through self-help groups, educational programs, advocacy and resource development. Newsletter, information and referral, assistance in starting groups. Dues $25/yr. Write: CODA, Box 30715, Santa Barbara, CA 93130. Call 805-682-0997 (Voice/TTY) (9am-9pm). *Website:* http://www.coda-international.org

Ear Foundation, The *National. 35 groups. Founded 1971.* Support and information for persons with Meniere's disease. Education regarding the condition, treatment and coping strategies. Newsletter. Group development guidelines, phone buddies, pen pals. Dues $25/yr. Write: The Ear Foundation, 955 Woodland St., Nashville, TN 37206. Call 1-800-545-4327; FAX: 615-627-2728. *Website:* http://www.earfoundation.org *E-mail:* amy@earfoundation.org

HLA (Hearing Loss Association of America) *International. 250 chapters and groups. Founded 1979.* Aim is to open the world of communication to people with hearing loss by providing information, education, support, referrals and advocacy. Bimonthly journal, online local group and chapters' listings. Assistance in starting groups. Write: HLA, 7910 Woodmont Ave., Suite 1200, Bethesda, MD 20814. Call 301-657-2248 (Voice) or 301-657-2249 (TTY); Fax: 301-913-9413. *Website:* http://www.hearingloss.org *E-mail:* info@hearingloss.org

National Association of The Deaf *National. 51 chapters. Founded 1880.* Federation of state associations, organizational and business affiliates that fights for the civil rights of deaf and hard-of-hearing Americans. Offers grassroots and youth leadership development and legal expertise across a broad spectrum of areas including, but not limited to, accessibility, education, employment, healthcare, mental health, rehabilitation, technology, telecommunications and transportation. Provides advocacy information and resources. Write: NAD, 8630 Fenton St., Ste. 820, Silver Spring, MD 20910-3819. Call 301-587-1789 (TTY); 301-587-1788 (Voice); Fax: 301-587-1791. *Website:* http://www.nad.org *E-mail:* nadinfo@nad.org

Rainbow Alliance of the Deaf *National. 23 affiliated chapters. Founded 1977.* Promotes the educational, economical and social welfare of deaf and hard-of-hearing gay, lesbian, bisexual, transgendered persons and their friends. Discussion of practical problems and solutions. Advocacy, conferences, newsletter, assistance in starting groups. Online information on contacting a local chapter. Write: RAD, c/o Steven Schumacher, 9804 Walker House Rd., # 4, Montgomery Village, MD 20886. *Website:* http://www.rad.org *E-mail:* president@rad.org

DEVELOPMENTAL DISABILITIES / DOWN SYNDROME

(see also parents of disabled, specific syndrome, toll-free helplines)

STATEWIDE

Arc of NJ, The Services and advocacy for children and adults with cognitive disabilities and their families. Parent support groups available at the chapter offices in each county. Membership dues vary for each chapter. Write: The Arc of NJ, 985 Livingston Ave., North Brunswick, NJ 08902. Call 732-246-2525 (day). *Website:* http://www.arcnj.org *E-mail:* info@arcnj.org

New Jersey Self-Advocacy Project, The Provides information on groups statewide. Helps people with developmental disabilities set up their own self-help groups. Groups have elected officers and a volunteer advisor. Members learn skills such as assertiveness, decision making. and effective communication. Write: NJ Self-Advocacy Project, 44 Stelton Rd., Suite 110, Piscataway, NJ 08854. Call Takeena Thomas 732-926-8010 (day). *Website:* http://www.arcnj.org

ATLANTIC

21 Down - Down Syndrome Awareness Group Inc. Support for families of a loved one with a developmental disability. Guest speakers. Meets 4 times a year. Call Susan 609-625-8141 (day). *Website:* http://www.21down.org *E-mail:* info@21down.org

CAPE MAY

21 Down - Down Syndrome Awareness Group, Inc. Support for families of a loved one with a developmental disability. Discusses educational, recreational and medical issues. Guest speakers and visitation. Under 18 welcome. Meets 4 times/ yr. Call Susan 609-625-8141 (day). *Website:* http://www.21down.org *E-mail:* info@21down.org

ESSEX

Down Syndrome Parent-To-Parent Support and current information to new parents and families of children with Down syndrome. Visitation, peer counseling, referrals. Meeting location rotates. Call 973-992-9830 (day). *Website:* http://www.arcessex.org

HUDSON

Family Support Group *(BILINGUAL)* Support for family and friends of people with developmental disabilities. Mutual sharing, socialization, education, lectures and advocacy for parents and others concerned about people with developmental disabilities. Meets 2nd Fri., 6-8pm, 405-09 36th St., Union City. Call Sandra Vasquez 201-319-9229 (day). *Website:* http://www.arcnj.org *E-mail:* svasquez@arcnj.org

HUNTERDON

Sharing and Caring of Bucks County Information and support for parents of children with autism, Asperger syndrome, mental retardation and related disorders. Discussion groups, guest speakers, sib-shop sibling support group, social and recreational activities. Meets 2nd Thurs., (except Jul/Aug), 7-9pm, St. Vincent DePaul Church, Education Building, Hatboro Rd., Richboro, PA. Call Holly 215-321-3202 (Mon.-Fri., 10am-6pm).

MERCER

Down Syndrome Association of Central NJ Mutual support for parents and family members of children with Down syndrome. Guest speakers, literature, newsletter, phone help and visitation. Meetings vary, The ARC of Mercer County, 180 Ewingville Rd., Ewing. Call Carron Morris 609-333-1077 (day/eve.), Kathy Cloyes 609-799-0187 (day/eve.) or 1-866-369-6796 (answering machine).

MIDDLESEX

Down Syndrome Family Support Group Support group for parents of children with Down syndrome. Meets in Edison. Call Children's Center 732-548-3356 (day). *E-mail:* anne.clark@cpamc.org

MONMOUTH

Down Syndrome Parent Support Group Mutual support for parents of children with Down syndrome. Meets quarterly, 8-11pm in members' homes. Call Susan Levine 732-747-5310 (day). *Website:* http://www.frainc.org

OCEAN

21 Down - Down Syndrome Awareness Group Inc. Support for families of a loved one with a developmental disability. Guest speakers. Meets 4 times a year. Call Susan 609-625-8141 (day). *Website:* http://www.21down.org *E-mail:* info@21down.org

SUSSEX

Self-Advocacy Group Fosters independence and responsibility in developmentally disabled adults. Education on advocating for one's own rights. Meetings vary, 112 Phil Hardin Rd., Fredon. Call 973-383-8574.

UNION

Adult Social Group Social activities club for developmentally disabled adults over 18. Discussions, films, recreation. Meets Wed., (except Jan., May, June, July, Aug.), 7pm, Kean University, University Center, Morris Ave., Union. Call Ina White 908-737-3857 (day).

Central NJ Down Syndrome Parent Advocacy Group Mutual support for parents of children with Down syndrome. Literature, guest speakers and phone help. Meets last Tues., 7pm, Children's Specialized Hospital, New Providence Rd., Mountainside. Call Janet 908-222-1281 (day). *E-mail:* janetcostello@verizon.net

WARREN

Down Syndrome Group of Northwest New Jersey, The Support for parents of children with Down syndrome to share information, experiences and provide education to new parents. Phone help, literature. Meetings vary in Washington. Call Melissa Ehrhardt 908-859-2747. *Website:* http://www.dsgnwnj.org

Go-Getters Self-advocacy group for persons with developmental disabilities. Peer counseling, guest speakers. Sponsored by the ARC. Meets in Washington. Call Bonnie Hill 908-689-7525 (day). *Website:* http://www.arcwarren.org

NATIONAL

Arc, The *National. 1100 chapters. Founded 1950.* Provides support for people with mental retardation and their families. Advocacy groups and direct services. Quarterly newspaper. Chapter development guidelines. Local group information on website. Write: The Arc, 1010 Wayne Ave., Suite 650, Silver Spring, MD 20910. Call 301-565-3842 (day); Fax: 301-565-5342. *Website:* http://thearc.org *E-mail:* info@thearc.org

National Down Syndrome Congress *National. 150+ parent group networks. Founded 1974.* Support, information and advocacy for families affected by Down syndrome. Promotes research and public awareness. Serves as clearinghouse and network for parent groups. Newsletter ($25/yr). Annual convention, phone support, chapter development guidelines. Write: National Down Syndrome Congress, 1370 Center Dr., Suite 102, Atlanta, GA 30338. Call 1-800-232-6372 or 770-604-9500; Fax: 770-604-9898. *Website:* http://www.NDSCcenter.org *E-mail:* info@NDSCcenter.org

People First *Model. 33 groups in Washington. 7 high school clubs. Founded 1977.* Self-help advocacy organization created by and for people with developmental disabilities. Provides help in starting new chapters. Quarterly newsletter. Write: People First, P.O. Box 648, Clarkston, WA 99403. Call 509-758-1123; Fax: 509-758-1289, TDD: 509-758-1123. *E-mail:* pfow@clarkston.com

Speaking For Ourselves *Model. 13 groups. Founded 1982.* Self-help advocacy for people with developmental disabilities. Monthly chapter meetings. Members help each other resolve problems, gain self-confidence and learn leadership skills. Chapter development guidelines. Newsletter. Write: Speaking For Ourselves, 502 W. Germantown Pike, Suite 105, Plymouth Meeting, PA 19462. Call 1-800-867-3330 or 610-825-4592; Fax: 610-825-4595. *Website:* http://www.speaking.org *E-mail:* info@speaking.org

Voice of the Retarded *National. 160 affiliated groups. Founded 1983.* Works to empower families of persons with mental retardation through information and advocacy. Weekly e-mail updates and quarterly newsletter for members. Networking, information and referrals, advocacy, phone support and conferences. Annual dues $25. Write: VOR, 5005 Newport Dr., Suite 108, Rolling Meadows, IL 60008. Call 847-253-6020 (day); Fax: 847-253-6054. *Website:* http://www.vor.net *E-mail:* vor@compuserve.com

ONLINE

Trisomy 21 Online Community *Online.* Offers support and information to those who have been touched by trisomy 21 (Down syndrome). Chat group and several forums. *Website:* http://www.trisomy21online.com

DISABILITIES (General) / SPINAL CORD INJURY

(see also parents of the disabled, specific disability, toll-free helpline)

STATEWIDE

Cerebral Palsy of New Jersey Provides services statewide to advance the independence of children and adults with all types of disabilities. Programs include: advocacy, employment services, family support, respite, assistive technology, substance abuse prevention, information and referral, personal assistance services and a technology lending center Write: CP of New Jersey, 354 S. Broad St., Trenton, NJ 08608. Call 609-392-4004 or 1-888-322-1918. 609-392-7044 (TTD). *Website:* http://www.cpofnj.org *E-mail:* info@cpofnj.org

Monday Morning Project, The Grassroots movement of people with disabilities, their families, friends and neighbors. Made up of advocacy networks in each county, it brings together ordinary citizens to work with local, state and federal officials on public policy issues important to people with disabilities. Some of the groups will help a new member with a personal advocacy issue. Meetings are held monthly in Bergen, Burlington, Camden, Cumberland, Essex, Gloucester, Hudson, Hunterdon, Mercer, Middlesex, Monmouth, Morris, Ocean, Passaic, Salem,

Somerset, Union and Warren counties. For information on your local county network call Luke Koppisch 609-777-3293 (day); 609-777-3228 (TDD) or Monday Morning Hotline 1-800-216-1199. *Website:* http://www.njddc.org

BERGEN

Big Wheels Mutual support for persons with physical disabilities to improve quality of life and enjoy outside activities. Group interacts with other state and Bergen County agencies. Monthly newsletters. Wheelchair transportation available with notice. Meets 2nd Thurs., 7pm, Pascack Valley Hospital, Old Hook Rd., Westwood. Call Tom Bengass 201-722-9537 (day) or Beverly Jensen 201-664-3581 (mornings).

Hip (Heightened Independence and Progress) Support groups, information, referrals, advocacy, peer counseling, recreational and other services for people of all types of disabilities with equipment and assistive devices. Meets various times, Heightened Independence and Progress, 131 Main St., Suite 120, Hackensack. Call Paula Walsh 201-996-9100 or TDD: 201-996-9424.

Post Stroke and Disabled Adult Program *(BERGEN COUNTY RESIDENTS ONLY)* Mutual support for post-stroke patients and disabled adults. Program functions include group discussions, various activities that promote physical fitness, arts and crafts, games, exercises and occasional recreational events. Meets various times/days, East Rutherford, Englewood, Oakland, Paramus, River Vale, and Maywood. Call Leo DePinto 201-336-6502 (day); TTY/TDD: 201-336-6505.

Women With Disabilities Support Group Discussion and education for disabled women. Meets 1st and 3rd Mon., 11am-1pm, Heightened Independence and Progress, 131 Main St., Suite 120, Hackensack. Call Paula Walsh 201-996-9100 (day) or 201-996-9424 (TDD). *Website:* http://www.hipcil.org

BURLINGTON

The Go Getters Support group for physically disabled adults. Socialization, awareness, recreation, phone help and rap sessions. Dues $20/yr. (can be waived). Meets 3rd Wed., 7pm, 315 Green St., Edgewater Park. Call Tammi Gauntt 609-261-2267.

ESSEX

Monday Morning Network of Essex County Advocacy support group organized by and for people with disabilities. Purpose is to provide and improve the quality of life for persons with disabilities by having a voice in government policy making and legislation. Helps members with individual advocacy issues. Family and friends welcome. Newsletter. Meets 2nd Thurs., 10am-noon, Opportunity Project, 60 East Willow St., Millburn. Call Frances Grant 973-470-8090 or Opportunity Project 973-921-1000 (day).

NJ Coalition on Women and Disabilities *(Essex County Chapter)* Support to empower, educate and motivate women with disabilities. Advocacy and guest speakers. Dues $12/yr. Meets 3rd Mon., 6:30-8:30pm, Pope John Paul Pavillion, 135 S. Center St., Orange. Call Cynthia De Souza 973-489-3228. *E-mail:* njcwd_essexchapter@verizon.net

Spinal Cord Injury Support Group Peer support group where individuals with spinal cord injuries share their experiences. Literature and buddy system. Meets 2nd and 4th Thurs., 6-7pm, Kessler Institute Rehabilitation, 1199 Pleasant Valley Way, New Building, SCI Day Room, 2nd Floor, West Orange. Call Sandy or Ron 973-243-6927 (day).

MERCER

Disability Support Group Support for persons with any disability to share feelings, thoughts and resources. Under 18 welcome. Phone help and newsletter. Meets monthly, Progressive Center for Independent Living, 1262 Whitehorse-Hamilton Square Rd., Suite 102, Hamilton. Before attending call Susan Jacobsen 609-581-4500 (day) or 609-581-4550 (TDD). *Website:* http://www.pcil.org *E-mail:* info@pcil.org

MIDDLESEX

Alliance For Disabled in Action Inc. Support for persons with any disability. Family members are welcome. Information, advocacy, education, referrals for housing, employment, transportation and assistive technology. Promotes barrier-free environments. Meets 3rd Thurs., 7pm, Brunswick Municipal Complex, 710 Hermann Rd., North Brunswick. Call Kathleen Orsetti 732-738-4388; TDD: 732-738-9644. *Website:* http://www.adacil.org *E-mail:* peersupport@adacil.org

MONMOUTH

NJ Coalition on Women and Disablities *(Monmouth County Chapter)* Support to empower, educate and motivate women with disabilities. Rap sessions, advocacy and guest speakers. Dues $10/yr. Meetings vary, 1-5pm, 384 2nd Ave., Community Room, Long Branch. For meeting information call Evelyn Wilson 732-229-2027 (day).

PASSAIC

DIAL, Inc. Center for Independent Living Provides people with disabilities with information and referral, peer counseling, advocacy and independent living skills program. Deaf and hard-of-hearing outreach services. Dues $15/yr./individual, $25/yr./family. Meets last Tues., 6:30-9:30pm, Clifton Center for Seniors and Citizens with Disabilities, Clifton. Call 973-470-8090 (day); TTY: 973-470-2521. *Website:* http://www.dial-cil.org *E-mail:* info@dial-cil.org

Monday Morning Project Support and advocacy for persons with a disability. Meets monthly, Wayne Public Library, 461 Valley Rd.,Wayne. Call 973-694-4272 ext. 5401.

SOMERSET

Alliance For Disabled in Action Inc. Support for persons with any disability. Family members are welcome. Information, advocacy, education, referrals for housing, employment, transportation and assistive technology. Promotes barrier-free environments. Meets 3rd Mon., 6:00pm, Bridgewater Library, 1 Vogt Dr., Bridgewater. Call Kathleen Orsetti 732-738-4388; TDD: 732-738-9644. *Website:* http://www.adacil.org *E-mail:* peersupport@adacil.org

Monday Morning Network Opportunity for persons with any type of disability to share their concerns, ideas and discuss the issues that affect them. Usually meets 3rd Mon., 7-9pm, Franklin Township Library, 485 Demott Lane, Somerset. Before attending call Jackie 908-561-6470. E-*mail:* jackeejackson@aol.com

UNION

Alliance For Disabled in Action, Inc. Support for persons with any disability. Family members are welcome. Information, advocacy, education, referrals for housing, employment, transportation and assistive technology. Promotes barrier-free environments. Meets last Thurs., 3:30pm, Runnells Specialized

Hospital, 40 Watchung Way, Berkeley Heights or 3rd Mon., 6pm, Rahway Public Library, Rahway. Call Kathleen Orsetti 732-738-4388 or 732-738-9644 (TDD). *Website:* http://www.adacil.org *E-mail:* peersupport@adacil.org

FOCAS Peer Support Group Mutual support for those with disabilities to enhance their daily living. Rap sessions and guest speakers. Meets 2nd Mon., 7-8:30pm, Elizabeth Public Library, 640 West Grand St., Elizabeth. Call 908-355-3299 (day). *E-mail:* susysnowflake2002@yahoo.com

SHARING Volunteer non-profit organization for disabled adults. Offers personal involvement, family support group, Second-Hand Shoppe and a free monthly newsletter. Call 908-508-0089 (day). *Website:* http://www.sharingnp.freeservers.com

WARREN

Totally Kids Network Support for siblings (ages 5-10) that have a sibling with a disability. Children are given the opportunity to share feelings in a relaxing, recreational atmosphere. Meets monthly on Sat., Phillipsburg and Columbia. For meeting information call 908-689-7525 ext. 209. *Website:* http://www.arcwarren.org

NATIONAL

Barn Builders Peer Support Group *National network. Founded 1979.* Provides peer support through networking for farmers and ranchers with disabilities. Connects recently injured individuals with persons with similar disability. Support through talking, correspondence and visitation. Write: Breaking New Ground, ABE Building, 225 South University St., West Lafayette, IN 47907-2093. Call 765-494-5088 (Voice/TTY) or 1-800-825-4264; Fax: 765-496-1356. *Website:* http://www.breakingnewground.info *E-mail:* bng@ecn.purdue.edu

National Spinal Cord Injury Association *National. 35 chapters and support groups. Founded 1948.* Provides information and referrals on many topics to persons with spinal cord injuries and diseases, their families and interested professionals. Group development guidelines, monthly newsletter, support groups, peer counseling. Online listing of local chapters. Write: NSCIA, 6701 Democracy Blvd., Suite 300-9, Bethesda, MD 20817. Call 1-800-962-9629; Fax: 301-990-0445. *Website:* http://www.spinalcord.org *E-mail:* info@spinalcord.org

Paralyzed Veterans of America *National. 34 chapters and 58 field service offices.* To ensure that spinal cord injured or diseased veterans achieve the highest quality of life possible. Membership is available solely to individuals who are American citizens with spinal cord dysfunction as a result of trauma or disease. Must have served on active duty and had an other than dishonorable discharge. Information and referrals, support groups, publications, VA benefits counseling, and magazine. Write: PVA, 801 18th St. NW, Washington, DC 20006. Call 1-800-424-8200 or 202-872-8200. *Website:* http://www.pva.org *E-mail:* info@pva.org

Project DOCC (Delivery Of Chronic Care) *International. 26 chapters. Founded 1994.* Provides education regarding the impact of chronic illness and/or disability on a family. Information, referrals, phone support, e-mail correspondence and "how-to" guides on developing a local group. Write: Project DOCC, One South Rd., Oyster Bay Cove, NY 11771. Call 1-877-773-8747; Fax: 516-498-1899. *Website:* http://projectdocc.org *E-mail:* projdocc@aol.com

Sibling Support Project *National. 200 affiliated groups. Founded 1990.* Organization dedicated to the life long concerns of brothers and sisters of children with special health, developmental and mental health concerns. Provides training and technical assistance regarding Sibshops and workshops for school-age siblings. Write: Donald Meyer, 6512 23rd Ave. NW, #213, Seattle, WA 98117. Call 206-297-6368; Fax: 509-752-6789. *Website:* http://www.siblingsupport.org *E-mail:* donmeyer@siblingsupport.org

United Spinal Association *National. Founded 1946.* To provide expertise, create access to resources and strengthen hope, thereby enabling people with spinal cord injuries and disorders to fulfill their potential as active members of their communities. Write: United Spinal Association, 75-20 Astoria Blvd., Jackson Heights, NY 11370-1177. Call 718-803-3782 ext. 1203.

ONLINE

Ability Online Support Network *Online. Founded 1992.* A family friendly monitored electronic message system that enables children and adolescents with disabilities or chronic illness (also parents/caregivers/siblings) to share experiences, information, encouragement, support and hope through messages. Write: Ability Online Support Network, 1120 Finch Ave. W., Suite 104, Toronto ON M3J 3H7 Canada. Call 1-866-650-6207 or 416-650-6207; Fax: 416-650-5073. *Website:* http://www.abilityonline.org *E-mail:* information@ablelink.org

Family Village *Online.* A global community that integrates information, resources and communication opportunities for persons with cognitive and other disabilities, their families and professionals. Broad range of discussion boards. *Website:* http://www.familyvillage.wisc.edu/ *E-mail:* familyvillage@waisman.wisc.edu

Quad-List *Online.* Provides a forum for quadriplegics (tetraplegics) to support and communicate with others who share the same condition. Not strictly a SCI (spinal cord injury) forum. Forum is for anyone who suffers a partial or full loss of function of all 4 extremities of the body, i.e. a quad due to any reason not just from a SCI. *Website:* http://www.makoa.org/quadlist.htm

LEARNING DISABILITY / ATTENTION DEFICIT DISORDER

(see also toll-free helplines)

STATEWIDE

ADDA (Attention Deficit Disorder Association) *National network. Founded 1989.* Mission is to provide information, resources and networking to adults with attention deficit hyperactivity disorder and to the professionals working with them. Aims to generate hope, awareness, empowerment and connections worldwide in the field of ADHD through bringing together science and the human experience. The information and resources provided to individual and families affected with ADHD focus on diagnosis, treatment, strategies and techniques for helping adults with ADHD lead better lives. Write: ADDA, 15000 Commerce Parkway, Suite C, Mount Laurel, NJ 08054. Call 856-439-9099; Fax: 856-439-0525. *Website:* http://www.add.org *E-mail:* mail@add.org

BERGEN

CHADD Support and education for adults and parents of children with attention deficit disorder. Membership $45/yr. Meets 3rd Wed., 7:30pm, (Oct.-June), Valley Hospital, Ridgewood. Call CHADD 201-664-1313. *Website:* http://www.chaddbc.org

CAMDEN

ADDventure for Adults To lend an attentative ear and helping hand to all who have adult ADD or a connection with someone who has adult ADD. Rap sessions, guest speakers, literature and speakers bureau. Dues $5/mtg. Meets 2nd Thurs.,

7:30-9pm, Barry D. Brown Health Education Center, Voorhees. Call 856-596-5520. *Website:* http://www.addventureforadults.org

CHADD of Southern NJ Support for adults and parents of children with attention deficit hyperactivity disorder. Membership dues $45/yr. Meetings vary, 7:30-9pm, (except Dec., July, Aug.), Barry D. Brown Health Education Center, Virtua West Jersey Hospital, 106 Carnie Blvd., Voorhees. Call Mary Fagnani or Linda Karanzalis 856-482-0756 (day). *Website:* http://www.chadd.org

ESSEX

ADD Action Group Information about alternative solutions for attention deficit disorder, learning disabilities, hyperactivity, dyslexia and autism. Educational series, guest speakers, literature, phone help. Usually meets 3rd Thurs., 7-8:45pm, Millburn Public Library, 200 Glen Ave., Millburn. Pre-registration required. Before attending call Lynne Berke 973-731-2189 (day/eve). *E-mail:* LTBerke@aol.com

Adult ADHD Support Group Provides support and education for adults who have attention deficit disorder or hyperactivity disorder. Family members welcome. Guest speakers, literature, phone help and buddy system. Meetings vary, Stepping Forward Counseling Center, 184 East Northfield Rd., Livingston. Before attending call Christine Robertello 973-533-6990 (day).

MERCER

CHADD Princeton-Mercer County Support and education for adults and parents of children with attention deficit disorder. Membership $45/yr. Meets 2nd Tues., (except July/Aug.), 7-9pm, Riverside Elementary School, 58 Riverside Dr., Princeton. Call Jane Milrod 609-683-8787 (day). *Website:* http://www.chadd.com *E-mail:* janemilrod@aol.com

MONMOUTH

Adult ADD Self-Help Support Group For adults who have attention deficit disorder or those who suspect that they may. Signifcant others welcome. Meets 4th Thurs., (except Aug.), (3rd Thurs. in Nov./Dec.), 7:30-9:30pm, Monmouth Medical Center, 300 2nd Ave., Long Branch. Pre-registration required. Before attending call Dr. Robert LoPresti 732-842-4553 (day). *Website:* http://www.drlopresti.com

MORRIS

Crossroads Community Satellite of CHADD Education and support for parents, teachers and friends of children and teens with attention deficit disorder and/or hyperactivity disorder. Guest speakers. Dues $1/mtg. Meets 2nd Fri., (except July, Aug., Dec.), 7:30-9pm, Crossroads Community Church, 104 Bartley Rd., Downstairs, Flanders. Call Rev. Paul Ingeneri 973-584-7149. *E-mail:* revpaul@optonline.net

Learning Disabilities Association of New Jersey Support and information for families of children with learning disabilities. Conferences, newsletters, literature. Dues $30/yr. Meets at various locations and times. Call Terry Cavanaugh 973-265-4303 (voice mail). *Website:* http://www.ldaamerica.org *E-mail:* info@ldaamerica.org

PASSAIC

Association for Special Children and Families Emotional support, resources and information for parents of children and young adults with any type of learning disability. Support groups, parenting classes, advocacy, social activities, library, phone help and guest speakers. Dues $35/yr. Call Julie Rikon 973-728-8744.

SOMERSET

Adults with Attention Deficit Disorder Provides support for adults who have attention deficit disorder. Meets 1st and 3rd Wed., 7:30-9:30pm, Somerset Medical Center, 110 Rehill Ave., ProKIDS Library, Community Health, South Fuld, Somerville. Call 908-685-2814 (day).

SUSSEX

Association for Special Children and Families Emotional support, resources and information for parents of children and young adults with any type of learning disability. Support groups, parenting classes, advocacy, social activities, library, phone help and guest speakers. Dues $35/yr. Call Julie Rikon 973-728-8744.

UNION

Adult ADHD Support Group Provides support and education for adults who have attention deficit disorder or hyperactivity disorder. Family members welcome. Guest speakers, literature, phone help and buddy system. Meetings vary, Stepping

Forward Counseling Center, 18 Bank St., Summit. Before attending call Christine Robertello 973-533-6990 (day).

Parents of ADD Children Support and casual discussion about the challenges and joys associated with raising a child with attention deficit disorder. Sharing of coping skills and resources. Meets 1st Mon., 7:30pm, Rustic Mill Diner, Cranford. Call Debbie Hargiss 908-272-2362 (eve). *E-mail:* dfhargiss@comcast.net

NATIONAL

ADDA (Attention Deficit Disorder Association) *National network. Founded 1989.* Mission is to provide information, resources and networking to adults with attention deficit hyperactivity disorder and to the professionals working with them. Aims to generate hope, awareness, empowerment and connections worldwide in the field of ADHD through bringing together science and the human experience. The information and resources provided to individual and families affected with ADHD focus on diagnosis, treatment, strategies and techniques for helping adults with ADHD lead better lives. Write: ADDA, 15000 Commerce Parkway, Suite C, Mount Laurel, NJ 08054. Call 856-439-9099; Fax: 856-439-0525. *Website:* http://www.add.org *E-mail:* mail@add.org

CHADD (Children and Adults with Attention-Deficit/Hyperactivity Disorder) *International. 200 chapters. Founded 1987.* Support network for parents and caregivers of children with attention deficit/hyperactivity disorder. Provides information for parents, adults, teachers and professionals. Bimonthly magazine, annual conference. Guidelines and assistance on starting self-help groups. Dues $45; student $35; healthcare professionals $100. Online listing of local support groups. Write: CHADD, 8181 Professional Pl., Suite 150, Landover, MD 20785. Call 1-800-233-4050 or 301-306-7070 (day); Fax: 301-306-7090. *Website:* http://www.chadd.org/

Feingold Association of the U.S. *National. Founded 1976.* Help for families of children with learning or behavior problems, including attention deficit disorder. Supports members in implementing the Feingold program. Generates public awareness re: food and synthetic additives. Newsletter. Phone support network. Write: Feingold Association of the US, 554 East Main St., Suite 301, Riverhead, NY 11901. Call 631-369-9340 or 1-800-321-3287 (US only). *Website:* http://www.feingold.org *E-mail:* help@feingold.org

GT/LD Network *National network. Founded 1984.* Mutual support and information for parents of gifted children who are also learning disabled. Open to students and educators. Newsletter, library information and referrals, advocacy, literature, conferences, online discussion support group and local meetings in Maryland. Dues $30. Write: GT/LD Network, P.O. Box 30239, Bethesda, MD 20824. *Website:* http://www.gtldnetwork.org *E-mail:* webmaster@gtldnetwork.org

ONLINE

Conduct Disorders Parent Message Board *Online. 6592 members. Founded 1995.* Support for parents living with a child with one of the many behavior disorders including: attention deficit hyperactivity disorder, oppositional defiance disorder, conduct disorder, depression and substance abuse. Parents with children of all ages welcome. *Website:* http://www.conductdisorders.com

Dyslexia Support 2 *Online. 341 members. Founded 2003.* Support list for parents of children who are dyslexic. Resource for parents to share ideas and exchange ways of helping. *Website:* http://health.groups.yahoo.com/group/dyslexiasupport2/ *E-mail:* dyslexiasupport2@yahoogroups.com

Dyslexia Talk *Online.* Support for anyone affected by dyslexia. Offers message board, open discussions and separate support group for parents. *Website:* http://www.dyslexiatalk.com

NLDA-In-Common *Online.* Opportunity for loved ones of people with non-verbal learning disabilities (NLD), adults with NLD and certain professionals to come together to communicate. Provides listserv support and information. Membership subject to approval. *Website:* http://www.groups.yahoo.com/group/NLD-In-Common/

Premature Baby - Premature Child *Online. Founded 1997.* Offers support for parents of premature babies that are age 4+ years old, for any of their special needs e.g., mental, physical, emotional or learning disability. Provides support, discussion listserv, prematurity forums, advocacy and educational links. Special children's show-and-tell section. *Website:* http://www.prematurity.org

FAMILY/PARENTING

ADOPTION

(see also parenting, toll-free helplines)

STATEWIDE

Foster and Adoptive Family Services Provides comprehensive information, education, training and support services to foster and adoptive parents. Advocates on behalf foster and adoptive parents and their children for improved foster care and adoption services. Information for persons wishing to become foster parents. Call 1-800-222-0047. *Website:* http://www.FAFSonline.org

NJ Families For Russian Ukranian Adoptions Support Group Support for people who have adopted or plan to adopt from Eastern Europe. Guest speakers, phone help, literature and newsletter. Dues $35/yr. Call Mirna Rucci 908-431-0318. *Website:* http://www.frua.org *E-mail:* mirucci@earthlink.net

BERGEN

Adoptive Parents Committee, Inc. Support and education for adoptive parents and those interested in adoption. Advocacy, social group, guest speakers, phone help, newsletter and annual conference. Dues $65/1st yr., $30/thereafter. Meets bimonthly, Sat. (Sept.-May), 7:30-10:30pm, Temple Beth Orr, Ridgewood Rd., Washington Township. Call Barbara Kalish 201-689-0995 (day/eve). *Website:* hhtp://www.adoptiveparents.org *E-mail:* apcconf2003@msn.com

Post Adoption Support Group of Northern NJ Mutual support and education for adoptees, adoptive and birth parents. Meets 2nd Mon., 7:30pm, Midland Park. For meeting information call Cindi Addesso 973-427-4521.

BURLINGTON

Birthmothers Support Group Support group for mothers who lost a child to adoption recently or decades ago. Adoptees welcome. Rap sessions. Meets 1st Thurs., 6:30-8:30pm, Pemberton Library, 16 Broadway Ave., Browns Mills. Call Irene Gendron 609-893-6086 (eve). *E-mail:* Eastwestig@aol.com

HUNTERDON

Adoptive Families Group NJ/PA Support, child and adult socialization, and education on various adoption issues for all adoptive families, including those considering adoption. Also open to adult adoptees, birthmothers who have made adoption plans for their children and any others who share an adoption connection. Monthly meetings in Hunterdon and Warren counties. Rap sessions, guest speakers, literature, phone help and buddy system. Call Patricia Blum 908-475-8944 (day). *E-mail:* pattypkb@earthlink.net

MIDDLESEX

Parents of Internationally Adopted Children Support Group Support, friendship and understanding for parents who have adopted children internationally. Issues include education, second language acquisition, etc. Group meets 4th Wed., 7:30pm, Woodbridge Public Library, George Frederick Plaza, Woodbridge. Call Deborah 732-642-5118.

MONMOUTH

Adoptive Parents Committee, Inc. Support, education and advocacy for adoptive parents and those interested in adopting. Social group, guest speakers and rap sessions. Dues $65/1st yr., $35/thereafter. Meets every other month (Sept.-June), St. Anselm's Church, 1028 Wayside Rd., Wayside. For meeting days and times call Susan 201-689-0995. *Website:* http://www.adoptiveparents.org

Monmouth/Ocean County Adoptive Parents Support Group Provides education, support and a network for all members of the adoption triad (pre- and post-adoption), especially those adopting transracially. Literature, guest speakers, phone help and buddy system. Dues $25/yr. Meets 3rd Fri., 7:30-9:30pm, St. Mary's Church, Spiritual Center, Phalanx Rd. and Route 34 North, Colts Neck. Call Danielle 732-845-0791 (day/eve) or Liz 732-473-9113 (day/eve). *E-mail:* webbymisha@hotmail.com or lgrudus@comcast.net

MORRIS

Concerned Persons for Adoption Organization working to support those who wish to adopt. Also, provides educational and networking resources to those who have adopted. Not an adoption agency. Social events and annual conference "Let's Talk Adoption." Membership dues $25/1st yr., $20/thereafter. Meetings are free. Meets 1st Mon. (except July/Aug.; 2nd Mon., Jan. and Sept.), 7:45pm, First

Presbyterian Church, 494 Route 10 West, Whippany. Call Joan Walsh 973-625-8440 or Kathleen Walz 973-625-5628. *Website:* http://www.cpfanj.org

NJ Coalition for Adoption Reform and Education Organization that supports honesty in adoption through educational outreach and legislative advocacy. Workshops. Links to statewide search/support groups. Meets Mon., 7pm, Presbyterian Church, Parish House, 65 South St., Morristown. Call Jane Nast 973-267-8698, Judy Foster 973-455-1268 or Pam Hasegawa 973-292-2440. *Website:* http://www.nj-care.org *E-mail:* janenast@compuserve.com

Post-Adoption Support Group Support and education for adoptees, adoptive parents, birth parents and professionals. Under 18 welcome. Donation $3. Guest speakers, advocacy, speakers bureau and search assistance. Meets 1st Sat., 1pm, Presbyterian Church Parish House, 65 South St., Morristown. Call Jane Nast 973-267-8698 or Judy Foster 973-455-1268. *Website:* http://www.nj-care.org *E-mail:* janenast@compuserve.com

SOMERSET

CHATS (Connected Hearts Adoption Triad Support) Seeks to involve and serve all members of the adoption triad i.e. adoptees, birth parents and adoptive parents, as well as others interested in adoption. Phone help, guest speakers, educational programs and sharing of stories. Meets 4th Mon., 7:15-9:15pm, Watchung Avenue Presbyterian Church, 170 Watchung Ave., North Plainfield. Call Alyce 732-227-0607 (day), Dot 908-755-6978 (eve) or Susan 908-561-9654 (eve). *Website:* http://www.chatsnj.com *E-mail:* alycemj@aol.com

WARREN

Adoptive Families Group NJ/PA Support, child and adult socialization, and education on various adoption issues for all adoptive families, including those considering adoption. Also open to adult adoptees, birthmothers who have made adoption plans for their children and any others who share an adoption connection. Monthly meetings in Hunterdon and Warren counties. Rap sessions, guest speakers, literature, phone help and buddy system. Call Patricia Blum 908-475-8944 (day) or Barbara Hurte 908-213-0184 (day). *E-mail:* pblum@netcarrier.com

NATIONAL

Adoption Crossroads *International. 475 affiliated groups. Founded 1990.* Mutual support for persons separated by adoption. Referrals to adoption search and support groups. Newsletter, phone support and conferences. Provides information and referrals to support group meetings. Assistance in starting groups. Write: Adoption Crossroads, c/o Joe Soll, 74 Lakewood Dr., Congers, NY 10920. Call 845-268-0283 (day/eve). Fax: 845-267-2736. *Website:* http://www.adoptioncrossroads.org *E-mail:* info@adoptioncrossroads.org

ALMA Society (Adoptees Liberty Movement Association) *International network. Founded 1971.* Provides moral support and guidance for adopted children in finding their birth parents and/or siblings. Also helps parents find the children they gave up for adoption. Open to foster children (ages 18+). International reunion registry. One-time tax deductible contribution $50. Write: ALMA Society, P.O. Box 85, Denville, NJ 07834. Call/fax 973-586-1358. *Website:* http://almasociety.org

Concerned United Birthparents, Inc. *National. 11 branches. Founded 1976.* Support for adoption-affected people in coping with adoption. Prevention of unnecessary separations. Online chat room. Quarterly newsletter. Dues $40/yr. Pen pals and phone network. Provides assistance starting local groups. Write: CUB, P.O. Box 503475, San Diego, CA 92150-3475. Call 1-800-822-2777; Fax: 858-712-3317. *Website:* http://www.Cubirthparents.org *E-mail:* info@CUBirthparents.org

Korean American Adoptee Adoptive Family Network *International.* Mission is to network groups or individuals related to Korean adoption. Offers support, e-mail newsletter and lists, resources, adoptee services, birth family search, etc. Write: KAAN, P.O. Box 5585, El Dorado Hills, CA 95762. Call 916-933-1447. *Website:* http://www.kaanet.com *E-mail:* KAANet@aol.com

North American Council on Adoptable Children *International (US/Canada). Founded 1974.* Focuses on special needs adoption. Provides referrals and maintains current listing of adoptive parent support groups which conduct a wide range of activities. Helps new groups get started and sponsors an annual adoption conference which features workshops for adoptive parents, prospective parents, foster parents, child welfare professionals and other child advocates. Newsletter. Membership $45/US and $60/Canada. Parent group manual ($10). Write: North American Council on Adoptable Children, 970 Raymond Ave., Suite 106, St. Paul,

MN 55114-1149. Call 651-644-3036 (day); Fax: 651-644-9848. *Website:* http://www.nacac.org *E-mail:* info@nacac.org

Stars of David, Inc. *International. 32+ chapters.* Support and advocacy group for Jewish or interfaith adoptive families, extended families, interested clergy, social service agencies and adoption professionals. Socials, phone help, literature, education, online listserv and newsletter. Online directory of local groups. Dues $50/family; $125/professional. Write: Stars of David, 3175 Commercial Ave., Suite 100, Norbrook, Il 60062-1915. Call 1-800-782-7349 or 847-274-1527. *Website:* http://www.starsofdavid.org

ONLINE

Parent Soup Message Boards *Online.* Offers a large variety of message boards which deal with parenting issues including infertility, pregnancy, parenting challenges, parents of disabled, pregnancy loss, newborn babies, toddlers, adoption, family issues, etc. *Website:* http://www.parentsoup.com/boards

CESAREAN BIRTH

(see also childbirth, premature/high risk infants)

BURLINGTON

ICAN of Burlington County Support for women healing from Cesarean birth. Encouragement and information for those wanting vaginal birth after previous Cesarean. Aims to lower the high Cesarean rate through prevention and education. Dues $35/yr. Guest speakers, literature and phone help. Meets 2nd and 3rd Thurs., 7-8:30pm, Evesham Library, Tuckerton Rd., Marlton. Call Janet Cappetta 856-810-9509 (day). *E-mail:* icanofburlington@aol.com

ONLINE

ICAN (International Cesarean Awareness Network), Inc. *Online.* Support for women healing from Cesarean birth. Encouragement and information for those wanting vaginal birth after previous Cesarean. Aims to lower the high Cesarean rate through prevention and education. Newsletter. Chapter development guidebook. Write: ICAN, 1304 Kingsdale Ave., Redondo Beach, CA 90278. Call 1-800-686-4226 or 310-542-6400; Fax: 310-697-3056. *Website:* http://www.ICAN-online.org *E-mail:* info@ICAN-online.org

CHILDBIRTH / PREGNANCY / BREASTFEEDING

(see also parenting, toll-free helplines)

BERGEN

La Leche League of Teaneck Education and support for pregnant and breastfeeding women. Discussion group, educational, mutual sharing, phone help and literature. Dues $36/yr. Meetings and locations vary, Teaneck. Call Carmen Clark 201-837-7646, Susan Esserman 201-385-2377 (day) or Julie Rosen 201-837-5910. *Website:* http://www.lalecheleaguenj.org

CAMDEN

Breastfeeding Support Group *Professionally-run.* Support and education for nursing mothers regardless of the age of the child. Meets every other Fri., 11:00am-12:30pm, Virtua Health's Barry D. Brown Health Education Center, 106 Carnie Blvd., Voorhees. Call 1-888-847-8823 (day).

ESSEX

Parenting Insights New mother education and support. Also offers breast feeding support. Group runs for four-weeks. Meetings vary at Saint Barnabas Medical Center, 94 Old Short Hills Rd., Livingston. For meeting information call 973-322-5360 (day).

HUDSON

TMS Support Group *Professionally-run.* Support and education for teenagers (under age 20) who are pregnant or recently gave birth. Guest speakers. Meets Thurs., 4pm, NHCAC, Jersey City Clinic, 324 Palisades Ave., 2nd Floor, Jersey City. Call Beatriz Amador 201-459-8888 ext. 3018 (day) or Rossetty Fernandez 201-876-8900 ext. 226. *E-mail:* BAmador@nhcac.org

HUNTERDON

Breastfeeding Support Group *Professionally-run.* Mutual support and education for women who are breastfeeding their infants. Moms welcome to bring lunch. Babies welcome. Meets 1st Thurs., noon-1pm, Hunterdon Medical Center, 2100 Westcott Dr., Flemington. Before attending call Jean Jamele, RN 908-788-6634 (day). *Website:* http://hunterdonhealthcare.org *E-mail:* jamele.jean@hunterdonhealthcare.org

MERCER

Pregnancy and Postpartum Support Group *Professionally-run.* Support for pregnant and new mothers adjusting to emotional issues such as blues, depression and anxiety. Children and significant others welcome. Meets 3rd Sat., 10:30am-noon, 60 Mt. Lucas Rd., Princeton. Pre-registration required. Before attending call Joyce 609-683-1000 or Hyla 609-936-1154.

MIDDLESEX

Breastfeeding Support Group Mutual support and education for women who are breastfeeding their infants. Moms welcome to bring bag lunch. Beverages provided. Babies are welcome. Expectant mothers may attend. Meets 1st and 3rd Wed., 12:15pm, Robert Wood Johnson University Hospital, Clinical Academic Building, Room 3405, New Brunswick. Call Community Education 732-418-8110.

Pregnant Again *Professionally-run.* Mutual support for anyone who has lost a child by miscarriage, stillbirth or infant death and are pregnant again. Literature and phone help. Meets 2nd Mon., 6-8pm, St. Peter's University Hospital, 254 Easton Ave., Conference Room 5, New Brunswick. Pre-registration required. Call Dawn Brady 732-745-8600 ext. 5214 (day).

MONMOUTH

Mother to Mother Support Group *Professionally-run.* Provides support and education to new mothers to help with topics such as feeding, sleeping, crying, recovery from childbirth and postpartum depression. Newborns to 6 months welcome. Meets Thurs., 10-11:30am, Monmouth Medical Center, Ronald McDonald Family Conference Room, Borden 2, Long Branch. Pre-registration required. Before attending call 732-923-6990 (day).

NATIONAL

La Leche League *International. 1269 chapters. Founded 1956.* Support and education for breastfeeding mothers. Group discussions, personal help, classes and conferences. Publishes literature on breastfeeding and parenting. Bi-monthly newsletter, quarterly abstracts and phone support network. Assistance with starting new groups. Write: La Leche League, 1400 N. Meacham Rd., P.O. Box 4079, Schaumburg, IL 60168-4079. Call 1-800-525-3243 (day) or 847-519-7730; Fax: 847-519-0035; TTY/TDD: 847-592-7570 *Website:* http://www.lalecheleague.org *E-mail:* LLLI@llli.org

Lamaze International *International. Founded 1960.* Dedicated to promoting normal, natural, healthy and fulfilling childbearing, breastfeeding and early parenting experiences through education, advocacy and reform. Newsletter and publications. Write: Lamaze International, 2025 M St., NW, Suite 800, Washington, DC 20036-3309. Call 1-800-368-4404; Fax: 202-367-2128. *Website:* http://www.lamaze.org *E-mail:* info@lamaze.org

National Association of Mothers' Centers *National. 40 sites. Founded 1975.* Discussion groups and other activities regarding parenting, pregnancy, childbirth and childrearing. Warm, welcoming environment of support. National and some local newsletters, conference and advocacy. Has up-to-date information on contacting local Mothers' Center programs, starting a center and how employers in NY/NJ/CT can offer a program for working parents. Write: NAMC, 64 Division Ave., Suite LL7, Levittown, NY 11756. Call 1-800-645-3828 or 516-520-2929; Fax: 516-520-1639. *Website:* http://www.motherscenter.org *E-mail:* info@motherscenter.org

ONLINE

Diabetic Mommies *Online. Founded 2001.* Support for all women with diabetes (type 1, type 1.5, type 2, gestational and pre-diabetes) at all stages of life whether already a mom, during pregnancy or trying to conceive. Articles, forum, chat room, surveys, networking and newsletters. *Website:* http://www.DiabeticMommy.com *E-mail:* editor@diabeticmommy.com

Expecting Parents Meetup Groups *Online.* Meet other new or expecting parents to exchange advice, support and laughs. Message boards. *Website:* http://newparents.meetup.com/

Parent Soup Message Boards *Online.* Offers a large variety of message boards which deal with parenting issues including infertility, pregnancy, parenting challenges, parents of disabled, pregnancy loss, newborn babies, toddlers, adoption, family issues, etc. *Website:* http://www.parentsoup.com/boards

Postpartum Hemorrhage Survivors *Online.* E-mail list for women who are supporting each other after a postpartum hemorrhage and hysterectomy. *Website:* http://health.groups.yahoo.com/group/pph-survivors/

Preeclampsia Foundation *Online.* Organization dedicated to funding research, raising public awareness, providing support and education for those whose lives have been touched by preeclampsia and other hypertensive disorders while pregnant. Forums. *Website:* http://www.preeclampsia.org

Pregnant Teen Support *Online.* E-mail list support group for teens (ages 12-20) facing an unplanned, unexpected or unwanted pregnancy. *Website:* http://health.groups.yahoo.com/group/Pregnant_Teen_Support

FOSTER FAMILIES

(see also toll-free helplines)

STATEWIDE

Foster and Adoptive Family Services Provides comprehensive information, education, training and support services to foster and adoptive parents. Advocates on behalf of foster and adoptive parents and their children for improved foster care and adoption services. Information for persons wishing to become foster parents. Call 1-800-222-0047. *Website:* http://www.FAFSonline.org

MORRIS

Morris County Foster Parents Association Self-help for foster and adoptive parents and their children to provide social and emotional support. Dues $20/yr. Meets 3rd Wed. (Sept.-June), 7pm, DYFS Morris Local Office, 855 Route 10 East, Randolph. Call Michele Cannaveno 908-850-8303 (day). *Website:* http://www.morrisfpa.org *E-mail:* webmaster@morrisfpa.org

NATIONAL

FACT (Fostered Adult Children Together) *Model. 1 group in MI. Founded 1999.* Provides mutual support for former foster children. Literature. Provides assistance in starting similar groups. Write: FACT, c/o Carol Lucas, 226 S. Burkhart Rd., Howell, MI 48843. Call 517-546-7818 (voice/fax). *Website:* http://www.factsupportgroup.com

National Foster Parent Association, Inc. *National. 50 affiliated groups. Founded 1972.* Support, education and advocacy for foster parents and their children. Resource center for foster care information. Quarterly newsletter, annual national conference and workshops. Chapter development guidelines. Write: National Foster Parent Association, 7512 Stanich Ave., #6, Gig Harbor, WA 98335. Call 1-800-557-5238 or 253-853-4000; Fax: 253-853-4001. *Website:* http://www.nfpainc.org *E-mail:* info@nfpainc.org

GRANDPARENTING

ATLANTIC

AtlantiCare Grandparents and Kin Support Group *(BILINGUAL) Professionally-run.* Provides information, advocacy and economic assistance to grandparents and kin raising other family members children. Families welcome. Rap sessions, guest speakers, literature, educational series and phone help. Meets 2nd Tues., 6-8pm, Uptown School Complex, 323 Madison Ave., Atlantic City. Call 609-345-1994 (day).

BERGEN

Grandparents Raising Grandchildren Monthly Support Group Mutual support, information and encouragement for grandparents raising grandchildren. Rap sessions and guest speakers. Meets one Thurs. per month, 10-11:30am, Liberty School, 12 Tenafly Rd., Englewood. Call Mildred Campbell 201-796-6209 or Lynn Bolson 201-796-6209 ext. 102.

BURLINGTON

BCCAP Headstart Grandparent Support Group Support for grandparents, great-grandparents, great-aunts/uncles, etc. who are raising grandchildren. Meets monthly (except July/Aug.), 7-9pm, Human Services Building, 795 Woodlane Rd., Mt. Holly. Call Sue Dietz 609-261-2323 (day).

CAMDEN

Grandparents Raising Grandchildren Support and education for women and men who are caring for their grandchildren struggling with emotional, behavioral and mental challenges. Guest speakers, literature, social, advocacy and buddy system. Meets 4th Mon., 6:30-8:30pm, Holy Trinity Lutheran Church, 325 South Whitehorse Pike, Audubon. Call Marge Varneke 856-547-1620 (eve) or Susan A. Doherty-Funke 856-662-2600 (day).

CAPE MAY

Grandparents Raising Grandchildren *Professionally-run.* Support and educational workshops for grandparents raising their grandchildren. Members share ideas, challenges and learn new skills. Newsletter. Meets monthly, Rutgers Cooperative Research and Extension, 355 Court House, South Dennis Rd., Cape

May Court House. For specific date and times call Marilou Rochford 609-465-5115.

ESSEX

Grandfamily Program *Professionally-run.* Mutual support for any family member or caregiver raising children. Rap sessions, literature, guest speakers, advocacy and phone help. Meets 1st Thurs., East Orange and 2nd Wed., Newark. Call 973-623-5959 ext. 207 (day).

MERCER

Grand-Parent Support Group *(MERCER COUNTY RESIDENTS ONLY) Professionally-run.* Provides support and education for grandparents who provide full-time or part-time care for grandchildren. On-going and short term groups. For meeting day, time and location call Barbara Stender 609-396-6788 ext. 241 (day). *E-mail:* addvantages@aol.com

MIDDLESEX

Middlesex County Grandparents Raising Grandchildren Coalition, Inc. Advocacy and support organization committed to providing kinship caregivers the tools necessary to provide a stable, nurturing and secure environment for each child in their care. Dues $10 per family. Children welcome. Childcare provided. Meets 2nd Mon., 7-9pm, Edison Senior Center, 2963 Woodbridge Ave., Edison. Call Jill Williams 732-248-8255. *E-mail:* DMWJAS@aol.com.

UNION

Grandparents Raising Grandchildren *(SPANISH) Professionally-run.* Support for grandparents raising grandchildren. Members share ideas, challenges, new skills and crafts. Meets Tues., 4:30-5:45pm, Josephine's Place, 638 Elizabeth Ave., Elizabeth. Call Sister Judy 908-436-0099 or 908-789-7625.

NATIONAL

GAP (Grandparents As Parents) *Model. 7 groups. Founded 1987.* Support network, sharing of experiences and feelings between grandparents and other relative caregivers who are raising their grandchildren for various reasons. Information and referrals, emergency services, phone support network and group member listings. Assistance in starting similar groups. Write: GAP, P.O. Box 964,

Lakewood, CA 90714. Call 818-264-0880; Fax: 818-264-0882. *E-mail:* ivyw@grandparentsasparents.com

MARRIAGE / FAMILY

BERGEN

As Life Changes *Professionally-run.* Self-help group designed to support seniors with interpersonal relationship problems. Opportunity for members to share feelings and experiences. Meets Tues., 1:15pm, Southeast Senior Center for Independent Living, 228 Grand Ave., Englewood. Call Laura, MSW 201-569-4080 (Tues. or Thurs.).

S.O.U.R.C.E., The *Professionally-run.* Support, information, networking and referrals for all family concerns. Phone help, drop-in center, guest speakers, groups for parents and kids. Meets various times, The Source Building, #1, West Plaza, Glen Rock. Call Jean Baker Wunder 201-670-4673 (day).

BURLINGTON

Recovering Couples Anonymous *(For couples only)* 12-Step. Fellowship of recovering couples who share their experience, strength and hope with each other that they may solve their common problems and help other recovering couples restore their relationships. The only requirement for membership is a desire to remain committed to each other and to develop new intimacy. Literature and phone help. Meets every other Thurs., 7:30-8:30pm, Prince of Peace Church, 61 Route 70 East, Marlton. Before attending call Jean and Joe 856-235-1553.

Third Option *Professionally-run.* Christian-focused group for persons with marital problems or couples who want to strengthen their marriages. Rap sessions, literature, lecture and education. Meets 1st and 3rd Thurs., 7-9pm, Fellowship Alliance Church, 199 Church Rd., Medford. Call Rev. Ed Stiegel 609-953-7333 ext. 129.

MORRIS

BAN (Beyond Affairs Network) Support for men and women who are dealing with a partner's affair. Opportunity to come together for strength, insight and mutual support. Not open to persons who have had affairs. Meets Thurs. evenings in area library. *Website:* http://www.dearpeggy.com *E-mail:* randolphnjBAN@yahoo.com (for meeting information)

NATIONAL

ACME (Association for Couples in Marriage Enrichment) *National network. Founded 1973.* Network of couples who want to enhance their own relationship, as well as help strengthen marriages of other couples. Local chapters sponsor support groups, retreats and workshops. Bi-monthly newsletter, leadership training and conferences. Write: ACME, P.O. Box 21374, Winston-Salem, NC 27120. Call 1-800-634-8325 or 336-724-1526; Fax: 336-721-4746. *Website:* http://www.bettermarriages.org *E-mail:* acme@bettermarriages.org

No Kidding! *International. 103 chapters in six countries. Founded 1984.* Mutual support and social activities for married and single people who either have decided not to have children, are postponing parenthood, are undecided or are unable to have children. Chapter development guidelines. Write: No Kidding!, Box 2802, Vancouver, BC, Canada V6B 3X2. Call 604-538-7736 (24 hr). *Website:* http://www.nokidding.net *E-mail:* info@nokidding.net

Recovering Couples Anonymous *National. 130 groups. Founded 1988.* 12-Step. Goal is to assist couples find freedom from dysfunctional patterns in their relationships. RCA is made up of couples committed to restoring healthy communication and developing a caring and functional relationship. Offers local support group information. Write: RCA, P.O. Box 11029, Oakland, CA 94611. Call 510-663-2312. *Website:* http://www.recovering-couples.org

ONLINE

After the Affair *Online.* Discussion forum to help persons recover after an extra-marital affair. *Website:* http://members3.boardhost.com/affair

G.I.F.T. (Getting Interracial/Cultural Families Together) *Online.* Support for biracial individuals, interracial/cultural couples, families, dating teens, transracial adoptive families and extended families of these groups. *Website:* http://groups.yahoo.com/group/njgift

PARENTING (GENERAL)

(see also parents of adolescents, childbirth and toll-free helplines)

STATEWIDE

Mocha Moms Support for stay-at-home mothers of color. Sponsors support group meetings, monthly moms-only events and community projects. There are presently

7 local groups in Bergen, Burlington, Essex, Gloucester, Mercer, Monmouth and Somerset counties. Visit their national website for contact information and details on status of NJ groups. *Website:* http://www.mochamoms.org

MOMS Club Support for stay-at-home moms. There are several groups that meet in NJ. Check website for local groups. *Website:* http://www.momsclub.org (scroll to bottom, then click on to chapter links).

MOPS (Mothers Of Preschoolers) Provides non-denominational Christian support for mothers of preschoolers. There are about 30 MOPS groups that meet in NJ. For information about a local chapter call 1-800-929-1287. *Website:* http://www.mops.org

Mothers and More Support groups for women who have altered their career paths to care for their children at home. 11 groups in NJ. Check website for listing of these chapters. Call 630-941-3553 (The national office in Illinois). *Website:* http://www.mothersandmore.org

Unschoolers Network Information and encouragement for families who educate their children at home. Guest speakers, literature and phone help. Quarterly newsletter $16 (optional). Annual conference. For local group information call Nancy Plent 732-938-2473. *E-mail:* UnNet@aol.com

ATLANTIC

Holistic Moms Network Mutual support for moms with an interest in natural health, alternative therapies and mindful parenting. Families welcome. Rap sessions and guest speakers. Dues $35/yr. Meets in Linwood. For monthly meeting information call 1-877-465-6667. *Website:* http://www.holisticmoms.org

MOPS (Mothers Of Pre-Schoolers) Support and encouragement for mothers of pre-schoolers. Program includes fellowship, lectures on Christian womanhood, discussion groups and crafts. Suggested $5/mtg. Meets 1st and 3rd Mon., 9:30-11:30am, Shore Fellowship Church, 1049 Ocean Heights Ave., Egg Harbor Township. Call Jennifer Christiansen 609-909-9702 or church 609-646-4693 (day).

BERGEN

Attachment Parenting International (API) of Bergen County Open to parents and all others interested in learning about the principles of attachment parenting.

Literature, newsletter and phone help. Dues $35/yr. Meets 4th Thurs., 10am-noon, Haworth. Call Susan Esserman 201-385-2377 (day) or Carole Blane 201-244-6758 (day). *Website:* http://www.attachmentparenting.org *E-mail:* susan@seventhmoon.net

Holistic Moms Network Mutual support for moms with an interest in natural health, alternative therapies and mindful parenting. Families welcome. Rap sessions and guest speakers. Dues $35/yr. Meets in Ramsey. For monthly meeting information call 1-877-465-6667. *Website:* http://www.holisticmoms.org

BURLINGTON

"I Can Problem Solve" Support Group *Professionally-run.* Mutual support for parents of children (ages 13 and under) to learn conflict resolution and problem solving skills. Advocacy, social, guest speakers and newsletter. Meets 2nd Mon., 6-8pm, Family Support Organization, 774 Eayrestown Rd., Lumberton. Call Maggie Kaupp 609-265-8838 (day).

Holistic Moms Network *(Tri-County Chapter)* Mutual support for moms with an interest in natural health, alternative therapies and mindful parenting. Families welcome. Rap sessions and guest speakers. Dues $35/yr. Meets in Pitman. For monthly meeting information call 1-877-465-6667. *Website:* http://www.holisticmoms.org

CAMDEN

Holistic Moms Network *(Tri-County Chapter)* Mutual support for moms with an interest in natural health, alternative therapies and mindful parenting. Families welcome. Rap sessions and guest speakers. Dues $35/yr. For meeting information call 1-877-465-6667. *Website:* http://www.holisticmoms.org

CUMBERLAND

Holistic Moms Network Mutual support for moms with an interest in natural health, alternative therapies and mindful parenting. Families welcome. Rap sessions and guest speakers. Dues $35/yr. Meets in Vineland. For monthly meeting information call 1-877-465-6667. *Website:* http://www.holisticmoms.org

ESSEX

Holistic Moms Network Mutual support for moms with an interest in natural health, alternative therapies and mindful parenting. Families welcome. Rap sessions and guest speakers. Dues $35/yr. Meets in Montclair. For monthly meeting information call 1-877-465-6667. *Website:* http://www.holisticmoms.org

MOPS (Mothers Of Preschoolers) Provides non-demoninational Christian support for mothers with children under school age. Education, group discussions, socials, guest speakers and crafts. For women with the desire to be the best mother they can be. Donation $6 (can be waived). Meets 4th Thurs., 9:30am-noon (except July/Aug.), Montclair Community Church, 143 Watchung Ave., Upper Montclair. Before attending call 973-746-0042. *Website:* http://www.mops.org

Parenting Insights New mother education and support. Also offers breast feeding support. Group runs for 4 weeks. Meetings vary at Saint Barnabas Medical Center, 94 Old Short Hills Rd., Livingston. For meeting information call 973-322-5360 (day).

GLOUCESTER

Bring-Along-Baby Morning *Professionally-run.* An informal support group for moms and their babies under 2 years of age. Fee $3/mtg. Meets Fri. (except July/Aug.), 9:30-11am, Central Baptist Church, West Centre St. and South Jackson St., Woodbury. Registration required. Before attending call 856-845-0100 ext. 2456 (day).

Holistic Moms Network *(Tri-County Chapter)* Mutual support for moms with an interest in natural health, alternative therapies and mindful parenting. Families welcome. Rap sessions and guest speakers. Dues $35/yr. Meets in Pitman. For monthly meeting information call 1-877-465-6667. *Website:* http://www.holisticmoms.org

Tag-Along-Toddler Morning *Professionally-run.* An informal support group for moms and their toddlers under 3 years of age. Fee $3/mtg. Meets Wed., (except July/Aug.), 9:30-11am, Central Baptist Church, West Centre St. and South Jackson St., Woodbury. Registration is required. Before attending call 856-845-0100 ext. 2456 (day).

HUDSON

TMS Support Group *Professionally-run.* Support and education for teenagers (under age 20) who are pregnant or recently gave birth. Guest speakers. Meets Thurs., 4pm, NHCAC, Jersey City Clinic, 324 Palisades Ave., 2nd Floor, Jersey City. Call Beatriz Amador 201-459-8888 ext. 3018 (day) or Rossetty Fernandez 201-876-8900 ext. 226. *E-mail:* BAmador@nhcac.org

HUNTERDON

Holistic Moms Network Mutual support for moms with an interest in natural health, alternative therapies and mindful parenting. Families welcome. Rap sessions and guest speakers. Dues $35/yr. Meets in Flemington. For monthly meeting information call 1-877-465-6667. *Website:* http://www.holisticmoms.org

MERCER

Hispanic Parenting Support Group *(SPANISH SPEAKING) Professionally-run.* Provides mutual support and education to Spanish-speaking parents. Rap sessions, guest speakers and literature. Life skills and parenting workshops. Also offers bilingual and multi-cultural parenting skills. Lunch provided. Meets Fri., 10am-1pm, Latinas Unidas, YWCA, 140 E. Hanover St., Trenton. Call Cecy Weeast 609-396-3040 (day).

Holistic Moms Network Mutual support for moms with an interest in natural health, alternative therapies and mindful parenting. Families welcome. Rap sessions and guest speakers. Dues $35/yr. Meets in Robbinsville. For monthly meeting information call 1-877-465-6667. *Website:* http://www.holisticmoms.org

Mercer County Mocha Moms Mutual support for full or part-time stay-at-home mothers of color. Encourages community activism among the membership. Advocacy, social, newsletter, guest speakers and online message board. Dues $34/yr. Meets 1st Sat., 9-10am, Panera Bread, 510 Nassau Park Blvd., West Windsor. Roslyn S. and Theresa G. can be contacted through e-mail address. *Website:* http://mercer.nj.mochamoms.tripod.com *E-mail:* mercer.nj.mochamoms@lycos.com

New Moms Group Support designed for moms with an infant from birth to one year. Offers mutual support discussing the ups and downs of a new baby on the family. Meets for 8 week sessions, 2-3 times per year, Jewish Center of Princeton,

435 Nassau St., Princeton. For dates and times call Debra Levenstein 609-987-8100 (eve).

MIDDLESEX

Holistic Moms Network Mutual support for moms with an interest in natural health, alternative therapies and mindful parenting. Families welcome. Rap sessions and guest speakers. Dues $35/yr. Meets in Metuchen. For monthly meeting information call 1-877-465-6667. *Website:* http://www.holisticmoms.org

MONMOUTH

Holistic Moms Network Mutual support for moms with an interest in natural health, alternative therapies and mindful parenting. Families welcome. Rap sessions and guest speakers. Dues $35/yr. Meets in Shrewsbury. For monthly meeting information call 1-877-465-6667. *Website:* http://www.holisticmoms.org

MOPS (Mothers Of Pre-Schoolers) Support and encouragement to mothers of preschoolers. Program includes fellowship, lectures on Christian womanhood, discussion groups and crafts. Suggested $4/mtg. Meetings vary (Sept.-May), 9-11am, First Presbyterian Church at Red Bank, 255 Harding Rd., Red Bank. Call 732-747-1348 (day) or Carol Andrews 732-671-0553 (day) to confirm meeting days.

Mother to Mother Support Group *Professionally-run.* Provides support and education to new mothers to help with topics such as feeding, sleeping, crying, recovery from childbirth and postpartum depression. Newborns to 6 months welcome. Meets Thurs., 10-11:30am, Monmouth Medical Center, Ronald McDonald Family Conference Room, Borden 2, Long Branch. Pre-registration required. Before attending call 732-923-6990 (day).

New Moms Network at Jersey Shore University Medical Center *Professionally-run.* Information and support for mothers of infants (age birth to 12 months). Rap sessions, guest speakers and phone help. Meets Thurs., 1-3pm, Jersey Shore University Medical Center, 1945 Route 33, Lance B 104, Neptune. Call Linda Carroll 732-776-4281 (day). *E-mail:* lcarroll@meridianhealth.com

Parent Linking Project Opportunity for parents to discuss parenting skills, child development and parent-child interaction. Some groups welcome young fathers and grandparents. Various meeting locations. For information call Jill Brown 732 246-8060 (day). *Website:* http://www.preventchildabusenj.org

MORRIS

Holistic Moms Network Mutual support for moms with an interest in natural health, alternative therapies and mindful parenting. Families welcome. Rap sessions and guest speakers. Dues $35/yr. Meets in Morris Plains. For monthly meeting information call 1-877-465-6667. *Website:* http://www.holisticmoms.org

PASSAIC

Holistic Moms Network Mutual support for moms with an interest in natural health, alternative therapies and mindful parenting. Families welcome. Rap sessions and guest speakers. Dues $35/yr. Meets in Wayne or Clifton. For monthly meeting information call 1-877-465-6667. *Website:* http://www.holisticmoms.org

SOMERSET

Holistic Moms Network Mutual support for moms with an interest in natural health, alternative therapies and mindful parenting. Families welcome. Rap sessions and guest speakers. Dues $35/yr. Meets in Bridgewater. For monthly meeting information call 1-877-465-6667. *Website:* http://www.holisticmoms.org

SUSSEX

Holistic Moms Network Mutual support for moms with an interest in natural health, alternative therapies and mindful parenting. Families welcome. Rap sessions and guest speakers. Dues $35/yr. Meets in Lafayette. For monthly meeting information call 1-877-465-6667. *Website:* http://www.holisticmoms.org

Project Self-Sufficiency *Professionally-run.* Support for single parents, teen parents, displaced homemakers and low-income families. Offers peer support groups for single parents and teen parents, loss recovery groups for children, parenting skills training and support. Also family activities, physical and emotional health educational seminars and job training and educational services designed to promote self-sufficiency. Meetings vary. Call Deborah Berry-Toon 973-383-5129 (day). *E-mail:* PSS@garden.net

UNION

Holistic Moms Network Mutual support for moms with an interest in natural health, alternative therapies and mindful parenting. Families welcome. Rap sessions and guest speakers. Dues $35/yr. Meets in Cranford. For monthly meeting information call 1-877-465-6667. *Website:* http://www.holisticmoms.org

Mother's Center of Central New Jersey, Inc. Support and discussion group for mothers. Education, information and referrals, workshops and newsletter. Semi-annual kids' toys/clothes exchange. Babysitting available. Dues $50/yr. Meets in Cranford. Call 908-561-1751 (taped message). *Website:* http://www.westfieldnj.com/mccnj *E-mail:* mccnj@westfieldnj.com

WARREN

Holistic Moms Network Mutual support for moms with an interest in natural health, alternative therapies and mindful parenting. Families welcome. Rap sessions and guest speakers. Dues $35/yr. Meets in Hackettstown. For monthly meeting information call 1-877-465-6667. *Website:* http://www.holisticmoms.org

NATIONAL

Attachment Parenting International *International. Founded 1994.* Offers parenting methods to create strong, healthy emotional bonds between parents and their child. Dues $35/yr. Offers support group referrals, newsletter, advocacy, literature, information and referrals. Write: Attachment Parenting International, P.O. Box 210208, Nashville, TN 37221. Call 615-298-4334; Fax: 615-646-7480. *Website:* http://www.attachmentparenting.org *E-mail:* info@attachmentparenting.org

Family Pride Coalition *National. 160+ local groups. Founded 1979.* Support, education and advocacy for gay/lesbian/transgendered parents and prospective parents. Families welcome. Information and referrals, phone support, family events, literature and newsletter. Assistance in starting groups. Write: Family Pride Coalition, P.O. Box 65327, Washington, DC 20035-5327. Call 202-331-5015; Fax: 202-331-0080. *Website:* http://www.familypride.org *E-mail:* info@familypride.org

Holistic Moms Network *International. Chapters in 32 States and Canada. Founded 2002.* Purpose is to provide awareness, education and support for holistic parenting, provides a nurturing, open-minded and respectful community for parents to share these ideals. Encourages moms and dads to parent naturally and educate themselves about alternative health, mindful parenting and natural healing. Assists persons in starting new chapters. Write: Holistic Moms Network, P.O. Box 408,

Caldwell, NJ 07006. Call 1-877-465-6667. *Website:*http://www.holisticmoms.org *E-mail:* info@holisticmoms.org

MAD DADS, Inc. (Men Against Destruction Defending Against Drugs and Social-disorder) *National. 60 affiliated groups in 17 states. Founded 1989.* Grassroots organization of fathers aimed at fighting gang and drug-related violence. Provides family and community activities and leadership, community education and mobilization, speaking engagements regarding goals and objectives and chapter formation. They present themselves as "surrogate fathers" who listen to and care about street teens. Provides assistance in starting chapters in hard-to-reach neighborhoods. Also, groups for kids, mothers and grandparents. Write: MAD DADS, Inc., 555 Stockton St., Jacksonville, FL 32204. Call 904-388-8171. *Website:* http://www.maddads.com *E-mail:* national@maddads.com

Mocha Moms Inc. *National. 100+ affiliated groups. Founded 1997.* Provides support for at-home mothers of color. Sponsors weekly support group meetings, monthly moms-only events, on-going community service and volunteer opportunities. Dues $20/year. Bulletins, information, assistance with starting local chapters and referrals to existing groups. Write: Mocha Moms, Inc., P.O. Box 1995 Upper Marlboro, MD 20773. Fax: 301-805-8147. *Website:* http://www.mochamoms.org *E-mail:* nationaloffice@mochamoms.org

MOMS Club *International. 1900+ affiliated groups. Founded 1983.* Mutual support for mothers-at-home. Groups provide at-home mothers of children of all ages emotional and moral support, as well as a wide variety of activities. Provides assistance in starting and maintaining or locating chapters through local coordinators (enclose $2 to cover postage). Write: MOMS Club, 1464 Madera Rd., N 191, Simi Valley, CA 93065. *Website:* http://www.momsclub.org *E-mail:* momsclub@aol.com

MOPS, International (Mothers Of Pre-Schoolers) *International. 3600 affiliated groups. Founded 1973.* Offers a non-denominational Christian support group for mothers with children from infancy to 6 years old. MOPS groups meet in churches throughout the U.S., Canada and 15 other countries. Provides assistance in starting local groups. Write: MOPS, International, 2370 South Trenton Way, Denver, CO 80231. Call 1-800-929-1287 or 303-733-5353 (group referrals); 1-888-910-6677 (to start a MOPS group); Fax: 303-733-5770. *Website:* http://www.mops.org *E-mail:* info@mops.org

Mothers and More *National. 180 chapters. Founded 1987.* Support and advocacy for women who have altered their career paths to care for their children at home. It is not about opposing mothers who work outside the home; rather it is about respecting, supporting and advocating for choice in how one combines working and parenting. Provides ongoing support for a woman's personal needs and interests with regard to active parenting. Also advocates for public and employment policies that accommodate stay-at-home mothers. Newsletter and chapter development guidelines. Write: Mothers and More, P.O. Box 31, Elmhurst, IL 60126. Call 630-941-3553; Fax: 630-941-3551. *Website:* http://www.mothersandmore.org *Email:* nationaloffice@mothersandmore.org

NATHHAN (National Challenged Homeschoolers) *National network. Founded 1990.* Christian, non-profit organization encouraging families with special needs, particularly those who home educate. Bi-annual magazine, lending library, family phone book, phone support, information and referrals. Dues $25/yr. Write: NATHHAN, P.O. Box 310, Moyie Springs, ID 83845. Call 208-267-6246. *Website:* http://www.nathhan.com *E-mail:* nathanews@aol.com

National Association of Mothers' Centers *National. 40 sites. Founded 1975.* Discussion groups and other activities regarding parenting, pregnancy, childbirth and childrearing. Warm, welcoming environment of support. National and some local newsletters, conferences and advocacy. Has up-to-date information on contacting local Mothers' Center programs, starting a center and how employers in NY/NJ/CT can offer a program for working parents. Write: National Association of Mothers' Centers, 64 Division Ave., Suite LL7, Levittown, NY 11756. Call 1-800-645-3828 or 516-520-2929; Fax: 516-520-1639. *Website:* http://www.motherscenter.org *E-mail:* info@motherscenter.org

PEP (Postpartum Education for Parents) *Model. 1 group in California. Founded 1977.* Volunteer-run group that provides emotional peer support for parents. Helps parents adjust to the changes in their lives that a baby brings. Education on basic infant care and parent adjustment. Monthly newsletter, online support group and phone help. Group development guidelines. Write: PEP, P.O. Box 6154, Santa Barbara, CA 93160. Call 805-564-3888. *Website:* http://www.sbpep.org *E-mail:* pepboard@gmail.com

ONLINE

Expecting Parents Meetup Groups *Online.* Meet other new or expecting parents to exchange advice, support and laughs. Message boards. *Website:* http://newparents.meetup.com/

G.I.F.T. (Getting Interracial/Cultural Families Together) *Online.* Support for biracial individuals, interracial/cultural couples, families, dating teens, transracial adoptive families and extended families of these groups and anyone supportive of interracial/cultural issues. *Website:* http://www.groups.yahoo.com/group/njgift

Jersey Dads *Online.* Support for stay-at-home dads to discuss parenting and household skills. *Website:* http://www.JerseyDads.com *E-mail:* NJDads@hotmail.com

Mothers of Freshmen *Online.* Support group for mothers of college freshmen where they share their various concerns unique to sending a child off to college, from how to support their child to coping with "Empty Nest Syndrome." Has a variety of topical message boards and evening chat sessions. *Website:* http://www.mofchat.com

Parent Empowerment Network *Online. Founded 1996.* E-mail group for parents with disabilities. *Website:* http://www.disabledparents.net *E-mail:* trish@disabledparents.net

Parent Soup Message Boards *Online.* Offers a large variety of message boards which deal with parenting issues including infertility, pregnancy, parenting challenges, parents of disabled, pregnancy loss, newborn babies, toddlers, adoption, family issues, etc. *Website:* http://www.parentsoup.com/boards

Conduct Disorders Parent Message Board *Online. 6592 members. Founded 1995.* Support for parents living with a child with one of the many behavior disorders including: attention deficit hyperactivity disorder, oppositional defiance disorder, conduct disorder, depression and substance abuse. Parents with children of all ages welcome. *Website:* http://www.conductdisorders.com

Slowlane.com *Online. Founded 1997.* Resource for stay at home fathers. Discussion forum, chat room, information and events. Write: Slowlane.com, 1216 East Lee St., Pensacola, FL 32503. Call 850-434-2626. *Website:* http://www.slowlane.com

Need help finding a specific group? Give us a call – we're here to help!
Call 1-800-367-6274

PARENTS OF CHILDREN WITH BEHAVIORAL PROBLEMS

(see also drugs, alcohol, parenting and toll-free helplines)

STATEWIDE

TOUGHLOVE America Mutual support for parents disturbed by their children's unacceptable behavior. Helps parents take a firm stand with their kids. Dues $5/wk. Membership $30/yr. Call Mary Cooke 609-883-1989.

ATLANTIC

Family Support Organization *"Parents Support Parents"* Provides education and advocacy for parents/caregivers of children with emotional and behavioral challenges. Rap sessions, guest speakers, buddy system, literature, speakers' bureau, newsletter and phone help. Meets 1st and 3rd Wed., 6:30-8:30pm, Atlantic Cape Family Support Organization, Northfield. Call Andrea Burleigh or Sondra Dublinsky 609-485-0575 (day).

BERGEN

Family Support Organization of Bergen County *Professionally-run.* Provides support and advocacy to families and caregivers of children with complex emotional and behavioral challenges. Educational lectures offered. Meets Wed., 7-8:30pm, Family Support Organization of Bergen County, 0-108 29th St., Fair Lawn. Before attending call Lynne Bolson, MSW or Karen Stack 201-796-6209 (day). *Website:* http://www.fsobergen.org

Parents in Crisis Mutual support for parents disturbed by their children's unacceptable behavior. Helps parents to take a firm stand with their kids. Meets Wed., 7:30pm, Community Church, 354 Rock Rd., Glen Rock. Call Jean Baker Wunder 201-652-8332 or The Source 201-670-4673.

BURLINGTON

B.I.L.Y. (Because I Love You) Mutual support to help parents with children, of any age, who have behavioral challenges. Guest speakers. Meets 1st and 3rd Thurs., 6:30-8:30pm, Sisterhood, Inc., 132-136 E. Broad St., Burlington. Call Deborah or Russ 609-265-8838 (day). *E-mail:* familyvoices@fsoburlco.org

CAMDEN

Grandparents Raising Grandchildren Support and education for women and men who are caring for their grandchildren struggling with emotional, behavioral and mental challenges. Guest speakers, literature, social, advocacy and buddy system. Meets 4th Mon., 6:30-8:30pm, Holy Trinity Lutheran Church, 325 South Whitehorse Pike, Audubon. Call Marge Varneke 856-547-1620 (eve) or Susan A. Doherty-Funke 856-662-2600 (day).

B.I.L.Y. (Because I Love You) Mutual support to help parents with children, of any age, who have behavioral challenges. Guest speakers, rap sessions, literature and phone help. Meets Tues., 6:30-8pm, Camden County Family Support Organization, 23 West Park Ave., Suite 103-104, Merchantville. Call Susan A. Doherty-Funke 856-662-2600 (day) or 856-261-0233 (eve). *Website:* http://www.camdenfso.org or http://www.becauseiloveyou.org *E-mail:* sdoherty-funke@camdenfso.org

CAPE MAY

Family Support Organization *"Parents Supporting Parents"* Support, education and advocacy for parents/caregivers of children with emotional and behavioral challenges. Rap sessions, guest speakers, buddy system, newsletter and phone support. Meets 4th Wed., 6:30-8:30pm, The Court House Church of Christ, 102 East Pacific Ave., Cape May Court House. Call Andrea Burleigh or Sondra Dublinsky 609-485-0575 (day). *Website:* http://www.famsupport.org *E-mail:* sdublinsky@famsupport.org

ESSEX

Family Support Organization of Essex County *Professionally-run.* Support for parents raising a child with emotional and behavioral challenges. Guest speakers, literature, newsletter, phone help and speakers' bureau. Meets Tues. and Thurs., 6-8pm, Family Support Organization of Essex County, 60 Evergreen Place, East Orange. Call Yvonne Rouse or Hazeline Pilgrim 973-395-1441 (day).

Parents Self-Help Group Mutual support for parents disturbed by their children's unacceptable behavior. Helps parents take a firm stand with their kids. Meets Tues., 7:30pm, Senior Community Center, Livingston. Call Debbie 973-533-1319 (day/eve), Helene and Jerry 973-994-4034 (day/eve) or Paul and Nancy 908-464-1590.

GLOUCESTER

Gloucester County Parent To Parent Coalition *Professionally-run.* Confidential meetings and focus on providing parents with support, information, resources, and referrals for dealing with substance abuse and related problems. Guest speakers, educational series and literature. Meets 2nd and 4th Mon., 7:30-9:30pm, Washington Township Municipal Building, 523 Egg Harbor Rd., Meeting Room C, Washington Township. Call 856-589-6446 (day).

HUDSON

F.S.O. - "I Need You, You Need Me" Parent Group *Professionally-run.* Support for parents raising a child with emotional and/or behavioral challenges. Educational series, advocacy, guest speakers, phone help, literature and buddy system. Meets 1st Tues., 6-8pm, Family Support Organization of Hudson County, 705 Bergen Ave., Jersey City. Call Roslyn Gibbs-Muse 201-915-5140 (day); Fax: 201-915-5142.

MERCER

Family Support Organization Women's Group Open discussion for mothers, caregivers and family members of children with emotional, behavioral and/or mental health challenges. Rap sessions. Meets Thurs., 6-7:30pm, YWCA, 127 Academy St., Trenton. Call Evangeline 609-581-6891 (day).

Parent Support Group *Professionally-run.* Support and information for parents of adolescents. Opportunity to share ideas, concerns, strategies, learn helpful parenting skills and techniques. Meets Wed., 6-7pm, Anchor House, 482 Centre St., Trenton. Call 609-396-8329.

TOUGHLOVE America Mutual support for parents disturbed by their children's unacceptable behavior. Dues $5 week per family. Meets Mon., 7pm, Unitarian Universalist Church, 90 Cherry Hill Rd., Princeton. Call Mary 609-883-1989.

MIDDLESEX

B.I.L.Y. (Because I Love You) Mutual support to help parents with children, of any age, who have behavioral challenges. Educational series, advocacy, speakers' bureau and literature. Meets for 6 weeks/6 times per year, Family Support Organization of Middlesex County, 1950 Route 27 North, Suite D., North

Brunswick. Call Dylys Koney 732-940-2837 (day). *E-mail:* dkfsomiddlesex9@msn.com

Family Support Organization of Middlesex County Support for parents raising children (ages 13 and above), with emotional and behavioral challenges. Guest speakers, literature, newsletter, phone help, buddy system and speakers' bureau. Meets Mon., 6:30-8:30pm, Family Support Organization of Middlesex County, 1950 Route 27, Suite D, North Brunswick. Call Bryn Schain or Lirie Mulaj 732-940-2837 (day). *Website:* http://www.njfamily.org

MONMOUTH

Parent Support Group Mutual support for parents whose children are experiencing emotional and behavioral problems. Childcare and limited transportation. Rap sessions, guest speakers, literature, phone help and newsletter. Before attending call 732-571-3272 (day).

Howell Meets Wed., 7-9pm, Church of the Master, 110 Salem Hill Rd.

Keansburg Meets Mon., 6:30pm, First United Methodist Church, 21 Church St.

Long Branch Meets Thurs., 7-9pm, Family Based Services Association, 279 Broadway, Suite 400.

Long Branch *(SPANISH)* Meets Wed., 7-9pm, Family Based Services Association, 279 Broadway, Suite 400. Call Ana Salgado 732-713-9027 (day).

TOUGHLOVE America Mutual support for parents disturbed by their children's unacceptable behavior. Dues $5/mtg - $30/yr. Meets Tues. 7:30pm, Church of the Master, 110 Salem Hill Rd., Howell. Call Susan Walters 732-431-1740.

OCEAN

Family Support Group *"Parents Supporting Parents"* Support, education and advocacy for parents/caregivers of children with emotional and behavioral challenges. Rap sessions and guest speakers. Meets 4th Tues., 7-9pm, Ocean County Family Support Organization, 44 Washington St., Suite 2A, Toms River. Call Maria Cruz 732-281-5770 (day).

"What do we live for if not to make life less difficult for each other."
–George Elloit

PASSAIC

Family Support Organization of Passaic County Support for parents and caregivers raising a child with emotional and behavioral challenges. Call 973-427-0100. *Website:* http://www.fso-pc.org

> **North Haledon** Meets 2nd and 4th Wed., 7-8:30pm, Family Support Organization of Passaic County, 810 Belmont Ave.
>
> **North Haledon** *(SPANISH)* Meets 1st and 3rd Tues., 7-8:30pm, Family Support Organization of Passaic County, 810 Belmont Ave., 2nd Floor.

TOUGHLOVE America Mutual support for parents disturbed by their children's unacceptable behavior. Helps parents take firm stand with their kids. Donation $5/week. Meets Thurs., 7:30-9:45pm, Pompton Lakes Reformed Church, Hamburg Turnpike, Pompton Lakes. Call Judy 973-838-8005.

NATIONAL

B.I.L.Y. (Because I Love You: The Parent Support Group) *National. 47 affiliated groups. Founded 1982.* Self-help groups for parents who have children of all ages with behavioral problems such as truancy, substance abuse or other forms of defiance of authority. Focus is on parents getting back their self-esteem and control of their home. Write: B.I.L.Y., P.O. Box 2062, Winnetka, CA 91396-2062. Call 818-884-8242; Fax: 805-493-2714. *Website:* http://www.becauseiloveyou.org *E-mail:* BILY1982@aol.com

Standup Parenting *National.* Offers mutual support, education, alternative strategies and practical solutions to family problems related to a child's out-of-control behavior. Local self-help groups in 10 states. Call 1-800-972-0416. *Website:* http://www.standup.org

TOUGHLOVE America *International. 43 affiliated groups. Founded 1979.* Self-help program for parents and kids in dealing with the out-of-control behavior of a family member. Parent support groups help parents take a firm stand to help kids take responsibility for their behavior. Groups listed at website. Newsletter. Group development guidelines. Write: TOUGHLOVE America, P.O. Box 491670, Los Angeles, CA 90049-1670. *Website:* http://www.toughlove.com

ONLINE

Conduct Disorders Parent Message Board *Online. 6592 members. Founded 1995.* Support for parents living with a child with one of the many behavior disorders including: attention deficit hyperactivity disorder, oppositional defiance disorder, conduct disorder, depression and substance abuse. Parents with children of all ages welcome. *Website:* http://www.conductdisorders.com

PARENTS OF CHILDREN WITH DISABILITIES / ILL CHILDREN

(see also specific disability and toll-free helplines)

STATEWIDE

S.P.A.N. (Statewide Parent Advocacy Network) *(BILINGUAL) Professionally-run.* Training, information, technical assistance, leadership development and support for parents concerning education and healthcare issues for children from birth to age 21. Special focus on children at risk due to disabilities, special healthcare or emotional needs, poverty, language or race. Workshops on laws, effective education practices and advocacy strategies. Assist parents of children with special health needs in medical and insurance advocacy. Newsletter, phone help and bilingual materials. Parent-to-Parent program call 1-800-372-6510 that matches families of children on a one-to-one basis with similar disabilities or other special health needs. The START Project helps parents of children who have special needs and are in public schools to find and/or start their own parent support groups there. Call 1-800-654-7726 (within NJ; voice/TDD) or 973-642-8100; Fax: 973-642-8080 (day). *Website:* http://www.spannj.org *E-mail:* span@spannj.org

BERGEN

Supporting Parents of Exceptional Children Provides education, resources and support to help families of children with special needs. Meets monthly on various days, 7:30-9pm, Pasack Valley Hospital, 250 Old Hook Rd., Westwood. For meeting dates call Lori Ruschman 201-358-0054 (day), Joanna 201-519-0340 (eve) or Elisa 201-723-2447.

BURLINGTON

Father's Group *Professionally-run.* Mutual support for fathers of children (any age) who have a developmental delay or disability. A great opportunity for dads to informally meet to discuss issues affecting themselves and their families. Meets 1st Sat. (except July/Aug.), 10am-noon, Early Intervention Program, 101 Burrs Rd., Suite B, Bldg. 2, Westampton. Before attending call Virtua 1-888-847-8823 (day).

HUDSON

MDA Parents Support Group *Professionally-run.* Mutual support for parents of children with muscular dystrophy. Sharing of information, experiences, ideas and resources. Usually meets 2nd Mon., 7-8:30pm, Liberty Health, Meadowlands Campus, 55 Meadowlands Parkway, Secaucus. Pre-registration required. Before attending call 201-843-4452 (day).

MERCER

Special Kids – Special Parents *(WEST WINDSOR RESIDENTS ONLY)* Community-based education, support and advocacy for parents of special needs children. Rap sessions, guest speakers, literature, activities, social events and phone help. Meetings vary, 7pm, West Windsor Library, 333 N. Post Rd., West Windsor. For meeting day call Judith 609-799-3344. *E-mail:* judith@wwpsksp.org

MIDDLESEX

High Expectations Parents and Friends Support Group Mutual sharing, socializing and advocacy for parents, friends and relatives of children with disabilities. Meets monthly in Iselin. Call Diane Heitmeyer 732-283-0925 (eve). *E-mail:* DianeHeit@aol.com

Special Kids – Special Parents *(PLAINSBORO RESIDENTS ONLY)* Community-based education, support and advocacy for parents of special needs children. Rap sessions, guest speakers, literature, activities, social events and phone help. Meetings vary, 7:45pm, Plainsboro Municipal Center, Plainsboro. For meeting day call Judith 609-799-3344. *E-mail:* judith@wwpsksp.org

MONMOUTH

Organization for Children with Profound Disabilities Mutual support for parents, grandparents and other caregivers of children (any age) with severe multiple handicaps or who are medically fragile. Rap sessions and advocacy. Group meets various times and locations. For information call Jane 732-866-9217. *E-mail:* janeye@verizon.net

Parents Of Children With Multiple Impairments *Professionally-run.* Suppport for parents of children with multiple impairments. Meets monthly, 7:30-9pm, Family Resource Associates, 35 Haddon Ave., Shrewsbury. Call Susan Levine 732-747-5310 (day).

PASSAIC

Parents Place/Club de Padres Catholic Family and Community Services *(BILINIGUAL)* Support for parents and families of children with disabilities. Meets 3rd Sat., 1:30-3:30pm, 26 DeGrasse St., Paterson. Information and referrals, translation and interpretation services available, educational issues, technical assistance, immigration assistance, advocacy, recreation, training, employment and respite care. Childcare and local transportation available. Call 973-523-8404 ext. 45 (day). *E-mail:* parentsplace26@aol.com

Supporting Special Families *Professionally-run.* Support for parents of children (ages birth - 21), with any type of disability. Buddy system, newsletter and phone help. Meets last Fri., 9:30am, Hillcrest Community Center, 1810 Macopin Rd., Room 25, West Milford. Pre-registration required. Before attending call Catherine Grisbacher 973-728-8744 (day).

SUSSEX

The Center for Families with Special Needs Parent-run organization that provides emotional support, information and literature for families of children with special needs. Referrals to local services, phone help and guest speakers. Newsletter $10/yr. Parent Support Network meets various Fri., 7:30-9:30pm, St. Thomas Church, Route 94, Vernon. Call Sheila McNally 973-827-4419 (Tues. and Thurs., 9am-1pm). *E-mail:* thecenter@nac.net

WARREN

North Warren Special Needs Advocacy Support and advocacy to parents/guardians of children with special needs. Rap sessions, guest speakers and phone help. Dues $10/yr. Meetings vary, Catherine Dickson Hofman Library, Blairstown. Call Margaret Scocozza 908-362-9066.

NATIONAL

Birth Defect Research for Children *National network. Founded 1982.* Provides information about birth defects, as well as services and resources that may be helpful to families. Links parents of children with similar birth defects for mutual sharing and support. Sponsors national birth defect registry. Maintains database on medical/scientific literature and research. Monthly electronic newsletter. Write: Birth Defect Research for Children, 930 Woodcock Rd., Suite 225, Orlando, FL

32803. Call 407-895-0802; Fax: 407-895-0824. *Website:* http://www.birthdefects.org *E-mail:* abdc@birthdefects.org

Family Voices *(BILINGUAL) National. 50 affiliated groups. Founded 1995.* Grassroots organization that speaks on behalf of children with special healthcare needs at the national, state and local levels. Encourages and supports families who want to play a role in their child's healthcare. Advocacy. Literature (Spanish and English). Write: Family Voices, 2340 Alamo SE, Suite 102, Albuquerque, NM 87106. Call 1-888-835-5669 or 505-872-4774; Fax: 505-872-4780. *Website:* http://www.familyvoices.org *E-mail:* kidshealth@familyvoices.org

MUMS National Parent-to-Parent Network *National. 36 affiliated groups. Founded 1979.* Mutual support and networking for parents or care providers of children with any disability, rare disorder, chromosomal abnormality or health condition using a database of over 20,000 families from 54 countries, covering 3400 disorders, very rare syndromes, or undiagnosed conditions. Referrals to support groups and provides assistance in starting groups. Newsletter ($15/parents; $25/ professionals). Matching services $5. Hyperbaric Oxygen Therapy as a Treatment for Brain Damage packet, $25 USA; $35 other countries. Other literature available. Write: MUMS National Parent-to-Parent Network, 150 Custer Court, Green Bay, WI 54301-1243. Call 1-877-336-5333 (parents only) or 920-336-5333 (day); Fax: 920-339-0995. *Website:* http://www.netnet.net/mums/ *E-mail:* mums@netnet.net

NATHHAN (National Challenged Homeschoolers) *National network. Founded 1990.* Christian, non-profit organization encouraging families with special needs, particularly those who home educate. Bi-annual magazine, lending library, family phone book, phone support, information and referrals. Dues $25/yr. Write: NATHHAN, P.O. Box 310, Moyie Springs, ID 83845. Call 208-267-6246. *Website:* http://www.nathhan.com *E-mail:* nathanews@aol.com

Parents Helping Parents *(MULTILINGUAL) Model. 22 groups. Founded 1976.* Parent-directed family resource center serving children with special needs (due to illness, accident, conditions of birth, learning differences or family stress), their families and the professionals who serve them. Information and referral, specialty programs, family support groups, peer counseling, training and library. Newsletter, group development guidelines and national resource directory online. Outreach in Spanish, Japanese and Vietnamese. Write: PHP, 3041 Olcott St., Santa Clara, CA 95054-3222. Call 408-727-5775; Fax: 408-727-0182. *Website:* http://www.php.com *E-mail:* info@php.com

Sibling Support Project *National. 200 affiliated groups. Founded 1990.* Organization dedicated to the life-long concerns of brothers and sisters of people with special health, developmental and mental health concerns. Provides training and technical assistance regarding Sibshops and workshops for school-age siblings. Write: Sibling Support Project, c/o Donald Meyer, 6512 23rd Ave. NW, #213, Seattle, WA 98117. Call 206-297-6368; Fax: 509-752-6789. *Website:* http://www.siblingsupport.org *E-mail:* donmeyer@siblingsupport.org

Washington PAVE *Model. 1 group in Washington. Founded 1979.* Parent-directed organization to increase independence, empowerment and opportunities for special needs children and their families through training, information, referrals and support. Newsletter, lending library of resources, networking between parents through internet, workshops on many issues, phone support and conferences on special education issues. Has special program that focuses on military family concerns. Write: Washington PAVE, 6316 S. 12th, Tacoma, WA 98465. Call 253-565-2266 (Voice/TTY) or 1-800-5-PARENT (Voice/TTY); Fax: 253-566-8052. *Website:* http://www.washingtonpave.org *E-mail:* wapave9@washingtonpave.com

Washington State Fathers Network *Model. 15 groups in Washington. Founded 1986.* Provides mutual support and resources for fathers and families raising children with special needs and developmental disabilities. Print newsletters, e-newsletter, web page with extensive links, photo album of men and children, articles by dads and materials for providers regarding family-centered, culturally competent care. Videos and monographs available. Statewide and regional conferences. Write: WSFN, 16120 N.E. Eighth St., Bellevue, WA 98008. Call Greg Schell 425-747-4004; Fax: 425-474-1069. *Website:* http://www.fathersnetwork.org *E-mail:* greg.schell@kindering.org

ONLINE

Mothers From Hell 2 *Online. National network. Founded 1992.* Support and advocacy for families of children with any type of disability. Mission is to improve the quality of the lives and education of persons with developmental and other disabilities. Seeks to promote understanding and acceptance of people with disabilities. Dues $10/yr. Newsletter, referral network and training packets. Assistance in starting local groups. Website and e-groups online. Write: Mothers From Hell 2, P.O. Box 62, Peru, IL 61354. Call 815-224-4568. *Website:* http://www.mothersfromhell2.org *E-mail:* mfh2_kim@sbcglobal.net

Parent Soup Message Boards *Online.* Offers a large variety of message boards which deal with parenting issues including infertility, pregnancy, parenting challenges, parents of disabled, pregnancy loss, newborn babies, toddlers, adoption, family issues, etc. *Website:* http://www.parentsoup.com/boards

Premature Baby - Premature Child *Online. Founded 1997.* Offers support for parents of premature babies that are age 4+ years old for any of their special needs e.g., mental, physical, emotional or learning disability. Provides support, discussion listserv, prematurity forums, advocacy and educational links. Special children's show-and-tell section. *Website:* http://www.prematurity.org

PARENTS OF PREMATURE / HIGH RISK INFANTS

(see also parents of twins and triplets, toll-free helplines)

NATIONAL

Sidelines High Risk Pregnancy Support *National network. Founded 1991.* Trained former high risk pregnancy moms provide support to current high risk patients and their families. Provides educational resources, advocacy and emotional support via phone and e-mail. Write: Sidelines National Support Network, P.O. Box 1808, Laguna Beach, CA 92652. Call 1-888-447-4754; Fax: 949-497-5598. *Website:* http://www.sidelines.org *E-mail:* sidelines@sidelines.org

ONLINE

Preemie-List *Online.* Mutual discussion forum of support for parents with children born six weeks or more before due date. Families and friends are welcome to join discussions. *Website:* http://groups.yahoo.com/group/preemie-list

Premature Baby - Premature Child *Online. Founded 1997.* Offers support for parents of premature babies that are age 4+ years old, for any of their special needs e.g., mental, physical, emotional or learning disability. Provides support, discussion listserv, prematurity forums, advocacy and educational links. Special children's show-and-tell section. *Website:* http://www.prematurity.org

"There is no such thing as 'them and us.' In a world this size there can only be 'we' – all of us working together." –Don Ward

PARENTS OF TWINS / TRIPLETS / MULTIPLES

BERGEN

Twins Mothers Club of Bergen County Provides support, advice and camaraderie for mothers of multiples. Rap sessions, guest speakers, literature and buddy system. Dues $35/yr. Meets 4th Wed., 7:15-10pm, (except June, July, Aug., Dec.), American Legion Hall, 33 West Passaic St., Rochelle Park. Call Megan Milner 973-835-3061 (day). *Website:* http://www.tmcofbc.com

CAMDEN

South Jersey Mothers of Multiples Moral support for mothers of multiple births. Hospital visits, clothing sales, childrens' activities, speakers and newsletters. Dues $30/yr. Meets 1st Wed., 7:30pm, Lions Lake Park Bldg., Route 73, Voorhees. Call Lisa 856-797-9863 (day).

MIDDLESEX

Twin Mothers Club of the Greater Plainfield Area Help and information for mothers of older multiples (ages 20 and older). Phone help, guest speakers, visitation and peer counseling. Dues $35/yr. Meets 2nd Wed., 8:30pm, Italian-American Club, Garibaldi Ave., South Plainfield. Call Carmela Ford 732-968-1503 (day/eve) or Kathy Gangemi 732-968-4351.

MONMOUTH

Mid-Jersey Mothers of Multiples Mothers of multiples share information and advice on dealing with their unique problems and joys. Guest speakers and activities for adults and children. Dues $35/yr. Meets 4th Tues., 8pm, Jackson Street Firehouse, Matawan. Call Lisa 732-238-7682 or Karen 732-765-1368 (day). *Website:* http://www.midjerseymoms.org

MORRIS

Twins and Triplets Mothers of Morris County Mothers of multiples share information and advice on dealing with their unique problems and joys. Newsletter. Dues $30/yr. Meets 2nd Thurs. (except summer), 7:30pm, Morristown Memorial Hospital, Jefferson B, Auditorium A, Madison Ave., Morristown. Call Cris Parente 973-257-0069 or Yvette Vieira 973-230-2386. *E-mail:* craftycrissy@aol.com

OCEAN

Mothers of Twins Club Support and education for mothers of multiples. Monthly local newsletter. Dues $30/yr. Meets 1st Thurs., 8pm (except July/Aug.), Knights of Columbus, Tennyson Ave., Toms River. Call Eileen Weiderspan 732-730-0573 (day/eve) or Chris Church 732-364-2790 (day/eve). *Website:* http://www.ocmotc.org

SOMERSET

Mothers and More Central Jersey Triplets And More Support for mothers of triplets and more. Offers mutual sharing, exchanging of experiences and helpful hints. Meets 2nd Tues., 7:30-10pm, Somerset Medical Center, Cafeteria, 110 Rehill Ave., Somerset. Call 908-685-2814 (day).

Raritan Valley M.O.M.S. Support for moms of multiples. Friendship, guest speakers and newsletter. Dues $25/yr. Meets 4th Mon. (except July, Aug., Dec.), 7:30pm, Somerset Medical Center, 110 Rehill Ave., Cafeteria, Somerville. Call Liz Pollard 908-575-9385 (day) or Medical Center 1-800-443-4605. *Website:* http://www.rvmom.net

NATIONAL

Conjoined Twins International *International network. Founded 1996.* Support for conjoined twins, their families and professionals. Offers peer support, professional counseling, crisis intervention, telephone helpline, pen pal network and videos. Information and referrals, peer counseling, speakers' bureau, registry of affected families and membership directory. Write: Conjoined Twins International, P.O. Box 10895, Prescott, AZ 86304-0895. Call 928-445-2777. *E-mail:* dwdegeraty@myexcel.org

M.O.S.T. (Mothers Of Super Twins) *International. Founded 1987.* Support network of families who are expecting, or already the parents of, triplets or more. Provides information, support, resources and empathy during pregnancy, infancy, toddlerhood and school age. Magazine, catalogue, networking, phone and online support. Specific resource persons for individual challenges. Help in starting groups. Write: M.O.S.T., P.O. Box 306, East Islip, NY 11730-0306. Call Maureen Boyle 631-859-1110; Fax: 631-859-3580. *Website:* http://www.MOSTonline.org *E-mail:* info@mostonline.org

National Organization of Mothers of Twins Clubs *National. 475 clubs. Founded 1960.* Opportunity for parents of multiple birth children (twins, triplets, quads) to share information, concerns and advice on dealing with their unique challenges. Literature, quarterly newspaper ($15/yr.), group development guidelines, educational materials, special needs and bereavement support and pen pal program. Membership through local chapters or as individual affiliate members. Write: NOMOTC, P.O. Box 700860, Plymouth, MI 48170-0955. Call 1-877-540-2200 (referrals) or 248-231-4480. *Website:* http://www.nomotc.org/ *E-mail:* nomotc@aol.com

Triplet Connection *International network. Founded 1983.* Network of caring and sharing for families with multiples. Emphasis is on providing quality information regarding pregnancy management and preterm birth prevention for high risk multiple pregnancies. Expectant parent's packet, new parent's packet, quarterly newsletter, phone support and area resources. Write: Triplet Connection, P.O. Box 429, Spring City, UT 84662. Call 435-851-1105; Fax: 435-462-7466. *Website:* http://www.tripletconnection.org *E-mail:* tc@tripletconnection.org

SEPARATION / DIVORCE

(see also men, women, single parenting and toll-free helplines)

STATEWIDE

Catholic Divorce - Ministry The Ministry of the North American Conference of Separated and Divorced Catholics Ministry serving individuals experiencing separation, divorce or death of a spouse. Offers leadership training conferences, resources, materials and social activities. Referrals to self-help groups statewide. Call Charlie Rauh 201-986-9676. *Website:* http://www.nacsdc.org (click into Region 3)

F.A.C.E. (Father's And Children's Equality) Support group for non-custodial mothers or fathers and their families. Concerned with gaining equal rights for mothers and fathers in parental separation. Networking, emergency housing referrals and advocacy for equal access to children regardless of parents marital status. Restores children's rights to two equal parents. Dues $75/yr. Write: F.A.C.E., P.O. Box 2471, Cinnaminson, NJ 08077. Call Hotline 856-786-3223. *Website:* http://www.facenj.org *E-mail:* faceinfo@facenj.org

Rainbows, Inc. *Professionally-run.* Time-limited support groups for children and teens (ages 4-17) who are grieving a loss due to death, divorce, abandonment or other life-altering experiences. Groups meet for a specific number of sessions and are held periodically. Some programs have concurrent groups for the parents. Helps implement programs throughout the state in schools, churches and social service agencies. *Website:* http://www.rainbowsnj.org *E-mail:* info@rainbowsnj.org

Central New Jersey (Covers Burlington, Mercer, Monmouth and Ocean counties) Write: Marilyn Schipp, Trenton Diocese Family Life Office, P.O. Box 5147, Trenton, NJ 08638-0147. For any upcoming group sessions planned call Marilyn Schipp 609-406-7400 ext. 5557 (day).

Northern New Jersey (Covers Bergen, Essex, Hudson, Hunterdon, Middlesex, Morris, Passaic, Somerset, Sussex, Union and Warren counties) Write: Rainbows, Inc., NJ State Chapter, 55 Woodland Ave., Summit, NJ 07901. For any upcoming group sessions planned call Alice Forsyth 908-608-0888 (day).

Southern New Jersey (Covers Atlantic, Camden, Cape May, Cumberland, Gloucester and Salem counties) Write: Sister Pat McGrenra, Gesu School, 1700 West Thompson St., Philadelphia, PA 19121. For any upcoming group sessions planned call Sister Pat McGrenra 215-763-3660 ext. 204 (day).

BERGEN

Healing Hope Support with a spiritual emphasis on helping those who suffer catastrophic loss including death, divorce, serious illness, etc. Meets 1st and 3rd Tues., 7:30-9pm, Cornerstone Christian Church, 495 Wyckoff Ave., Wyckoff. Call Kris 201-847-8107 (eve).

New Beginnings *Professionally-run.* Support group for separated or divorced persons. Meets Tues., 7:30pm, Montvale Evangelical Free Church, 141 W. Grand Ave., Montvale. Call Dr. Brian Cistola 845-353-1433 (day/eve) or 201-391-6233 (day).

Rainbows Peer Support Group *Professionally-run.* Peer support for children (ages 4 - teens) who experienced a family loss because of separation, divorce, death or abandonment. Goals are to provide peer support, furnish an understanding of the grief experience, assist in building a stronger sense of self-esteem and teach appropriate coping mechanisms. Parents' group meets concurrently. Meets Tues., 7-8pm (Sept.-Dec.) and Wed., 7-8pm (Jan.-Apr.), Ridgewood YMCA, 112 Oak St., Ridgewood. Registration required. Call Kathy Meding 201-444-5600 ext. 332 (day). For any other new group sessions planned, call regional representative, Alice Forsyth 908-608-0888 (day). *E-mail:* kmeding@ridgewoodym.org

Separated, Divorced and Bereaved Catholics Referrals to groups for emotional/spiritual support and social activities for separated, divorced or bereaved men and women. Groups are sponsored by various churches throughout the county and are open to people of any faith. For information call Family Life Ministry, Newark Archdiocese 973-497-4327.

BURLINGTON

Initial Care/Divorce Recovery Support Group *Professionally-run.* Christian-based psychoeducation and support group for persons going through divorce. Open to people of any faith. Facilitators have gone through divorce. Rap sessions. Meets Wed., 7:30-9pm, Fellowship Alliance Chapel, 199 Church Rd., Room C-9, Medford. Call Rev. Ed Stiegel 609-953-7333 (day).

Separated and Divorced Catholics Mutual support for separated or divorced men and women. Open to people of any faith. Various meeting locations and times. See group listings and contacts online at: http://www.dioceseoftrenton.org/church/consolation.asp (scroll down to "Support Groups for Separated and Divorced") or call Office of Family Life, Trenton Diocese 609-406-7400 ext. 5557 (day).

CAMDEN

Grief Management of St. Rose of Lima Mutual support for anyone grieving the loss of a significant person in their life due to death, separation or divorce. Families welcome. Meets Thurs. (for 12 week sessions), 7:30-9:30pm, St. Rose of Lima, 300 Kings Highway, Parish Lounge, Haddon Heights. Before attending call Sister Eucharista Johnson 856-310-1770. *Website:* http://www.strosenj.com

CUMBERLAND

DivorceCare Christian support group that helps in recovery from separation and divorce. Sharing of experiences, video showings, education, guest speakers and phone help. Meets Thurs., 6:30-7:45pm, Vineland Nazarene Church, 2725 North Delsea Dr., Vineland. Call Sandy Bohren 856-697-4945 (day/eve). *Website:* http://www.vinelandnaz.com

ESSEX

Rainbows, Inc. *Professionally-run.* Peer support for children and adolescents (kindergarten - eighth grade) who are grieving a loss due to death, divorce or abandonment. For any other new group session planned call the regional representative, Alice Forsyth 908-608-0888 (day).

Livingston Meets Mon., 5:30-6:30pm, Linda and Rudy Slucker Center for Women, 513 West Mt. Pleasant Ave. Call 973-994-4994 (day). *Website:* http://www.centerforwomennj.org *E-mail:* centerforwomen@jwessex.org

Verona Meets Mon., (Spring and Fall; 7 week sessions), First Presbyterian Church, 10 Fairview Ave. Call Barbara 973-857-0626 (day).

Separated, Divorced and Bereaved Catholics *Professionally-run.* Emotional and spiritual support for separated, divorced or bereaved men and women. Groups are held at various churches throughout the diocese and are open to people of any faith. For information call Family Life Ministry, Newark Archdiocese 973-497-4327.

Women Coping with Separation and Divorce Support for women coping with separation and divorce. Groups start periodically and run for 6 weeks. Registration fee $45. Meets at Linda and Rudy Slucker NCJW Center for Women, Livingston. Call Project GRO 973-994-4994 (day). *Website:* http://www.centerforwomennj.org *E-mail:* centerforwomen@ncjwessex.org

GLOUCESTER

Banana Splits Children's Divorce Group *(WASHINGTON TOWNSHIP RESIDENTS ONLY)* Support for children going through the separation or divorce of their parents. Call 856-589-6446 (day).

Center for People in Transition *Professionally-run.* Assists displaced homemakers to become emotionally and economically self-sufficient through life skills training, career decision making, education or vocational training and supportive services. Evening divorce and bereavement support groups open to men and women. For information call 856-415-2222 (Mon.-Fri.). *E-mail:* peopleintransition@gccnj.edu

Single Again Support and Recovery Group *Professionally-run.* Christian support, encouragement and healing for those separated, in the process of divorce and/or trying to transition from being part of a couple to single life. Families and friends welcome. Education and buddy system. Meets Thurs., 7pm, St. John's United Methodist Church, 149 Ganttown Rd., Turnersville. Call Nancy 856-589-2208 (eve).

HUDSON

Rainbows, Inc. *Professionally-run.* Peer support for children and adolescents (kindergarten - eighth grade) who are grieving a loss due to death, divorce or abandonment. Parent group meets concurrently. Meets Thurs., 7-8pm (Oct.-Dec.), St. Anne's School, Parish Center, Jersey City. Call Sister Alberta 201-656-2490. For any other new group sessions planned, call the regional representative, Alice Forsyth 908-608-0888 (day). *Website:* http://www.stanncsjc.com

Separated, Divorced and Bereaved Catholics *Professionally-run.* Emotional and spiritual support for separated, divorced or bereaved men and women. Groups are sponsored by various churches throughout the county and are open to people of any faith. For information call Family Life Ministry, Newark Archdiocese 973-497-4327.

HUNTERDON

Separated and Divorced Catholics Mutual support and social events for separated or divorced men and women. Open to people of any faith. Various meeting times and locations. For information call the Office of Family Life, Metuchen Diocese 732-562-1990 ext. 1624 (day).

MERCER

Divorce Recovery Program *Professionally-run.* Support and education seminar for separated or divorced persons. Support group meets 1st and 4th Fri., 7:30pm; seminar meets 2nd Fri., 7:30pm, Princeton Church of Christ, 33 River Rd., Princeton. Call Phyllis Rich 609-581-3889 (eve). *Website:* http://www.princetonchurchofchrist.com/divorcerecovery.shtml *E-mail:* divorcerecovery@softhome.net

Separated and Divorced Catholics Mutual support for separated or divorced men and women. Open to people of any faith. Various meeting locations and times. See group listings and contacts online at: http://www.dioceseoftrenton.org/church/consolation.asp (scroll down to "Support Groups for Separated and Divorced") or call Office of Family Life 609-406-7400 ext. 5557 (day).

Separated and Divorced Support Group Helps people through the pain and trauma of separation and divorce to grow into well-adjusted, self-sufficient, whole single people. Encourages sharing and support among members with an end towards friendship (not for singles seeking dates). Meets Thurs., 7:30-9:30pm, Hopewell Presbyterian Church, 80 W. Broad St., Hopewell. Call 609-466-0758 ext. 1 (day).

MIDDLESEX

CONCORDS Mutual support for divorced and separated people. Literature. Meets 2nd Wed. (except July/Aug.), 8pm, Our Lady of Fatima Roman Catholic Church, 501 New Market Rd., Rectory Meeting Room #2, Piscataway. Call Mel 732-926-1963 (day/eve) or Lucy 732-968-4093.

Passages Support for separated or divorced persons to help them regain self-esteem, confidence and the ability to go on with their lives. Donation $3 per mtg. Rap session, guest speakers and social group. Meets Tues., 7:30-9:30pm, St. Peter's Episcopal Church, 505 Main St., Spotswood. Call Robin 732-238-7822 (eve) or Alan 732-828-5880 (day/eve). *Website:* http://www.passagesnj.com *E-mail:* passages@excite.com

Separated and Divorced Catholics Mutual support for recently separated or divorced men and women. Open to people of any faith. Various meeting times and locations. For information call the Family Life Office, Metuchen Diocese 732-562-1990 ext. 1624 (day).

MONMOUTH

Separated / Divorced / Widows and Widowers Support Group Support for persons who have lost their spouse due to separation, divorce or death (past the bereavement stage) to help members get on with their lives. Not for crisis situations. Not intended as a social group. Meets Tues., 7:30pm, St. Veronica's Rectory Cellar, Route 9 North, Howell. Call Ree 732-431-0446 or Cookie 732-577-6964 (day). *Website:* http://www.divorceheadquarters.com *E-mail:* Reegroup@aol.com

Separated and Divorced Catholics Mutual support for separated or divorced men and women. Open to people of any faith. Various meeting locations and times. See group listings and contacts online at: http://www.dioceseoftrenton.org/church/consolation.asp (scroll down to "Support Groups for Separated and Divorced") or call Office of Family Life, Trenton Diocese 609-406-7400 ext. 5557 (day).

Transitions Support for persons in all stages of separation and divorce to provide comfort, support and recovery. Rap sessions. Meets Tues., 7:30-8:45pm, Monmouth County Library, 125 Symmes Dr., Manalapan. Call David Nasoff 732-888-4440 (day/eve).

Women's Support Group Helps women who are displaced homemakers (facing the loss of their primary source of income due to separation, divorce, disability or death of spouse). Issues addressed include self-sufficiency, career development, assertiveness, self-esteem, divorce, separation, widowhood and other related topics. Groups are set-up as needed in Asbury Park, Long Branch, West Keansburg and Lincroft. Call Robin Vogel 732-495-4496 (day) or Mary Ann O'Brien 732-229-8675.

MORRIS

Crossroads Support for separated and divorced persons. Open to anyone who has experienced the pain of a broken marriage. Meets Sun., 7-8:30pm, St. Peter the Apostle Church, Convent, 189 Baldwin Rd., Parsippany. Call Nick DelMedico 973-334-8373 (eve). *E-mail:* ndmedico@yahoo.com

Rainbows and Prism Peer support for children and adolescents (kindergarten - eighth grade) who are grieving the loss of a parent due to death or divorce. Parent group meets concurrently. Meets Tues., 7:15-8pm (Sept.-Jan.), Our Lady of Magnificent, 2 Miller Rd., Kinnelon. Call Claudette Meehan 973-492-9406 (eve) or Peggy Tana 973-838-7265. For any upcoming group sessions planned call Alice Forsyth 908-608-0888 (day).

Rainbows, Inc. *Professionally-run.* Peer support for children and adolescents (kindergarten - eighth grade) who are grieving a loss due to death, divorce or abandonment. Group runs for 14 weeks in winter; and 7 weeks in summer. Meets Tues., 7-7:45pm, St. Francis Residential Community, 122 Diamond Spring Rd., Denville. Before attending call Diane 973-627-2134 (day/eve). For any other new group sessions planned, call the regional representative, Alice Forsyth 908-608-0888 (day).

Separation, Divorce, and Bereavement Support Group Emotional and spiritual support for men and women in all stages of separation, divorce, bereavement and other emotional pain. Phone help, pen pals and buddy system. Meets Thurs., 6:30pm, Morris County Library, 30 E. Hanover Ave., Whippany. Call Laura 973-581-1636 (day/eve) or Eric 201-247-6582 (day/eve).

OCEAN

DivorceCare Support Group Christian support group for those going through separation or divorce. Video showings followed by discussion. Meets Mon., 7-9pm, (13 week sessions, 2 times year), Shore Vineyard Church, 320 Compass Ave., Beachwood. Call 732-244-3888. *E-mail:* shorevineyard@comcast.net

Kids and Divorce Support Group *Professionally-run.* Support for children (ages 7-12) who have experienced a separation or divorce in their family. Rap sessions. Meets 2nd Thurs., 5:30-6:30pm, Center for Kids and Family, 591 Lakehurst Rd., Toms River. Call 732-505-5437 (day).

Separated and Divorced Catholics Mutual support for separated or divorced men and women. Open to people of any faith. Various meeting locations and times. See group listings and contacts online at: http://www.dioceseoftrenton.org/church/consolation.asp (scroll down to "Support Groups for Separated and Divorced") or call Office of Family Life, Trenton Diocese 609-406-7400 ext. 5557 (day).

St. Barnabas Ministry to Separated/Divorced and Remarried Catholics Provides a safe haven for people who are separated, divorced or after a civil divorce. Provides a confidential informal setting where adults can engage in peer-to-peer discussions. Meets Thurs., 7:15-8:45pm, St. Barnabas Church, Father Rucki Hall, Room 8, Bayville. Call Mary Alice Laird 732-269-2020 (eve) or Deacon Michael Taylor 732-269-2208 (day). *E-mail:* deaconmike@stbarnabasbayville.com or marala2020@aol.com

PASSAIC

Circle of Friendship Mutual support for those who are separated and divorced. Phone help, social and guest speakers. Meets Thurs., 7:30pm, St. Mary's School, Conference Room, 17 Pompton Ave., Pompton Lakes. Call Christine Scott 973-335-9880, Donna White 973-831-8825 or church 973-835-0374.

Separation and Divorce Support Group Mutual support and education to help women through the emotional, legal, financial and family issues which arise during the divorce process. Meetings vary, Women In Transition, 1022 Hamburg Turnpike, Wayne. Before attending call Kate McAteer 973-694-9215 (day).

SOMERSET

JANUS Bereavement Group *Professionally-run.* Support and education for anyone who has experienced a loss such as a separation/divorce, death, retirement, loss of a job, health or relocation. Helps individuals accept and adjust to the loss. Meets 2nd Tues., 7:30-9pm, in Bridgewater and Branchburg. Call Barbara Ronca, LCSW 908-218-9062 (Mon.-Fri., 9am-3pm).

M.A.S.H. Group for Separated and Divorced Men and Women Support, education and discussion. Social activities between meetings. Donation $3/mtg. Meets Mon., 7:30-9pm, St. Luke's Roman Catholic Church, 300 Clinton Ave., North Plainfield. Call 908-889-7243 or 732-548-6580. *E-mail:* passages@excite.com

Separated and Divorced Catholics Mutual support and social events for separated or divorced men and women. Open to people of any faith. Various meeting times and locations. For information call the Office of Family Life, Metuchen Diocese 732-562-1990 ext. 1624 (day).

Single Senior Women Support for women (age 60+) who are divorced, separated, widowed, never married or who have a spouse who is ill. Recreational activities. Meets 2nd and 4th Thurs., 10am-noon, Office on Aging, 92 East Main St., 1st Floor, Conference Room, Somerville. Call Erin 908-704-6339 (day).

SUSSEX

Separated and Divorced Support Group *Professionally-run.* Support, discussion and encouragement for separated and divorced people. Donation $5. Meets Wed., 7:30-9:30pm, Partnership for Social Services, 48 Wyker Rd., Franklin. Call 973-827-4702. *Website:* http://www.partnershipforsocialservice.org *E-mail:* psocsert@warwick.net

UNION

DivorceCare *Professionally-run.* Christian support group for persons recovering from a separation or divorce. Offers video program and mutual sharing. Meets Tues., 7:30-9pm (11 week sessions, several times a year), Presbyterian Church, New Providence. Call Colleen 908-665-0050. *Website:* http://www.pcnp.org *E-mail:* fletcher@pcnp.org

Separated, Divorced and Bereaved Catholics *Professionally-run.* Emotional and spiritual support for separated, divorced or bereaved men and women. Groups are sponsored by various churches throughout the county and are open to people of any faith. For information call Family Life Ministry, Newark Archdiocese 973-497-4327.

WARREN

Separated and Divorced Catholics Mutual support and social events for separated or divorced men and women. Open to people of any faith. Various meeting times and locations. For information call the Office of Family Life, Metuchen Diocese 732-562-1990 ext. 1624 (day).

NATIONAL

ACES (Association for Children for Enforcement of Support) *National. 400 affiliated groups. Founded 1984.* Information and support for parents who have custody of their children and have difficulty collecting child support payments. Location service on non-payers. Assistance in starting local support groups. Newsletter, information and referrals. Write: ACES, P.O. Box 7842, Fredericksburg, VA 22404. Call 1-800-738-2237; Fax: 540-582-3386. *Website:* http://www.childsupport-aces.org *E-mail:* aces@childsupport-aces.org

Beginning Experience *International. 112 teams. Founded 1974.* Support programs for divorced, widowed, separated adults and their children enabling them to work through the grief of a lost marriage. Write: The Beginning Experience, c/o International Ministry Center, 1657 Commerce Dr., South Bend, IN 46628. Call 574-283-2079 or 1-866-610-8877; Fax: 574-283-0287. *Website:* http://www.beginningexperience.org *E-mail:* jan@beginningexperience.org

Children's Rights Council *International. 53 chapters in 37 states, 8 countries. Founded 1985.* Concerned parents provide education and advocacy for reform of the legal system regarding child custody. Offers help with visitation, mediation, custody and support groups. Newsletter, information and referrals, directory of parenting organizations, neutral drop-off and pick-up centers for children and supervised access in various states, catalog of resources, conferences and group development guidelines. Write: CRC, c/o David L. Levy, CEO, 6200 Editors Park Drive, Hyattsville, MD 20782-4900. Call 301-559-3120; Fax: 301-559-3124. *Website:* http://www.gocrc.com *E-mail:* crcdc@erols.com

DivorceCare *International. 9000+ affiliated groups. Founded 1993.* Network of Christian support groups, often run for 13 week sessions, to help people recover from separation or divorce. Videos are shown at meetings, followed by group discussion and members' use of workbooks. Write: DivorceCare, 250 S. Allen Rd., P.O. Box 1739, Wake Forest, NC 27588. Call 1-800-489-7778; Fax: 919-562-2114. *Website:* http://www.divorcecare.org *E-mail:* info@divorcecare.org

EX-POSE (Ex-Partners Of Servicemembers for Equality) *National membership. Founded 1981.* Disseminates information concerning military divorce. Lawyer referral. Quarterly newsletter. Membership dues $20. Offers list of questions to ask an attorney during the attorney selection process. Write: EX-POSE, P.O. Box 11191, Alexandria, VA 22312. Call 703-941-5844 (Mon.-Fri., 11am-3pm EST). *Website:* http://ex-pose.org *E-mail:* ex-pose@juno.com

Grandparents Rights Organization *National. Founded 1984.* Advocates and educates on behalf of grandparent-grandchild relationships, primarily with respect to grandparent visits. Assists in the formation of local support groups dealing with the denial of grandparent visitation by custodial parent or guardian. Newsletter, conferences, information and referrals. Donations $40/yr. Write: Grandparents Rights Organization, 100 W. Long Lake Rd., Suite 250, Bloomfield Hills, MI 48304. Call 248-646-7191 (day); Fax: 248-646-9722. *Website:* http://www.grandparentsrights.org *E-mail:* RSVlaw@aol.com

Joint Custody Association *International network. Founded 1979.* Assists divorcing parents and their families to achieve joint custody. Disseminates information concerning family law research and judicial decisions. Advocates for legislative improvement of family law in state capitals. Referrals to local self-help groups. Write: Joint Custody Association, c/o James A. Cook, 10606 Wilkins Ave., Los Angeles, CA 90024. Call 310-475-5352; Fax: 310-475-6541. *Website:* http://www.jointcustody.org

North American Conference of Separated and Divorced Catholics *International. 3000+ groups. Founded 1974.* Religious, educational and emotional aspects of separation, divorce, remarriage and widowhood are addressed through self-help groups, conferences and training programs. Families of all faiths are welcome. Group development guidelines. Newsletter. Membership dues starting at $35 (includes newsletter, discounts and resources). Write: NACSDC, P.O. Box 10, Hancock, MI 49930. Call 906-482-0494; Fax: 906-482-7470. *Website:* http://www.nacsdc.org *E-mail:* office@nacsdc.org

RAINBOWS *International. 8300 affiliated groups. Founded 1983.* Establishes peer support groups in churches, schools or social agencies for children and adults who are grieving a death, divorce or other painful transition in their family. Groups are led by trained adults. Online newsletter, information and referrals. Write: RAINBOWS, 2100 Golf Rd., Suite 370, Rolling Meadows, IL 60008-4231. Call 1-800-266-3206 or 847-952-1770; Fax: 847-952-1774. *Website:* http://www.rainbows.org *E-mail:* info@rainbows.org

SINGLE PARENTING

(see also parenting, divorce/separation and widows/widowers)

STATEWIDE

Parents Without Partners Devoted to the interests and welfare of single parents over 18 and their children. Provides recreational, educational and social activities. Rap sessions. Membership dues $25-40/yr. 18 chapters throughout NJ. Call 1-800-637-7974 (day). *Website:* http://www.parentswithoutpartners.org

ATLANTIC

Parents Without Partners Devoted to the interests and welfare of single parents over 18 and their children. Provides recreational, educational and social activities. Rap sessions, guest speakers and phone help. Membership dues $40/yr. Meets 2nd Fri., 8:30pm, VFW, Bethel Rd., Somers Point. Call 609-653-7000 (day/eve). *Website:* http://www.pwp181.00go.com/homepage.htm

BERGEN

Parents Without Partners Mutual support for single parents. Provides educational, social and recreational activities.

Oakland Membership $33/yr. Dues $8 mtg/members; $10 mtg/guests. Meets 2nd and 4th Sat., orientation 7:00pm, meeting 7:30pm, American Legion Hall, Oak St. Call Betty McKenzie 973-831-1535 (9am-8pm).

Paramus (*Chapter #962)* Dues $35/yr. Members $6/mtg. and guests $10/mtg. Meets Thurs., 7:30pm orientation, 8pm meeting, Elks Club, Route 17 North. Call Amy 201-641-1116. *Website:* http://www.pwp962.org

Park Ridge (*Pascack Valley Chapter)* Dues $30/yr. Meets Sun., 7pm, Park Ridge Elks Club, Sulak Lane. Call 201-573-9510.

ESSEX

Women Parenting Alone Mutual support for single mothers. Group starts periodically and runs for 6 weeks. Registration fee $45. Meets at Linda and Rudy Slucker NCJW Center for Women, 513 W. Mount Pleasant Ave., Suite 325, Livingston. Call Project GRO 973-994-4994. *Website:* http://www.centerforwomennj.org *E-mail:* centerforwomen@ncjwessex.org

GLOUCESTER

Single Parents Society Devoted to the interests and welfare of single parents and their children. Various events scheduled throughout the year. Open to parents who are separated, divorced, widowed or never married. Dues $25/yr. Meetings $7/members; $8/guests. Newsletter. Meets Fri., 8:30pm, American Legion Post, Clayton. Call Fran 856-845-6810 (day). *Website:* http://www.singleparentsoc.com *E-mail:* marynzub@zoominternet.net

MORRIS

Parents Without Partners Mutual support and education for single parents. Provides recreational, educational and social activities for single parents and their children. Dues $40/yr. All children's activities are subsidized. Meets 2nd and 4th Sat., various meeting locations and times. For more information call Parents Without Partners 973-539-5523. *Website:* http://www.parentswithoutpartners.org

SOMERSET

Parents Without Partners - Chapter #236 Mutual support for single parents and their children. Provides educational, social and recreational activities for children and adults. Rap sessions, guest speakers and phone help. Dues $45/yr. Meets 1st Sun., 2:30pm, Hillsborough Municipal Complex, 379 South Branch Rd., Hillsborough. Call 908-393-2006.

SUSSEX

Project Self-Sufficiency *Professionally-run.* Support for single parents, teen parents, displaced homemakers and low-income families. Offers peer support groups for single parents and teen parents, loss recovery groups for children, parenting skills training and support, family activities, physical and emotional health educational seminars, comprehensive job training and educational services designed to promote self-sufficiency. Meetings vary. Call Deborah Berry-Toon 973-383-5129 (day). *E-mail:* PSS@garden.net

NATIONAL

National Organization of Single Mothers *National. 3 affiliated groups. Founded 1991.* Networking system helping single mothers meet the challenges of daily life with wisdom, dignity, confidence and courage. Information and referrals. Dues $15.97/yr. Assistance in starting new groups. Write: NOSM, P.O. Box 68, Midland, NC 28107. Call 704-888-5437. *Website:* http://www.singlemothers.org *E-mail*: info@singlemothers.org

Parents Without Partners *National. 225+ chapters/5 affiliates. Founded 1957.* Educational organization of single parents (either divorced, separated, widowed or never married). Online chat room, single parent magazine, chapter development guidelines and personal growth/self-help articles from various authors. Local chapter activities for families and parents only. Annual convention. Membership dues $30-50. Write: Parents Without Partners, 1650 S. Dixie Highway, Suite 510, Boca Raton, FL 33432. Call 1-800-637-7974 or 561-391-8833; Fax: 561-395-8557. *Website:* http://www.parentswithoutpartners.org

Single Mothers By Choice *National. 25 chapters. Founded 1981.* Support and information to mature single women, who have chosen or who are considering, single motherhood. "Thinkers" workshops, quarterly newsletter, brochure and list of back issues of newsletter available. Write: SMC, P.O. Box 1642 Gracie Square Station, New York, NY 10028. Call 212-988-0993. *Website:* http://www.singlemothersbychoice.com *E-mail:* smc-office@pipeline.com

Single Parent Resource Center *International. 7 affiliated groups. Founded 1975.* Support and discussion group for single fathers. Refers single parents to helpful programs in New York City and nationwide, assists new single parent organizations informing, offers skills-building workshops, a relapse-prevention program for single parents in recovery from substance abuse and a family reunification program for children and parents in the first year after incarceration. Write: Single Parent Resource Center, 228 East 45th St., 2nd Floor, New York, NY, 10017. Call 212-951-7030; Fax: 212-951-7037. *Website:* http://www.singleparentusa.com

STEPFAMILIES

MERCER

Stepfamily Support Group Emotional support and encouragement for persons in stepfamily situations. Group usually meets one Sat. per month, Hickory Corner Library, East Windsor. For information call Lisa 609-448-8823.

ONLINE

StepTogether *Online. Founded 1998.* Provides virtual support for stepfamilies through moderated message board and scheduled real-time chat meetings. *Website:* http://www.steptogether.org *E-mail:* steptogether@steptogether.org

"HE DREW A CIRCLE THAT SHUT ME OUT –
HERETIC, REBEL, A THING TO FLOUT.
BUT LOVE AND I HAD A WILL TO WIN;
WE DREW A CIRCLE THAT TOOK HIM IN."
-- Edwin Markham

PRIORITIES

A philosophy professor stood before his class and had some items in front of him. When the class began, wordlessly he picked up a large empty mayonnaise jar and proceeded to fill it with rocks right to the top, rocks about 2" in diameter. He then asked the students if the jar was full. They agreed it was.

So the professor then picked up a box of pebbles and poured them into the jar. He shook it lightly. The pebbles of course, rolled into the empty area between the rocks. The students laughed. He asked his students if the jar was full. They agreed it was. The professor then picked up a box of sand and poured it into the jar. Of course, the sand filled up everything else. "Now," said the professor, "I want you to recognize that this is your life. The rocks are the important things: your family, your partner, your health, your children and anything that is so important to you that if it were lost, you would be nearly destroyed.

The pebbles are the other things in life that matter, but on a smaller scale. The pebbles represent your job, your house and your car. The sand is everything else. The small stuff. If you put sand or the pebbles in the jar first, there would be no room for the rocks. The same goes for your life. If you spend all your energy and time on the small stuff, material things, you will never have room for the things that are truly important."

Pay attention to the things that are critical in your life.
Play with your children.
Take your partner out dancing.
There will always be time to go to work, clean the house, give a dinner party and fix the disposal.
Take care of the rocks first, the things that really matter.
SET YOUR PRIORITIES.
"The rest is just pebbles and sand."

--Author Unknown

HEALTH

AIDS / HIV INFECTION

(see also toll-free helplines)

STATEWIDE

AIDS Coalition of Southern New Jersey *Professionally-run.* To ensure the quality of care and continuity of vital resources for persons affected by AIDS/HIV. Provides support groups, direct services and education. Newsletter, speaker's bureau, phone help and guest speakers. Serves Burlington, Camden, Gloucester and Salem counties. Write: AIDS Coalition of Southern NJ, 100 Essex Ave., Suite 300, Bellmawr, NJ 08031. Call 856-933-9500 (day). *Website*: http://www.acsnj.org

Hyacinth AIDS Foundation Support groups and information for anyone affected by AIDS or HIV+ (patients, families, partners, friends). Provides support groups, advocacy, legal services, public education and training, short-term emergency services and hotline. All services are confidential. Serves Northern and Central NJ. Write: Hyacinth AIDS Foundation, 317 George St., Suite 203, New Brunswick, NJ 08901. For information call 1-800-433-0254 (9am-7pm) or Admin. 732-246-0204 (day). *Website*: http://www.hyacinth.org *E-mail*: info@hyacinth.org

ATLANTIC

HIV Support Group *Professionally-run.* Support for persons with HIV. Families and friends welcome. Social group, literature and buddy system. Meets 3rd Mon., 5:30-7:30pm, Access One, 730 Shore Rd., Somers Point. Call Michele Keenan 609-927-6662 ext. 14 (day). *E-mail*: HIVaccess@aol.com

South Jersey A.I.D.S. Alliance *Professionally-run.* Support, education and information for anyone affected by AIDS (patients, families, partners, friends). Buddy system. Support centers in Atlantic City 609-347-1085, Bridgeton 856-455-5125, Cape May County 609-523-0024 or Hotline 1-800-281-2437. *Website*: http://www.southjerseyaidsalliance.org

BERGEN

AIDS Interfaith Network Networking and support for clergy and laypersons of any age on the issue of AIDS. Meetings vary, Ridgewood. Call Rev. Jan Philips 201-670-1610 (day).

Double Jeopardy Peer Support Group *Professionally-run.* Emotional support and information for men and women who have HIV/HCV and substance abuse issues. Meets Thurs., 6:30-8pm, Buddies of New Jersey, 149 Hudson St., Hackensack. Call Susan 201-489-2900 (10am-6pm).

New Jersey Buddies *Professionally-run.* Provides support and education to people infected with or affected by HIV/AIDS. Support groups for HIV positive women, gay men, men and women and substance abusers, as well as a group for those who have engaged in risky activities, but have not been tested. Meetings held at Buddies of New Jersey, 149 Hudson St., Hackensack. Call 201-489-2900 (9am-5pm). *Website*: http://www.njbuddies.org *E-mail*: njbuddies@aol.com

S.E.L.F. (Support, Education, Learning, Friendship) Mutual support and education for HIV+ gay men. Rap sessions and guest speakers. Meets Mon., 7-8:30pm, Buddies of New Jersey, Inc., 151 B Hudson St., Hackensack. Call Steve Scheuermann 201-489-2900 (day). *E-mail*: njbuddies@aol.com

CAPE MAY

South Jersey A.I.D.S. Alliance *Professionally-run.* Support, education and information for anyone affected by AIDS (patients, families, partners, friends) and prevention case management. Buddy system. Support centers in Atlantic City 609-347-1085, Bridgeton 856-455-5125, Cape May County 609-523-0024 or Hotline 1-800-281-2437. *Website*: http://www.southjerseyaidsalliance.org

CUMBERLAND

South Jersey A.I.D.S. Alliance *Professionally-run.* Support, education and information for anyone affected by AIDS (patients, families, partners, friends) and prevention case management. Buddy system. Support center in Atlantic City 609-347-1085, Bridgeton 856-455-5125, Cape May County 609-523-0024 or Hotline 1-800-281-2437. *Website*: http://www.southjerseyaidsalliance.org

ESSEX

Double Trouble *Professionally-run.* Support for HIV+ persons who are also substance abusers. Group meets Wed., noon-2pm, North Jersey Community Research Initiative, 393 Central Ave., 2nd Floor, Newark. Call 973-483-3444. *Website*: http://www.njcri.org

Gay Men's HIV+ Support Group *Professionally-run.* Support group for gay men who are HIV+. Provides support, information and newsletter. Meets Thurs.,

2:30-4:30pm, North Jersey Community Research Initiative, 393 Central Ave., 2nd Floor, Newark. Call 973-483-3444.

HIV Support Group *(SPANISH SPEAKING) Professionally-run.* Support for men and women who have HIV. Meets every other Thurs., noon-2pm, North Jersey Community Research Initiative, 393 Central Ave., 2nd Floor, Newark. Lunch provided. Call 973-483-3444 (day).

Men's HIV+ Support Group *Professionally-run.* Offers support for men who are HIV+. Meets Tues., noon-2pm, 393 Central Ave., 2nd Floor, Newark. Lunch provided. Call Christopher Wilson 973-483-3444 (day).

New Hope Baptist Church HIV/AIDS Support Ministry *Professionally-run.* Mutual support for persons diagnosed with AIDS, their caregivers, families, and friends. Rap sessions and guest speakers. Provides information on new medications. Meetings vary, New Hope Baptist Church, 144 Norman St., East Orange. Call Sister Mary Frazier 973-675-5174, Gary Haith 973-375-2768 (eve) or church 973-678-6710.

Our Other Place *Professionally-run.* Offers support for persons infected and affected by HIV/AIDS in a safe, confidential environment. Under 18 welcome. Meets Thurs., 7-9pm, Verona. Before attending call Ilene Palent, COPE Center 973-783-6655.

Our Place *Professionally-run.* Provides a safe and confidential environment to offer support for persons infected with the HIV virus, their loved ones and caregivers. Meets Tues. evenings in Montclair. For meeting information call Ilene Palent, COPE Center 973-783-6655. *Website*: http://www.copecenter.net *E-mail*: info@copecenter.net

Women's HIV+ Support Group *Professionally-run.* Support for women who are HIV+. Meets Fri., noon-2pm, North Jersey Community Research Initiative, 2nd Floor, Newark. Guests welcome. Lunch provided. Call 973-483-3444 (day). *Website*: http://www.njcri.org

HUDSON

Hyacinth Foundation Support Group Mutual support for anyone infected/affected by AIDS or HIV+. Patients, families, friends and partners welcome. Meets Thurs., 6:30-8:30pm, Hyacinth AIDS Foundation, 880 Bergen Ave., Suite 102, Jersey City. Call 201-432-1134 or Hyacinth Foundation 1-800-433-0254 (10am-6pm). *Website*: http://www.hyacinth.org

Hyacinth Foundation Support Group Mutual support for persons who are infected with AIDS or HIV+. Wellness Community meets Wed. and Thurs., 1-3:30pm and Treatment support group meets Tues., 4-6pm, Men's Wellness group meets 2nd and 3rd Thurs., 4-6pm, 82 Summit Ave., Jersey City. Call 201-432-1134 or the Hyacinth Foundation 1-800-433-0254 (10am-6pm). *Website*: http://www.hyacinth.org

Living Beyond HIV (GAY MALE HUDSON COUNTY RESIDENTS ONLY) *Professionally-run.* Mutual support for gay men who are HIV+. Rap sessions, guest speakers, literature and buddy system. Meets Thurs., 7-9pm, Jersey City. Call 201-963-4779.

MIDDLESEX

HIV Infected/Affected Group *Professionally-run.* Mutual support and education for persons infected or affected by HIV. Rap sessions and literature. Meets Mon., 6-8pm, Raritan Bay Medical Center, 530 New Brunswick Ave., Perth Amboy. Before attending call Sandra Nilsson, Early Intervention Program 732-324-5022.

Support Group for HIV+ Gay Men *Professionally-run.* Support for gay men who are HIV+. Rap sessions. Meets 3rd Tues., 6-7:30pm, E.B. Chandler Health Center, 277 George St., New Brunswick. Call Chas White 908-595-2674 (day).

MONMOUTH

HIV Support Group Mutual support for individuals infected/affected by HIV/AIDS. Family and friends welcome. Guest speakers. Meets Thurs., 6-8pm, Riverview Medical Center, Jane Booker Building, 2nd Floor, Red Bank. Call Elise Millea 732-450-2863.

Positive and Beautiful *Professionally-run.* Support for women diagnosed HIV positive. Meets 1st and 3rd Tues., 11am, Monmouth Medical Center, Alexander Pavilion, Long Branch. Call Xiomara Pino, CSW 732-923-7138.

MORRIS

Gay Men's Support Group *Professionally-run.* Provides emotional support for gay men who are HIV+ or have AIDS. Under 18 welcome. Meets Wed., 7-8:30pm, Hope House, 19-21 Belmont Ave., Dover. Call Allison Sisko 973-361-5565 ext. 151 (day). *Website*: http://www.hopehousenj.org

HIV Support Group *Professionally-run.* Offers support for men and women with HIV+/AIDS. Meets Wed., 6-7:30pm, Hope House, 19-21 Belmont Ave., Dover. Call Allison Sisko 973-361-5565 ext. 151 (day).

OCEAN

HIV / AIDS Infected/Affected Group *Professionally-run.* Support to persons who are infected or affected by HIV/AIDS. Members build a support network and share knowledge. Guest speakers and literature. Meets Tues., 7-8pm, Ocean County Department of Health, 175 Sunset Ave., Toms River. Call Patricia Brown 732-341-9700 ext. 7603, Anne McBride 732-341-9700 ext. 7633 (day) or TDD: 1-800-852-7899. *E-mail*: amcbride@ochd.org

PASSAIC

HIV / AIDS Support Group (*BILINGUAL*) *Professionally-run.* Mutual support and education for adult persons with HIV/AIDS and their family members. Case management, massage therapy and grocery vouchers. Meetings vary, Paterson Division of Health, 176 Broadway, Paterson. Call Robert or Paul 973-321-1277 ext. 2732 (day).

SOMERSET

Ryan White Support Group *Professionally-run.* Provides support and education for those affected by HIV disease. Guest speakers. Meets 1st and 3rd Thurs., 6-8pm, Somerset Medical Center, 110 Rehill Ave., Conference Room A and B, Somerville. Call 908-685-2814 (day).

Somerset Treatment Services Activity Group Mutual support for anyone living with HIV/AIDS. Dinner discussion group with hot meal provided. Meets Wed., 5:30-8pm, Somerset Treatment Services, 118 W. End Ave., Somerville. Call Grace Wosu 908-722-1232 ext. 3015 (day).

NATIONAL

National Association of People With A.I.D.S. *National. Founded 1986.* Network of persons with AIDS. Sharing of information and collective voice for health, social and political concerns. Phone, mail and electronics network, speakers bureau, quarterly newsletter and free publications. Write: NAPWA, 8401 Colesville Rd., Suite 750, Silver Spring, MD 20910. Call 240-247-0880 (day); Fax: 240-247-0574. *Website*: http://www.napwa.org *E-mail*: info@napwa.org

One Day At A Time *Model. 10 affiliated groups in Pennsylvania. Founded 1987.* To help people with HIV infection become aware of and make use of services provided. To encourage self-empowerment by providing a source of support given by other HIV+ people. Also provides drug and alcohol addiction and homeless shelter services, community outreach, prevention and education. Newsletter and group development assistance. Write: One Day At A Time, 2532 North Broad St., Philadelphia, PA 19132. Call 215-226-7860; Fax: 215-226-7869. *Website*: http://www.odaat.us *E-mail*: info@odaat.us

ONLINE

HIV Anonymous *Online.* Provides support through message board and regularly scheduled chats. Newsletter and free informational packets containing information on starting local groups are available. Write: HIV Anonymous, Inc., 129 W. Canada, San Clemente, CA 96272. Call 949-264-4170 (hotline and general information). *Website*: http://www.hivanonymous.com *E-mail*: info@hivanonymous.com

ALLERGY

ESSEX

Allergy Asthma Support Group To help families manage issues regarding food allergies and asthma. Promotes awareness and education. Rap sessions, advocacy, guest speakers and literature. Dues $20/yr. Meetings vary, St. Barnabas Ambulatory Care Center, Livingston. Call Susan DiAnthony 973-514-1654 (eve) or Anna Fusaro 973-228-8919 (eve). *E-mail:* palkidz@aol.com

MERCER

Allergy Asthma Support Group Support and education for adults and parents of children with food allergies and asthma. Guest speakers and literature. Dues $20/yr. Meets 1st Wed., 7-9pm, Buckingham Place, 155 Raymond Rd., Princeton. Call Dina 732-821-0567. *E-mail:* bmwlaw123@aol.com

NATIONAL

Asthma and Allergy Foundation of America *National. 100+ affiliated groups and 10 chapters. Founded 1953.* Serves persons with asthma and allergic diseases through the support of research, advocacy patient and public education. Newsletter, support and education groups. Assistance in starting and maintaining groups. Books, videos and other educational resources. Write: AAFA, 1233 20th St. NW,

Suite 402, Washington, DC 20036. Call 1-800-727-8462 or 202-466-7643 (Mon.-Fri. 10am-3pm EST); Fax: 202-466-8940. *Website:* http://www.aafa.org *E-mail:* info@aafa.org

FAAN (Food Allergy Anaphylaxis Network) *National network. 30 groups. Founded 1991.* Mission is to increase public awareness about food allergies and anaphylaxis, provide advocacy, education and advance research on behalf of all those affected by food allergies and anaphylaxis, a severe life-threatening reaction that can result in hives, swelling, unconsciousness and possibly death. Information and referrals, conferences, literature, phone support, booklets, newsletters and educational videos. Guidelines available for starting a similar group. Write: The Food Allergy Anaphylaxis Network, 11781 Lee Jackson Highway, Suite 160, Fairfax, VA 22033. Call 1-800-929-4040 or 703-691-3179; Fax: 703-691-2713. *Website:* http://www.foodallergy.org *E-mail:* faan@foodallergy.org

ALZHEIMER'S DISEASE / DEMENTIA

(see also caregivers, toll-free helplines)

STATEWIDE

Alzheimer's Association Delaware Valley Chapter *Professionally-run.* Sponsors support groups for caregivers of persons with Alzheimer's and related dementias in Southern Jersey. Information, referrals, education, newsletter, advocacy, patient and family service programs. Serves Atlantic, Burlington, Camden, Cape May, Cumberland, Gloucester and Salem counties. Write: Alzheimer's Association, Delaware Valley Chapter, 3 Eves Dr., Suite 310, Marlton, NJ 08053. Call 856-797-1212 or 1-800-272-3900 (day). *Website*: http://www.alz-delawarevalley.org

Alzheimer's Association Greater NJ Chapter *Professionally-run.* Sponsors support groups throughout 14 counties in Greater NJ. Information and referral service, education, advocacy, patient and family service programs. Write: Alzheimer's Association, 400 Morris Ave., Suite 251, Denville, NJ 07834. Call Alzheimer's Helpline 1-800-883-1180 or 973-586-4300 (day). *Website*: http://www.alznj.org

ATLANTIC

Alzheimer's Caregivers Support Group *Professionally-run.* Offers support to families and caregivers coping with Alzheimer's disease. Guest speakers and literature. Meets 3rd Mon., 2pm, Herman Pogachefsky Senior Services Pavilion, 1102 Atlantic Ave., Atlantic City. Call Adrienne Epstein 609-345-5555 (day).

Alzheimer's Support Group *Professionally-run.* Support for anyone affected by someone with Alzheimer's. Rap sessions, guest speakers, literature and mutual sharing. Meets last Wed., 3:45pm, Brandall Estates, 432 Central Avenue, Linwood. Call Shannon Datig 609-926-5635 (day) or Eileen Bennett 609-926-4663 (day). *E-mail*: datigs@brandycare.com

BERGEN

Alzheimer's Association Family Support Group Support for caregivers of persons with Alzheimer's disease and related dementias. Group provides opportunity to share practical information, exchange community resources, solve problems and learn ways to cope with dementia-related issues. *Website*: http://www.alznj.org

Dumont Meets 3rd Wed., 7-8:30pm, Northern Valley Adult Day Health Center, 2 Park Ave. Call Rose Marie Dudas or Nancy Bortinger 201-384-7734.

New Milford Meets 4th Wed., 5:30-7:30pm, Wood Crest Center, 800 River Rd. Call Karen Angrist 201-358-3092.

Paramus Meets 1st Wed., 7-9pm, Bergen Regional Medical Center, Bldg. 14, Room E 007, 230 East Ridgewood Ave. Before attending call Fred Meyer 201-797-3421. *Website*: http://www.alz.org/gnj

Ramsey Meets 3rd Tues., 8pm, St. John's Episcopal Church, Main St. and Franklin Turnpike. Call Caregiver Helpline 1-800-883-1180.

Rockleigh Meets 1st Wed., 10am and 3rd Tues., 7pm, Gallen Adult Day Care Center, 10 Link Dr. Call Shelley Steiner 201-784-1414 ext. 5340.

Rutherford Meets 2nd Thurs., 1pm, 55 KIP Center, 55 KIP Ave. Call Caregiver Helpline 1-800-883-1180 (day).

Tenafly Meets 2nd Wed., 7:30pm and 4th Thurs., 11am, Adult Reach Center, 411 E. Clinton Ave. Call Vivian Green Korner 201-569-7900 ext. 461.

Westwood Meets 1st Wed., 7pm, Pascack Valley Hospital, 250 Old Hook Rd. Call Karen Angrist 201-358-3092.

Caregivers Family Support Group *Professionally-run.* Support for caregivers and family members of persons with Alzheimer's or related disorders. Meets 3rd Thurs., 1:30-3pm, Community Services Building, 327 E. Ridgewood Ave., Room 208, Paramus. Call first if requesting professional supervision on frail family member. Call Diana Shapiro 201-634-2822 (day).

BURLINGTON

Caregivers Support Group *Professionally-run.* Support for anyone caring for an individual with progressive supranuclear palsy, Alzheimer's or Parkinson's disease. Meets 1st Tues., 6:30-7:30pm, Care One at Evesham, 870 East Route 70, Marlton. Call Carol Solomon 856-985-1180 (day).

Families Who Are Hurting Mutual support and encouragement for families who are hurting due to an addiction of a loved one, loss of a spouse or for those caring for a loved one with dementia. Meets 1st Sat., 6pm, Rose of Sharon Lutheran Church, Route 528, Jacobstown. Call Bill Millet 609-758-2746.

CAMDEN

Alzheimer's Support Group - South Jersey *Professionally-run.* Support and information for families and friends of persons with Alzheimer's disease and related disorders. Meets 2nd Tues., 7:30-9:30pm, Cadbury Retirement Center, 2150 Route 38, Cherry Hill. Call 856-797-1212 (eve). *Website*: http://www.alz-delawarevalley.org *E-mail*: mary.washart@alz.org

Alzheimer's Support Group *Professionally-run.* Offers support to families and caregivers of dementia patients. Guest speakers, literature and phone help. Meets 1st Thurs., 7pm, Voorhees Center, 3001 Evesham Rd., Voorhees. Call Joan Cunningham 856-751-1600 (day).

Promise Alternative Care Support and information to Alzheimer's patients and their families. Guest speakers, literature and newsletter. Meets last Mon., (except July, Aug., Dec.), 7:30-9pm, Promise Alternative Care, 1149 Marlkress Rd., Cherry Hill. Call Kathy Licardo 856-751-4884 (day). *E-mail*: klicardo@comcast.net

Senior Care of Haddon Heights *Professionally-run.* Offers support for persons caring for someone with Alzheimer's. Guest speakers, education, advocacy and literature. Meets 3rd Tues., 6:30-7:30pm, Senior Care of Haddon Heights, 607 South Whitehorse Pike, Audubon. Call Kim Lahr 856-546-0005 (day).

CAPE MAY

Alzheimer's Caregiver Support Group of Cape May County Offers support for caregivers of those with Alzheimer's disease. Meets 2nd Tues., 10am-noon, Chapin House, 1042 Route 47, Rio Grande. Call Marie Giansante 609-884-7670 (day).

CUMBERLAND

Alzheimer's Support Group of Cumberland County Information, discussions and guest speakers for families and friends of persons with Alzheimer's disease and related disorders. Meets 3rd Thurs., 7pm, Genesis Elder Care, 54 Sharp St., Millville. Call Ray Gage 856-451-8383 (day).

ESSEX

Alzheimer's Association Family Support Group. Support for caregivers of persons with Alzheimer's disease. Provides opportunity to share practical information, exchange community resources, solve problems and learn new ways of coping with dementia.

East Orange Meets 4th Wed., 5pm, Good Life Adult Day Center, The Great Room, 515 North Arlington Ave. Call Grace Ann Kelly 973-674-2700 ext. 2276.

East Orange Meets 1st Tues., 7pm, St. Mark AME Church, 587 Springdale Ave. Call church office 973-674-5859.

Montclair *Professionally-run.* Meets 1st Tues., 2-3pm and 1st Mon., 7-9pm, Senior Care Activities Center, 46 Park St. Call Fran Moravick 973-783-5589 (day). *Website*: http://www.Sencare.org

Newark Meets 3rd Wed., 4:30pm, Newark Beth Israel, 156 Lyons Ave. Call Sara Thompson 973-926-7489 or 973-926-3004.

West Caldwell Meets 3rd Tues., 7pm, Crane's Mill Assisted Living Center, 459 Passaic Ave. Call Chaplain George Lofmark 973-276-6700 ext. 3008.

Alzheimer's Caregiver Support Group *Professionally-run.* Support for persons caring for someone with Alzheimer's or related memory impairment. Group sessions, guest speakers, literature and educational series. Meets 3rd Wed., 7:30pm, Arden Courts-Manorcare Health Services, 510 Prospect Ave., West Orange. Call Gail Kuchavik or Bill Milianes 973-736-3100 ext. 205 (day). *Website*: http://www.hcrmanorcare.com

GLOUCESTER

Alzheimer's Support Group Mutual support for family or friends caring for persons afflicted with Alzheimer's or dementia. Meets 3rd Mon., 7-9pm, Underwood Memorial Hospital, Medical Arts Building, Suite 14, 509 N. Broad St., Woodbury. Call Karen Rodemer 856-853-2114 (day).

HUDSON

Alzheimer's Association Family Support Group *Professionally-run.* Support for caregivers of persons with Alzheimer's disease and related dementias. Opportunity to share practical information, exchange community resources, solve problems and learn ways to cope with dementia-related issues. Meets 4th Thurs., 2pm, Meadowlands Hospital Medical Center, Meadowlands Pkwy., Secaucus. Call Edna Mondadori 201-865-8542 (day).

HUNTERDON

Alzheimer's Association Family Support Group *Professionally-run.* Support for caregivers of persons with Alzheimer's disease and related dementias. Opportunity to share practical information, exchange community resources, solve problems and learn ways to cope with dementia-related issues. Meets 2nd Wed., 7-9pm, Hunterdon Medical Center, 4th Floor Conference Room, Flemington. Call Chris Stevens 908-788-6401.

Dementia Caregivers' Group *Professionally-run.* Mutual support and education for caregivers of persons with any type of dementia. Meets 2nd Tues., 1-3pm, Hunterdon County Division of Senior Services (Office on Aging), Route 31, Flemington. Call 908-788-6401 ext. 3149.

MERCER

Alzheimer's Association Family Support Group *Professionally-run.* Support for caregivers of persons with Alzheimer's disease and related dementias. Opportunity to share practical information, exchange community resources, solve problems and learn ways to cope with dementia-related issues. Meets 3rd Thurs., 6:30pm, St. Mark United Methodist Church, 465 Paxson Ave., Room 303, Hamilton Square. Call Kathy Wooley or Karin Rentschler 609-514-1180 (day). *Website*: http://www.alznj.org

Princeton Support Groups *Professionally-run.* Support for caregivers of persons with Alzheimer's disease and related dementias. Opportunity to share practical information, exchange community resources, solve problems and learn ways to cope with dementia-related issues. Meets 3rd Sat., 2pm, Woodlands Professional Building, Suite 6, 256 Bunn Dr., Princeton. Call Eileen 609-514-1180 (day). *Website*: http://www.alznj.org

MIDDLESEX

Alzheimer's Association Family Support Group Support for caregivers and family members of Alzheimer's and related disorders. Occasional educational programs with guest speakers.

Edison *Professionally-run.* Meets 1st Wed., 7pm, Jewish Family and Vocational Service of Middlesex County, 515 Plainfield Ave., Suite 201. Call Marnie Kean 732-777-1940.

Iselin *Professionally-run.* Meets 3rd Tues., 6:30pm, Woodbridge Public Library, 1081 Green St. Call Rosemary Oarlsey or Joan Fuhr 732-324-6005.

Monroe Township *Professionally-run.* Meets 1st Thurs., 7pm, Cranbury Center, 292 Applegarth Rd. Call Linda Silverstein or Marilyn Magan 609-860-2500.

Old Bridge *Professionally-run.* Meets 1st Mon., 6:30pm, Old Bridge Medical Center, Route 9 and Route 18 on Ferry Rd., One Hospital Plaza. Call Wanda Forys 732-324-4930.

Alzheimer's Support Group Support for caregivers of persons with Alzheimer's disease and related dementias. Opportunity to share practical information, exchange community resources, solve problems and learn ways to cope with dementia-related issues. Meets 1st Sat., 10:30am, JFK Hartwyck Adult Medical Day Center, Lifestyle Building, 2050 Oak Tree Rd., Edison. Call Mary Buglio or Michelle Charme 732-548-9770.

COPSA Spouse Support Group *Professionally-run.* Mutual support and understanding for spouses of persons with any type of memory loss (Alzheimer's, Parkinson's, vascular disease, stroke, head injury, dementia, etc.). Meets 1st and 3rd Mon., 9:30-11am, UBHC, 671 Hoes Lane, Piscataway. Call Mary Catherine Lundquist 732-235-2858 (day). *Website*: http://vbhcweb/ (then go to Aging-COPSA) E-mail: lindqumc@umdnj.edu

Young Wives' Support Group Mutual support and understanding for young women caring for a spouse with dementia. Meets 3rd Tues., 4:30-6pm, UBHC, 667 Hoes Lane, Piscataway. Call Meredith Doll, MSW 732-235-4910.

"There is great comfort and inspiration in the feeling of close human relationships, and its bearing on our mutual fortunes – a powerful force, to overcome the 'tough breaks' which are certain to come to most of us from time to time." -- Walt Dinsney

MONMOUTH

Alzheimer's Association Family Support Group. Support for caregivers of persons with Alzheimer's disease and related dementias. Opportunity to share practical information, exchange community resources, solve problems and learn ways to cope with dementia-related issues.

Allenwood *Professionally-run.* Meets 3rd Wed., 6:30pm, Geraldine Care Center, Hospital Rd. Call Bonnie Lamont 732-938-5350.

Atlantic Highlands Meets 1st Wed. 6:30pm, Royal Senior Care, 1041 State Highway 36. Call Rita Torres 732-291-0710 ext. 14.

Freehold Meets 3rd Tues., 7pm, First United Methodist Church, 91 West Main St. Call Eileen Doremus or Lucinda Seares Monica 609-514-1180.

Freehold *Professionally-run.* Meets 2nd Thurs., 2-3pm, Applewood Estates, Gully Rd. Call Heleyne Gladstein 732-363-5150. *Website*: http://www.alznj.org

Holmdel *Professionally-run.* Meets 3rd Tues., 7-9pm, Bayshore Hospital, Conference Room B. Call Carol Auletto 732-914-9306. *Website*: http://www.alznj.org

Middletown *Professionally-run.* Meets 4th Thurs., 7pm, Brighton Gardens, 620 Highway 35 South. Call Pearl Kaufman 732-275-0790.

Tinton Falls Meets 4th Mon., 10:30am and 2nd Wed., 7-8:30pm, Kensington Court, 864 Shrewsbury Ave. Call Kathleen Geren or Maryann Frantz 732-784-2406.

Wall Meets last Mon., 6pm, Allaire Center Senior Day Care, Wall Circle Park, Route 34 South. Call Cheryl Fenwick 732-974-7666 or Phyllis Noviello 732-918-1960.

MORRIS

Alzheimer's Association Family Support Group Support for caregivers of persons with Alzheimer's disease and related dementias. Opportunity to share practical information, exchange community resources, solve problems and learn ways to cope with dementia-related issues.

Chatham *Professionally-run.* Meets 3rd Thurs., 7:30pm, Chatham United Methodist Church, Route 24. Call Phyllis Flemming 973-635-2266 (day).

Dover Meets 1st Thurs., 2pm, Saint Clare's Hospital, 400 West Blackwell St. Call Diane Wood 973-989-3228.

Pompton Plains *Professionally-run.* Meets 2nd Wed., 7-8:30pm, Chilton Memorial Hospital, Collins Pavilion, Classroom B, 2nd Floor, 97 West Parkway. Call Joan Beloff 973-831-5167 (day). *E-mail*: joan.beloff@chiltonmemorial.org

Alzheimer's Association Support Group Support and education for caregivers and friends of individuals afflicted with Alzheimer's. Support, guest speakers and educational materials. Meets 4th Mon., 10am, Alzheimer's Association, 400 Morris Ave., Denville. Call Alzheimer's Association 973-586-4300.

Male Caregivers - Alzheimer's Support Group Support for male caregivers of persons with Alzheimer's disease and related dementias. Opportunity to share practical information, exchange community resources, solve problems and learn ways to cope with dementia-related issues. Meets 1st Thurs., 7pm, St. Lawrence Church Hall, Main St. (Route 24), Chester. Call Pete 908-665-1613 (day).

OCEAN

Alzheimer's Association Family Support Group *Professionally-run.* Support for caregivers of persons with Alzheimer's disease and related dementias. Opportunity to share practical information, exchange community resources, solve problems and learn ways to cope with dementia-related issues.

Jackson Meets last Tues., 10am, Bella Terra Retirement Community, 2 Kathleen Dr. Call Paula Douglass 732-730-9500.

Lakewood Meets 2nd Thurs., 7-9pm, Kimball Medical Center, Center for Healthy Living, 198 Prospect St. Call Eileen Doremus or Dolores Rosen 609-514-1180 (day).

Lakewood Meets 4th Tues., 10am, Wellsprings Adult Day Program, 515 Route 70. Call Dawn Matthews or Rita Sason 732-942-1610.

Manhawakin Meets 2nd Mon., 2pm, (Feb., May, Aug., Nov.), Southern Ocean County Hospital, Wellness Center, 1140 Route 72 West. Call Robyn Ciangetti 609-978-3559.

Toms River Meets 1st and 3rd Mon., 9:15am, Visiting Homemaker Service Day Care, Conference Room. Call Michelle Mahieu 732-244-5565.

Toms River Meets 2nd Tues., 6pm, Country Manor Nursing and Rehabilitation Center, 16 Whitesville Rd. Call Lilly Ballance 732-341-1600.

Toms River Meets 3rd Sat., 10am, Magnolia Gardens Assisted Living, 1935 Lakewood Rd. Call Cathy Vakulchik or Amy Palazzo 732-557-6500 ext. 0.

Toms River Meets 3rd Thurs., 2pm, Bey Lea Nursing Home, 1351 Old Freehold Rd. Call Edward Mount 732-240-0090.

Tuckerton Meets 2nd Thurs., 2pm, (July, Sept., Oct., Dec.) Seacrest Village, 1001 Center St. Before attending call Robyn Ciangetti 609-296-9292 (day).

Whiting Meets 2nd Wed., 10:30am, St. Elizabeth Ann Seton Church, Parish Hall, School House Rd. Call Marion Ariemma 732-350-8688.

Ocean Alzheimer's Caregivers Support Group Support for caregivers of those afflicted with Alzheimer's or dementia. Advocacy, guest speakers, mutual sharing, phone help, literature and educational information. Meets Wed., 1:30-3:30pm, First Aid Squad Building, Colonial Drive, Manchester Township. Call Therese 732-818-1992 (day/eve) or Lynn Clair 732-780-0998.

PASSAIC

Alzheimer's Association Family Support Group *Professionally-run.* Support for caregivers of persons with Alzheimer's disease or other related dementias. Opportunity to share practical information, exchange community resources, solve problems and learn ways to cope with dementia-related issues.

Clifton Meets 2nd Mon., 7:30-9pm, Clifton Family Medicine, 716 Broad St. Call Diane Lesko 973-904-5000 (day).

Hawthorne Meets 3rd Thurs., 7pm, Van Dyk Park Place (Assisted Living), 644 Goffle Rd. Call 973-648-4062.

SOMERSET

Alzheimer's Association Family Support Group *Professionally-run.* Support for caregivers of persons with Alzheimer's disease or related dementias. Opportunity to share practical information, exchange community resources, solve problems and learn ways to cope with dementia-related issues.

Bridgewater Meets 1st Wed., 6pm, Harborside Healthcare Woods Edge, 875 Route 202/206 North. Call Margaret McArdle 908-526-8600.

Hillsborough Meets 1st Thurs., 7pm, Summerville Senior Living, 600 Auten Rd. Call Allison Elkow Lazicky 908-431-1300.

SUSSEX

Alzheimer's Association Family Support Group *Professionally-run.* Support for caregivers of persons with Alzheimer's disease and related dementias. Opportunity to share practical information, exchange community resources, solve problems and learn ways to cope with dementia-related issues. Meets 4th Wed., 1pm, The Homestead, 129 Morris Turnpike, County Route 655, Newton. Call Liz Shuster or MaryLou Schnurr 973-948-5400.

Alzheimer's Support Group *Professionally-run.* Support for caregivers of persons with Alzheimer's disease or related dementias. Opportunity to share practical information, exchange community resources, solve problems and learn ways to cope with dementia-related issues. Meets 2nd Wed., 7-9pm, Visiting

Nurse Association of Saint Clares, Sparta Plaza, 191 Woodport Rd., Sparta. Call Linda Schurmann 973-729-7078 (day).

UNION

Alzheimer's Association Family Support Group Support for caregivers of persons with Alzheimer's disease and related dementias. Opportunity to share practical information, exchange community resources, solve problems and learn ways to cope with dementia-related issues.

Berkeley Heights *Professionally-run.* Meets 3rd Thurs., 1-2pm, Runnells Specialized Hospital, Room C 318, Third Floor, 40 Watchung Way. Call Liz Carabuena, LSW 908-771-5828 (day).

Cranford Meets 1st Wed., 7pm, Family Resource Center, 300 North Ave. Call Ruth 908-994-7313.

Summit *Professionally-run.* Meets 2nd and 4th Thurs., 7-9pm, Overlook Hospital, 99 Beauvoir Ave. Call Jack Becker 908-719-2276. *E-mail*: thinkjk1@verizon.net

WARREN

Alzheimer's Association Family Support Group Support for caregivers of persons with Alzheimer's disease and related dementias. Opportunity to share practical information, exchange community resources, solve problems and learn ways to cope with dementia-related issues. Meets 2nd Tues., 7pm, Day Break, Daybreak Adult Day Care Center, 443 Schooley's Mountain Rd. (Route 24), Hackettstown. Call Valerie Hart 908-852-7300 (day).

NATIONAL

Alzheimer's Association *National. 80+ chapters. Founded 1980.* Information and assistance for caregivers of Alzheimer's patients. Quarterly newsletter and literature. Online message board. Write: Alzheimer's Assn., 225 N. Michigan Ave., Suite 1700, Chicago, IL 60601. Call 1-800-272-3900 or 312-335-8700; TDD: 312-335-8882; Fax: 866-699-1246 *Website*: http://www.alz.org *E-mail*: info@alz.org

Can't find an appropriate group in your area? The Clearinghouse helps people start groups. Give us a call at 1-800-367-6274

AMYOTROPHIC LATERAL SCLEROSIS (ALS / Lou Gehrig's Disease)

ATLANTIC

ALS Resource Group "Lou Gehrig's Disease" *Professionally-run.* Mutual support for patients and families to learn how to cope with the daily changes associated with ALS. Guest speakers and literature. Meets 1st Tues., 6-7:30pm, Holy Redeemer Health System, 6727 Delilah Rd., Egg Harbor Township. Call Stephanie Hand-Kowchak 609-909-3509 (day). *Website:* http://www.alsphiladelphia.org

BERGEN

MDA/ALS Support Group *Professionally-run.* Mutual support for individuals with muscular dystrophy or ALS. Families and caregivers welcome. Sharing of information, experiences, ideas and resources. Usually meets 3rd Thurs., 4-6pm, Jewish Community Center on the Palisades, 411 East Clinton Ave., Tenafly. Pre-registration required. Before attending call 201-843-4452 (day).

MERCER

ALS Resource Group "Lou Gehrig's Disease" *Professionally-run.* Mutual support for patients and families to learn how to cope with the daily changes associated with ALS. Guest speakers and literature. Meets 1st Sat., 1-3pm, Lawrence Township Municipal Building, Public Meeting Room, 2207 Lawrenceville Rd., Lawrenceville. Call Cathe Frierman 609-394-3556 (day) or Rick van den Heuvel 609-883-6784 (day). *Website:* http://www.alsphiladelphia.org

MIDDLESEX

A.L.S. Association *Professionally-run.* Mutual support for patients and families to learn to cope with A.L.S. Under 18 welcome. Meetings vary, Robert Wood Johnson University Hospital, New Brunswick. For meeting information call 732-235-7331.

MONMOUTH

Joan Dancy and People with ALS Support Group *Professionally-run.* Mutual support for patients and families to cope with ALS. Guest speakers. Meets 1st Tues., 6:30pm, Riverview Medical Center, Administrative Board Room, Red Bank. Call Patricia Schaeffer, RN 732-450-2677 (day).

NATIONAL

A.L.S. Association *National. 75+ chapters and support groups. Founded 1984.* Dedicated to finding the cause, prevention, and cure of amyotrophic lateral sclerosis, and to enhance quality of life for ALS patients and their families. Quarterly newspaper and chapter development guidelines. Write: A.L.S. Association, 27001 Agoura Rd., Suite 150, Calabasas Hills, CA 91301. Call 818-880-9007 or 1-800-782-4747 (information and referral); Fax: 818-880-9006. *Website*: http://www.alsa.org *E-mail*: alsinfo@alsa-national.org

ANEMIA

NATIONAL

Aplastic Anemia and MDS International Foundation, Inc. *International. Founded 1983.* Emotional support and worldwide support groups, free educational materials, information about current research, clinical trials and financial assistance for persons with aplastic anemia, myelodysplastic syndromes, paroxysmal nocturnal hemoglobinuria and other bone marrow failure diseases. Financially supports research. Write: Aplastic Anemia and MDS International Foundation Inc., P.O. Box 613, Annapolis, MD 21404. Call 1-800-747-2820 or 410-867-0242; Fax: 410-867-0240. *Website:* http://www.aamds.org *E-mail:* help@aamds.org

Cooley's Anemia Foundation *National. 16 chapters. Founded 1954.* Offers education and networking for families affected by Cooley's anemia (thalassemia). Fund-raising for research. Newsletter, annual seminars, research grants, patient support group, patient services and chapter development guidelines. Write: Cooley's Anemia Foundation, 330 Seventh Ave., Suite 900, New York, NY, 10001. Call 1-800-522-7222 or 212-279-8090; Fax: 212-279-5999. *Website:* http://www.cooleysanemia.org *E-mail:* info@cooleysanemia.org

ONLINE

Myelodysplastic Syndromes Foundation *Online.* Unmoderated forums for patients and professionals dealing with myelodysplastic syndromes, a group of bone marrow diseases. Also has referrals to treatment centers. Call 1-800-637-0839 (US), 609-298-6746 (Outside US); Fax 609-298-0590. Write: MDS Foundation, P.O. Box 353, Crosswicks, NJ 08515. *Website:* http://www.mds-foundation.org *E-mail:* patientliaison@mds-foundation.org

APHASIA

BERGEN

Aphasia Support Group Mutual support for persons suffering from aphasia and their families. Disseminates information and group discussions. Dues $12yr./$2 wk. Meets Fri. (except Aug.), 10:30am-noon, Kip Center, 55 Kip Ave., Rutherford. Call Donna Hyduk 973-472-4676 (eve) or Kip Center 201-460-1600 (day).

Caregiver Aphasia Support Group Support for people with aphasia and their caregivers. Group is primarily for individuals who have had a stroke, but also includes those with head injury or other brain trauma. Lecture series, social group and guest speakers. Meets Wed., 10:45-11:45am, Adler Aphasia Center, 60 West Hunter Ave., Maywood. Call Karen Tucker 201-368-8585 (day). *E-mail:* ktucker@adleraphasiacenter.org

UNION

Kean University Aphasia Support Group Mutual support for persons suffering from aphasia and their families. Disseminates information, group discussions, rap sessions and guest speakers. Meetings vary, Kean University, CSI, Bldg. 101, 1000 Morris Ave., Union. Before attending call Dr. Mary Jo Santo Pietro 908-737-5409 (day).

NATIONAL

National Aphasia Association *National umbrella organization. 350 Groups. Founded 1987.* Educates the public about aphasia. Provides educational information to patients and their families about coping with aphasia. Listing of state representatives and support groups. Write: National Aphasia Association, 7 Dey St., Suite 600, New York, NY 10007. Call 1-800-922-4622; Fax: 212-267-2812. *Website:* http://www.aphasia.org *E-mail:* naa@aphasia.org

ARTHRITIS

STATEWIDE

Arthritis Foundation NJ Chapter Mutual support and education for people with arthritis and their families. Call the Arthritis Foundation State Headquarters, Iselin. Call 1-888-467-3112 or 732-283-4300 (day). *Website:* http://www.arthritis.org

BERGEN

Juvenile Arthritis Group *Professionally-run.* Mutual support and education for teens with arthritis and other rheumatic conditions. Concurrent group for parents. Meets regularly, Hackensack University Medical Center, Children's Arthritis Center, Dept. of Pediatrics, 30 Prospect St., Hackensack. For meeting information call Katie Rosenthal 201-336-8241.

BURLINGTON

Arthritis Foundation NJ Chapter Mutual support and education for people with arthritis and their families. Meets 3rd Tues., 1pm, Willingboro Senior Citizen Center, Room 302, 429 JFK Way, Willingboro. Call 1-888-847-8823.

CAMDEN

Arthritis Foundation Support Group Mutual support and education for people with arthritis and their families. Meets 1st Wed., 1pm, (except Jan., Feb., July, Aug., Sept.), Virtua Health's Barry D. Brown Health Education Center, 106 Carnie Blvd., Voorhees. Call Virtua 1-888-847-8823.

ESSEX

Arthritis Foundation NJ Chapter Mutual support and education for people with arthritis and their families. Meets 2nd Mon., 10:30am, St. Mary's Life Center, 135 South Center Street, Orange. Call 973-266-3000 or 1-888-467-3112 (day). *Website*: http://www.arthritis.org

North Jersey Regional Arthritis Center Support Group *Professionally-run.* Mutual support and education for persons with arthritis and their families. Aim is to raise quality of life for those with arthritis through group discussions, educational programs, mutual sharing and guest speakers. Offers phone help, speakers' bureau and literature. Meets 2nd Mon., 2-3pm (except July/Aug.), Verona Community Center, 880 Bloomfield Ave., Verona. For meeting information call NJRAC 1-877-973-6500.

HUDSON

North Jersey Regional Arthritis Center Support Group *Professionally-run.* Mutual support and education for persons with arthritis and their families. Aim is to raise quality of life for those with arthritis through group discussions, educational programs, mutual sharing and guest speakers. Offers phone help, speakers' bureau and literature. Meets 2nd Tues., 11:30am-noon, Community Crossing, 488 Broadway, Bayonne. Call Community Crossing 201-437-4100.

HUNTERDON

Arthritis Foundation NJ Chapter Mutual support and education for people with arthritis and osteoporosis, their families. Meets 2nd Mon., 1-3pm, Hunterdon Medical Center, 2100 Wescott Drive, Flemington. Call 908-788-6373 or The Arthritis Foundation 1-888-467-3112 (day). *Website*: http://www.arthritis.org

MERCER

Arthritis Support Group *Professionally-run.* Support and education for people with all types of arthritis, and their families. Meets various days, Capital Health Systems, Mercer Campus, 446 Bellevue Ave., Trenton. Call 609-394-4000 or Arthritis Foundation 1-888-467-3112. *Website*: http://www.arthritis.org.

Arthritis Support Group Support and education for people with all types of arthritis. Meets 3rd Wed., 7pm, Robert Wood Johnson University Hospital at Hamilton, 1 Hamilton Health Place, Hamilton. Call Arthritis Foundation 609-584-5900 or 1-888-467-3112. *Website*: http://www.arthritis.org

MONMOUTH

Arthritis Foundation NJ Chapter Mutual support and education for persons with arthritis and their families. Meets 4th Thurs., 6:30pm, Wall Township Library, 2700 Allaire Rd., Wall. Call 732-449-2733.

MORRIS

North Jersey Regional Arthritis Center Support Group *Professionally-run.* Mutual support and education for persons with arthritis and their families. Aim is to raise quality of life for those with arthritis through group discussions, educational programs, mutual sharing and guest speakers. Offers phone help, speakers' bureau and literature.

Rockaway Meets various days and times, Rockaway Township Municipal Building, 65 Mt. Hope Rd., Conference Room. For meeting information call Rockaway Health Dept. 973-983-2899.

Whippany Meets 2nd Thurs., 10:30am-12pm, Morris County Library, 30 E. Hanover Ave. Call NJRAC 1-877-973-6500.

PASSAIC

Arthritis Support Group *Professionally-run.* Support and education for persons (age 50+) with arthritis. Guest speakers and literature. Meets 4th Tues., 10:30-11:30am, Renaissance Subacute Care Center, 493 Black Oak Ridge Rd., Wayne. Call Joan Beloff 973-831-5167 (day) or Kathy Ferrara 973-831-5175 (day).

North Jersey Regional Arthritis Center Support Group *Professionally-run.* Mutual support and education for persons with arthritis or fibromyalgia and their families. Aim is to raise quality of life for those with arthritis or fibromyalgia through group discussions, educational programs, mutual sharing and guest speakers. Offers phone help, speakers' bureau and literature. Meets 1st Tues., 1:30-2:30pm, Main Memorial Library, 292 Piaget Ave., Clifton. Call NJRAC 1-877-973-6500.

SALEM

Arthritis Foundation NJ Chapter Mutual support and education for people with arthritis and their families. Meets at South Jersey Healthcare, Elmer Division, 8 West Front St., Elmer. For meeting information call 856-363-1585. *Website*: http://www.arthritis.org

SUSSEX

North Jersey Regional Arthritis Center Support Group Mutual support and education for people with arthritis and their families. Aim is to raise quality of life for those with arthritis through group discussions, educational programs, mutual sharing and guest speakers.

Lafayette *Professionally-run.* "Lunch and Chat" group meets 1st Tues., 11:30am-1:30pm, Lafayette House. Call NJRAC 1-877-973-6500.

Newton Meets 3rd Tues., 1-2pm, Newton Memorial Hospital, NJ cafeteria Conference Room. Call NJRAC 1-877-973-6500.

UNION

North Jersey Regional Arthritis Center Support Group *Professionally-run.* Mutual support and education for persons with arthritis and their families. Aim is to raise quality of life for those with arthritis through group discussions, educational programs, mutual sharing and guest speakers. Offers phone help, speakers' bureau and literature. Meets 2nd Wed., 9:30-11am, Westfield YMCA, East Broad Street Branch, 422 East Broad St., Westfield. Call Westfield YMCA 908-233-2700 or NJRAC 1-877-973-6500.

WARREN

Arthritis Foundation NJ Chapter Education for people with arthritis and their families. For meeting information call the Arthritis Foundation 1-888-467-3112 (day). *Website*: http://www.arthritis.org

NATIONAL

American Juvenile Arthritis Organization *National. 50 Chapters. Founded 1981.* Council of the Arthritis Foundation devoted to serving the special needs of children, teens and young adults with childhood rheumatic diseases (including juvenile rheumatoid arthritis, systemic lupus erythematosus and ankylosing spondylitis) and their families. Provides information, advocacy, educational materials, programs and conferences. Offers online support and local chapter locator. Dues $20 (for Arthritis Foundation). Write: AJAO, 1330 West Peachtree St., Suite 100, Atlanta, GA 30309. Call 404-872-7100 ext. 7538; Fax: 440-872-9559. *Website*: http://www.arthritis.org

Arthritis Foundation *National. 64 chapters. Founded 1948.* Mission is to improve lives through leadership in the prevention, control and cure of arthritis and related diseases. Offers education, support and activities for people with arthritis, their families and friends. Self-help instruction programs. Land and water exercises. Provides community-based public health, public policy and nationwide research funding. Bimonthly magazine. Write: Arthritis Foundation, 1330 West Peachtree St. NW, Atlanta, GA 30309. Call 1-800-568-4045 or 404-872-7100. *Website*: http://www.arthritis.org *E-mail*: help@arthritis.org

BONE MARROW / STEM CELL TRANSPLANT

BERGEN

Post-Bone Marrow/Stem Cell Transplant Support Group Provides emotional support to post-bone marrow or stem cell transplant patients, their family and friends. Facilitator is a transplant recipient. Guest speakers and education. Meetings vary, Hackensack University Medical Center, 20 Prospect Ave., 4th Floor, Waiting Room, Hackensack. Call Renee Stein-Goetz 201-336-8290 (day/eve).

NATIONAL

Blood Marrow Transplant Information Network *Resource. Founded 1990.* Transplant center database has information about 220 transplant programs in U.S. and Canada, a resource directory, attorney referral service and a patient-to-survivor link service. Resources include "Blood Marrow Transplant Newsletter" for bone marrow, peripheral stem cell, cord blood transplant patients; "Bone Marrow and Blood Stem Cell Transplants: A Guide for Patients" which describes the physical and emotional aspects of marrow and stem transplantation. Also a 208-page book "Autologous Stem Cell Transplant: A Handbook for Patients." Write: BMT Information Network, 2310 Skokie Valley Rd., Suite 104, Highland Park, IL 60035. Call 847-433-3313 or 1-888-597-7674; Fax: 847-433-4599. *Website:* http://www.bmtinfonet.org *E-mail:* help@bmtinfonet.org

BRAIN TUMOR

(see also toll-free helpline)

STATEWIDE

Acoustic Neuroma Association of NJ Support and information for pre- and post - operative patients. Quarterly meetings present programs of interest to acoustic neuroma patients and their families. Dues $25/yr. (optional). Quarterly newsletter. Ongoing programs to create public awareness. Write: ANA/NJ, Inc., 291 Nassau St., Princeton, NJ 08540. Call Wilma Ruskin 609-683-4650 (eve); Fax: 609-279-9295. *E-mail:* ananjinc@aol.com *Website:* http://www.ananj.org

ESSEX

Acoustic Neuroma Association Northern NJ Mutual support to assist those diagnosed with, or receiving post-treatment for, acoustic neuromas. Rap sessions, guest speakers, literature and phone help. Meets 4 times/yr., Montclair. Call Jon Bonesteel 973-783-8723 (day/eve). *E-mail:* bonestee@verizon.net

Support For Children With Brain and Spinal Cord Tumors Support groups for children with brain and spinal cord tumors. Parents and siblings are welcome. Group meets monthly, 10-11am, Jewish Community Center, 769 Northfield Ave., West Orange. For meeting information call Lissa Parsonnet, PhD 973-921-9629. *Website:* http://www.makingheadway.org *E-mail:* info@makingheadway.org

MIDDLESEX

Brain Tumor (Tu-Mor Helping Hands) Support Group Support and education for individuals and their families recovering from, or who will be undergoing, brain tumor surgery. Guest speakers, phone help, literature. Meets 2nd Mon., 7:00pm,

Robert Wood Johnson University Hospital, One Robert Wood Johnson Place, BMSCH Conference Room, New Brunswick. Call 732-418-8110 (day).

MONMOUTH

Monmouth and Ocean County Brain Tumor Support Group Provide support for patients and family members of those affected by all types of brain tumors. Guest speakers, literature and speakers bureau. Meets 1st Sat., 3-4:45pm, (except July/Aug., 1st Thurs., 7pm), Wall Township Branch of the Monmouth County Library, 2700 Allaire Rd., Wall. Call Bruce 609-758-0806. *Website:* http://www.njbt.org *E-mail:* Mngioma634@aol.com

OCEAN

Brain Tumor Support Group Emotional support and education for persons with a brain tumor, their families and friends. Guest speakers and literature. Meets 3rd Mon., 3pm, Community Medical Center, 99 Highway 37 West, Toms River. Call Sherry 732-557-8270 (day).

SOMERSET

Brain Tumor Resources And Support Center Support for brain tumor patients and their families. Meets 1st Thurs., 7pm, St. Luke's Church, 300 Clinton Ave., North Plainfield. Call Patty Anthony 732-321-7000 ext. 68998 (day), Stan or Virginia 908-685-0917 (day). *Website:* http://www.njbt.org *E-mail:* info@njbt.org

UNION

Brain Tumor Support Group Mutual support for patients with brain tumors and/or their family members. Meets various days and times, Overlook Hospital, 99 Beauvoir Ave., Summit. Call Kristen Scarlett, LPC, NCC 908-522-5255 (day).

NATIONAL

Acoustic Neuroma Association *National. 53 affiliated groups. Founded 1981.* Support and information for patients who have been diagnosed with acoustic neuroma, a benign tumor affecting the 8th cranial nerve. Quarterly newsletter ($35/yr), nationwide support group network, biennial national symposium and patient information booklets. Write: ANA, 600 Peachtree Parkway, Suite 108, Cumming, GA 30041-6899. Call 1-877-200-8211 or 770-205-8211; Fax: 1-877-202-0239. *Website:* http://www.anausa.org *E-mail:* info@anausa.org

American Brain Tumor Association *National. Founded 1973.* Dedicated to eliminating brain tumors by funding and encouraging research and providing free patient education, materials and resource information. Pen pal program, newsletter, publications, resource listings. Support group referrals. Assistance in starting groups Write: American Brain Tumor Association, 2720 River Rd., Suite 146, Des Plaines, IL 60018. Call 847-827-9910; or 1-800-886-2282 (patient services); Fax: 847-827-9918. *Website:* http://www.abta.org *E-mail:* info@abta.org

Brain Tumor Society *National. Founded 1989.* Committed to finding a cure for brain tumors. Improves the quality of life for brain tumor patients, survivors and caregivers through research, education, support programs and services. Maintains a database of brain tumor support groups. Funds research. Publishes free newsletter, e-newsletter, comprehensive resource guide and brain tumor Fact Sheets. Write: Brain Tumor Society, 124 Watertown St., Suite 3-H, Watertown, MA 02472-2500. Call 1-800-770-8287 or 617-924-9997; Fax: 617-924-9998. *Website:* http://www.tbts.org *E-mail:* info@tbts.org

Children's Brain Tumor Foundation, Inc. *(BILINGUAL) National network. Founded 1988.* Provides a Parent-to-Parent Network to link parents of a child with a brain or spinal cord tumor with another parent with similar experiences for information and support. Offers free resource guide (English/Spanish), Parker's Brain Storm (a book for children), Brain Tumor Week at Camp Sunshine, newsletter, annual teleconferences (available for replay on website) and funds research. Write: Children's Brain Tumor Foundation, 274 Madison Ave., Suite 1004, New York, NY 10016. Call 1-866-228-4673 or 212-448-9494; Fax: 212-448-1022. *Website:* http://www.cbtf.org *E-mail:* info@cbtf.org

Musella Foundation *National.* Provides emotional support and exchange of information for patients with various brain tumors and their families. Information on research, medication and clinical trials. Chat rooms, support groups, video library and other resources. Write: Musella Foundation, 1100 Peninsula Blvd., Hewlett, NY 11557. Call 1-888-295-4740 or 516-295-4740; Fax: 516-295-2870. *Website:* http://www.virtualtrials.com *E-mail:* musella@virtualtrials.com

National Brain Tumor Foundation *National. 150+ affiliated groups. Founded 1981.* Support and information for persons with brain tumors. Provides funding for research as well as client services for brain tumor patients and family members. Offers support group listings, a quarterly newsletter, information and referrals, conferences, literature and support line. Assistance in starting and maintaining support groups. Write: NBTF, 22 Battery Street, Suite 612, San Francisco, CA 94111-5520. Call 1-800-934-2873 or 415-834-9970; Fax: 415-834-9980. *Website:* http://www.braintumor.org *E-mail:* nbtf@braintumor.org

ONLINE

BRAIN TRUST, The Healing Exchange *Online. Founded 1993.* Mission is to exchange information and support people affected by brain tumors and related conditions including patient-survivors, families, caregivers and health professionals. Online support groups cover a large range of brain tumors, acquired injuries and other special interests. Write: T.H.E. BRAIN TRUST, 186 Hampshire St., Cambridge, MA 02139-1320. Call 617-876-2002 or 1-877-252-8480; Fax: 617-876-2332. *Website:* http://www.braintrust.org *E-mail:* info@braintrust.org

Brain Tumour Foundation of Canada *Online. Founded 1982.* Virtual support group includes online chat room, message board and moderated chat events. Support groups meet monthly in many Canadian communities. Write: Brain Tumour Foundation of Canada, 620 Colborne St., Suite 301, London, Ontario, Canada N6B 3R9. Call 519-642-7755 or 1-800-265-5106; Fax: 519-642-7192. *Website:* http://www.braintumour.ca *E-mail:* braintumour@braintumour.ca

Spouses of Brain Tumor Patients *Online.* Support for spouses of brain tumor patients. Opportunity to connect with others who understand the emotions and frustrations involved with a spouse who has a brain tumor. Message board and chat room. *Website:* http://www.bradsupdates.com/care.html

BREAST CANCER

(see also cancer, toll-free helpline)

BERGEN

Breast Cancer Support Group *Professionally-run.* Support group for breast cancer patients. Family and friends welcome. Meets various evenings, Hackensack University Medical Center, 20 Prospect Ave., Reception Area, Suite 400, Hackensack. Registration required. Call Joan Managhan 201-996-4942 (day).

Sisters Network of Central New Jersey Mutual support for female African American breast cancer survivors. Aim is to increase awareness of the impact of breast cancer. Literature and phone help. Meets 3rd Sat., 10am-noon, Gilda's Club Northern New Jersey, 575 Main St., Hackensack. Call Cheryl Walters 973-279-6070.

Support Group For Breast Cancer *(SPANISH SPEAKING)* Support for women with breast cancer. Mutual sharing, educational and guest speakers.

Meetings vary, Latin America Institute, 10 Banta Place, Hackensack. Call 201-525-1700 (day). *E-mail*: ssdeber05@hotmail.com

Tennis For Life Mutual support for women with breast cancer. Peer-led rap sessions, guest speaker and a free tennis lesson. Meets in Ridgewood. To register call Melissa Donahue 201-996-5836 (day).

BURLINGTON

Speak Easy Breast Cancer Support Group *Professionally-run.* Mutual support and information to breast cancer survivors. Guest speakers, phone help and literature. Meets 1st Tues., 7-9pm (except July/ Aug.), Lourdes Medical Center of Burlington County, 218A Sunset Rd., Willingboro. Call Maxine Mayer 856-662-5474 (day).

CAMDEN

Pink Ribbon Poetry Breast Cancer Support Group Support for breast cancer survivors that uses poetry as a tool for reflection. Meets 1st and 3rd Thurs., 7-9pm, Barry D. Brown Health Education Building, 106 Carnie Blvd., Voorhees. Before attending for the first time call 1-888-847-8823 (day).

Women Supporting Women Through Breast Cancer *Professionally-run.* Mutual support for breast cancer patients and those currently under treatment. Meets 2nd and 4th Wed., 6:30-8pm, Virtua Health, William G. Rohrer Center for Health Fitness, 2309 Evesham Rd., Voorhees. Before attending call Virtua Health 1-888-847-8823 (day).

ESSEX

Circle of Women *Professionally-run.* Networking group to support women diagnosed with breast cancer. Rap sessions and mutual sharing. Meets 2nd and 4th Tues., 7-8:30pm, Mountainside Hospital, Harries Pavilion, Cancer Center, 1 Bay Ave., Montclair. Call Sara Duphiney, LSW 973-429-6038 (day).

Primary Breast Cancer Support Group *Professionally-run.* Mutual support for women with breast cancer to share their concerns and experiences with other women facing the same illness and treatments. Meeting dates and times vary, St. Barnabas Medical Center, 94 Old Short Hills Rd., Livingston. Call Patti Conlin, LSW 973-322-8405 (day).

HUNTERDON

Breast Cancer Support Group *Professionally-run.* Offers support and education for women with breast cancer. Rap sessions, guest speakers, phone help and literature. Meets 3rd Thurs., 7:30-9pm, Hunterdon Regional Cancer Center, Flemington. Call 1-800-227-2345 ext. 2 (day).

MERCER

Advanced Breast Cancer Support Group *Professionally-run.* Provides support for women living with stage IV breast cancer. Sharing of experiences, solutions, triumphs and concerns. Meets 1st and 3rd Mon., 7:30-9pm, YWCA Princeton, 59 Paul Robeson Place, Bramwell House Living Room, Princeton. Call 609-497-2100. *Website*: http://www.bcrcnj.org *E-mail*: bcrc@ywcaprinceton.org

Breast Cancer Support Group *Professionally-run.* Mutual support and guidance for women with breast cancer. Rap sessions, guest speakers, phone help and literature. Meets alternate Wed., 1-2pm, Capital Health System at Mercer, 446 Bellevue Ave., Trenton. Call Oncology Social Worker 609-394-4228 (day).

Breast Cancer Support Group *Professionally-run.* Support for breast cancer patients. Families welcome. Meets 1st and 2nd Tues., 6:30-8pm, The Cancer Institute of NJ, RWJU Hospital Hamilton, 2575 Klockner Road, Hamilton. Call Trish Tatrai for 1st Tues. meeting 609-584-2836 and Lois Glasser for 2nd Tues. meeting 1-800-813-4673 ext. 107.

Breast Cancer Support Group Provides peer support to anyone diagnosed with breast cancer at any stage of treatment or recovery. Share questions, concerns and coping strategies in a caring, understanding environment. Meets 4th Wed., 11:45am-1pm and 3rd Tues., 7:30-9pm, YWCA Princeton, 59 Paul Robeson Place, Bramwell House Living Room, Princeton. Call 609-497-2100 ext. 346 or Breast Cancer Helpline 609-497-2126. *Website*: http://www.bcrcnj.org *E-mail*: bcrc@ywcaprinceton.org

Young Women Breast Cancer Support Group *Professionally-run.* Support for young women (ages 45 and under) with breast cancer. Meets 3rd Tues., 6:30-8pm, The Cancer Institute of NJ, RWJU Hospital Hamilton, 2575 Klockner Road, Hamilton. Call Trish Tatrai 609-584-2836.

Young Women's Breast Cancer Support Group *Professionally-run.* Provides support to women (ages 45 and under) diagnosed with breast cancer. Addresses issues such as fertility, dating, self-image, coping with treatment side effects, raising young children and recent marriage. Meets 1st Wed., 7:30-9pm, YWCA Princeton, 59 Paul Robeson Place, Bramwell House Living Room, Princeton. Call Kara Stephenson 609-497-2100 ext. 346. *Website*: http://www.bcrcnj.org *E-mail*: bcrc@ywcaprinceton.org

MIDDLESEX

Breast Cancer Support Group Mutual support and education for women with breast cancer and their family members. Guest speakers. Meets 1st and 3rd Mon., 7-8:30pm, CARES, St. Peter's University Hospital, 3rd Floor, Conference Room, New Brunswick. Call Linda Mathew, LSW 732-235-8799 (day).

Voices of Healing *Professionally-run.* Helps women with breast cancer to decrease their feelings of isolation and provides a sense of purpose and belonging. Empowerment, body image and family roles are discussed. Members are encouraged to discover the strength of their own inner resources. Meets 1st Tues., 6:30-8pm, Haven Hospice, JFK Medical Center, 65 James St., Edison. Call Elaine Murphy 732-321-7769 (day).

MONMOUTH

After Hours Breast Cancer Support Group *Professionally-run.* Designed for working women who have been diagnosed with breast cancer. Meets 1st Tues., 7-8pm, Jersey Shore Medical Center, 1945 Corlies Ave., Neptune. Before attending call 732-776-2380.

Breast Cancer Support Group *Professionally-run.* Support and education for mastectomy and lumpectomy patients. Peer-counseling and guest speakers. Meets 1st Tues., 7:00pm, Riverview Medical Center, 1 Riverview Plaza, Red Bank. Call 732-530-2382 (day).

Breast Cancer Support Group *Professionally-run.* Support and education for those diagnosed with breast cancer. Guest speakers. Meets for 6 week sessions, Jersey Shore University Medical Center, Ambulatory Care Center, Cancer Center Conference Room, Neptune. Call 732-776-4432 (day). *Website*: http://www.meridianhealth.com

Breast Cancer Support Group *Professionally-run.* Support, information and mutual sharing for breast cancer survivors. Rap sessions and phone help. Meets 1st Mon., 7:30-9pm, Health Awareness Center, 65 Gibson Pl., Freehold. Call Stephanie O'Neil 732-308-1850 (day).

Breast Cancer Support Group Support for any woman with breast cancer. Psycho-Social workshop. Meets Tues., 2-4pm, Breast Care Center at Jersey Shore Medical Center, Ambulatory Care Pavilion, Cancer Center Conference Room, 1945 Corlies Ave., Neptune. Before attending call Breast Care Center 732-776-4432.

Living with Early Stage Breast Cancer Support Group *Professionally-run.* Opportunity for women diagnosed with breast cancer to obtain information, support and coping skills. Meets 2nd and 4th Tues., 7:15-9pm, Monmouth Medical Center, Comprehensive Center, 300 Second Ave., Long Branch. Must pre-register. Call Jan Tryba 732-923-7711 (day).

Living with Metastic Breast Cancer Support Group *Professionally-run.* Support for women facing the challenge of recurrent or metastic breast cancer. A place to share information and receive support. Meets 1st and 3rd Tues., 1-2:30pm, Monmouth Medical Center, Comprehensive Breast Center, 300 Second Ave., 4th Floor, Long Branch. Must pre-register. Call Jan Tryba 732-923-7711 (day).

Metastic and Recurrent Breast and Ovarian Cancer Group *Professionally-run.* Designed for women diagnosed with metastic or recurrent breast, ovarian, cervical, endometrial or uterine cancer. Meets 3rd Tues., 4:30pm, Jersey Shore Medical Center, 1945 Corlies Avenue, Neptune. Before attending call 732-776-2380.

Partners in Healing Support Group *Professionally-run.* Mutual support for spouses/significant others of women diagnosed with breast cancer, cervical, endometrial ovarian, and uterine cancer. Meets 3rd Tues., 7:-8:30pm, Cancer Center Conference Room, Ambulatory Care Pavilion, Jersey Shore Medical Center, Neptune. Before attending call 1-800-560-9990 (day).

Young Women with Breast Cancer Support Group *Professionally-run.* Support and education for young women with breast cancer. Peer-counseling and guest speakers. Meets 4th Thurs., 7:00pm, Riverview Medical Center, 1 Riverview Plaza, Red Bank. Call 732-530-2382 (day).

Younger Generation *Professionally-run.* Mutual support for individuals with breast cancer up to the age of 40. Rap sessions and guest speakers. Meets 1st Tues., 6pm, Jersey Shore Medical Center, Ambulatory Care Pavilion, Cancer Center Conference Room, 1945 Corlies Avenue, Neptune. Before attending call Breast Care Center 732-776-4432.

MORRIS

Breast Cancer Support Group *Professionally-run.* Information and support to women with breast cancer. Meets 1st and 3rd Tues., 7-8:30pm, Morristown Memorial Hospital, Carol G. Simon Cancer Center, 100 Madison Ave., Conference Room, Morristown. Call Jean Marie 973-971-6514.

Breast Cancer Support Group *Professionally-run.* Mutual support for women diagnosed with breast cancer. Meets Thurs., Morristown Memorial Hospital, Carol G. Simon Cancer Center, Women's Cancer Center, 100 Madison Ave., Morristown. Registration required. For meeting information call Sharing Village 908-234-0334 (day).

Together *Professionally-run.* Education and sharing for women who are undergoing (or have undergone) treatment for breast cancer. Rap sessions and guest speakers.

Denville Meets 1st and 3rd Wed., 7-8:30pm, Saint Clare's Hospital, Urban 2 Conference Room, 25 Pocono Rd. Before attending call 973-625-6176. *E-mail*: Bjohnson@saintclares.org

Dover Meets twice monthly, Mon., 1-2pm, Saint Clare's Hospital, Conference Room. For meeting information call 973-625-6176. *E-mail*: Bjohnson@saintclares.org

OCEAN

Breast Cancer Support Group *Professionally-run.* Education and sharing for women diagnosed with breast cancer. Rap sessions and occasional guest speaker. Meets last Wed., Community Medical Center, 99 Hwy. 37 West, Radiation Oncology, Ground Floor, Toms River. Before attending call Tracie Barberi, LCSW or Rose Cowen, CSW 732-557-8076 (day).

Breast Cancer Support Group *Professionally-run.* Support and education for persons afflicted with breast cancer. Meets 2nd Tues., 7-8pm, Ocean Club, 700 Route 9 South, Stafford Township. Call 609-978-3559.

PASSAIC

Breast Cancer Support Group - Embracing Life Self-help for women coping with breast cancer.

Clifton Meetings vary, St. Joseph's Regional Medical Center, 1135 Broad St. Registration is required. Before attending call Marie Marrinan 973-569-6329.

Paterson *(SPANISH SPEAKING)* Meets 1st and last Wed., 5-6pm, St. Joseph's Regional Medical Center, Xavier Bldg., 4th Floor, 703 Main St. Registration is required. Before attending call Victoria Pacheco 973-616-0514.

Post-Mastectomy/Lumpectomy Program *Professionally-run.* Support and exercise for women who have had breast surgery. Meets periodically in the spring and fall, 199 Scoles Ave., Clifton. For information call Ellen Cannel 973-890-5633 or American Cancer Society 973-696-1885. *Website*: http//www.cancer.org

SOMERSET

Breast Cancer Networking Group *Professionally-run.* Provides an opportunity for individuals with a breast cancer diagnosis to discuss and exchange information. Meets 3rd Wed., 6:30-8pm, The Wellness Community of Central New Jersey, 3 Crossroads Dr., Bedminster. Call Karen Larsen, LCSW 908-658-5400 (day).

Inflammatory Breast Cancer Networking Group *Professionally-run.* Provides an opportunity for individuals with an inflammatory breast cancer diagnosis to discuss and exchange information. Meetings vary, The Wellness Community of Central New Jersey, 3 Crossroads Dr., Bedminster. Call Ellen Levine, LCSW 908-658-5400 (day).

Post-treatment Breast Cancer Support Group *Professionally-run.* Support for women who have had surgery, radiation and/or chemotherapy. Meets Wed., Sharing Village, 161 Main St., Peapack. Registration required. Before attending call 908-234-0334 (day).

Sisters Network of Central New Jersey Mutual support for female African American breast cancer survivors. Aim is to increase awareness of the impact of breast cancer. Literature and phone help. Meets 2nd Mon., 7-8:30pm, Somerset. Call Dorothy Reed 732-246-8300 (day). *Website*: http://www.sistercentral.com *E-mail*: sistercentral@aol.com

SUSSEX

Breast Cancer Support Support and information for women at any stage of breast cancer. Meets 2nd Tues., 6:30pm, Sparta Health and Wellness Center, 89 Sparta Ave., Sparta. Call Community Benefits Education 973-579-8340 (day).

UNION

Breast Cancer Support Group *Professionally-run.* Support for women with breast cancer, diagnosed at any age and any stage of diagnosis and treatment, where resources and coping strategies are shared. Literature, newsletter and phone help. Meets Thurs., 10:30-11:45am and Wed., 7:15-8:30pm, Pathways, 79 Maple St., Summit. Pre-registration required. Before attending call 908-273-4242 ext. 154 (day).

Recurrent Breast Cancer Support Group *Professionally-run.* Support for women with recurrent breast cancer. Focuses on facing change while finding meaning and value in a challenging time. Literature, newsletter and phone help. Meets 1st and 3rd Mon., 12:30-1:45pm, Pathways, 79 Maple St., Summit. Pre-registration required. Before attending call 908-273-4242 ext. 154 (day).

Wednesday Night Family Focus Group *Professionally-run.* Support for family and friends of women with breast and gynecological cancers. Provides an opportunity to discuss and share feelings, concerns and resources with one another. Literature, newsletter and phone help. Meetings vary, Pathways, 79 Maple St., Summit. Pre-registration required. Before attending call 908-273-4242 ext. 154 (day).

Young Women's Breast Cancer Support Group *Professionally-run.* Support for women (ages 40 and under) dealing specifically with the issues that are generated by being diagnosed with breast cancer. Literature, newsletter and phone help. Meets Tues., noon-1:15pm, Pathways, 79 Maple St., Summit. Pre-registration required. Before attending call 908-273-4242 ext. 154 (day).

WARREN

Breast Cancer Support Group Mutual support and encouragement for women with breast cancer. Meets alternate Mon. evenings, Joan Knechel Cancer Center at Hackettstown Regional Medical Center, 651 Willow Grove St., Hackettstown. For information call Joan Runfola, ACSW, LCSW 908-441-1503.

Women's Cancer Group Mutual support and encouragement for women with any type of cancer and for those women in recovery from cancer. Meets 1st

Thurs., 7-8:30pm, Lutheran Church of the Good Shepherd, 168 Route 94, Blairstown. Call Kathy 908-362-6344.

NATIONAL

AABCA (African American Breast Cancer Alliance) *Model. 1 group in Minnesota. Founded 1990.* Education, support group and advocacy for Black women and men with breast cancer and their families. Provides information and referrals, education and a support group for patients and survivors to discuss issues and concerns. Open to anyone interested in supporting and working with this grass-roots organization. Write: AABCA, P.O. Box 8981, Minneapolis, MN 55408. Call 612-825-3675; Fax: 612-827-2977. *Website*: http://www.aabcainc.org *E-mail*: aabcainc@yahoo.com

Breast Cancer Support and Reach to Recovery Discussion Group *National.* Local outgrowth of Reach to Recovery Program which in most areas is a one-to-one visitation program but in some areas is a support group. Contact your local or state chapter of American Cancer Society at 1-800-227-2345 to determine availability of such groups and availability of trained volunteers. *Website*: http://www.cancer.org (click on "survivors," then click on "support programs")

Mothers Supporting Daughters with Breast Cancer *Model. Founded 1995.* Offers emotional support to the mothers of daughters newly diagnosed with breast cancer to help them to be better "care partners" to their daughters. Helps mothers cope with stress, learn about breast cancer treatment and promote breast cancer awareness. Literature, advocacy, phone support and online message board. Write: MSDBC, c/o Charmayne Dierker, 25235 Foxchase Dr., Chestertown, MD 21620. Call 410-778-1982; Fax: 410-778-1411. *Website*: http://www.mothersdaughters.org *E-mail*: msdbc@verizon.net

SHARE: Self-Help for Women with Breast or Ovarian Cancer (*BILINGUAL*) *Model. 18 sites in NY Metro Area. Founded 1976.* Provides support to women with breast or ovarian cancer, their families and friends. Support groups led by trained survivors. Cutting edge educational forums, mind/body workshops and advocacy activities held throughout the five boroughs of New York City. Write: SHARE, 1501 Broadway, Suite 704A, New York, NY 10036. Call 1-866-891-2392; Fax: 212-869-3431; Breast Hotline: 212-382-2111; Ovarian Hotline: 212-719-1204; Latina Hotline (Spanish): 212-719-4454; Toll-free (outside NYC): 1-866-891-2392; New York State Ovarian Hotline (toll-free): 1-866-537-4273. *Website*: http://www.sharecancersupport.org

Sisters Network Inc. *National. 40 affiliated chapters. 3000 members. Founded 1994.* A national African American breast cancer survivors organization that promotes the importance of breast health through empowerment, support, breast education programs, resource information and clinical trials. Write: Sisters Network Inc., 8787 Woodway Dr., Suite 4206, Houston, TX 77063. Call 1-866-781-1808 or 713-781-0255; Fax: 713-780-8998. *Website*: http://www.sistersnetworkinc.org *E-mail*: infonet@sistersnetworkinc.org

Y-ME National Breast Cancer Organization (*BILINGUAL*) *National. 9 affiliate groups. Founded 1978.* Mission is to decrease the impact of breast cancer, create and increase breast cancer awareness, and ensure through information, empowerment and peer support that no one faces breast cancer alone. Information and peer support for breast cancer patients and their families during all stages of the disease. Offers 24-hour hotlines (English and Spanish), a Latino Outreach program, a Men's Match program for husbands and partners of women with breast cancer, support groups, a Teen Education program and Advocacy Network to increase funding for research, publications, wig and prosthesis bank and newsletter. Group development guidelines. Write: Y-ME, 212 W. Van Buren St., Chicago, IL 60607-3908. Call 1-800-221-2141 (English; 24 hrs) or 1-800-986-9505 (Spanish; 24 hrs) ; Fax: 312-294-8598. *Website*: http://www.y-me.org/

ONLINE

FORCE (Facing Our Risk of Cancer Empowered) *Online. Founded 1999.* Support and education for women whose family history and genetic status put them at high risk of getting ovarian or breast cancer. Open to family members. Provides resources for women to determine if they are at high risk. Forums, chats, bulletin boards and member profiles. Phone support network. Write: FORCE, c/o Sue Friedman, 16057 Tampa Palms Blvd. W., #373, Tampa, FL 33647. Call 954-255-8732 or 1-866-824-7475. *Website*: http://www.facingourrisk.org/ *E-mail*: info@facingourrisk.org

MaleBC *Online. Founded 1997.* Brings men together who have been diagnosed with male breast cancer so they can share experiences, gain information and support each other. *Website*: http://www.acor.org (once there, click on A-Z cancers, then select "breast," then "MaleBC")

CANCER

(see also breast cancer, life threatening, toll-free helplines)

ATLANTIC

Gilda's Club South Jersey *Professionally-run.* Emotional and social support for anyone touched by cancer. Separate support groups, workshops, lectures and social events for family members. Programs for children also. Meetings vary, Gilda's Club, 300 Shore Rd., Linwood. Before attending call 609-926-2699. *Website*: http://www.gildasclubsouthjersey.org *E-mail*: erin@gildasclubsouthjersey.org

"Man to Man" Prostate Cancer Support Group An educational, information sharing and emotional support group designed to meet the challenge of living with prostate cancer for men and their partners. Educational series, literature and guest speakers. Meets 2nd Tues. (except June/July/Aug.), 7-9pm, Shore Memorial Cancer Center, 2nd Floor, Brighton Ave. and Shore Rd., Somers Point. Call Burnett Watson 609-641-7907 (day/eve).

BERGEN

Cancer Care (*BILINGUAL*) *Professionally-run.* Various support groups for cancer patients and their families. Groups also include bereavement, telephone and internet groups. Groups start periodically and run for 8 weeks. Groups meet in Ridgewood. For meeting information 1-800-813-4673 or 201-444-6630 (day). *Website*: http://www.cancercare.org

CARE (Cancer Alternatives Research Exchange) Mutual support for persons with cancer and their families. Explores any type of treatment that may be of benefit with a focus on integrated medicine. Supportive environment for whichever treatment is chosen. Guest speakers and literature. Donation $5. Meets 4 times/yr., Ridgewood United Methodist Church, 100 Dayton St., Ridgewood. For meeting dates send e-mail or call Ed Van Overloop 201-391-5931 (Mon.-Fri., 9am-noon). *E-mail*: wasub@optonline.net

Caregivers of Cancer Patients *Professionally-run.* Mutual support and education for caregivers of cancer patients. Guest speakers. Meets 2nd and 4th Mon., 2:30-4pm, Cancer Center, 20 Prospect Ave., Hackensack. Call Melissa Donahue 201-996-5836 (day).

DongGueRaMee Mutual support and education for Korean patients who have cancer, as well as cancer survivors. Families welcome. Guest speakers. Meets 1st Fri., 10am-12:30pm, Korean Community Center, 15 Ver Valen St., Closter. Call Hei Young 201-594-4848 (day).

Gastrointestinal/Colorectal Cancer Mutual support for patients, families and friends affected by gastrointestinal/colorectal cancer. Rap sessions, guest speakers and literature. Meets 2nd Thurs., 10:30am-noon, Medical Plaza, 20 Prospect Ave., Hackensack. Call Melissa Donahue 201-996-5836 (day).

Gilda's Club Northern NJ *Professionally-run.* Support groups for individuals, family members and friends touched by cancer. Programs for children also. Meetings vary, Gilda's Club, 575 Main St., Hackensack. Call 201-457-1670 (day). *Website*: http://www.gildasclubnnj.org *E-mail*: info@gildasclubnnj.com

Living With Cancer Mutual support for patients, families and friends who are affected by cancer. Rap sessions, guest speakers and literature. Meets 4th Thurs., 10:30am-noon, Medical Plaza, 20 Prospect Ave., Hackensack. Call Melissa Donahue 201-996-5836 (day).

Lung/Thoracic Cancer Mutual support for patients, families and friends affected by lung/thoracic cancer. Rap sessions, guest speakers and literature. Meets 1st Thurs., 10:30am-noon, Medical Plaza, 20 Prospect Ave., Hackensack. Call Melissa Donahue 201-996-5836 (day).

Multiple Myeloma *Professionally-run.* Mutual support for patients, families and friends affected by multiple myeloma. Rap sessions, guest speakers and literature. Meets 3rd Thurs., 10:30am-noon, Medical Plaza, 20 Prospect Ave., Hackensack. Call Melissa Donahue 201-996-5836 (day).

Northern NJ Chapter Leukemia and Lymphoma Society *Professionally-run.* Emotional support for adult patients and family members where there has been a diagnosis of leukemia, lymphoma, Hodgkins disease or multiple myeloma. Mutual sharing, guest speakers and education. Meets 10:30am, 6 week sessions, 3 times/yr., Cancer Center, Hackensack University Medical Center, Hackensack. Pre-registration required. Call Deborah Halpern, MSW, ACSW 908-654-9445 ext. 12 (day). *Website*: http://www.lls.org/nj *E-mail*: deborah.halpern@lls.org

On Treatment Families *Professionally-run.* Support and education for patients, parents and siblings who have cancer or serious blood disorders. Also groups for children and families who have completed treatment. Meetings vary, Hackensack University Medical Center, Reuten Clinic, Hackensack. For meeting information call Judy Solomon 201-996-5437 (day).

Prostate Cancer Support Group *Professionally-run.* Support and education for prostate cancer patients and their families. Meets 3rd Wed., 10am-noon, Hekemian Conference Center, Hackensack University Medical Center, 30 Prospect Ave., Hackensack. Call Melissa Donahue 201-996-5836 (day).

Prostate Cancer Support Group Support and education for people affected by prostate cancer. Families and caregivers welcome. Guest speakers and literature. Meets 2nd Wed., 7-9pm, Pascack Valley Hospital, 250 Old Hook Rd.,

Westwood. Call Ray 201-670-0586 or Health Information Resource 201-358-6000 (day).

Survivorship After Treatment *Professionally-run.* Mutual support and education for patients who have undergone cancer treatment. Rap sessions and guest speakers. Meets various times and days, Medical Plaza, 20 Prospect Ave., Hackensack. Call Melissa Donahue 201-996-5836 (day).

Us Too *Professionally-run.* Support and education for persons diagnosed with prostate cancer and their significant others. Meets 3rd Fri., 10am-noon, Daniel and Gloria Blumenthal Cancer Center, 2nd Floor, Meeting Room, One Valley Health Plaza, Paramus. Call 201-634-5339 (day).

BURLINGTON

Living with Lung Cancer *Professionally-run.* Mutual support and encouragement for anyone with lung cancer. Meets 1st Wed., 11:30am-12:30pm, Virtua Memorial Hospital of Burlington County, Conference Center, 175 Madison Ave., Mt. Holly. Before attending for the first time call Virtua Memorial Hospital 1-888-847-8823 (day).

"Man to Man" Prostate Cancer Support Group *Professionally-run.* An educational, information sharing and emotional support group designed to meet the challenge of living with prostate cancer. Meets 3rd Tues., 7-8:30pm, Virtua Memorial Hospital of Burlington County, Conference Room B, 175 Madison Ave., Mt. Holly. Call 1-800-227-2345 (day). *Website*: http://www.cancer.org *E-mail*: natalie.sheldrick@cancer.org

CAMDEN

Cancer Adjustment Program *Professionally-run.* Mutual support for cancer patients and their families. Meets Mon., 7:30pm, 1851 Old Cuthbert Rd., Cherry Hill. Call American Cancer Society 1-800-227-2345 (day). *Website*: http://www.cancer.org *E-mail*: natalie.sheldrick@cancer.org

Leukemia Society of America - Eastern Pennsylvania Chapter *Professionally-run.* Support and education for families to help cope with the emotional and personal issues of lymphoma, leukemia and multiple myeloma. Meets 4th Thurs., 7-8:30pm, Einstein Center One, Suite 206, 9880 Bustleton Ave., Philadelphia. Free parking. Call Anne Waldman 215-456-3822 (day). *E-mail*: mclaughlin@lls.org

Women's Cancer Connection *Professionally-run.* Mutual support for women with ovarian, cervical or uterine cancer. Meets 1st Tues., 7-8:30pm, Virtua Health's William G. Rohrer Center for Health Fitness, 2309 Evesham Rd., Voorhees. Before attending for the first time call Virtua Health 1-888-847-8823 (day).

CAPE MAY

Cancer Support Group *Professionally-run.* Mutual support and education for men and women who have cancer. Separate group for spouses and significant others. Guest speakers, literature. Both groups meet 2nd and 4th Thurs., 7pm, Burdette Tomlin Memorial Hospital, Maruchi Room, Cape May Court House. Call 609-463-2367 (day) or 609-463-2298.

ESSEX

Abrazos de Carino (Caring Hugs) *(SPANISH SPEAKING) Professionally-run.* Opportunity for men and women who have been diagnosed with cancer to come together to offer strength, experience and hope. Provides a supportive environment where persons can express feelings and concerns with others who share a common experience. Meditation offered after meeting. Meets Mon., 11am-1pm, Cathedral Regional Cancer Center, Saint Michael's Medical Center, Conference Room, Central Ave., Newark. Before attending call Joanne Rodriguez 973-877-2967 (day).

Beyond Primary Cancer *Professionally-run.* Group provides a supportive environment to share thoughts, concerns, gain practical information and emotional support for patients coping with recurrent or metastic cancer. Meeting days vary, Saint Barnabas Medical Center, 94 Old Short Hills Rd., Livingston. Before attending call Angela McCabe 973-322-2668.

Caring Arms *Professionally-run.* Opportunity for men and women who have been diagnosed with cancer to come together to offer strength, experience, and hope. Provides a supportive environment where persons can express feelings and concerns with others who share a common experience. Meditation offered after meeting. Meets Mon., 12:30pm, Cathedral Regional Cancer Center, Saint Michael's Medical Center, Conference Room, Central Ave., Newark. Before attending call Joanne Rodriguez 973-877-2967 (day).

Expressive Arts Group *Professionally-run.* Support for patients who are undergoing cancer treatment. Meeting days and times vary, St. Barnabas Medical Center, 94 Old Short Hills Rd., Livingston. Call Stephanie Buck, MPS, ATR 973-322-2171 (day).

Gynecological Cancer Support Group *Professionally-run.* Mutual support for women with any type of gynecological cancer. Opportunity to talk and share with one another. Meets 3rd Tues., 6-7pm, Mountainside Hospital Cancer Center, Harries Pavilion, Conference Room, 1 Bay Ave., Montclair. Call Sara Duphiney 973-429-6038 (day) or Kathy Morelli 973-429-6009 (day).

Healing Stitches *Professionally-run.* Mutual support for cancer patients to gather weekly to chat, knit or crochet while interacting and creating projects. Families and caregivers welcome. Meets Wed., 1-3pm, Mountainside Hospital, Cancer Center, 1 Bay Ave., Montclair. Call Sara Duphiney, LSW 973-429-6038 (day).

"Us Too" Prostate Cancer Support Group *Professionally-run.* Information and support for men with prostate cancer and their families.

Livingston Meets 2nd Tues., 7-8:30pm, St. Barnabas Medical Center, Dept. of Radiation, Oncology Room 1749, 94 Old Short Hills Rd. Call Angela McCabe 973-322-2668 (day). *Website*: http://www.sbhcs.com

Montclair Meets 1st Thurs. (except July), 7-8:30pm, Mountainside Hospital, Harries Pavilion, Cancer Center, Conference Room, 1 Bay Ave. Before attending call Sara Duphiney, LSW 973-429-6038 (day).

GLOUCESTER

Leukemia and Lymphoma Support Group *Professionally-run.* Emotional support, education, and discussion of common issues for people with leukemia, lymphomas and related disorders, as well as for their families and loved ones. Rap sessions and guest speakers. Meets 3rd Tues., 7-9pm, Gloucester County Dept. of Education, Tanyard Rd., Sewell. Call Leukemia Society 856-869-0200 or Libby Maurer 856-468-1167.

HUDSON

Cancer Support Group (*BILINGUAL*) *Professionally-run.* Support for cancer patients and their families. Literature and guest speakers. Meetings vary, 3-4pm, Columbus Health Center, 115 Columbus Dr., 1st Floor, Jersey City. Call Janet Richman, LCSW 201-946-6807 (day). *E-mail*: jrichman@libertyhcs.org

HUNTERDON

Us Too! Prostate Cancer Support Group *Professionally-run.* Provides support and education for those with prostate cancer and their spouse. Guest speakers, phone help and literature. Meets 2nd Thurs., 6-7:30pm, Hunterdon Regional

Cancer Center, Conference Room, 2100 Westcott Dr., Flemington. Call 908-237-2337.

MERCER

Sharing Your Journey Through Cancer *Professionally-run.* Peer support for persons with cancer to share experiences. Families welcomed. Phone help and literature. Meets 1st and 3rd Thurs., 6:30-8pm, The Cancer Institute of NJ at Hamilton, Campus of RWJU Hospital, Conference Room, 2575 Klockner Road, Hamilton. Call Connie Stallone, MSW, LCSW 609-584-6680 (day).

Thyroid Cancer Survivors Support Group Support group for thyroid cancer survivors. Families are welcome. Literature, guest speaker and phone help. Meets 3rd Sat., 10-11:30am, Capitol Health System at Hamilton, 1445 Whitehorse-Mercerville Rd., Mercerville. Call Michael Dubrow 1-877-588-7904 (eve). *E-mail*: centraljersey@thyca.org

MIDDLESEX

Cancer Support Group (*BILINGUAL*) Support for cancer survivors and their loved ones to provide an opportunity to meet with others who may be experiencing similar issues. Guest speakers, literature and speakers bureau. Meets 1st Tues., 6-7:30pm, Raritan Bay Medical Center, 530 New Brunswick Ave., Perth Amboy. Call Teresa Madden 732-324-5173 (day) or Sandra Nilsson 732-324-5079 (day).

Coping With Cancer *Professionally-run.* Provides a safe environment for cancer patients and their families to share their feelings and concerns. Helps patients become educated partners in their healthcare through information on diagnosis and treatment. Meets 4th Tues., 2-3:30pm, JFK Medical Center, 65 James St., Edison. Call Mary Aloia 732-321-7769 (day).

Healing Journey: Relaxation for Cancer Patients/Families, The *Professionally-run.* Support for those afflicted with cancer to develop relaxation and visualization skills. Families welcome. Educational and experiential group. Meets 3rd Tues., 6-7:30pm, Haven Hospice, JFK Medical Center, 65 James St., Edison. Call Erika Kalb 732-321-7769 (day).

Lesbians with Cancer Support Group *Professionally-run.* Mutual support, sharing and education. Partners welcome. Meets 2nd Wed., 7pm, The Cancer Institute of NJ, 195 Little Albany St., New Brunswick. Call Rebecca Pick, MSW, LSW 732-235-7011 (day).

Living with Cancer Support Group *Professionally-run.* Mutual support for anyone who has been diagnosed with cancer to help them gain control over their lives through better knowledge of the disease. Family and friends welcome. Meets 2nd and 4th Wed., 7pm, Cancer Institute of NJ, 195 Little Albany St., 2nd Floor Waiting Room, New Brunswick. Must register first. Call 732-235-7557 (day).

Northern NJ Chapter Leukemia and Lymphoma Society *Professionally-run.* Emotional support for adult patients and family members where there has been a diagnosis of leukemia, lymphoma, Hodgkin's disease or multiple myeloma. Mutual sharing, guest speakers and education. Meets 2nd Mon., 1pm, Cancer Institute of NJ, New Brunswick. Pre-registration required. Call Deborah Halpern, MSW, ACSW 908-654-9445 ext. 12. *Website*: http://www.lls.org/nj *E-mail*: deborah.halpern@lls.org

STEPS (Skills To Empower People) *Professionally-run.* Educational program for cancer patients, families and friends that focuses on ways to cope with various aspects of dealing with cancer. Guest speakers, literature and newsletter. Meeting days and times vary, The Cancer Institute of NJ, 195 Little Albany St., New Brunswick. For meeting information call Nursing Education Dept. 732-235-8784 (day). *Website*: http://www.cinj.org/Patients/Education/support-education.htm

Strength For Caring *Professionally-run.* Support, education and coping skills to families caring for a loved one with cancer. Meets 4th Tues., 7pm, Cancer Institute, 195 Little Albany St., 2nd Floor Learning Room, New Brunswick. To register call 732-235-6027 (day).

MONMOUTH

Cancer Caregivers Support Group *Professionally-run.* Mutual support for caregivers of cancer patients. Offers encouragement and coping skills. Meets 2nd Mon., 7:30-9pm, Riverview Medical Center, Booker Cancer Center, 1 Riverview Plaza, Red Bank. Pre-registration required. Call 732-530-2382 (day).

Cancer Patient and Family Support *Professionally-run.* Mutual support and education for persons with all types of cancer and their families. Exchange of coping skills. Meets 2nd Mon., 3-4:30pm, CentraState Medical Center, 901 W. Main St., Freehold. Call Karen Sherman, RN 732-303-5098 (day) or Deb Turi-Smith, BACSW 732-294-2842 (day). *E-mail*: ksherman@centrastate.com

Coping with Chemotherapy *Professionally-run.* Mutual support for persons who are undergoing chemotherapy or radiation treatments, their families and caregivers. Meets various times and days, Jersey Shore Medical Center, 1945 Corlies Ave., Neptune. Before attending call 732-776-2346.

Inner Circle *Professionally-run.* Mutual support for cancer patients, survivors, their families, and caregivers. Meets 1st and 3rd Wed., 7-9pm, Jersey Shore University Medical Center, Ambulatory Care Center, 1945 Route 33, Neptune. Call 1-888-538-8314.

Kids Need Support, Too *Professionally-run.* Support for children and adolescents who have a family member diagnosed with cancer or other serious illness. Meets 1st Wed., 7pm, Monmouth Medical Center, 300 Second Ave., Long Branch. Pre-registration required. Before attending call 732-923-6990 (day).

Leukemia and Lymphoma Support Group *Professionally-run.* Emotional support, education and discussion of common issues for people with leukemia, lymphomas and related disorders, as well as for their families and loved ones. Rap sessions and guest speakers. Meets 1st Wed., 7pm, Centra State Medical Center, 901 W. Main St., Freehold. Call Leukemia Society 1-888-920-8557.

Metastic and Recurrent Breast and Ovarian Cancer Group *Professionally-run.* Designed for women diagnosed with metastic or recurrent breast, ovarian, cervical, endometrial or uterine cancer. Meets 3rd Tues., 4:30pm, Jersey Shore Medical Center, 1945 Corlies Ave., Neptune. Before attending call 732-776-2380.

Ovarian Cancer Support Group Support for women with ovarian, cervical, uterine and endometrial cancer. Meets 1st and 3rd Tues., 11:30am-1:30pm, Jersey Shore University Medical Center, Ambulatory Care Center, Cancer Conference Room, 1945 Corlies Ave. (Route 33), Neptune. Call 732-776-4432.

Partners in Healing Support Group *Professionally-run.* Mutual support for spouses/significant others of women diagnosed with breast, cervical, endometrial, ovarian or uterine cancer. Meets 3rd Tues., 7:00-8:30pm, Cancer Center Conference Room, Ambulatory Care Pavilion, Jersey Shore Medical Center, Neptune. Before attending call 732-776-2380.

"Us Too" Prostate Cancer Support Group Mutual support for men who have prostate cancer. Family members are welcome.

> **Long Branch** Meets 1st Thurs., 7-9pm, Monmouth Medical Center. Registration required. Before attending call Cancer Services 732-923-6575.

Neptune Meets 3rd Thurs., 7-9pm, Neptune Housing Authority, 19 Davis Ave., Community Rm. Call Jersey Shore Cancer Center 1-888-538-8314 (day).

Young People Have Feelings Too *Professionally-run.* Support group held in a family setting for youth (ages 5-17) who have an immediate family member with cancer. Meets 1st Tues., 7-8pm, for 8 consecutive sessions in Neptune. Before attending call 1-888-538-8314.

MORRIS

Children's Group *Professionally-run.* Provides support to children (ages 6-12) dealing with family issues of cancer. Group meets for 8 week sessions. Parents group meets concurrently. For information call Brandy Johnson 973-625-6176 (day).

Head And Neck Cancer Support for any person afflicted with head and neck cancer. Meets 3rd Wed., 1:30-3pm, Carol G. Simon Cancer Center, Morristown Memorial Hospital, 100 Madison Ave., Morristown. Call Catherine Owens, LCSW 973-971-5169.

Living with Cancer *Professionally-run.* Support and information for people with cancer, their families and supportive friends to help them adjust. Meets 2nd and 4th Wed., 7-8:30pm, Saint Clare's Hospital, 25 Pocono Rd., Urban 2 Conference Room, Denville. Call Brandy 973-625-6176 (day). *E-mail*: bjohnson@saintclares.org

Lung Cancer Support Group Support for people at any stage of lung cancer. Spouses are welcome. Meets 4th Wed., 2-3:30pm, Carol G. Simon Cancer Center, Morristown Memorial Hospital, Morristown. Call Catherine Owens, LCSW 973-971-5169.

Northern NJ Chapter Leukemia and Lymphoma Society *Professionally-run.* Emotional support for adult patients and family members where there has been a diagnosis of multiple myeloma. Mutual sharing, guest speakers and education. Meetings vary, Morristown Memorial Hospital, Carol G. Simon Conference Center, Morristown. Pre-registration required. Call Deborah Halpern, MSW, ACSW 908-654-9445 ext. 12 (day). *Website*: http://www.lls.org/nj *E-mail*: deborah.halpern@lls.org

Tri-County New Voice Laryngectomee Support Group of Morris/Sussex/Warren Counties Mutual support and social activities for laryngectomees. Also includes neck, head and/or oral cancers. Hospital visitation for new laryngectomees. Family and friends are welcome. Meets 2nd Mon. (except Jan., Feb., Mar., July, Aug.), 7:15pm, Saint Clare's Hospital, Silby Hall, 25 Pocono Rd., Denville. Call Tom Beneventine 973-694-8417 (day/eve).

"Us Too" Prostate Cancer Support Group *Professionally-run.* Education and support for prostate cancer survivors and their supportive family members and friends.

Denville Meets 2nd Tues. (except July/ Aug.), 7:30-9pm, Saint Clare's Hospital, Silby Cafeteria, 25 Pocono Rd., Denville. Before attending call Ron 973-927-0534.

Morristown Meets 1st Tues., 7:30-9:30pm, Morristown Memorial Hospital, Malcolm Forbes Amphitheater, 100 Madison Ave. Call Bill Grassmyer 973-895-2135 or Catherine Owens, LCSW 973-971-5169 (day).

Woman to Woman Mutual support for women living with cancer. Meets 1st and 3rd Tues., 2-3:30pm, Chilton Memorial Hospital, Collins Pavilion, 97 West Parkway, Pompton Plains. Call 973-831-5311 (Tues.-Thurs.); TTY: 973-831-5000.

OCEAN

Cancer Concern Center Support for those coping with cancer. Family and friends welcome. Yoga, meditation and wigs. Phone help available. Meets Tues., noon-1pm and Wed., 6:30pm, 1101 Richmond Ave., Route 35 South, Point Pleasant. Call 732-701-0250.

Colorectal Cancer Support Group *Professionally-run.* Mutual support for persons with colorectal cancer. Family and friends welcome. Guest speakers and phone help. Meets 2nd Wed., 3pm, Community Medical Center, 99 Route 37 West, Radiation - Oncology Dept., Toms River. Call Sherry 732-557-8270 (day).

Prostate Cancer Support Group Provides support and education for men diagnosed with prostate cancer and their families. Meets 3rd Thurs., 2pm, The Lighthouse, 591 Lakehurst Rd., Toms River. Call 1-800-621-0096 (day).

SPOHNC (Support for People with Oral and Head and Neck Cancer) *Professionally-run.* Support for persons with oral, head and neck cancer. Families welcome. Guest speakers, newsletter and phone help. Meets last Thurs., 3pm, Community Medical Center, 99 Route 37 West, Radiation - Oncology Dept., Toms River. Call Sherry 732-557-8270 (day). *Website:* http://www.spohnc.org

SOMERSET

Cancer Support Group *Professionally-run.* Provides support for cancer patients to share thoughts, feelings and information with others diagnosed with cancer. Meets Thurs., 10-11:30am, The Wellness Community of Central New Jersey, 3 Crossroads Dr., Bedminster. Pre-registration is required. Before attending call Karen Larsen, LCSW 908-658-5400 (day).

Caregiver Support Group *Professionally-run.* Support for family members and friends who are caring for a person with cancer. Share thoughts, feelings and information. Meets Thurs., 10-11:30am, The Wellness Community of Central New Jersey, 3 Crossroads Dr., Bedminster. Pre-registration required. Before attending call Ellen Levine, LSCW 908-658-5400 (day).

Colorectal Cancer Networking Group *Professionally-run.* Provides an opportunity for individuals with colorectal cancer diagnosis to discuss and exchange information. Meets 1st Wed., 6:30-8pm, The Wellness Community of Central New Jersey, 3 Crossroads Dr., Bedminster. Call Karen Larsen, LCSW 908-658-5400 (day).

Gynecological Cancer Networking Group *Professionally-run.* Provides an opportunity for individuals with a gynecological cancer diagnosis to discuss and exchange information. Meets 4th Wed., 6:30-8pm, The Wellness Community of Central New Jersey, 3 Crossroads Dr., Bedminster. Call Karen Larsen, LCSW 908-658-5400 (day).

Kids Connect / Parents Connect *Professionally-run.* Support for children (ages 7-17) to help them cope with a parent's cancer diagnosis. Children participate in creative activities to help them express their feelings. Parents develop skills to talk with children about their cancer. Meetings vary, 10am-noon, The Wellness Community of Central New Jersey, 3 Crossroads Dr., Bedminster. Pre-registration required. Before attending call Karen Larsen, LCSW 908-658-5400 (day).

Lung Cancer Networking Group *Professionally-run.* Provides an opportunity for individuals with a lung cancer diagnosis and their caregivers to discuss and exchange information. Meets 2nd Wed., 6:30-8pm, The Wellness Community of Central New Jersey, 3 Crossroads Dr., Bedminster. Call Karen Larsen, LCSW 908-658-5400.

SUSSEX

Blood Cancer Family Support Group *Professionally-run.* Support for patients affected by leukemia, lymphoma, myeloma. Families and friends welcome. Rap sessions and guest speakers. Meets last Wed., 6:30-8pm, Sparta Cancer Center, Sparta. To register call Deborah Halpern 908-654-9445 ext. 12. Before attending each session call Kathryn Cramer or Nina Sullivan 973-726-0005 (day). *Website*: http://www.LLS.org/nnj *E-mail*: halpernd@lls.org

Life After Cancer Support Group *Professionally-run.* Support and education for those with cancer at any stage, their families and friends. Meets last Tues., 6:30pm, Newton Memorial Hospital, 175 High St., Newton. Call Social Work Dept. 973-579-8620.

"Man to Man" Prostate Cancer Support Group An educational, information sharing and emotional support group designed to meet the challenge of living with prostate cancer for men and their partners. Educational series, literature and guest speakers. Meets 3rd Tues., 6:30-8:30pm, Sparta Health and Wellness Center, 89 Sparta Ave., Sparta. Call Michele Capossela 973-331-3794 ext. 118 (day). *E-mail*: Michele.capossela@cancer.org

Northern NJ Chapter Leukemia and Lymphoma Society *Professionally-run.* Emotional support for adult patients and family members where there has been a diagnosis of blood cancer. Mutual sharing, guest speakers and education. Meets last Wed., 6:30-8pm, Sparta Cancer Center, 89 Sparta Ave., Sparta. Pre-registration required. Call Deborah Halpern, MSW, ACSW 908-654-9445 (day). *Website*: http://www.lls.org/nnj *E-mail*: deborah.halpern@lls.org

UNION

Gynecological Cancer Support Group *Professionally-run.* Support for women afflicted with gynecological cancers at any stage of diagnosis and treatment, where resources and coping strategies are shared. Meets Tues., noon-1:15pm, Faith Lutheran Church, South St., New Providence. Pre-registration required. Before attending call 908-273-4242 ext. 154.

Hearts and Hands *Professionally-run.* An open drop-in cancer support group offering patients and caregivers the opportunity to support each other. Members may knit, crochet or do other crafts while meeting. Meets Thurs., 2-4pm, Overlook Hospital, 99 Beauvoir Ave., Conference Room 1, Summit. Call Lee Anne Caffrey 908-522-5349 (day) or Kristen Scarlett 908-522-5255 (day).

Insight *Professionally-run.* Support for cancer patients and their families to talk about problems and issues in dealing with cancer. Meets 3rd Thurs., 7-9pm, Jewish Community Center, 1391 Martine Ave., Scotch Plains. Call Mary Aloia 908-668-2248 (day) or JCC 908-889-8800.

N.J. Chapter – Metro New York Carcinoid Support Group Provides help and education to patients and caregivers. Discusses experiences and options for those with carcinoid or other neuroendocrine tumors. Meets 1st Sun. (except Feb., Apr., July, Aug., Oct.), 1:30pm, Crossroads Christian Fellowship, 2815 Morris Ave., Union. Call Jim Weiveris 609-812-9294 (day/eve.) or Judy Golz 201-891-2259 (eve.). *Website*: http://www.carcinoid.us *E-mail:* Caring4noids@aol.com

Wednesday Night Family Focus Group *Professionally-run.* Support for family and friends of women with breast and gynecological cancers. Provides an opportunity to discuss and share feelings, concerns and resources with one another. Literature, newsletter and phone help. Meetings vary, Pathways, 79 Maple St., Summit. Pre-registration required. Before attending call 908-273-4242 ext. 154 (day).

WARREN

Women's Cancer Group Mutual support and encouragement for women with any type of cancer and for those women in recovery from cancer. Meets 1st Thurs., 7-8:30pm, Lutheran Church of the Good Shepherd, 168 Route 94, Blairstown. Call Kathy 908-362-6344.

NATIONAL

Cancer Care, Inc. *National. Founded 1944.* Support for cancer patients and their families. Financial assistance, information and referrals, community and professional education. On-going telephone, online and in-person support groups. Free counseling. Write: Cancer Care, Inc., 275 Seventh Ave., New York, NY 10001. Call 1-800-813-4673; Fax: 212-719-0263. *Website*: http://www.cancercare.org *E-mail*: info@cancercare.org

Candlelighters Childhood Cancer Foundation *International. 300+ groups (32 in U.S.). Founded 1970.* Support for parents of children and adolescents with cancer, their families, adult survivors of childhood cancer and the professionals working with them. Links parents, families and groups. Provides psychosocial support, educational resource materials and advocates on behalf of childhood cancer. Newsletter, youth newsletter, educational materials and publication list. Write: Candlelighters Childhood Cancer Foundation, P.O. Box 498, Kensington,

MD 20895-0498. Call 1-800-366-2223 or 301-962-3520; Fax: 301-962-3521. *Website*: http://www.candlelighters.org *E-mail*: staff@candlelighters.org

Colorectal Cancer Network *National. Founded 1999.* 5 affiliated groups. Support, education and advocacy for colorectal cancer survivors and their caregivers. Peer-to-peer support groups, extensive website library of online links and resources. Write: Colorectal Cancer Network, P.O. Box 182, Kensington, MD 20895-0182. Group development guidelines available. Call 301-879-1500; Fax: 267-821-7080. *Website*: http://www.colorectal-cancer.net *E-mail*: ccnetwork@colorectal-cancer.net

DES Cancer Network *National. Founded 1983.* Mutual support and education for DES-exposed women, with a special focus on DES cancer issues. Provides research, advocacy and medical/legal resources. Newsletter. Write: DES Cancer Network, 2925 Garber St., Berkeley, CA 94705. *Website*: http://www.descancer.org *E-mail*: desnetwrk@aol.com

IMPACC (Intestinal Multiple Polyposis And Colorectal Cancer) *National network. Founded 1986.* Support network to help patients and families dealing with familial polyposis and hereditary colon cancer. Provides information and referrals, encourages research, educates professionals and public. Phone support network, correspondence and literature. Write: IMPACC, c/o Ann Fagan, P.O. Box 11, Conyngham, PA 18219. Call Ann Fagan 570-788-1818 (day) or 570-788-3712 (eve); Fax: 570-788-4046. *E-mail*: impacc@epix.net

International Myeloma Foundation *International network. Helps support over 89 myeloma support groups in the US. Founded 1990.* Mission is to improve the quality of life of myeloma patients while working toward a prevention and a cure. Educational and supportive programs, information packets, phone support and newsletter. Networks patients together for mutual support. Referrals to self-help groups nationwide. Guidelines offered to assist those interested in starting a group. Write: International Myeloma Foundation, 12650 Riverside Dr., Suite 206, North Hollywood, CA 91607. Call 818-487-7455 or 1-800-452-2873; Fax: 818-487-7454. *Website*: http://www.myeloma.org *E-mail*: TheIMF@myeloma.org

Kidney Cancer Association *National. Founded 1990.* Provides information about kidney cancer to patients and doctors. Sponsors research and advocates on behalf of patients. E-newsletter, information and referrals, literature and conferences. Write: Kidney Cancer Assn., 1234 Sherman, Suite 203, Evanston, IL 60202. Call 1-800-850-9132 or 847-332-1051; Fax: 847-332-2978. *Website*: http://www.curekidneycancer.org *E-mail*: office@curekidneycancer.org

Kids Konnected *National. 17 affiliated groups. Founded 1993.* Opportunity for children who have a parent with cancer to connect with other children in similar situations for support and understanding. Groups are headed by youth leaders and co-facilitated by professionals. Hotline, Youth Leadership program, monthly meetings, information and referrals, newsletter and summer camps. Call 1-800-899-2866 or 949-582-5443 (24 hr). *Website*: http://www.kidskonnected.org *E-mail*: info@kidskonnected.org

Leukemia and Lymphoma Society, The *National. 66 chapters. Founded 1949.* Provides educational materials, patient financial aid, support services for patients, families and friends coping with leukemia, lymphoma, myeloma and other blood cancers. Support group meetings schedule depends on location. Consult local chapter. Live help online 10am-5pm EST. Write: LLS, 1311 Mamaroneck Ave., Suite 310, White Plains, NY 10605. Call 1-800-955-4572 or 914-949-5213; Fax: 914-949-6691. *Website*: http://www.lls.org *E-mail*: infocenter@lls.org

Lymphoma Research Foundation (*BILINGUAL*) *National. 20 chapters. Founded 1991.* Provides information and emotional support for lymphoma patients and their families. Offers free educational materials, lymphoma helpline, national buddy program, quarterly newsletter, annual patient educational forum and local seminars. Fundraises for research. Advocacy. Devoted to funding lymphoma research and providing patients and healthcare professionals with critical information on the disease. Some materials available in Spanish and Chinese. Write: Lymphoma Research Foundation, 8800 Venice Blvd., Suite 207, Los Angeles, CA 90034. Call 310-204-7040 or 1-800-500-9976; Fax: 310-204-7043. *Website*: http://www.lymphoma.org or http://www.lymphomafacts.org *E-mail*: LRF@lymphoma.org

Man To Man Program *National. 300 affiliated groups. Founded 1990.* Support and education for men with prostate cancer to enable them better understand their options and to make informed decisions. Phone support, information and referrals, support group meetings, education and support visitation program. Newsletter. Some chapters invite wives and partners. Other chapters have wives and partners meet separately. Assistance available for starting new groups. Call the American Cancer Society 1-800-227-2345. *Website*: http://www.cancer.org

Mautner Project, the National Lesbian Health Organization *Model. Several groups in Washington, DC. Founded 1990.* Cancer support and survivorship groups for lesbian, bisexual and transgender women who partner with women (WPWs), their partners and caregivers. Bereavement support groups for WPWs who have lost a partner, friend or loved one. Smoking cessation groups for the lesbian, gay, bisexual and transgender community. Health self-empowerment groups for black WPWs. Provides phone and online support to WPWs outside the DC-Metro area. Provides LGBT cultural competency training to health care professionals and their staff members. Educates the lesbian/WPW community about health issues. Advocacy, information and referrals, phone support, literature, newsletter. Write: Mautner Project, 1707 L St. NW, Suite 230, Washington, DC 20036. Call 1-866-628-8637 or 202-332-5536 (day); TDD: 202-332-5536. *Website*: http://www.mautnerproject.org *E-mail*: mautner@mautnerproject.org

National Coalition for Cancer Survivorship *National network. Founded 1986.* Grassroots network that works on behalf of persons with any type of cancer. Mission is to advocate for quality of cancer care for all Americans by leading and strengthening the survivorship movement, empowering cancer survivors and advocating for policy issues affecting survivors' quality of life. Provides information on employment and insurance issues, referrals and publications. Newsletter. Guidelines available to help start a similar group. Write: NCCS, 1010 Wayne Ave., Suite 770, Silver Spring, MD 20910. Call 301-650-9127; Fax: 301-565-9670. *Website*: http//:www.canceradvocacy.org or http://www.cancersurvivaltoolbox.org *E-mail*: info@canceradvocacy.org

National Ovarian Cancer Coalition *National. 80 affiliated divisions. Founded 1995.* Promotes education and awareness regarding ovarian cancer for patients, families and medical community. Information and referrals, networking, conferences, literature, and phone support. Helps develop statewide divisions. Write: National Ovarian Cancer Coalition, 500 NE Spanish River Blvd., Suite 8, Boca Raton, FL 33431. Call 1-888-682-7426 or 561-393-0005; Fax: 561-393-7275. *Website*: http://www.ovarian.org *E-mail*: nocc@ovarian.org

PAACT (Patient Advocates for Advanced Cancer Treatment) *International. 150 affiliated groups. Founded 1984.* Provides support and advocacy for prostate cancer patients, their families and the general public at risk. Information relative to the advancements in the detection, diagnosis, evaluation and treatment of prostate cancer. Information, referrals, phone help, conferences and newsletter. Group development guidelines. Write: PAACT, P.O. Box 141695, Grand Rapids, MI 49514-1695. Call 616-453-1477; Fax: 616-453-1846. *Website*: http://www.paactusa.org *E-mail*: paact@paactusa.org

People Living Through Cancer *Model. 35 groups in New Mexico. Founded 1983.* Helps cancer survivors and their loved ones make informed choices and improve the quality of life by sharing in a community of people who have "been there." Newsletter, information and referrals, support groups and advocacy. Dues $35/yr. (includes subscription to journal). Conducts national training for American Indians and Alaskan natives who are interested in developing cancer survivorship programs based on a grassroots program serving Pueblo Indians. Write: People Living Through Cancer, 3939 San Pedro Blvd. NE, Suite C-8, Albuquerque, NM 87110. Call 505-242-3263; Fax: 505-242-6756. *Website*: http://www.pltc.org *E-mail*: pltc@pltc.org

Pregnant with Cancer Network *National. Founded 1997.* Created by three women who were diagnosed with cancer while pregnant. Mission is to let women know that they are not alone facing cancer and pregnancy. Links women together who have a similar diagnosis. Newsletter. Write: The Pregnant with Cancer Support Group, P.O. Box 1243, Buffalo, NY 14220. Call 1-800-743-4471. *Website*: http://www.pregnantwithcancer.org

SHARE: Self-Help for Women with Breast or Ovarian Cancer *(BILINGUAL) Model. Founded 1976.* Provides support to women with breast or ovarian cancer, their families and friends. Support groups led by trained survivors. Cutting edge educational forums, mind/body workshops and advocacy activities held throughout the five boroughs of New York City. Write: SHARE, 1501 Broadway, Suite 704A, New York, NY 10036. Call 1-866-891-2392; Fax: 212-869-3431; Breast Hotline: 212-382-2111; Ovarian Hotline: 212-719-1204; Latina Hotline (Spanish): 212-719-4454; Toll-free (outside NYC): 1-866-891-2392; New York State Ovarian Hotline (toll-free): 1-866-537-4273. *Website*: http://www.sharecancersupport.org

SPOHNC (Support for People with Oral and Head and Neck Cancer) *National. 54 affiliated groups. Founded 1991.* Patient-directed self-help program offering information, encouragement, support, acceptance and self-expression for persons with oral, head and neck cancer. National Survivor Volunteer Network offering one-on-one support, phone support, educational programs and publications. Assistance in starting groups. Membership dues $25 (includes 9 newsletters). Write: SPOHNC, P.O. Box 53, Locust Valley, NY 11560-0053. Call 1-800-377-0928; Fax: 516-671-8794. *Website*: http://www.spohnc.org *E-mail*: info@spohnc.org

ThyCa: Thyroid Cancer Survivors' Association, Inc. *National.* Support, education and communication for people with all types of thyroid cancer, as well as caregivers. Outreach to the public for thyroid cancer awareness and early detection. Nine online support groups, local support groups, free online newsletter, free downloadable low-iodine cookbook, free regional workshops, annual international conference, free thyroid cancer awareness brochures, Thyroid Cancer Awareness Month, funding for research and educational website. Write: ThyCa: Thyroid Cancer Survivors' Association, Inc., P.O. Box 1545, New York, NY 10159-1545. Call 1-877-588-7904; Fax: 630-604-6078. *Website*: http://www.thyca.org *E-mail*: thyca@thyca.org

"Us Too" International Prostate Cancer Education and Support Net *International. 300 affiliated groups. Founded 1990.* Education and support provided for men and their families with fellowship and peer counseling. Timely, personalized, unbiased and reliable information about prostate cancer. Monthly newsletter distributed through support groups and also on website. Write: Us Too Int'l Prostate Cancer Education and Support, 5003 Fairview Ave., Downers Grove, IL 60515-5286. Call 1-800-808-7866 or 630-795-1002 (day); Fax: 630-795-1602. *Website*: http://www.ustoo.org *E-mail*: ustoo@ustoo.org

ONLINE

ACOR (Association of Cancer Online Resources) *Online.* Provides information related to different types of cancer, with an emphasis on rare types of cancer. ACOR also provides contacts for caregivers and hosts a large collection of patient websites. Write: ACOR, 173 Duane St., Suite 3A, New York, NY 10013-3334. Call 212-226-5525; Fax: 212-219-3109. *Website*: http://www.acor.org

Bladder Cancer Advocacy Network *Online. Founded 2005.* National advocacy organization dedicated to improving public awareness and increasing research. Weekly online support chats. Plans to help start local chapters nationwide. Write: BCAN, 4813 St. Elmo Ave., Bethesda, MD 20814. Call 301-215-9099. *Website*: http://www.bcan.org *E-mail*: dzquale@bcan.org

Cancer and Careers *Online.* A resource for working women with cancer, their employers, coworkers and caregivers. Offers first-hand experiences and articles for working women with cancer. Provides resource information and publications via the website. Also provides extensive information for employers, coworkers, families and caregivers. *Website*://http://www.cancerandcareers.org *E-mail*: ksweeney@cew.org

FORCE (Facing Our Risk of Cancer Empowered) *Online. Founded 1999.* Support and education for women whose family history and genetic status put them at high risk of getting ovarian or breast cancer. Open to family members. Provides resources for women to determine if they are at high risk. Forums, chats, bulletin boards, member profiles. Phone support network. Write: FORCE, c/o Sue Friedman, 16057 Tampa Palms Blvd. W., #373, Tampa, FL 33647. Call 954-255-8732 or 1-866-824-7475. Fax: 954-827-2200. *Website*: http://www.facingourrisk.org/ *E-mail*: info@facingourrisk.org

Group Loop *Online.* Support for teens with cancer and their parents. Weekly scheduled online support groups with professionals, discussion boards, resources, information and news about many types of cancers and their affect on teens. *Website*: http://www.grouploop.org

Johns Hopkins Disease Information *Online*. Provides information and support to cancer patients and their families. Specific cancer websites include: colon, pancreas, ovarian, gallbladder, and bile duct. Also has message boards for Barrett's esophagus and non-cancerous conditions. *Website*: http://www.pathology2.jhu.edu/ department/patientcare.cfm, select condition from drop down menu.

CELIAC SPRUE / GLUTEN INTOLERANCE

BERGEN

American Celiac Society - Bergen County Chapter Phone support for people with celiac disease. Call Laurie Schlussel 201-573-0397 (day/eve). *E-mail:* fit4us1227@aol.com

Celiac Disease Support Group for Parents Information, sharing, mutual support and education for parents of children with celiac disease. Families welcome. Rap sessions, guest speakers, literature and quarterly newsletter. Meetings vary, Don Imus Pediatric Center, Hackensack University Medical Center, Hackensack. Call Joseph Chan 201-336-8845 (day).

CAMDEN

Celiac Sprue Association *(Southern New Jersey Chapter)* Mutual support information to persons diagnosed with celiac sprue (gluten sensitive enteropathy), dermatitis herpetiformis and parents of celiac children. Guest speakers, rap sessions, literature and phone help. Annual dues $20/yr. new members; $15/yr./thereafter. Meets 1st Sun. (except July/Aug.), 2pm, West Jersey Hospital, Barry Brown Health Education Center, Evesham Rd. and Carnie Blvd., Voorhees. Call Patti Townsend 856-854-5508 (eve) or Bill Lucas 609-387-7139. *Website:* http://www.home.earthlink.net/~celiac9/index.html *E-mail:* celiac9@earthlink.net

ESSEX

ROCK (Raising Our Celiac Kids) Support for parents of children with celiac sprue. Guest speakers, literature and phone help. Activities events for children and young adults. Meetings vary, Millburn Library, 200 Glen Ave., Millburn. For meeting information call Ellie Fried 973-912-0253 (day/eve). *Website:* http://www.celiackids.com

MIDDLESEX

Central NJ Celiac Sprue and Dermatitis Herpetiformis Support Group Dietary support for persons with celiac sprue and dermatitis herpetiformis. Also Cel-Kids Network. Dues $20/yr. Meetings vary, East Brunswick Library, East Brunswick. Before attending call Diane Paley 732-679-6566 (day/eve). *Website:* http://www.csaceliacs.org

MONMOUTH

ROCK (Raising Our Celiac Kids) Support group for parents of children with celiac sprue. Events planned and activities for school-aged children. Meetings vary, 7-8:45pm, Monmouth County Library, Symmes Rd., Manalapan. Call Elissa 732-677-2700.

WARREN

Celiac Sprue Association/Gluten Free 101 Support Group Support group dedicated to helping those with celiac disease and its complication, dermatitis herpetiformis, learn to live safely on the gluten free diet. Literature, speakers bureau, advocacy, social and phone help. Meets 2nd Wed., 7:30-9:30pm, Warren Hospital, Farley Education Center, Phillipsburg. Call Gary Powers 610-438-0205 (eve). *Website:* http://www.csaceliacs.org *E-mail:* gppowers14@earthlink.net

NATIONAL

American Celiac Society / Dietary Support Coalition *National. 78 affiliated chapters. Founded 1976.* Mutual support and information for celiac-sprue patients, families and health care professionals. Newsletter, buddy system, visitation, phone help system and participation in educational efforts. Also supports dermatitis herpetiformis, Crohn's disease, lactose intolerance and other food allergies. Write: American Celiac Society, c/o Annette Bentley, P.O. Box 23455, New Orleans, LA 70183-0455. Call Annette Bentley 504-737-3293. *Website:* http://www.americanceliacsociety.org *E-mail:* americanceliacsociety@yahoo.com

Celiac Disease Foundation *National. Founded 1990.* Creates awareness and provides services and support for patients and professionals seeking information about celiac disease/dermatitis herpetiformis. Free information packets. Annual membership $35.00. Handbook "Guidelines For a Gluten-Free Lifestyle" sold separately or is included with annual membership, which also includes a quarterly newsletter. Basic brochure and quick start diet available in Spanish. Write: Celiac Disease Foundation, 13251 Ventura Blvd., Suite 1, Studio City, CA 91604. Call

818-990-2354 (day); Fax: 818-990-2379. *Website:* http://www.celiac.org *E-mail:* cdf@celiac.org

Celiac Sprue Association/United States of America, Inc. *National. 100 chapters and 60 resource units. Founded 1969.* Provides educational materials on celiac sprue, dermatitis herpetiformis and basics for the gluten-free diet for patients, parents of children with celiac sprue and professionals. Children's camp in August in Rhode Island. Provides opportunities for support groups and networking with patients and professionals. Newsletter and annual conference. Group development guidelines. CelKids network. Write: Celiac Sprue Association USA, P.O. Box 31700, Omaha, NE 68131-0700. Call 1-877-272-4272 or 402-558-0600; Fax: 402-558-1347. *Website:* http://www.csaceliacs.org *E-mail:* celiacs@csaceliacs.org

Gluten Intolerance Group of North America *National network. 30+ affiliated groups. Founded 1974.* Mission is to increase awareness by providing accurate and up-to-date information, education and support to persons with gluten intolerance, celiac disease/dermatitis herpetiformis, their families, health care professionals and the public. Offers News magazine ($35), information and referral, conferences, guidance to those starting groups, group development guidelines and cookbooks. Write: Gluten Intolerance Group, 31214 124th Ave. SE, Auburn, WA, 98092. Call 253-833-6655; Fax: 253-833-6675. *Website:* http://www.gluten.net *E-mail:* info@gluten.net

"How can we communicate love? I think three things are involved. We must reach out to a person, make contact. We must listen with the heart, be sensitive to the other's needs. We must respond in a language that the person can understand. Many of us do all the talking. We must learn to listen and to keep on listening."

--Princess Pale Moon

CHRONIC FATIGUE SYNDROME

STATEWIDE

NJ Chronic Fatigue Syndrome Association, Inc. Support for people with chronic fatigue syndrome. All are welcome. Educational series, guest speakers, speakers' bureau, advocacy, social group, literature, medical conferences and phone help. Newsletter $25/yr. Support groups throughout New Jersey in Atlantic, Bergen, Mercer, Middlesex, Monmouth and Union counties. Call Lon Smith 609-219-0662. *Website:* http://www.njcfsa.org

ATLANTIC

Atlantic County Chronic Fatigue Syndrome Support Group Offers emotional support and sharing of the latest information on chronic fatigue syndrome for those afflicted, as well as their families. Under 18 welcome. Doctor referrals available. Rap sessions, guest speakers and phone help. Meets 2nd Sun., 2-4pm (except July/Aug.), AtlanticCare Regional Medical Center, Mainland Division, Jimmie Leeds Rd., Pomona. Call Betty Mc Connell 609-748-3559 (eve). *Website:* http://www.njcfsa.org

BERGEN

Chronic Fatigue Syndrome Association Support Group Education support and mutual assistance for patients with chronic fatigue syndrome, their family, friends and interested professionals. Meets 3rd Sun. (Sept.-May) (2nd Sun. in June), 2pm, Pascack Valley Hospital, Old Hook Rd., Westwood. Call Pat 201-385-4194 (day). *Website:* http://www.njcfsa.org (click on support groups)

MERCER

Chronic Fatigue Syndrome Support Group of Mercer County Mutual support, education and sharing of resources for persons with chronic fatigue syndrome, their families, caregivers and friends. Literature and some social activities. Meets 2nd Sun., 2-4pm, Robert Wood Johnson University Hospital at Hamilton, 1 Hamilton Health Place, Outpatient Services Building, Auditorium, Hamilton. For information call 609-584-5900 (ext. 1).

MIDDLESEX

Chronic Fatigue Syndrome Group Support and education for chronic fatigue syndrome patients and their families. Meets 2nd Sun., 12:30pm, Robert Wood Johnson University Hospital, Board Room, New Brunswick. Call 732-418-2110.

MONMOUTH

Chronic Fatigue Syndrome Support Group *Professionally-run.* Provides support for chronic fatigue syndrome patients, their families, friends and significant others. Guest speakers. Meets 3rd Tues., 7-8:30pm, Monmouth Medical Center, 300 Second Ave., Long Branch. Pre-registration required. Call 732-923-6990 (day).

WARREN

Fibromyalgia / Chronic Fatigue Support Group Provides education and support for those with fibromyalgia or chronic fatigue syndrome. Meets 1st Thurs., 7pm (Apr., July, Oct., Jan.), Warren Hospital, 185 Roseberry St., Farley Education Center, Phillipsburg. Before attending call 908-859-6735 (day).

NATIONAL

CFIDS Association, Inc. *National. Founded 1987.* Advocacy, information and encouragement for persons with chronic fatigue immune dysfunction syndrome. Publisher of the CFIDS Chronicle newsletter ($35/US; $45/Canada; $60/Overseas/Air) and research newsletter. Write: CFIDS Association, P.O. Box 220398, Charlotte, NC 28222-0398. Call 704-365-2343 (resources); *Website:* http://www.cfids.org *E-mail:* cfids@cfids.org

CLEFT PALATE

MONMOUTH

Cleft Palate Support Group *Professionally-run.* Support group for parents of children with cleft palates or cleft lips. Provides a forum for discussing shared concerns and exploring resources. Meets 2nd Thurs., various times, Monmouth Medical Center, Long Branch. Registration required. Call Helene Henkel 732-923-7653.

NATIONAL

Cleft Palate Foundation *National network. Founded 1973.* Provides information and referrals to individuals with cleft lip and palate or other craniofacial anomalies. Referrals to local cleft palate/craniofacial teams for treatment and to local parent support groups. Free information on various aspects of clefting for parents and individuals. Write: Cleft Palate Foundation, 1504 E. Franklin St., Suite 102, Chapel Hill, NC 27514. Call 1-800-242-5338 or 919-933-9044; Fax: 919-933-9604. *Website:* http://www.cleftline.org *E-mail:* info@cleftline.org

Prescription Parents, Inc. *Model. Founded 1973.* Support group for families of children with cleft lip and palate. Education for parents of newborns, presentations by professionals, family social events, phone support network and group development guidelines. Write: Prescription Parents, Inc., P.O. Box 920554, Needham, MA 02492. Call 617-499-1936. *Website:* http://www.prescriptionparents.org *E-mail:* info@prescriptionparents.org

ONLINE

cleftAdvocate *Online.* Resource for educational materials, cleft/craniofacial team information, emotional support and more. Local and regional family networking for parents, kids, teens and adults. cleftAdvocate hosts the North American Craniofacial Family Conference for individuals and families dealing with all craniofacial conditions, including acquired facial differences (trauma, illness and disease). Write: cleftAdvocate, P.O. Box 751112 Las Vegas, NV 89136. Call 702-769-9264; Fax: 702-341-5351. *Website:* http://www.cleftadvocate.org *E-mail:* debbie@cleftadvocate.org

Wide Smiles *Online.* Support, inspiration, information and networking for families dealing with the challenges associated with clefting. Sharing of struggles, joys and triumphs. Referrals to doctors. Write: Wide Smiles, P.O. Box 5153, Stockton, CA 95205-0153. Call 209-942-2812; Fax: 209-464-1497. *Website:* http://www.widesmiles.org

Need help finding a specific group?
Give us a call – we're here to help!
Call 1-800-367-6274

CYSTIC FIBROSIS

STATEWIDE

New Jersey CF Family Network Telephone network that provides mutual support for parents of children with cystic fibrosis. Up-to-date news regarding all aspects of CF including new treatments, equipment and physicians. Call Jean Gaito 973-492-3868 (day/eve) or Carol Russo 201-265-3503. *E-mail:* jcgaito@msn.com

NATIONAL

Cystic Fibrosis Foundation *National. 80 affiliated groups. Founded 1955.* Provides information and referrals to patients, families, caregivers and the general public. Accredits more than 115 care centers throughout the United States. Fund-raising. Provides grants to researchers. Newsletter, literature and conferences. Write: Cystic Fibrosis Foundation, 6931 Arlington Rd., Bethesda, MD 20814. Call 1-800-344-4823 or 301-951-4422; Fax: 301-951-6378. *Website:* http://www.cff.org *E-mail:* info@cff.org

DIABETES

(see also transplants)

STATEWIDE

American Diabetes Association (Northern NJ Area Office) *Professionally-run.* Support and educational programs for persons with diabetes, their families, professionals and public. Referrals to local groups and education programs. Adult and youth discussion groups. Fund-raising for research. Write: American Diabetes Association, 19 Schoolhouse Rd., Somerset, NJ 08873. Call 732-469-7979; Fax: 908-722-4887. *Website*: http://www.diabetes.org

Juvenile Diabetes Research Foundation Support and educational programs for parents of children with type 1 diabetes. Referrals to local chapter support groups. *Website*: http://www.jdrf.org

> **Central Jersey Chapter** Covers Essex, Union, Monmouth, Ocean. Write: Juvenile Diabetes Research Foundation, 740 Broad St., Shrewsbury, NJ 07702. Call 732-219-6654. *Website*: http://www.jdrf.org/chapters/nj/central-jersey *E-mail*: centraljersey@jdrf.org

> **Mid-Jersey Chapter** Covers Hudson, Hunterdon, Mercer, Middlesex, Morris, Somerset. Buddy system and phone help. Quarterly newsletter. Write: C.A.R.E.S., c/o Juvenile Diabetes Research Foundation, 28

Kennedy Blvd., Suite 180, East Brunswick, NJ 08816-1248. Call Jennifer Byram 732-296-7171. *E-mail*: midjersey@jdrf.org

Northern NJ Chapter Covers Bergen, Passaic, Sussex, Warren, Rockland. Write: Juvenile Diabetes Research Foundation, 560 Sylvan Ave., Englewood Cliffs, NJ 07632. Call 201-568-4838.

ATLANTIC

Adult Diabetes Support *Professionally-run.* Provides information and support to individuals with diabetes. Education, guest speakers and literature. Meets 2nd Mon., 6-7pm, Shore Memorial Hospital, 1 East New York Ave., Somers Point. Call Meaghan Kim 609-653-3489 (day) or Fran Jerome 609-653-4516 (day).

BERGEN

Diabetes Support for Children and Their Families *Professionally-run.* Support for children up to age 18 with diabetes. Family members welcome. Discusses nutrition, school issues and new treatments. Guest speakers, rap sessions and education. Meets 2nd Tues., 7-9pm (except July/Aug.), Valley Home Care, 15 Essex Rd., Paramus. Call Leslie Schifrien, MS, RD, CDE 201-291-6000 ext. 7116 (day) or Judy Brewer 201-447-6293 (day). *E-mail*: j.brewer.cde@gmail.com

Diabetes Support Group of Englewood Hospital and Medical Center *Professionally-run.* Support and education for persons with diabetes, their families and significant others. Teaches members to become self-sufficient in the daily management of their diabetes. Meets 4th Tues., 7-8:30pm, Englewood Hospital and Medical Center, 350 Engle St., Englewood. Call Diabetes Educator 201-894-3335 (day).

Holy Name Hospital Diabetes Program *Professionally-run.* Provides support and education for people with diabetes and their families. Meets 1st Wed., 7:30-9pm, Holy Name Hospital, 718 Teaneck Rd., Teaneck. Call Community Health Services 201-833-3371 (day).

Molly Diabetes Center Support Group *Professionally-run.* Mutual support for individuals with diabetes. Guest speakers. Meets 1st Mon. (except July/Aug.), 6-7pm, Hackensack University Medical Center, Diabetes Center, 211 Essex St., Suite 101, Hackensack. Call Judith Shanberg 201-968-0585 (day).

BURLINGTON

Diabetes Friends Support and education for those who have diabetes. Guest speakers, weight management, stress management, nutrition and mutual aid. Meets 1st Tues. (except July/Aug.), 7-8:30pm, Virtua Memorial Hospital, Conference Center, 175 Madison Ave., Mt. Holly. For meeting information call 1-888-847-8823 (day).

CAMDEN

Diabetes Friends Voorhees Support and education for people with diabetes. Guest speakers, weight management, stress management, nutrition and mutual aid. Meets 2nd Tues. (except Jan., July, Aug.), 7-8:30pm, Virtua Health's Education Center, 106 Carnie Blvd., Voorhees. Call 1-888-847-8823 (day).

Diabetes Support Group *Professionally-run.* Group deals with daily life challenges related to having diabetes (both type 1 and 2). Focuses on problem-solving, improving self-image and coping skills. Meets 4th Mon., 1:30-3:00pm, Kennedy Center, 1099 White Horse Road, Voorhees. Call Tanya Donovan 856-566-2096 (day) or 1-800-522-1965.

Diabetes Support Group *Professionally-run.* Mutual support and education for adults with diabetes. Also has children and teens groups. Meets the 1st Tues., 7-9pm, Virtua Memorial Hospital, 175 Madison Ave., Mt. Holly or 2nd Tues., 7-9pm, Virtua Health's Barry D. Brown Health Education Center, 106 Carnie Blvd., Voorhees. Call Lois J. Gerst, RN 1-888-847-8823 (day). *Website*: http://www.virtua.org

Kids Club and Parents Korner Mutual support for children with diabetes to help them better deal with their disease. Parent group runs concurrently. Meets 2nd Wed., (except July/Aug.), 6:30-7:30pm, Virtua Health's Barry D. Brown Health Education Center, 106 Carnie Blvd., Voorhees. Call 1-888-847-8823 (day).

Teen Diabetes Support Group Support for teens (ages 13-19) with diabetes. Meets 4 times/yr. Virtua Health's Barry D. Brown Health Education Center, 106 Carnie Blvd., Voorhees. Call 1-888-847-8823 (day).

CUMBERLAND

Adult Diabetes Support Group *Professionally-run.* Mutual support for adults with type 1 or type 2 diabetes, their families, friends and caregivers. Phone help, guest speakers and rap sessions. Meets 1st Wed., 2pm, South Jersey Healthcare,

1505 West Sherman Ave., Vineland. Call Cathy Giovinazzi 856-641-7542. *E-mail*: giovinazzic@sjhs.com

Pediatric Diabetes Support Group *Professionally-run.* Mutual support and education for children under the age of 12 who have diabetes. Meets 1st Wed., 6:45pm, Sept.-June, Regional Medical Center, 1505 West Sherman Ave., Vineland. Before attending call Cathy Giovinazzi 856-641-7542 (day). *E-mail*: giovinazzic@sjhs.com

ESSEX

Diabetes at Newark Beth Israel Medical Center Support Group *Professionally-run.* Support group for people of all ages with any type of diabetes. Offers an open format for educational and emotional concerns. Meets monthly, Newark Beth Israel Medical Center, 201 Lyons Ave., Newark. Must pre-register. Call 973-926-3218 (day).

GLOUCESTER

Diabetes Support Group *Professionally-run.* Support and education for those who have diabetes. Families welcome. Guest speakers, literature and phone help. Meets 4th Thurs. (3rd Thurs., Nov.; 2nd Thurs., Dec.), 6:45-8:45pm, Underwood-Memorial Hospital, 509 N. Broad St., Woodbury. Call Nancy Edwards 856-845-2476 (day).

HUDSON

Diabetes Support Group of Bayonne *Professionally-run.* Support and education for people of all ages and ethnic backgrounds with type 1 and type 2 diabetes, as well as their families. Rap sessions and guest speakers. Meets 3rd Tues., 7pm, Community Crossings, 488 Broadway, Bayonne. Call 201-858-5219 (day).

Diabetes Support Group *Professionally-run.* Provides support and education for adults with diabetes. Rap sessions and guest speakers. Meetings vary, Meadowlands Hospital, Secaucus. Before attending call Karen 201-392-3531 (day).

HUNTERDON

Diabetes Education Series *Professionally-run.* Support and education in a comfortable environment for those with diabetes and their families to share feelings, listen and learn. Literature and guest speakers. Meets 2nd Thurs. 7-

8pm, (except July/Aug.), Diabetes Health Center, 190 Highway 31, Suite 300, Flemington. Call Alicia Dougherty 908-788-6136 (day). *Website*: http://www.hmcdiabetes.org

Insulin Pump Support Group *Professionally-run.* Support for anyone, including friends and family, interested in or using insulin pump therapy as a treatment for diabetes. Meets 3rd Tues., 6-7pm, Diabetes Health Center, 190 Highway 31, Suite 300, Flemington. Call 908-788-6136 (day). *Website*: http://www.hmcdiabetes.org

MIDDLESEX

Adults with Diabetes *Professionally-run.* Support and education for persons with diabetes, their families and friends. Meets 1st Wed., 5-6:30pm, St. Peter's University Hospital, CARES Building, 4th Floor Conference Room, New Brunswick. Call Fansie Connelly 732-745-8600 ext. 8704 (day).

Diabetes Support Group Support, discussion and problem solving for persons with diabetes and their families. Rap sessions, literature and guest speakers. Meets various days, 7:30-8:30pm, Raritan Bay Medical Center, Perth Amboy and Old Bridge. For meeting information call Diabetes Center 732-360-4155 (day).

Diabetes Type 2 Support Group *Professionally-run.* Support for people affected with type 2 diabetes. Meets 1st Wed., 1:30pm and 7pm; Weight management meets 2nd and 4th Wed., 1:30pm and 7pm; Insulin pump group meets 2nd Tues., 7:15pm, JFK Medical Center, Edison. Registration required. Before attending call 1-800-991-6668 (day).

Stay On Target With Our Children Pump Group *Professionally-run.* Support and education for children with diabetes on or interested in insulin pumps (ages 11 and under). Parents are welcome. Meets monthly, 6:30-7:30pm, Saint Peter's University Hospital, Ground Floor, MOB Conference Rooms, New Brunswick. Call Donna 732-745-8574 option # 5.

Teen Support Group For Teens With Pumps *Professionally-run.* Support and education for teens with diabetes or interested in insulin pumps. Meets once a month, Saint Peter's Medical Center, New Brunswick. Call Donna 732-745-8574 option # 5.

MONMOUTH

Central Jersey Chapter Juvenile Diabetes Foundation Mutual support for insulin-dependent children and their parents to discuss solutions to the problems of day-to-day living with the disease. Phone help and peer counseling. Meets 3rd Wed. (every other month except Jul/Aug.), 7-8:30pm, Jersey Shore Medical Center, 2nd Floor, Ackerman Bldg., Conference Room 4, Neptune. For meeting information call 732-219-6654 (day). *Website*: http://www.jdrf.org *E-mail*: centraljersey@jdrf.org

Diabetes Insulin Pump Support Group *Professionally-run.* Support and mutual aid for any person on an insulin pump or contemplating using a pump. Meets 1st Wed. (Jan., Mar., May, July, Sept., Nov.), 7:30-9pm, Monmouth Medical Center, Long Branch. Pre-registration required. Before attending call 732-923-6990.

Diabetes Support Group *Professionally-run.* Mutual support and education for people with diabetes. Family and friends welcome. Meets 3rd Wed., 7:30-9pm, Monmouth Medical Center, Long Branch. Pre-registration required. Before attending call 732-923-6990 (day).

Diabetes Support Group *Professionally-run.* Mutual support for persons with diabetes who are on insulin injections and/or insulin pump. Learn about technology, discuss issues that affect their lives, educational series, literature and guest speakers. Meets Jan., Mar., May, July, Sept., and Nov., 10-11am and 7-8pm, Health Awareness Center, 65 Gibson Place, Freehold. Before attending call Suzanne Khanna 732-294-2574 (day).

Diabetes Support Group *Professionally-run.* Mutual support for seniors with diabetes. Family and friends welcome to attend. Offers guest speakers, literature, social and educational series. Meets 3rd Mon., 10-11am, Health Awareness Center, 65 Gibson Place, Freehold. Call Suzanne 732-294-2574.

Diabetes Support Group *Professionally-run.* Support and education for adults with diabetes. Guest speakers. Meets 2nd Thurs., 7-8pm, Jersey Shore University Medical Center, 1945 State Route 33, Room B-105, Neptune. Call Loretta 732-776-4195 (day).

Pediatric Insulin Pump Support Group *Professionally-run.* Support group for children using an insulin pump. Families and caregivers welcome. Meets 1st Wed., (Jan., Mar., May, July, Sept., Nov.), 6:30-7:30pm, Monmouth Medical Center, Long Branch. Pre-registration required. Before attending call 732-932-7790.

MORRIS

Diabetes Support Group *Professionally-run.* Mutual support for adults with diabetes and their families. Rap sessions, guest speakers, phone help and literature. Groups meet 1st and 3rd Wed., 7:30-9pm and last Thurs., 10-11am, Saint Clare's Regional Diabetes Center, 400 W. Blackwell St., Dover. Call to confirm meeting times 973-989-3603 (day).

Diabetes Support Group *Professionally-run.* Spanish-speaking support group for persons with any type of diabetes. Meets 1st Thurs., 10am-noon, Sister Catherine Health Center (building next to Women's Health Center/St. Clare's Hospital), Basement Level Community Room, Dover. Before attending call Alberto Olarte 973-537-3855 (day).

Diabetes Type 2 Support Group *Professionally-run.* Education and support for people (age 60+) with type 2 diabetes. Guest speakers and literature. Meets 1st Wed., 10-11am, Chilton Memorial Hospital, Collins Pavilion, 97 West Parkway, Pompton Plains. Call Joan Beloff 973-831-5167 (day) or Kathy Ferrara 973-831-5175 (day).

Insulin Pump Support Group *Professionally-run.* Mutual support for diabetics who use an insulin pump. Families and professionals are welcome. Rap sessions, phone help, literature and guest speakers. Meets last Mon., 7:30-9pm, Saint Clare's Regional Diabetes Center, 400 W. Blackwell St., Dover. Before attending call 973-989-3603 (day).

Pump Continuing Education Group *Professionally-run.* Support for people living with diabetes. Mutual sharing, education and updates on current medical treatments. Meets 1st Thurs., every other month, 7-8pm, Morristown Hospital Diabetes Center, Morristown. Call Donna Naturale 973-971-5524.

Type 2 Continuing Education *Professionally-run.* Support for people living with diabetes. Mutual sharing, education and updates on current medical treatments. Meets 3rd Wed., 7-8pm, Morristown Hospital Diabetes Center, Bldg. B, Morristown. Call Donna Naturale 973-971-5524.

OCEAN

Center for Diabetes Support Group *Professionally-run.* Support, on-going education and social interaction for adults with type 1 or 2 diabetes and their caretakers. Rap sessions and guest speakers. Meets once per month, Center for Diabetes, 731 Lacey Rd., Suite 1, Forked River. Call Kathleen Siciliano 732-349-5757.

Diabetic Support Group *Professionally-run.* Education and sharing for people with diabetes and their families. Meets 1st Thurs., 2pm, Ocean Club, 700 Route 9 South, Stafford Township. Call Barbara 609-978-3491 (day). *Website*: http://www.soch.org

Parents of Children with Diabetes Support Group *Professionally-run.* Support and information for parents of children with diabetes. Literature. Meets 3rd Wed., alternate months, 7-8:30pm, Center For Diabetes Education, 731 Lacey Rd., Suite 1, Forked River. Call Kathleen Siciliano 732-349-5757 (day).

PASSAIC

Diabetes Support Group *Professionally-run.* Provides support and education for people with diabetes. Meets 2nd Tues., 7pm, Barnert Hospital, Ivor Conference Room, 680 Dr. Martin Luther King, Jr. Way, Paterson. Call Patti Keller, RN, CDE 973-977-6683.

St. Joseph's Wayne Hospital Diabetes Support *Professionally-run.* Provides support and education for those with diabetes and their families. Monthly lectures by health professionals related to diabetes. Meets 3rd Thurs. (except July/Aug./Dec.), St. Joseph's Wayne Hospital, 224 Hamburg Turnpike, Wayne. For meeting time call Mary Schneider 973-720-6733 (day). *E-mail*: diabetes@sjwh.org.

SALEM

Adult Diabetes Support Group *Professionally-run.* Mutual support for adults with type 1 or type 2 diabetes, their families, friends and caregivers. Phone help, guest speakers and rap sessions. Meets 2nd Tues., 2-3:30pm, South Jersey Healthcare Elmer Hospital, 501 West Front St., Elmer. Call Cathy Giovinazzi 856-641-7542 (day). *E-mail*: giovinazzic@sjhs.com

Insulin Pump Support Group *Professionally-run.* Mutual support and education for adolescents or adults who use insulin pumps. Meetings vary, South Jersey Healthcare, Elmer. For meeting information call Cathy Giovinazzi 856-641-7542 (day).

SOMERSET

Living Well With Diabetes Support Group *Professionally-run.* Mutual support and information for adults with diabetes and for adults with type 1 or 2 diabetes. Meets quarterly, Somerset Medical Center, 110 Rehill Ave., Somerville. For meeting information call 908-685-2846 (day).

SUSSEX

Insulin Pump Support Group *Professionally-run.* Mutual support and education for adults who use insulin pumps. Families welcome. Rap sessions, education and guest speakers. Meets 2nd Tues. (Mar., June, Sept., Dec.), 7-9pm, Newton Memorial Hospital, 175 High St., Newton. Call Chris Orr 973-579-8340 (day).

Support Group for Those with Diabetes *Professionally-run.* Provides educational enrichment and emotional support for those with diabetes. Also offers rap sessions and guest speakers. Meets 1st Wed., 10am and 4th Tues. (Sept., Nov., Jan., Mar.), 7pm, Newton Memorial Hospital, 175 High St., Newton. Before attending call Chris Orr 973-579-8340 (day). *E-mail*: corr@nmhnj.org

UNION

Diabetes Support Group *Professionally-run.* Mutual support and education for persons with type 2 diabetes, their family and friends. Guest speakers and rap sessions. Meets 1st Tues., 7-9pm, Robert Wood Johnson University Hospital at Rahway, 865 Stone St., Basement Education Center, Rahway. Before attending call 732-499-6166 (day).

Diabetes Support Group *Professionally-run.* Share personal experiences and discuss new ideas for living well with diabetes. Families welcome. Meets 1st Mon., 7-8:30pm, Overlook Hospital, 99 Beauvoir Ave., Conference Room # 2, Summit. Before attending call 908-522-5277 (Mon.-Fri., 8am-4pm).

Parents or Caregivers of Children/Adolescents with Diabetes *Professionally-run.* Support and education for parents or caregivers of children/adolescents with diabetes. On-site play area for children available during the meeting time. Guest speakers and rap sessions. Meets various days, noon-1:30pm, Rahway Hospital, 865 Stone St., Rahway. For information call Angela Bacque' 732-499-6175 (day).

WARREN

Diabetes Support Group *Professionally-run.* Support and education for people with diabetes, their friends, family and caregivers. Usually meets last Tues., 3pm (except Dec.), Warren Hospital, Farley Education Center, 185 Roseberry St., Phillipsburg. For more information call Education Dept. 908-859-6777 (day).

NATIONAL

American Diabetes Association (*BILINGUAL*) *National. 100+ affiliates. Founded 1940.* Seeks to prevent and cure diabetes and to improve the lives of people affected by diabetes. Referrals to local support groups, offices and chapters. Dues $28 (includes magazine). Write: American Diabetes Association, 1701 N. Beauregard St., Alexandria, VA 22311. Call 1-800-342-2383 (Mon.-Fri., 8:30am-8pm); *Website*: http://www.diabetes.org *E-mail*: askADA@diabetes.org

Juvenile Diabetes Research Foundation International *International. 110 chapters in North America; 11 international affiliates. Founded 1970.* Supports and funds research to find a cure for diabetes and its complications. Individual chapters offer support groups and other activities for families affected by diabetes. Awards research grants and sponsors a variety of career development and research training programs. International conferences and workshops for researchers. Chapter development guidelines. Online listing of local chapters. Write: JDF International, 120 Wall St., 19th Fl., New York, NY 10005-4001. Call 212-785-9500 or 1-800-533-2873; Fax: 212-785-9595. *Website*: http://www.jdrf.org *E-mail*: info@jdrf.org

ONLINE

Diabetic Mommies *Online.* Support for all women with diabetes (type 1, type 1.5, type 2, Gestational, pre-diabetes) at all stages of life whether already a mom, during pregnancy or trying to conceive. Articles, forum, chat room, surveys, networking and newsletters. *Website*: http://www.diabeticmommy.com *E-mail*: editor@diabeticmommy.com

EATING DISORDERS

(see also overweight, toll-free helplines)

STATEWIDE

Eating Disorders Association of New Jersey *Professionally-run.* Support for persons with eating disorders, their families, friends and interested professionals. Dues $5/mtg. Membership $50/yr. Various meeting locations throughout NJ. Call 1-800-522-2230 (voice mail). *Website*: http://www.edanj.org

"Serenity isn't freedom from the storm; it is peace within the storm."
--Author Unknown

BERGEN

Eating Disorders Association of New Jersey *Professionally-run.* Support for persons with anorexia, bulimia or compulsive overeating and their families. Newsletter. Donation $5 per family. Meets 3rd Sat., 10-11:30am, Hackensack Medical Center, Hekemian Conference Center Building, Hackensack. Call Pia Jacangelo, ACSW 973-882-4099 (day). *Website*: http://www.edanj.org

ESSEX

ANAD (Anorexia Nervosa and Associated Disorders) of Northern NJ *Professionally-run.* Support for people with anorexia, bulimia or compulsive overeating. Concurrent groups for family and friends. Under 18 welcome. National newsletter. Donation $5 (optional). Meets 1st Sat. (2nd Sat. for major holidays), 9:30-11am, Saint Barnabas Ambulatory Care Center, 200 S. Orange Ave. (across from the Livingston Mall), Livingston. Call Barbara Reese, MSW, LCSW 973-783-2292. *Website*: http://www.anad.org

Eating Disorders Association of NJ *Professionally-run.* Support group for people with anorexia, bulimia or compulsive overeating. Meets 2nd Sun., 10-11:30am, Mountainside Hospital, Main Bldg., 1st Floor, Montclair. Donation $5. Call Maureen Kritzer-Lange, MSW, LCSW 973-313-1691, Ilene Fishman, MSW, LCSW 973-509-1400 or 1-800-522-2230 (day). *Website*: http://www.edanj.org

Reformers Anonymous Faith-based group to help people find freedom from addictions: alcohol, debt, drugs, eating disorders, gambling, internet, sex/love addiction, smoking, etc. Literature, newsletter and phone help. Meets Fri., 7-9pm, First Baptist Church, 257 Bloomfield Ave., Caldwell. Call Pastor Eli Miranda 201-724-9208 (day) or church 973-226-1004 (day).

HUNTERDON

Eating Disorders Association of New Jersey *Professionally-run* Support for those with anorexia, bulimia, or compulsive eating and their families. Under 18 welcome also. Rap sessions. Membership $50/yr. or $5 donation per week. Meets 4th Sat., 10-11:30am, Clarence Dillon Library, 2336 Lamington Rd., Bedminster. Call Kim Leatherdale 908-256-4779 (day / eve.).

MIDDLESEX

Eating Disorders Association of NJ *Professionally-run.* Support group for people with anorexia, bulimia or compulsive overeating. Meets 2nd Sat.,

10:30am-noon, East Brunswick Library, Civic Center Dr. and Ryder Lane, East Brunswick. Call Tina Weishaus 732-572-0461 (day), Ann Chicchi, MS, RD 732-254-7896 or 1-800-522-2230 (day). *Website*: http://www.edanj.org

SMART Recovery (Self-Management And Recovery Training) *Professionally-run.* Self-help group for individuals wanting to gain their independence from addictive behaviors (drugs, including alcohol and nicotine, and other compulsive behaviors including gambling, eating disorders). SMART is an abstinence program based on cognitive-behavioral education and principles, especially those of rational-emotive behavior therapy. Meets Mon., 6-7:30pm, Rutgers University, Busch Campus, Psychology Building, Room A224, Piscataway. Call Tom Morgan 732-445-0902. *Website*: http://www.smartrecovery.org

MONMOUTH

Eating Disorder Support Group *Professionally-run.* Support group for people with anorexia or bulimia and their families. Under 18 welcome. Meets 4th Sat., 10:30am-noon, Riverview Medical Center, 1 Riverview Plaza, Board Room, Red Bank. Call Monmouth Psychological Associates 732-530-9029 (day; ask for free support group).

MORRIS

SMART Recovery (Self-Management And Recovery Training) Self-help group for individuals wanting to gain their independence from addictive behaviors (drugs, including alcohol and nicotine, and other compulsive behaviors including gambling, eating disorders). SMART is an abstinence program based on cognitive-behavioral education and principles, especially those of rational-emotive behavior therapy. Meets Thurs., 7-8:30pm, 152 Speedwell Ave., Morristown. Call Rich 973-983-8755. *Website*: http://www.smartrecovery.org

SOMERSET

Anorexia/Bulimia Family and Friend Support Group *Professionally-run.* Support and education for family and friends of those with anorexia or bulimia to help understand the disorder. Guest speakers and quarterly newsletter. Meets Tues., 7:30-9pm, Somerset Medical Center, 110 Rehill Ave., Emergency Dept. Conference Room, Lobby Level, Somerville. Call Eating Disorders Unit 908-685-2847 (day).

Eating Disorders Association of New Jersey *Professionally-run* Support for those with anorexia, bulimia, or compulsive eating and their families. Under 18 welcome also. Rap sessions. Membership $50/yr. or $5 donation per week. Meets 4th Sat., 10-11:30am, Clarence Dillon Library, 2336 Lamington Rd., Bedminster. Call Kim Leatherdale 908-256-4779 (day / eve.).

Eating Disorders Support Group *Professionally-run.* Provides mutual support for those suffering from an eating disorder. Under 18 welcome. Members share information and experiences. Meets Tues., 7:30-9pm, Somerset Medical Center, Eating Disorder Conference Room, 110 Rehill Ave., 1st Floor, Room 197, Somerville. Call Eating Disorders Unit 908-685-2847.

NATIONAL

Eating Addictions Anonymous - SANE Fellowship *National. 6 affiliated chapters.* 12-Step. Recovery program for men and women recovering from all forms of eating and body image addictions. Includes anorexia, bulimia, binge eating, overeating, exercise bulimics, etc. Focuses on internal growth and reclaiming bodies rather than weight or appearance. Write: E.A.A., P.O. Box 8151, Silver Spring, MD 20907-8151. Call 202-882-6528. *Website*: http://www.eatingaddictionsanonymous.org *E-mail*: 12n12@tidalwave.net

Eating Disorders Anonymous *International. Founded 2000.* Fellowship of men and women who share their experience, strength and hope with each other that they may solve their common problems and help others to recover from their eating disorders. Focuses on the solution; not the problem. EDA endorses sound nutrition. Information and referrals, pen pals, phone support and literature. Assistance in starting groups. Offers online referrals to local groups. Write: General Service Board of EDA, P.O. Box 55876, Phoenix, AZ 85078-5876. *Website*: http://www.4EDA.org *E-mail*: info@EatingDisordersAnonymous.org

National Association of Anorexia Nervosa and Associated Disorders, Inc. *International. Founded 1976.* Telephone hotline for victims of eating disorders, their families and friends. Provides information on over 250+ free ANAD support groups, referrals to therapists and treatment centers that specialize in eating disorders. Quarterly newsletter. Assistance with insurance discrimination and parity issues. Free eating disorders education program for middle and high schools. Write: ANAD, P.O. Box 7, Highland Park, IL 60035. Call 847-831-3438 (Mon.-Fri., 9am-5pm CST); Fax: 847-433-4632. *Website*: http://www.anad.org *E-mail*: anad20@aol.com or Anadadvocacy@aol.com

Overcomers In Christ *International. Founded 1987.* Recovery program that deals with every aspect of addiction and dysfunction (spiritual, physical, mental, emotional and social). Uses Overcomers goals which are Christ-centered. Literature, resources, information and referrals. Assistance in starting new groups. Write: Overcomers In Christ, P.O. Box 34460, Omaha, NE 68134-04604. Call 402-573-0966; Fax: 402-573-0960. *Website*: http://www.OvercomersInChrist.org *E-mail*: OIC@OvercomersInChrist.org

Overcomers Outreach, Inc. *International. 700 affiliated groups. Founded 1985.* Christ-centered support group for persons with any compulsive behavior, as well as their families and friends. Uses 12-steps of A.A. and applies them to the Scriptures. Uses Jesus Christ as "higher power." Supplements involvement in other 12-step groups. Newsletter, group development guidelines and conferences. Write: Overcomers Outreach, P.O. Box 2204, Oakhurst, CA 93644. Call 1-800-310-3001. *Website*: http://www.overcomersoutreach.org *E-mail*: info@overcomersoutreach.org

Recoveries Anonymous *International. 50 chapters.* Spiritual recovery group for anyone seeking a solution from any kind of addiction, problem or behavior. Family and friends welcome. "How To Begin..." guides and "Start A Group" kit can be downloaded free from the website. Write: RA, P.O. Box 1212, East Northport, NY 11731. *Website*: http://www.r-a.org *E-mail*: raus@r-a.org

ONLINE

BDD Central *Online.* Provides resources, information and support for body dysmorphic disorder (BDD). Support through two email lists, chat room and a message board. Information available for family, friends and professionals. DVD, newsletter and doctor lists available. *Website*: http://www.bddcentral.com *E-mail*: Brit@bddcentral.com

ECZEMA

NATIONAL

National Eczema Association *National network. Founded 1988.* Provides support for persons with atopic dermatitis as well as other forms of eczema. Promotes education and research. Offers newsletter, networking information and referrals. Donations accepted. Write: National Eczema Association, 4460 Redwood Highway, Suite 16-D, San Rafael, CA 94903-1953. Call 1-800-818-7546 or 415-499-3474; Fax: 415-472-5345. *Website:* http://www.nationaleczema.org *E-mail:* info@nationaleczema.org

ENDOMETRIOSIS

NATIONAL

Endometriosis Association *International. 170 groups. Founded 1980.* Offers group support to those affected by endometriosis. Educates the public and medical community about the disease. Funds and promotes research projects. Newsletters, books, literature, support group information, teen programs and network. Brochures in 29 languages. Chapter development guidelines. Online support group, crisis call listeners and e-mail support. Write: Endometriosis Association, 8585 N. 76th Pl., Milwaukee, WI 53223. Call 1-800-992-3636 or 414-355-2200; Fax: 414-355-6065. *Website:* http://www.endometriosisassn.org or www.killercramps.org *E-mail:* endo@EndometriosisAssn.org

Endometriosis Research Center *International. 50+ support groups worldwide. Founded 1997.* Maintains and offers a vast database of materials on every aspect of endometriosis to all those interested in the disease. Education, research and advocacy. Write: Endometriosis Research Center, 630 Ibis Dr., Delray Beach, FL 33444. Call 1-800-239-7280 or 561-274-7442; Fax: 561-274-0931. *Website:* http://www.endocenter.org *E-mail:* EndoFL@aol.com Support Network Listserv: http://groups.yahoo.com/group/erc

ONLINE

EndoCenter of Northern NJ *Online.* Support and discussion for women suffering from endometriosis in the Northern New Jersey area. *Website:* http://www.groups.yahoo.com/group/EndoCenterNJ *E-mail:* endocenternj@gmail.com

EPILEPSY / CONVULSIVE DISORDERS

(see also toll-free helplines)

STATEWIDE

Epilepsy Foundation of New Jersey Support, information and referrals for people of any age with epilepsy and their families. Support groups, employment services, pharmaceutical plan, respite care, camp, family services and education. Dues $25/yr. Write: Epilepsy Foundation of NJ, 429 River View Plaza, Trenton, NJ 08611-3420. Call Trenton: 609-392-4900 (day); Westmont: 856-858-5900 (day); Parsippany: 973-244-0850 (day); Brick: 732-262-8020 (day) or 1-800-336-5843 *Website*: http://www.efnj.com

ATLANTIC

Atlantic - Cape Epilepsy Support Group *Professionally-run.* Mutual support and education for persons with epilepsy or related seizure disorder. Open to parents, caregivers and other interested persons. Rap sessions. Meets 4th Sat., 10am-noon, Shore Memorial Hospital, New York Ave., Jenkins Room, 2nd Room, Somers Point. Call Marian 609-822-8783 (day/eve) or 609-823-8023 (day). *E-mail*: amrein@ix.netcom.com

BERGEN

Bergen/Passaic County Epilepsy Support Group For those age 16 and over to talk with others who are afflicted directly or indirectly with epilepsy to show them that they are not alone and educate all about the disorder. Meets 3rd Mon., 7-8:30pm, Valley Hospital, 223 N. Van Dien Ave., Conference Room, First Floor, Ridgewood. Call Michael Hickey 973-962-0625. *Website*: http://www.efnj.com *E-mail*: mjhickey@att.com

GLOUCESTER

Epilepsy Support Group Mutual support and education for anyone with epilepsy, their families and friends. Guest speakers, advocacy and literature. Meets 2nd Tues., 7-9pm, Wedgewood County Club, Hurffville Rd., Dining Room, Turnersville. Call Shelby Myers 856-401-0445 (day/eve).

MIDDLESEX

Epilepsy Support Group Support and education for persons with epilepsy. Buddy system, guest speakers and phone help. Transportation available. Meets last Tues., 7:30pm (except July/Aug.), Robert Wood Johnson University Hospital, Board Room, New Brunswick. Call 732-418-8110.

MORRIS

Epilepsy Support Group Support for anyone with epilepsy and their families. Coping skills discussed. Occasional guest speakers. Meets 3rd Thurs. (except Dec.), 7:30-8:30pm, Morristown Memorial Hospital, 100 Madison Ave., Conference Room 3, Level B, Morristown. Call Pat 908-612-9093 (day). *Website*: http://www.efnj.com

Pediatric Epilepsy Support Group *Professionally-run.* Provides support network and education for parents of children with epilepsy. Guest speakers and literature. Meets 1st Thurs. (every other month), 7-8:30-pm, Saint Clare's

Hospital, 25 Pocono Rd., Auditorium, Denville. Pre-registration required. Before attending call Karoline Neumann 973-625-6199 (day).

UNION

Epilepsy Adult Support Group *Professionally-run.* Mutual support for adults with epilepsy and their caregivers. Share experiences on how to best live with this sometimes puzzling disorder. Guest speakers, literature, phone help and buddy system. Meets 2nd Thurs., 6:30-8pm, Overlook Hospital, Neuroscience Conference Center, 99 Beauvoir Ave., Summit. Call Ann Marie Bezuyen 845-695-6885 (day). *Website:* http://www.epilepsygroup.com *E-mail:* abezuyen@epilepsygroup.com

NATIONAL

Epilepsy Foundation *(ENGLISH/SPANISH) National. 60+ affiliates. Founded 1967.* Information and support for people with epilepsy, their families and friends. Publishes Epilepsy USA magazine and a wide range of informational materials for people of all ages. Referrals to local affiliates (many of which have employment related programs). Information and referrals. Write: Epilepsy Foundation, 8301 Professional Place East, Landover, MD 20785. Call 301-459-3700; Professional Library: 1-800-332-4050; Consumer Infoline: 1-888-886-3745; Fax: 301-577-4941. *Website*: http://www.epilepsyfoundation.org *E-mail*: postmaster@efa.org

ONLINE

Pyridoxine Dependent Kids *Online. 149 members. Founded 1998.* Support group for parents of children with pyridoxine dependency, or parents who are using B6 as an anticonvulsant. Offers public and subscribers only message boards. *Website*: http://groups.yahoo.com/group/b6children

Can't find an appropriate group in your area? The Clearinghouse helps people start groups. Give us a call at 1-800-367-6274

FIBROMYALGIA

MONMOUTH

Fibromyalgia Support Group of Western Monmouth County Mutual support for people suffering from fibromyalgia. Also welcome are their families, friends and professionals interested in learning about the disease. Offers phone help, group sessions, rap sessions and guest speakers.

> **Manalapan** Meets 1st Thurs., 7-9pm, Manalapan Library, Symms Rd. Call Tania Kanthal 732-462-6656.
>
> **Wall** Meets 4th Thurs. (except Dec. Jan.), 6:30pm, Wall Township Library, 2700 Allaire Rd. Call Linda 732-449-2733.

MORRIS

North Jersey Regional Arthritis Center Fibromyalgia Support Group *Professionally-run.* Provides support resources for those age 16 and over who are diagnosed with fibromyalgia. Mutual sharing and literature. Meets 1st Thurs., 11am-noon, Atlantic Rehabilitation Institute (RIMM), 95 Mt. Kemble Ave., 3rd Floor Chapel, Morristown. Call Dr. Michael Horowitz 973-971-4515 (day).

PASSAIC

North Jersey Regional Arthritis Center Support Group *Professionally-run.* Mutual support and education for persons with arthritis or fibromyalgia and their families. Aim is to raise quality of life for those with arthritis or fibromyalgia through rap sessions, educational programs, mutual sharing and guest speakers. Offers phone help, speakers' bureau and literature. Meets 1st Tues., 1:30pm, Clifton Main Memorial Library, 292 Piaget Ave., Clifton. For information call Anne Marie Leveto 973-365-4752 or Alicia 973-470-5773.

WARREN

Fibromyalgia Chronic Fatigue Support Group Provides education and support for those with fibromyalgia or chronic fatigue syndrome. Meets 1st Thurs., 7pm (Apr., July, Oct. Jan.), Warren Hospital, 185 Roseberry St., Farley Education Center, Phillipsburg. Before attending call Health Education Dept. 908-859-6735 (day).

NATIONAL

National Fibromyalgia Association *National network.* Organization to develop and execute programs dedicated to improving the quality of life for people with fibromyalgia. Patient assistance and information programs, awareness outreach, support group directory and magazine. Write: National Fibromyalgia Association, 2200 North Glassell St., Suite A, Orange, CA 92865. Call 714-921-0150; Fax: 714-921-6920. *Website:* http://www.FMaware.org *E-mail:* aquinn@fmaware.org

GRAVES' DISEASE

National Graves' Disease Foundation *National. 32 affiliated groups in 25 states. Founded 1990.* Aim is to establish patient-based Graves exclusive support groups to provide better treatment and to increase public awareness. Participates in research. Newsletter, information and referrals, phone support, national conferences, internet bulletin board and weekly online chat room. Each group has medical back-up/resource. Guidelines available to assist in starting a similar group. Write: National Graves' Disease Foundation, c/o Dr. Nancy Patterson, P.O. Box 1969, Brevard, NC 28712. Call 828-877-5251. *Website:* http://www.ngdf.org *E-mail:* nancyngdf@yahoo.com

HEADACHES

NATIONAL

ACHE (American Council for Headache Education) Support Group *National. 23 affiliated groups. Founded 1990.* An opportunity for headache sufferers to decrease their feeling of isolation, to help them learn more about headaches and enhance their coping skills. Information and referrals, group meetings. Online quarterly newsletter available soon. Assistance in starting groups. Write: ACHE, 19 Mantua Rd., Mt. Royal, NJ 08061. Call 856-423-0258 option 1; Fax: 856-423-0082. *Website:* http://www.achenet.org *E-mail:* achehq@talley.com

National Headache Foundation *National. 30+ affiliated groups. Founded 1970.* Mutual support for chronic headache sufferers and their families. Education on how to deal with chronic head pain. Group meetings, phone support, e-mail pen pals and group development guidelines. Public awareness seminars, funds research, newsletter, brochures and information on diets. Write: National Headache Foundation, 820 N. Orleans, Suite 217, Chicago, IL 60610-3132. Call

1-888-643-5552 (day); Fax: 312-640-9049. *Website:* http://www.headaches.org *E-mail:* sbarron@headaches.org

ONLINE

OUCH (Organization for Understanding Cluster Headaches) *Online.* Offers information and support for cluster headache suffers worldwide. Provides message board, newsletter and informative links. Support research to improve treatments. Holds annual conference. *Website:* http://www.ouch-us.org *E-mail:* contact_ouch@ouch-us.org

HEART DISEASE

(see also specific disorder, toll-free helplines, transplants)

BERGEN

Mended Hearts, Inc. Help, encouragement and education for those anticipating or recovering from heart surgery and/or other heart disease. Family and friends welcome. Professional speakers. Meets 3rd Thurs., "meet and greet" at 7pm; meeting follows, Hackensack Medical Center, Cafeteria, Hackensack. Call Barbara Cecco 201-265-9296 (day). *E-mail*: bobbi0530@aol.com

BURLINGTON

Zapper Club *Professionally-run.* Support group for patients with implantable defibrillators and their families. For meeting information call Laura Gebers 609-893-1200 ext. 5258 (day). *Website*: http://www.deborah.org *E-mail*: gebersl@deborah.org

Zipper Club Mutual support for persons coping with heart disease or heart surgery. Meets 9 times/yr., 1st Thurs., Deborah Heart and Lung Center, Browns Mills. Call Laura 609-893-1200 ext. 5258 (day/eve). *Website*: http://www.zipperclub.com *E-mail*: zipperclub@juno.com

CAMDEN

Heart And Soul Cardiac Support Group Mutual support and education for persons with any type of heart disease. Meets 3rd Thurs. (except July/Aug.), 7:30-8:30pm, Virtua Health, Barry D. Brown Health Education Center, 106 Carnie Blvd., Voorhees. Call 1-888-847-8823 (day).

HUDSON

Circle of Hearts *Professionally-run.* Group provides support and education for patients with heart problems as well as their spouses and families. Rap sessions and guest speakers. Meets various days, every other month, 7pm, Meadowlands Hospital, 55 Meadowlands Pkwy., Secaucus. Call Dan Lange or Louise Sallustio 201-392-3531 (day).

Women's Cardiac Support Group *Professionally-run.* Mutual support and discussion for women to share experiences and concerns regarding heart disease and other related problems. Meets 3rd Wed., 12:30-1:30pm, Meadowlands Hospital, 55 Meadowlands Pkwy., Secaucus. Call Louise Sallustio or Nancy Braddell 201-392-3531 (day).

MIDDLESEX

COPSA Spouse Support Group *Professionally-run.* Mutual support and understanding for spouses of persons with any type of memory loss (Alzheimer's, Parkinson's, vascular disease, stroke, head injury, dementia, etc.). Meets 1st and 3rd Mon., 9:30-11am, UBHC, 671 Hoes Lane, Piscataway. Call Mary Catherine Lundquist 732-235-2858 (day). *Website*: http://vbhcweb/ (then go to Aging-COPSA) E-mail: lindqumc@umdnj.edu

MONMOUTH

Cardiac Support Group *Professionally-run.* Mutual support and education for cardiac patients. Families and friends welcome. Literature. Meets 3rd Wed., 2-3pm, Centra State Medical Center, Cardiac Rehab Center, 901 West Main St., 3rd Floor, East Tower, Freehold. Before attending call 732-294-2918 (day).

ICD Patient/Family Support and Education Group *Professionally-run.* Provides support, education and a mechanism for networking for patients and families having implantable cardioverter defibrillators. Rap sessions, guest speakers, phone help, and literature. Meets Jan., Mar., May, July, Sept., Nov., Jersey Shore Medical Center, Neptune. Call 732-775-5500 ext. 5249.

Mended Hearts Support and encouragement for heart patients and their families. Visitation, guest speakers, newsletter and phone help. Dues $22 1st yr.; $17/yr. thereafter. Meetings vary, Brick, Neptune and Red Bank. For meeting information call Bill 732-367-3648 (day). *Website*: http://www.heartsofjersey.org

MORRIS

ICD Support Group *Professionally-run.* Provides education and psycho-social support to those with implantable cardioverter defibrillators as well as their significant others. Mutual sharing, guest speakers, literature and newsletter. Meets various times, Morristown Memorial Hospital, 100 Madison Ave., Morristown. Call Sheri Raquet 973-971-7939 (day) or Myra Hoffman 973-971-4261 (day).

OCEAN

Mended Hearts Support and encouragement for heart patients and their families. Visitation, guest speakers, newsletter and phone help. Dues $22 1st yr.; $17/yr. thereafter. Meetings vary, Brick, Neptune and Red Bank. For meeting information call Bill 732-367-3648 (day). *Website*: http://www.heartsofjersey.org

UNION

Cardiac Support Group *Professionally-run.* Support and education for cardiac patients and their families. Meets 1st Mon., 7-8:30pm, Robert Wood Johnson University Hospital at Rahway, 865 Stone St., Rahway. Call Helen Peare 732-499-6073 (day).

Mended Hearts Support and encouragement for heart patients and their families. Visitation, guest speakers, socials and newsletter. Dues $19-31/yr. Meets 3rd Tues., 7:30pm, Springfield First Aid Squad Building, North Trivett Ave., Springfield. Call Dan Kalem 973-376-0582 (day/eve) or Tom 973-762-7648 (day).

WARREN

Healthy Heart Self-help for those who have heart disease. Family members and significant others welcome. Provides emotional support and education. Meets 3rd Thurs. (except Jan.), 1pm, Warren Hospital, Farley Education Center, 185 Roseberry St., Phillipsburg. Before attending call Sue Himmelreich 908-859-6700 ext. 2180 (day).

NATIONAL

Adult Congenital Heart Association *National. 25 affiliated groups. Founded 1998.* Seeks to improve the quality of life and extend the lives of adults with congenital heart defects. Education, outreach, advocacy and promotion of research. On-line support, quarterly newsletter, regional and national conferences. Write: ACHA, 6757 Greene St., Philadelphia, PA 19119. Call 215-849-1260 or 1-800-921-2242; Fax: 245-849-1261. *Website*: http://www.achaheart.org *E-mail*: info@achaheart.org

Arrhythmia Alliance (The Heart Rhythm Charity) *International network. Founded 2004*. A network of sufferers, medical professionals, various UK based charities and related industry promoting better understanding, diagnosis, treatment and quality of life for individuals with cardiac arrhythmias. Write: Arrhythmia Alliance, P.O. Box 3697, Stratford upon Avon Warwickshire CV37 8YL United Kingdom. Call +44 (0) 17890450787; Fax: +44 (0) 1789 450682. *Website*: http://www.arrhythmiaalliance.org.uk *E-mail*: info@arrhythmiaalliance.org.uk

CHASER (Congenital Heart Anomalies-Support, Education, Resources) *National network. Founded 1992*. Opportunity for parents of children born with heart defects to network with other parents with similar needs and concerns. Education on hospitalization, surgeries, medical treatments, etc. Newsletter, phone support, information and referral. Heart surgeons and facilities directory. Write: CHASER, 2112 N. Wilkins Rd., Swanton, OH 43558. Call Jim and Anita Myers 419-825-5575 (day); Fax: 419-825-2880.

Kids With Heart *National. 3 affiliated groups. Founded 1985*. Mutual support for families and adults affected by congenital or acquired heart defects. Also provides bereavement services. Matches persons together for support, referrals to local support groups nationwide. Books and assistance in starting groups. Write: Kids With Heart NACHD, Inc., 1578 Careful Dr., Green Bay, WI 54304. Call 1-800-538-5390 or 920-498-0058 (Voice/Fax). *Website*: http://www.kidswithheart.org *E-mail*: michelle@kidswithheart.org

Little Hearts, Inc. *National*. Provides support, resources, networking and hope to families affected by congenital heart defects. Provides newsletter, literature, phone support, annual picnic and advocacy. Call 1-866-435-4673; Fax: 860-635-0006. *Website*: http://www.littlehearts.org *E-mail*: info@littlehearts.org

Mended Hearts *National. 285 chapters. Founded 1951*. Mutual support for persons who have heart disease, their families, friends and other interested persons. Quarterly magazine. Chapter development kit. Write: Mended Hearts, 7272 Greenville Ave., Dallas, TX 75231. Call 1-888-432-7899 or 214-360-6149; Fax: 214-360-6145. *Website*: http://www.mendedhearts.org *E-mail*: info@mendedhearts.org

SADS Foundation *International. 5 affiliated groups. Founded 1992.* International organization working to save the lives of young persons who are predisposed to sudden death due to cardiac arrhythmia. Offers networking, newsletter, literature, advocacy, information, phone support and referrals. Write: SADS Foundation, 508 E. South Temple, Suite 20, Salt Lake City, UT 84102. Call 1-800-786-7723 or 801-531-0937; Fax: 801-531-0945. *Website*: http://www.sads.org *E-mail*: sads@sads.org

ONLINE

Children's Cardiomyopathy Foundation *Online*. Provides support and information on pediatric cardiomyopathy. Offers online discussion forum and biannual newsletter. Working on plans to start community support groups. Write: Children's Cardiomyopathy Foundation, P.O. Box 547, Tenafly, NJ 07670. Call 1-866-808-2873 or 201-227-8852. *Website*: http://www.childrenscardiomyopathy.org *E-mail*: info@childrenscardiomyopathy.org

Congenital Heart Information Network *Online*. Offers information, support and resources to families of children with congenital heart defects, acquired heart disease and adults with congenital heart defects. Also open to interested professionals. *Website*: http://www.tchin.org

Pacemaker Club *Online. Founded 2000.* Regular exchange of messages, listserv and newsgroup. Chat meetings. E-mail pen pal program to support new members. Offers support, information and encouragement in a fun and interactive environment. Also information on local groups. *Website*: http://www.pacemakerclub.com *E-mail*: info@pacemakerclub.com

SVT (Supra Ventricular Tachycardia) Support *Online. Founded 2002.* E-mail list support. Mutual aid support from and for persons with supra ventricular tachycardia or any type arrhythmia. Newsletter. *Website*: http://groups.yahoo.com/group/SVTSupport/

HEPATITIS

HUDSON

Hepatitis C Support Group Mutual support and education for persons with Hepatitis C. Families friends welcome. Rap sessions, guest speakers and literature. Meets 1st Mon., 7-8pm, Meadowlands Hospital Medical Center, 55 Meadowlands Parkway, Secaucus. For meeting information call 201-392-3266 (day).

MERCER

Mercer County Survivors of Liver Disease/Hepatitis Support and education for those afflicted with liver disease or hepatitis. Family, friends and professionals welcome. Lectures, guest speakers, advocacy, rap sessions and social group. Meets 1st 3rd Sun., 7-9pm, Robert Wood Johnson at Hamilton, 1 Hamilton Place, Hamilton. Call Peggy Goodale 609-903-8524 or Tammy Leigh 609-584-2166 (day).

MONMOUTH

Hepatitis C Support Group Mutual support for persons with hepatitis C. Families welcome. Guest speakers. Meets 3rd Thurs., 7pm, Meridian Life Fitness, 2020 Route 33, Neptune. Registration required. For meeting information call 732-974-5797.

OCEAN

Hepatitis C Support Group Mutual support for persons with hepatitis C. Families welcome. Guest speakers. Meets 1st Tues., 7-8:45pm, Ocean Medical Center, 425 Jack Martin Blvd., Brick. For meeting information call 732-974-5797.

NATIONAL

Hepatitis B Foundation *International network. Founded 1991.* Mutual support and information for persons affected by hepatitis B. Dedicated to finding a cure for hepatitis B. Supports research. Advocacy, information and referrals, educational literature, conferences, confidential phone and e-mail support, newsletter. Referrals to liver specialists. Suggested donation $40. Write: Hepatitis B Foundation, 3805 Old Easton Rd., Doylestown, PA 18902. Call 215-489-4900; Fax: 215-489-4920. *Website:* http://www.hepb.org *E-mail:* info@hepb.org

Hepatitis Foundation International *International network. Founded 1995.* Grassroots support network for persons with viral hepatitis. Provides education about the prevention, diagnosis and treatment of viral hepatitis. Phone support network and literature. Referrals to local support groups. Quarterly newsletter. Some materials available in Spanish, Mandarin and Vietnamese. Write: Hepatitis Foundation International, 504 Blick Dr., Silver Springs, MD 20904 Call 1-800-891-0707 (day); Fax 301-622-4702. *Website:* http://www.hepfi.org *E-mail:* hfi@comcast.net

ONLINE

HCV: Hepatitis C Anonymous *Online.* 12-Step. Provides support through message board and regularly scheduled chats. Has articles, newsletters and matching program. Offers informational packets containing information on starting local groups. Hotline and general information call 949-264-4175. Write: HCV Anonymous, Inc., 129 W. Canada, San Clemente, CA 92672 *Website:* http://www.hcvanonymous.com . *Email:* info@hcvanonymous.com

Hepatitis Neighborhood *Online.* An online educational resource to help individuals understand hepatitis, treatment options, find support, message boards and chat rooms. *Website:* http://www.hepatitisneighborhood.com *E-mail:* hn_admin@priorityneighborhoods.com

HERPES / SEXUALLY TRANSMITTED DISEASES

(see also toll-free helplines)

NATIONAL

ASHA's STI Resource Center *National network. 85+ groups. Founded 1914.* Emotional support and education for persons with herpes and other sexually transmitted infections. Referrals to HELP (herpes) support groups, which provide a safe, confidential environment in which to obtain accurate information and share experiences with others. Support group development guidelines. Book ($26.95) and quarterly journal ($25). Write: Herpes Resource Center, P.O. Box 13827, Research Triangle Park, NC 27709. Call 919-361-8488 (hotline: 9am-6pm EST); 919-361-8486 (for starting groups) or 919-361-8400 (ASHA); Fax: 919-361-8425. *Website*: http://www.ashastd.org *E-mail*: hsvnet@ashastd.org

ONLINE

PickingUpThePieces *Online. Founded 1998.* Support and educational group open to anybody interested in learning more about Herpes Simplex Virus (HSV) or Human Papillomavirus (HPV). Group message board available to share your story and ask questions. *Website*: http://health.groups.yahoo.com/group/pickingupthepieces/

We can't help everyone, but everyone can help someone. –Dr. Loretta Scott

HIGH BLOOD PRESSURE / HYPERTENSION

ONLINE

High Blood Pressure (Hypertension) Online Support *Online.* E-mail list for those suffering from high blood pressure/hypertension who are looking for others suffering from high blood pressure or hypertension. *Website:* http://curezone.com/diseases/cardiovascular/hypertensionpage.html E-mail: http://health.groups.yahoo.com/group/hypertension

HIP REPLACEMENT

ONLINE

Totally Hip *Online. Founded 1996.* Support to help relieve the fear of total hip replacement surgery, share experiences and offer moral as well as spiritual support to patients. Helps answer questions on hip replacement. Also discuss other joint problems. Click on bulletin board at website for message exchange. *Website:* http://www.totallyhip.org *E-mail:* Linda@totallyhip.org

HUMAN PAPILLOMA VIRUS

NATIONAL

HPV Resource Center *National. 15 affiliated support groups. Founded 1999.* Provides a safe, confidential environment in which to share support and experiences with others who also have the human papilloma virus (aka genital warts and cervical dysplasia). Information and referrals, bi-monthly news journal ($25/yr.), pamphlets, assistance in starting new groups and how-to materials. HPV message boards available free of charge at website. Write: ASHA/HPVRC, c/o Fred, P.O. Box 13827, Research Triangle Park, NC 27709-3827. Call 919-361-8486; Fax: 919-361-8425. *Website:* http://www.ashastd.org or http://www.hpvnews.com *E-mail:* hpvnet@ashastd.org

ONLINE

Club HPV *Online.* Opportunity for people with human papilloma virus (genital warts) to share experiences and information with others. *Website:* http://groups.yahoo.com/group/clubhpv

HUNTINGTON'S DISEASE

STATEWIDE

Huntington's Disease Society of America Education and support for afflicted families. Fund-raising, visitation and phone help. Meets various times at various locations throughout NJ. Call HDSA 609-448-3500 (day) or Family Service Center 732-235-5993 (day). *Website:* http://www.HDSAnj.org *E-mail:* info@hdsanj.org

CAMDEN

Huntington's Disease Support Group Support and education for persons who have Huntington's disease, their caregivers, relatives and those at risk. Meets 3rd Tues., 6:30-8pm, University Doctors Pavilion, 42 E. Laurel Rd., Room 1013, Stratford. Call Nancy Alterman, LCSW 856-566-7078.

MIDDLESEX

Huntington's Disease Support Group Support and education for persons who have Huntington's disease, caregivers, relatives and those at risk. Meets 4th Wed., 6:30pm, 667 Hoes Lane, Piscataway. Call Christine Hogan 732-235-5993 (day).

OCEAN

Huntington's Disease Support Group Support and education for persons who have Huntington's Disease, their caregivers, relatives and those at risk. Meets 2nd Wed., 6:30-8pm, Leisure Chateau Care Center, 962 River Ave., Lakewood. Call Judy 732-370-8600.

UNION

Huntington's Disease Support Group Support for caregivers of individuals with Huntington's disease. Guest speakers, literature and phone help. Meetings vary, 6:30-7:30pm, Hartwyck at Cedar Brook, 1340 Park Ave., Plainfield. Registration required. Before attending call Kathy Little 908-754-3100 (day).

"The value of compassion cannot be over-emphasized. Anyone can criticize. It takes a true believer to be compassionate. No greater burden can be borne by an individual than to know no one cares or understands." –Arthur H. Stainback

NATIONAL

Huntington's Disease Society of America *National. 28 chapters/10 affiliates. Founded 1967.* Provides information and referrals to local chapters, support groups, social workers, local health care professionals and other resources. Supports and funds research for treatment and cure of Huntington's disease. Provides written and audiovisual materials. Publishes three newsletters. Write: Huntington's Disease Society of America, 505 8th Ave., Suite 902, New York, NY 10018. Call 1-800-345-4372 or 212-242-1968. *Website:* http://www.hdsa.org *E-mail:* hdsainfo@hdsa.org

INCONTINENCE

STATEWIDE

T.I.S. Group (Tri-State Incontinence Support) Provides on-going educational and emotional support. Offers networking opportunities for persons with bladder control problems. Includes children with bladder control problems and their parents. Buddy system. Write: TIS, 51 Nassau Ave., Brooklyn, NY 11222. Call Bob Goddard 718-599-0170 (eve). *Website:* http://www.tis-group.org

NATIONAL

Continence Restored Inc. *International. 8 affiliated groups. Founded 1984.* Forum where persons with incontinence, their families and friends can express concerns and receive assistance. Disseminates information on bladder control. Phone support. Assistance in starting groups. Write: Continence Restored Inc., 407 Strawberry Hill Ave., Stamford, CT 06902. Call 203-348-0601. *E-mail:* as4young@optonline.net

Pull-thru Network, The *International network. Founded 1988.* Support and information for the families with children born with anorectal, colorectal, or urogenital disorder and any of the associated disease. Disorders include cloaca, bladder exstrophy, imperforate anus, VATER/VACTERL association, anal stenosis, cloacal exstrophy and Hirschsprung's Disease. Maintains a database for personal networking. Quarterly magazine. Online discussion group. Weekly chat for members. Phone support and literature. Dues $30/year - can be waived upon request. Write: Pull-thru Network, 2312 Savoy St., Hoover, AL 35226-1528. Call 205-978-2930. *Website:* http://www.pullthrough.org *E-mail:* info@pullthrough.org

Simon Foundation for Continence *National. Professionally facilitated. 500+ affiliated groups. Founded 1983.* Support and advocacy for people suffering from incontinence. Quarterly newsletter, pen pals, books, videos and group development guidelines. Write: Simon Foundation for Continence, P.O. Box 835, Wilmette, IL 60091. Call 1-800-237-4666; Fax: 847-864-9758. *Website:* http://www.simonfoundation.org *E-mail:* cbgartley@simonfoundation.org

INFERTILITY / CHILDLESSNESS

(see also women's health)

STATEWIDE

RESOLVE *Professionally-run.* Provides education, support and resources (medical, therapeutic and adoption professionals) for individuals and couples experiencing infertility. Information on current medical treatments and adoption. Bi-monthly newsletter. Membership dues $55/yr. Educational meetings. Support group meetings also held throughout NJ counties. Write: Northeast Region of RESOLVE, P.O. 189, Eatontown. Call 1-888-765-2810. *Website*: http://www.northeast.resolve.org *E-mail*: info@northeast.resolve.org

ESSEX

Infertility Support Group *Professionally-run.* Offers a variety of individual and couple support groups for those struggling with the stress of infertility. Topics include male and female infertility, pregnancy loss, the use of donors, etc. Meets 2nd and 4th Wed., 7-8:30pm, St. Barnabas, IRMS, East Wing, Livingston. Register before attending. Call 973-322-5356. *Website*: http://www.sbivf.com

NATIONAL

NINE (National Infertility Network Exchange) *National. Founded 1988.* Support for persons and couples with impaired fertility and the professionals who serve them. Support system to help understand, cope and reach a resolution. Monthly educational meetings, newsletter, talk line and professional referral. Guidelines to assist others start a similar group. Dues $40/yr. Write: NINE, P.O. Box 204, East Meadow, NY 11554. Call 516-794-5772; Fax: 516-794-0008. *Website*: http://www.nine-infertility.org *E-mail*: NINE204@aol.com

No Kidding! *International. 103 chapters in six countries. Founded 1984.* Mutual support and social activities for married and single people who either have decided not to have children, are postponing parenthood, are undecided or are unable to have children. Chapter development guidelines. Write: No

Kidding!, Box 2802, Vancouver, BC, Canada V6B 3X2. Call 604-538-7736 (24 hr). *Website:* http://www.nokidding.net *E-mail:* info@nokidding.net

Organization of Parents Through Surrogacy *National. Founded 1988.* Educational, support and advocacy organization for families built through surrogate parenting. Members work together to address legislative bills on surrogacy. Information, networking, referrals, e-mail chat room, phone support, and literature. Dues $50/parents and surrogates. $100/professionals. Write: OPTS, P.O. Box 611, Gurnee, IL 60031. Call 847-782-0224; Fax: 847-782-0240. *Website*: http://www.opts.com *E-mail*: bzager@msn.com

RESOLVE, The National Infertility Association *National. 50+ chapters. Founded 1974.* Emotional support and medical referrals for infertile couples. Support groups, education for members and public. Quarterly magazine and publications. Chapter development guidelines. Write: RESOLVE, Inc., 7910 Woodmont Ave., Suite 1350, Bethesda, MD 20814. Call 1-888-623-0744 (helpline) or 301-652-8585 (office). *Website*: http://www.resolve.org *E-mail*: Info@Resolve.org

ONLINE

Fertile Thoughts *Online.* Provides support for infertile couples through chat rooms and forums. Issues include: general infertility, primary vs. secondary infertility, over 35, overweight, grief, polycystic ovarian syndrome, male infertility, adoption and parenting. *Website*: http://www.fertilethoughts.net

INCIID (International Council on Infertility Information Dissemination) *Online.* Dedicated to helping infertile couples find their best family-building options. Includes treatment and prevention of infertility and pregnancy loss. Guidance for those seeking to adopt. Provides free in-vitro fertilization scholarships to couples in need. Offers message boards on a variety of issues including fertility after forty, men, recurrent pregnancy loss, legal and insurance-related issues, grief, alternative therapies, medical issues and other online resources. *Website*: http://www.inciid.org

Parent Soup Message Boards *Online.* Offers a large variety of message boards which deal with parenting issues including infertility, pregnancy, parenting challenges, parents of disabled, pregnancy loss, newborn babies, toddlers, equipment, adoption, family issues, etc. *Website*: http://www.parentsoup.com/boards

TASC (The American Surrogacy Center) *Online*. Cybercommunity of friends and acquaintances who have a personal interest or experience concerning surrogacy issues. Various email discussions, password protected bulletin boards, live chats and monthly virtual seminars. Topics include: surrogate parents, egg donation, miscarriages, DES daughters, sperm donation and Mayer-Rokitansky-Kustur-Hauser syndrome. *Website*: http://www.surrogacy.com *E-mail*: info@surrogacy.com

INFLAMMATORY BOWEL DISEASE / IRRITABLE BOWEL SYNDROME / CROHN'S

STATEWIDE

Crohn's and Colitis Foundation of America, Inc. Greater NJ Chapter *Professionally-run.* Provides support and education for persons with inflammatory bowel disease, Crohn's or ulcerative colitis and their families. Does not include irritable bowel syndrome. Fund-raising for support, education and research. Membership dues $30/yr. Various meeting locations throughout NJ. Write: NJ Chapter CCFA, 45 Wilson Ave., Manalapan, NJ 07726. Call 732-786-9960 (Mon.-Fri., 9am-5pm). *Website*: http://www.ccfa.org *E-mail*: newjersey@ccfa.org

BERGEN

Crohn's and Colitis Support Group Support and education for people with Crohn's and colitis. Rap sessions. Meetings vary, Hackensack Hospital, Hackensack. For information call Carolyn Zorn 201-488-2668 (eve).

Inflammatory Bowel Disease Support for Parents *Professionally-run.* Provides support and education for parents of children with inflammatory bowel disease. Families welcome. Rap sessions, guest speakers, literature and quarterly newsletter. Meetings vary, Don Imus Pediatric Center, Hackensack University Medical Center, Hackensack. Call Joseph Chan, LCSW 201-336-8840 (day).

MERCER

Crohn's and Colitis Support Group *Professionally-run.* Support and education for people with Crohn's and colitis. Family and friends welcome. Guest speakers, literature, phone help, buddy system and educational series. Meetings vary, Robert Wood Johnson Hospital, Hamilton. For meeting information call Bill 609-587-7215 (day/eve).

MIDDLESEX

Crohn's Disease and Colitis Support Group *Professionally-run.* Support and education for people with Crohn's disease and colitis. Meets last Tues., 7pm, Robert Wood Johnson Medical School, Medical Education Bldg., Room 492, New Brunswick. Call Mark 732-381-7369.

NATIONAL

American Celiac Society / Dietary Support Coalition *National. 78 affiliated chapters. Founded 1976.* Mutual support and information for celiac-sprue patients, families and health care professionals. Newsletter, buddy system, visitation, phone help system and participation in educational efforts. Also supports dermatitis herpetiformis, Crohn's disease, lactose intolerance and other food allergies. Write: American Celiac Society, c/o Annette Bentley, P.O. Box 23455, New Orleans, LA 70183. Call Annette Bentley 504-737-3293. *E-mail*: americanceliacsociety@yahoo.com (please do not send attachments) or amerceliacsoc@netscape.net

Crohn's and Colitis Foundation of America *National. 42 chapters. Founded 1967.* Offers educational programs and supportive services for people with Crohn's disease or ulcerative colitis, as well as their family and friends. Funds research that seeks a cure for these illnesses. Membership benefits include: newsletter, a national magazine and discounts on books. Brochures available free of charge. Dues: individual $30/family $60/yr. Write: CCFA, 386 Park Ave. South, 17th Fl., New York, NY 10016. Call 1-800-932-2423. *Website*: http://www.ccfa.org *E-mail*: info@ccfa.org

International Foundation for Functional Gastrointestinal Disorders *International network. Founded 1990.* Educational and research organization that provides information, assistance and support for people affected by functional gastrointestinal disorders, irritable bowel syndrome, gastroesophageal reflux disease and bowel incontinence. Publishes quarterly journal addressing digestive disorders in adults and children. Many other fact sheets and educational publications are available. Write: IFFGD, P.O. Box 170864, Milwaukee, WI 53217-8076. Call 1-888-964-2001 or 414-964-1799; Fax: 414-964-7176. *Website*: http://www.iffgd.org *E-mail*: iffgd@iffgd.org

Irritable Bowel Syndrome Self Help and Support Group *International. Groups in USA and Canada. Founded in 1987.* Mutual support for persons with irritable bowel syndrome, their families, and health care professionals. Literature, advocacy and assistance in starting similar groups. Write: IBS Self-

Help and Support Group, 1440 Whalley Ave., #145, New Haven, CT 06515. *Website*: http://www.ibsgroup.org *E-mail*: ibs@ibsgroup.org

Reach Out for Youth with Ileitis and Colitis, Inc. *Model. 2 local groups. Founded 1979*. Provides support and education to patients and their families. Networking, literature, advocacy, information and referrals, phone support, conferences, regular group meetings and pen pals. Promotes research and sponsors fund raising activities. Write: Reach Out for Youth with Ileitis and Colitis, Inc., 84 Northgate Circle, Melville, NY 11747. Call 631-293-3102; Fax: 631-293-3103. *Website*: http://www.reachoutforyouth.org *E-mail*: reachoutforyouth@reachoutforyouth.org

INTERSTITIAL CYSTITIS

CAMDEN

Camden County ICA Support and information for persons with interstitial cystitis or painful bladder, their families and friends. Rap sessions, guest speakers, phone help and National ICA newsletter ($40). Meets bi-monthly, Sat., 1-3pm, West Jersey Hospital, Voorhees. Call Linda Benecke 856-667-5842 (day) or Virtua 1-888-847-8823 (day).

NATIONAL

Interstitial Cystitis Association *National. Founded 1984.* Provides education, information support for persons with interstitial cystitis, their spouses and families. Quarterly newsletter. Dues $45/yr. Write: ICA, 110 N. Washington St., Suite 340, Rockville, MD 20850-2239. Call 1-800-435-7422 or 301-610-5300; Fax: 301-610-5308. *Website:* http://www.ichelp.org *E-mail:* icamail@ichelp.org

ONLINE

North Jersey IC Support Group *Online.* Support for persons with interstitial cystitis, friends and family members. Exchange coping skills. *Website:* http://health.groups.yahoo.com/group/njicsupportgroup

We can also refer callers to over 100 individuals who are seeking others to help start new support groups throughout NJ. Give us a call for more information.

1-800-367-6274

KIDNEY DISEASE

(see also specific illness, transplants)

ESSEX

Kidney Transplant Recipient Support Group *Professionally-run.* Provides a forum for transplant recipients to discuss their common concerns and experiences after a transplant. Meets once monthly, St. Barnabas Medical Center, 94 Old Short Hills Rd., Livingston. For information call Adriane Shaw, MSW 973-322-2204 (day).

Parents' Night Out *(BILINGUAL) Professionally-run.* Support for families of young children (up to age 8) with kidney disease. Group includes families with children on dialysis, pre- or post- kidney transplant. Guest speakers, phone help and buddy system. Meetings vary, 4 times/yr., St. Barnabas Medical Center, Livingston. For meeting day and time call Jennifer Boyd, MSW 973-322-5264 (day).

MORRIS

Kidney Korner, The *Professionally-run.* Support and education for dialysis and transplant patients. Meets every other month, 7pm, Roxbury Library, Main St., Succasunna. Call 973-584-1117.

NATIONAL

American Association of Kidney Patients *National. 14 chapters. Founded 1969.* Patient organization dedicated to helping renal patients and their families deal with the physical, emotional and social impact of kidney disease. Aim is to inform and inspire patients and their families to better understand their condition, adjust more readily to their circumstances and assume more normal, productive lives. Provides education and support for kidney patients, including those with reduced kidney function, on dialysis and transplant patients. Offers various educational materials, a bimonthly and quarterly magazine, two electronic newsletters and an annual convention. Chapter development guidelines available. Write: AAKP, 3505 East Frontage Rd., Suite 315, Tampa, FL 33607. Call 1-800-749-2257 or 813-636-8100; Fax: 813-636-8122. *Website*: http://www.aakp.org *E-mail*: info@aakp.org

Kidneeds *National network. Founded 1997.* Grassroots support network for parents of children with membranoproliferative glomerulonephritis type 2 (aka dense deposit disease), a rare kidney disorder. Provides money for research on MPGN type 2. Offers phone support, newsletter and advocacy. For grant information please see website. Write: Kidneeds, P.O. Box 1324, Iowa City, IA 52240. Call 319-338-6404. *Website*: http://www.medicine.uiowa.edu/kidneeds *E-mail*: kidneedsMPGN@yahoo.com

PKD Foundation for Research in Polycystic Kidney Disease *International. 65 volunteer friends chapters. Founded 1982.* Funds research and provides emotional support and education for persons with polycystic kidney disease and their families. Promotes public awareness. Holds medical seminars and fund-raisers. Conferences, phone support, newsletter and assistance in starting new groups. Write: PKD Foundation, 9221 Ward Parkway, Suite 400, Kansas City, MO 64114-3367. Call 1-800-753-2873 or 816-931-2600; Fax: 816-931-8655. *Website*: http://www.pkdcure.org *E-mail*: daves@pkdcure.org

LARYNGECTOMY

BERGEN

Lost Cords - Laryngectomee Association Mutual support for laryngectomees. Pre-op and post-op visitation offered. Meets 1st Thurs., 7pm, American Cancer Society, 20 Mercer St., Hackensack. Call American Cancer Society 201-343-2222 (day) or Michael Lobosco 973-956-0278 (day). *Website*: http://www.cancer.org

BURLINGTON

Laryngectomy Club (Nu-Voice Program) Support for laryngectomy patients and their families. Meets 2nd Thurs., 7pm (except July/Aug.), Raphael Meadows Health Center, Woodlane Rd., Mt. Holly. Before attending call 1-800-227-2345. *Website*: http://www.cancer.org

CAMDEN

Laryngectomy Club (Nu-Voice Program) Support group for laryngectomy patients and their families. Meets 1st Tues., 7pm, American Cancer Society, 1851 Old Cuthbert Rd., Cherry Hill. Before attending call 1-800-227-2345 (day). *Website*: http://www.cancer.org

"The deepest need of man is the need to overcome his separateness, to leave the prison of his aloneness." –Eric Fromm, PhD

MIDDLESEX

Laryngectomee Support Group *Professionally-run.* Support for patients who have undergone a laryngectomee. Families welcome. Guest speakers. Meets 3rd Mon. (except July/Aug.), 2-3pm, JFK Medical Center, Dept. of Speech and Audiology, 65 James St., Edison. Pre-registration required. Before attending call Patricia 732-321-7063 (day).

MONMOUTH

Garden State Nu-Voice Club Dedicated to the education, rehabilitation, safety and welfare of laryngectomees. Mutual support and encouragement. Meets 1st and 3rd Sat., 9:30-11am, Riverview Medical Center, Red Bank. Call James 732-257-6927.

MORRIS

Tri-County New Voice Laryngectomee Support Group of Morris/Sussex/Warren Counties Mutual support and social activities for laryngectomees. Also includes anyone with neck, head, and/or oral cancers. Hospital visitation for new laryngectomees. Family and friends are welcome. Meets 2nd Mon. (except Jan., Feb., Mar., July, Aug.), 7:30pm, Saint Clare's Hospital, Silby Hall, 25 Pocono Rd., Denville. Call Tom Beneventine 973-694-8417 (day/eve).

OCEAN

International Association of Laryngectomees Ocean County Nu-Voice Club Self-help for people who have had a laryngectomy. Newsletter. Dues $3. Meets 1st Mon., 10am, The Lighthouse, 591 Lakehurst Rd., Toms River. Call 1-800-621-0096.

SOMERSET

Miracle Voice Club, The *Professionally-run.* Support and encouragement for laryngectomy patients and their families. Meets 1st Thurs., 1pm, American Cancer Society, 600 First Ave., Raritan. Call American Cancer Society 908-725-4664 ext. 3 (day).

"There are only two ways to approach life – as a victim or as a gallant fighter – and you must decide if you want to act or react." --Anonymous

NATIONAL

International Association of Laryngectomees *International. 200 chapters. Founded 1952.* Acts as a bridge starting before laryngectomy surgery through rehabilitation. Provides practical and emotional support. Newsletter. Chapter development guidelines. Write: International Association of Laryngectomees, P.O. Box 12036, Jacksonville, NC 28546. Call 1-866-831-8525; Fax: 910-455-1855. *Website*: http://www.larynxlink.com *E-mail*: IALhq@larynxlink.com

LIFE THREATENING / CHRONIC ILLNESS

(see also cancer, specific illness, toll-free helplines)

BERGEN

Healing Hope Support with a spiritual emphasis on helping those who suffer catastrophic loss including death, divorce, serious illness, etc. Meets 1st and 3rd Tues., 7:30-9pm, Cornerstone Christian Church, 495 Wyckoff Ave., Wyckoff. Call Kris 201-847-8107 (eve).

MIDDLESEX

Especially For You – Support for the Caregiver *Professionally-run*. Support group exclusively for caregivers, friends, families and spouses who care for someone who is chronically ill. Meets 1st Tues., 7pm, Robert Wood Johnson University Hospital, 1 Robert Wood Johnson Place, BMSCH Conference Room, New Brunswick. Call Community Education 732-418-8110 (day). E-mail: esp4yousupport@aol.com

MONMOUTH

Art Therapy for Children with a Chronically Ill Loved One *Professionally-run.* Support for children (ages 4 1/2-13) who have a family member with a chronic or terminal illness. Uses art therapy to help children express their feelings. Meets periodically for 7 weeks, Riverview Medical Center, 1 Riverview Plaza, Red Bank. For information call Jane Weinheimer 732-530-2382 (day).

NATIONAL

Center for Attitudinal Healing, The *National. 130+ affiliates. Founded 1975.* Emotional and spiritual support programs for children, youth and adults facing their own or a family member's life-threatening illness, long-term diagnosis or bereavement. Offers group guidelines for starting a local group. Also open to anyone wishing to change their perception of their lives. Workshops and trainings. Website contains information on centers and contacts around the world. Write: Center for Attitudinal Healing, 33 Buchanan Drive, Sausalito, CA 94965. Call 415-331-6161; Fax: 415-331-4545. *Website*: http://www.attitudinalhealing.org *E-mail*: home123@aol.com

Project DOCC (Delivery Of Chronic Care) *International. 26 chapters. Founded 1994.* Provides education regarding the impact of chronic illness and/or disability on a family. Information, referrals, phone support, e-mail correspondence and "how to" guides on developing a local group. Write: Project DOCC, 1 South Rd., Oyster Bay Cove, NY 11771. Call 1-877-773-8747; Fax: 516-498-1899. *Website*: http://projectdocc.org *E-mail*: projdocc@aol.com

Rest Ministries *National. 275 affiliated groups. Founded 1997.* Christian ministry for people who live with chronic pain or illness and their families. Quarterly magazine, daily devotionals, share and prayer email support mailing list, online chat, etc. Information and resources manual for starting groups ($15) or complete kit available. Assistance to churches in setting up support groups, teaches church awareness and trains church leadership on how to outreach to the chronically ill effectively. Write: Rest Ministries, Inc., P.O. Box 502928, San Diego, CA 92150. Call 1-888-751-7378 or 858-486-4685; Fax: 1-800-933-1078. *Website*: http://www.hopekeepers.org or http://www.restministries.org *E-mail*: rest@restministries.org

ONLINE

Ability Online Support Network *Online.* A family friendly monitored electronic message system that enables children and adolescents with disabilities or chronic illness (also parents/caregivers/siblings) to share experiences, information, encouragement, support and hope through messages. Write: Ability Online Support Network, 1120 Finch Ave. W., Suite 104, Toronto ON M3J 3H7 Canada. Call 1-866-650-6207 or 416-650-6207; Fax: 416-650-5073; *Website*: http://www.abilityonline.org *E-mail*: information@ableline.org

LIVER DISEASE

(see also hepatitis, specific illness)

STATEWIDE

American Liver Foundation (Greater NY Chapter; Covers northern NJ counties) *Professionally-run.* Support for persons with hepatitis or any other liver disease. Advocacy, education, guest speakers, phone help and literature.

Family, friends and concerned professionals welcome. Meeting day and times vary. Call 1-877-307-7507 (day). *Website*: http://www.liverfoundation.org

CAMDEN

South Jersey Liver Opportunity for persons with any liver disease, including hepatitis C, to share coping skills. Buddy system, guest speakers and phone help. $3/mtg. Meets 2nd Tues. (except June, July, Aug., Dec.), 7-9:30pm, West Jersey Hospital, Barry Brown Health Education Center, 316 Carnie Blvd., Voorhees. Call Harry Hagar Jr. 856-983-8247 or Marlene Reid 856-468-2883. *Website*: http://www.geocities.com/SJLDSG

MERCER

Mercer County Survivors of Liver Disease/Hepatitis Support and education for those afflicted with liver disease or hepatitis. Family, friends and professionals welcome. Lectures, guest speakers, advocacy, rap sessions and social group. Meets 1st and 3rd Sun, 7-9pm, Robert Wood Johnson University Hospital, 1 Hamilton Place, Hamilton. Call Peggy Goodale 609-903-8524 (day) or Tammy Leigh 609-584-2166 (day).

NATIONAL

American Liver Foundation *National. 25 chapters. Founded 1976.* Dedicated to the prevention, treatment and cure of liver disease (including hepatitis), through research, education, and advocacy. Members include patients, families, professionals and supporters. Chapters organized and operated by lay volunteers and staff. Offers guidelines for starting groups. Online local chapter locator. Write: American Liver Foundation, 75 Maiden Lane, Suite 603, New York, NY 10038-4810. Call 1-800-465-4837; Fax: 212-483-8179. *Website*: http://www.liverfoundation.org

CLASS (Children's Liver Association for Support Services) *Model. Founded 1995*. Dedicated to addressing the emotional, educational and financial needs of families with children with liver disease or liver transplantation. Telephone hotline, newsletter, parent matching, literature and financial assistance. Supports research and educates public about organ donations. Write: CLASS, 27023 McBean Pkwy., Suite 126, Valencia, CA 91355. Call 1-877-679-8256 or 661-263-9099; Fax: 661-263-9099. *Website*: http://www.classkids.org

ONLINE

Autoimmune Liver Disease Support Group *Online*. Support and sharing for those who have been afflicted with autoimmune liver disease of all forms. Message board. *Website*: http://health.groups.yahoo.com/group/LiverSupport-L/

LUPUS

(see also toll-free helplines)

STATEWIDE

Lupus Foundation of America - South Jersey Support and education for persons with lupus and their families. Social activities, fund-raising, guest speakers, newsletter, phone help and literature. Dues $20yr/individual, $25yr/family. Support group in Cherry Hill. Write: Lupus Foundation of South Jersey, Heritage Executive Complex, 1873 Rt. 70 East, Suite 110F, Cherry Hill, NJ 08003. Call 856-424-0255 (day). *Website*: http://www.sjlupus.org *E-mail*: sjlupus@verizon.net

Lupus Foundation of America, Inc. - North Jersey Chapter *Professionally-run*. Monthly support group meetings in 16 counties (see local county listings). Professional staff, volunteers and peer counselors assist and support lupus patients and their families. Information and referral, resource library, pen pals and seminars. Monthly newsletter to members. Dues $20/individual, $30/family. Provides speakers for public and professional education. Write: Lupus Foundation of America, Inc., NJ Chapter, P.O. Box 1184, 150 Morris Ave., Suite 102, Springfield, NJ 07081. Call 1-800-322-5816. *Website*: http:www.lupusnj.org

BERGEN

Lupus Foundation of America Support and information for lupus patients and their families. Promotes education and public awareness. Dues $20yr/individual, $30yr/family. Meets 4th Mon. (except Jan., Mar., July, Aug., Oct., Dec.), 7:30pm, Kessler Institute for Rehabilitation, 300 Market St., Conference Room B, 4th Floor, Elmwood Park. Call 1-800-322-5816. *Website*: http://www.lupusnj.org

CAMDEN

Lupus Foundation of South Jersey Support and information for lupus patients and their families. Promotes education and public awareness. Dues $20yr/individual, $25yr/family. Meets 3rd Wed., 7-8:30pm, Heritage Office

Park, 1873 Route 70 E., Suite 110F, Conference Room, Cherry Hill. Call Marjorie 856-424-0255. *Website*: http://www.sjlupusnj.org

HUDSON

Lupus Foundation of America Support and information for lupus patients and their families. Promotes education and public awareness. Dues $20yr/individual, $30yr/family. Meets 4th Thurs. (except Jan., July, Aug. Dec.), 7:30pm, St. Anne's Church, 3545 Kennedy Blvd., Jersey City. Call 1-800-322-5816. *Website*: http://www.lupusnj.org

MERCER

Lupus Foundation of America Support and information for lupus patients and their families. Promotes education and public awareness. Dues $20yr/individual, $30yr/family. Meets 3rd Wed. (except Jan., July, Aug., Dec.), 7:30pm, Mercer County Library, 2751 Brunswick Pike, Lawrenceville. Call 1-800-322-5816. *Website*: http://www.lupusnj.org

MORRIS

Lupus Foundation of America Support and information for lupus patients and their families. Promotes education and public awareness. Dues $20yr/individual, $30yr/family. Meets 2nd Wed. (except Jan., Feb., July and Aug.), 7:30pm, Saint Clare's Hospital, 1st Floor, Conference Room C, D, and E, 400 W. Blackwell St., Dover. Call 1-800-322-5816. *Website*: http://www.lupus.org

OCEAN

Lupus Foundation of America Support and information for lupus patients and their families. Promotes education and public awareness. Dues $20yr/individual, $30/family. Meets 2nd Thurs., alternate months, Brick Hospital, Brick. For meeting schedule call 1-800-322-5816. *Website*: http://www.lupusnj.org

UNION

Lupus Foundation of America *Professionally-run.* Support and information for lupus patients and their families. Promotes education and public awareness. Dues $20yr/individual, $30yr/family. Meets 2nd Sat. (except Jan., July, Aug.), 11am, Muhlenberg University Medical Center, Park Ave. and Randolph Rd., Plainfield. Call 1-800-322-5816. *Website*: http://www.lupus.org

NATIONAL

Lupus Foundation of America, Inc., The (*BILINGUAL*) *National. 50 chapters. Founded 1977.* Provides information and materials about lupus, and services to people with lupus and their families. Conducts education and supports research programs. Membership and newsletter available through local chapters. Write: Lupus Foundation of America, 2000 L Street, N.W., Suite 710, Washington, DC 20036. Call 1-800-558-0121 or 202-349-1155; Spanish: 1-800-558-0231; Fax: 202-349-1156. *Website*: http://www.lupus.org *E-mail*: info@lupus.org

LYME DISEASE

BURLINGTON

Lyme Disease Information Group Offers emotional support and education for those with Lyme disease. Meets 1st Wed., 7-8:30pm, Burlington County Library, Cinnaminson Branch, Riverton Rd., Cinnaminson. Call Sue Huesken 856-461-3369.

MORRIS

Long Valley Lyme Disease Association Support, information and networking for people with Lyme disease. Social group, educational series and advocacy. Meets 3rd Wed., 7-9pm, Our Lady Of The Mountain Church, Springtown Schooley's Mountain Rd., Long Valley. Call Nancy Braithwaite 908-852-5937 (eve). *E-mail:* dabrai@comcast.net

Morristown Lyme Support Group Support and education for Lyme disease victims and their families. Meets 3rd Tues., 7pm, The Presbyterian Parish House, 65 South St., Morristown. Call Anita Glick 973-267-8858.

OCEAN

Lyme Disease Association Inc. Very active group that focuses on education, prevention and research for Lyme disease. Referrals to health professionals and other health care. For meeting information call 1-888-366-6611. *Website:* http://www.lymediseaseassociation.org or http://www.lymenet.org *E-mail:* lymeliter@aol.com

NATIONAL

Lyme Disease Network *National network. Founded 1991.* Support, information and referrals for victims of Lyme disease and their families. Maintains computer information system. Write: Lyme Disease Network, 43 Winton Rd., E. Brunswick, NJ 08816. *Website:* http://www.lymenet.org *E-mail:* jenifer@lymenet.org

LYMPHEDEMA

ATLANTIC

Living with Lymphedema Support for any type of lymphedema. Families welcome, guest speakers, education and literature. Meets 2nd Thurs., 7-8:30pm, Shore Memorial Hospital, Cancer Center, Shore Rd. and Brighton Ave., Somers Point. Call Jennifer Hay 609-653-3512 (day). Write: Living with Lymphedema, Shore Memorial Hospital, 1 East NY Ave, Somers Point, NJ 08244

ESSEX

Saint Barnabas Lymphedema Education/Support Group Support and education for persons with lymphedema. Offers phone help, guest speakers and literature. Family and friends are welcome. Meets 2nd Wed., 6:30-8pm (except July/Aug.), St. Barnabas Ambulatory Care Center, 200 S. Orange Ave., Livingston. Call Rita Loew 973-322-7293 (day).

NATIONAL

National Lymphedema Network Inc. *National. Founded 1988.* Support groups and information regarding primary and secondary lymphedema for patients and professionals. Newsletter, telephone infoline, conferences, pen pal program, referrals to treatment centers and physicians. Assistance in starting new groups. Dues $45. Write: National Lymphedema Network, 1611 Telegraph Ave., Suite 1111, Oakland, CA 94612. Call 1-800-541-3259 (recording) or 510-208-3200; Fax: 510-208-3110. *Website:* http://www.lymphnet.org *E-mail:* nln@lymphnet.org

"The best thing about information is that we learn more when we share it with others, and less when we keep it to ourselves." –Robert Greene

MITRAL VALVE PROLAPSE

NATIONAL

National Society for MVP and Dysautonomia *National. 54 affiliated groups. Founded 1987.* Assists individuals suffering from mitral valve prolapse syndrome and dysautonomia to find support and understanding. Education on symptoms and treatment. Newsletter, literature. Write: Nat'l Soc. for MVP and Dysautonomia, 880 Montclair Rd., Suite 370, Birmingham, AL 35213. Call 205-592-5765 (day) or 1-800-541-8602 (day); Fax: 205-592-5707. *Website*: http://www.mvprolapse.com *E-mail*: staff@MVProlapse.com

Society for Mitral Valve Prolapse Syndrome *International. 23 affiliated groups. Founded 1991.* Provides support and education to patients, families and friends about mitral valve prolapse syndrome. Newsletter, phone support, literature, conferences and support group meetings. Publishes "Survival Guide." Offers guidelines to start similar groups. Write: Society for MVP Syndrome, P.O. Box 431, Itasca, IL 60143-0431. Call 630-250-9327; Fax: 630-773-0478. *Website*: http://www.mitralvalveprolapse.com *E-mail*: bonnie0107@aol.com

MULTIPLE MYELOMA

NATIONAL

International Myeloma Foundation *International network. Founded 1990. 89 groups.* Goal is to improve the quality of life of myeloma patients while working toward prevention and a cure, the IMF operates a Myeloma Hotline, disseminates comprehensive printed and online information about myeloma, treatment options and disease management. Seminars and workshops for the patient community and medical professionals. Write: International Myeloma Foundation, 12650 Riverside Dr., Suite 206, North Hollywood, CA 91607. Call 818-487-7455 or 1-800-452-2873; Fax: 818-487-7454. *Website:* http://www.myeloma.org *E-mail:* TheIMF@myeloma.org

"If we all tried to make other people's paths easy, our own feet would have a smooth even place to walk on." – *Myrtle Reed (A Weaver of Dreams)*

MULTIPLE SCLEROSIS

(see also physical disability, toll-free helplines)

STATEWIDE

Multiple Sclerosis Association of America Mutual support and education for persons with multiple sclerosis. Offers phone support, information and referrals, networking program, support group meetings, lending library, home modification program, equipment distribution program and more. Assistance in starting local support groups. Write: MSAA, 706 Haddonfield Rd., Cherry Hill, NJ 08002. Call 1-800-532-7667 (Mon-Thurs. 8:30am-8pm; Fri. 8:30am-5pm EST); Fax: 856-488-8257. *Website*: http://www.msaa.com *E-mail*: msaa@msaa.com

National Multiple Sclerosis Society Local support groups, resource centers and lending library information, education programs, national research and much more.

Greater Delaware Valley Serving South Jersey, Greater Delaware Valley Area, Lehigh Valley and Reading. Write: National Multiple Sclerosis Society/Greater Delaware Valley, 1 Reed St., Suite 200, Philadelphia, PA 19147. Call 1-800-548-4611. *Website*: http://www.nationalmssociety.org/pae/home

Greater Northern Jersey Chapter Serving Bergen, Essex, Hudson, Morris, Passaic, Union, Warren and Sussex counties. Write: National Multiple Sclerosis Society, 1 Kalisa Way, Suite 205, Paramus, NJ 07652-3550. Call 1-800-833-0087 or 201-967-5599 (day). *Website*: http://www.njbnmss.org *E-mail*: pat@njb.nmss.org

Mid-Jersey Chapter Serving Monmouth, Ocean, Middlesex, Mercer, Somerset and Hunterdon counties. Write: National Multiple Sclerosis Society, Mid-Jersey Chapter, 246 Monmouth Rd., Oakhurst, NJ 07755. Call 732-660-1055 (day). *Website*: http://www.nationalmsssociety.org *E-mail*: irc@njm.nmss.org

ATLANTIC

Pomona MS Group Provides support and education for persons with multiple sclerosis. Rap sessions, guest speakers and literature. Meets 1st Tues., 6-8pm, Galloway Library, 306 East Jimmie Leeds Rd., Galloway. Call Barbara 609-164-1916 (day) or Phyllis 609-266-1497 (day).

BERGEN

National "Friends" M.S. Society Support group for persons with multiple sclerosis and their families. Occasional guest speakers. Meets 1st Thurs., 7pm, Holy Name Hospital, Teaneck. Call Sister Mary 201-967-5599. *Website*: http://www.njbnmss.org *E-mail*: pat@njb.nmss.org

National MS Society C.O.P.E. (Concern Over People's Emotion) Peer support, information and socialization for persons with multiple sclerosis. Meets last Thurs., 11am-1pm, Cornell Surgical Supply, 30 New Bridge Rd., Bergenfield. Before attending call Joan 201-837-7790. *Website*: http://www.njbnmss.org *E-mail*: pat@njb.nmss.org

National MS Society T.M. (Twice Monthly) Support and education for persons diagnosed with multiple sclerosis, their families and friends. Guest speakers. Meets 1st and 3rd Mon., 7pm, Trinity Presbyterian Church, 650 Pascack Rd., Paramus. Call Joe 201-797-3386. *Website*: http://www.njbnmss.org *E-mail*: pat@njb.nmss.org

CAPE MAY

Cape May County MS Group Provides support and education for persons with multiple sclerosis. Rap sessions, guest speakers, literature and phone help. Meets 4th Thurs., 5-7pm, Burdette Tomlin Hospital, 2 Stone Harbor Blvd., Mariucci Room, Cape May Courthouse. Call Ron 609-861-0711 (day).

ESSEX

National M.S. Society Support group for persons with multiple sclerosis and their families. *Website*: http://www.njbnmss.org *E-mail*: pat@njb.nmss.org

> **Livingston** Meets 2nd Mon., 7pm, Livingston Library. Always a guest speaker. Call Marlene 973-992-5313 or Roy 973-338-9693.
> **Newark** Meets 3rd Thurs., noon, University of Medicine and Dentistry, Newark. Lunch provided. Before attending call Linda 973-923-6912
> **Nutley** Meets 3rd Thurs., 7pm, Vincent United Methodist Church. Call Gary 973-667-5209.

National MS Gay/Lesbian Support Group *Professionally-run.* Mutual support for gay/lesbians with multiple sclerosis. Family and friends welcome. Rap sessions. Meets 2nd Thurs., 7pm, Vincent United Methodist Church, 100 Vincent Place, Nutley. Call Laura 973-509-8567. *Website*: http://www.njbnmss.org *E-mail*: pat@njb.nmss.org

GLOUCESTER

Gloucester County MSAA Client Support *Professionally-run.* Provides fellowship and support to persons with multiple sclerosis. Education, guest speakers, rap sessions and socials. Meets 4th Wed., 6:30-8:30pm, Johnson Wood Library, Highland Ave., Deptford. Call Shirley 856-228-8474.

Washington-Gloucester Twp. MS Self-Help Mutual support for persons with multiple sclerosis, their families and friends. Rap sessions and guest speakers. Meets 3rd Mon., 11am-1pm, Cardinal Retirement Home, 455 Hurffville-Crosskey Rd, Sewell. Call Denise Savarese 856-627-6401 or Joyce Nealon 856-374-9273 (12-8pm). *Website*: http://www.pae.nmss.org *E-mail*: deeanns53@comcast.net

HUDSON

National MS Society - Hudson County Self-Help Group Mutual support and education for persons with multiple sclerosis, their families and friends. Guest speakers, phone help and social activities. Meets periodically, Newport Rehabilitation Center, Jersey City. For meeting information call Christine 201-332-3417 (day). *Website*: http://www.njbnmss.org *E-mail*: pat@njb.nmss.org

National Multiple Sclerosis Society/Bayonne Support Group Mutual support for persons with multiple sclerosis. Rap sessions and guest speakers. Meets 4th Mon., 1pm, Jewish Community Center, 44th St. and Kennedy Blvd., Bayonne. Call Helen 201-858-3999. *Website*: http://www.njbnmss.org *E-mail*: pat@njb.nmss.org

HUNTERDON

MS Hunterdon Support Group Support for multiple sclerosis patients. Family and friends welcome. Discussions, exchange of coping skills, guest speakers, literature and phone help. Meets 2nd Fri., 7:30pm (except Jan., Feb., July, Aug.), Our Lady of Lourdes Church, White House Station. Call Peggy 908-806-4920, Joan 732-828-1263 (day) or NMSS Chapter 732-660-1005 (day). *E-mail*: joan_simons@hotmail.com

New Hope/Lambertville MS Self-Help Group Mutual support, education and encouragement for persons with multiple sclerosis and their families. Guest speakers. Meets 1st Thurs., 6:30-8pm, St. Martin of Tours Church, New Hope, PA. Call Angela Jacobs 609-915-7208 (day) or Robyn Beer 267-617-7104 (eve).

MERCER

MS Support of Mercer County Support, information and open discussions on living and managing the physical and emotional aspects of multiple sclerosis. Also open to family members. Meets 4th Sun., 2-4pm (except July/Aug.), Morris Hall, 1 Bishop's Court and Route 546, Lawrenceville. Call Mike 609-588-0902. *Website*: http://www.nationalmssociety.org

MIDDLESEX

Metuchen Multiple Sclerosis Peer Group Mutual help for persons with multiple sclerosis. Meets 3rd Tues. (except June, July, Aug.), 10am-1pm, First Presbyterian Church, Social Center, Woodbridge Ave. and Home St., Metuchen. Call Bob 732-249-0480 (day), Camille 732-634-4104 or Sonya 732-826-7754. *Website*: http://www.nationalmssociety.org

Multiple Sclerosis "Mild Symptoms" Mutual support for persons with multiple sclerosis who have mild symptoms. Meets 3rd Wed., 7-9pm, North Brunswick Fire House, Cozzens Lane, North Brunswick. Call Susan 732-238-0864 or Heather 732-422-1391. *Website*:http://www.nationalmssociety.org

Multiple Sclerosis Support Group/Central Jersey Chapter Mutual support for people with multiple sclerosis, their families, and friends. Transportation available. Meets 3rd Wed., 7-9pm, East Brunswick Public Library, 2 Civic Center Dr., East Brunswick. Before attending call Elihu 732-613-5080 (day/eve). *Website*: http://www.nationalmssociety.org

MONMOUTH

Eastern Monmouth County Multiple Sclerosis Self-Help Phone support and networking for persons with multiple sclerosis and their families. Call Evelyn Wilson 732-229-2027 (day).

Multiple Sclerosis Support Group Mutual support for persons with multiple sclerosis. Families and friends welcome.

> **Freehold** *Professionally-run.* Meets 3rd Mon., 1-3pm, Centra State Hospital, Health Awareness Center, Gibson Pl. Call Michele 732-294-2505 ext. 6 (day).
>
> **Marlboro** Meetings vary, Marlboro Public Library, Library Ct. Call Lorraine 732-671-9384 or Dianne 732-536-3033. *E-mail*: lolo391064@aol.com

National MS Society Support Group Mutual support for person with multiple sclerosis. Meets 2nd Tues., noon-2pm, MS Society, 246 Monmouth Rd., Oakhurst. Call Lori 732-229-2259. *Website*: http://www.nationalmssociety.org

MORRIS

M.S. Dinner Group Mutual support and social events for singles and young adults with multiple sclerosis. Phone help and rap sessions. Meets various times and days at local restaurants. For information call Marcia Lutwin 973-625-8981 (day/eve).

Montville Multiple Sclerosis Support Group *Professionally-run.* Fellowship of persons with multiple sclerosis. Provides information, networking and a creative exchange of ideas. All ages welcome. Meets 2nd Thurs., 10am, Youth Center, Changebridge Rd., Montville. Call Roseann 973-334-8434. *Website*: http://www.njbnmss.org *E-mail*: pat@njb.nmss.org

National Multiple Sclerosis Morristown Support Group Fellowship of M.S. patients that meet for information, networking and creative exchange of ideas. All ages welcome. Guest speakers, discussions and socials. Meets 1st Tues., 7pm, Presbyterian Parish House, 65 South St., Morristown. Call Mary Ellen 973-299-1778. *Website*: http://www.njbnmss.org *E-mail*: pat@njb.nmss.org

OCEAN

Multiple Sclerosis Support Group (Sponsored by MSAA) Mutual support for multiple sclerosis patients, their families and friends. Meets 3rd Sat., 1pm (except June/July/Aug.), Epiphany Roman Catholic Church, All Purpose Room, Thiele Rd., Brick. Before attending call Gene Van Severen 732-920-3641 (day).

National M.S. Society Support Group Support group for persons with multiple sclerosis and their families. Occasional guest speakers. *Website*: http://www.njbnmss.org

Brick Meets last Mon., 10:30am-noon, Ocean Medical Center, Jack Martin Blvd., 1st Floor Atrium. Call Fran 732-701-1593, Alice 732-244-8332 or Jan 732-840-2186.

Manahawkin Meets 3rd Fri., 10:30am-12:30pm, Lutheran Church of the Holy Spirit, 333 N. Main St. Call Jill 609-607-8720 or Gail 609-978-1268.

Toms River Family and Friends Support Group Provides support and education for family and friends of individuals with multiple sclerosis. Rap sessions, guest speakers and phone help. Meets 4th Fri. (except July and Aug.),

7-9pm, Community Care Center, 591 Lakehurst Rd., Toms River. Call Pat 732-244-7523. *Website*: http://www.nationalmssociety.org

Toms River Support Group Provides education, rap sessions, guest speakers, phone help, support and camaraderie for people with multiple sclerosis. Meets 4th Fri. (except July/Aug.), 7-9pm, The Lighthouse, 591 Lakehurst Rd., Toms River. Call Pat 732-244-7523 or Dianne 732-892-2230. *Website*: http://www.nationalmssociety.org

PASSAIC

National M.S. Society - OUI MS Self-Help Group Support group for persons with multiple sclerosis and their families. Guest speakers. Meets 3rd Mon., 7pm, Packanack Lake Church, 120 Lake Drive East, Wayne. Call Michael 973-628-8991. *Website*: http://www.njbnmss.org *E-mail*: pat@njb.nmss.org

National M.S. Society - Working with MS Support group for persons with multiple sclerosis who are still working. Guest speakers, rap sessions, literature and buddy system. Meets 2nd Thurs., 7-9pm, Clifton Public Library, Piaget Ave., Clifton. Call Pat Evertz 201-967-5599 ext. 205 or Susan Rueda 973-667-1316 (eve). *Website*: http://www.njbnmss.org *E-mail*: goostersmom@hotmail.com

National MS Society - "Squeaky Wheels" Caring and sharing support group for persons with multiple sclerosis and their families. Information and advocacy. Meets 4th Wed., noon, Hillcrest Center, Macopin Rd., West Milford. Call Janice 973-728-1282 (day) or Mary 973-835-2565. *Website*: http://www.njbnmss.org *E-mail*: pat@njb.nmss.org

SOMERSET

Multiple Sclerosis Support Group Information and open discussions on living with and managing physical and emotional aspects of multiple sclerosis for both the person with M.S. and their significant others. Meets 4th Thurs., 7-9pm (except July/Aug.), Summerville At Hillsborough Assisted Living Complex, 600 Auten Rd., Hillsborough. Call Wendy 908-359-4514 (day) or Doug 908-369-4609 (before 8pm). *Website*: http://www.nationalmssociety.org

SUSSEX

National Multiple Sclerosis - Sussex County Support Group Fellowship of M.S. patients meeting for information, networking and creative exchange of ideas. Guest speakers, discussions and socials. Meets 1st Wed., 7pm, CFCS

Adult Day Care Center, 55 Mill St., Newton. Call Marie 973-209-2420, Debbie 973-948-6586 or Anita 973-875-0626. *Website*: http://www.njbnmss.org *E-mail*: pat@njb.nmss.org

UNION

Bridges for Life Support group for minorities who are challenged with multiple sclerosis. Mutual support, sharing of ideas, education and guest speakers. Meets 3rd Sat., 10am-12:30pm, Steve Sampson Senior Center, 800 Anna St., Elizabeth. Call Tina Smith 908-354-1481 (day).

Building Bridges: A Group for Minorities Peer support, information and socialization for people with multiple sclerosis. Meets 4th Sat., 1pm, Muhlenberg Medical Center, Park Ave. and Randolph Rd., Plainfield. Call Tennille 973-207-4191. *Website*: http://www.njbnmss.org *E-mail*: pat@njb.nmss.org

National MS Society - Clark Support Group Peer support, information and socialization for people with multiple sclerosis. Meets 1st Tues., 7pm, Clark Town Hall, 430 Westfield Ave., Clark. Call Beth 732-388-9409. *Website*: http://www.njbnmss.org *E-mail*: pat@njb.nmss.org

WARREN

Sharing and Caring Mutual support for persons with multiple sclerosis. Guest speakers. Meets 2nd Mon., 7:30pm, Hackettstown Hospital, Willow Grove St., Hackettstown. Call Cindy 973-786-5382 or Helen 908-979-0984. *Website*: http://www.njbnmss.org *E-mail*: pat@njb.nmss.org

NATIONAL

Multiple Sclerosis Association of America *National. 6 regional U.S. offices. Founded 1970.* Mutual support and education for persons with multiple sclerosis. Offers phone support, information and referrals, networking program, support group meetings, MRI funding, lending library, home modification program, cooling equipment program and more. Write: MSAA, 706 Haddonfield Rd., Cherry Hill, NJ 08002. Call 1-800-532-7667 (Mon.-Thurs. 8:30am-8pm; Fri. 8:30am-5pm EST); Fax: 856-488-8257. *Website*: http://www.msaa.com *E-mail*: msaa@msaa.com

National Multiple Sclerosis Society *National. 1800 self-help groups. Founded 1946.* Funds research in multiple sclerosis, provides information and referrals, support groups for patients and families, professional education, and newsletter. Write: National MS Society, 733 Third Ave., New York, NY 10017. Call 1-800-344-4867. *Website*: http://www.nationalmssociety.org

ONLINE

MS Moms (Managing Our Multiple Sclerosis) *Online.* Support for mothers living, parenting and managing with their multiple sclerosis. *Website*: http://www.msmoms.com

MUSCULAR DYSTROPHY

BERGEN

MDA/ALS Support Group Mutual support for individuals with muscular dystrophy or ALS. Families and caregivers welcome. Sharing of information, experiences, ideas and resources. Usually meets 3rd Thurs., 4-6pm, Jewish Community Center on the Palisades, 411 East Clinton Ave., Tenafly. Pre-registration required. Before attending call 201-843-4452 (day).

CAMDEN

Muscular Dystrophy Association Support Group *(Southern NJ Residents)* Mutual support for individuals with muscular dystrophy. Families welcome. Guest speakers. Sharing of information, experiences, ideas and resources. Meets 3rd Tues., 7pm, Town Plaza, Centennial Crescent Rd., Voorhees. Pre-registration required. Before attending call 856-356-4467 (day).

ESSEX

Muscular Dystrophy Support Group Mutual support for individuals with muscular dystrophy. Families welcome. Sharing of information, experiences, ideas and resources. Guest speakers. Usually meets 2nd Tues., 7-8:30pm, Jewish Community Center Metrowest, 760 Northfield Ave., Meeting Room M3, West Orange. Before attending call 201-843-4452 (day).

HUDSON

MDA Parents Support Group Mutual support for parents of children with muscular dystrophy. Sharing of information, experiences, ideas and resources.

Usually meets 2nd Mon., 7-8:30pm, Liberty Health, Meadowlands Campus, 55 Meadowlands Parkway, Secaucus. Pre-registration required. Before attending call 201-843-4452 (day).

MORRIS

Muscular Dystrophy Association Caregivers Support Group Mutual support for caregivers of persons with muscular dystrophy. Sharing of information, experiences, ideas and resources. Usually meets 1st Mon., 7-8:30pm, St. Clare's Hospital, 400 West Blackwell St., Dover. Pre-registration required. Before attending call 201-843-4452 (day).

NATIONAL

Muscular Dystrophy Association *National. 200+ chapters. Founded 1950.* Provides comprehensive medical services to persons with neuromuscular disease. Supports research into the causes, cures and treatments of neuromuscular disorders. Support programs include self-help groups, phone friends, pen pals and scheduled online chat sessions. Write: Muscular Dystrophy Association, 3300 E. Sunrise Dr., Tucson, AZ 85718-3299. Call 1-800-572-1717; Fax: 520-529-5454. *Website:* http://www.mda.org *E-mail:* mda@mdausa.org

Parent Project for Muscular Dystrophy Research, Inc. *International network. Founded 1994.* Support for parents of children with Duchenne and Becker muscular dystrophy. Goal is to improve the treatment, quality of life and long-term outlook for all individuals affected by DMD through research, advocacy, education and compassion. Provides user-friendly website with online forums, scientific and legislative conferences, newsletters, information on newest diagnosis, standards of care and research strategies. Write: Parent Project for Muscular Dystrophy, 158 Linwood Plaza, Fort Lee, NJ 07024. Call 1-800-714-5437 or 201-944-9985; Fax: 201-944-9987. *Website:* http://www.parentprojectmd.org *E-mail:* info@parentprojectmd.org

S.M.D.I. International (Society for Muscular Dystrophy Information) *International network. Founded 1983.* Purpose is to share and encourage the exchange of non-technical, neuromuscular and disability-related information. Referrals to support groups via networking website. Write: SMDI, International, P.O. Box 479, Bridgewater, NS Canada B4V 2X6. Call 902-685-3962 (voice/fax). *Website:* http://www.societyneuromuscularinfo.org *E-mail:* smdi_intl@mail_auracom.com

NEUROPATHY

BERGEN

Northern New Jersey Peripheral Neuropathy Support Group Support, information advocacy to persons with peripheral neuropathy. Guest speakers, educational series, phone help and literature. Dues $15/yr. Meets 3rd Thurs., 7:30-9:30pm (except Jan., July, Aug.), Englewood Hospital, 350 Engle St., Englewood. Call Tom 201-692-9313. For directions to Englewood Hospital call 201-894-3000.

MERCER

Peripheral Neuropathy Support Group Support for person with nerve damage as a result of neuropathy. Family and friends are welcome. Offers guest speakers, mutual sharing, educational series, rap sessions, literature and phone help. Meetings vary, Robert Wood Johnson Hospital, Hamilton Square. For meeting information call Bill 609-587-7215.

MONMOUTH

Monmouth/Ocean Neuropathy Support Group Support and information to those afflicted with neuropathy. Mutual sharing, guest speakers, literature and phone help. Dues $15 yr. Meets 3rd Sat., every other month, 1-3pm, Rehabilitation Hospital of Tinton Falls, 2 Centre Plaza, Tinton Falls. Before attending call Fontaine 908-233-9709. *E-mail:* FontaineGatti@msn.com or Fontaine.D.Gatti@aexp.com

NATIONAL

Neuropathy Association *International. 214 affiliated groups. Founded 1995.* Provides support, education and advocacy for persons with peripheral neuropathy. Promotes and funds research into the cause and cure. Phone support, newsletter, literature, information and referrals. Online bulletin board, referrals to support groups and doctors. Medical surveys. Write: Neuropathy Association, 60 E. 42nd St., Room 942, New York, NY 10165. Call 212-692-0662; Fax: 212-692-0668. *Website:* http://www.neuropathy.org *E-mail:* info@neuropathy.org

OSTEOPOROSIS

BERGEN

Arthritis Foundation Osteoporosis Support Group Provides those with osteoporosis, their family and friends an opportunity to discuss their problems, offer mutual respect and exchange ideas to help cope with the disease. Rap sessions, guest speakers, phone help and literature. Meetings vary, 10-11am, Pascack Valley Hospital, Auditorium, Old Hook Rd., Westwood. Registration required. Call 201-358-6000 or 845-426-5505.

ESSEX

Osteoporosis Support Group Support education for people with osteoporosis, their families and friends. Discussions, guest speakers and literature. Meets 2nd Thurs., 11:30am-1pm, St. Barnabas Ambulatory Care Center, 200 S. Orange Ave., Conference Room A/B, Livingston. Call Susan Allison 973-322-7830 (day). *E-mail:* sallison@sbhcs.com

HUNTERDON

Arthritis Foundation NJ Chapter Mutual support and education for people with arthritis, osteoporosis and their families. Meets 2nd Mon., 1-3pm, Hunterdon Medical Center, Meeting Room A and B, 2100 Wescott Drive, Flemington. Call 908-788-6373 ext. 1.

MORRIS

Osteoporosis Support Group Provides those with osteoporosis, their family and friends an opportunity to discuss their problems, offers mutual respect and exchange ideas to help cope with the disease. Meets 3rd Thurs., 10:30am-noon, Madison YMCA, 111 Kings Rd., Madison. Call Angele Thompson 908-898-0055 (day).

OCEAN

Osteoporosis Self-Help Organization Support and education for persons with osteoporosis. Meets 1st Fri., 2:30pm, The Lighthouse, Community Medical Center, 591 Lakehurst Rd., Toms River. Call Sherlynn 732-349-8239 or The Lighthouse 1-800-621-0096 (day).

NATIONAL

National Osteoporosis Foundation *National. 80+ affiliated support groups. Founded 1984.* Dedicated to reducing the widespread prevalence of osteoporosis through programs of research, education and advocacy. Provides referrals to existing support groups, educational materials, as well as free resources and materials to assist people to start groups. Newsletter, information and referrals, conferences. Write: National Osteoporosis Foundation, 1232 22nd St., NW, Washington, DC 20037-1202. Call 202-223-2226 or 1-800-223-9994; Fax: 202-223-2237. *Website:* http://www.nof.org *E-mail:* jeffrey@nof.org

OSTOMY

BURLINGTON

United Ostomy Associations of America Education and encouragement for ostomy patients, those with related surgery. Families are welcome. Visitation, peer-counseling and newsletter. Meets 3rd Mon., 7-9pm, Virtua Memorial Hospital of Burlington County, 175 Madison Ave., Conference Center, Mt. Holly. Call Ken Aukett 856-854-3737 (10am-10pm). *Website*: http://www.ostomyburlco.org *E-mail*: kenaukett@uoaa.org

ESSEX

United Ostomy Associations of America Education and encouragement for ostomy patients and their families. Outreach, peer-counseling, phone help and newsletter. Meets monthly (except July/Aug.), St. Barnabas Ambulatory Care Center, 200 S. Orange Ave., Livingston. Call Paula Von Rosendahl 973-239-1616, Harold 973-992-8241 (day) or Margaret Tretola 973-743-9550 (visitor coordinator).

HUNTERDON

Ostomy Support Group *Professionally-run.* Education and support for ostomy patients and their families. Guest speakers, lecture series and literature. Meets 3rd Tues., 7-9pm, Hunterdon Medical Center, 2100 Wescott Dr., Flemington. Call Beverly Phillips 908-237-5427 (day/eve).

MIDDLESEX

United Ostomy Associations of America Education and encouragement for ostomy patients and their families. Outreach, visitation, phone help and newsletter. Dues $15/yr. Meets 1st Wed. (except Jan., July, Aug., Sept.), 7pm,

Magyar Reformed Church, Somerset St. and Division St., New Brunswick. Call 732-572-3298. *E-mail*: medicamm@verizon.net

MORRIS

United Ostomy Associations of America Education and encouragement for ostomy patients and their families. Provides outreach, visitation, peer-counseling and newsletter. Meets 3rd Wed., 7:30-9:00pm, Morristown Memorial Hospital, Carol G. Simon Cancer Center, Conference Room, Morristown. Call Toni McTigue, RN, 973-971-5522 (day).

OCEAN

United Ostomy Association Education and encouragement for ostomy patients and their families. Visitation, peer-counseling and newsletter. Dues $5/yr. Meets 4th Fri., (except July/Aug.), 7pm, Toms River Presbyterian Church, 1070 Hooper Ave., Toms River. Call Tom 732-901-9411 (day) or American Cancer Society 732-914-1000 (day/eve).

SOMERSET

United Ostomy Association Education and encouragement for ostomy patients and their families. Outreach visitation, guest speakers, phone help and newsletter. Meets 3rd Tues., (except June/July/Aug./Dec.), 7:30-9pm, Somerset Medical Center, South Fuld, Conference Room C and D, 110 Rehill Ave. Somerville. Call Joyce Hoffman 908-685-2814 (day).

UNION

Ostomy Support Group *Professionally-run.* Sharing and support for any ostomate and their families with questions and concerns related to living with an ostomy. Guest speakers. Meets one Tues., every other month, 2pm, Overlook Hospital, 99 Beauvoir Ave., Summit. Call Stephanie D'Andrea 908-522-5552.

WARREN

Warren County Ostomy Club (United Ostomy Association) *Professionally-run.* Dedicated to serving and educating persons before and after surgery for a colostomy, ileostomy or urostomy. Families welcome. Education, visitation and socials. Meets 3rd Sun., 2pm, Warren Hospital, Farley Education Room, Warren. Dues $15/yr. Call Cathy Kiley 610-252-4777.

NATIONAL

Pull-thru Network, The *International network. Founded 1988.* Support and information for families with children born with anorectal, colorectal, or urogenital disorders and any of the associated diagnoses. Disorders include cloacal, bladder exstrophy, imperforate anus, VATER/VACTERL association, anal stenosis, cloacal exstrophy and Hirschsprung's disease and associated diagnoses. Maintains a database for member networking. Quarterly magazine, online discussion group, weekly chat for members, phone support and literature. Dues $30/year - free membership upon request. Write: The Pull-thru Network, 2312 Savoy St., Hoover, Al 35226-1528. Call 205-978-2930. *Website*: http://www.pullthrough.org *E-mail*: info@pullthrough.org

United Ostomy Associations of America *National. 217 affiliates. Founded 2005.* Dedicated to helping every person with an ostomy and related surgeries return to normal living. Also has support groups for parents of children with ostomies, teens, young adults, gay, lesbian and transgender and those who have had a continent diversion. Provides education, support to local groups, national identity and affiliate development help, visitation program and quarterly magazine. Chapter development help. Local group directory on website. Write: United Ostomy Associations of America, P.O. Box 66, Fairview, TN 37062. Call 1-800-826-0826 or 949-660-8624; Fax: 615-799-5915. *Website*: http://www.uoaa.org *E-mail*: info@uoaa.org

OVEREATING / OVERWEIGHT

(see also eating disorders, toll-free helplines)

STATEWIDE

Overeaters Anonymous 12-Step. Fellowship of men, women and children who meet to help one another understand and overcome their common problem of compulsive overeating. Follows the O.A. 12-step program. Meetings throughout New Jersey.

Central New Jersey Intergroup Covers Hunterdon, Mercer, Middlesex, Monmouth, Somerset and Union counties. Write: Overeaters Anonymous, P.O. Box 284, Woodbridge, NJ 07095. Call 908-253-3464 or Kim 732-634-6695. *Website*: http://www.oa-centraljersey.org

Jersey Shore Intergroup Covers Atlantic, Cape May and Ocean counties. Write: Overeaters Anonymous, P.O. Box 571, Manahawkin, NJ 08050. Call Jersey Shore Intergroup 609-698-0244 (day/eve). *Website*: http://www.oa.org

North Jersey Intergroup Covers Bergen, Essex, Hudson, Morris, Passaic, Sussex, Union and Warren counties. $2 donation. Write: Overeaters Anonymous, P.O. Box 827, Fairlawn, NJ 07410-0827. Call 973-746-8787 (day/eve). *Website*: http://www.njioa.org

South Jersey Intergroup Covers Atlantic, Burlington, Camden, Cumberland, Gloucester and Salem counties. Write: Overeaters Anonymous, South Jersey Intergroup, P.O. Box 766, Voorhees 08044. Call South Jersey Intergroup 609-239-0022. *Website*: http://www.southjerseyoa.org

T.O.P.S. (Take Off Pounds Sensibly) Helps overweight persons lose weight through medical supervision, competition and group process. Open to children 7 years and older. Phone network, buddy system, peer-counseling and newsletter. Dues $20/yr. Meetings throughout NJ. For information call Jane 973-875-7649. (leave message) Check website for local meetings. *Website*: http://www.tops.org

ATLANTIC

Overeaters Anonymous 12-Step. Fellowship who meet to help one another understand and overcome their common problem of compulsive overeating. For information on local meetings call Jersey Shore Intergroup 609-698-0244.

BERGEN

Food Addicts in Recovery Anonymous 12-Step. Fellowship of those recovering from the disease of food addiction, obesity, anorexia and bulimia.

Paramus Meets Thurs., 6:30-8pm, Kraft Center, 15 Essex Rd. Call Joe S. 973-243-8807.

Westwood Meets Sun., 8-9:30am, Pascack Valley Hospital, 250 Old Hook Rd. Call Naomi 201-265-6917.

Gastric Bypass Support Group *Professionally-run.* Mutual support and education for persons who have had bariatric surgery (gastric stapling or lap band) within the last year or are considering the procedure. Education, guest speakers and phone help. Meets 3rd Tues., 5:30-7pm, Englewood Hospital, Learning Center, Conference Room A and B, 350 Engle St., Englewood. Before attending call 201-227-5534 (day).

Gastric Bypass Support Group *Professionally-run.* Mutual support and education for persons who have had bariatric surgery (gastric stapling) over a year past surgery. Education, guest speakers and phone help. Meets 3rd Tues., 5:30pm, Englewood Hospital, 350 Engle St., Englewood. Before attending call 201-227-5534 (day). *E-mail*: bergenbariatric@yahoo.com

Gastric Bypass Support Group *Professionally-run.* Mutual support and education for persons who have had bariatric surgery (gastric stapling or lap band) or are considering the procedure. Education, guest speakers and phone help. Meets 4th Tues., 5:30pm, Holy Name Hospital, 718 Teaneck Rd., Teaneck. Before attending call 201-227-5534 (day).

Lap Band Support Group *Professionally-run.* Mutual support and education for persons who have had lap band surgery or are considering the procedure. Meets 4th Tues., 5:30pm, Englewood Hospital, 350 Engle St., Englewood. Before attending call 201-227-5534 (day).

Overeaters Anonymous 12-Step. Fellowship who meet to help one another understand and overcome their common problem of compulsive overeating. For local meeting information by day of week call 973-746-8787.

T.O.P.S. (Take Off Pounds Sensibly) Helps overweight persons lose weight through medical supervision, competition and group process. Open to children 7 years and older. Phone network, buddy system, peer-counseling and newsletter. Membership $20/yr. Dues $1/wk. For meeting information call Jane 973-875-7649 (leave message). Check website for local meetings. *Website*: http://www.tops.org

BURLINGTON

Overcomers 12-Step. Christian-focused recovery group for anyone suffering from any type of addiction, dependency or compulsive disorder. Meets Thurs., 7:30-9pm, Fellowship Alliance Chapel, 199 Church Rd., Medford. Call 609-953-7333 (day).

Overeaters Anonymous 12-Step. Fellowship who meet to help one another understand and overcome their common problem of compulsive overeating. For local meetings call the Overeaters Anonymous South Jersey Intergroup 609-239-0022.

T.O.P.S. (Take Off Pounds Sensibly) Helps overweight persons lose weight through medical supervision, competition and group process. Open to children 7 years and older. Phone network, buddy system, peer-counseling and newsletter. Membership $20/yr. Dues $1/wk. For meeting information call Dave 609-724-9328 (eve). Check website for local meetings. *Website*: http://www.tops.org

CAMDEN

Overeaters Anonymous 12-Step. Fellowship who meet to help one another understand and overcome their common problem of compulsive overeating. For local meetings call the Overeaters Anonymous South Jersey Intergroup 609-239-0022.

T.O.P.S. (Take Off Pounds Sensibly) Helps overweight persons lose weight through medical supervision, competition and group process. Open to children 7 years and older. Phone network, buddy system, peer-counseling and newsletter. Membership $20/yr. Dues $1/wk. For meeting information call DJ 609-758-6471 (eve). Check website for local meetings. *Website*: http://www.tops.org

CAPE MAY

Overeaters Anonymous 12-Step. Fellowship who meet to help one another understand and overcome their common problem of compulsive overeating. For local meetings call the Overeaters Anonymous Jersey Shore Intergroup at 609-698-0244.

T.O.P.S. (Take Off Pounds Sensibly) Helps overweight persons lose weight through medical supervision, competition and group process. Open to children 7 years and older. Phone network, buddy system, peer-counseling and newsletter. Membership $20/yr. Dues $1/wk. For meeting information call Jane 973-875-7649 (leave message). Check website for local meetings. *Website*: http://www.tops.org

CUMBERLAND

Gastric Bypass Support Group Mutual support for those who have or are planning to have gastric bypass surgery (under 18 welcome). Rap sessions. Meets 4th Wed., 7pm, South Jersey Healthcare, Fitness Connection, 1430 W. Sherman Ave., Vineland. For information call 856-451-7533 (day).

Overeaters Anonymous 12-Step. Fellowship who meet to help one another understand and overcome their common problem of compulsive overeating. For local meetings call the Overeaters Anonymous South Jersey Intergroup 609-239-0022.

T.O.P.S. (Take Off Pounds Sensibly) Helps overweight persons lose weight through medical supervision, competition and group process. Open to children 7 years and older. Phone network, buddy system, peer-counseling and newsletter.

Membership $20/yr. Dues $1/wk. For meeting information call Jane 973-875-7649 (leave message). Check website for local meetings. *Website*: http://www.tops.org

ESSEX

Food Addicts Anonymous 12-Step. Fellowship to recover from food addiction. Primary purpose is to maintain abstinence from sugar, flour and wheat. Meets Sun., 7:30-8:30pm, St. Peter's Episcopal Church, 94 East Mount Pleasant Ave., Livingston. Call Roger 908-403-6535 (day/eve) or Lisa 973-403-0333 (day).

Overeaters Anonymous 12-Step. Fellowship who meet to help one another understand and overcome their common problem of compulsive overeating. For local meeting information by day of week call 973-746-8787.

Reformers Anonymous Faith-based group to help people find freedom from addictions: alcohol, debt, drugs, eating disorders, gambling, internet, sex/love addiction, smoking, etc. Literature, newsletter and phone help. Meets Fri., 7-9pm, First Baptist Church, 257 Bloomfield Ave., Caldwell. Call Pastor Eli Miranda 201-724-9208 (day) or church 973-226-1004 (day).

T.O.P.S. (Take Off Pounds Sensibly) Helps overweight persons lose weight through medical supervision, competition and group process. Open to children 7 years and older. Phone network, buddy system, peer-counseling and newsletter. Membership $20/yr. Dues $1/wk. For meeting information call Jane 973-875-7649 (leave message). Check website for local meetings. *Website*: http://www.tops.org

GLOUCESTER

Overeaters Anonymous 12-Step. Fellowship who meet to help one another understand and overcome their common problem of compulsive overeating. For information on local meetings call the Overeaters Anonymous South Jersey Intergroup 609-239-0022.

South Jersey Bariatric Support System Support for persons who have had gastric bypass or are considering the procedure. Families welcome. Rap sessions, online support and literature. Meets every other Fri., 7pm, Church of the Nazarene, Broadway, Pitman. For meeting information call Chrissie 856-256-9066 (day). *Website*: http://www.yahoogroups.com/sjbss *E-mail*: sjbss@verizon.net

T.O.P.S. (Take Off Pounds Sensibly) Helps overweight persons lose weight through medical supervision, competition and group process. Open to children 7 years and older. Phone network, buddy system, peer-counseling and newsletter. Membership $20/yr. Dues $1/wk. For meeting information call DJ 609-758-6471 (eve). Check website for local meetings. *Website*: http://www.tops.org

HUDSON

Overeaters Anonymous 12-Step. Fellowship who meet to help one another understand and overcome their common problem of compulsive overeating. There is one group in Hudson County on Sun. For local meeting information by day of week call 973-746-8787.

HUNTERDON

Overeaters Anonymous 12-Step. Fellowship who meet to help one another understand and overcome their common problem of compulsive overeating. For local meeting information call the Overeaters Anonymous Central Intergroup 908-253-3464 or 732-634-6695.

T.O.P.S. (Take Off Pounds Sensibly) Helps overweight persons lose weight through medical supervision, competition and group process. Open to children 7 years and older. Phone network, buddy system, peer-counseling and newsletter. Membership $20/yr. Dues $1/wk. For meeting information call Jane 973-875-7649 (leave message). Check website for local meetings. *Website*: http://www.tops.org

MERCER

NJ Bariatrics Support Group Mutual support and education for persons who have had bariatric surgery (gastric stapling or lap band) or are considering the procedure. Education, guest speakers, literature and phone help. Meetings vary, N.J. Bariatrics, 4250 US Route 1 North, Suite 1, Monmouth Junction. Before attending call 732-274-3434 (day).

Overeaters Anonymous 12-Step. Fellowship who meet to help one another understand and overcome their common problem of compulsive overeating. For local meetings call the Overeaters Anonymous Central Intergroup 732-634-6695.

T.O.P.S. (Take Off Pounds Sensibly) Helps overweight persons lose weight through medical supervision, competition and group process. Open to children 7 years and older. Phone network, buddy system, peer-counseling and newsletter.

Membership $20/yr. Dues $1/wk. For meeting information call DJ 609-758-6471 (eve). Check website for local meetings. *Website*: http://www.tops.org

Together We Can 12-Step. Fellowship of men and women who share their experience, strength and hope with each other that they may solve their common problem of alcoholism and/or overeating. Meets Mon. and Thurs., 7pm, Trinity Church, 33 Mercer St., Princeton. Call Janet 609-273-6955.

MIDDLESEX

Bariatric Angels *Professionally-run.* Mutual support for bariatric surgery patients using a 12-step program. Education, advocacy, rap sessions, buddy system, socials, newsletter and phone help. Pre-surgery individuals are welcome 1st meeting of each month. Meets Sat., 10:30am (surgery less than 3 months) and 11am (surgery more than 3 months), Bayshore Wellness Center, Conference Room, 1044 US Highway 9, Parlin. Registration required. Before attending call Kate Fenimore, RN 908-685-2200 ext. 3167 (day) or 732-203-2322 (eve).

Overeaters Anonymous 12-Step. Fellowship who meet to help one another understand and overcome their common problem of compulsive overeating. For local meeting information call the Overeaters Anonymous Central Intergroup 908-253-3464 or 732-634-6695.

SMART Recovery (Self-Management and Recovery Training) *Professionally-run.* Self-help group for individuals wanting to gain their independence from addictive behaviors (drugs, including alcohol and nicotine, and other compulsive behaviors i.e. gambling, eating disorders). SMART is an abstinence program based on cognitive-behavioral education and principles, especially those of rational-emotive behavior therapy. Meets Mon., 6-7:30pm, Rutgers University, Busch Campus, Psychology Building, Room A224, Piscataway. Call Tom Morgan 732-445-0902. *Website*: http://www.smartrecovery.org

T.O.P.S. (Take Off Pounds Sensibly) Helps overweight persons lose weight through medical supervision, competition and group process. Open to children 7 years and older. Phone network, buddy system, peer-counseling and newsletter. Membership $20/yr. Dues $1/wk. For meeting information call Dave 609-724-9328 (eve). Check website for local meetings. *Website*: http://www.tops.org

MONMOUTH

Bariatric Angels *Professionally-run.* Mutual support for bariatric surgery patients using a 12-step program. Education, advocacy, rap sessions, buddy system, socials, newsletter and phone help. Meets Fri., 7:30pm, Angels Cove Retreat, 164 West Front St., Keyport. Registration required. Before attending call Kate Fenimore, RN 908-685-2200 ext. 3167 (day) or 732-203-2322 (eve).

Overeaters Anonymous 12-Step. Fellowship who meet to help one another understand and overcome their common problem of compulsive overeating. For local meeting information call the Overeaters Anonymous Central Jersey Intergroup 908-253-3464 or 732-634-6695.

T.O.P.S. (Take Off Pounds Sensibly) Helps overweight persons lose weight through medical supervision, competition and group process. Open to children 7 years and older. Phone network, buddy system, peer-counseling and newsletter. Membership $20/yr. Dues $1/wk. For meeting information call Dave 609-724-9328 (eve). Check website for local meetings. *Website*: http://www.tops.org

MORRIS

Band Support Group *Professionally-run.* Mutual support for those who have had, or are planning to have, adjustable gastric band surgery. Families welcome. Rap sessions, advocacy and guest speakers. Meets 2nd and last Wed., 7-8pm, 147 Columbia Turnpike, Suite 301, Florham Park. Call Jennifer Levine, Kim Manzo or Linda R. Lens, NP-C 973-410-9700 (leave message).

Food Addicts in Recovery Anonymous 12-Step. Fellowship of those recovering from the disease of food addiction, obesity, anorexia and bulimia. Meets Sat., 10-11:30am, Saint Clares Health System, 400 West Blackwell St., Conference Room C, Dover. Call Sheila 973-243-8807 or Barbara 973-600-4449 (day). *Website*: http://www.foodaddicts.org

Gastric Bypass Support Group *Professionally-run.* For those who have undergone, or are considering, gastric bypass surgery. Literature and phone help. Meets 4th Wed., 5:30-6:30pm, Hilton Garden Inn, 375 Mount Hope Ave., Rockaway. Call Patti Smith 973-989-3644 (day).

Lap Band Support Group *Professionally-run.* For those who have undergone, or are considering, lap band surgery. Literature and phone help. Meets 4th Wed., 7-8pm, St. Clare's Hospital, Cafeteria, Dover. Call Patti Smith 973-989-3644 (day).

Overeaters Anonymous 12-Step. Fellowship who meet to help one another understand and overcome their common problem of compulsive overeating. For local meeting information by day of week call 973-746-8787.

SMART Recovery (Self-Management And Recovery Training) Self-help group for individuals wanting to gain their independence from addictive behaviors (drugs, including alcohol and nicotine, and other compulsive behaviors i.e. gambling, eating disorders). SMART is an abstinence program based on cognitive-behavioral education and principles, especially those of rational-emotive behavior therapy. Meets Thurs., 7-8:30pm, Beginnings, 65 Spring St., Morristown. Call Rich 973-983-8755. *Website*: http://www.smartrecovery.org

T.O.P.S. (Take Off Pounds Sensibly) Helps overweight persons lose weight through medical supervision, competition and group process. Open to children 7 years and older. Phone network, buddy system, peer-counseling and newsletter. Membership $20/yr. Dues $1/wk. For meeting information call Jane 973-875-7649 (leave message). Check website for local meetings. *Website*: http://www.tops.org

OCEAN

Bariatric Angels *Professionally-run.* Mutual support for post-bariatric surgery patients using a 12-step program. Education, advocacy, rap sessions, buddy system, socials, newsletter and phone help. Pre-surgery individuals are welcome 1st meeting of each month. Meets Thurs., 7pm (surgery less than 3 months) and 8pm (surgery more than 3 months), Community Medical Center, Conference Room B, 99 Route 37 West, Toms River. Registration required. Before attending call Kate Fenimore, RN 908-685-2200 ext. 3167 (day) or 732-203-2322 (eve).

Checkpoint Support to help overcome dependencies and addictions through accountability, encouragement and spiritual development. Meets Thurs., 7-8:30pm, Shore Vineyard Church, 320 Compass Ave., Beachwood. Call 732-244-3888 (day).

Overeaters Anonymous 12-Step. Fellowship who meet to help one another understand and overcome their common problem of compulsive overeating. For information on local meetings call Jersey Shore Intergroup 609-698-0244.

T.O.P.S. (Take Off Pounds Sensibly) Helps overweight persons lose weight through medical supervision, competition and group process. Open to children 7 years and older. Phone network, buddy system, peer-counseling and newsletter. Membership $20/yr. Dues $1/wk. For meeting information call DJ 609-758-6471 (eve). Check website for local meetings. *Website*: http://www.tops.org

PASSAIC

Food Addicts in Recovery Anonymous 12-Step. Fellowship of those recovering from the disease of food addiction, obesity, anorexia and bulimia. Meets Tues., 6:45-8:15pm, St. Joseph's Hospital, 224 Hamburg Turnpike, Wayne. Call Barbara 973-600-4449.

Overeaters Anonymous 12-Step. Fellowship who meet to help one another understand and overcome their common problem of compulsive overeating. For local meeting information by day of week call 973-746-8787.

T.O.P.S. (Take Off Pounds Sensibly) Helps overweight persons lose weight through medical supervision, competition and group process. Open to children 7 years and older. Phone network, buddy system, peer-counseling and newsletter. Membership $20/yr. Dues $1/wk. For meeting information call Jane 973-875-7649 (leave message). Check website for local meetings. *Website*: http://www.tops.org

SALEM

Overeaters Anonymous 12-Step. Fellowship who meet to help one another understand and overcome their common problem of compulsive overeating. For information on local meetings call the Overeaters Anonymous South Jersey Intergroup 609-239-0022 or Bobbie S. 856-346-2336 (day/eve).

T.O.P.S. (Take Off Pounds Sensibly) Helps overweight persons lose weight through medical supervision, competition and group process. Also open to children 7 years and older. Phone network, buddy system, peer-counseling and newsletter. Membership $20/yr. Dues $1/wk. For meeting information call Jane 973-875-7649 (leave message). Check website for local meetings. *Website*: http://www.tops.org

SOMERSET

Bariatric Angels *Professionally-run.* Mutual support for post-bariatric surgery patients using a 12-step program. Education, advocacy, rap sessions, buddy system, socials, newsletter and phone help. Pre-surgery individuals are welcome 1st meeting of each month. Meets Tues., 7pm (surgery less than 3 months) and 8pm (surgery more than 3 months), Presbyterian Church of Bound Brook, 950 Mountain Ave. and Route 28 (Union Ave.), Bound Brook. Registration required. Before attending call Kate Fenimore, RN 908-685-2200 ext. 3167 (day) or 732-203-2322 (eve).

Gastric Bypass Support Group *Professionally-run.* Mutual support for those who have had, or are planning to have, gastric bypass surgery. Families welcome. Rap sessions, advocacy and guest speakers. Meets 4th Thurs., 6:30-7:30pm, The Olde Mill Inn, 225 Route 202, Basking Ridge. Call Lynn Elsayed 973-410-9700 (day).

Overeaters Anonymous 12-Step. Fellowship who meet to help one another understand and overcome their common problem of compulsive overeating. For local meeting information call Overeaters Anonymous Central Intergroup 908-253-3464 or 732-634-6695.

SUSSEX

Overeaters Anonymous 12-Step. Fellowship who meet to help one another understand and overcome their common problem of compulsive overeating. For local meeting information by day of week call 973-746-8787.

T.O.P.S. (Take Off Pounds Sensibly) Helps overweight persons lose weight through medical supervision, competition and group process. Open to children 7 years and older. Phone network, buddy system, peer-counseling and newsletter. Membership $20/yr. Dues $1/wk. For meeting information call Jane 973-875-7649 (leave message). Check website for local meetings. *Website*: http://www.tops.org

UNION

Food Addicts Anonymous 12-Step. Mutual support meetings for recovery from food addiction. Primary purpose is to maintain abstinence from sugar, flour and wheat. Meets Mon. and Fri., 8pm, Cranford United Methodist Church, 201 Lincoln Ave., Cranford. Call Phyllis 732-244-4324 (Mon. group) and Dorene 908-377-7939 (Fri. group). *Website*: http://www.foodaddictsanonymous.org

Overeaters Anonymous 12-Step. Fellowship who meet to help one another understand and overcome their common problem of compulsive overeating. For local meeting information by day of week call 908-253-3464.

WARREN

Bariatric Angels *Professionally-run.* Mutual support for bariatric surgery patients using a 12-step program. Education, advocacy, rap sessions, buddy system, socials, newsletter and phone help. Pre-surgery individuals are welcome 1st meeting of each month. Meets Wed., 7pm (surgery less than 3 months) and 8pm (surgery more than 3 months), Grace Lutheran Church, 300 Roseberry St.,

Phillipsburg. Registration required. Before attending call Kate Fenimore, RN 908-685-2200 ext. 3167 (day) or 732-203-2322 (eve).

Overeaters Anonymous 12-Step. Fellowship who meet to help one another understand and overcome their common problem of compulsive overeating. There is only one group in Warren County on Sun. For local meeting information by day of week call 973-746-8787.

T.O.P.S. (Take Off Pounds Sensibly) Helps overweight persons lose weight through medical supervision, competition and group process. Open to children 7 years and older. Phone network, buddy system, peer-counseling and newsletter. Membership $20/yr. Dues $1/wk. For meeting information call Jane 973-875-7649 (leave message). Check website for local meetings. *Website*: http://www.tops.org

NATIONAL

Compulsive Eaters Anonymous - H.O.W. *International. 500 affiliated groups. Founded 1985.* 12-Step. Fellowship to share experience, strength and hope in order to help themselves and others who suffer from the self destruction of compulsive eating. H.O.W. (Honesty, Open-mindedness and Willingness) groups use a food plan which includes an abstinence of sugar and flour, and allows only three weighed and measured meals per day. Write: CEA-HOW, 5500 E. Atherton St., Suite 227 B, Long Beach, CA 90815-4017. Call 562-342-9344 (day); Fax: 562-342-9346. *Website*: http://www.ceahow.org *E-mail*: gso@ceahow.org

Eating Addictions Anonymous - SANE Fellowship *National. 6 affiliated chapters.* 12-Step. Recovery program for men and women recovering from all forms of eating and body image addictions. Includes anorexia, bulimia, binge eating, overeating, exercise bulimics, etc. Focuses on internal growth and reclaiming bodies rather than weight or appearance. Write: Eating Addictions Anonymous, P.O. Box 8151, Silver Spring, MD 20907-8151. Call 202-882-6528 *Website*: http://www.eatingaddictionsanonymous.org *E-mail*: 12n12@tidalwave.net

Eating Disorders Anonymous *International. Founded 2000.* Fellowship of men and women who share their experience, strength and hope with each other that they may solve their common problems and help others to recover from their eating disorders. Focuses on the solution; not the problem. EDA endorses sound nutrition. Literature, information and referrals, pen pals and phone support. Assistance in starting groups. Offers local support group referrals online. Write: General Service Board of EDA, P.O. Box 55876, Phoenix, AZ

85078-5876. *Website*: http://www.4EDA.org *E-mail*: info@EatingDisordersAnonymous.org

Food Addicts Anonymous *International. 146 affiliated groups worldwide. Founded 1987.* 12-Step. Fellowship of men and women who are willing to recover from the disease of food addiction. Primary purpose is to maintain abstinence from sugar, flour and wheat. Information and referral, pen pals, online contacts and conferences. Assistance in starting groups. Online listing of local support groups. Write: Food Addicts Anonymous, 4623 Forest Hill Blvd., Suite 109-4, W. Palm Beach, FL 33415. Call 561-967-3871; Fax: 561-967-9815. *Website*: http://www.foodaddictsanonymous.org *E-mail*: info@foodaddictsanonymous.org

Food Addicts In Recovery Anonymous *International. Founded 1998.* 12-Step. Fellowship addressing all forms of food addiction, e.g. undereating, overeating and bulimia through purging and/or exercise. FA members are all ages and walks of life. Literature, phone support, assistance in starting new groups and on-line listing of meetings. Write: Food Addicts Anonymous, 6 Pleasant St., Room 402, Malden, MA 02148. Call 781-321-9118; Fax: 781-321-9223. *Website*: http://www.foodaddicts.org *E-mail*: fa@foodaddicts.org

I.C.A.P. (Intercongregational Addictions Program) *International. Founded 1979.* Network of recovering alcoholic women in religious orders. Helps Roman Catholic women who are or have been members of religious orders and are alcoholic or chemically dependent, compulsive eaters, compulsive gamblers, etc. Information, referrals, assistance in meeting other members, phone support, conferences and e-newsletters. Write: Intercongregational Addictions Program, 7777 Lake Street, Suite 115, River Forest, IL 60305-1734. Call 708-488-9770; Fax: 708-488-9774. *Website*: http://www.2icap.org *E-mail*: lclose1@core.com

National Association to Advance Fat Acceptance (NAAFA) *National. 50 chapters. Founded 1969.* Fights size discrimination and provides fat people with the tools for self-empowerment. Public education regarding obesity. Provides a forum for peer support and activism. Dues $35 (includes newsletter), educational materials, group development guidelines and annual convention. Special interest groups include: youth, families, gays, diabetics, men, women, sleep apnea, military, mental health professionals and couples. Write: National Association to Advance Fat Acceptance, P.O. Box 22510, Oakland, CA 94609. Call 916-558-6880. *Website*: http://www.naafa.org

Overcomers In Christ *International. Founded 1987.* Recovery program that deals with every aspect of addiction and dysfunction (spiritual, physical, mental, emotional and social). Uses Overcomers Goals which are Christ-centered.

Literature, resources, information and referrals. Assistance in starting new groups. Write: Overcomers In Christ, P.O. Box 34460, Omaha, NE 68134-04604. Call 402-573-0966; Fax: 402-573-0960. *Website*: http://www.OvercomersInChrist.org *E-mail*: OIC@OvercomersInChrist.org

Overcomers Outreach, Inc. *International. 700 affiliated groups. Founded 1985*. 12-Step. Christ-centered support group for persons with any compulsive behaviors, as well as their families and friends. Uses the 12-steps of A.A. and applies them to the Scriptures. Uses Jesus Christ as "higher power." Supplements involvement in other 12-step groups. Newsletter, group development guidelines and conferences. Write: Overcomers Outreach, P.O. Box 2204, Oakhurst, CA 93644. Call 1-800-310-3001. *Website*: http://www.overcomersoutreach.org *E-mail*: info@overcomersoutreach.org

Overeaters Anonymous *International. 6,500 groups. Founded 1960.* 12-Step. Fellowship of men and women who meet to help one another understand and overcome compulsive eating. Also groups and literature for young persons and teens. Monthly magazine, literature and group development guidelines. Write: Overeaters Anonymous, P.O. Box 44020, Rio Rancho, New Mexico 87174-4020. Call 505-891-2664 or look in white pages for local number; Fax: 505-891-4320. *Website*: http://www.oa.org *E-mail*: info@oa.org

Recoveries Anonymous *International. 50 chapters.* Spiritual recovery group for anyone seeking a solution for any kind of addiction, problem or behavior. Family and friends welcome. "How To Begin..." guides and "Start A Group" kit can be downloaded free from the website. Write: Recoveries Anonymous, P.O. Box 1212, East Northport, NY 11731. *Website*: http://www.r-a.org *E-mail*: raus@r-a.org

T.O.P.S. (Take Off Pounds Sensibly) *International. 10,000 chapters. Founded 1948*. Members use professionally prepared materials on menu planning, food exchanges, motivation and exercise. Promotes a sensible approach to managing weight as a life choice. Weekly meetings emphasize recognition and support. Newsletter, tools for weight management and chapter development. New chapters may be started by a minimum of four people. Support group locations available online. Dues $24/USA; $30/Canada. Write: TOPS, P.O. Box 070360, 4575 South 5th St., Milwaukee, WI 53207. Call 1-800-932-8677. *Website*: http://www.tops.org

ONLINE

Gastric Bypass Family Support *Online*. Support for those who expect to have, or have had, gastric bypass surgery. Family and friends are included. Offers an e-mail discussion group. *Website*: http://health.groups.yahoo.com/group/Gastric_Bypass_Family/

PAIN, CHRONIC

ATLANTIC

Atlantic Chronic Pain Support Group Mutual support for individuals dealing with a chronic pain situation. Meets Wed., 6:30-8:30pm, Bacharach Institute for Rehabilitation, Board Room, Pomona. Call Bob 609-266-1198 (day).

BURLINGTON

Reflex Sympathetic Dystrophy Chronic Pain Support Group 12-Step. Support for persons with reflex sympathetic dystrophy or chronic pain, their families and friends. Helps members maintain as normal and pain free life as possible. Guest speakers, educational programs, pen pals, rap sessions, literature, phone help and advocacy. Call Ursula Weed 856-304-6682 (day). *E-mail:* sula25@msn.com

> **Mt. Holly** Meets 2nd Wed., 7-9pm, Virtua Hospital, 175 Madison Ave., Conference Room, 1st Floor. Call Kathy Henson 609-268-1565 (day). *E-mail:* bepainfree2000@aol.com
>
> **Mt. Laurel** Meets 4th Tues., 6-8pm, YMCA, 5001 Centerton Rd. Call Lisa Yabey 609-877-0213 (day).

CAMDEN

American Chronic Pain Association *"Help and Hope"* Support for those suffering from chronic pain and their families. A helping hand and friendly ear for those chronic pain sufferers willing to help themselves. Rap sessions, guest speakers and literature. For meeting information call Philip Elting 856-489-4383.

Chronic Pain Support Group Provides support for those living with chronic pain. Meets 2nd Fri., 10:30-11:30am, New Seasons Assisted Living, 501 Laurel Oak Rd., Voorhees. Call Tanya Donovan at Elder Med 1-800-522-1965.

MERCER

American Chronic Pain Association *"Help and Hope"* Support for people suffering from chronic pain. Offers support, education, resources and understanding to those living with chronic pain. Meets 1st and 3rd Mon., 1-3pm, University

Medical Center at Princeton, Lambert House, 253 Witherspoon St., Classroom #4, Princeton. Call Anne 609-799-4681. *Website:* http://www.theacpa.org

MORRIS

American Chronic Pain Association Support Group *Professionally-run.* Support and education for people and their families living with chronic pain. Rap sessions, guest speakers and literature. Meetings vary in Mine Hill and Dover. For meeting information and to register call Pat Merritt 973-347-7470 or Pat Santoro 973-366-8765. *Website:* http://www.theacpa.org *E-mail:* merrittspnb@aol.com

New Hope and Healing Support for adults experiencing pain in their lives. Offers mutual support, sharing coping skills, guest speakers, education workshops, seminars and retreats. Meets in Morris County. Call Christine 973-927-4719 (day).

WARREN

American Chronic Pain Association Support Group *Professionally-run.* Support and education for people and their families living with chronic pain. Rap sessions, guest speakers and literature. Meetings vary in Hackettstown. For meeting information and to register call Pat Merritt 973-347-7470 or Pat Santoro 973-366-8765. *Website:* http://www.theacpa.org *E-mail:* merrittspnb@aol.com

NATIONAL

American Chronic Pain Association, Inc. *National. 400+ affiliated chapters. Founded 1980.* Provides peer support and education for individuals with chronic pain and their families so that they may live more fully in spite of their pain. Aim is to raise awareness among health care community, policy makers and the public about issues of living with chronic pain. Workbooks for self-help recovery,. quarterly newsletter, group development guidelines, phone network and outreach program to clinics. Write: American Chronic Pain Association, P.O. Box 850, Rocklin, CA 95677. Call 1-800-533-3231 or 916-632-0922; Fax: 916-632-3208. *Website:* http://www.theacpa.org *E-mail:* ACPA@pacbell.net

Rest Ministries *National. 275 affiliated groups. Founded 1997.* Christian ministry for people who live with chronic pain or illness and their families. Quarterly magazine, daily devotionals, share and prayer e-mail support mailing list, online chat, etc. Information and resources manual for starting groups ($15) or complete kit available. Assistance to churches in setting up support groups, teaching church awareness and training church leadership on how to outreach to the chronically ill effectively. Write: Rest Ministries, Inc., P.O. Box 502928, San Diego, CA 92150.

Call 1-888-751-7378 or 858-486-4685; Fax: 1-800-933-1078. *Website:* http://www.hopekeepers.org or http://www.restministries.org *E-mail:* rest@restministries.org

PARKINSON'S DISEASE

(see also toll-free helplines)

STATEWIDE

American Parkinson's Disease Association NJ Chapter Provides literature, speakers' bureau, educational programs and physician referrals. Referrals to support groups. Write: NJ APDA Information and Referral Center, Robert Wood Johnson University Hospital., 1 Robert Wood Johnson Place, New Brunswick, NJ 08901. Call 732-745-7520.

BERGEN

Parkinson's Support Group Mutual support and education for individuals diagnosed with Parkinson's disease. Families and caregivers welcome. Rap sessions, guest speakers, literature and phone help.

Englewood Meets Fri., 1-3pm, Englewood Southeast Center for Independent Living, 228 Grand Ave. Call Ilse Heller 201-265-4946 (day) or Pat Marshall 201-224-8816. *E-mail*: pkmarshall4@msn.com

Haworth Meets 1st Sat. (except July/Aug.), 1-2:30pm (Easy yoga exercise at 12:15pm), First Congregational Church, Haworth Ave. Call Ilse Heller 201-265-4976 (day/eve).

Wyckoff *Professionally-run.* Meets 1st Thurs. (separate groups for patients and caregivers), 7:30pm and 3rd Thurs. (except Dec.), regular meeting at 7:30pm (optional exercise at 7pm), Cedar Hill Christian Reformed Church, Cedar Hill Ave. Call Marion Arenas 201-670-0083 (day) or Gene Provost 973-875-8429 (day).

BURLINGTON

Caregivers Support Group *Professionally-run.* Support for anyone caring for an individual with progressive supranuclear palsy, Alzheimer's or Parkinson's disease. Meets 1st Tues., 6:30-7:30pm, Care One at Evesham, 870 East Route 70, Marlton. Call Carol Solomon 856-985-1180 (day).

Parkinson Disease Support *Professionally-run.* Support for persons afflicted with Parkinson's disease and their families. Meets 3rd Wed. (except Dec.), 7-8:30pm, Virtua Health and Rehab Center, 62 Richmond Ave., Mt. Holly. Call

Virtua Health 1-888-847-8823 (day) or Virginia Hedges 609-261-7040 (day). *Website*: http://www.virtua.org

CAPE MAY

Parkinson's Support Group of Cape May County Mutual support for Parkinson's disease patients and their families. Meets 2nd Thurs. (except July/Aug.) 1pm, Victoria Commons, Town Bank Rd., North Cape May. Call Rita 609-886-2455 (day).

ESSEX

Parkinson Disease Support Group *Professionally-run.* Provides emotional support and education for those diagnosed with Parkinson's disease, their family members and caregivers. Guest speakers. Meets 1st Wed., 11am-12:30pm, Care One, 76 Passaic Ave., Livingston. Before attending call Carol Carlson, PhD 973-627-4087.

Parkinson Support Group of North Jersey Mutual support and exchange of information for persons with Parkinson's, families and caregivers. Discussions and guest speakers. Meets 3rd Sat., 10am-noon, Mountainside Hospital, Bay Ave., Montclair. Call 973-376-3365 or Ted 973-338-4745.

GLOUCESTER

Parkinson's Support Group of Southern New Jersey *Professionally-run.* Support, education and social events for Parkinson's patients and their families. Occasional guest speakers. Meets 1st Wed., 7pm, Woodbury Mews, 122 Green Ave., Woodbury. Call Diane Gruszewski 856-582-1419 (day).

HUNTERDON

Hunterdon County Parkinson's Support Group *Professionally-run.* Support for persons with Parkinson's and their caregivers. Patients and caregivers meet both together and separately. Meets 4th Fri., 1:30-3:30pm, Hunterdon County Div. of Senior Services, Office on Aging, Route 31 South, Flemington. Call Barbara Burgard 908-788-6401 ext. 3149 (day).

MERCER

Parkinson's Support Group of Central Delaware Valley Support and information for Parkinson's patients and families. Guest speakers and educational programs. Meets 3rd Wed. (except July/Aug./Jan./Feb.), 1pm,

Lawrenceville Presbyterian Church, 2688 Main St., Route 206, Lawrenceville. Call John Wicoff 609-737-3364 (day/eve). *E-mail*: JRWicoff@comcast.net

MIDDLESEX

COPSA Spouse Support Group *Professionally-run*. Mutual support and understanding for spouses of persons with any type of memory loss (Alzheimer's, Parkinson's, vascular disease, stroke, head injury, dementia, etc.). Meets 1st and 3rd Mon., 9:30-11am, UBHC, 671 Hoes Lane, Piscataway. Call Mary Catherine Lundquist 732-235-2858 (day). *Website*: http://vbhcweb/ (then go to Aging-COPSA) E-mail: lindqumc@umdnj.edu

JFK Johnson Rehab Institute Parkinson's Group Support, education and coping skills for individuals with Parkinson's disease. Families welcome. Literature, rap sessions and guest speakers. Meets 1st Wed., 1-2:30pm, Monroe Township Office on Aging, Municipal Complex, Perrineville Rd., Monroe Township. Pre-registration required. Call Jennifer 732-521-6111 (day) or Janice Dibling 732-321-7063 (day).

Parkinson's Disease Patient and Family Support Group Mutual support and education for those with Parkinson's, their families and caregivers. Patients and caregivers meet both separately and together. Meets 3rd Thurs., 12:30pm, New Brunswick. Call NJ Parkinson Disease Information and Referral Center 732-745-7520 (day).

Young Onset Parkinson's Patient and Family Support Group *Professionally-run*. Support and education for Parkinson's patients under 60 years old, their families and caregivers. Meets 3rd Wed., 7pm, New Brunswick. For meeting location call NJ Parkinson Disease Information and Referral Center 732-745-7520 (day).

MONMOUTH

Parkinson's Support Group Mutual support for Parkinson's patients and their families. Guest speakers. Light refreshments. Meets 3rd Tues., 11:15am-12:15pm, Manalapan Senior Center, Route 522, Manalapan. Call Seniors First 732-780-3013 (day).

"No one is useless in the world who lightens the burden of others."
--Charles Dickens

MORRIS

Parkinson Disease Support Group *Professionally-run.* Provides emotional support and education for those diagnosed with Parkinson's disease, their family members and caregivers. Guest speakers.

Parsippany Meets 3rd Mon., 1:45-3pm, Care One at Morris, 200 Mazda Brook Road. Before attending call Richard Petruce, LCSW or Carol Carlson, PhD 973-627-4087 (day).

Morristown Meets 1st Mon., 11am-12:30pm, Care One, 151 Madison Ave. Before attending call Carol Carlson, PhD 973-627-4087 (day).

OCEAN

Parkinson's Support Group Support and education for patients with Parkinson's, their families and caregivers. Meets 2nd Wed., 1-2:30pm, Community Medical Center, The Lighthouse, Toms River. Call Andrea Brandsness 1-800-621-0096.

SUSSEX

Eleanore Chaplin Memorial Parkinson Support Group Mutual support and exchange of information for persons with Parkinson's, their families and caregivers. Rap sessions, phone help and newsletter. Meets 3rd Fri., 1-2:30pm, Senior Center (Lower Level), La Bonce Dr., Franklin Boro. Call Bob Cummings 973-334-1591 (eve; before 8pm) or Anita Navara 973-948-3329 (eve).

UNION

Parkinsonian Support Group In Westfield, The Provides support and education to persons with Parkinson's disease as well as their caregivers, including former caregivers who have lost a family member to Parkinson's. Handicapped accessible. Meets 2nd Mon. (except July/Aug./Oct.), 1:30-3pm, Presbyterian Church in Westfield, 140 Mountain Ave., Westfield. Call Church office 908-233-0301 (day).

Parkinson's Support Group *Professionally-run.* Support and education for patients of all ages with Parkinson's disease. Literature, buddy system and guest speakers. Meets 2nd Wed., 1-3pm, Robert Wood Johnson University Hospital at Rahway, Stone St., Rahway. Call Dr. Paul Abend 732-516-1042 (day).

WARREN

Lehigh Valley Parkinson's Support Group, The Mutual support and encouragement for Parkinson patients, their families and friends. Guest speakers. Meets 4th Tues., 10:30am-noon, Muhlenberg Hospital, Banko Building, Schoenersville Rd., Bethlehem, PA. Call Geraldine 610-868-3510.

NATIONAL

American Parkinson Disease Association, Inc. *National. 59 chapters. Founded 1961.* Network of 300 support groups for patients and families. Chapter development guidelines and quarterly newsletter. Promotes research. Fifty-nine information and referral centers nationwide. Also offers online booklets, referrals and support. Write: American Parkinson Disease Association, 135 Parkinson Ave., Staten Island, NY 10305. Call 718-981-8001 or 1-800-223-2732; Fax: 718-981-4399. *Website*: http://www.apdaparkinson.org

National Parkinson Foundation *National. 1,000 groups*. Provides information, support and education for persons with Parkinson's, their families and health care professionals. Funds research. Seeks to improve quality of life for both patients and their caregivers. Includes Young Onset Parkinson network. Helps to start groups. Write: National Parkinson Foundation, 1501 N.W. Ninth Ave., Miami, FL 33136. Call 1-800-327-4545 or 305-547-6666; Fax: 305-243-5595. *Website*: http://www.parkinson.org *E-mail*: contact@parkinson.org

POLIO

STATEWIDE

Polio Network of NJ Support and information for NJ polio survivors and their families. Optional $10/yr donation. For information on support groups in your area call the Polio Network of NJ 201-845-6860 (day). *Website:* http://www.njpolio.org *E-mail:* NJPN10@hotmail.com

ATLANTIC

Atlantic County Post-Polio Support Group Support and information on the late effects of polio, for post-polio survivors, their families and friends. Dues $15 yr. Meets 4th Sat. (except July/Aug.), 10:00am-noon, Atlantic Township Library, Mays Landing. Before attending call Marge 609-909-1518 (day). *E-mail:* kittystamp@comcast.net

BERGEN

Bergen County Polio Support Group Support network information on late effects of polio and polio survivors. Peer-counseling, phone network and guest speakers. Meets 1st Sat., 10:30am, Maywood Senior Center, 145 Magnolia Ave., Maywood. Before attending call Heather Broad 201-845-6317. *E-mail:* hbroad@netzero.com

CAMDEN

South West Jersey Polio Support Group Support and information on the late effects of polio for post-polio survivors, their families and friends. Dues $15/yr. Meets 4th Sat., 10:30am-noon, Kennedy Conference Center, 30 E. Laurel Rd., Stratford. Call Ann 856-784-7741 (day).

MONMOUTH

Monmouth County Post-Polio Support Group Support for persons suffering from post-polio syndrome, in need of pain management, or who need help controlling their lives, through meetings, referrals, discussions, guest speakers, social events and networking. Families and friends welcome. Phone help. Dues $15/yr. Meeting days and locations vary. Call Antoinette Wilczewski (President) 732-229-9343 or Arthur Siegfried 908-722-7212 (day). *Website:* http://www.njpolio.org

MORRIS

Morris County Polio Network Mutual support for post-polio survivors, their families and friends. Information on the late-effects of polio. Rap sessions. Newsletter. Dues $10/yr. Meets 3rd Mon., Charlie Brown's Restaurant, Route 46 East, Denville. However in Mar., July, Aug. and Dec. meets 3rd Wed., 7pm, Zeris Inn, Route 46 East, Mountain Lakes. Call Marion Rosenstein 201-585-8125 or Vincent Avantagiato, D.C. 973-769-0075 (day). *E-mail:* Marion618R@msn.com

OCEAN

Ocean County Post-Polio Support Group Support information sharing for polio survivors. Networking with professionals and other groups. Phone help, guest speakers, literature and buddy system. Meets 3 to 4 times per year, Health South, 14 Hospital Dr., Toms River. Call Susan Gato 732-864-0998 (day) or Kevin Marie Moore 732-240-4272 (day). *Website:* http://www.tomsrivernjpolio.org

SOMERSET

Raritan Valley Post-Polio Support Group Support information sharing for post-polio survivors. Networking with professionals other groups. Phone help, speakers, monthly newsletter. Dues $10/yr. Meets 1st Sat. (Oct., Nov., Dec., Mar., Apr.), Manville Library, Manville. Call Arthur Siegfried 908-722-7212 (eve). *Website:* http://www.njpolio.org/rvppsg

NATIONAL

Post-Polio Health International *National network. Founded 1958.* Information on late effects of polio for survivors and health professionals. International conferences. Quarterly newsletter (free to donor members who contribute $25), annual directory $8. Guidelines and workshops for support groups. Handbook on late effects ($11.50). Write: Post-Polio Health International, 4207 Lindell Blvd., Suite 110, St. Louis, MO 63108-2930. Call 314-534-0475; Fax: 314-534-5070. *Website:* http://www.post-polio.org *E-mail:* director@post-polio.org

POLYCYSTIC OVARIAN SYNDROME

NATIONAL

Polycystic Ovarian Syndrome Association *International. Founded 1997.* Provides emotional support and information for women with polycystic ovarian syndrome. Provides information on various treatments and diagnosis. Newsletter, phone support, literature, conferences, regional symposiums and advocacy. Online chats and e-mail lists. Assistance in starting local groups. Dues $40. Write: PCOSA, P.O. Box 3403, Englewood, CO 80111. *Website:* http://www.pcosupport.org *E-mail:* info@pcosupport.org

PSORIASIS

NATIONAL

National Psoriasis Foundation *National. Founded 1968.* Support and information for people who have psoriasis and psoriatic arthritis, their families and friends. Education to increase public awareness of these disorders. Fund-raising for research. Bi-monthly magazine, educational booklets and physician directory. Offers online message board and chat rooms. Write: National Psoriasis Foundation, 6600 SW 92nd Ave., Suite 300, Portland, OR 97223. Call 503-244-7404 or

1-800-723-9166 (free packet of information); Fax: 503-245-0626. *Website:* http://www.psoriasis.org *E-mail:* getinfo@psoriasis.org

REFLEX SYMPATHETIC DYSTROPHY

STATEWIDE

Reflex Sympathetic Dystrophy Syndrome Association *Southern NJ Chapter* Aims to meet the practical emotional needs of reflex sympathetic dystrophy syndrome patients and their families. Promotes research into the cause and cure of RSDS. Offers education to the public professionals. Call Jim Everett 856-456-2107 (day).

BURLINGTON

Reflex Sympathetic Dystrophy Chronic Pain Support Group 12-Step. Support for persons with reflex sympathetic dystrophy or chronic pain, their families and friends. Helps members maintain as normal and pain free life as possible. Guest speakers, educational programs, pen pals, rap sessions, literature, phone help and advocacy. Meets 2nd Wed., 7-9pm, Virtua Hospital, 175 Madison Ave., Conference Room, 1st Floor, Mt. Holly. Call Kathy Henson 609-268-1565 (day) or Ursula Weed 856-304-6682 (day). *E-mail:* bepainfree2000@aol.com

Reflex Sympathetic Dystrophy Chronic Pain Support Group 12-Step. Support for persons with reflex sympathetic dystrophy or chronic pain, their families and friends. Helps members maintain as normal and pain free life as possible. Guest speakers, educational programs, pen pals, rap sessions, literature, phone help and advocacy. Meets 4th Tues., 6-8pm, YMCA, 5001 Centerton Rd., Mt. Laurel. Call Ursala Weed 856-304-6682 (day) or Lisa Yabey 609-877-0213 (day). *E-mail:* sula25@msn.com

PASSAIC

Moving Forward with RSD Support Group Mutual support, information and encouragement for persons with reflex sympathetic dystrophy (aka complex regional pain syndrome) and their families. Meets 4th Tues., 7:30pm, St. Joseph Regional Medical Center, 6th Floor, Room 114 CN6, Paterson. Call Gloria 973-743-1985. *E-mail:* movingfrwd@aol.com

SOMERSET

Living with RSDA/CRPS, Inc. Offers education and support for persons afflicted with reflex sympathetic dystrophy (chronic regional pain syndrome). Families and friends are welcome. Meets 1st Tues., 7-9pm, Somerset Medical Center, 110 Rehill Ave., Somerville. Call 908-575-7737 (answering machine). *Website:* http://www.livingwith rsds.com *E-mail:* slweiner@hotmail.com

NATIONAL

Reflex Sympathetic Dystrophy Syndrome Association *National. 100 independent groups. Founded 1984.* Aims to meet the practical and emotional needs of reflex sympathetic dystrophy syndrome (aka complex regional pain syndrome) patients and their families. RSDS is a disabling disease involving nerve, skin, muscle, blood vessels and bones. The only common symptom in all patients is pain. Promotes research, educates public and professionals. Quarterly newsletter. Group development guidelines available. Write: RSDS Association, P.O. Box 502, Milford, CT 06460. Call 1-877-662-7737. *Website:* http://www.rsds.org *E-mail:* info@rsds.org

RESPIRATORY DISEASE / EMPHYSEMA

(see also toll-free helplines)

STATEWIDE

American Lung Association of New Jersey *Professionally-run.* Refers callers to regional resources for information on lung health, asthma, smoking and environment. Referrals to support groups for persons with chronic lung disorders (emphysema, chronic bronchitis, asthma, pulmonary problems, etc.). Write: American Lung Association of New Jersey, 1600 Route 22 East, Union, NJ 07083. Call 908-687-9340 (day); Fax: 908-851-2625. *Website*: http://www.lungusa.org *E-mail*: info@alanewjersey.org

BURLINGTON

Better Breathers Club *Professionally-run.* Support for those with lung disease and their families. Meets 1st Wed., 10am, Deborah Heart and Lung Center, 200 Trenton Rd., Browns Mills. For schedule call Patient Care Services Dept. 609-893-1200 ext. 5618 (day). *Website*: http://deborah.org *E-mail*: gebersl@deborah.org

Breathe Better Mutual support for patients with chronic lung disease to share problems, solutions and experiences. Families welcome. Lecture series, guest speakers and phone help. Meets 3rd Wed., 7:30-9pm, Lourdes Medical Center of Burlington County, 218 Sunset Rd., Willingboro. Call Linda Booth 609-387-4146 (eve) or Doris King 856-764-3019 (day).

ESSEX

Allergy and Asthma Support Group Helps families manage issues regarding food allergies and asthma. Promotes awareness and education. Rap sessions, advocacy, guest speakers and literature. Dues 20/yr. Meetings vary, St. Barnabas Ambulatory Care Center, Livingston. Call Susan DiAnthony 973-514-1654 (eve) or Anna Fusaro 973-228-8919 (eve). *E-mail*: palkidz@aol.com

HUDSON

Second Wind *Professionally-run.* Group provides support and education to those with any type of lung disease. Rap sessions and guest speakers. Meetings vary, 12:30-1:30pm, Meadowlands Hospital, 55 Meadowlands Pkwy., Secaucus. Call 201-392-3531 (day).

MERCER

Allergy and Asthma Support Group Support and education for adults and parents of children with food allergies and asthma. Guest speakers and literature. Dues $20/yr. Meets 1st Wed., 7-9pm, Buckingham Place, 155 Raymond Rd., Princeton. Call Dina 732-821-0567. *E-mail*: bmwlaw123@aol.com

Better Breathers Club Mutual support for people with chronic obstructive pulmonary disease (bronchitis, emphysema, fibrosis, asthma, post-lung cancer, etc.) their family and friends. Rap sessions and guest speakers. Princeton Medical Center, 253 Witherspoon St., Princeton. For meeting times call 908-687-9340. *Website*: http://www.lungusa.com

MONMOUTH

Monmouth Easy Breathers *Professionally-run.* Support group for adults (ages 60 and over) with COPD, emphysema, chronic asthma, asthma or bronchitis. Families welcome. Registration required. Meets 2nd Tues. (except June, July, Aug.), 10:30am-noon, Monmouth Medical Center, Elizabeth Benjamin Care Center, Conference Room, 300 Second Ave., Long Branch. Pre-registration required. Before attending call 732-923-6990 (day).

MORRIS

IPF Support Group Mutual support for patients with idiopathic pulmonary fibrosis and their caregivers. Family members welcome. Rap sessions and phone help. Meets last Wed., 7-9pm, Morristown Memorial Hospital, 100 Madison Ave., Morristown. Before attending call Barbara Murphy 908-276-3394 (eve). *E-mail*: bjmurphy21@comcast.net

Lung Talk *Professionally-run.* Support group for patients with chronic lung disease (COPD). Families welcome. Educational series, rap sessions, literature and guest speakers. Meets 3rd Fri., 2-3pm, Chilton Memorial Hospital, 97 West Parkway, Board Room, Pompton Plains. Call William McCarthy 973-831-5070 (day) or Gail Klaus 973-831-5070 (day).

WARREN

Better Breathers Club *Professionally-run.* Support for those with breathing problems, their families and friends. Education, lecture series, socials and guest speakers. Meets last Wed., 1-2pm, Warren Hospital, 185 Roseberry St., Phillipsburg. Call Judy Reed 908-859-8716 (day).

NATIONAL

Alpha 1 Association *International. 54 affiliated groups. Founded 1988.* Support, advocacy and information for persons with alpha-1 antitrypsin deficiency and their families. Networking of members through newsletter and support groups across the country. Sharing of current information on treatments and research. Newsletter, group development guidelines, educational materials and advocacy information. Write: Alpha-1 Association, 2937 SW 27th Ave., Miami, FL 33133. Call 1-800-521-3025 or 305-648-0088; Fax: 305-648-0089. *Website*: http://www.alpha1.org *E-mail*: info@alpha1.org

American Lung Association *National. Founded 1904.* Refers callers to regional resources for information on lung health, smoking and environment. Local chapters can provide referrals to support groups for persons with chronic lung disorders (emphysema, chronic bronchitis, asthma, pulmonary problems, etc.) if available. These groups use names such as "Easy Breathers" or "Family Asthma Support Group." Write: American Lung Association, 61 Broadway, 6th Floor, New York, NY 10006. Call 1-800-586-4872 or 212-315-8700. *Website*: http://www.lungusa.org

Asthma and Allergy Foundation of America *National. 100+ affiliated groups and 10 chapters. Founded 1953.* Serves persons with asthma and allergic diseases through advocacy, the support of research, patient and public education. Newsletter and support/education groups. Assistance in starting and maintaining groups. Books, videos and other educational resources. Write: Asthma and Allergy Foundation of America, 1233 20th St. NW, Suite 402, Washington, DC 20036. Call 1-800-727-8462 or 202-466-7643 (M-F 10am-3pm EST); Fax: 202-466-8940. *Website*: http://www.aafa.org *E-mail*: info@aafa.org

Coalition for Pulmonary Fibrosis *National. 35 affiliated groups. 11,000 members. Founded 2001.* Information, resources, educational materials and support for patients with pulmonary fibrosis. Write: Coalition for Pulmonary Fibrosis, 1659 Branham Lane, Suite F, #227, San Jose, CA 95118. Call 1-888-222-8541. *Website*: http://www.coalitionforpf.org *E-mail*: info@coalitionforpf.org

SAY (Support for Asthmatic Youth) *National. 30 affiliated groups. Founded 1989.* Provides an atmosphere of support, reassurance and fun for children (ages 9-17) with asthma and allergies. Exchanging of personal experiences and concerns. Education, information and referrals, phone support, conferences, newsletter, advocacy and literature. Write: SAY, Attn: Renee Theodorakis, 1080 Glen Cove Ave., Glen Head, NY 11545. Call 516-625-5735 (day); Fax: 516-625-2976. *E-mail*: ReneeTheo1@aol.com

White Lung Association *National. Founded 1979.* Educational support and advocacy for the general public, provided in part by asbestos victims and their families. Provides public education on health hazards of asbestos and the education of workers on safe work practices. Part of the global effort to ban asbestos. Assistance provided in starting new groups. Dues $25/yr. Write: White Lung Association, P.O. Box 1483, Baltimore, MD 21203. Call 410-243-5864. *Website*: http://www.whitelung.org *E-mail*: jfite@whitelung.org

ONLINE

Bronchiectasis Support and Information *Online.* Provides information and support to fellow sufferers and caregivers. Bronchiectasis is a condition where some bronchi and smaller bronchioles in lungs are permanently dilated. Message board. *Website*: http://health.groups.yahoo.com/group/Bronchiectasis_support/

COPD-Support, Inc. *Online.* Provides a variety of online self-help support programs for chronic obstructive pulmonary disease patients, caregivers and interested medical personnel. Programs include: moderated mailing lists, forums, chats, a weekly newsletter and "COPD-Watch" for those living alone,

"Smoke No More" for help in quitting smoking and "Let's Get Fit" exercise program. *Website*: http://copd-support1.com *E-mail*: management@copd-support1.com

EFFORTS *Online*. Support for persons afflicted with emphysema. Offers information on local support groups. Forum for sharing ideas and help in dealing with emphysema. Advocacy for research. Listserv. Write: EFFORTS, 239 NE Hwy 69, Suite D, Claycomo, MO 64119. Fax: 816-413-0176. *Website*: http://www.emphysema.net/bindex.html

Huff-n-Puff *Online. 1,000+ members*. Provides support for people with any type of interstitial lung disease (including pulmonary fibrosis). Opportunity to meet others with similar conditions, experiences and knowledge. *Website*: http://www.huff-n-puff.net

SCLERODERMA

STATEWIDE

Scleroderma Foundation of the Delaware Valley *(Serves southern/central NJ/Delaware/Penn)* Support and education for persons with scleroderma. Funds research. Seeks to increase public awareness, provides patient education and support programs. Phone support, networking, newsletter, information, and referral. $25 annual membership dues, meetings are free. Several meeting locations. Write: Scleroderma Foundation, 385 Kings Highway North, Cherry Professional Building, Cherry Hill, NJ 08034. Call 856-779-7225 (day) or 1-866-675-5545 (Mon.-Fri., 9am-5pm). *Website:* http://www.scleroderma.org *E-mail:* sfdvl@verizon.net

Scleroderma Foundation of Tri-State Chapter *(Serves northern NJ, NY, CT)* Promotes the welfare of scleroderma patients and their families. Provides education, support groups, phone help, referrals. Fund-raising for research. Newsletter, resource library and other educational materials. Group development guidelines. Annual dues $25. Several meeting locations in the tri-state area. Write: Scleroderma Foundation, 59 Front St., Binghamton, NY 13905. Call Rosemary Markoff 1-800-867-0885; Fax: 607-723-2039. *Website:* http://www.scleroderma.org *E-mail:* sdtristate@aol.com

We can also refer callers to over 100 individuals who are seeking others to help start new support groups throughout NJ. Call us for more information.
1-800-367-6274

CAMDEN

Camden County Scleroderma Support Group Provides support and education to scleroderma patients, their families and friends. Rap sessions, guest speakers and literature. Meetings vary, Haddon Heights. Call Laurie Rabin 856-231-0221. *E-mail:* laurierabin@yahoo.com

CUMBERLAND

Vineland Scleroderma Support Group Provides support and education to scleroderma patients, their families and friends. Rap sessions, guest speakers and literature. Meetings vary, 6-7:30pm, YMCA, Vineland. Call Tina Mullins 856-405-0758. *E-mail:* tinamarie31@comcast.net

GLOUCESTER

Southwest New Jersey Scleroderma Support Group Provides support and education to scleroderma patients, their families and friends. Rap sessions, guest speakers and literature. Meets 1st Tues., 7-9pm, Underwood Memorial Hospital, Dining Room, 1st Floor, Woodbury. Call Mary Nuzzo 856-582-6456. *E-mail:* marynuzz@msn.com

MIDDLESEX

New Brunswick Scleroderma Support Group Provides support and education to scleroderma patients, their families and friends. Guest speakers and literature. Meets 3rd Thurs., 6:30-8pm, Robert Wood Johnson Hospital, Medical Education Building, 108A, New Brunswick. Call 908-489-3092.

MORRIS

Northern New Jersey Scleroderma Support Group Provides support and education to scleroderma patients, their families and friends. Guest speakers, rap sessions and literature. Meets 2nd Tues. (Jan., Mar., May, July, Sept., Nov.), 7-9pm, St. Clare's Hospital, Route 46 West, Dover. Call Kitsa Jobeless 973-328-2627 (eve) or Margaret Paxos 973-584-9607. *E-mail:* munchkit@optonline.com

OCEAN

Scleroderma Ocean County Support Group Provides support and education to scleroderma patients, their families and friends. Rap sessions, guest speakers and literature. Meets 2nd Tues. (Feb., May, Aug., Nov.), 4:30-6pm, The Lighthouse Community Medical Center, Toms River. Call Karyn Arnold 908-489-3092 (day). *E-mail:* support@sclerodermadv.org

NATIONAL

Scleroderma Foundation, Inc. *National. 22 chapters, 170 affiliated groups. Founded 1970.* Dedicated to providing emotional support to people with scleroderma and their families. Provides scleroderma education and public awareness and funds research. Referrals to local support groups and physicians. Advocacy and conferences. Online chatrooms. Dues $25. Write: Scleroderma Foundation, 330 Rosewood Dr., Suite 105, Danvers, MA 01923. Call 1-800-722-4673 or 978-463-5843; Fax: 978-463-5809. *Website:* http://www.scleroderma.org *E-mail:* sfinfo@scleroderma.org

Scleroderma Research Foundation *National. Founded 1987.* Mission is to find a cure for scleroderma by funding and facilitating the most promising research. Provides scleroderma information online and via "Insights" scleroderma newsletter. Write: Scleroderma Research Foundation, 220 Montgomery St., Suite 1411, San Francisco, CA 94104. Call 1-800-441-2873; Fax: 415-834-9177. *Website:* http://www.sclerodermaresearch.org *E-mail:* info@sclerodermaresearch.org

SCOLIOSIS

CUMBERLAND

Scoliosis Association of South Jersey Mutual support for people suffering from scoliosis. Family members are welcome. Literature, phone help, education and guest speakers. Meets 2nd Tues., 7:30-9pm, Rehabilitation Hospital of South Jersey, 1237 West Sherman Ave., Vineland. Call Tiffany Patterson 856-981-2161 (eve). *Website:* http://www.scoliosis-assoc.org *E-mail:* pattersonsky81@aol.com

NATIONAL

National Scoliosis Foundation *International. 5 affiliated groups. Founded 1976.* Dedicated to helping children, parents, adults and health care providers deal with the complexities of spinal deformities such as scoliosis. Whether the issue is early detection and screening programs, treatment methods, pain management or patient care, NSF strives to promote public awareness, provide reliable information, encourage on-going research and educate and support the scoliosis community. Bi-annual newsletter, information packets, pen pals, conferences and phone support. Assistance in starting local groups. Write: National Scoliosis Foundation, 5 Cabot Pl., Stoughton, MA 02072. Call 1-800-673-6922 or 781-341-6333 (Mon.-Thurs., 9am-5pm); Fax: 781-341-8333. *Website:* http://www.scoliosis.org *E-mail:* NSF@scoliosis.org

Scoliosis Association, Inc. *National. 50 chapters. Founded 1974.* Information support network for scoliosis patients and parents of children with scoliosis. Establishes local patient and parent self-help groups. Encourages school screening programs. Supports research. Newsletter. Membership contribution $20. Guidelines for starting chapters. Write: Scoliosis Association Inc., c/o Stanley Sacks, Chair C.E.O., P.O. Box 811705, Boca Raton, FL 33481-1705. Call 1-800-800-0669; Fax: 561-994-2455. *Website:* http://www.scoliosis-assoc.org

SLEEP APNEA

MERCER

A.W.A.K.E. (American Sleep Apnea Association) Network Groups Support and education to individuals and their families suffering from sleep apnea. Rap sessions, guest speakers and phone help. For meeting information call George Evans 609-278-6990 (day) or Robert Perro 609-394-4167 (day). *E-mail:* Rbrooks@chsnj.org

MORRIS

Sleep Apnea Support Group of Northwest New Jersey Support group for persons afflicted by sleep apnea. Family members welcome. Exchanges information and experiences. Guest speakers, education and mutual sharing. Meets at St. Clare's Hospital, Dover. Before attending call Sleep Center 973-989-3477 (option # 2).

SOMERSET

Somerset County Snoozers A.W.A.K.E. Support for person afflicted with sleep apnea. Family and friends welcome. Lecture series, education, mutual sharing, guest speakers, rap sessions and advocacy. Meetings vary, 7-10pm, Somerset Medical Center, 110 Rehill Ave., Somerville. Call 908-685-2450 or Medical Center 1-800-443-4605.

NATIONAL

A.W.A.K.E. (American Sleep Apnea Association) Network Groups *National. 200+ affiliated groups. Founded 1990.* Provides education, support and social interaction for persons with sleep apnea, their families and friends. Membership dues $25/year. Assistance and guidelines for starting groups ($30). Write: A.W.A.K.E. Network Groups, 1424 K St., NW, Suite 302, Washington, DC 20005. Call 202-293-3650; Fax: 202-293-3656. *Website:* http://www.sleepapnea.org *E-mail:* asaa@sleepapnea.org

SPINA BIFIDA

(see also disabilities general, parents of disabled, toll-free helplines)

STATEWIDE

Spina Bifida Association Support for persons with spina bifida and their families. Peer-counseling, advocacy, newsletter, conferences, family support coordination and continence management assistance. Various meeting times and places. Also has several telephone support groups. Write: Spina Bifida Association, 84 Park Ave., Flemington, NJ 08822. Call 908-782-7475 (9am-4pm); Fax: 908-782-6102. *Website*: http://www.sbatsr.org *E-mail*: info@sbatsr.org

NATIONAL

Spina Bifida Association of America *National. 62 chapters. Founded 1972.* Encourages educational and vocational development of patients. Promotes public awareness, advocacy and research. Newsletter, chapter development guidelines, national resource center, scholarships and film/videotapes. Write: Spina Bifida Association of America, 4590 MacArthur Blvd. NW, Suite 250, Washington, DC 20007. Call 1-800-621-3141 or 202-944-3285; Fax: 202-944-3295. *Website*: http://www.sbaa.org *E-mail*: sbaa@sbaa.org

STROKE

(see also caregivers, physical disabilities)

ATLANTIC

Bacharach Stroke Club *Professionally-run.* Support and education for stroke survivors, their families and friends. Rap sessions, social activities, guest speakers, literature and phone help. Meets last Wed., 3pm, Bacharach Institute for Rehabilitation, 61 West Jimmy Leads Rd., Pomona. Call 609-748-5420 (day).

BERGEN

New Jersey Stroke Activity Center Support and recovery of long-term stroke survivors, sound and movement therapy, networking and socialization. Families welcome. Rap sessions, guest speakers, phone help and newsletter. Call Mary Jo Schreiber 973-450-4114. *Website*: http://www.njsac.org *E-mail*: maryjo@njsac.org

> **Paramus** Meets 2nd and 4th Tues., 11:30am, Care One at the Cupola, 100 West Ridgewood Ave.
>
> **Saddle Brook** Meets 1st and 3rd Tues., Kessler Institution for Rehabilitation, 300 Market St.

Post Stroke and Disabled Adult Program *Professionally-run.* (BERGEN COUNTY RESIDENTS ONLY) Mutual support for post-stroke patients and disabled adults. Program functions include group discussions, various activities that promote physical fitness, arts and crafts, games, exercises and occasional recreational events. Meets various times and days, E. Rutherford, Englewood, Oakland, Paramus, River Vale and Maywood. Call Leo DePinto 201-336-6502 (day); TTY/TDD: 201-336-6505.

Post Stroke Support Group *Professionally-run.* Mutual support for post-stroke individuals. Meets Fri., 9am-12:30pm, 228 Grand Ave., Englewood. Before attending call Frieda Wells 201-569-4080 (day). *E-mail*: lyd228@aol.com

BURLINGTON

Stroke Club *Professionally-run.* Promotes the well-being of stroke patients and families through educational and social programs and sharing of concerns. Meets 4th Tues. (except Nov./Dec.), 7-9pm, Virtua Health and Rehabilitation Center, 62 Richmond Ave., Mt. Holly. Before attending call 1-888-847-8823 (day).

Stroke Support Group Mutual support for stroke patients and their families. Meets 2nd Fri., 10-11:30am, Lourdes Health System, 218 A Sunset Rd., Willingboro. Call 609-835-5813 (day).

MERCER

St. Lawrence Stroke Support Group *Professionally-run.* Promotes the well-being of stroke patients and families through educational and social programs and sharing of concerns. Discussions and guest speakers. Meets 1st Wed., 6:30-8pm, St. Lawrence Rehab Center, 2381 Lawrenceville Rd., Cafeteria,

Lawrenceville. Call Annette Murphy, MSW, LSW 609-896-9500 ext. 2591 (day).

MIDDLESEX

COPSA Spouse Support Group *Professionally-run.* Mutual support and understanding for spouses of persons with any type of memory loss (Alzheimer's, Parkinson's, vascular disease, stroke, head injury, dementia, etc.). Meets 1st and 3rd Mon., 9:30-11am, UBHC, 671 Hoes Lane, Piscataway. Call Mary Catherine Lundquist 732-235-2858 (day). *Website*: http://vbhcweb/ (then go to Aging-COPSA) E-mail: lindqumc@umdnj.edu

JFK Stroke Wives Group Support for women who are married to men who have had strokes. Mutual sharing, rap sessions and social group. Meets 3rd Tues., 7-8:30pm, JFK Hospital, James St., Edison. Call Rosemarie 732-752-2644. *E-mail*: crossingladynj@aol.com

Middlesex County Stroke Support Group *Professionally-run.* Promotes the well-being of stroke patients and families through educational programs and sharing of concerns. Dues $1 mtg. Meets 1st Wed., 7:15pm, JFK Rehab Institute, 65 James St., Edison. Call Frank Roche 732-969-2097 (day).

Stroke Club Support Group Support and education for stroke patients, their families and friends. Guest speakers. Meets last Fri., 12:30-2pm (except July, Aug., Nov.), Robert Wood Johnson University Hospital, New Brunswick. Call 732-418-8110 (day).

MONMOUTH

New Jersey Stroke Activity Center Support and recovery of long-term stroke survivors, sound and movement therapy, networking and socialization. Families welcome. Rap sessions, guest speakers, phone help, newsletter and speakers' bureau. Meets 1st and 3rd Wed., 2pm, Health South Rehabilitation Hospital, 2 Centre Plaza, Tinton Falls. Call Mary Jo Schreiber 973-450-4114. *Website*: http://www.njsac.org *E-mail*: maryjo@njsac.org

Stroke Support Group Mutual support for stroke patients and their families. Education, guest speakers, lecture series and literature. Meets 2nd Wed. (except July/Aug.), 2-4pm, Rehabilitation Hospital of Tinton Falls, 2 Centre Plaza, Tinton Falls. Call Lara Latzsch 732-460-5377 (day).

MORRIS

North Jersey Stroke Discussion Group Promotes the well-being of stroke patients and families through educational programs and sharing of concerns. Meets 2nd and 4th Tues. (except July/Aug.), 1pm, Grace Episcopal Church, Library, Route 24, Madison. Call George 973-543-6386.

Stroke Discussion Group *Professionally-run.* Mutual support and education for stroke survivors and their families. Exchange of coping skills. Meets 1st and 3rd Tues., 1-2:30pm, Care One, 151 Madison Ave., Morristown. Pre-registration required. Before attending call 973-714-7652.

OCEAN

Stroke of Luck *Professionally-run.* Mutual support for stroke survivors and caregivers. Family and friends welcome. Lecture series, guest speakers and literature. Meets last Wed., Health South Rehabilitation Hospital, 14 Hospital Dr., Toms River. Call Marianne Harms 732-286-5688 (day).

Stroke Support Group *Professionally-run.* Mutual support and education for stroke patients, their families and caregivers. Guest speakers. Meets 2nd Mon., 2-4pm, West Lake Community Club House, 1 Pine Lake Circle, Jackson. Call 732-780-3013 (day).

Stroke Support Group *Professionally-run.* Purpose of group is to educate and support individuals and families associated with stroke related issues. Rap sessions and guest speakers. Under 18 welcome. Meets 4th Tues. (except Dec./Jan./Feb.), 2pm, Shore Rehab Institute, 425 Jack Martin Blvd., Brick. Call Lisa Wazeka or Tami Pindulic 732-836-4528 or 4527.

SOMERSET

Stroke Club of Somerset County *Professionally-run.* Mutual support for stroke patients and their families. Meets 1st Tues., 1:30-3:30pm, Somerset Medical Center, 110 Rehill Ave., Somerville. Call 908-685-2814 (day) for more information.

SUSSEX

Stroke Support Group *Professionally-run.* Offers support for persons recovering from a stroke. Caretakers welcomed. Meets 4th Tues., 7:30pm, Newton Memorial Hospital, Rehabilitation Lounge, 175 High St., Newton. Call Carolyn Matzal 973-579-8816.

UNION

Stroke Club, The *Professionally-run.* Support and socialization for stroke survivors and their families. Rap sessions, guest speakers and educational series. $1 donation (optional). Meets 2nd Thurs., 12:30-2pm, Rahway Hospital, 865 Stone St., Rahway. Pre-registration required, before attending call Rehabilitation Dept. 732-499-6012 (day).

NATIONAL

American Stroke Association, Division of American Heart Association *National. 1,800 groups. Founded 1979.* Maintains a listing of support groups for stroke survivors, their families, friends and interested professionals. Publishes bimonthly magazine. Provides information and referrals to groups and general resources. Write: Stroke Connection, 7272 Greenville Ave., Dallas, TX 75231-4596. Call 1-888-478-7653 (day). *Website*: http://www.StrokeAssociation.org *E-mail*: strokeconnection@heart.org

National Stroke Association *National. 9 chapters. Founded 1984.* Dedicated to reducing the incidence and impact of stroke through prevention, medical treatment, rehabilitation, family support and research. Professional publications, Stroke Smart magazine, information and referrals to local groups. Guidance for starting stroke clubs and groups. Write: National Stroke Association, 9707 E. Easter Lane, Suite B, Englewood, CO 80112-3747. Call 303-649-9299 or 1-800-787-6537; Fax: 303-649-1328. *Website*: http://www.stroke.org *E-mail*: info@stroke.org

Stroke Clubs International *International. 900+ clubs. Founded 1968.* Organization of persons who have experienced strokes, their families and friends for the purpose of mutual support, education, social and recreational activities. Provides information and assistance to Stroke Clubs (which are usually sponsored by local organizations). Newsletter, videotapes and group development guidelines. Write: Stroke Clubs International, 805 12th St., Galveston, TX 77550. Call Ellis Williamson 409-762-1022. *E-mail*: strokeclubs@earthlink.net

ONLINE

Brain Injury Information NETwork, The (TBINET) *Online.* Various support group email lists for brain injury, stroke and other "medical" related issues. Has lists for caregivers, family and friends. *Website*: http://www.tbinet.org

THYROID CONDITIONS

MERCER

Thyroid Cancer Survivors Support Group Support group for thyroid cancer survivors. Families welcome. Literature, guest speaker and phone help. Meets 3rd Sat., 10-11:30am, Capitol Health System at Hamilton, 1445 Whitehorse-Mercerville Rd., Mercerville. Call Michael Dubrow 1-877-588-7904 (eve.). *E-mail:* centraljersey@thyca.org

OCEAN

Thyroid Support Group Support for anyone affected by a thyroid problem. Mutual support, mutual sharing, guest speakers and video viewing. Meets 2nd Mon., 1-3pm, Lighthouse, 63 Lacey Rd., Whiting. Call Lighthouse 732-849-4610 or Stefanie 732-350-2904.

NATIONAL

ThyCa: Thyroid Cancer Survivors' Association, Inc. *National.* Support, education and communication for people with all types of thyroid cancer, as well as caregivers. Outreach to the public for thyroid cancer awareness and early detection. Nine online support groups, more than 60 local support groups, free online newsletter, free downloadable low-iodine cookbook, free regional workshops, annual international conference, free thyroid cancer awareness brochures, Thyroid Cancer Awareness Month, funding for research and educational website. Write: ThyCa: Thyroid Cancer Survivors' Association, Inc., P.O. Box 1545, New York, NY 10159-1545. Call 1-877-588-7904; Fax: 630-604-6078. *Website:* http://www.thyca.org *E-mail:* thyca@thyca.org

TRANSPLANT, ORGAN

ATLANTIC

Cape Atlantic Transplant Support Group Mutual support and education for organ transplant recipients and candidates. Families welcome. Guest speakers. Meets 4th Wed., 4:30-6pm, Shore Memorial Hospital, Pitman Room, 1 East New York Ave., Somers Point. Call Kathleen 609-653-3667 (day).

CAMDEN

Second Chance Heart Transplant Support Group Mutual support for pre- and post-heart transplant patients, their families, friends and caregivers. Rap sessions and guest speakers. Meets 2nd Tues., 11am, Hahnemann University Hospital, Broad & Vine, Philadelphia, PA. Call Renard Petronzio 856-346-9030.

ESSEX

SPK Recipient/Family Support Group Emotional support and education to kidney pancreas recipients, their families and friends. Social group, advocacy, literature, rap sessions and guest speakers. Meets various Tuesdays, 7-9pm, (except July/Aug.), St. Barnabas Medical Center, 3rd Floor, East Wing, Old Short Hills Rd., Livingston. Before attending call Marcia Rower 973-322-8461 (day).

Transplant Patient Family Support Group Emotional support education for all kidney transplant recipients, their families and friends. Social group, advocacy, rap sessions, guest speakers, literature. Usually meets once a month, St. Barnabas Medical Center, 3rd Floor, Board Room, East Wing, Old Short Hills Rd., Livingston. For information call Debbie Hopkins 973-322-5890 (day).

MERCER

Circle of Hope Mutual support for recipients of organ transplants. Guest speakers, advocacy, literature and phone help. Meets 3rd Wed., (except July/Aug.), 7:00-9pm, Robert Wood Johnson University Hospital at Hamilton, One Hamilton Health Place, Hamilton. Call Chaplain Jeff Pierfy 609-631-6980 (day). *E-mail:* jpierfy@rwjuhh.edu

MIDDLESEX

Kidney Pancreas Support Group Mutual support for pre- and post-kidney and pancreas transplant patients. Family and relatives welcome. Guest speakers, literature, educational series and social group. Meets 3rd Mon., 7pm, Robert Wood Johnson University Hospital, 1 Robert Wood Johnson Place, Board Room, New Brunswick. Call 732-235-8987 (day).

Second Chance Mutual support for heart transplant patients and their families. Meets 1st Thurs., 2pm, Robert Wood Johnson University Hospital, 1 Robert Wood Johnson Place, BMSCH Conference Room, New Brunswick. Call 732-418-8110.

MONMOUTH

Central Jersey Transplant Lifeline Support for persons who have had, or are waiting for, an organ transplant. Open to family, friends or anyone interested in organ donations. Rap sessions, mutual sharing and phone help. Meets 2nd Tues., 7-9pm, Riverview Medical Center, 1st floor, Little Silver. Call Virginia O'Keefe 732-450-1271.

MORRIS

Lung Transplant Support Group Mutual support for persons who have received a lung transplant or are considering it. Sharing of information and concerns. Families welcome. Rap sessions. Meetings vary, 2:30-4pm, Dover General Campus of St. Clares Hospital, 400 West Blackwell St., Dover. Before attending call Jean Wiarda, RN 973-989-3128 (day).

Organ Transplant Recipient Support Group Provides mutual support and education to persons who have undergone an organ transplant or are considering having one. Family and friends welcome. Meets 1st Sat., 10-11:30am, Denville Library, Meeting Room, 121 Diamond Spring Rd., Denville. Call Barbara 973-335-7112 (day).

NATIONAL

Second Wind Lung Transplant Association, Inc. *International network. Founded 1995.* Developed by transplant patients. Opportunity for persons who have undergone, or who will undergo, lung transplants to share their stories on a web page. Newsletter available. Write: Second Wind Lung Transplant Association, c/o Kathryn Flynn, Vice President, 2509 Old NC 10, Hillsborough, NC 27278. Call 1-888-855-9463 or 919-732-0851. *Website:* http://www.2ndwind.org *E-mail:* sarika@mindspring.com

TRIO (Transplant Recipients International Organization) *International. 43 chapters. Founded 1983.* Works to improve the quality of life of transplant candidates, recipients, donors and their families. TRIO serves its members in the areas of donor awareness, support, education and advocacy. Annual conference, bi-monthly newsletter, monthly membership update, support network and chapter development assistance. Offers information online on finding local chapters. Write: TRIO, 2100 M St., NW, Suite 170-353, Washington, DC 20037. Call 1-800-874-6386. *Website:* http://www.trioweb.org *E-mail:* info@trioweb.org

VACCINE

HUNTERDON

NJ Alliance for Informed Choice in Vaccinations Support group of parents concerned about the safety of vaccines and the right to informed consent. Literature, advocacy and phone help. Professionals welcome to attend. Meetings vary. Call Renee Foster 1-800-613-9925 (answering machine). *E-mail:* njaicv@aol.com

OCEAN

HANDIN (Health Natural Decisions for Immunity Network) Provides support, research aid information on the freedom of vaccine choice. Mutual sharing, guest speakers and literature. Dues $3/family. Telephone support network. For information call Cathy Millet 732-892-4852 (eve). *E-Mail:* handin@comcast.net

NATIONAL

National Vaccine Information Center *National. 20 affiliated groups. Founded 1982.* Support, information and advocacy group for parents whose children were adversely affected by vaccines. Advocates for safety reforms in the mass vaccination system and safer vaccines. Promotes education for parents and professionals. Various literature. Dues $25/yr. Write: National Vaccine Information Center, 204 Mill St., Suit B-1, Vienna, VA 22180. Call 703-938-DPT3; Fax: 703-938-5768. *Website:* http://www.nvic.org *E-mail:* Kathi@nvic.org

WOMEN'S HEALTH

(see also breast cancer, specific illness, toll-free helplines)

BURLINGTON

Midpoint *Professionally-run.* Support and discussion for women to share their feelings, fears and concerns in coping with menopause and mid-life issues. Phone help and speakers. Meets 4th Wed., 7:30-9:30pm (except July/Aug.), Lourdes Medical Center of Burlington County, Wellness Center, 218 A Sunset Rd., Willingboro. Call Hospital 609-835-5813 or Lorraine 856-663-7862 (eve).

NATIONAL

Black Women's Health Imperative *International. 15 chapters. Founded 1981.* Grassroots organization aimed at improving the health of Black women by providing wellness education, services, self-help group development, leadership development, health information and advocacy. Assists in the development of new local affiliate groups. Self-help brochure, quarterly newsletter and annual news magazine. Membership dues vary. Write: Black Women's Health Imperative, 1420 K St., NW, Suite 1000, 10th Fl., Washington, DC 20005. Call 202-548-4000; Fax: 202-543-9743. *Website*: http://www.blackwomenshealth.org *E-mail*: nbwhp@nbwhp.org

DES Cancer Network *National. Founded 1983.* Mutual support and education for DES-exposed women, with a special focus on DES cancer issues. Provides research advocacy and medical/legal resources. Newsletter ($25). Annual conferences. Write: DES Cancer Network, 2925 Garber St., Berkeley, CA 94705. *Website*: http://www.descancer.org *E-mail*: desnetwrk@aol.com

International Premature Ovarian Foundation *National network. 8 affiliated groups. Founded 1995.* Mutual support for women who have prematurely entered menopause. Phone support, literature, information and referrals. Assistance in starting groups. Write: IPOFA, P.O. Box 23643, Alexandria, VA 22304. Call 703-913-4787. *Website*: http://www.pofsupport.org *E-mail*: info@pofsupport.org

ONLINE

iVillage Health Message Boards *Online.* Provides various message boards concerning all aspects of health, including menopause, breast cancer, addictions, allergies, arthritis, heart, immune disorders, vision, disabilities, diabetes, caregivers, brain disorders, infertility, respiratory, mental health, pain, parenting, thyroid and medications. Mailing lists, message boards, chats and newsletters. *Website*: http://www.ivillage.com/boards

Mullerian Anomalies of the Uterus *Online.* Support and information for those with mullerian anomalies of the uterus such as bicornuate, septate, unicornauate, hypoplastic and didelphys uteria. Weekly chat, email list and message board. *Website*: http://health.groups.yahoo.com/group/MullerianAnomalies/

Postpartum Hemorrhage Survivors *Online.* E-mail list for women who are supporting each other after a postpartum hemorrhage and hysterectomy. *Website*: http://health.groups.yahoo.com/group/pph-survivors/

Power Surge *Online.* Provides support and information for women going through menopause. Online interactive chats, message boards, information, newsletters and weekly gab sessions. Some pages require flash. *Website*: http://power-surge.com

MENTAL HEALTH

ANXIETY ATTACKS / PHOBIAS / AGORAPHOBIA

(see also mental health general, mental health consumers, toll-free helplines)

STATEWIDE

GROW A mutual self-help group to prevent and recover from depression, anxiety and other mental health problems. Caring and sharing community to attain emotional maturity, personal responsibility and recovery. Meets in various counties in NJ. Write: GROW Center, 4A Iowa Dr., Whiting, NJ 08759. Call 732-350-4800.

BERGEN

Recovery, Inc. Self-help method of will training. Offers techniques for controlling temperamental behavior and changing attitudes toward nervous symptoms, anxiety, depression and fears. Call 201-612-8153. *Website:* http://www.recovery-inc.org

> **Hasbrouck Heights** Meets Wed., 8pm, First Reformed Church, Washington Place and Burton Ave.
>
> **Ridgewood** Meets Fri., 1:30pm, Christ Church, Cottage Place and Franklin Ave.

BURLINGTON

Recovery, Inc. Self-help method of will training. Offers techniques for controlling temperamental behavior and changing attitudes toward nervous symptoms, anxiety, depression and fears. Call 856-848-8715. *Website:* http://www.recovery-inc.org

> **Marlton** Meets Mon., 7pm and Thurs., 7pm, Prince of Peace Lutheran Church, 61 Route 70 East.
>
> **Westampton** Meets Tues., 7pm, Hampton Hospital, Cafeteria, Rancocas Rd. Call John 856-983-7291.

CAMDEN

Depression / Anxiety Support Group For anyone suffering from anxiety and/or depression to support one another in an effort to remain healthy and to share common problems and concerns (under 18 welcome). Rap sessions, phone help and literature. Meets 3rd Mon., 7:15-9pm, Marie Fleche Library, White Horse Pike, Berlin. Call Nancy 856-768-1258 (eve) or Rhonda 856-768-2030 (day/eve).

New Beginnings Support Group - A Chapter of DBSA Mutual support and education for persons with mood disorders and their families. Also open to persons with anxiety, dual diagnosis and schizo-affective disorder. Opportunity to discuss successes in dealing with various symptoms. Meets Mon., 7-9pm and Wed., 11am-1pm, Holy Trinity Lutheran Church, 214 N. Warwick Rd., Magnolia. Call Maribel 856-232-3181. *Website:* http://www.njnb.org *E-mail:* newbeginningsnj@gmail.com

Recovery, Inc. Self-help method of will training. Offers techniques for controlling temperamental behavior and changing attitudes toward nervous symptoms, anxiety, depression and fears. Call 856-848-8715. *Website:* http://www.recovery-inc.org

> **Magnolia** Meets Wed., 9:45am, Holy Trinity Lutheran Church, 501 N. Warwick Rd.
>
> **Westmont** Meets Sat., 11:30am, Starting Point, 215 Highland Ave.

CUMBERLAND

GROW A mutual self-help group to prevent and recover from depression, anxiety and other mental health problems. Caring and sharing community to attain emotional maturity, personal responsibility and recovery.

> **Vineland** Meets Thurs., 7pm, Church of Christian/Missionary Alliance, Main Rd. and Harding Ave., Board Room. Before attending call Rip 856-293-9061.
>
> **Vineland** Meets 3rd Thurs., 3:30pm, New Horizons Self-Help Center, 63 S. Myrtle St. Before attending call Chris 856-794-2986.

Overcomer's Outreach *(Shiloh Faith Meeting)* Christian 12-Step. Fellowship to overcome any type of addiction or compulsive behavior, anxiety, depression or loneliness using God's word as a basis of recovery. Discussion, Bible study, prayer, phone help. Meets Thurs., 7-8pm, Shiloh Seventh Day Baptist Church, East Ave., Shiloh. Call Rev. Chrowiger 856-455-0488 (day) or Frank B. Mulford 856-451-8698 (day). *E-mail:* ahfarm@hotmail.com

ESSEX

GROW A mutual self-help group to prevent and recover from depression, anxiety and other mental health problems. Caring and sharing community to attain emotional maturity, personal responsibility and recovery. Meets Mon., 4:30pm, 570 Belleville Ave., Belleville. Before attending call Caroline 732-575-5765.

Recovery, Inc. Self-help method of will training. Offers techniques for controlling temperamental behavior and changing attitudes toward nervous symptoms, anxiety, depression and fears. Meets Tues., 8pm, Prospect Presbyterian Church, 646 Prospect St., Maplewood. Call 201-612-8153. *Website:* http://www.recovery-inc.org

GLOUCESTER

Recovery, Inc. Self-help method of will training. Offers techniques for controlling temperamental behavior and changing attitudes toward nervous symptoms, anxiety, depression and fears. Families welcome. Meets Fri., 10-11am, James Johnson Library, 670 Ward Dr., Deptford. Call 856-848-8715. *Website:* http://www.recovery-inc.org

MERCER

GROW A mutual self-help group to prevent and recover from depression, anxiety and other mental health problems. Caring and sharing community to attain emotional maturity, personal responsibility and recovery. Meets Thurs., 6pm, Reach Out/Speak Out, 2100 E. State St., Hamilton. Before attending call Caroline 732-575-5765.

New Perspectives Mutual support for persons with depression, bipolar disorder, anxiety or panic attacks. Meets every other Mon., 7:30pm, Unitarian Universalist Church, Washington Crossing. Call David Hughes 609-818-0177 (eve). *E-mail:* David.Hughes419@att.net

P.U.S.H. (Phobics Using Self-Help) Mutual support and encouragement for persons suffering from agoraphobia or panic attacks. Donation $1/week. Meets Mon., 7pm, St. Mark's United Methodist Church, Paxtson Ave., Hamilton Square. For information call 609-291-0095 (answering machine).

MIDDLESEX

Overcomer's Outreach Christian 12-Step. Fellowship to overcome any type of addiction or compulsive behavior, anxiety, depression or loneliness using God's word as a basis of recovery. Discussion, Bible study, prayer, phone help. Meets Thurs., 7-8:30pm, Metuchen Assembly of God, Rose and Whitman St., Metuchen. Call Janet 732-388-2856 (eve) or Pat 732-321-6896.

MONMOUTH

GROW A mutual self-help group to prevent and recover from depression, anxiety and other mental health problems. Caring and sharing community to attain emotional maturity, personal responsibility and recovery. Before attending call Nancy 732-350-4800.

Freehold Meets Wed., 5:30pm, Freehold Self-Help Center, 17 Bannard St.

Freehold Meets Wed., 7pm, 11 Spring St.

Ocean Grove Meets Thurs., 6:45pm, St. Paul's Methodist Church, 80 Enbury St., Stokes Room. Before attending call Caroline 732-575-5765.

MORRIS

Anxiety Support Group Mutual support and encouragement to people suffering from anxiety and phobias. Meets 1st and 3rd Mon., 7-8:30pm, United Methodist Church, 903 South Beverwyck Rd., Parsippany. Call Flora 973-257-7023 (eve).

OCEAN

GROW A mutual self-help group to prevent and recover from depression, anxiety and other mental health problems. Caring and sharing community to attain emotional maturity, personal responsibility and recovery.

Brick Meets Tues., 6:30pm, Brick Presbyterian Church, 111 Drum Point Rd. Before attending call Lisa 732-575-5766.

Manchester Meets Thurs., 7:30pm, Redeemer Lutheran Church, 2309 Route 70. Before attending call Nancy 732-350-4800.

Toms River Meets Tues., 5:30pm, Brighter Days Self-Help Center, Route 37 West. Before attending call Nancy 732-350-4800.

Toms River Meets Thurs., 4pm, Presbyterian Church of Toms River, River Room, Hooper Ave. and Chestnut St. Before attending call Lisa 732-575-5766.

P.H.O.B.I.A. (People Helping Others Become Independent Again) Support group for people with panic attacks, anxiety, phobias, depression and agoraphobia. Families welcome. Guest speakers, literature and phone help. Meets Wed., 7-9pm, St. Stephen's Church, Route 9, Waretown. Call Cathy 609-971-9110. *Website:* http://www.members.tripod.com/~phobiagroup/index.html *E-mail:* phobia@verizon.net

Recovery, Inc. Self-help method of will training. Offers techniques for controlling temperamental behavior and changing attitudes toward nervous symptoms, anxiety, depression and fears. Meets Mon., 7:30pm, Presbyterian Church of Toms River, Hooper Ave. and Chestnut St., Toms River. Call 201-612-8153. *Website:* http://www.recovery-inc.org

SOMERSET

P.A.C.T. (Phobics with Anxiety Coping Together) Self-help group for persons with panic attacks and/or agoraphobia. Meets Mon., 7-8:30pm, Somerset Medical Center, 110 Rehill Ave., Somerville. Call Diane 908-393-2719 (2-6pm), Violet 908-369-3892 or Marti 908-218-8919.

UNION

GROW A mutual self-help group to prevent and recover from depression, anxiety and other mental health problems. Caring and sharing community to attain emotional maturity, personal responsibility and recovery. Before attending call Caroline 732-575-5765.

Elizabeth Meets Wed., 4pm, New Beginnings Self-Help Center, 60 Prince St., Lower Level.

Plainfield Meets Wed., 3:30pm, Self-Help Center, 333 Park Ave.

Overcomer's Outreach Christian 12-Step. Fellowship to overcome any type of addiction or compulsive behavior, anxiety, depression or loneliness using God's word as a basis of recovery. Discussion, Bible study, prayer, phone help. Call Carmen 908-245-2788.

Cranford Meets Mon., 7pm, Harvest Training Center at Calvary Tabernacle, 69 Myrtle St.

Elizabeth Meets Tues., 7:30pm, Mount Teman AME Church, 160 Madison Ave.

Elizabeth Meets Thurs., 7:30pm, Union Baptist Church, 1088 E. Grand St.

Need help finding a specific group?
Give us a call – we're here to help!
Call 1-800-367-6274

Recovery, Inc. Self-help method of will training. Offers techniques for controlling temperamental behavior and changing attitudes toward nervous symptoms, anxiety, depression and fears. Call 201-612-8153. *Website:* http://www.recovery-inc.org

Summit Meets Wed., 7:45pm, Central Presbyterian Center, Morris Ave. and Maple St. (parking lot entrance).

Westfield Meets Fri., 8pm, Union County Community Services Building, 300 North Ave. East, 2nd Floor, Conference Room (rear parking lot entrance).

NATIONAL

ABIL (Agoraphobics Building Independent Lives), Inc. *National. 15+ groups/contacts. Founded 1986.* Mutual support, encouragement, hope, goal setting and education for persons with agoraphobia, anxiety or panic-related disorders, their families and friends. Provides information and referrals, phone support, newsletter, assistance in starting new groups. Also offers online message board. Write: ABIL, Inc., 2501 Fox Harbor Ct., Richmond, VA, 23235. Call 804-353-3964; Fax: 804-353-3964. *Website:* http://www.anxietysupport.org *E-mail:* abil1996@yahoo.com

Agoraphobics In Motion *National. 7 groups. Founded 1983.* Self-help group that uses specific behavioral and cognitive techniques to help people recover from anxiety disorders. Relaxation techniques, small group discussions and field trips. Group development guidelines ($2.50). Write: AIM, 1719 Crooks, Royal Oak, MI 48067-1306. Call 248-547-0400. *Website:* http://www.aim-hg.org *E-mail:* anny@ameritech.net

Anxiety Disorders Association of America *National network. 197 groups. Founded 1980.* Promotes the diagnosis and treatment of all anxiety and related disorders including obsessive compulsive disorder, post-traumatic stress disorder, panic disorder, specific phobia, social anxiety disorder and generalized anxiety disorder. Listing of state-by-state local support groups, brochures, information about anxiety disorders, local listing of healthcare professionals providing treatment for anxiety disorders and a national listing of clinical trials provided free. Write: Anxiety Disorders Association of America, 8730 Georgia Ave., Suite 600, Silver Spring, MD 20910. Call 240-485-1001; Fax: 240-485-1035. *Website:* http://www.adaa.org

GROW in America *International. 143 groups. Founded in 1957.* 12-step group that offers mutual help, friendship, community, education and leadership. Focuses on recovery and personal growth. Open to all including those with mental health issues, depression, anxiety, grief, fears, etc. Write: GROW in America, P.O. Box 3667, Champaign, IL 61826. Call 1-888-741-4760. *E-mail:* growil@sbcglobal.net

International Paruresis Association, Inc. *International network. 35 affiliated groups. Founded 1996.* Provides emotional support and information for persons with paruresis (shy or bashful bladder). Supports research to develop effective treatments. Information, referrals, literature, phone support, workshops, conferences and advocacy. Assistance in starting similar groups. Write: International Paruresis Association, P.O. Box 65111, Baltimore, MD 21209. Call 1-800-247-3864. *Website:* http://www.paruresis.org *E-mail:* ssoifer@ssw.umaryland.edu

Recovery, Inc. *International. 640+ groups. Founded 1937.* Mental health self-help organization that offers weekly group meetings for people suffering from various emotional and mental conditions. Principles parallel those found in cognitive-behavioral therapy. Teaches people how to change their thoughts, reactions and behaviors that cause their physical and emotional symptoms. Write: Recovery, Inc., 802 N. Dearborn St., Chicago, IL 60610. Call 312-337-5661; Fax: 312-337-5756. *Website:* http://www.recovery-inc.org

Selective Mutism Foundation Inc *National. Founded 1992.* Pioneering group that offers mutual support for professionals and parents of children with selective mutism or social phobia (a psychiatric anxiety disorder in which children are unable to speak in social situations). Includes social anxiety and shyness. Also open to adults who had or have outgrown, the disorder. Provides information and online support. Website contains DSM revisions, research studies, printable brochures, literature and publications. Write: Carolyn Miller, P.O. Box 13133, Sissonville, WV 25360 or Sue Newman Mercado, P.O. Box 936165, Margate, FL, 33093. *Website:* http://www.selectivemutismfoundation.org *E-mail:* sue@selectivemutismfoundation.org or carolyn@selectivemutismfoundation.org

"To understand any living thing,
you must creep within and feel the beating of its heart."
-- W. Macneile Dixon

Social Phobics Anonymous *International. 6 groups.* 12-Step. Face-to-face and telephone group that provides support for people who suffer from social phobia, social anxiety disorder, shyness problems, avoidant personality disorder or paruresis. Assists others in starting local groups. Support group meets by telephone Wed., 9pm (EST) and Sat., 5pm (EST). To obtain access code for conference call you must first email or call 303-404-3747 (leave a message with a good time to get back to you). *Website:* http://www.geocities.com/seanphilib/spaleftframe.html *E-mail:* healsocialanxiety@hotmail.com

ONLINE

Alt.Support.Shyness.FAQ *Online. Founded 1994.* Support for shyness. Offers information on understanding shyness, tackling shyness, job hunting, overcoming shyness and developing assertiveness. Includes shyness/dating, children who are shy and general self-help. Message board and newsgroup. *Website:* http://members.aol.com/cybernettr/shyness.html

Panic Center, The *Online.* Offers online scheduled support group meetings, forums and email list. Addresses various types of anxiety, panic attacks and phobias. *Website:* http://www.paniccenter.net

Panic Survivor *Online.* Support group for persons who suffer from anxiety, panic attacks, social anxiety, generalized anxiety, post traumatic stress disorder, obsessive compulsive disorder, hypochondria or any other form of anxiety. Focus is on recovery and day-to-day survival with a "can do" attitude. *Website:* http://panicsurvivor.com/

Selective Mutism Group, The *Online.* Devoted to educating and promoting awareness on selective mutism and other related childhood anxiety disorders. Online support group for parents, teachers and professionals dealing with selective mutism. *Website:* http://selectivemutism.org *E-mail:* sminfo@selectivemutism.org

"Taking Flight" Fear of Flying Support *Online.* Mutual help group created by and for fearful fliers for their own recovery. Message boards, information and a variety of resources. *Website:* http://www.takingflight.us *E-mail:* info@takingflight.us

"Remember there's no such thing as a small act of kindness. Every act creates a ripple with no logical end." -- Scott Adams

DEPRESSION / BIPOLAR DISORDER / POSTPARTUM DEPRESSION

STATEWIDE

DBSA (Depression and Bipolar Support Alliance) of NJ *16 chapters throughout New Jersey.* Education and support for persons with depression or bipolar disorder, their families and friends. Peer support groups and educational programs. Call 609-812-5219.

GROW A mutual self-help group to prevent and recover from depression, anxiety and other mental health problems. Caring and sharing community to attain emotional maturity, personal responsibility and recovery. Meets in various counties in NJ. Write: GROW Center, 4A Iowa Dr., Whiting, NJ 08759. Call 732-350-4800.

ATLANTIC

Persons with Depression, Bipolar Disorder Support Group Mutual support and encouragement for persons suffering from depression or bipolar disorder and their families. Meets Fri., 7-9pm, St. Mark All Saints Episcopal Church, Pitney Rd., Galloway. Call Barbara 609-404-1984.

BERGEN

DBSA (Depression and Bipolar Support Alliance) Mutual support for persons with bipolar or unipolar disorders. Families and friends welcome. Phone help, guest speakers, rap sessions and literature. Donation $1. Meets Thurs., 7:15pm, Bergen Regional Medical Center, 230 E. Ridgewood Ave., Psych Pavilion, Room E007, Paramus. Call Cecily 973-423-4394 or 1-888-622-3272. *Website:* http://www.dbsabergennj.org/ *E-mail:* bergendmda@aol.com

Post Partum Depression Support Group Professionally-run. Mutual support and encouragement for women who are suffering from post partum depression. Meets 2nd and 4th Tues, 7pm, Luckow Pavillion, Winters Ave. (behind the Fashion Center), Ridgewood. Call Trudy Heerema 201-447-8539 (day).

Recovery, Inc. Self-help method of will training. Offers techniques for controlling temperamental behavior and changing attitudes toward nervous symptoms, anxiety, depression and fears. Call 201-612-8153. *Website:* http://www.recovery-inc.org

> **Hasbrouck Heights** Meets Wed., 8pm, First Reformed Church, Washington Place and Burton Ave.
>
> **Ridgewood** Meets Fri., 1:30pm, Christ Church, Cottage Place and Franklin Ave.

BURLINGTON

Recovery, Inc. Self-help method of will training. Offers techniques for controlling temperamental behavior and changing attitudes toward nervous symptoms, anxiety, depression and fears. Call 856-848-8715. *Website:* http://www.recovery-inc.org

> **Marlton** Meets Mon., 8pm and Thurs., 7pm, Prince of Peace Lutheran Church, 61 Route 70 East.
>
> **Westampton** Meets Tues., 7pm, Hampton Hospital, Cafeteria, Rancocas Rd. Call John 856-983-7291.

CAMDEN

Depression / Anxiety Support Group For anyone suffering from anxiety and/or depression to support one another in an effort to remain healthy and share common problems and concerns. Under 18 welcome. Rap sessions, phone help and literature. Meets 3rd Mon., 7:15-9pm, Marie Fleche Library, Berlin. Call Nancy 856-768-1258 (eve) or Rhonda 856-768-2030 (day).

Manic-Depressives Anonymous Self-help group to guide persons with manic-depression, their families and friends. Rap sessions. Meets Wed., 8-9pm, Cherry Hill. Call Jackie 856-667-3485 (day).

New Beginnings Support Group - A Chapter of DBSA Mutual support and education for persons with mood disorders and their families. Also open to persons with anxiety, dual diagnosis and schizo-affective disorder. Opportunity to discuss successes in dealing with various symptoms. Meets Mon., 7-9pm, and Wed., 11am-1pm, Holy Trinity Lutheran Church, 214 N. Warwick Rd., Magnolia. Call Maribel 856-232-3181. *Website:* http://www.nbgroup.org *E-mail:* newbeginningsnj@gmail.com

Recovery, Inc. Self-help method of will training. Offers techniques for controlling temperamental behavior and changing attitudes toward nervous symptoms, anxiety, depression and fears. Call 856-848-8715. *Website:* http://www.recovery-inc.org

Magnolia Meets Wed., 9:45am, Holy Trinity Lutheran Church, 501 N. Warwick Rd.

Westmont Meets Sat., 11:30am, Starting Point, 215 Highland Ave.

South Jersey Depression and Bipolar Support Group Opportunity for persons with depression or bipolar disorder to exchange coping skills, treatment options and develop a network of friends. Rap sessions. Meets Wed., 7-8:45pm, Virtua Hospital, 101 Carnie Blvd., Mohrfeld Room, Voorhees. Call Regis 856-673-0619 (day/eve). *Website:* http://www.depression.meetup.com/291 *E-mail:* DBsupport-SJ@comcast.net

TLC for Moms (Postpartum Depression Support Group) Mutual support and education for women experiencing postpartum depression. Babies are welcome. Meets Thurs., 10:30am-noon also 2nd and 4th Tues., 7-8:30pm, Virtua Health, Barry D. Brown Health Education Center, 106 Carnie Blvd., Voorhees. Call 1-888-847-8823 (day).

CUMBERLAND

Depression Support Group Mutual support for persons suffering from depression or any other mental illness. Provides a safe and comfortable environment where persons can share with others who also suffer from depression. Meets Thurs. 6:30-9pm, in Millville. For meeting information call 856-825-3521 (after 10am).

GROW A mutual self-help group to prevent and recover from depression, anxiety and other mental health problems. Caring and sharing community to attain emotional maturity, personal responsibility and recovery.

Vineland Meets Thurs., 7pm, Church of Christian/Missionary Alliance, Main Rd. and Harding Ave., Board Room. Before attending call Rip 856-293-9061.

Vineland Meets 3rd Thurs., 3:30pm, New Horizons Self-Help Center, 63 S. Myrtle St. Before attending call Chris 856-794-2986.

"With the gift of listening comes the gift of healing."
--Catherine de Hueck Doherty (Poustinia)

Overcomer's Outreach *(Shiloh Faith Meeting)* Christian 12-Step. Fellowship to overcome any type of addiction or compulsive behavior, anxiety, depression or loneliness using God's word as a basis of recovery. Discussion, Bible study, prayer, phone help. Meets Thurs., 7-8pm, Shiloh Seventh Day Baptist Church, East Ave., Shiloh. Call Rev. Chrowiger 856-455-0488 (day) or Frank B. Mulford 856-451-8698 (day). *E-mail:* ahfarm@hotmail.com

ESSEX

Comfort Zone, The Provides mutual support for people suffering from depression and bipolar disorder. Meets 2nd and 4th Fri., noon-1:30pm, Mental Health Association of Essex County, 33 South Fullerton Ave., Montclair. Call Mary Ann Forster 973-509-9777 (day). *E-mail:* mforster@mhaessex.org

DBSA (Depression and Bipolar Support Alliance) Mutual support and sharing of information for individuals diagnosed with depression or bipolar disorder. Family members welcome. Rap sessions, guest speakers, educational programs, literature, phone help and email.

> **Montclair** Meets Mon. and Thurs., 7:30-9pm, First Congregational Church, 40 South Fullerton Ave. (enter via parking lot door from Plymouth St.). Call Margo Atwell 973-744-5230 or Tom B. 201-998-5751. *Website:* http://www.dbsanewjersey.org/essexcounty *E-mail:* margo.atwell@gmail.com
>
> **Newark** Meets Fri., 7:00-8:30pm, UMDNJ-University Hospital, Behavioral Health Sciences Bldg., 183 S. Orange Ave. Call Kevin 973-848-1859. *E-mail*: newarksupport@hotmail.com

GROW A mutual self-help group to prevent and recover from depression, anxiety and other mental health problems. Caring and sharing community to attain emotional maturity, personal responsibility and recovery. Meets Mon., 4:30pm, 570 Belleville Ave., Belleville. Before attending call Caroline 732-575-5765.

Postpartum Depression Support Group *Professionally-run.* Support group for pregnant women and new mothers experiencing anxiety and/or depression. Meets Tues., 10-11:30am, St. Barnabas Ambulatory Care Center, 200 South Orange Ave., Livingston. Call Dr. Lauren Meisels, PhD. 973-762-4147.

Recovery, Inc. Self-help method of will training. Offers techniques for controlling temperamental behavior and changing attitudes toward nervous symptoms, anxiety, depression and fears. Meets Tues., 8pm, Prospect Presbyterian Church, 646

Prospect St., Maplewood. Call 201-612-8153. *Website:* http://www.recovery-inc.org

GLOUCESTER

Recovery, Inc. Self-help method of will training. Offers techniques for controlling temperamental behavior and changing attitudes toward nervous symptoms, anxiety, depression and fears. Families welcome. Meets Fri., 10-11am, James Johnson Library, 670 Ward Dr., Deptford. Call 856-848-8715. *Website:* http://www.recovery-inc.org

HUDSON

DBSA (Depression and Bipolar Support Alliance) Mutual support for persons with depression and bipolar depression.

Bayonne Meets 2nd and 4th Fri., 7-9pm, Community Mental Health Center, 597 Broadway. Call 201-387-0091.

Jersey City Meets 2nd and 4th Mon., 5pm, Hudson County Self-Help Center, 880 Bergen Ave., Suite 605. Call Debbie or Carol 201-420-8013.

Postpartum Depression *Professionally-run.* Support for new mothers and their families. Meetings vary, Meadowlands Hospital, 55 Meadowlands Parkway, Secaucus. Call Kate Waldron 201-392-3180 (day).

HUNTERDON

DBSA (Depression and Bipolar Support Alliance) Mutual support for persons suffering from depression or bipolar depression. Rap sessions and literature. Suggested donation $1 or $2 for DBSA literature. Meets Mon., 7:30pm, 51 Main St., Suite 12, Clinton. Before attending call Lyn Siegel, LCSW 908-586-3254 (day). *Website:* http://www.dbaslliance.org (click on "Find support") *E-mail:* lynsiegel@patmedia.net

"To refer your patient to a support group, you don't need to find the correct ICD Code, nor obtain approval from an insurance carrier. You can just say: 'You're not alone. There are other people out there who have gone through this.'"
-- Kathleen A. Gaioni, M.D.

Postpartum Depression Support Group *Professionally-run.* Mutual support and education for women experiencing postpartum depression. Babies welcome. Meets 1st and 3rd Fri., 10:30-11:30am, Hunterdon Medical Center, 2100 Westcott Dr., Flemington. Before attending call Jean Jamele, RN 908-788-6634 (day).

MERCER

DBSA (Depression and Bipolar Support Alliance) An informal forum for education, support and socialization among patients diagnosed with depression, bipolar disorder or related disorders. Families, friends and interested others welcome. Meets Tues. and Wed., 7:30-9:30pm, Lambert House, 253 Witherspoon St., Room 1, Princeton. Call 609-716-9829 *Website:* http://www.dbsanewjersey.org/princeton

GROW A mutual self-help group to prevent and recover from depression, anxiety and other mental health problems. Caring and sharing community to attain emotional maturity, personal responsibility and recovery. Meets Thurs., 6pm, Reach Out/Speak Out, 2100 East State St., Hamilton. Before attending call Caroline 732-575-5765.

New Perspectives Mutual support for persons with depression, bipolar disorder, anxiety or panic attacks. Meets every other Mon., 7:30pm, Unitarian Universalist Church, Washington Crossing. Call David Hughes 609-818-0177 (eve). *E-mail:* David.Hughes419@att.net

Pregnancy and Postpartum Support Group *Professionally-run.* Support for pregnant women and new mothers adjusting to emotional issues such as blues, depression and anxiety. Meets 3rd Sat., 10:30am-noon, 60 Mt. Lucas Rd., Princeton. Pre-registration required. Before attending call Joyce 609-683-1000 or Hyla 609-936-1154.

MIDDLESEX

DBSA (Depression and Bipolar Support Alliance) Support and information for manic-depressive/depressive sufferers. Meets Fri., 7:45pm, Robert Wood Johnson University Hospital, Auditorium, Main Floor, New Brunswick. Call 1-888-226-6437. *Website:* http://www.moodgarden.org/middlesex.htm *E-mail:* dbsamsex@hotmail.com

Overcomer's Outreach Christian 12-Step. Fellowship to overcome any type of addiction or compulsive behavior, anxiety, depression or loneliness using God's word as a basis of recovery. Discussion, Bible study and prayer, phone help. Meets Thurs., 7-8:30pm, Metuchen Assembly of God, Rose and Whitman St., Metuchen. Call Janet 732-388-2856 (eve) or Pat 732-321-6896.

MONMOUTH

DBSA (Depression and Bipolar Support Alliance) Support for persons affected by depression and bipolar disorder. Families and interested professionals are welcome. Guest speakers, phone help and mutual sharing. Meets Mon. and Thurs., 7:30-9pm, St. Mary's Church, Route 34 and Phalanx Rd., Colts Neck. Call Rick 732-919-7739 (eve). *Website:* http://www.moodgarden.org/coltsneck.htm *E-mail:* Antwon82763@aol.com

GROW A mutual self-help group to prevent and recover from depression, anxiety and other mental health problems. Caring and sharing community to attain emotional maturity, personal responsibility and recovery.

> **Freehold** Meets Wed., 5:30pm, Freehold Self-Help Center, 17 Bannard St.
>
> **Freehold** Meets Wed., 7pm, 11 Spring St. Before attending call Nancy 732-350-4800.
>
> **Ocean Grove** Meets Thurs., 6:45pm, St. Paul's Methodist Church, 80 Enbury St., Stokes Room. Before attending call Caroline 732-575-5765.

MORRIS

DBSA (Depression and Bipolar Support Alliance) Education and support for persons with depression or bipolar disorder, their families and friends. Peer support groups and educational programs.

> **Morristown** Peer support group meets Tues., 7:30-9pm, except holidays, suggested donation $2. Lecture/educational series meets last Wed., 7:30pm, earlier dates in Nov./Dec., suggested donation $3 non-members, Morristown Unitarian Fellowship, 21 Normandy Heights Rd. Call Linda 973-994-1143 (after 6pm) for lecture schedule and weather cancellation or Ron 908-377-5245 (after 6pm) for peer group schedule and weather cancellation. *Website:* http://dbsanewjersey.org/morristownarea *E-mail:* lsb1@panix.com
>
> **Succasunna** Rap group meets 1st and 3rd Thurs., 7:15-9pm and 4th Tues., 10:30am-noon. Lecture/educational series meets 2nd Thurs., 7:15pm, Temple Shalom, 215 South Hillside Ave. Call Bonnie 973-361-5456 or Ann Kays 973-927-3810 (day). *Website:*

http://www.dbsanewjersey.org/succasunna2 *E-mail:* bonnie@therosenthals.net

Postpartum Support Group *Professionally-run.* Provides support for new mothers experiencing postpartum depression. Meets 1st and 3rd Tues., 7-8pm, Saint Clare's Behavioral Health Center, 50 Morris Ave., Denville. Before attending call 1-888-626-2111 (ask for mom's support group).

OCEAN

DBSA Long Beach Island (Depression and Bipolar Alliance) Mutual support and education for persons diagnosed with depression or bipolar disorder, their families and friends.

Brant Beach Meetings vary, St. Francis Community Center, Seniors' Luncheon Room, 47th and Long Beach Blvd. Call Salvina 609-812-5219; for families and friends call Catherine 609-494-3931. *Website:* http://www.dbsanewjersey.org/LBI *E-mail:* sivan710@comcast.net

Stafford Meets 1st and 3rd Fri., 7:15-9pm, Ocean Club, Family Resource Center, Route 9. Call Salvina 609-812-5219.

Toms River Meets Wed. and Fri., 7:30-9:30pm, Community Medical Center, 99 Route 37 West, Auditorium B (Wed.), Auditorium C (Fri.). Call 1-888-226-6437. *Website:* http://www.moodgarden.org/ocean.htm *E-mail:* ss_njdbsa@hotmail.com

GROW A mutual self-help group to prevent and recover from depression, anxiety and other mental health problems. Caring and sharing community to attain emotional maturity, personal responsibility and recovery.

Brick Meets Tues., 6:30pm, Brick Presbyterian Church, 11 Drum Point Rd. Before attending call Lisa 732-575-5766.

Manchester Meets Thurs., 7:30pm, Redeemer Lutheran Church, 2309 Route 70. Call Nancy 732-350-4800.

Toms River Meets Tues., 5:30pm, Brighter Days Self-Help Center, Route 37 West. Before attending call Nancy 732-350-4800.

Toms River Meets Thurs., 4pm, Presbyterian Church of Toms River, River Room, Hooper Ave. and Chestnut St. Before attending call Lisa 732-575-5766.

Postpartum Depression Support Group *Professionally-run.* Mutual support, encouragement and education for women who are experiencing postpartum depression. Meets one Sat. per month, 10-11am, Southern Ocean County Hospital,

Conference Room 2, 140 Route 72 West, Manahawkin. For meeting information call SOCH Connect 609-978-3400 or Kristen Castro 609-978-3165.

Recovery, Inc. Self-help method of will training. Offers techniques for controlling temperamental behavior and changing attitudes toward nervous symptoms, anxiety, depression and fears. Meets Mon., 7:30pm, Presbyterian Church of Toms River, Hooper Ave. and Chestnut St., Toms River. Call 201-612-8153. *Website:* http://www.recovery-inc.org

SUSSEX

DBSA (Depression and Bipolar Support Alliance) Sussex County Support and education for persons suffering from depression or bipolar depression. Rap sessions and guest speakers. Family and friends welcome. Meets Wed., 7:30-9pm, Redeemer Lutheran Church, 37 Newton-Sparta Rd., Newton. Call Dan 973-948-6999 or Jean 973-383-3808. *Website:* http://www.scdbsa.org *E-mail:* dan@dancarter.net

UNION

DBSA (Depression and Bipolar Support Alliance) Education and support for persons with depression or bipolar disorder (manic depression), their families and friends. Rap sessions. Call Theldora Hawkins 908-233-7074 (day/eve). *Website:* http://www.dbsanewjersey.org/essexcounty

> **Summit** Meets 1st and 3rd Thurs., 7:30-9pm, Overlook Hospital, Conference Room # 1. Also offers Saturday meeting.
>
> **Westfield** Meetings vary, First Baptist Church (accessible by bus # 59), 170 Elm St.

GROW A mutual self-help group to prevent and recover from depression, anxiety and other mental health problems. Caring and sharing community to attain emotional maturity, personal responsibility and recovery.

> **Elizabeth** Meets Wed., 4pm, New Beginnings Self-Help Center, 60 Prince St., Lower Level. Before attending call Caroline 732-575-5765.
>
> **Plainfield** Meets Wed., 3:30pm, Self-Help Center, 333 Park Ave.

"Action conquers fear." -- Peter Nivio Zarlenga

Overcomer's Outreach Christian 12-Step. Fellowship to overcome any type of addiction or compulsive behavior, anxiety, depression or loneliness using God's word as a basis of recovery. Discussion, Bible study, prayer and phone help. Call Carmen 908-245-2788.

Cranford Meets Mon., 7pm, Harvest Training Center at Calvary Tabernacle, 69 Myrtle St.

Elizabeth Meets Tues., 7:30pm, Mount Teman AME Church, 160 Madison Ave.

Elizabeth Meets Thurs., 7:30pm, Union Baptist Church, 1088 E. Grand St.

Recovery, Inc. Self-help method of will training. Offers techniques for controlling temperamental behavior and changing attitudes toward nervous symptoms, anxiety, depression and fears. Call 201-612-8153. *Website:* http://www.recovery-inc.org

Summit Meets Wed., 7:45pm, Central Presbyterian Center, Morris Ave. and Maple St. (parking lot entrance).

Westfield Meets Fri., 8pm, Union County Community Services Building, 300 North Ave. East (rear parking lot entrance), 2nd Floor, Conference Room.

WARREN

Depression and Bipolar Disorder Support Group Mutual support and encouragement for persons with depression and bipolar disorder. Rap sessions. Meets Tues. (except 1st Tues.), 6-7:30pm, Better Futures Self-Help Center, 21 W. Washington Ave., Washington. Call Bruce 908-835-0055 (day/eve).

NATIONAL

Dep-Anon *National. Founded 1999.* 12-Step. Fellowship for men, women and children whose lives have been affected by a family member's depression. Members share hope, strength and experience in order to grow emotionally and spiritually. Write: Dep-Anon, P.O. Box 17414, Louisville, KY 40217. Call Hugh S. 502-569-1989. *Website:* http://www.depressedanon.com *E-mail:* info@depressedanon.com

Depressed Anonymous *International. 50 affiliated groups. Founded 1985.* 12-Step. Program to help depressed persons believe and hope they can feel better. Newsletter, phone support, information and referrals, workshops, conferences and seminars. Information packet. Assistance starting a similar group. Write: D.A.P.,

Box 17414, Louisville, KY 40217. Call Hugh 502-569-1989. *Website:* http://www.depressedanon.com *E-mail:* info@depressedanon.com

Depression After Delivery *National. Founded 1985.* Support and information for women who have suffered from postpartum depression. Volunteer phone support in most states, some local support groups, newsletter and group development guidelines. *Website:* http://www.depressionafterdelivery.com

Depression and Bipolar Support Alliance *National. 1,000+ affiliated groups. Founded 1986.* Mutual support and information for persons with depressive and manic-depressive illness and their families. Provides public education on the nature of depressive illnesses. Advocacy for research and improved access to care. Annual conference, chapter development guidelines and quarterly newsletter. Write: DBSA, 730 N. Franklin, Suite 501, Chicago, IL 60610. Call 1-800-826-3632 or 312-642-0049; Fax: 312-642-7243. *Website:* http://www.dbsalliance.org

DRADA (Depression and Related Affective Disorders Association) *International. 73 affiliated groups. Founded 1986.* Aims to alleviate the suffering arising from depression and manic-depression by assisting self-help groups. Provides education, information and supports research. Also offers newsletter, literature and phone support. Assistance in starting new groups, training for group leaders and peer support programs. Young People's Outreach Project. Write: DRADA, 8201 Greensboro Drive, Suite 300, McLean, VA 22102. Call 703-610-9026. *Website:* http://www.drada.org *E-mail:* info@drada.org

GROW in America *International. 143 groups. Founded in 1957.* 12-step group that offers mutual help, friendship, community, education and leadership. Focuses on recovery and personal growth. Open to all including those with mental health issues, depression, anxiety, grief, fears, etc. Write: GROW in America, P.O. Box 3667, Champaign, IL 61826. Call 1-888-741-4769. *E-mail:* growil@sbcglobal.net

Postpartum Support International *International. 600+ members; support networks in 48 states; 25 countries. Founded 1987.* Goal is to increase the awareness of the emotional changes women often experience during pregnancy and after the birth of a baby. Information on diagnosis and treatment of postpartum depression. Provides education, advocacy and annual conference. Encourages formation of support groups. Helps strengthen existing groups. Phone support, referrals, literature and newsletter. Write: Postpartum Support International, 927 N. Kellogg Ave., Santa Barbara, CA 93111. Call 805-967-7636; Fax: 805-967-0608. *Website:* http://www.postpartum.net *E-mail:* psioffice@postpartum.net

Recoveries Anonymous *International. 50 chapters.* Spiritual recovery group for anyone seeking a solution for any kind of addiction, problem or behavior. Family and friends welcome. "How To Begin..." guides and "Start A Group" kit can be downloaded free from the website. Write: RA, P.O. Box 1212, East Northport, NY 11731. *Website:* http://www.r-a.org *E-mail:* raus@r-a.org

Recovery, Inc. *International. 640 groups. Founded 1937.* Mental health self-help organization that offers weekly group meetings for people suffering from various emotional and mental conditions. Principles parallel those found in cognitive-behavioral therapy. Teaches people how to change their thoughts, reactions and behaviors that cause their physical and emotional symptoms. Write: Recovery, Inc., 802 N. Dearborn St., Chicago, IL 60610. Call 312-337-5661; Fax: 312-337-5756. *Website:* http://www.recovery-inc.org

ONLINE

BPSO (Bipolar Significant Others) Bulletin Board *Online.* Provides support and information for families and friends of persons with bipolar disorder (aka manic-depression). Opportunity to communicate online with others in similar situations. Website offers chat, forums, email list and over 3000 pages of information. *Website:* http://www.bipolarworld.net/ *E-mail:* bipolarworld@yahoo.com

Child and Adolescent Bipolar Foundation *Online.* Site provides information posted by members to provide support to families of children or teens with bipolar disorder. Offers message boards, support group information, community center and general information. *Website:* http://www.bpkids.org

Conduct Disorders Parent Message Board *Online. 6592 members. Founded 1995.* Support for parents living with a child with one of the many behavior disorders including: attention deficit hyperactivity disorder, oppositional defiance disorder, conduct disorder, depression and substance abuse. Parents with children of all ages welcome. *Website:* http://www.conductdisorders.com

We can also refer callers to over 100 individuals who are seeking others to help start new support groups throughout NJ. Give us a call for more information.
1-800-367-6274

MENTAL HEALTH CONSUMERS

(see also other mental health sections)

STATEWIDE

COMHCO (Coalition Of Mental Health Consumer Organizations) Information, support and advocacy on mental health issues. Speakers and workshops. Membership $5/yr. For meeting time and location, call Annette Wright 973-778-8810 (after 1pm). *E-mail:* comhco@aol.com

Consumer Connections Support Network Regional support group meetings for consumers who work in mental health/social services. Groups focus on work-related issues only. Write: Consumer Connections - MHA in NJ, 88 Pompton Ave., Verona, NJ 07044. Call Ray Cortese 973-571-4100 (day); Fax: 973-857-1777. *Website:* http://www.mhanj.org

CSP (Collaborative Support Programs) of NJ, Inc. Assists statewide in the development and networking of mental health consumer/psychiatric survivor groups. Workshops, quarterly newsletter, conferences, system advocacy, funding of consumer-run self-help centers, community services, technical assistance and supportive housing. Brochures available. Write: CSP, 11 Spring St., Freehold, NJ 07728. Call 1-800-227-3729 or 732-780-1175 (day); Fax: 732-780-8977. *Website:* http://www.cspnj.org

NAMI CARE (Consumers Advocating Recovery through Empowerment) Support for anyone afflicted with any type of psychiatric disorder. Follows a national model, based upon shared insights and empathy. Groups are affiliated with local NAMI groups for education and advocacy. Offers trained peer facilitators. Help in forming CARE groups. Call Jay Yudof, NAMI NJ Consumer Outreach Liaison 1-866-464-3267. *Website:* http://www.naminj.org *E-mail:* jyudof@hotmail.com

ATLANTIC

ICE Self-Help Center Consumer-run self-help center that provides an environment of support and empowerment that provides wellness. Offers self-help groups and recreational activities for mental health consumers. For information call ICE Self-Help Center 609-272-0928 or Karen Turner 609-272-1700 ext. 302.

BERGEN

For Us/By Us Consumer-run self-help center that brings together consumers of mental health services. Center provides support, socializing, recreational activities and advocacy. Open Mon.-Fri., 3-7pm and Sun., noon-5pm, For Us/By Us Self-Help/Drop In Center, 40 North Van Brunt St., Englewood. Call 201-541-1221.

Mental Health Support Group *Professionally-run.* Support for mental health consumers. Meets 1st Thurs., 7pm, Community Services Building, 327 E. Ridgewood Ave., Paramus. Call 201-635-9595 (day).

NAMI en Espanol of Bergen County *(SPANISH)* Advocacy and support for family and friends of those with a mental illness and for mental health consumers who attend. Meets 3rd Mon., 6:30-8pm, Latin America Institute, 10 Banta Pl., Suite 101, Hackensack. Call Martha Silva 1-888-803-3413. *Website:* http://www.naminj.org *E-mail:* naminjenespanol@msn.com

On Our Own Self-Help Center Consumer-run self-help center that offers support groups, socializing, recreational activities and advocacy to bring together consumers of mental health services. Open Mon-Fri., noon-7pm; Sat and Sun., 1-6pm; support group meets 1st and 3rd Thurs., 6-8:30pm, On Our Own Self-Help Center, 179 Main St., 2nd Floor (entrance on Mercer St.), Hackensack. Call 201-489-8402.

BURLINGTON

RITE (Realizing Independence Through Empowerment) Center, The Consumer-run self-help center that provides opportunities for sharing, recreation and advocacy. Offers rap sessions, literature, socialization and outside activities. Open Tues., Wed., Thurs., Fri., 1-6:30pm and Sat., 10:30am-4pm, The RITE Center, 693 Main St., Bldg. C, Lumberton. Call 609-518-7292.

Riverbank Self-Help Center Consumer-run self-help center that provides self-help, mutual support, advocacy and social activities for mental health consumers. Open Wed., 5-9pm, every other Fri., 6:30-9pm and Sun., noon-4pm, Riverbank Self-Help Center, 114 Delaware Ave., Burlington. Call 609-239-1786. *Website:* http://www.riverbankshc.com *E-mail:* riverhelps@comcast.net

Recovery Center, 4404 Pacific Ave., Wildwood. For meeting information call 609-523-7100.

CUMBERLAND

New Horizons Consumer-run self-help center that provides mutual support, special events, socializing, recreational activities and advocacy for mental health care consumers. Open Mon., Wed., Thurs., Fri., 11am-4pm and Tues., 10am-4pm, New Horizons, 63 S. Myrtle St., Vineland. For information call 856-696-8921.

ESSEX

East Essex Self-Help Center Consumer-run self-help center that offers support, discussions, computers, speakers, socializing and self-help groups for mental health consumers. Open Mon.-Wed., 3-7pm; Fri., 3-6pm and Sat., 1-4pm, East Essex Self-Help Center, 570 Belleville Ave. (entrance on Franklin Ave.), Belleville. Call 973-450-0347.

Spirituality Group Support for mental health consumers fostering an awareness of spirituality and a sense of being a part of a much larger powerful entity. Offers mutual sharing, education, rap sessions, social, phone help and advocacy. Meets Tues., 4pm, Where Peaceful Waters Flow, 47 Cleveland St., Orange. Call Celine 973-677-7700 (eve).

Thursdays *Professionally-run.* Drop-in center that provides mutual support for mental health care consumers. Opportunity to socialize, guest speakers and trips. Meets Thurs., 6:30-9pm, MHA of Essex, 33 South Fullerton Ave., Montclair. Call Judi Fiederer 973-509-9777.

Where Peaceful Waters Flow Consumer-run self-help center that offers support and advocacy for mental health consumers. Provides resources, socialization, rap sessions, recreational activities, literature and phone help. Open Mon.-Thurs., 2-7pm and Sat., 9am-4pm, Where Peaceful Waters Flow, 47 Cleveland St., Orange. Call 973-677-7700 (eve).

Youth Partnership Group Adult supervised activities for youth (ages 13-21) with complex emotional, mental health or behavioral issues to help them express what they have been through and share concerns. Rap sessions, guest speakers, literature, newsletter and phone help. Meets Tues., 6-8pm, Family Support Organization of Essex County, 60 Evergreen Place, East Orange. Call Yvonne Rouse or Hazeline Pilgrim 973-395-1441 (day).

Youth Partnership Group Adult supervised activities for youth (ages 13-2. complex emotional, mental health or behavioral issues to help them express they have been through and share concerns. Rap sessions. Meets T 6:30-8:30pm, Family Support Organization of Burlington County, 774 Eayres Rd., Lumberton. Call Jamison Gsell 609-265-8838 (day).

CAMDEN

Donald Mays Jr. Self-Help Center, The Consumer-run center offers supp recreational activities and advocacy for mental health consumers. Open Mo 2-8pm; Wed., 1-7pm; Fri., 1-8pm and Sat. 11am-6pm, The Donald Mays Jr., Colby Ave., Suite 16, Stratford. Call 856-346-9043.

New Beginnings Support Group - A Chapter of DBSA Mutual support and education for persons with mood disorders and their families. Also open to persons with anxiety, dual diagnosis and schizo-affective disorder. Opportunity to discuss successes in dealing with various symptoms. Meets Mon., 7-9pm,and Wed., 11am-1pm, Holy Trinity Lutheran Church, 214 N. Warwick Rd., Magnolia. Call Maribel 856-232-3181. *Website:* http://www.njnb.org *E-mail:* newbeginningsnj@gmail.com

Pink and Blues Peer Support Group (Gay and Lesbian) Support group for sexual and gender minority people living with a mental illness. Meets Wed., 7pm, St. Luke's and the Epiphany Church, 330 S. 13th St., Philadelphia, PA. Call Mark Davis 215-546-0300 ext. 3301 (day) or 215-627-0424 (eve). *E-mail:* Mark.Davis@Phila.Gov

Youth Partnership Group Adult supervised activities for youth (ages 13-21) with complex emotional, mental health or behavioral issues to help them express what they have been through and share concerns. Rap sessions. Call 856-662-2600 (day).

> <u>Atco</u> Meets Wed., 6:30-8pm, Winslow High School, 10 Coopers Folly Rd.
>
> <u>Merchantville</u> Meets Thurs., 6:30-8pm, Camden County Family Support Organization, 23 W. Park Ave., Ste. 103-104.

CAPE MAY

Learning Recovery Center Consumer-run self-help center that provides mutual support, advocacy, social and recreational activities for mental health consumers Open Wed., 6:30-8:30pm; Thurs., 1-7pm; Fri., 1-9pm; Sat., 11am-5pm, Learnin

GLOUCESTER

Schizophrenics Anonymous Mutual support for persons with schizophrenia. Literature. Meets alternate Sat., 10am-noon, Underwood Memorial Hospital, Broad St. and Red Bank Ave., Dining Room B, Woodbury. Before attending call Community Relations 856-853-2011.

Up Your Alley Self-Help Center Consumer-run self-help center that provides socialization, support, advocacy, rap sessions and guest speakers. Open Mon. and Tues., 3-8pm; Wed., 1-6pm and Sat., 11am-4pm, Up Your Alley Self-Help Center, 8 Liberty St., Glassboro. Call 856-881-2204. *E-mail:* gloucestershc@snip.net

HUDSON

Hudson County Self-Help Center Consumer-run self-help center that provides socialization, recreation and advocacy for mental health consumers. Open Mon., Tues., Wed., Fri., 2-7pm and Sat., noon-5pm, Hudson County Self-Help Center, 880 Bergen Ave., Suite 605, Jersey City. Call 201-420-8013.

NAMI NJ en Espanol of Hudson County *(SPANISH)* Advocacy and support for family and friends of those with a mental illness and for mental health consumers who attend. Meets 1st Wed. (except Aug.), 6:30-8pm, Catholic Community Service Office, 2201 Bergenline Ave., 2nd Floor, Union City. Call Martha Silva 1-888-803-3413. *E-mail:* naminjenespanol@msn.com

Schizophrenics Anonymous Fellowship for persons diagnosed with any schizophrenia-related disorder. Focuses on recovery, using a 6-step program, along with medication and professional help. Meets 1st and 3rd Tues., 4:30pm, Hudson County Self-Help Center, 3000 Kennedy Blvd., Suite 305, Jersey City. Call Anthony or Barbara 201-420-8013 (eve).

HUNTERDON

Getting Together Self-Help Center Drop-in center for mental health consumers. Educational series, support groups, social and advocacy. Open Sun., noon-4pm; occasional Mon.; Tues., 4:30-6pm; Wed., 5-8pm; Fri., 4-8pm and Sat., 5-8pm, Getting Together Self-Help Center, 162A Route 31 N., Flemington. Call Eileen 908-806-8202. *E-mail:* outreach31@earthlink.net

Living Your Life Opportunity for persons with mental illness to work on life goals and learn the steps necessary to achieve them. Focus is not on mental illness but on what members want and can do with their lives. Meets Mon., 4:30-6pm, Getting Together Self-Help Center, 162A Route 31 North, Flemington. Before attending call Juliette, Eileen or Paul 908-806-8202.

NAMI Hunterdon - Peer Support Group Peer-based mutual support group for anyone diagnosed with a mental illness. Program is designed to help individuals share experiences in a positive, supportive and understanding atmosphere. Opportunity to learn from each other in a safe and confidential environment. Rap sessions and literature. Meets 2nd and 4th Thurs., 7:30-9pm, Getting Together Self-Help Center, 162A Route 31 North, Flemington. Call Walt 908-638-8034. *E-mail:* dudzinski@net-lynx.com

MERCER

NAMI CARE (Consumers Advocating Recovery through Empowerment) Self-help group run by and for consumers. Meets 2nd and 4th Mon., 6-7pm, Nami Mercer, Lawrence Commons, 3371 Brunswick Pike, Lawrenceville. Call 609-799-8994 (day). *Website:* http://www.namimercer.org *E-mail:* home@namimercer.org

Reachout / Speakout Consumer-run self-help center that offers mutual support and socialization for mental health consumers. Advocacy, education, social activities and referrals. Open Tues., Wed., Thurs., 2-8pm; Fri., 5-6:30pm and Sat., 10am-4pm, Reachout-Speakout Self-Help Center, 2100 E. State St., Hamilton. Call 609-586-2551 or 732-682-2555.

MIDDLESEX

CAMHOP-NJ (Chinese Mental Health Self-Help Group) *(BILINGUAL) Professionally-run.* Mutual support group for families and individuals of Chinese origin with mental illnesses. Meets 3rd Tues., 7-8:45pm, Stelton Baptist Church, 334 Plainfield Ave., Edison. Call Maggie Luo 732-940-0991 (day). *Website:* http://www.naminj.org/programs/camhop/camhop.html *E-mail:* namichinesegroup@yahoo.com

Member To Member Rap Group Support and confidential discussion of concerns for mental health consumers. Meets Wed., 4pm, and Thurs., 4:30pm, Moving Forward, 35 Elizabeth St., 2nd Floor, Suite B, New Brunswick. Call Moving Forward 732-317-3893 (day). *Website:* http://www.cspnj.org

Moving Forward Consumer-run self-help center that offers socialization and support for adults with a mental health issue or other special needs. Includes Peer Employment, Wellness and Recovery Support Groups and others. Handicapped accessible. Open Mon.-Thurs., 3-7pm; Fri., 3-8pm; Sat., 1-5pm, 35 Elizabeth Street, 2nd Floor, Suite B, New Brunswick. Call 732-317-3893. *Website:* http://www.cspnj.com

Rap Group Offers a safe supportive environment for consumers to express and share their feelings about mental health issues. Meets Wed. and Thurs., 3-7pm; Sat., 1-5pm, Moving Forward, 35 Elizabeth St., 2nd Floor, Suite B, New Brunswick. Call 732-317-3893 (day) or Carey 732-656-9288 (eve).

Schizophrenics Anonymous Mutual support for persons with schizophrenia or schizophrenia-related disorders. Guest speakers, literature. Meets 1st and 3rd Tues., 4pm, Moving Forward, 35 Elizabeth St., 2nd floor, Suite B, New Brunswick. Call Integrated Case Management Services 732-235-6184 (day), Moving Forward 732-317-3893 (day) or Attila 732-220-1671 (eve).

Youth Partnership Group Adult supervised activities for youth (ags 13-21) with complex emotional, mental health or behavioral issues to help them express what they have been through and share concerns. Educational series, advocacy, social group, newsletter, phone help and buddy system. Meets Fri., 6-8pm, Family Support Organization of Middlesex County, 1950 Route 27 North, Suite D, North Brunswick. Call Dylys Koney or Sam Hartman 732-940-2837 (day). *E-mail:* dkfsomiddlesex9@msn.com

MONMOUTH

C.A.R.E. Center (Consumer Advocacy Recreation Exchange) Self-help center for mental health consumers to provide support and socialization. Open Mon., noon-7pm; Tues., 10am-4pm; Wed. and Thurs., noon-7pm, Fri., 10am-4pm and Sat., 11am-5pm, CARE Center, 80 Steiner Ave., Neptune City. Call 732-774-0288 (day).

Freehold Self-Help Center Consumer-run drop-in center that offers support for mental health consumers. Consumer resource center, rap sessions, social, educational and employment resources for persons with disabilities. Open Mon., noon-4pm; Wed., 3-9pm; Thurs., 3-9pm; Fri., 3-9pm and Sat., 1-7pm, Freehold Self-Help Center, 17 Bannard St., Suite 22, Freehold. Call 732-625-9485.

NAMI CARE (Consumers Advocating Recovery through Empowerment) Support and advocacy group for mental health consumers. Meets 3rd Tues., 7-8:45pm, Lutheran Church of the Good Shepherd, 112 Middletown Rd., Holmdel. Call Jay 732-531-7624. *E-mail:* jyudof@hotmail.com

MORRIS

CAP (Consumer Advocacy Program) Advocacy group and drop-in center for mental health consumers. Consumer resource center group meets last Tues., 10am-2pm, Mental Health Association, 100 Route 46 E., Bldg. C, Mountain Lakes. Call Christa Utz 973-334-3496 (day).

M.O.M.M.I.E.S. Group (Mothers Overcoming Medical Mental Illnesses Eternal Support), The Support for mothers with mental illnesses who have children of all ages. Rap sessions, education, guest speakers, newsletter, literature, buddy system and phone help. Meets Fri., 6-7pm, Saint Clare's Hospital, 130 Powerville Rd., Community Room, Boonton Township. Call Kim-Marie De Lauro 973-257-9585 (day).

Morris Self-Help Center Consumer-run drop-in center that provides socialization for mental health consumers. Handicapped accessible. Open Mon.-Fri., 3-7pm; Sat. and Sun., 1-5pm, Morris Self-Help Center, 1259 Route 46 East, Bldg. 4, Entrance 4D, Parisppany. Call 973-334-2470.

Schizophrenics Anonymous Fellowship, support and information for persons with schizophrenia or related disorders. Focuses upon recovery, using a 6-step program, along with medication and professional help. Meets 1st and 3rd Wed., 7pm, Mental Health Association, 100 Route 46 E., Bldg. C, Mountain Lakes. Call Christa Utz 973-334-3496.

OCEAN

Brighter Days Self-Help Mutual Aid Center Consumer-run self-help center that offers mutual support and discussion for mental health consumers. Rap sessions, advocacy, socials and special celebrations. Open Mon., 2-9pm; Tues. 2-8pm; Wed., 4-9pm; Thurs., 2-9pm and Sat., 11am-7pm, S&F Plaza, 2008 Route 37 East, Suite 6, Toms River. Call Brighter Days at 732-270-6061.

PASSAIC

Social Connections Consumer-run self-help center that provides support for mental health consumers. Rap groups, social activities and meeting new friends. MICA (mental illness chemically addicted) self-help group. Open Tues. and Thurs., 2-5pm; Wed. and Fri., 4-9pm and Sun., 11am-4pm, Social Connections, 1 Westervelt Ave., Vanderhoef House, Weaslebrook Park, Clifton. Call Annette Wright 973-778-8810.

SALEM

NAMI CARE (Consumers Advocating Recovery thru Empowerment) Support and advocacy group for mental health consumers. Meets 2nd and 4th Wed., 7-8:30pm, First Baptist Church, 117 S. Main St., Woodstown. Call Kathleen Chance 856-299-4012. *Website:* http://www.naminj.org *E-mail:* JYudof@hotmail.com

New Dimensions Consumer-run self-help center that provides socialization for mental health consumers. Handicapped accessible. Arts, crafts, mental health education and lending library. Open Tues., Wed., Thurs., Sat., 3:30-9pm, New Dimensions, 316A Merion Ave., Carneys Point. Call 856-351-9100 (day).

SOMERSET

Freedom Trail Self-Help Center Consumer-run self-help center that provides socializing, advocacy and support for mental health consumers. Open Mon., Wed., Fri., 9am-2pm and Tues., Thurs., Sat., 6-11pm, Third Reformed Church, 10 W. Somerset St., Rear 2nd Floor, Raritan. Call 908-722-5778.

SUSSEX

A Way To Freedom Consumer-run drop-in center where mental health consumers can support each other. Advocacy, education, socialization and recreation. Mutual sharing, rap sessions, literature, guest speakers, phone help, food bank, MICA (mental illness chemically addicted) support group and part time consumer employment opportunities. Meets Mon., Wed., Thurs. and Fri., 3-7:30pm; Sat., 11am-4pm, A Way To Freedom, 69 Water St., Newton. Call Ann Lovell or Betty 973-300-0830.

UNION

Esperanza Self-Help Center *(SPANISH) Professionally-run.* Mutual support, social and recreational activities for Latino mental health consumers to provide positive interpersonal relationships. Open Mon.-Thurs., 9am-1pm, Esperanza Self-Help Center, 361-363 Monroe Ave., Kenilworth. Call Marta 908-272-5296.

NAMI Union County Provides education, information, support and advocacy for persons suffering from mental illness, their families and friends. Meets 4th Tues., 7:30-9:30pm, Osceola Presbyterian Church, 1689 Raritan Rd., Clark. Call NAMI Union 908-233-1628. *E-mail:* nami.union.nj@nami.org

New Beginnings Self-Help Center Consumer-run self-help center that provides support for mental health consumers to establish a social network to share experiences, resource information, encouragement and companionship. Recreational and social activities, self-help group discussions. Open Mon., Wed., Thurs., Fri., 3-8pm and Sun., 2-7pm, New Beginnings Self-Help Center, 60 Prince St., Lower Level, Elizabeth. Call Joyce Haberer or Kenneth Quigley 908-352-7830 (day).

Park Avenue Self-Help Center Consumer-run self-help center for mental health consumers to provide support and socialization. Offers Peer Employment Support Group among others. Open Mon., 1-4pm; Wed., 3-7pm; Thurs., 3-6pm and Sat., 12:30-4pm, Park Avenue Self-Help Center, 333 Park Ave., Plainfield. Call 908-757-1350.

Youth Partnership Group Adult supervised activities for youth (ages 13-21) with complex emotional, mental health or behavioral issues to help them express what they have been through and share concerns. Rap sessions. Meets 2nd and 4th Wed., 6:30-8:30pm, Family Support Organization, 137 Elmer St., 1st Floor, Westfield. Also girls group age (13-17) in Elizabeth. Call Kathy Wagner 908-789-7625 (day).

WARREN

Better Future Self-Help Center Consumer-run self-help drop-in center for persons with a mental illness. Various support groups are offered. Meals offered Mon.-Fri. Transportation provided. Open Mon., Wed, Fri., 3-9pm; Tues. and Thurs., 5-9pm; Sat.-Sun., 1-5pm, Better Future Self-Help Center, 21 West Washington Ave., Washington. Call 908-835-1180.

NATIONAL

CONTAC (Consumer Organization and Networking Technical Assistance Center) *Resource.* Center for mental health consumers and consumer-run organizations nationwide that promotes self-help, recovery and empowerment. Provides technical assistance for organizing and maintaining self-help groups. Conducts leadership training. listserv, electronic library, online peer support. Write: CONTAC, P.O. Box 11000, Charleston, WV 25339. Call 1-888-825-8324 or 304-345-7312; Fax: 304-345-7303. *Website:* http://www.contac.org *E-mail:* usacontac@contac.org

National Mental Health Consumers Self-Help Clearinghouse *Resource. Founded 1986.* Provides information and recovery-oriented services for mental health consumers. Assistance in self and system advocacy, on-site consultations, training and educational events. Assistance in starting groups. Also provides technical assistance to consumer-run groups. Maintains a database of consumer support and advocacy groups. Write: Nat'l MH Consumers Self-Help Clearinghouse, 1211 Chestnut St., Suite 1207, Philadelphia, PA 19107-4103. Call 1-800-553-4539; Fax: 215-636-6312; TDD: 215-751-9655. *Website:* http://www.mhselfhelp.org *E-mail:* info@mhselfhelp.org

Schizophrenics Anonymous *International. 160 groups. Founded 1985.* Organized and run by people with a schizophrenia-related disorder. Offers fellowship, support and information. Focuses on recovery, using a 6-step program, along with medication and professional help. Weekly meetings and newsletters. Provides assistance in starting and maintaining groups. Write: Schizophrenics Anonymous, c/o National Schizophrenia Foundation, 403 Seymour St., Suite 202, Lansing, MI 48933. Call 517-485-7168 or Consumer Line 1-800-482-9534; Fax: 517-485-7180. *Website:* http://www.nsfoundation.org *E-mail:* info@nsfoundation.org

ONLINE

BPDWORLD *Online.* Mutual support for individuals with borderline personality disorder (BPD) provided through message boards. Started by a person with BPD in England, who has developed the online organization as a non-profit. To view the message boards, click on "How we can help" at top, then "User Forums." *Website:* http://www.bpdworld.org

MENTAL HEALTH FAMILY SUPPORT

(see also mental health consumers, general mental health, toll-free helplines)

STATEWIDE

NAMI NJ (National Alliance on Mental Illness New Jersey) Dedicated to improving the quality of life for people with mental illness and their families. Provides self-help groups, education and advocacy. Provides an array of public education and mental illness awareness activities to create understanding and eradicate the stigma associated with mental illness. For information call 732-940-0991 (day) or 1-866-626-4437. *Website:* http://www.naminj.org *E-mail:* info@naminj.org

ATLANTIC

Family Support Group *Professionally-run.* Mutual support for parents and families of persons diagnosed with both a mental illness and chemical addiction. Sharing of emotional and practical coping skills. Guest speakers. Meets 2nd Thurs., 10am and 4th Thurs., 4:30pm, Mental Health Association, 1127 North New Rd., Absecon. Call Christine Gromadzyn, MSW 609-272-1700 (day). *Website:* http://www.mhaac.org

Family Support Organization *"Parents Supporting Parents"* Provides education and advocacy for parents/caregivers of children with emotional and behavioral challenges. Rap sessions, guest speakers, buddy system, literature, speakers' bureau, newsletter and phone help. Meets 1st and 3rd Wed., 6:30-8:30pm, Atlantic Cape Family Support Organization, Northfield. Call Andrea Burleigh or Sondra Dublinsky 609-485-0575 (day).

Intensive Family Support Services *Professionally-run.* Education and support for families dealing with a family member diagnosed with mental illness. Guest speakers. Meets 2nd Thurs., 10:30am and 4th Thurs., 5:30pm, Mental Health Association, 1147 North New Rd., Absecon. Call 609-272-1700 ext. 301 (day). *Website:* http://www.mhaac.info *E-mail:* cgromadzyn@mhanj.org

NAMI Atlantic County Support and advocacy for families of persons with chronic psychiatric disorders. Offers a 12 week "Family-to-Family" education series. Support group meets 1st Tues., 7pm, Pleasantville Presbyterian Church, 1311 S. Main St., Pleasantville. Call Gary 609-748-9558 (eve) or Gail 609-927-0215 (eve).

BERGEN

Family Support Organization of Bergen County *Professionally-run.* Provides support and advocacy to families and caregivers of children with complex emotional and behavioral challenges. Educational lectures offered. Meets Wed., 7-8:30pm, Family Support Organization of Bergen County, 0-108 29th St., Fair Lawn. Before attending call Lynne Bolson, MSW or Karen Stack 201-796-6209 (day). *Website:* http://www.fsobergen.org

Intensive Family Support Service *Professionally-run.* Support, education, and advocacy for family members of those diagnosed with mental illness. Meets Wed., 7pm, in Oradell. Family Education Workshops meets 3 times/yr., Paramus. Call Nadine Venezia 201-646-0333 (day). *Website:* http://www.cbhcare.com

NAMI Bergen County Support, education, advocacy, information and referral for families of those diagnosed with mental illness. Newsletter. Membership $20/yr. Meets 1st Mon., 8pm, Community Services Building (Museum Building), 327 Ridgewood Ave., Paramus. Call Al Supino 201-635-9595 (day). *Website:* http://www.namibergen.org *E-mail:* namibergen@namibergen.org

NAMI en Espanol of Bergen County *(SPANISH)* Advocacy and support for family and friends of those with a mental illness and for mental health consumers who attend. Meets 3rd Mon., 6:30-8pm, Latin America Institute, 10 Banta Pl., Suite 101, Hackensack. Call Martha Silva 1-888-803-3413. *Website:* http://www.naminj.org *E-mail:* naminjenespanol@msn.com

NAMI Family Organization of Bergen County *Professionally-run.* Provides support, information, education and advocacy to families of those diagnosed with mental illness. Membership $30/year. Guest speakers. Meets 1st Wed., 7-9pm, Care Plus Mental Health Center Inc., 610 Valley Health Plaza, Paramus. Call 201-797-3579 (day).

SMG ~ CAN Connections *Professionally-run.* Provides support and education for parents and professionals involved with a selectively mute child. Rap sessions, guest speakers, literature and phone help. Dues $45/yr. Meets 4th Mon., 12:45-2:30pm, Manito School, 111 Manito Ave., Oakland. Call Gail Kervatt 973-208-1848 (day/eve). *Website:* http://www.selectivemutism.org *E-mail:* kervatt@optonline.net

BURLINGTON

AACT-NOW! of Southern Jersey (African American Community Takes New Outreach Worldwide) Support, education and advocacy for African-American families affected by the mental illness of a loved one. Sponsored by NAMI-NJ. Meets 3rd Wed., 7:30-9:30pm, Parkway Baptist Church, 4 Pennypacker Dr., Willingboro. Call Winifred 609-265-0746 (day).

"I Can Problem Solve" Support Group *Professionally-run.* Support group for parents to help children think and make logical decisions independently. Meets 2nd Mon., 6-8pm, Family Support Organization of Burlington, 774 Eayrestown Rd., Lumberton. Call Russ 609-265-8838.

Intensive Family Support Services *Professionally-run.* Support, information and advocacy for family members and caregivers of an adult relative diagnosed with mental illness. Meets 3rd Thurs., 1:30-3pm, Riverbank Building, Catholic Charities, 114 Delaware Ave., Burlington or 1st Wed., 6-7:30pm, Virtua Memorial Hospital of Burlington County, 175 Madison Ave., Mt. Holly. Call Emmanuel Estacio 609-386-8653 (day).

NAMI Burlington FACE (Family And Consumer Exchange) Mutual support for families and friends of those diagnosed with mental illness. Education, information and referrals. Dues $25 (includes newsletter). Meets 2nd and 4th Mon., 7:30pm, First Presbyterian Church, Moorestown. Call Lucille Klein 609-877-4260, Larry Joyce 856-461-3339 (day) or 609-914-0933 (office). *E-mail:* NAMIFACENJ@aol.com

CAMDEN

Grandparents Raising Grandchildren Support and education for women and men who are caring for their grandchildren struggling with emotional, behavioral and mental challenges. Guest speakers, literature, social, advocacy and buddy system. Meets 4th Mon., 6:30-8:30pm, Holy Trinity Lutheran Church, 325 South Whitehorse Pike, Audubon. Call Marge Varneke 856-547-1620 (eve) or Susan A. Doherty-Funke 856-662-2600 (day).

NAMI - Visions for Tomorrow Workshop and Support Group Workshops and parent support group providing up-to-date information and support to family members with children with mental health challenges. Guest speakers, literature/workbooks and phone support. Meets Mon., 6:30-8:30pm, Camden County Family Support Organization, 23 W. Park Ave., Suite 103-104,

Merchantville. Call Susan A. Doherty-Funke 856-662-2600 (day). *Website:* http://www.nami.org *E-mail:* kbirmingham@camdenfso.org

NAMI of Camden County Support for families and friends of those diagnosed with mental illness. Advocacy, phone help and guest speakers. Meets 2nd and 4th Tues., 7pm, Steininger Behavioral Care Services, 19 East Ormond Ave., Cherry Hill. Call Barbara 856-783-2518 (day) or Gale 856-854-2165. *E-mail:* namiccinj@comcast.com

New Beginnings Support Group - A Chapter of DBSA Mutual support and education for families of persons with mood disorders. Opportunity to discuss successes in dealing with various symptoms. Group meets 1st and 3rd Mon., 7-9pm, Holy Trinity Lutheran Church, 214 N. Warwick Rd., Magnolia. Call Karen 856-451-1240.

CAPE MAY

Family Support Organization *"Parents Supporting Parents"* Support, education, and advocacy for parents/caregivers of children with emotional and behavioral challenges. Rap sessions, guest speakers, buddy system, newsletter and phone support. Meets 4th Wed., 6:30-8:30pm, The Court House Church of Christ, 102 East Pacific Ave., Cape May Court House. Call Andrea Burleigh or Sondra Dublinsky 609-485-0575 (day). *Website:* http://www.famsupport.org *E-mail:* sdublinsky@famsupport.org

IFSS Family Support Group Support and advocacy for families and friends of those diagnosed with mental illness. Rap sessions and guest speakers. Meets 2nd Thurs., 6-7:30pm, Cape Counseling Services, 217 N. Main St., Suite 202, Cape May Court House. Call Samantha Knocke 609-463-0014 ext. 17.

CUMBERLAND

Intensive Family Support Services *Professionally-run.* Information, support and advocacy for family members and caregivers of an adult with major mental illness. Guest speakers and phone help. Meets Thurs., 10am-noon or 2nd, 4th and 5th Tues., 7-9pm, Cumberland County Guidance Center, 2038 Carmel Rd., Millville. Call Diana White 856-825-6810 ext. 286 or Daniel Rickets 856-825-6810 ext. 278 (day).

NAMI Cumberland County *Professionally-run.* Support for families and friends of persons with mental illness. Mutual sharing, education, advocacy, literature, phone help and guest speakers. Dues $23/yr. Meets 3rd Wed., 7:15pm, First Presbyterian Church, 8th and Landis Ave., Vineland. Call 856-691-9234 or 856-794-9987.

ESSEX

Family Resource Center, The *Professionally-run.* Support for family members and significant others of persons with chronic mental/emotional illness. Groups for parents of adults with mental illness. Support groups for siblings and adult offspring meet on a time limited basis. Children and adolescents who have a family member diagnosed with mental illness attend Kids Cope in age appropriate groups at various locations. Meet various times and days. Call 973-509-9777 (day). *Website:* http://www.mhaessex.org

Family Support Organization of Essex County *Professionally-run.* Support for parents raising a child with emotional and behavioral challenges. Guest speakers, literature, newsletter, phone help and speakers bureau. Meets Tues. and Thurs., 6-8pm, Family Support Organization of Essex County, 60 Evergreen Place, Suite 410, East Orange. Call Yvonne Rouse or Hazeline Pilgrim 973-395-1441 (day).

NAMI Essex County Help for families of persons with mental illness by sharing ideas and experiences in a caring atmosphere. Guest speakers, phone help and newsletter. Dues $30/yr. Meets 4th Mon., 7:30pm, 67 S. Fullerton Ave., Montclair. Call Betsy 973-623-7878 (day).

GLOUCESTER

NAMI Gloucester County Mutual support and education for families and friends of persons with mental illness. Advocacy, phone help, literature and professional speakers. Dues $30/yr. Meets 2nd Wed., 7pm, Newpoint Behavioral Health, 1070 Main St., Sewell. Call Domenica Grant 856-423-1217. *Website:* http://community.nj.com/cc/NAMIgloucestercounty

"It is one of those beautiful compensations of this life that no one can sincerely try to help another without helping himself." -- Ralph Waldo Emerson

HUDSON

F.S.O. "I Need You, You Need Me" Parent Group *Professionally-run.* Support for parents raising a child with emotional and/or behavioral challenges. Educational series, advocacy, guest speakers, phone help, literature and buddy system. Meets 1st Tues., 6-8pm, Family Support Organization of Hudson County, 705 Bergen Ave., Jersey City. Call Roslyn Gibbs-Muse 201-915-5140 (day).

NAMI Hudson County Advocacy and support for family and friends of those diagnosed with mental illness. Meets 2nd Tues., 6:30-9pm (except Aug.), 3040 Kennedy Blvd. (entrance on Huron Ave., behind St. John's Church), Jersey City. Before attending call Martha Silva 201-861-0614 or 1-888-803-3413. *E-mail:* NamiHudson@msn.com

NAMI NJ en Espanol of Hudson County *(SPANISH)* Advocacy and support for family and friends of those with a mental illness and for mental health consumers who attend. Meets 1st Wed. (except Aug.), 6:30-8pm, Catholic Community Service Office, 2201 Bergenline Ave., 2nd Floor, Union City. Call Martha Silva 1-888-803-3413. *E-mail:* naminjenespanol@msn.com

HUNTERDON

Families of Persons with Mental Illness Opportunity for families of persons with mental illness to share experiences. Rap sessions, mutual sharing, psycho-education and encouragement. Meets 4th Mon., 6-8pm, Hunterdon Medical Center, 2100 Wescott Dr., 5th Floor, Conference Room, Flemington. Call Cris Maglione 908-788-6401 ext. 3006 or Elaine Howe 908-788-6401 ext. 3029.

Family Support Group Provides support, information and education for families of children and adults with mental illness. Meets 1st and 3rd Mon., 7-8:30pm, Clinton Presbyterian Church, Center St., Clinton. Call Walt Dudzinski 908-638-8034.

Family Support Group *Professionally-run.* Support for parents and caregivers raising a child with emotional and behavioral challenges. Meetings days and times vary, Family Support Organization, 4 Minneakoning Rd., Flemington. Call Stanley Croughter 908-788-8585 (day). *Website:* http://www.fsohsw.org

NAMI Hunterdon County Support and advocacy for persons with mental illness, their families and friends. Dues $30/yr. Meets 2nd Wed., 7pm, Getting Together Center, 162 Route 31, Flemington. Call Walt Dudzinski 908-638-8034.

MERCER

Family Support Organization Women's Group Open discussion for mothers, caregivers and family members of children with emotional, behavioral and/or mental health challenges. Rap sessions. Meets Thurs., 6-7:30pm, YWCA, 127 Academy St., Trenton. Call Evangeline 609-581-6891 (day).

IFSS Family Support Group *Professionally-run.* Support for family members and caregivers of any adult with a mental illness. Guest speakers, phone help and literature. Call Amy Layng 609-396-6788 ext. 236 or Amandalynn Salzman 609-396-6788 ext. 206.

> **Lawrenceville** Meets Mon., 5:30-7pm, Lawrence Road Presbyterian Church, 1039 Lawrence Rd.
>
> **Lawrenceville** Meets Tues., 5:30-7pm, NAMI Mercer, Lawrence Commons, 3371 Brunswick Pike, Suite 124.

NAMI C.A.R.E.S. Kids Support for caregivers of children and adolescents with brain disorders. Rap sessions, guest speakers, educational series, phone help, workshops, literature and newsletter. Families are welcome. Meets 1st Wed., 7:30-9pm, Lawrence Commons, 3371 Brunswick Pike, Suite 124, Lawrenceville. Also 3rd Sat. (call for time and location). Call 609-799-8994 (day). *Website:* http://www.namimercer.org *E-mail:* home@namimercer.org

NAMI Mercer County *Professionally-run.* Mutual support, education and advocacy for families and friends of persons with mental illness. Guest speakers, helpline and newsletter. Dues $38/yr per family/associate member. Meets 3rd Tues., 7:30pm, Lawrenceville Library, Darrah Lane, Lawrenceville. Call 609-799-8994. *Website:* http://www.namimercer.org *E-mail:* home@namimercer.org

MIDDLESEX

CAMHOP-NJ (Chinese Mental Health Self-Help Group) *(BILINGUAL) Professionally-run.* Mutual support group for families and individuals of Chinese origin with mental illnesses. Meets 3rd Tues., 7-8:45pm, NAMI New Jersey, 1562 Route 130, North Brunswick. Call Maggie Luo or Aruna Rao 732-940-0991 (day). *Website:* http://www.naminj.org/programs/camhop/camhop.htm. *E-mail:* namichinesegroup@yahoo.com

Family Support Organization of Middlesex County Support for parents raising a child, age 13 and above, with emotional and behavioral challenges. Guest speakers, literature, newsletter, phone help and buddy system. Meets Mon., 6:30-8:30pm, Family Support Organization of Middlesex County, 1950 Route 27, Suite D, North Brunswick. Call Bryn Schain or Lirie Mulaj 732-940-2837 (day). *Website:* http://www.njfamily.org

NAMI Middlesex County For persons with mental illness and their families to promote improved quality of life for people with severe mental illness. Dues $25/person and $35/family per/yr. Education and advocacy program meets 1st Mon., 7pm, University Behavioral Mental Health Center, 671 Hoes Lane, Room C 101, Piscataway. Coping meeting meets 2nd Thurs., 7pm, IFSS, 1440 How Lane, Suite 2 A, North Brunswick. Call Elizabeth Golden 908-753-1753 or Carol Piekarski 732-297-4959 (eve). *Website:* http://www.naminj.org

NAMI NJ en Espanol of Middlesex County *(SPANISH) Professionally-run.* Support and advocacy for families of those with a mental illness. Call Marti Eisner 732-940-0991. *E-mail:* mceisner@optonline.net

> **New Brunswick** Meets last Thurs., 6:30-8pm, The First Baptist Church of New Brunswick, 226 Hale St.
>
> **Perth Amboy** Meets 3rd Thurs., 6:30-8pm, Christian Centers Ministry, 299 Barclay St. Call Nancy Felix 732-343-3409.

MONMOUTH

Family Support Group Support group for family members of persons age 18+ with a psychiatric diagnosis. Meets twice a month, 6-7:30pm, Community Connections, 75 N. Bath Ave. and Second Ave., Long Branch. Registration required. Call Ron Collier 732-923-5226.

Monmouth Family and Friends Group *Professionally-run.* Mutual help and support group for families and friends of persons who are psychiatrically disabled. Discussions, learning and advocacy for improved services. Educational workshops. Meets 1st and 3rd Tues., noon-1:30pm or 2nd and 4th Tues., 7:30-9pm, Mental Health Association, 59 Broad St., Eatontown. Call 732-542-6422 (day). *Website:* http://www.mentalhealthmonmouth.org *E-mail:* mhamonmouth@verizon.net

NAMI Greater Monmouth Support, education and advocacy for consumers and their families. Guest speakers, literature and mutual sharing. Meets 3rd Tues., 7pm, Lutheran Church of the Good Shepherd, 112 Middletown Rd., Holmdel. Call 732-449-2356.

Parent Support Group Mutual support for parents whose children are experiencing emotional and behavioral problems. Childcare and limited transportation. Rap sessions, guest speakers, literature, phone help and newsletter. Before attending call 732-571-3272.

Howell Meets Wed., 7-9pm, Church of the Master, 110 Salem Hill Rd.

Keansburg Meets Mon., 6:30pm, First United Methodist Church, 21 Church St.

Long Branch Meets Thurs., 7-9pm, Family Based Services Association, 279 Broadway, Suite 400.

Long Branch *(SPANISH)* Meets Wed., 7-9pm, Family Based Services Association, 279 Broadway, Suite 400. Before attending call Ana Salgado 732-713-9027 (day).

Shore Family and Friends for Mental Health *Professionally-run.* Mutual support and education for families and friends of individuals with mental illness. Meets 1st and 3rd Tues., 7:30-9pm, Jersey Shore Medical Center, 1945 Hwy. 33, Neptune. Call Linda Ballin, RNC 732-776-4777 (day) or Dennis Broschart, LCSW 732-776-4176 (day). *E-mail:* lballin@meridianhealth.com

MORRIS

IFSS Family Support Group *Professionally-run.* Support and education for family members or caretakers of individuals with a mental illness. Meets Wed., 7:00pm, Saint Clare's Behavioral Health Center, 50 Morris Ave., Room 320, Denville. Call 973-625-7131 (day).

IFSS Parent Support Group Education and support for parents of adults with depression or bipolar illness. Meets 4th Thurs., 7pm, Saint Clare's Behavioral Health Center, 50 Morris Ave., Room 320, Denville. Call 973-625-7095 (day).

Kids Cope *Professionally-run.* Support for children (ages 3-17) whose lives have been impacted by a family member with a mental illness. Children groups are separated into different age groups. Groups provide mutual sharing, art and games to encourage social interaction. Groups are time limited. Meets at St. Clare's Behavioral Health Center, Room 320, 50 Morris Ave., Denville. Call 973-625-7069.

NAMI Concerned Families of Greystone *Professionally-run.* Advocacy and support for family and friends of persons with mental illness. Provides literature, advocacy, guest speakers and mutual sharing. Dues $5/yr. Meets 4th Tues. (except July/Aug.), 6:30-8:30pm, Greystone Hospital, Main Building, Boardroom, Central Ave., Greystone Park. Call Dorothy Thaller 973-386-1845.

NAMI Morris County Support and advocacy for families of persons with chronic psychiatric disorders. Educational series. Meets 3rd Mon., 7:30pm, St. Francis Residential, 122 Diamond Spring Rd., Community Room, Denville. Call Eileen Griffith 908-879-5687.

Parents Connecting Mutual support for parents of children up to the age of 22 with juvenile bipolar, anxiety and other mood disorders. Families welcome. Rap sessions and guest speakers. Meets 1st and 3rd Mon., 7:15-9pm, Redeemer Lutheran Church, 203 Eyland Ave. and Unneberg Ave., Succasunna. Call 973-927-0383. *E-mail:* parentsconnecting@yahoo.com

OCEAN

Family Support Organization *"Parents Supporting Parents"* Support, education and advocacy for parents/caregivers of children with emotional and behavioral challenges. Rap sessions and guest speakers. Meets 4th Tues., 7-9pm, Ocean County Family Support Organization, 44 Washington St., Suite 2A, Toms River. Call Maria Cruz 732-281-5770 (day).

NAMI Ocean County *Professionally-run.* Support, education, socialization, advocacy, coping and support for families and friends of those diagnosed with mental illness. Dues $23/yr (can be waived). Meets 2nd Wed., 6:30pm (speaker) and 8-9pm (group), Ocean County Complex, Hooper Ave. and Madison Ave., 2nd Level Cafeteria, Toms River. Call Mary 732-886-7461 (day).

PASSAIC

Family Circle Support Group *Professionally-run.* Mutual support for families living with a relative who has a mental illness. Provides an opportunity to share experiences with others. Guest speakers. Meets 2nd and 4th Wed., 7-8:30pm, Mental Health Association, 404 Clifton Ave., Clifton. Call Julia Miller 973-478-4444 ext. 13.

Family Support Organization of Passaic County Support for parents and caregivers raising a child with emotional and behavioral challenges. Call 973-427-0100. *Website:* http://www.fso-pc.org

North Haledon *(SPANISH)* Meets 1st and 3rd Tues., 7-8:30pm, Family Support Organization of Passaic County, 810 Belmont Ave., 2nd Floor.

North Haledon Meets 2nd and 4th Wed., 7-8:30pm, Family Support Organization of Passaic County, 810 Belmont Ave., 2nd Floor.

NAMI - Families In Quest *Professionally-run.* For families and friends of persons with mental illness. Mutual support, advocacy and exchange of information. Meets 1st Tues., 7:30pm, Mental Health Association, 404 Clifton Ave., 1st Floor, Clifton. Call 973-478-4444 (day) or Edward 973-773-5112.

NAMI NJ en Espanol of Passaic County *(SPANISH)* Mutual support for Latino families of persons with mental illness. Meets 3rd Tues., 6:30pm, St. Anthony of Padua Church, 101-103 Myrtle Ave, Passaic. Call Martha Silva 1-888-803-3413.

SALEM

NAMI Salem County Mutual sharing, understanding, discussion of problems and education for families of those diagnosed with mental illness. All welcome. Meets 1st Wed., 7pm, Union Presbyterian Church, Carneys Point. Call Virginia 856-769-2492 (day/eve). *E-mail:* saullnami@aol.com

SOMERSET

AACT-NOW! of Central Jersey (African American Community Takes New Outreach Worldwide) Support, education and advocacy for African-American families affected by the mental health illness of a loved one. Sponsored by NAMI-NJ. Meets 4th Thurs., 6-8pm, First Baptist Church of Lincoln Gardens, 771 Somerset St., Somerset. Call Cynthia Miles 732-490-0991 (day).

NAMI Somerset County Education, advocacy and mutual support for families of persons with mental illness. Dues $25/yr. Meets 1st Thurs., business meeting, 7pm and Coping meeting, 7:30pm, Richard Hall Mental Health Center, Bridgewater. Call Sonja Peterson 908-781-2071 (day) or Helen Campbell 908-359-0321.

SAMHAJ Support for South Asians Mutual support for South Asian (Indians, Pakistanis, Bangladeshi Sri Lankan) families affected by mental illness. Educational series, guest speakers and literature. Meets 1st Thurs., 7-9pm, 84 Cortelyou Lane, Somerset. Call Aruna Rao 732-940-0991 (day). *E-mail:* arao@naminj.org

SUSSEX

NAMI Sussex County Support for families dealing with a loved one's mental illness. Dues $25/yr. Meets 1st Mon., 7pm, Newton Memorial Hospital, Sussex House, Meeting Room, Newton. Call Jane Blackburn 973-875-7802.

UNION

Family Support Group *Professionally-run.* Provides support, information and education for families of adults with mental illness. Meets 1st and 3rd Wed., 7:30pm, Mental Health Association in NJ, 363 Monroe Ave., Kenilworth. Call Joyce Benz 908-272-5309 ext. 106 (day). *Website:* http://www.mhanj.org *E-mail:* jbenz@mhanj.org

NAMI NJ en Espanol of Union County *(SPANISH)* Education, advocacy and support for families of persons with mental illness. Meets 3rd Mon., 6:30pm, Trinitas Hospital, 655 E. Jersey St., 6th Floor, Elizabeth. Call Martha Silva 1-888-803-3413.

NAMI Union County Provides education, information, support and advocacy for persons with mental illness, their families and friends. Meets 4th Tues., 7:30-9:30pm, Osceola Presbyterian Church, 1689 Raritan Rd., Clark. Call NAMI Union 908-233-1628. *E-mail:* nami.union.nj@nami.org

Sibling Support Group *Professionally-run.* Support, information and education for siblings of adults with mental illness. Meets 2nd Wed., 7:30-9pm, Mental Health Association in NJ, 363 Monroe Ave., Kenilworth. Call Joyce Benz 908-272-5309 ext. 106 (day). *Website:* http://www.mhanj.org *E-mail:* jbenz@mhanj.org

Spouse and Partner Support Group Support, information and education for spouses and partners of people with mental illness. Meets 4th Wed., 7:30-9pm, Mental Health Association in NJ, 363 Monroe Ave., Kenilworth. Call Joyce Benz 908-272-5309 ext. 106 (day). *Website:* http://www.mhanj.org *E-mail:* jbenz@mhanj.org

WARREN

IFSS Family Support Group *Professionally-run.* Provides families and friends of adults and youths with a mental illness. Support, mutual sharing, education and guest speakers. Meets 2nd and 4th Tues., 7-8:30pm, Family Guidance Center, 492 Route 57 West, Washington. Call Suzette 908-689-1000 ext. 331 (day).

NAMI Warren County Mutual support and advocacy for families and friends of persons with a mental illness. Dues $25/yr. (can be waived). Meets 1st Wed., 7:30-9pm, St. Joseph Church, 200 Carlton Ave., Washington. Call 908-859-4368 (eve/weekend). *E-mail:* NAMI_Warren_county@NAMI.org

NATIONAL

Adult Children of Multiplicity *International. Founded 1998.* Mission is to provide companionship and back up support for adult children (18+) who had or have a parent with Multiple Personality Disorder or Dissociative Identity Disorder (MPD/DID). Call 415-585-6352 (11am-11:30pm PST). Write: Adult Children of Multiplicity, P.O. Box 12376, San Francisco, CA 94112.

Attachment Disorder Network *National network. Founded 1997.* Support and information for parents and professionals dealing with children with attachment issues or reactive attachment disorder. Newsletter, phone and online support, and referrals. Dues $25 (includes newsletter). Write: ADN, P.O. Box 4104, Overland Park, KS 66204. Call 785-624-6364. *Website:* http://www.radzebra.org *E-mail:* info@radzebra.org

Federation of Families for Children's Mental Health *National. 137 affiliated groups. Founded 1989.* Parent-run organization focused on the needs of children and youth with emotional, behavioral or mental disorders and their families. Guidelines available to help start similar groups. Provides information, advocacy, newsletter and conferences. Local support group information available at website. Write: Federation of Families for Children's Mental Health, 9605 Medical Center Dr., Suite 280, Rockville, MD 20850. Call 240-403-1901; Fax: 240-403-1909. *Website:* http://www.ffcmh.org *E-mail:* ffcmh@ffcmh.org

NAMI (National Alliance on Mental Illness) *National. 1100 groups. Founded 1979.* Has local self-help groups for family members and others affected by serious mental illness; NAMI-CARE groups for mental health consumers; and online community message boards. Focuses on education, advocacy, research and support. Quarterly newsletter. Write: NAMI, Colonial Place Three, Suite 300, 2107

Wilson Blvd., Arlington, VA 22201-3042. Call 1-800-950-6264 (helpline) or 703-524-7600 (day); Fax: 703-524-9094. *Website:* http://www.nami.org

Relatives Project, The *National. 3 affiliated groups. Founded 1994.* Offers self-help groups for families and friends of persons with mental or emotional problems. Helps families and friends deal with troublesome relationships. Teaches coping skills and techniques to manage stress in order to create a peaceful domestic environment. Assistance in starting new groups. Write: Relatives Project, c/o Phyllis Berning, Abraham A. Low Institute, 550 Frontage Rd., Suite 2797, Northfield, IL 60093. Call 847-441-0445; Fax: 847-441-0446. *Website:* http://lowinstitute.org *E-mail:* lowinstitute@aol.com

Schizophrenia Society of Canada *(ENGLISH and FRENCH) National. 110 societies. Founded 1979.* Information, support and advocacy for families and friends of persons with schizophrenia. Public awareness campaigns, advocacy and fund-raising. Newsletters. Guidelines and assistance for starting self-help groups. Information and referrals, phone help, conferences, brochures, handbooks and videos. Write: Schizophrenia Society of Canada, 50 Acadia Ave., Suite 205, Markham, Ontario, L3R OB3, Canada. Call 905-415-2007; Fax: 905-415-2337. *Website:* http://www.schizophrenia.ca *E-mail:* info@schizophrenia.ca

Selective Mutism Foundation Inc *National. Founded 1992.* Pioneering group that offers mutual support for professionals and parents of children with selective mutism or social phobia (a psychiatric anxiety disorder in which children are unable to speak in social situations). Includes social anxiety and shyness. Also open to adults who had or have outgrown, the disorder. Provides information and online support. Website contains DSM revisions, research studies, printable brochures, literature and publications. Write: Carolyn Miller, P.O. Box 13133, Sissonville, WV 25360 or Sue Newman Mercado, P.O. Box 936165, Margate, FL, 33093. *Website:* http://www.selectivemutismfoundation.org *E-mail:* sue@selectivemutismfoundation.org or carolyn@selectivemutismfoundation.org

Sibling Support Project *National. 200 affiliated groups. Founded 1990.* Organization dedicated to the life long concerns of brothers and sisters of children with special health, developmental and mental health concerns. Provides training and technical assistance regarding Sibshops and workshops for school-age siblings. Write: Donald Meyer, 6512 23rd Ave. NW, #213, Seattle, WA 98117. Call 206-297-6368; Fax: 509-752-6789. *Website:* http://www.siblingsupport.org *E-mail:* donmeyer@siblingsupport.org

ONLINE

Adult Children of Narcissists *Online.* Email-based support group for children of narcissistic parents. Offers safe, supportive, nurturing environment to discuss past and present concerns about being raised with a narcissistic parent. *Website:* http://health.groups.yahoo.com/group/AdultChildrenofNarcissists

Attachment Disorder Support Group *Online.* Provides an interactive supportive website for parents, families, friends and professionals concerned with a child's troublesome behavior. Offers message forum, email listserv, general information, educational material and helpful links. *Website:* http://adsg.syix.com

BPD Central *Online.* Provides links to online groups for persons dealing with a loved one with borderline personality disorder. Several mailing lists given for parents, siblings, grandparents and others close to someone with BPD and one group for persons with BPD themselves (BorderPD). *Website:* http://www.bpdcentral.com

Conduct Disorders Parent Message Board *Online. 6592 members. Founded 1995.* Support for parents living with a child with one of the many behavior disorders including: attention deficit hyperactivity disorder, oppositional defiance disorder, conduct disorder, depression and substance abuse. Parents with children of all ages welcome. *Website:* http://www.conductdisorders.com

North American Society for Childhood Onset Schizophrenia (NASCOS) *Online. Founded 2004.* Provides families of children with childhood-onset schizophrenia (onset before age 13) with access to information, discussion forum, email list and a geographical locator in order to find other members in your region. Families and caregivers of older patients, whose onset was during childhood, as well as interested professionals are welcome to join. Write: NASCOS, 88 Briarwood Drive E., Berkeley Heights, NJ 07922. *Website:* http://www.nascos.org; *Email:* info@nascos.org

Selective Mutism Group, The *Online.* Devoted to educating and promoting awareness on selective mutism and other related childhood anxiety disorders. Online support group for parents, teachers and professionals dealing with selective mutism. *Website:* http://selectivemutism.org *E-mail:* sminfo@selectivemutism.org

MENTAL HEALTH (GENERAL)

(see also mental health consumers, specific disorder, toll-free helplines)

STATEWIDE

GROW A mutual self-help group to prevent and recover from depression, anxiety and other mental health problems. Caring and sharing community to attain emotional maturity, personal responsibility and recovery. Meets in various counties in NJ. Write: GROW Center, 4A Iowa Dr., Whiting, NJ 08759. Call 732-350-4800.

BERGEN

Emotions Anonymous 12-Step. Fellowship sharing experiences, hopes and strengths in order to gain better emotional health. Deals with anxiety, fears, anger, depression, etc. Donation $2/mtg. Call Joseph 201-678-3289 (day) or Sam 201-962-8038 (day).

> **Hackensack** Meets Tues. and Thurs., 7:30pm, First Presbyterian Church, 64 Passaic St. and Vanderbeck (use right side entrance), 1st Floor.
>
> **Hackensack** Meets Sat., noon and Sun., 7pm, 200 Passaic St. and Vanderbeck, 3rd Floor (rear entrance).
>
> **Westwood** Meets Mon., 7:30pm, Pascack Valley Hospital, Old Hook Rd., 1st Floor (behind Cafeteria). Call Lea 201-666-1009.

Recovery, Inc. Self-help method of will training. Offers techniques for controlling temperamental behavior and changing attitudes toward nervous symptoms, anxiety, depression and fears. Call 201-612-8153. *Website:* http://www.recovery-inc.org

> **Hasbrouck Heights** Meets Wed., 8pm, First Reformed Church, Washington Place and Burton Ave.
>
> **Ridgewood** Meets Fri., 1:30pm, Christ Church, Cottage Place and Franklin Ave.

"There is more than anger, there is more than sadness, more than terror. There is hope."
--L. Davis & E. Bass, from their book, The Courage to Heal

BURLINGTON

Recovery, Inc. Self-help method of will training. Offers techniques for controlling temperamental behavior and changing attitudes toward nervous symptoms, anxiety, depression and fears. Call 856-848-8715. *Website:* http://www.recovery-inc.org

Marlton Meets Mon., 7pm and Thurs., 7pm, Prince of Peace Lutheran Church, 61 Route 70 East.

Westampton Meets Tues., 7pm, Hampton Hospital, Cafeteria, Rancocas Rd. Call John 856-983-7291.

CAMDEN

Recovery, Inc. Self-help method of will training. Offers techniques for controlling temperamental behavior and changing attitudes toward nervous symptoms, anxiety, depression and fears. Call 856-848-8715. *Website:* http://www.recovery-inc.org

Magnolia Meets Wed., 9:45am, Holy Trinity Lutheran Church, 501 N. Warwick Rd.

Westmont Meets Sat., 11:30am, Starting Point, 215 Highland Ave.

CUMBERLAND

GROW A mutual self-help group to prevent and recover from depression, anxiety and other mental health problems. Caring and sharing community to attain emotional maturity, personal responsibility and recovery.

Vineland Meets Thurs., 7pm, Church of Christian/Missionary Alliance, Main Rd. and Harding Ave., Board Room. Before attending call Rip 856-293-9061.

Vineland Meets 3rd Tues., 1pm, New Horizons Self-Help Center, 63 S. Myrtle St. Before attending call Chris 856-696-8921.

ESSEX

GROW A mutual self-help group to prevent and recover from depression, anxiety and other mental health problems. Caring and sharing community to attain emotional maturity, personal responsibility and recovery. Meets Mon., 4:30pm, 570 Belleville Ave., Belleville. Before attending call Caroline 732-575-5765.

Recovery, Inc. Self-help method of will training. Offers techniques for controlling temperamental behavior and changing attitudes toward nervous symptoms, anxiety, depression and fears. Meets Tues., 8pm, Prospect Presbyterian Church, 646

Prospect St., Maplewood. Call 201-612-8153. *Website:* http://www.recovery-inc.org

GLOUCESTER

Recovery, Inc. Self-help method of will training. Offers techniques for controlling temperamental behavior and changing attitudes toward nervous symptoms, anxiety, depression and fears. Families welcome. Meets Fri., 10-11am, James Johnson Library, 670 Ward Dr., Deptford. Call 856-848-8715. *Website:* http://www.recovery-inc.org

MERCER

GROW A mutual self-help group to prevent and recover from depression, anxiety and other mental health problems. Caring and sharing community to attain emotional maturity, personal responsibility and recovery. Meets Tues., 5:45pm, Reach Out/Speak Out, 121 North Broad St., Trenton. Before attending call Caroline 732-575-5765.

MIDDLESEX

Emotions Anonymous 12-Step. Fellowship sharing experiences, hopes and strengths with each other in order to gain better emotional health. Phone help. Donation. Meets Wed., 7:15pm, Community Presbyterian Church, 75 Glenville Rd. at Blvd. of the Eagles, Edison. Call Paul 908-685-1335 (day/eve) or Carolyn 732-723-1960 (day).

MONMOUTH

Emotions Anonymous Fellowship sharing experiences, hopes and strengths, following the 12-step program, in order to gain better emotional health. Donation $1-2 per week. Meets Sat., noon, Port Monmouth. Call Chris or Lillian 732-495-7453 (day). *E-mail:* graye22@netzero.net

GROW A mutual self-help group to prevent and recover from depression, anxiety and other mental health problems. Caring and sharing community to attain emotional maturity, personal responsibility and recovery.

Freehold Meets Wed., 5:30pm, Freehold Self-Help Center, 17 Bannard St.

Freehold Meets Wed., 7pm, 11 Spring St. Before attending call Nancy 732-350-4800.

Ocean Grove Meets Thurs., 6:45pm, St. Paul's Methodist Church, 80 Embry St., Stokes Room. Before attending call Caroline 973-575-5765.

Youth Partnership Group Peer support and advocacy to empower youth (ages 13-21) with emotional or behavioral challenges. Rap sessions, guest speakers, literature, phone help and newsletter. Meets Tues., 6-8pm, Family Based Services Association, 279 Broadway, Suite 400, Long Branch. Call Tamara 732-571-3272 (day).

OCEAN

GROW A mutual self-help group to prevent and recover from depression, anxiety and other mental health problems. Caring and sharing community to attain emotional maturity, personal responsibility and recovery.

Brick Meets Thurs., 4pm, Brick Presbyterian Church, 111 Drum Point Rd. Before attending call Lisa 732-575-5766.

Manchester Meets Thurs., 7:30pm, Redeemer Lutheran Church, 2309 Route 70. Before attending call Nancy 732-350-4800.

Toms River Meets Tues., 5:30pm, Brighter Days Self-Help Center, Route 37 West. Before attending call Nancy 732-350-4800.

Toms River Meets Thurs., 11:30am, Presbyterian Church of Toms River, Hooper Ave. and Chestnut St., River Room. Before attending call Lisa 732-350-4800.

Recovery, Inc. Self-help method of will training. Offers techniques for controlling temperamental behavior and changing attitudes toward nervous symptoms, anxiety, depression and fears. Meets Mon., 7:30pm, Presbyterian Church of Toms River, Hoopers Ave. and Chestnut St., Toms River. Call 201-612-8153. *Website:* http://www.recovery-inc.org

SUSSEX

New Beginning *Professionally-run.* Mutual support to create more peace and balance in your daily living. Donation $5 towards refreshments, literature and space rental. Group meets Tues., 7:30-9:30pm, Partnership for Social Services Family Center, 48 Wyker Rd., Franklin. Call 973-827-4702. *Website:* http://www.partnershipforsocialservices.org

Self-Enhancement Support Group *Professionally-run.* Support for men and women who want to make improvements in their personal lives. Meets Tues.

(except June/July/Aug.), 7:30-9:30pm, Partnership for Social Services Family Center, 48 Wyker Rd., Franklin. Call Dr. Thomasina Gebhard 973-827-4702 (day).

UNION

GROW A mutual self-help group to prevent and recover from depression, anxiety and other mental health problems. Caring and sharing community to attain emotional maturity, personal responsibility and recovery. Before attending call Caroline 732-575-5765.

Elizabeth Meets Wed., 4pm, New Beginnings Self-Help Center, 60 Prince St., Lower Level.

Plainfield Meets Wed., 3:30pm, Self-Help Center, 333 Park Ave.

Recovery, Inc. Self-help method of will training. Offers techniques for controlling temperamental behavior and changing attitudes toward nervous symptoms, anxiety, depression and fears. Call 201-612-8153. *Website:* http://www.recovery-inc.org

Summit Meets Wed., 7:30pm, Central Presbyterian Center, Morris Ave. and Maple St. (parking lot entrance).

Westfield Meets Fri., 8pm, Union County Community Services Building, 300 North Ave. East, 2nd Floor, Conference Room (rear parking lot entrance). Call 201-612-8153. *Website:* http://www.recovery-inc.org

NATIONAL

C.A.I.R. (Changing Attitudes In Recovery) *Model. 30 groups. Founded 1990.* Self-help "family" sharing a common commitment to gain healthy esteem. Includes persons with relationship problems, addictions, mental illness, etc. Offers new techniques and tools that lead to better self-esteem. Assistance in starting groups. Handbook ($9.95), audio tapes and leader's manual. Write: CAIR, c/o Psych. Assoc. Press, 706 13th St., Modesto, CA 95354. Call 209-577-1667 (day); Fax: 209-577-3805. *Website:* http://www.cairforyou.com

Emotions Anonymous *International. 904 chapters. Founded 1971.* Fellowship for people experiencing emotional difficulties. Uses the 12-step program for sharing experiences, strengths and hopes in order to improve emotional health. Books and literature available to new and existing groups. Guidelines available to help start a similar group. Write: E.A., P.O. Box 4245, St. Paul, MN 55104-0245. Call 651-647-9712; Fax: 651-647-1593. *Website:* http://www.emotionsanonymous.org *E-mail:* info@emotionsanonymous.org

GROW in America *International. 143 groups. Founded in 1957.* 12-step group that offers mutual help, friendship, community, education and leadership. Focuses on recovery and personal growth. Open to all including those with mental health issues, depression, anxiety, grief, fears, etc. Write: GROW in America, P.O. Box 3667, Champaign, IL 61826. Call 1-888-741-4760. *E-mail:* growil@sbcglobal.net

HE/SHE Anonymous *National. Founded 1997.* 12-Step. Fellowship that helps members recover from any addictive or abusive behavior. Helps members stay emotionally sober. Groups for adults and adolescents. Deals with any addiction, compulsion, abusive behavior or dysfunction. Write: HE/SHE World Service, P.O. Box 1752, Keene, NH 03431. Call 802-447-4736 (eve). *E-mail:* heshe@adelphia.net

International Association for Clear Thinking *International. 100 chapters. Founded 1970.* Support for people interested in living their lives more effectively and satisfactorily. Uses principles of clear thinking and self-counseling. Offers group handbook, chapter development kit, audio tapes, facilitator leadership training and self-help materials. Write: IACT, P.O. Box 1011, Appleton, WI 54912. Call 920-739-8311; Fax: 920-582-9783.

Pathways To Peace *International. 11 groups. Founded 1998.* Self-help group program for anger management. Offers peer support, education, workbook ($19.95) and assists with starting groups. Write Pathways To Peace, P.O. Box 259, Cassadaga, NY 14718. Call 1-800-775-4212 or 716-595-3886 (voice/fax). *Website:* http://www.pathwaystopeaceinc.com/index.htm#1 *E-mail:* transfrm@netsync.net

Recovery, Inc. *International. 640 groups. Founded 1937.* Mental health self-help organization that offers weekly group meetings for people suffering from various emotional and mental conditions. Principles parallel those found in cognitive-behavioral therapy. Teaches people how to change their thoughts, reactions and behaviors that cause their physical and emotional symptoms. Write: Recovery, Inc., 802 N. Dearborn St., Chicago, IL 60610. Call 312-337-5661; Fax: 312-337-5756. *Website:* http://www.recovery-inc.org

ONLINE

Anger Management Live Chat *Online.* Message board. Offers support and understanding. *Website:* http://www.angermgmt.com

OBSESSIVE-COMPULSIVE DISORDER

STATEWIDE

NJ Affiliate of the OCF, Inc. Mutual support for anyone concerned with obsessive compulsive disorder. Provides quarterly newsletter, referrals to professionals, speakers' bureau, fund-raising, education, socials, support group network, phone help and literature. Provides assistance in starting new groups. Call Ina Spero 732-828-0099 or Dr. Allen Weg 732-390-6694. *Website:* http://www.njocf.org *E-mail:* julina@patmedia.net

BURLINGTON

OCD Support Group Support for persons who suffer from obsessive compulsive disorder. Family members and friends are welcome to attend. Meets 2nd and 4th Mon., 7:30-9pm, Virtua West Hospital, Howe Room, 90 Brick Rd., Marlton. Call Betty 856-751-1957.

ESSEX

Obsessive-Compulsive Support Group Support for persons with obsessive compulsive disorder. Meets 1st and 3rd Thurs., 8-10pm, Mountainside Hospital, Schering-Plough Conference Room #3, 1 Bay Ave., Montclair. Call Nancy 973-472-8215 (eve).

GLOUCESTER

OCD Families Support Group Mutual support and coping skills for families and friends of children and adolescents who suffer from obsessive compulsive disorder. Rap sessions. Meets 1st Sun., 6:30-7:30pm, Underwood Memorial Hospital, Medical Arts Building, Suite 14, 509 North Broad St., Woodbury. Call Rich Bellamente 856-853-2011 (day).

MIDDLESEX

Central NJ Affiliate of the Obsessive Compulsive Foundation Support for any persons concerned with OCD. Provides guest speakers, phone help, literature, newsletter and annual conference. Meets 2nd Mon., (Mar., June, Sept., Dec.), 7-9pm, Robert Wood Johnson Hospital, Medical Education Building, New Brunswick. For meeting information call Ina Spero 732-828-0099.

Rutgers OCD Support Group *Professionally-run.* Group provides support and education for individuals with obsessive compulsive disorder, their families and friends. Donation $1. Meets 1st and 3rd Wed., 7-8:30pm, Rutgers University, 797 Hoes Lane West, Piscataway. Call 732-445-5384 (day).

MONMOUTH

OCA Obsessive-Compulsive Anonymous 12-Step. Fellowship for persons affected by obsessive compulsive disorder. Offers mutual sharing and rap sessions and stories from the Big Book. Meets Wed., 8:15-9:30pm, Prince of Peace Lutheran Church, E. Aldrich Rd., Howell Twp. Call Ron 848-702-5044 (day/eve). *E-mail:* RonnyHugs@aol.com

MORRIS

OCD Support Group Mutual support for persons with obsessive compulsive disorder. Family members are also welcome to attend. Opportunity to discuss techniques and solutions to overcome the disorder. Rap sessions, phone help and literature. Meets 2nd and 4th Wed., 7:45pm, Saint Clare's Hospital, Boonton. Call Diane Walker 862-268-6397 (day/eve). *E-mail:* dewalker@optonline.net

OCEAN

Obsessive Compulsive Anonymous 12-Step. Provides mutual support for individuals recovering from obsessive compulsive disorder. Meets Fri., 8-9:30pm, St. Paul's Methodist Church, 714 Herbertsville Rd., Room # 6, Brick. Call John 732-691-3200.

SOMERSET

Obsessive - Compulsive Disorder Support Group *Professionally-run.* Support, education and coping skills for persons suffering with, or recovering from, obsessive compulsive disorder (including trichotillomania). Families welcome. Meets 3rd Thurs., 7:30pm, Somerset Medical Center, Hamilton Wing, Conference Room, Somerville. Call Joseph Donnellan, M.D. 908-725-5595 (day).

OCD Support Group Mutual support for children and adolescents with obsessive compulsive disorder and their families. Meets 2nd Wed., 7-8:30pm, Richard Hall Community Mental Health Center, 500 North Bridge St., Bridgewater. Call Barbara 908-229-1367. *E-mail:* OCDhelp4kids@yahoo.com

UNION

Obsessive Compulsive Anonymous 12-Step. Provides relief or recovery from obsessive compulsive disorder. Sufferers find fellowship and support by sharing experience, strength and hope. Must have obsessive compulsive disorder to attend meetings. Donations optional. Meets Mon., 7:45-9:15pm, Diamond Hill United Methodist Church, Diamond Hill Rd., Berkley Heights. Call Jim 201-941-8143. *Website:* http://hometown.aol.com/west24th/index.html

NATIONAL

Anxiety Disorders Association of America *National network. 197 groups. Founded 1980.* Promotes the diagnosis and treatment of all anxiety and related disorders including obsessive compulsive disorder, post-traumatic stress disorder, panic disorder, specific phobia, social anxiety disorder and generalized anxiety disorder. Listing of state-by-state local support groups, brochures, information about anxiety disorders, local listing of healthcare professionals providing treatment for anxiety disorders and a national listing of clinical trials provided free. Write: Anxiety Disorders Association of America, 8730 Georgia Ave., Suite 600, Silver Spring, MD 20910. Call 240-485-1001; Fax: 240-485-1035. *Website:* http://www.adaa.org

Obsessive-Compulsive Anonymous *National. 50 affiliated groups. Founded 1988.* 12-Step. Self-help group for people with obsessive-compulsive disorders. Assistance and guidelines available for starting groups. Write: OCA, P.O. Box 215, New Hyde Park, NY 11040. Call 516-739-0662. *Website:* http://members.aol.com/west24th/index.html

Obsessive-Compulsive Foundation, Inc. *International. 9 chapters. Founded 1986.* Support and education for people with obsessive-compulsive and related disorders, their families, friends and professionals. Listings of treatment providers and support groups on the website. Supports research into the causes and effective treatments of these disorders. Bimonthly newsletter, referrals to support groups and treatment centers, annual conference, books, audio and video tapes. Trains mental health professionals in the latest treatment techniques. Write: OCF, P.O. Box 9573, New Haven, CT 06535. Call 203-401-2070 (day); Fax: 203-401-2076. *Website:* http://www.ocfoundation.org *E-mail:* info@ocfoundation.org

Trichotillomania Learning Center *International. Founded 1991.* Information and support to patients, families and professionals about trichotillomania (compulsive hair pulling). Newsletter, information and referrals, annual retreat, conferences, phone support, pen pals and literature. Assistance in starting similar groups. Write: TLC, 207 McPherson St., Santa Cruz, CA 95060. Call 831-457-1004; Fax: 831-426-4383. *Website:* http://www.trich.org *E-mail:* info@trich.org

ONLINE

OCD and Parenting List *Online. Over 1260 families.* Mutual support and information for parents of children with obsessive compulsive disorder through an e-mail discussion group. Professional advisors who respond to questions. Also has an extensive listing of web links. *Website:* http://health.groups.yahoo.com/group/ocdandparenting/ *E-mail:* louisharkins@yahoo.com or louisharkins@gmail.com

Panic Survivor *Online.* Support group for persons who suffer from anxiety, panic attacks, social anxiety, generalized anxiety, post traumatic stress disorder, obsessive compulsive disorder, hypochondria or any other form of anxiety. Focus is on recovery and day-to-day survival with a "can do" attitude. *Website:* http://panicsurvivor.com/

"Each of us is connected to all living things,
whether we are aware of this beautiful fact or not.
And should you ever begin to feel that you are becoming separated from the world,
you are simply self-deceived, for you could no more do this than a wave could separate itself from the ocean and still be a wave."

--Gerald Jampolsky

MISCELLANEOUS

ACCIDENT VICTIMS

NATIONAL

ACCESS (AirCraft Casualty Emotional Support Services) *National network. Founded 1996.* Matches persons who have lost a loved one in an aircraft related tragedy to volunteers who previously experienced a similar loss. Goal is to help fill the void that occurs when the emergency and disaster relief organizations disband, the initial shock subsides and the natural grieving process intensifies. Offers guidelines to help start a similar group. Persons communicate through email or by phone. Online newsletter. Write: ACCESS, 1202 Lexington Ave., #335, New York, NY, 10028. Call 1-877-227-6435. *Website:* http://www.accesshelp.org *E-mail*: info@accesshelp.org

Wings of Light, Inc. *National. 3 support networks. Founded 1995.* Support and information network for individuals whose lives have been touched by aviation accidents. Separate networks for airplane accident survivors, families and friends of persons killed in airplane accidents. Helps individuals involved in the rescue, recovery and investigation of crashes. Information and referrals, phone support. Write: Wings of Light, PMB 448, 16845 N. 29th Ave., Suite 1, Phoenix, AZ 85053. Call 623-516-1115. *Website:* http://www.wingsoflight.org

ONLINE

CRASH Foundation (Citizens for Reliable And Safe Highways) *Online.* Dedicated to providing immediate compassionate support to truck crash survivors and families of truck crash victims. Referrals to grief counseling, medical services and truck crash experts. Phone support, conferences, advocacy, First Response Program and survivors network. Write: CRASH, P.O. Box 14380, Washington, DC 20044-4380. Call 1-888-353-4572; Fax: 202-232-4661. *Website:* http://www.trucksafety.org/ *E-mail*: crash@trucksafety.org

We can also refer callers to over 100 individuals who are seeking others to help start new support groups throughout NJ. Give us a call for more information.
1-800-367-6274

AGING / OLDER PERSONS

(see also caregivers, toll-free helplines)

STATEWIDE

AARP A membership organization for people age 50 and over. Provides information, resources, advocacy, newsletter, offers a wide range of benefits and services for our members. National membership $12.50/yr. Write: AARP - NJ State Office, 101 Rockingham Row, Princeton, NJ 08540-5739. Call 1-866-542-8165 (Mon.-Fri., 9am-5pm). *Website:* http://www.aarp.org/nj

DOROT/University Without Walls Telephone Support Teleconference support groups for persons age 59+ who are coping with vision loss, caregiving, aging issues, etc. There is a $10 registration fee and $15 tuition per support group. Scholarships are available. Write: DOROT, 171 W. 85th St., New York, NY 10024. Call 1-877-819-9147. *Website:* http://www.dorotusa.org

BERGEN

As Life Changes *Professionally-run.* Self-help group designed to support seniors with interpersonal relationship problems. Opportunity for members to share feelings and experiences. Meets Tues., 1:15pm, Southeast Senior Center for Independent Living, 228 Grand Ave., Englewood. Call Laura, MSW 201-569-4080 (Tues. or Thurs.).

Transitions Discussions *Professionally-run.* Support for seniors 60+ to discuss problems of aging, relocation, loss of spouse, friends, health, relationships and children.

Midland Park Meets Mon., 12:30-2pm, Northwest Senior Center. Call 201-445-5690 (day).

Wallington Meets Mon., 10-11:30am, Wallington Senior Center, 24 Union Blvd. Call 973-777-5815 (day).

CAMDEN

70+ Club Support group for men and women age 70+ to enhance coping skills for later life changes. Meets 2nd Tues., 10:30am-noon, Kennedy Center at Voorhees, 1099 White Horse Rd., Voorhees. Call Tanya 856-566-2096 (day) or 1-800-522-1965 (day).

ESSEX

Single in the Suburbs Mutual support for women of any age who are living alone. Group starts periodically and runs for 6 weeks. Registration fee $45. Meets at Linda and Rudy Slucker NCJW Center for Women, Livingston. Call Project GRO 973-994-4994. *Website:* http://www.centerforwomennj.org *E-mail*: centerforwomen@ncjwessex.org

HUDSON

Healthy Aging in Jersey City *Professionally-run.* Education, wellness workshops, health screening, alcohol and substance prevention for women and men age 55 and over. Meets various days and times in Jersey City. Call Crystal 201-795-8178 (day).

OCEAN

Gay and Lesbian Senior Support Group Mutual support for lesbian and gay seniors age 50+ to share common concerns and challenges to reduce sense of isolation. Meets 2nd and 4th Thurs., 5-6:30pm, Community Medical Center, 99 Route 37 West, Toms River. Call 1-800-621-0096 (day). *Website:* http://www.yahoo.com/group/galesseniorsupport *E-mail*: galeseniorsupport@yahoo.com

Senior Support Group *Professionally-run.* Mutual support to share experiences, resources, coping skills and topics of interest for the elderly. Call Rita Sason or Carol Powell 732-363-8010 (Mon.-Thur.). *E-mail*: jfcs@ocjf.org

Brick Social and guest speakers. Meets Thurs., 10-11:30am, Temple Beth Or, 200 Van Zile Rd.

Lakewood Meets Wed., 1-2:30pm, Jewish Family and Children's Services, 301 Madison Ave.

NATIONAL

AARP *National. 4000 chapters. Founded 1958.* Organization for people age 50 and older. Addresses needs and interests through information, education, advocacy and community service which are provided by a network of local chapters and experienced volunteers throughout the country. Offers members a wide range of special benefits and services, including "AARP Magazine" and the monthly "Bulletin." Write: AARP, 601 E St., NW, Washington, DC 20049. Call 1-888-687-2277. *Website:* http://www.aarp.org

Gray Panthers *National. 47 chapters. Founded 1970.* Multigenerational education and advocacy movement/organization which works to bring about fundamental social changes including a national health care system, elimination of all forms of discrimination and economic justice. Newsletter and newspaper. Chapter development guidelines. Dues $20/US; $35/Organization; $40/Internationl. Online site offers referrals to local chapters and useful links. Write: Gray Panthers, 733 15th St., NW, Suite 437, Washington, DC 20005. Call 1-800-280-5362 or 202-737-6637; Fax: 202-737-1160. *Website:* http://www.graypanthers.org *E-mail*: info@graypanthers.org

Older Women's League *National. 60+ chapters. Founded 1980.* Membership organization that advocates on behalf of various economic and social issues for midlife and older women (social security, pension rights, employment, caregiver support, elder abuse, etc.). Newsletter and chapter development guidelines. Dues $25/yr. Write: OWL, 3300 North Fairfax Dr., Suite 218, Arlington, VA 22201. Call 1-800-825-3695; Fax: 703-812-0687. *Website:* http://www.owl-national.org *E-mail*: owlinfo@owl-national.org

ARTISTIC CREATIVITY

CAPE MAY

ARTS Anonymous (Artists Recovering Through the Twelve Steps) A spiritual program based on the 12-steps and 12-traditions of A.A. The only requirement for membership is a desire to fulfill creative potential. Meets Thurs., 9:30am, Cape May County Library, Lower Cape Branch, 2600 Bayshore Rd., Villas. Call Don T. 718-251-3828.

MONMOUTH

ARTS Anonymous (Artists Recovering Through the Twelve Steps) A spiritual program based on the 12-steps and 12-traditions of A.A. The only requirement for membership is a desire to fulfill creative potential. Meets Fri., 10:30am, Monmouth Beach Cultural Center, 128 Ocean Ave., Rte. 36, Monmouth Park. Call Don T. 718-251-3828.

NATIONAL

ARTS Anonymous (Artists Recovering Through the Twelve Steps) *International. 150 affiliated groups. Founded 1984.* Supports individuals in identifying and overcoming challenges to their artistic expression. Through a mix of traditional 12-step tools, literature, weekly meetings, artist-to-artist fellowship, innovative ArtShares and Annual Fellowship Convention, ARTS establishes a safe haven in which to grow, explore, take risks and celebrate the many facets of creativity. Meeting start-up guidelines available. Include self-addressed stamped envelope. Write: ARTS Anonymous, P.O. Box 230175, New York, NY 10023. (For requests outside of NY/NJ/CT area, include $2 with name of nearby cities). For NY/NJ/CT group information, call 212-873-7075 (need a touch tone phone). *Website:* http://www.artsanonymous.org *E-mail*: artseasternregion@yahoo.com

CAREGIVERS / FAMILIES OF NURSING HOME RESIDENTS

(see also alzheimer's, toll-free helplines, specific illness)

STATEWIDE

DOROT/University Without Walls Telephone Support Teleconference support groups for persons age 59+ who are coping with vision loss, caregiving, aging issues, etc. There is a $10 registration fee and $15 tuition per support group. Scholarships are available. Write: DOROT, 171 W. 85th St., New York, NY 10024. Call 1-877-819-9147. *Website:* http://www.dorotusa.org

BERGEN

ARC (Adult Reach Center) *Professionally-run.* Provides emotional support, information and referrals for caregivers. Guest speakers. Meets 2nd Wed., 7:30pm (except Aug.), and 4th Thurs., 11am, JCC on the Palisades, 411 E. Clinton Ave., Tenafly. Call Vivian Green Korner 201-569-7900 ext. 461 (day). *Website:* http://jcconthepalisades.org *E-mail*: Vkorner@jcconthepalisades.org

Caregiver Support Group *Professionally-run.* Provides mutual support for people caring for an ill relative (age 60+). Meets Tues., 10-11am, Northwest Senior Center, 46-50 Center St., Midland Park. Call Sheila Brogan 201-447-5695 (Tues./Wed., 9am-3pm). *E-mail*: sbrogan.nwsrctr@verizon.net

Caregivers Family Support Group *Professionally-run.* Support for caregivers and family members of persons with Alzheimer's or related disorders. Meets 3rd Thurs., 1:30-3pm, Community Services Building, 327 E. Ridgewood Ave., Room 208, Paramus. Call first if requesting professional supervision for frail family member. Call Diana Shapiro 201-634-2822 (day).

Caregivers of the Disabled or Elderly *Professionally-run.* Mutual support, sharing of coping skills and education for persons who are caregivers of elderly or disabled adults. Meets 1st Wed., 1pm, Day-A-Way, Holy Name Hospital,

Community Services Building, 725 Teaneck Rd., Teaneck. Call Ann Marie Cecere, LCSW 201-833-3757 (afternoon).

Well Spouse Group Self-help group for spouses or partners of persons with any type of illness or chronic disability.

Nyack, NY Meets 2nd and 4th Tues., 3:30pm, Nyack Hospital. Call Jeanmarie Grahn 845-634-6885 (day). *E-mail*: norina_o@verizon.net

Teaneck The only way to learn details about meetings is to *E-mail*: anitabluestone@msn.com

BURLINGTON

Caregiver Support Group *Professionally-run.* Support and education for caregivers of older adults. Family, friends and professionals are welcome to attend. Guest speakers, literature and mutual sharing. Meets last Thurs., 7-8:30pm, Senior Care of Delran, 8008 Route 130 N., Building B, Suite 300, Delran. Call Janine Brown 856-461-1700 (day).

Caregivers Support Group *Professionally-run.* Support for anyone caring for an individual with progressive supranuclear palsy, Alzheimer's or Parkinson's disease. Meets 1st Tues., 6:30-7:30pm, Care One at Evesham, 870 East Route 70, Marlton. Call Carol Solomon 856-985-1180 (day).

Families Who Are Hurting Mutual support and encouragement for families who are hurting due to an addiction of a loved one, loss of a spouse or for those caring for a loved one with dementia. Meets 1st Sat., 6pm, Rose of Sharon Lutheran Church, Route 528, Jacobstown. Call Bill Millet 609-758-2746.

CAMDEN

Promised Partners Support Group *Professionally-run.* Support for any caregiver focused on their ongoing needs. Rap sessions, guest speakers, literature and mutual sharing. Meets last Mon. (except July/Aug.), 7pm, Promise Adult Day Health Center, 1149 Marlkress Rd., Cherry Hill. Call Kathy Licardo or Denise Pletcher 856-751-4884 (day).

Senior Care of Voorhees Caregiver Support Group *Professionally-run.* Offers information and support for families or caregivers of any senior. Lecture series, mutual sharing, education and guest speakers. Meets last Thurs., 6-7pm, Senior Care at Voorhees, 1000 Voorhees Dr., Voorhees. Call 856-784-4000 (day).

Well Spouse Association, The Support for a spouse or partner who care for a chronically-ill spouse (MS, Parkinson's, emphysema, diabetes, etc.) to share common feelings and concerns. Meets 2nd Thurs., 7:30pm, Kennedy Memorial Hospital, Chapel Ave. and Cooper Landing Rd., Cherry Hill. Call Judy Baumbach 609-654-5618 (day/eve). *E-mail*: JEBaumbach@JUNO.com

CAPE MAY

Caring for You, Caring for Me *Professionally-run.* Support for those who provide care for family or friends. Discussion, activities, speakers and refreshments. Meets 1st Tues., 1-3pm and 3rd Wed., 7:30-9pm, Burdette Tomlin Memorial Hospital, Two Stone Harbor Blvd., Maruchi Room, Cape May Courthouse. Call Bonnie Kratzer, RN 609-463-4043 (day).

ESSEX

Caregivers of Stroke, Parkinson's and Alzheimer's Patients *Professionally-run.* Mutual support for caregivers of stroke, Parkinson's disease or Alzheimer's disease patients. Sharing of coping skills. Meets 3rd Wed., 1:30-3pm, Care One, 76 Passaic Ave., Livingston. Call Carol Carlson, PhD 973-627-4087 (day).

Caring for an Aging Spouse *Professionally-run.* Discuss complex and emotional caregiving issues with others who share your experience, gain coping skills and take time for you. Meets Fri., 1-2:15pm, Daughters of Israel, 1155 Pleasant Valley Way, West Orange. Call Liz Klapman, LSW 973-467-3300 ext. 231 (day).

Senior Care and Activities Center Support Group *Professionally-run.* Support, education and training for caregivers. Also various special activities series. Meets 1st Tues., 2-3pm or 1st Mon., 7-9pm; also well spouse group meets 2nd Tues., 2-3pm, Senior Care and Activities Center, 110 Greenwood Ave., Montclair. Call Fran Moravick 973-783-5589 (day). *Website:* http://www.seniorcarecenter.org

GLOUCESTER

Circle of Caring *Professionally-run.* Promotes the well-being of caregivers through emotional support and information. Families welcome. Phone help, guest speakers and literature. Meets last Fri., 10am-noon, County Offices at Five Points, 211 County House Rd., Sewell. Call 856-232-4646 ext. 4931 (day).

HUNTERDON

Caregivers Support Group *Professionally-run.* Support for family caregivers of the frail elderly. Meets 1st Thurs., 1-3pm and 3rd Wed., 7-9pm, Hunterdon Medical Center, 4th Floor, Conference Room, 2100 Westcott Drive, Flemington. Also meets 3rd Thurs., 1-3pm, Hunterdon County Library, Clinton. Call 908-788-6401 ext. 3149.

MERCER

Caregiver Support Group *Professionally-run.* Support for those caring for an older adult. Any type of care, including Alzheimer's, Parkinson's, stroke, heart, COPD or other illnesses of aging. Meets 2nd Mon., 1-2:30pm, Princeton Senior Resource Center, Suzanne Patterson Building (behind Borough Hall), 45 Stockton St., Princeton. Call Susan Hoskins 609-924-7108 (day).

Caregivers Support Group *Professionally-run.* (MERCER COUNTY RESIDENTS ONLY) Provides support and education for caregivers who are caring for family members or friends with a serious chronic disease. On-going and short term groups. For meeting day, time and location call Barbara Stender 609-396-6788 ext. 241 (day). *E-mail*: bstender@gtbhc.org

Caregivers Support Group *Professionally-run.* Mutual support for any caregiver. Opportunity to meet others in similar situations, gain valuable information, resources and get emotional support. Guest speakers. Meets 1st Wed., 4-5pm, Saint Lawrence Rehabilitation Center, Outpatient Dept., Room 117, 2381 Lawrenceville Rd., Lawrenceville. Call Doug Behan 609-896-9500 ext. 2279.

Children of Aging Parents *Professionally-run.* Information, education and peer support for adult children who are caring for aging parents near or far. Literature and guest speakers. Meets 3rd Wed., 4:30-6pm, Princeton Senior Resource Center, Suzanne Patterson Bldg. (behind Borough Hall), 45 Stockton St., Princeton. Call Susan Hoskins 609-924-7108 (day).

MIDDLESEX

EARS (Educate, Advocate, Reduce Stress for Caregivers) *Professionally-run.* Mutual support for caregivers of the elderly. Rap sessions, guest speakers, educational series and phone help. Meets 2nd Wed., 1-3pm, UBHC, 100 Metroplex Dr. (on Plainfield Ave.), Suite 200, Edison. Call Susan Schwartz 1-866-300-3277 (day).

Especially For You – Support for the Caregiver *Professionally-run.* Support group exclusively for caregivers, friends, families and spouses who care for someone who is chronically ill. Meets 1st Tues., 7pm, Robert Wood Johnson University Hospital, 1 Robert Wood Johnson Place, BMSCH Conference Room, New Brunswick. Call Community Education 732-418-8110 (day). *E-mail*: esp4yousupport@aol.com

Spouses Caregiver Support Group *Professionally-run.* Mutual support for elderly persons caring for a spouse. Meets 2nd Thurs., 1:30-3pm, St. Peter's Adult Daycare Center, Pondview Plaza, 200 Overlook Dr., Monroe. Call Stephanie Fitzsimmons 1-800-269-7508 ext. 8662 (day).

Strength For Caring Provides support and education to families coping with the emotional strain of caring for a loved one with cancer. Offers literature and mutual sharing. Meets 4th Tues., Cancer Institute of NJ, 195 Little Albany St., New Brunswick. Registration required. Call Brenda Bly 732-235-6027.

MONMOUTH

Well Spouse Association Provides peer-to-peer emotional support for spousal caregivers or significant others who care for a chronically ill or disabled spouse. Quarterly newsletter. Dues $25/yr. Meets 2nd Tues., 7pm, Freehold. Call Donna 732-577-8899 or 1-800-838-0879 (day). *Website:* http://www.wellspouse.org *E-mail*: info@wellspouse.org

MORRIS

Caregivers Support Group *Professionally-run.* Support and sharing of experiences for persons who are caring for the elderly. Rap sessions, guest speakers and educational series. Meets 1st Thurs., 5:30-7:30pm, Morris View Nursing Home, 540 W. Hanover Rd., Morris Plains. Call Carolann Roberto 973-326-7288 (day).

Evening Caregivers Support Group *Professionally-run.* To provide support, information and education to caregivers of dependent adults. Mutual sharing sessions. Meets 2nd Wed., 7-9pm, Time Out Adult Care Center, 4 Division Ave., Madison. Call Ellen Brody 973-822-8006 (day). *Website:* http://www.fsmc.org

"You give but little when you give of your possessions. It is when you give of yourself that you truly give." -- Kahlil Gibran

Muscular Dystrophy Association Caregivers Support Group *Professionally-run.* Mutual support for caregivers of persons with muscular dystrophy. Sharing of information, experiences, ideas and resources. Usually meets 1st Mon., 7-8:30pm, St. Clares Hospital, 400 West Blackwell St., Dover. Pre-registration required. Before attending call 201-843-4452 (day).

Your Aging Parent and You *Professionally-run.* Support and education for those caring for their aging parents. Mutual sharing, education, guest speakers and literature. Fee $15. Meets evenings for 5 week sessions, 2 times per year, Chilton Memorial Hospital, 97 West Parkway, Pompton Plains. Call Joan Beloff 973-831-5167 (day).

OCEAN

Caregiver Support Group Mutual support and encouragement for caregivers of any kind. Provides an opportunity for caregivers to share problems and solutions with others in the same circumstances. Families are welcome. Meets 3rd Tues., 4pm, Sunrise Leisure Village, 1400 Route 70 East, Lakewood. Call Rita Sason or Carol Powell 732-363-8010 (Mon.-Thurs.). *E-mail*: jfcs@ocjf.org

Caregiver Support Group *Professionally-run.* Mutual support for persons who are caring for the elderly or disabled. Literature available. Meets 4th Mon., 7pm, Adult Day Care Center, 591 Lakehurst Rd., Toms River. Call Lisa 732-505-9420 (day).

Caregiver Support Group *Professionally-run.* Provide caregivers with a place to share problems and solutions with others in the same circumstance. Families welcome. Lecture series, rap sessions and guest speakers. Meets 4th Tues., 10-11am, Wellsprings, 525 State Highway 70, Lakewood. Call Rita Sason or Carol Powell 732-363-8010 (Mon.-Thurs.). *E-mail*: jfcs@ocjf.org

PASSAIC

Caregiver's Support Group *Professionally-run.* Mutual support for individuals and families who are the primary caregiver of anyone with any type of dementia. Rap sessions and guest speakers. Lunch provided. Meets last Tues., 11am-12:30pm, Daughters of Miriam, 155 Hazel St., Rothenberg Bldg., Clifton. Call 973-253-5709 (day).

"Do your little bit of good where you are; it's those little bits of good put together that overwhelm the world." -- Desmond Tutu

SALEM

Caregivers Cafe *Professionally-run.* Support through discussions, education, sharing and referrals for caregivers of the aged or disabled at home. Guest speakers. Meets 3rd Wed., 4:30-6:30pm, Fenwick Plaza, Broadway and Walnut St., Salem. Call Melinda Lodge 856-878-6035 (day).

SOMERSET

F.A.R.E. (Friends And Relatives of the Elderly) *Professionally-run.* Mutual support for emotional and practical concerns facing those taking care of an elderly or chronically disabled adult. Call Respite Care 908-766-0180 (day) or FARE Hotline: 908-766-0180 ext. 241. *Website:* http://www.visitingnurse.org

Basking Ridge Meets 4th Mon., 1:30pm, Somerset Hills Adult Day Center, 510 Mt. Airy Rd.

Bridgewater Meets 2nd Wed., 6-7:30 pm, Arbor Glen, 100 Monroe St. Bring your own dinner, dessert and drinks provided.

Well Spouse Group Mutual support for spouses or partners of those with a chronic illness or disability. Rap sessions. Meets 3rd Tues., 7:30pm, Cafe Verona, 53 Mountain Blvd., Warren. Call Mary 908-212-1921 (day).

UNION

Caregivers Support Mutual sharing and support for caregivers of the elderly. Meetings vary, Muhlenberg Regional Medical Center, Adult Day Health Center, Park Ave. and Randolph Rd., Plainfield. Call MRMC Adult Day Health Center 908-668-2328.

Caretakers of the Elderly Support Group Mutual support for people responsible for caring for an elderly family member. Assists through group discussions. Meets 1st Mon., 8pm, St. Helen's Parish Center, 1600 Rahway Ave., Westfield. Call Marilyn Ryan 908-232-1867 (day).

C.O.O.P. (Children Of Older Parents) Mutual support for adult children of elderly persons. Information, sharing, discussions of feelings and problems. Guest speakers and phone help. Meets last Wed., 7pm, Cranford Community Center, Walnut Ave., Cranford. Call Jo D'Arcangelo 908-276-9206 (day) or Reggi Bleemer 908-272-6731. *E-mail*: regmel@aol.com

Engel Center Support Group *Professionally-run.* Support group for caregivers of the elderly. Sharing of information and experiences. Meets 2nd Wed., noon-1:30pm, 505 South Ave. East, Cranford. Call Hazel Garlic 908-497-3945 or 908-497-3944 (day).

P.R.E.P. (People Responsible for Elderly Persons) *Professionally-run.* Mutual support and education for caregivers of elderly people. Meets 3rd Wed., 7-9pm, SAGE Eldercare, 290 Broad St., Summit. Call Ellen McNally 908-598-5509 (day). *Website:* http://www.sageeldercare.org

NATIONAL

CAPS (Children of Aging Parents) *National. 65 groups. Founded 1977.* Non-profit membership organization dedicated to the needs of caregivers of the elderly. National network of support and offers information, referral and counseling. Write: CAPS, P.O. Box 167 Richboro, PA, 18954. Call 1-800-227-7294 or 215-355-6611. *Website:* http://www.CAPS4caregivers.org *E-mail*: admin@caps4caregivers.org

ElderCare Rights Alliance *Statewide model. Founded 1972.* Promotes the principles of justice and dignity in the long-term care system through education, advocacy and action. Individual advocacy, crime victim support, family caregiver training, nursing home Resident and Family Councils and community education. Write: ElderCare Rights Alliance, 2626 E. 82nd St., Suite 230, Bloomington, MN 55425. Call 1-800-893-4055 or 952-854-7304; Fax: 952-854-8535. *Website:* http://www.eldercarerights.org *E-mail*: thyder@eldercarerights.org

National Family Caregivers Association *National. Founded 1992.* Dedicated to improving the quality of life for family caregivers through support and validation, education, information, public awareness and advocacy. Information and referrals, quarterly newsletter, resources and literature. Write: National Family Caregivers Association, 10400 Connecticut Ave., Suite 500, Kensington, MD 20895-3944. Call 301-942-6430 or 1-800-896-3650. *Website:* http://www.thefamilycaregiver.org *E-mail*: info@thefamilycaregiver.org

Well Spouse Association *International. 60+ affiliated groups. Founded 1988.* Provides emotional support and information to spousal caregivers of the chronically ill and/or disabled through support groups, round robins, mentor programs, online chat forum, respite weekends, national conference and a quarterly newsletter. $25/yr but can be waived. Guidelines and assistance available for starting new groups. Write: Well Spouse Association, 63 West

Main St., Suite H, Freehold, NJ 07728. Call 1-800-838-0879 or 732-577-8899; Fax: 732-577-8644. *Website:* http://www.wellspouse.org *E-mail*: info@wellspouse.org

ONLINE

ElderCare *Online. Founded 1997.* Provides daily support for caregivers. Biweekly email newsletter includes articles, news releases, self-care tips, etc. Online chats and message boards covering a broad range of topics. Some chat rooms are run by authors and professionals. Offers software for medical planners and taxes. *Website:* http://www.ec-online.net *E-mail*: rich@ec-online.net or info@ec-online.net

Family Caregiver Alliance *Online.* Unmoderated listserv for caregivers to share strategies, information, education, support and ideas with each other. Provides free fact sheets, newsletter. Write: Family Caregiver Alliance, 180 Montgomery St., Suite 1100, San Francisco, CA 94104. Call 1-800-445-8106; Fax: 415-434-3508. *Website:* http://www.caregiver.org *E-mail*: info@caregiver.org

CRIME VICTIMS / OFFENDERS

(see also toll-free helplines, spouse abuse, sexual abuse)

STATEWIDE

MADD (Mothers Against Drunk Driving) Mission is to stop drunk driving and prevent underage drinking. Offers support for the victims of this violent crime. Has 11 chapter locations in NJ. Call 609-585-7233 (day), the victim hotline 1-800-448-6233 (day) or the 24 hour helpline 1-877-683-3435. Write: MADD, P.O. Box 5085, Trenton, NJ 08638. *Website:* http://www.madd.org/nj

BERGEN

END DWI Support for victims of drunk driving crashes in Bergen/Hudson counties. Aims to prevent drunk driving crashes. Helps victims through the court system. Phone support. Regular membership dues $20/individual; $35/family; $10/senior citizens; free for victims. Meets 1st Thurs., Bogota. Call 201-525-5414 (day). *Website:* http://www.enddwi.com

Need help finding a specific group? Give us a call – we're here to help!
Call 1-800-367-6274

BURLINGTON

Helping Hand Grief Support Group Christian-based support for someone bereaving the loss of a loved one (including death of a child, loss to homicide, or suicide) through education, encouragement, counseling and understanding. Families welcome. Meets 1st and 3rd Mon. 7-9pm, (10 week sessions), Fellowship Alliance Chapel (log house in back of church), 199 Church Rd., Medford. Call Wanda and George Stein 609-953-7333 ext. 309 (day/eve).

ESSEX

Prisoners Resource Center (ESSEX COUNTY RESIDENTS ONLY) Provides support for prisoners, ex-offenders and their families. Assists ex-offenders with resolving issues of re-entry, employment, educational and vocational opportunities, counseling, advocacy, detoxification programs, resume writing and family crisis intervention. Meets Mon., 10am, 89 Market St., 6th Floor, Newark. Call Prisoners Resource Center 973-643-2205 (day).

RAP (Reality After Prison) Group *Professionally-run.* Rap group for ex-offenders to discuss issues relating to re-entry struggles and living healthy lives in the community. Guest speakers and literature. Meets 2nd Wed., 5-7pm, 155 Washington St., Newark. Call 1-800-433-0254 (day).

HUDSON

Keeping It Real Community Outreach Mutual support program to aid females in their transition from incarceration or addiction to productive lifestyles. Rap sessions, literature, phone help, speakers' bureau, newsletter and guest speakers. Meetings vary, Jersey City. Call Marsha 201-433-9113 (eve); Fax: 201-433-8295.

HUNTERSON

Parents of Murdered Children Support for parents who have survived murder or homicide to come together and share their experiences and pain. Meets 3rd Thurs., 7-9pm, Family Support Organization, 4 Minneakoning Rd., 2nd Floor, Flemington. Call 732-227-1023. *E-mail*: stanley184@patmedia.net

"There is no power greater than right action in the present moment."
-- Yaga Vasistha

MONMOUTH

New Jersey CASA (Cleptomaniacs And Shoplifters Anonymous) Provides a safe, confidential and non-judgmental space for compassion, understanding and recovery from "addictive-compulsive" dishonest behavior, primarily shoplifting. Meets Tues., in Freehold. *E-mail*: casanj@aol.com

MORRIS

Shoplifters Anonymous Support for recovering shoplifters and other persons suffering from dishonesty related to fraud, stealing or cheating. Meetings vary, 7-8:30pm, Saint Clare's Hospital, 400 West Blackwell St., 1st Floor, Conference Room, Dover. Call Elsie 973-691-5857.

PASSAIC

Life Support Discussion Spiritual group to help victims of violence reclaim their lives. Goal is to reach out to all victims (including sexual assault, domestic violence, families of incarcerated and homicide victims) to provide words of encouragement to help them become survivors; then advocates. Meets alternate Sat., 4-6pm, Paterson. For meeting information call Elizabeth 973-881-2500 (day); 973-264-5032 (cell) or Rose 973-696-1493 (eve).

SOMERSET

Parents of Murdered Children Support group for parents who have survived murder or homicide to come together, share their experiences and pain. Meets 1st Mon., 7-9pm, Somerset Baptist Church, 9 Pershing Ave., Somerset. Call 732-227-1023. *E-mail:* stanley184@patmedia.net

UNION

Homicide Survivors *Professionally-run.* Provides support to family members and friends of homicide victims. Rap sessions and guest speakers. Meets 3rd Mon. (except July/Aug.), 7:15-9pm, Robert Wood Johnson Hospital, Rahway. Call Elaine O'Neal 908-527-4596 (day).

Outmate Outreach Support, discussions and sharing of information for wives and girlfriends of prison inmates. Meets 3rd Sat., 9-11am, Resurrection Temple Church, 1229 Spruce St., Roselle. Call Reverend Holmes 908-620-0470 (day) or 908-456-3928 (eve).

Parents of Murdered Children Support for parents who have survived murder or homicide to come together and share their experiences and pain. Meets 2nd Tues., 7-9pm, First Baptist Church, 100 High St., Cranford. Call 732-227-1023. *E-mail:* stanley184@patmedia.net

NATIONAL

C.A.S.A. (Cleptomaniacs And Shoplifters Anonymous) *National. Founded 1992.* 12-Step. Secular support group for recovering shoplifters, kleptomaniacs and other persons suffering from dishonesty related to fraud, stealing or cheating. Pen pals, information, referrals and phone support. Offers online chat room and e-group. Assistance in starting similar groups. Include self-addressed stamped envelope. Write: C.A.S.A, c/o Terry S., P.O. Box 250008, Franklin, MI 48025. Call 248-358-8508. *Website:* http://www.shopliftersanonymous.com or http://www.shopacholicsanonymous.org *E-mail*: SA2006V@aol.com

MADD (Mothers Against Drunk Driving) *National. 600+ chapters. Founded 1980.* Mission of MADD is to stop drunk driving, support victims of this violent crime and prevent underage drinking. Write: MADD, 511 E. John Carpenter Freeway, Suite 700, Irving, TX 75062-8187. Call 214-744-6233; 1-800-438-6233 (general information); 1-877-623-3435 (victim/survivor hotline); Fax: 972-869-2206. *Website:* http://www.madd.org

Molesters Anonymous *Founded 1985.* Provides support with anonymity and confidentiality for men who molest children. Use of "thought stoppage" technique and buddy system. Groups are initiated by a professional but become member-run. Group development manual $9.95. Write: Jerry Goffman, PhD, 1040 S. Mt. Vernon Ave., G-306, Colton, CA 92324. Call Dr. Jerry Goffman 951-312-1041; Fax: 909-370-0438. *E-mail*: jerrygoffman@hotmail.com

National Organization for Victim Assistance *National. 2300 members. Founded 1975.* Support and advocacy for victims and survivors of violent crimes and disasters. Newsletter, information, referrals, phone help, conferences, crisis response training and group development guidelines. Referrals to local self-help groups. Dues $35/ind; $125/org. Write: NOVA, 510 King St., Suite 424, Alexandria, VA 22314. Call 703-535-6682 or 1-800-879-6682 (victim referral line); Fax: 703-535-5500. *Website:* http://www.try-nova.org *E-mail*: nova@try-nova.org

National Organization of Parents of Murdered Children *National. 230 chapters in the US, Canada and Costa Rica. Founded 1978.* Provides self-help groups to support persons who survived the violent death of someone close. Newsletter and guidelines for starting local chapters. Court accompaniment also provided in many areas. Parole Block Program and Second Opinion Service are also available. Write: POMC, 100 E. 8th St., B-41, Cincinnati, OH 45202. Call 1-888-818-7662 or 513-721-5683 (office); Fax: 513-345-4489. *Website:* http://www.pomc.com *E-mail*: NatlPOMC@aol.com

RID (Remove Intoxicated Drivers) *National. 152 chapters in 41 states. Founded 1978.* Citizens' project organized to advocate against drunk driving, educate the public, reform legislation and aid victims of drunk driving. Newsletter. Chapter information kit ($20). For descriptive pamphlet send self-addressed stamped envelope. Write: RID, c/o Doris Aiken, P.O. Box 520, Schenectady, NY 12301. Call 518-370-4917; Fax: 518-370-4917. *Website:* http://www.rid-usa.org *E-mail*: dwi@rid-usa.org

ONLINE

Families-of-Inmates *Online. 752 members. Founded 1998.* Email list for people with loved ones in jail or prison, who "support each other through the rough times." Offers public and subscribers only chat rooms. *Website:* http://groups.yahoo.com/group/Families-of-inmates

Prison Talk *Online. 87,000+ members.* Support for families of inmates. Also offers support to the incarcerated. Offers advocacy, education and mutual support. *Website:* http://www.prisontalk.com/forums/

Take Root *Online. Founded 2000.* Peer support for adult children (age 18+) who were abducted as a child by a parent or family member. Offers literature, information, referrals, newsletter, peer support and advocacy. Write: Take Root, P.O. Box 930, Kalama, WA 98625. Call 1-800-766-8674. *Website:* http://www.takeroot.org *E-mail*: liss@takeroot.org

CULTS

STATEWIDE

Cult Information Service Public education about destructive mind control cults. Mutual support for families and friends of cult members and teenagers involved. Group meets in Teaneck. Helps cult members return to society. Write: Cult Information Service, P.O. Box 867, Teaneck, NJ 07666. Call 201-833-1212 (day) or 201-833-0817.

"Clinging to the past is the problem. Embracing change is the answer."
-- Gloria Steinem

NATIONAL

reFOCUS (recovering FOrmer CUltists Support) *National network. Founded 1984.* Support for former members of closed, high demand groups, relationships or cults. Referrals to other former cult members by group and/or area, support groups, therapists and services. Literature, free internet newsletter, recovery workshops and conferences. Write: reFOCUS, P.O. Box 2180, Flagler Beach, FL 32136. Call 386-439-7541; Fax: 386-439-7537. *Website:* http://www.refocus.org *E-mail*: refocuscarol@att.net

EMPLOYMENT / RETIREMENT

(see also toll-free helplines, women)

BERGEN

Employment Peer Support Provides support to those that are unemployed. Meets Mon., 8pm, Church of the Presentation, 271 West Saddle River Rd., Upper Saddle River. Call 201-327-1313.

Job Support Group *Professionally-run.* Exchange of job hunting experience, "hands-on" skills of resume development, networking, interviewing and prayer support. Meets Thurs., 7:30-9pm, 228 Vittorio Court, Park Ridge. Call Bob Miller 201-391-0657 (day/eve). *E-mail*: RJJMiller@optonline.net

Professional Service Group *Professionally-run.* Mutual support to help unemployed and underemployed professional-level job seekers develop leads, learn effective job search techniques and network. Meets various times, NJ State Employment Service, 60 State St., Hackensack. Call Bruce Lauber 201-329-9600 ext. 5755 (day); Fax: 201-996-8884. *Website:* http://wnjpin.net

ESSEX

Job Seekers of Montclair Mutual support and education for people seeking a new job or in career transition.. Meets Wed., 7:30-9:15pm, St. Luke's Church, 73 South Fullerton Ave., Montclair. Call 973-783-3442. *Website:* http://www.jobseekersofmontclair.org

HUDSON

Women's Project Groups *Professionally-run.* Education, support, workshops and groups to help women on subjects such as self-esteem, domestic violence, employment and stress management. Meets various days and times, Christ

Hospital, 176 Palisade Ave., Jersey City. Call Michele Bernstein 201-795-8375 ext. 8416 (day).

MERCER

Jobseekers Education, support and networking for unemployed people and those who are changing jobs or careers. Meets Tues., 7:30pm, Trinity Church, 33 Mercer St., Princeton. Call the church office 609-924-2277 (day). *Website:* http://www.trinityprinceton.org (click on "Job Seekers")

MORRIS

Professional Services Group *Professionally-run.* Self-help organization, sponsored by the New Jersey Department of Labor, for professional-level job seekers. Meets Wed., 9am (new member orientation Wed., 1pm), Dover Employment Service, 107 Bassett Highway, Dover. Call 973-361-1034 (9am-4pm) or Cindy 973-361-9050. *Website:* http://www.wnjpin.net

SOMERSET

JANUS Bereavement Group *Professionally-run.* Support and education for anyone who has experienced a loss such as a loss of a job, retirement, relocation, separation/divorce or death. Helps individuals accept and adjust to the loss. Meets 2nd Tues., 7:30-9pm, in Bridgewater and Branchburg. Call Barbara Ronca, LCSW 908-218-9062 (Mon.-Fri., 9am-3pm).

Jobseekers *Professionally-run.* Mutual support and encouragement for persons who are unemployed, underemployed or seeking a career change. Guest speakers and literature. Meets monthly, 7-9pm, Jewish Family Service, 150-A West High St., Somerville. Call Elise Prezant 908-725-7799 (day). *E-mail*: elise.prezant@verizon.net

Somerset Hills YMCA - Career Forum Mutual support for individuals seeking a career/job change or early retirement. For those who are underemployed or unemployed. Meets Tues., 7:30pm, Somerset Hills YMCA, 140 Mt. Airy Rd., Basking Ridge. Call 908-766-7898 (day).

"If you keep on doing what you've always done, you'll keep on getting what you've always got." -- *W.L. Bateman*

SUSSEX

OLL Job Networking Group Provides job seeking skills, strategies, networking contacts, leads, referrals, tips and techniques to aid in job search. For those who are unemployed, underemployed or concerned about current job. Also for human resource, managing or hiring professionals interested in sharing helpful advice and experiences. Guest speakers and phone help. Meets 2nd Wed., 6:30pm, Our Lady of the Lake Parish, 294 Sparta Ave., Conference Room, Sparta. Call Frank 973-300-1010 (day). *Website:* http://www.ourladyofthelake.org

NATIONAL

9 to 5, National Association of Working Women *National. 24 chapters. Founded 1973.* Support, advocacy and legislative assistance on issues that affect women who work. Job problem counselors can advise women on how to make changes on their jobs. Dues $25/yr. Phone support, conferences, newsletters and referrals to local groups. Group development guidelines. Write: 9 to 5, 207 E. Buffalo St., #211, Milwaukee, WI 53202. Job Survival Hotline 1-800-522-0925. Call 414-274-0925; Fax: 414-272-2870. *Website:* http://www.9to5.org *E-mail*: 9to5@9to5.org

Business and Professional Women/USA *National. 1300 chapters. Founded 1919.* Organization comprised of working women, who promote workplace equity and provide networking opportunities. Lobbying efforts, tri-annual magazine, periodic publications, resource center and grassroots community action projects. Annual national convention. Local group information available online. Write: Business and Professional Women/USA, 1900 M St., NW, Suite 310, Washington, DC 20036. Call 202-293-1100; Fax: 202-861-0298. *Website:* http://www.bpwusa.org *E-mail*: memberservices@bpwusa.org

Employment Support Center *Model. 1 group in Washington, DC. Founded 1984.* Provides technical assistance for self-help groups for the unemployed, underemployed and persons in transition. Provides leadership training for groups. Sets up new groups and coalitions of job clubs with training and materials. Newsletter. Extensive network of group leaders, employment professionals and job seekers. Provides job bank, consultations, network meetings and programs, small business seminars, self-help and job search sessions. Trains facilitators and provides assistance in starting new groups. "Self-Help Bridge to Employment" manual ($25 pre-paid). Dues $50. Write: ESC, 1556 Wisconsin Ave. NW, Washington, DC 20007. Call 202-628-2919. *Website:* http://www.angelfire.com/biz/jobclubs *E-mail*: escjobclubs@yahoo.com

FOOD BORNE INFECTIOUS DISEASES

ONLINE

S.T.O.P. (Safe Tables Our Priority) *Online. Founded 1993.* Offers support, education and advocacy for victims and family of victims of food borne infectious diseases (E.coli, salmonella listeria, shigella, vibrio and many others). Phone and online networking, newsletter and annual meeting. *Website:* http://www.safetables.org *E-mail*: mail@safetables.org

HOLOCAUST SURVIVORS

BERGEN

Second Generation: Children of Holocaust Survivors Support for children of survivors to discuss and share common experiences. New topic focus every month, discussion, seminar group and guest speaker. Meets 2nd or 3rd Thurs., 7-8:30pm, Jewish Family Service, 1485 Teaneck Rd., Teaneck. Before attending call Amy Bolton or Melody Sandor 201-837-9090 (day). *E-mail*: thelivingroom@jfsbergen.org

HOUSING

STATEWIDE

New Jersey Tenants Organization Works for pro-tenant state legislation. Helps organize local tenants associations. Gives legal guidance to members and fights for tenants' rights. Membership dues $22/individual; different for groups. Membership meeting once a year in alternating towns. Call Bonnie Shapiro 201-342-3775 (day). *Website:* http://www.njto.org *E-mail*: info@njto.org

LANDMINE SURVIVORS

NATIONAL

Landmine Survivors Network *International network. Founded 1997.* Created by and for landmine survivors. Links victims in mine-affected countries to a range of rehabilitative services. Provides peer counseling and direct assistance. Promotes social and economic reintegration. Strives to protect future generations from the scourge of landmines. Maintains database of medical facilities, prosthetic clinics and rehabilitation projects who work with landmine survivors and their families. Provides active support network online. Write: Landmine Survivors Network, 2100 M St., NW, Suite 302, Washington, DC 20037. Call

202-464-0007; Fax: 202-464-0011. *Website:* http://www.landminesurvivors.org *E-mail*: info@landminesurvivors.org

LIGHTNING / SHOCK SURVIVORS

NATIONAL

Lightning Strike and Electric Shock Survivors Int'l, Inc. *International network. Founded 1989.* Mutual support for survivors of lightning or electric shock, their families and families of non-survivors. Studies the long-term after-effects. Information and referrals, phone support, annual conferences, help in starting support groups. Newsletter. Books and tapes available. Write: LS and ESSI Inc., P.O. Box 1156, Jacksonville, NC 28541-1156. Call Steve Marshburn, Sr. 910-346-4708; Fax: 910-346-4708. *Website:* http://www.lightning-strike.org *E-mail*: lightning1@ec.rr.com or smarshburnsr@yahoo.com

ONLINE

Lightning Strike Survivor List *Online. Founded 1999.* Online e-mail support group whose members have been affected by a lightning strike. Group members include survivors, family members of survivors, caregivers, doctors and others who want or need a way to share with people who can understand because they have been there. *Website:* http://health.groups.yahoo.com/group/lightningstrike/

MEN'S ISSUES

(see also separation/divorce)

MIDDLESEX

Men's Group Offers mutual support for men. Opportunity for men to discuss issues that are important in their lives. Meets twice a month in various members' homes in Southern Middlesex County. Call Frank Foulkes 609-655-0059 (eve).

MORRIS

Men-To-Men Mutual support for men in transition. Topics include divorce, anger, parenting, health, aging, relationships, etc. Offers networking, phone support and guest speakers. Donation $10 per meeting. Meets Wed., Xavier Center, College of Saint Elizabeth, Convent Station. Before attending call Dale Leffler 732-494-8198. *Website:* http://www.men-to-men.themenscenter.com

SOMERSET

Men Mentoring Men A men's center dedicated to the sharing of a man's unique experience in a complex world through organizing and facilitating peer led men's discussion groups. Literature. Suggested donation $15/mtg. Meets twice a month, 7:30pm, 125 West End Ave., Somerville. Call Richard Horowitz or Jerry Zipkin 908-707-0774. *Website:* http://www.menmentoringmen.org *E-mail*: questions@mthree.org

NATIONAL

Bald-Headed Men of America *National. 6 affiliated groups. Founded 1973.* Self-help group instilling pride in being bald. Offers opportunity to exchange feelings and experiences through group discussions which may lead to acceptance of being bald. "We believe the best cure for baldness is to promote a positive mental attitude...with humor." Newsletter. Write: Bald Headed Men of America, 4102 Plantation Rd., Morehead City, NC 28557. Call 252-726-1823. *Website:* http://www.baldusa.org *E-mail*: jcapps4102@aol.com

NORM (National Organization of Restoring Men) *International. 20 affiliated groups. Founded 1989.* (meetings for *MEN ONLY*; information for all) Provides a safe environment in which men can, without fear of being ridiculed, share their concerns about circumcision/restoration and their desire to be intact and whole again. Confidential discussions of goals and methods of foreskin restoration. Information and referrals, phone support, assistance in starting new groups. Write: NORM, c/o R. Wayne Griffiths, 3205 Northwood Dr., #209, Concord, CA 94520. Call 925-827-4077 (eve). *Website:* http://www.norm.org *E-mail*: waynerobb@aol.com

ONLINE

Menstuff *Online Resource. Founded 1982.* Provides information on variety of local men's groups in USA, Canada and a few other countries. Provides references for guides to starting a group, other resources and links. *Website:* http://www.menstuff.org (click on "Groups" within menu list on left side. Then click on "Men's Groups - Peer Led" or other group). *E-mail*: gordonclay@aol.com

Can't find an appropriate group in your area? The Clearinghouse helps people start groups. Give us a call at 1-800-367-6274

MESSINESS

BERGEN

Clutterers Anonymous 12-Step. Support for persons who have a problem with clutter. Opportunity to share experience, strength and hope with one another in the hope of solving this common problem and helping each other to recover. Meets Mon., 7:30pm, Bogart Memorial Reformed Church, Larch Ave. and West Fort Lee Rd., Bogota. Call Laraine 201-836-5149.

CAMDEN

Clutterers Anonymous 12-Step. Support for persons who have a problem with clutter. Opportunity to share experience, strength and hope with one another in the hope of solving this common problem and helping each other to recover. Meets 1st and 3rd Sat., 11:30am, St. Bartholmew's Church, 1989 Route 70 East, Cherry Hill. Call 1-866-800-3881.

ESSEX

Clutterers Anonymous 12-Step. Support to help overcome compulsive saving, pack ratting, procrastination and cluttering. Donation. Meets Mon., 7:30pm, 21 Dodd St., Bloomfield. Call Aloma 973-748-0423 (day).

MIDDLESEX

Clutterers Anonymous 12-Step. Support for persons who have a problem with clutter. Opportunity to share experience, strength and hope with one another in the hope of solving this common problem and helping each other to recover. Meets Sun., 5pm, St. Luke's Episcopal Church, Middlesex and Oak Ave., Parish Hall, Metuchen. Call Richard 732-548-1419.

PASSAIC

Clutterers Anonymous 12 Step. Support for persons who have a problem with clutter. Opportunity to share experience, strength and hope with one another in the hope of solving this common problem and helping each other to recover. Meets Thurs., 6pm, St. Michael's Episcopal Church, 1219 Ratzer Rd., Room 1, Wayne. Call Peter 908-875-3881.

UNION

Clean Slate Club, The *Professionally-run.* Support and discussion group for individuals struggling with issues relating to clutter. Rap sessions, education and literature series. Meets 2nd Thurs., 7:30-9pm, Mountainside Public Library, Constitution Plaza, Mountainside. Call Ellen 908-403-6217 (day). *E-mail:* clean.slate@att.net

Clutter Club *Professionally-run.* Mutual support for persons who have a problem with clutter. Rap sessions, literature, phone help, newsletter and buddy system. Meets 3rd Mon., 7:30-9pm, Barnes and Noble, Raritan Rd., Clark. Call Jamie 1-866-294-9900. *E-mail*: jamie@jamienovak.com

NATIONAL

Clutterers Anonymous *National. 59 affiliated chapters.* 12-Step. 12-Traditions. Fellowship of individuals who share experience, strength and hope with each other that they may solve their common problem with clutter and help others recover. Based on suggestion, interchange of experience, rotation of leadership and service. The only requirement for membership is a desire to eliminate clutter and bring order into your life. Call 908-875-3881 (EST). *Website:* http://www.clutterersanonymous.net *E-mail*: cla@clutterfreeworld.net

Clutterless Recovery Groups Inc. *National. 6 affiliated groups. Founded 2000.* Support for those persons that find it difficult to discard unwanted possessions. Group uses psychological principles to change behavior. Provides newsletter, literature, information, referrals, conferences and group meeting locations. Also offers online networking. Offers information on starting similar groups. Write: Clutterless, 5413 N. 32nd St., McAllen, TX 78504. Call 512-351-4058. *Website:* http://www.clutterless.org

Messies Anonymous (*MULTILINGUAL*) *National. 100 groups. Founded 1981.* 12-Step. Group that aims to improve the quality of life of disorganized homemakers. Provides motivation and a program for change to help members improve self-image as control of house and life is obtained. Optional donation at meetings. Online newsletter: "The Organizer Lady." Interactive online group. Books and materials available in English, German and Spanish. Send a self-addressed stamped envelope when writing. Write: Messies Anonymous, 5025 SW 114th Avenue, Miami, FL 33165. Call Sandra 305-271-8404; Fax and automated order line: 786-243-2793. *Website:* http://www.messies.com *E-mail*: nestbuilder@earthlink.net

NEAR DEATH EXPERIENCE

NATIONAL

International Association for Near-Death Studies *International. 43 affiliated groups. Founded 1981.* Support and interest groups for anyone who has had a near-death or near-death-like experience or who has personal or professional interest in such experiences. Newsletter, group development guidelines. Write: IANDS, P.O. Box 502, E. Windsor Hill, CT 06028-0502. Call 860-882-1211; Fax: 860-882-1212. *Website:* http://www.iands.org *E-mail*: services@iands.org

NETWORKING FOR ILL / DISABLED

NATIONAL

MUMS National Parent-to-Parent Network *National. 36 affiliated groups. Founded 1979.* Mutual support and networking for parents or care providers of children with any disability, rare disorder, chromosomal abnormality or health conditions using a database of over 20,000 families from 54 countries, covering 3400 disorders, very rare syndromes or undiagnosed conditions. Provides referrals to support groups and assistance in starting groups. Newsletter ($15/parents; $25/professionals). Matching services $5. "Hyperbaric oxygen therapy as a treatment for brain damage" packet, $25. Other literature available. Write: MUMS National Parent-to-Parent Network, 150 Custer Crt., Green Bay, WI 54301-1243. Call 1-877-336-5333 (parents only) or 920-336-5333 (day); Fax: 920-339-0995. *Website:* http://www.netnet.net/mums/ *E-mail*: mums@netnet.net

PATIENT RIGHTS

NATIONAL

New England Patients' Rights Group *Model. Founded 1992.* Mutual support for health care consumers, many of whom are suffering because of deficiencies or negligence in the system. Advocates for consumer empowerment, quality, accurate information, informed consent, insurance needs, patients' rights and protection. Newsletter. Write: New England Patients Rights Group, P.O. Box 141, Norwood, MA 02062. Call 781-769-5720. *Website:* http://www.newenglandpatientsrights.org *E-mail*: neprg@verizon.net

POLICE OFFICERS

ESSEX

Wounded Officers Support Group of NJ *Professionally-run.* Provides support to officers who were wounded in the line of duty. Guest speakers and buddy system. Meets 3rd Wed., 9:30-11:30am, Fraternal Order of Police Building, Lodge #12, 51 Rector St., 2nd Floor Conference Room, Newark. Call Joe Orgo or Fred Mitchell 1-866-267-2267 (day).

PREJUDICE

NATIONAL

Recovering Racists Network *National. Groups in CA, MO and MI. Founded 1997.* Mutual support to help people overcome their everyday racism and prejudice. Newsletter, literature, phone support, conferences, advocacy, anti-racism training, high school Race Awareness Program, online support, information and referral. Assistance in helping others to start similar groups. Write: RRN, c/o John Mc Kenzie, 517 Loon Dr., Petaluma, CA 94954. Call 707-789-9505 or 415-577-8331. *Website:* http://www.rrnet.org *E-mail*: john@jmckenzie.com

PROSTITUTION / SEX INDUSTRY

NATIONAL

PRIDE (from PRostitution to Independence, Dignity and Equality) *Model. One group in Minnesota. Founded 1978.* Provides PRIDE support groups and other services to assist women and children in escaping the sex industry (including prostitution, pornography and stripping). Write: PRIDE, c/o Family and Children Service, 4123 E. Lake St., Minneapolis, MN 55406. Call 612-728-2080. *Website:* http://www.fcsmn.org/pride/

Sexworkers Anonymous *International. 3 affiliated groups. Founded 1987.* 12-Step. Fellowship of men and women who have a desire to leave commercial sex work behind (including prostitution, escorting, pimping, pornography, stripping, phone sex, etc.). Online chat room. Assistance in starting local chapters. Books and videotapes. Write: Sex Workers Anonymous, 3395 S. Jones Blvd., Suite 217, Las Vegas, NV 89146. Call JW 702-987-0239. *Website:* http://www.sexworkersanonymouswso.com *E-mail*: sexworkrecovery@yahoo.com

SELF-ABUSE / SELF-MUTILATION

MORRIS

BSSI (Breaking the Silence of Self-Injury) Christian-based group to provide support for those who cut, burn, or harm their body as a way of coping with overwhelming emotions, thoughts and circumstances. Purpose is to realize that a life can be lived without self-injurious behavior. Guest speakers, discussions, literature and newsletter. Meets 1st and 3rd Fri., 7:15-9:15pm, Living Praise Church, Room 205, 37 Vreeland Rd., Florham Park. Call Vicki Duffy 973-224-4144. *Website:* http://www.endallthepain.com *E-mail*: vicki@endallthepain.com

NATIONAL

Inspiration Support Group *Model.* Support for people who self-injure themselves by cutting or other injury to the body without the intention of ending their life. Helps members recognize "triggers", control their thoughts and solve their problems. Manual and CD with exercises and education materials available. Consultation on group development guidelines ($65 postpaid). Write: Safe In Canada, 611 Wonderland Rd. N., Suite 224, London, Ontario, Canada N6H-5N7. Call 519-657-6570. *Website:* http://www.safeincanada.ca *E-mail*: bjthom_6@yahoo.ca

Self Mutilators Anonymous (SMA) *National. 10 affiliated groups.* 12-Step. Fellowship of men and women who share their experience, strength and hope with each other, that they may solve their common problem and help others recover from physical self mutilation. Information resources. Online self-help group meeting available. *Website:* http://www.selfmutilatorsanonymous.org

ONLINE

Secret Shame: Self Injury Information and Support *Online.* Extensive information resource on self-injury and self-abuse. Resources for how to deal with self-abuse and the self-abuse of family members or friends. Offers web board and separate email lists for self-injurers, their family and friends (email lists are named BUS for "bodies under siege" and are located in the right hand column). Web Board: http://buslist.org *Website:* http://www.selfharm.net

"Don't be afraid if things seem difficult in the beginning. That's only the initial impression. The important thing is not to retreat; you have to master yourself."
-- Olga Korbut

SEPTEMBER 11TH

(see also bereavement, crime victims)

STATEWIDE

Sky Help Inc. "Hope and Healing after Tragedy" Trauma intervention workshops will be offered for any individual or family member directly affected by the Sept. 11th tragedy. The workshops are for anyone who has been extremely impacted by terrorist incidents. Military personnel, emergency service personnel, survivors, witnesses, family members and loved ones of the victims. Confidential three-four day workshops to help cope with the trauma will be offered free of charge (room, meals and activities). Workshops will be in Long Beach Island, NJ. For information or to register call 1-877-759-4357. *Website:* http://www.skyhelp.org

WTC United Family Group, Inc. Support for families who lost a loved one in the World Trade Center attacks and for W.T.C. survivors. Online e-mail groups for both. Families and survivors can register online or write: W.T.C. United Family Group, Inc., 2640 Highway 70, Bldg. 1A, Manasquan, NJ 08736. Call 732-292-2910. *Website:* http://www.wtcufg.org *E-mail*: info@wtcufg.org

BERGEN

W.T.C. Bereavement Support Group *Professionally-run.* Provides emotional support for working through the mourning process of those directly affected by the W.T.C. disaster. Open to anyone affected. Guest speakers, mutual sharing, phone help and literature. Meets Fri., 7-9pm, Pastoral Center, 2nd Floor, Conference Room, St. Catherine's Church, 905 South Maple Ave., Glen Rock. Call Deborah Van Alstine, M.A. 201-444-4915 (eve). *Website:* http://mysite.verizon.net/vze8lw19/ *E-mail*: debvanalstine@optonline.net

MERCER

Sept. 11th Family Support Group Mutual support for adults who lost a family member in the September 11th attacks. Meetings vary, Princeton Junction. Call Carol 609-936-0579.

MORRIS

Healing Hands *Professionally-run.* Art workshop for children (ages 4-11) who have lost a parent or relative in the World Trade Center tragedy. Meetings vary, Morristown. Before attending call Tammy Rosenthal 973-538-5260.

OCEAN

World Trade Center Disaster Victims Support Group Offers support to help focus on the grief process, recovery skills and how recovery is impacted by being a victim of terrorism. Meets at St. Francis Center, 4700 Long Beach Blvd., Brant Beach. Registration required. Call Sue Crane 609-494-1554.

Young Widows' Support Group Provides support and information for young women who lost their husband. Meets 3rd Wed., 7-9pm, Church of St. Luke, 1674 Old Freehold Rd., Toms River. Call Sharyn Cartnick 732-286-2222.

NATIONAL

COPS (Concerns of Police Survivors, Inc.) *National. 48 chapters. Founded 1984.* Provides resources for the surviving families of law enforcement officers killed in the line of duty according to federal criteria. Also offers law enforcement training. Quarterly newsletter, departmental guidelines, peer support. Provides annual National Police Survivors' Conference each May during National Police Week. Special hands-on programs for survivors. Summer camp for children ages 6-14 and their parent/guardian, parents' retreats, spouse get-aways, Outward Bound experiences for young adults ages 15-20, sibling retreat and adult children's retreat. Write: COPS, P.O. Box 3199, South State Highway 5, Camdenton, MO 65020. Call 573-346-4911; Fax: 573-346-1414. *Website:* http://www.nationalcops.org *E-mail*: cops@nationalcops.org

Wings of Light, Inc. *National. 3 support networks. Founded 1995.* Support and information network for individuals whose lives have been touched by aviation accidents. Separate networks for airplane accident survivors, families and friends of persons killed in airplane accidents and persons involved in the rescue, recovery and investigation of crashes. Information and referrals, phone support. Write: Wings of Light, PMB 448, 16845 N. 29th Ave., Suite 1, Phoenix, AZ 85053. Call 623-516-1115. *Website:* http://www.wingsoflight.org

ONLINE

Gift From Within *Online. (WOMEN ONLY)* Offers a one-on-one email//pen pal support network for women who are experiencing post-traumatic stress disorder. Female victims of specific trauma can be matched with survivors of similar PTSD. *Website:* http://www.giftfromwithin.org *E-mail*: Joyceb3955@aol.com

SEXUAL ORIENTATION / GENDER IDENTITY

(see also toll-free helplines, battered lesbian hotline)

STATEWIDE

Gay and Lesbian Political Action and Support Group Provides opportunity for individuals in isolated areas to be politically active and establish support groups where they are needed. Write: GLPASC, P.O. Box 11406, New Brunswick, NJ 08906-1406. For information call 732-744-1370 (day). *Website:* http://www.gaypasg.org *E-mail*: gaypasg@att.net

Rainbow Families of New Jersey Provides support, advocacy and education for gay and lesbian parents, their families and prospective parents. Social activities and quarterly newsletter. Membership dues $35/yr. Write: Rainbow Families of NJ, P.O. Box 1385, Maplewood, NJ 07040. For further information call 973-763-8511 (day/eve). *Website:* http://www.rainbowfamiliesofnj.org

BERGEN

P-FLAG (Parents, Families and Friends of Lesbians and Gays) Support and discussion groups to help people understand and accept homosexuality. Educates society and advocates for full human rights for all, regardless of sexual orientation. Speakers, newsletter and phone help. Membership dues $30/yr. (includes monthly newsletter). All welcome. Meets 3rd Tues., 8pm (7:30pm newcomers), Washington Twp. Call 201-287-0318 (eve). *Website:* http://www.pflag-bergennj.org *E-mail*: info@bergenpflag.org

Straight Spouse Support Network Supports anyone whose current or former partner/spouse is gay, lesbian, transgender or bisexual. Mutual sharing, rap sessions, resources, phone help, regular email correspondence and newsletter (3 times/yr). Donations accepted. Meets 2nd Fri., 6:30-9pm, 61 North Bayard Lane, Mahwah. Call Kathryn Callori 201-825-7512 (eve). *Website:* http://www.ssnetwk.org *E-mail*: SSSNNJ@aol.com

CAMDEN

Coming Out and Family Support Group *Professionally-run.* Mutual support and encouragement for gay, lesbian, bisexual, transgender and questioning individuals. Families welcome. Dinner served. Separate groups for youth-only and general coming out/family groups. Meets bimonthly on various Thurs. (general group on last Thurs.), 6pm, Planned Parenthood of Southern NJ, 317 Broadway, Camden. Call 856-365-3519 ext. 232. *Website:* http://www.ppsnj.org

Keeping It Safe Support for gay, lesbian, bisexual, transgender and questioning individuals under the age of 20 to discuss social, educational, health and sexuality issues in a relaxed environment. Meets Wed., 6-9pm, Camden Area Health Education Center, 514 Cooper St., Camden. Call Damon L. Humes 856-963-2432 (day). *Website*: http://www.camden-ahec.org *E-mail*: humes_d@camden-ahec.org

Pink and Blues Peer Support Group (Gay and Lesbian) Support group for sexual and gender minority people living with a mental illness. Meets Wed., 7pm, St. Luke's and the Epiphany Church, 330 S. 13th St., Philadelphia, PA. Call Mark Davis 215-546-0300 ext. 3301 (day) or 215-627-0424 (eve). *E-mail*: Mark.Davis@Phila.Gov

South Jersey Lesbians of Color Discussion and social support group for lesbians of color (age 21+) in Southern New Jersey. Rap sessions, social and guest speakers. Dues $3 per meeting. Meets 3rd Fri., 7:30-9pm, The Starting Point, 215 Highland Ave., Suite C, Westmont. Call Woo 856-465-6186 (eve). *Website:* http://www.groups.yahoo.com/group/sjloc2006 *E-mail*: sjloc2006-owner@yahoogroups.com

CAPE MAY

Gables of Cape May County Provides support to gays, lesbians and bisexuals, as well as their family and friends. Rap sessions, guest speakers and newsletter. Dues $20/yr. Meets 1st and 3rd Mon., Cape May. Call 609-861-1848 (answer machine). *Website:* http://www.gablescapemay.com *E-mail*: gables00@email.com

ESSEX

Dignity Organization of lesbian, gay and bisexual Catholics, their family and friends. Socials and rap sessions. Meets 1st and 3rd Sun., 4pm, St. George's Episcopal Church, 550 Ridgewood Rd., Maplewood. Call 973-857-4040 (day). *E-mail*: dignitymetronj@msn.com

P-FLAG (Parents, Families and Friends of Lesbians and Gays) Support and discussion groups to help people understand and accept homosexuality. Educates society and advocates for full human rights for all, regardless of sexual orientation. Speakers, newsletter and phone help. All welcome. Membership dues $25/yr individual; $35/yr family. Meets 2nd Sun., 2:30-4:30pm (newcomers 1:30pm), South Orange. Call P-FLAG hotline 973-267-8414. *Website:* http://www.pflagnorthjersey.org

HUDSON

GLITZ (Girls Living In the Transgender Zone) Peer support for women dealing with transgender issues. Rap sessions, guest speakers, literature and phone help. Meets Tues., 6:30-8:30pm, Jersey City. Call Vanessa 201-963-4779.

Youth Connect *Professionally-run.* Support groups and drop-in hours for lesbian, gay, bisexual, transsexual and questioning youth. Guest speakers, social activities, mutual support, rap sessions and literature. Online email discussion group. LGBTQ Youth Support Group meets Fri. and Sat., 3:30-8pm, Jersey City Connections, 34-36 Tones St., Jersey City. Call Guido Sanchez 201-963-4779 (day). *Website:* http://www.hudsonpride.org *E-mail*: jcconnections@aol.com

MERCER

"First and Third" *Professionally-run.* Educational and social support for gay, lesbian, bisexual and transgender youth. Rap sessions, phone help, guest speakers and mutual sharing. Meets 1st and 3rd Sat., 2:30-4:30pm, 21 Wiggins St., Princeton. Call Corrine 609-683-5155 ext. 217 (day). *Website:* http://www.hitops.org *E-mail*: corrine@hitops.org

MIDDLESEX

Lesbian/Bisexual Women in Heterosexual Marriages Support for lesbian/bisexual women who are married to men to deal with feelings of loneliness, guilt and depression. Rap sessions. Meets 3rd Wed., 7:30pm, The Pride Center of NJ, 1048 Livingston Ave., North Brunswick. For meeting information call 732-846-2232. *Website:* http://www.pridecenter.org *E-mail*: info@pridecenter.org

Lesbians and Gay Men of New Brunswick Social and educational group for lesbian women and gay men. Guest speakers and social activities. Meetings $2 donation. Meets 2nd and 4th Tues., 8pm, The Pride Center, 1048 Livingston Ave., North Brunswick. Call 732-846-2232. *Website:* http://www.pridecenter.org *E-mail*: njrj@aol.com

Men's Coming Out Rap Group Assists men dealing with issues pertaining to coming out. Dues $2. Meets Wed., 7:30-9pm, The Pride Center, 1048 Livingston Ave., North Brunswick. Call Gary P. 732-846-2232 (day). *Website:* http://www.pridecenter.org *E-mail*: info@pridecenter.org

Orthodykes - NJ *Professionally-run.* Mutual support for Orthodox Jewish lesbians as they attempt to integrate these two identities. Rap sessions and newsletter. Dues $3. Meets 1st Sun., 7:30-8:30pm, North Brunswick. Call Elissa 732-650-1010 (mailbox # 5). *E-mail*: info@njhav.org

OWLs (Older Wilder Lesbians) Group of mature lesbians who meet for support and socialization. Meets 3rd Fri., 8pm, The Pride Center, 1048 Livingston Ave., North Brunswick. Call 732-846-2232 (day). *Website:* http://www.pridecenter.org *E-mail*: info@pridecenter.org

Together We Can Support and social group for the lesbian, gay, bisexual, transgender and intersex community (age 18+). Provides a safe, honest, open and supportive setting for people dealing with all types of issues. Meets Tues., 7-8:30pm, The Pride Center of NJ, 1048 Livingston Ave., North Brunswick. Call Patricia Hepp, MSW 732-846-2232 or Robert Lord-Taylor, PhD. 732-220-9137. *Website:* http://www.pridecenter.org *E-mail*: info@pridecenter.org

Under the Rainbow Support and socials for lesbian, gay, bisexual, transgender, intersex and questioning young adults (ages 18-25). Meets 1st Wed., 7:30-9pm, The Pride Center, 1048 Livingston Ave., North Brunswick. Call 732-846-2232. *Website:* http://www.pridecenter.org *E-mail*: info@pridecenter.org

Youth Drop-In Center Support and socials for lesbian, gay, bisexual, transgender, intersex and questioning youth (ages 17 and under) and their allies. Meets 2nd and 4th Sat., The Pride Center, 1048 Livingston Ave., North Brunswick. Call 732-846-2232. *Website:* http://www.pridecenter.org *E-mail*: info@pridecenter.org

MORRIS

Gay Activist Alliance in Morris County Educates the lesbian and gay community through speakers and programs, socials and political involvement. Monthly newsletter and speakers' bureau. Publishes resource book. Membership $40/yr. Dues $4/member; $6/non-member. Meets Mon., 8:30pm (7:30pm separate discussion groups for men/women), Morristown Unitarian Fellowship, 21 Normandy Heights Rd., Morristown. *Website:* http://www.gaamc.org *E-mail*: info@gaamc.org

"The best way to cheer yourself up is to try to cheer somebody else up."
-- Mark Twain

OCEAN

Gay and Lesbian Senior Support Group Mutual support for lesbian and gay seniors age 50+ to share common concerns and challenges to reduce sense of isolation. Meets 2nd and 4th Thurs., 5-6:30pm, Community Medical Center, 99 Route 37 West, Toms River. Call 1-800-621-0096 (day). *Website:* http://www.yahoo.com/group/galesseniorsupport *E-mail*: galeseniorsupport@yahoo.com

P-FLAG (Parents, Families and Friends of Lesbians and Gays) Jersey Shore Chapter Support and discussion group to help people understand and accept variance in sexual orientation and gender identity. Educates and advocates for full human rights for all, including sexual minorities. Speakers, literature and phone help. All welcome. Meets 2nd Wed., 7-9pm, United Church of Christ, 1681 Ridgeway Rd. (Route 571), Toms River. Call 908-814-2155 (day). *Website:* http://www.jerseyshorepflag.org or http://www.tomsriverucc.org/directions.htm (for directions) *E-mail*: jerseyshorepflag@yahoo.com

SOMERSET

Transit Fellowship of transsexual men and women who share their experience, strength and hope with each other, that they may solve their common problems and help others heal from the effects of gender identity conflicts. Offers an informal support group. Meets Sun., 1pm, in Bridgewater. For directions call Dr. Aviva Sinvany Nubel 908-722-9884 (day). *Website:* http://www.tgdoctor.com *E-mail*: avivanubel@yahoo.com

UNION

On Q A free, confidential support group for gay, lesbian, bisexual, transgender, queer, questioning and intersex teens between the ages of 14 and 18. Rap groups and literature. Meets Sat., 1-3pm, Summit Oaks Hospital, 19 Prospect St., 1st Floor Group Room, Summit. Call Steph Furness 908-277-9071 (day).

"Respect your fellow human beings, treat them fairly, disagree with them honestly, enjoy their friendship, explore your thoughts about one another candidly, work together for a common goal and help one another achieve it. No destructive lies. No ridiculous fears. No debilitating anger." -- *Bill Bradley*

NATIONAL

COLAGE (Children Of Lesbians And Gays Everywhere) *International. 40 affiliated groups. Founded 1990.* Mission of COLAGE is to connect and empower people to make the world better for children of lesbian, gay, bisexual and transgender parents. Information and referrals, conferences, pen pals, literature and newsletter. Various online programs. Write: COLAGE, 1550 Bryant St., Suite 830, San Francisco, CA 94103. Call 415-861-5437; Fax: 415-255-8345. *Website:* http://www.colage.org *E-mail*: colage@colage.org

COURAGE *International. Over 95 groups. Founded 1980.* Provides spiritual support and fellowship for men and women with same-sex attractions who are striving to live chaste lives in accordance with the Roman Catholic Church's teachings. The companion group, EnCourage, is for families and friends of persons with same-sex attractions. Newsletter, phone help, conferences and assistance in starting groups. Write: COURAGE, c/o St. John the Baptist, 210 W. 31st St., New York, NY 10001. Call 212-268-1010. *Website:* http://www.couragerc.net *E-mail*: NYCourage@aol.com

Dignity/USA *National. 50 chapters. Founded 1969.* Organization of gay, lesbian, bisexual and transgender Catholics, their families and friends. Concerned with spiritual development, feminism, education and advocacy. Newsletter and chapter development guidelines. Write: Dignity/USA, 1500 Massachusetts Ave., NW, #08, Washington, DC 20005. Call 1-800-877-8797; Fax: 202-429-9808. *Website:* http://www.dignityusa.org *E-mail*: info@dignityusa.org

Family Pride Coalition *National. 160+ local groups. Founded 1979.* Support, education and advocacy for gay, lesbian and transgender parents, prospective parents and their families. Information and referrals, phone support, family events, literature and newsletter. Assistance in starting groups. Write: Family Pride Coalition, P.O. Box 65327, Washington, DC 20035-5327. Call 202-331-5015; Fax: 202-331-0080. *Website:* http://www.familypride.org *E-mail*: info@familypride.org

Homosexuals Anonymous *National. 40 chapters. Founded 1980.* Christian fellowship of men and women who have chosen to help each other to live free from homosexuality. Group support through weekly meetings. Online groups. Newsletter, chapter manual. Write: Homosexuals Anonymous, P.O. Box 7881, Reading, PA 19603. Call 610-779-2500 or 1-800-288-4237. *Website:* http://members.aol.com/hawebpage

International Foundation for Gender Education *International. Founded 1978.* Support and educational services for and about gender variant persons (including transsexuals, cross-dressers, intersex androgynes, non-gendered and multi-gendered persons). Services include referrals to local support groups and to medical and psychological professionals. Speakers program, publication of "Transgender Tapestry" magazine, synchronicity bookstore and national outreach. Write: IFGE, P.O. Box 540229, Waltham, MA 02454-0229. Call 781-899-2212; Fax: 781-899-5703. *Website:* http://www.ifge.org *E-mail*: info@ifge.org

Mautner Project, the National Lesbian Health Organization *Model. Several groups in Washington, DC. Founded 1990.* Cancer support and survivorship groups for lesbian, bisexual and transgender women who partner with women (WPWs), their partners and caregivers. Bereavement support groups for WPWs who have lost a partner, friend or loved one. Smoking cessation groups for the lesbian, gay, bisexual and transgender community. Health self-empowerment groups for black WPWs. Provides phone and online support to WPWs outside the DC-Metro area. Provides LGBT cultural competency training to health care professionals and their staff members. Educates the lesbian/WPW community about health issues. Information and referrals, phone support, literature, newsletter and advocacy. Write: Mautner Project, 1707 L St. NW, Suite 230, Washington, DC 20036. Call 1-866-628-8637 or 202-332-5536 (day); TDD: 202-332-5536. *Website*: http://www.mautnerproject.org *E-mail*: mautner@mautnerproject.org

National Gay and Lesbian Task Force *National. Founded 1973.* Advocates and organizes for the rights of gay, lesbian, bisexual and transgender people. Technical assistance for state and local organizers. Publications, materials and newsletter. Write: National Gay and Lesbian Task Force, 1325 Massachusetts Ave., NW, Suite 600, Washington, DC 20005. Call 202-393-5177; Fax: 202-393-2241. *Website:* http://www.thetaskforce.org *E-mail*: ngltf@ngltf.org

PFLAG (Parents, Families and Friends of Lesbians and Gays) *International. 490 chapters worldwide. Founded 1981.* Helps families understand and accept gay, lesbian, bisexual and transgender family members. Offers help in strengthening families, support groups for families and friends, educational outreach, newsletter, chapter development guidelines, grassroots advocacy, information and referrals. Also has a Transgender Network (PFLAG TNET). Write: P-FLAG, 1726 M Street, NW, Suite 400, Washington, DC 20036. Call 202-467-8180; Fax: 202-467-8194. For information about TNET call Karen Gross 216-691-4357 or e-mail imatmom@aol.com *Website:* http://www.pflag.org *E-mail*: info@pflag.org

Rainbow Room *Model. Founded 1979.* Adult-facilitated support group for gay, lesbian, bisexual, transgender and questioning youth (ages 13-21). Provides a safe space for youth to talk about the issues that affect their daily lives. Write: Rainbow Room, c/o Hartford Gay and Lesbian Health Collective, P.O. Box 2094, Hartford, CT 06145. Call 860-278-4163; Fax: 860-278-5995. *E-mail*: info@hglhc.org

Renaissance Transgender Association, Inc. *National. 6 chapters and 6 affiliates. Founded 1987.* Mutual support for both transvestites and transsexuals. Provides education about transgender issues for the public and the transgender community. Networking with other support groups, information and referrals, phone support and pen pals. Assistance in starting new groups. Write: Renaissance Transgender Association, 987 Old Eagle School Rd., Suite 719, Wayne, PA 19087. Call 610-975-9119 (day/eve). *Website:* http://www.ren.org *E-mail*: info@ren.org

Society for the Second Self (Tri-Ess International) *National. 30 chapters. Founded 1976.* Provides informational and educational resources to promote the understanding of crossdressing. Offers support equally for heterosexual crossdressers, their spouses, partners and families. Emphasizes security and confidentiality, full expression of both masculine and feminine elements, the balance and integration of these traits into the whole personality and relationship-building. Pen pals and Big Sister programs, quarterly journal and newsletter, membership directory. Online forums. Annual conventions for crossdressers, spouses, partners and couples. Write: Society for Second Self, P.O. Box 980638, Houston, TX 77098-0638. Call 713-349-8969 (eve). *Website:* http://www.tri-ess.org *E-mail*: TRIESSINFO@aol.com

Straight Spouse Network (SSN) *International network. 75 groups* and *61 state/country contacts. Founded 1986.* Confidential personal support network serving current or former heterosexual spouses or partners, current or former, gay, lesbian, bisexual or transgender mates and mixed-orientation couples. Helps straight spouses or partners cope constructively and promotes understanding between spouses, within families and with the larger community through education and collaboration. Resource information, research-based publications, referrals, reading and media references and newsletter. Guideline available for starting new groups. Numerous confidential internet lists. Write: SSN, 33 Linda Ave., # 33, Oakland, CA 94611-4820. Call 510-595-1005. *Website:* http://www.straightspouse.org *E-mail*: dir@straightspouse.org

SHORT / TALL

STATEWIDE

Little People of America - Garden State Chapter Mutual support for short-statured people (infants - adults) and parents of short-statured children. Guest speakers, social get-togethers and fund-raisers. Spring and Fall regional conferences and national conventions. Dues $50/yr. per household. Call Helen Finkle 732-780-3827 or Robin Thibault 973-822-3665 (day/eve). *Website:* http://www.lpaonline.org

NATIONAL

Adult Growth Hormone Deficiency *National network. Founded 1989.* Provides public education and networking for adults with growth-related disorders. Information and referrals, phone support, pen pals, annual convention and conferences. Newsletter. Write: The MAGIC Foundation, 6645 W. North Ave., Oak Park, IL 60302. Call 1-800-362-4423; Fax: 708-383-0899. *Website:* http://www.magicfoundation.org *E-mail*: mary@magicfoundation.org

Growth Hormone Deficiency Support Network *National network. Founded 1989.* Network and exchange of information for families of children with growth hormone deficiency disorders. Information and referrals, phone support, pen pals, conferences, literature, annual convention and membership newsletter ($35/US, $40/Canada, $45/overseas). Write: Growth Hormone Deficiency Support Network, c/o MAGIC Foundation, 6645 W. North Ave., Oak Park, IL 60302. Call 1-800-3-MAGIC-3 or 708-383-0808; Fax: 708-383-0899. *Website:* http://www.magicfoundation.org *E-mail*: mary@magicfoundation.org

Human Growth Foundation *National. 31 chapters. Founded 1965.* Local groups provide members the opportunity to meet other parents of children with growth related disorders. Mutual sharing of problems, research and public education. Monthly and quarterly newsletter. Parent-to-parent support and networking program. Annual conference. Also offers Internet support list for parents and adults. Write: Human Growth Foundation, 997 Glen Cove Ave., Glen Head, NY 11545-1564. Call 516-671-4041 or 1-800-451-6434; Fax: 516-671-4055. *Website:* http://hgfound.org *E-mail*: hgf1@hgfound.org

We can also refer callers to over 100 individuals who are seeking others to help start new support groups throughout NJ. Give us a call for more information.
1-800-367-6274

Little People of America (*BILINGUAL*) *National. 68 chapters. Founded 1957.* Provides mutual support to people of short stature (4'10" and under) and their families. Information on physical and developmental concerns, employment, education, disability rights, medical issues, adaptive devices, etc. Newsletter. Provides educational scholarships and medical assistance grants, access to medical advisory board and assistance in adoption. Local, regional and national conferences and athletic events. Online chat room and email list serve. Dues $50/year, $10/year seniors, $500/lifetime. Write: LPA, 5289 NE Elam Young Parkway, Suite F-100, Hillsboro, OR 97124-6440. Call 1-888-572-2001. *Website:* http://www.lpaonline.org *E-mail*: info@lpaonline.org

MAGIC Foundation for Children's Growth *National network. Founded 1989.* Provides public education and networking for families of children with growth-related disorders. MAGIC Foundation has 11 divisions including: growth hormone deficiency, congenital adrenal hyperplasia, Turner's syndrome, precocious puberty, McCune Albright syndrome, panhypopituitarism, adult growth hormone deficiency, Russell Silver Syndrome, thyroid disorders, chronic renal insufficiencies and septo optic dysplasia. Information and referrals, phone support, pen pals, annual convention and conferences. Newsletters for children and adults. Write: The MAGIC Foundation, 6645 W. North Ave., Oak Park, IL 60302. Call 1-800-362-4423; Fax: 708-383-0899. *Website:* http://www.magicfoundation.org *E-mail*: mary@magicfoundation.org

Tall Clubs International *International. 65+ groups. Founded 1938.* Social support for tall persons (men at least 6'2", women at least 5'10"). Also advocacy for clothing and other special needs of tall people. Skywriters and TALLrific for persons under 21. Group development guidelines, information and referrals, conferences, newsletters and social gatherings. Write: Tall Clubs International, P.O. Box 1811, Cincinnati, OH 45201. Call 1-888-468-2552. *Website:* http://www.tall.org *E-mail*: admin@tall.org

SINGLES

(see also separation/divorce, widowhood)

CAMDEN

Friendly Singles Fifty Plus Club, Inc. Provides social activities for singles, age 50 and over. Barbeques, house parties, bus trips, dances, hay rides and weenie roasts. Dues $20/yr. Dances $7/members; $8/non-members. Meets Fri., 8-11pm, VFW, Chestnut Ave., Berlin. Call Lori 856-228-1039 (day).

ESSEX

Single in the Suburbs Mutual support for single women. Groups start periodically and run for 6 weeks. Registration fee $45. Meets at Linda and Rudy Slucker NCJW Center for Women, 513 West Mount Pleasant Ave., Suite 325, Livingston. Call Project GRO 973-994-4994. *Website:* http://www.centerforwomennj.org *E-mail*: centerforwomen@ncjwessex.org

GLOUCESTER

Joyful Singles Provides a safe environment where singles over the age of 35 can find trust, support, significance and purpose through discussions, encouragement, accountability and prayer. Meets 3rd Thurs., 7-8:30pm, Hope House, Lincoln Ave., Pitman. Call JoAnne 856-863-0401 or Jim 856-256-0940.

SOMERSET

Single Senior Women Support for women (age 60+) who are divorced, separated, widowed, never married or have a spouse who is ill. Recreational activities. Meets 2nd and 4th Thurs., 10am-noon, Office on Aging, 92 East Main St., Somerville. Call Erin 908-704-6339 (day).

SPEECH / STUTTERING

(see also toll-free helplines)

STATEWIDE

Toastmasters International Mutual help for people to improve speaking skills, express themselves more effectively and to gain confidence. For those who are hesitant to speak before an audience. Membership fees. Monthly magazine. See website for location of the nearest group. *Website*: http://www.toastmasters.org

BERGEN

Speak Easy International Foundation, Inc. Self-help group for people who stutter. Must have speech dysfunction or phobia. Phone network, peer-counseling, newsletter and yearly conference. Dues $80/yr. Meets alternate Tues., 7:30pm, Cerebral Palsy Center, Fair Lawn. Call Bob 201-262-0895.

Toastmasters International Club Mutual support for people to improve speaking skills, express themselves more effectively and to gain confidence. For those who are hesitant to speak before an audience.

Haworth - Valley Chapter Dues $70 (includes workbook and monthly magazine). Meets 1st and 3rd Mon., 8-10pm, First Congregational United Church of Christ, 276 Haworth Ave. Call Adam Strobel at 201-385-2514. *Website:* http://www.valleytoastmasters.org

Ramsey - Park Chapter. Dues $44/yr. Newsletter. Meets 2nd and 4th Fri., 7:15pm, Ramsey Library, 30 Wyckoff Ave. Call Ira Goodman 845-480-5446.

Rutherford Dues $24/semi-yearly. Meets Sat. (except July and Aug.), 9-11am, Rutherford Public Library, Park Ave. and Chestnut St. Call Sylvia Schaja 973-773-4998 (day). *Website:* http://www.toastmaster.org *E-mail*: fairleighearlybirds@yahoo.com

CAMDEN

National Stuttering Association - New Jersey Division To provide support to and promote fluency for stutterers. Meets 2nd and 4th Thurs., 7-9pm, John F. Kennedy Hospital, Stratford. Call Kathy Filer 609-706-4098. *Website:* http://www.nsastutter.org *E-mail*: katfiler@aol.com

CAPE MAY

Toastmasters International Boardwalk Chapter Support and education to improve communication, leadership, social and public speaking skills. Dues $56/yr.; $21 initiation. Meets 1st and 3rd Wed., Chatterbox Restaurant, Ninth and Central Ave., Ocean City. Call Ted Armstrong or Karol Armstrong 856-691-7748 (day) or Rich Catando 609-652-9169 (day). *Website:* http:www.boardwalktoastmasters.com

ESSEX

Speak Easy Toastmasters Club Provides mutual support and a positive learning environment in order for members to develop communication and leadership skills. Meets 1st and 3rd Thurs., 12:30-1:30pm, Formosa Plastics Corp., Training Room, 9 Peach Tree Hill Rd., Livingston. Call Prokopis 973-716-7284 (day). *Website:* http://www.27.brinkster.com/njtoastmasters/

"Come to the edge," He said. They said, "We are afraid." "Come to the edge," He said. They came. He pushed them ... and they flew. – G. Apollinaire

MERCER

First Amendment of Princeton Meets to practice air-flow speech technique to overcome stuttering. Under 18 welcome. Prior speech therapy required. Meets odd Mon., 7:30pm, Princeton Medical Center, Merwick Unit, Rt. 206, Princeton. Call Elliot Dennis 609-275-3806 (day/eve). *E-mail*: elliotdennis@yahoo.com

UNION

Summit Toastmasters Support and education to improve communication, leadership, social and public speaking skills. Guest speakers and speakers' bureau. Dues $34 twice a year. Meets Wed., 8-10pm, St. John's Church, 587 Springfield Ave., Summit. Call Kevin Moulton 1-877-854-5014 (day). *Website:* http://www.summittoastmasters.com

NATIONAL

International Foundation for Stutterers, Inc. *International. 6 Chapters. Founded 1980.* Aims to eliminate stuttering through speech therapy in conjunction with self-help groups. Education for public and professionals about stuttering and self-help. Newsletter, speakers, phone help system and guidelines on forming self-help groups. Write: International Foundation for Stutterers, 304 Hampshire Dr., Plainsboro, NJ 08536. Call Elliot Dennis 609-275-3806 (eve). *E-mail*: elliotdennis@yahoo.com

National Stuttering Association *National.* 80 *groups. Founded 1977.* Provides information about stuttering. Self-help chapter meetings provide supportive environment where people who stutter can learn to communicate more effectively. Network of groups. Referrals, advocacy, monthly newsletter and group development guidelines. Dues $35; $20 (senior, student, low income). Write: National Stuttering Association, 119 West 40th St., 14th Floor, New York, NY 10018. Call 1-800-364-1677; Fax: 212-944-8244. *Website:* http://www.WeStutter.org *E-mail*: info@WeStutter.org

Speak Easy International Foundation, Inc. *International. 6 chapters. Founded 1977.* Self-help group for adult and adolescent stutterers. Must have speech dysfunction or phobia. Phone network, peer counseling and newsletter. Offers assistance starting new groups. Annual national symposium and Fall retreat in Madison, CT (contact Brian Baik: 860-292-2040). Dues $80/yr. Write: Speak Easy International, c/o Bob Gathman, 233 Concord Dr., Paramus, NJ 07652. Call Bob 201-262-0895. *E-mail*: speakezusa@juno.com

Toastmasters International *International. 10,000 chapters. Founded 1924.* Mutual help for people to improve speaking and leadership skills to express themselves more effectively and to gain confidence. For those who are hesitant to speak before an audience. Leadership training. Membership fees. Monthly magazine. Write: Toastmasters Int'l, P.O. Box 9052, Mission Viejo, CA 92690-7052. Call 949-858-8255; Fax: 949-858-1207. *Website:* http://www.toastmasters.org *E-mail*: tminfo@toastmasters.org

U.S. Society for Augmentative and Alternative Communication *National. 30 affiliated groups. Founded in 1986.* Addresses the needs of persons who are severely speech impaired or unable to speak. Works to improve services and products. Dues $63 (includes newsletter). Information and referrals, conferences, advocacy, literature and networking. Write: USSAAC, P.O. Box 10906, Baltimore, MD, 21234. Call 1-877-887-7222. *Website:* ussaac.org *E-mail*: info@ussaac.org

ONLINE

Latetalkers *Online.* Email group to discuss developmental speech delays caused by apraxia, dyspraxia, phonological disorders, autism spectrum disorders, learning disabilities or other causes. Aim is to help children attain intelligible speech. Open to families, speech language pathologists, medical professionals, students and educators. *Website:* http://groups.yahoo.com/group/latetalkers

SPIRITUALITY / MEDITATION

ESSEX

Spiritual Sisters With a Purpose *(WOMEN ONLY)* A spiritual support group to help members lift each other up and find a purpose to connect their spirits to a higher power. Meets 4th Sat., 5-7pm, 827 S. 14th St., Newark. Before attending call Deborah 973-596-0896 (eve) or Yvonne 973-313-9329 (eve). *E-mail*: millard43@msn.com or ydbanks@msn.com

Spirituality Group Support for mental health consumers fostering an awareness of spirituality and a sense of being a part of a much larger powerful entity. Offers mutual sharing, education, rap sessions, social, phone help and advocacy. Meets Tues., 4pm, Where Peaceful Waters Flow, 3-5 Vose Ave., 2nd Floor, S.Orange. Call Celine or Jacqueline 973-677-7700 (eve).

TRAUMA

ONLINE

Gift From Within *Online. (WOMEN ONLY)* Offers a one-on-one PTSD e-mail/Pen Pal support network, where female victims of specific trauma can be matched with survivors of similar PTSD. *Website:* http://www.giftfromwithin.org *E-mail*: joyceb3955@aol.com

Trauma Anonymous *Online.* Provides information on trauma and post-traumatic stress disorder. Information on symptoms and treatment. Chat rooms for veterans, victims of domestic violence and survivors of sexual abuse. Message board for victims. *Website:* http://www.bein.com/trauma/index.html

VETERANS / MILITARY

(see also toll-free helplines)

STATEWIDE

Vet Center Support Groups *Professionally-run. Four Veteran Centers.* Support groups and related services for both combat veterans of all wars (Iraq, Afghan, Vietnam, WWII) and their families to deal with PTSD and other readjustment issues. Write: Ann Talmage, Vet Center, 2 Broad St., Suite 703, Bloomfield, NJ 07003. For group types and times, contact the closest center: Bloomfield (Essex) 973-748-0980; Jersey City (Hudson) 201-748-4467; Trenton (Mercer) 609-882-5744; Ventnor (Atlantic) 609-487-8387. *Website:* http://www.va.gov/rcs *E-mail*: ann.talmage@med.va.gov

HUNTERDON

Balkan Military Support Group Informal support network for families and friends of American troops in Persian Gulf, Bosnia, Kosovo and staging areas. For information call 908-782-6722.

MIDDLESEX

Army and Air National Guard Family Support Offers support for any family member of military personnel. Mutual support to discuss or share any issues of concern. Family member does not have to be on active duty. For meeting information call 732-937-6290.

MORRIS

Vets4Vets Mutual support for veterans returning and adapting to civilian life. Families welcome. Meets Tues., 5-6pm, Morris County Library, 30 East Hanover Ave., Hanover. Before attending call Stacy 973-627-4120. *Website:* http://www.vets4vets.us

NATIONAL

Blinded Veterans Association *National. 54 regional groups. Founded 1945.* Information, support and outreach to blinded veterans, including those who were blinded in combat and those suffering from age-related macular degeneration and other eye diseases. Help in obtaining prosthetic devices and accessing the latest technological advances to assist the blind. Information on benefits and rehabilitation programs. Quarterly newsletter. Regional meetings. Write: BVA, 477 H St., NW, Washington, DC 20001. Call 202-371-8880 or 1-800-669-7079; Fax: 202-371-8258. *Website:* http://www.bva.org *E-mail*: bva@bva.org

EX-POSE (Ex-Partners of Servicemembers for Equality) *National membership. Founded 1981.* Lobbies for changes in military divorce laws. Disseminates information concerning military divorce. Lawyer referral. Quarterly newsletter. Publishes "Guide for Military Separation and Divorce." Membership dues $15. Write: EX-POSE, P.O. Box 11191, Alexandria, VA 22312. Call 703-941-5844 (day); Fax: 703-212-6951. *Website:* http://ex-pose.org *E-mail*: ex-pose@juno.com

National Gulf War Resource Center, Inc. *National. 61 affiliated groups. Founded 1995.* Supports the efforts of grassroots organizations that assist veterans affected by the Persian Gulf War illnesses. Also provides advocacy and support for Gulf War veterans, veterans of Afghanistan and Iraq and their families. Conducts research into the causes of Gulf War Syndrome. Information and referrals, media assistance, provides congressional testimony, advocacy, literature and self-help guides. Write: National Gulf War Resource Center, 3027 Walnut St., Kansas City, MO 64108. Call 1-866-531-7183; Fax: 816-531-7184. *Website:* http://www.ngwrc.org *E-mail*: ngwrc@sbcglobal.net

Paralyzed Veterans of America *National. 34 chapters and 58 field service offices.* To ensure that spinal cord injured or diseased veterans achieve the highest quality of life possible. Membership is available solely to individuals who are American citizens with spinal cord dysfunction as a result of trauma or disease. Must have served on active duty and had an other than dishonorable discharge. Information and referrals, support groups, publications, VA benefits counseling and magazine. Write: PVA, 801 18th St. NW, Washington, DC

20006. Call 1-800-424-8200 or 202-872-8200. *Website:* http://www.pva.org *E-mail*: info@pva.org

Society of Military Widows *National. 27 chapters. Founded 1968.* Support and assistance for widows/widowers of members of all U.S. uniformed services. Help in coping with adjustment to life on their own. Promotes public awareness. Bimonthly magazine/journal. Dues $12. Chapter development guidelines. Online listing on local chapters. Write: Society of Military Widows, 5535 Hempstead Way, Springfield, VA 22151. Call 253-750-1342 or 1-800-842-3451 (press 5). *Website:* http://www.militarywidows.org *E-mail*: hgrant@naus.org

TAPS (Tragedy Assistance Program for Survivors) *National network.* Provides support for persons who have lost a loved one while serving in the armed forces (Army, Air Force, Navy, Marine Corps, National Guard, Reserves, Service Academies, Coast Guard or contractors serving beside the military). Networking, crisis information, problem solving assistance and liaison with military agencies. TAPS youth programs and annual seminar. Write: TAPS, 1621 Connecticut Ave., NW, Suite 300, Washington, DC 20009. Call 1-800-959-8277 or 202-588-8277; Fax: 202-588-0784. *Website:* http://www.taps.org *E-mail*: info@taps.org

United Spinal Association *National. Founded 1946.* To promote independence for paralyzed veterans, enhance their health and medical care and protect the civil rights of the disabled. Write: United Spinal Association, 75-20 Astoria Blvd., Jackson Heights, NY 11370-1177. Call 718-803-3782 ext. 203.

Vietnam Veterans of America, Inc. *National. 600+ chapters. Founded 1978.* Devoted to the needs and concerns of Vietnam era veterans and their families. Provides leadership and advocacy in all areas that have an impact on veterans, with an emphasis on Agent Orange related problems and post traumatic stress disorder. Bimonthly newspaper. Write: VVA, 8605 Cameron St., Suite 400, Silver Spring, MD 20910-3710. Call 1-800-882-1316 or 301-585-4000; Fax: 301-585-0519. *Website:* http://www.vva.org

"Nothing liberates our greatness like the desire to help, the desire to serve."
-- Marianne Williamson

ONLINE

Aftermath of War: Coping with PTSD Support Group *Online.* Support service with various message boards for loved ones of those suffering from combat-related PTSD. Wives, daughters and mothers of war veterans come together to share information, support and friendship. Their aim is "in the aftermath of war, may we find peace in understanding this disorder." *Website:* http://groups.msn.com/AftermathOfWarCopingWithPTSDtoo *E-mail*: Combatptsd@aol.com

Kathy's Military Links *Online resource.* Lists about 150 online sites for family members of military. In addition to many online groups for wives, mothers and girlfriends of those in the military, other listed groups address special situations, such as pregnant marine wives or interracial military marriages. *Website:* http://geocities.com/kathysmilitarylinks/mom.html

Marine Moms Online *Online.* Discussion forum. Offers support, information, questions, answers and chat room. There is also a forum for dads. *Website:* http://mmo.proboards10.com/index.cgi

Support4militarywives *Online.* Support for military wives. Provides online chat room and some useful links. *Website:* http://www.groups.yahoo.com/group/support4militarywives/

WOMEN'S ISSUES

(see also toll-free helplines)

STATEWIDE

N.O.W. - N.J. (National Organization for Women of N.J.) Political advocacy for women's equality in society. Dedicated to eliminating sexism and racism. Political advocacy for reproductive rights, older women's rights, homemakers rights, women in the work force, lesbian rights, etc. Information and referrals about chapters, groups and services throughout NJ. Dues $35/yr. Write: N.O.W - NJ, 110 W. State St., Trenton, NJ 08608. Call 609-393-0156 (day). *Website:* http://www.nownj.org

ESSEX

Project G.R.O. Various support groups dealing with women's issues (including separation/divorce, women living alone, parenting, widows, singles, etc.). Groups start periodically and run for 6 weeks. Registration fee $45. Meets at Linda and Rudy Slucker NCJW Center for Women, 513 West Mt. Pleasant

Ave., Suite 325, Livingston. Call Project Gro 973-994-4994. *Website:* http://www.centerforwomennj.org *E-mail*: centerforwomen@ncjwessex.org

GLOUCESTER

Center for People in Transition *Professionally-run.* Assists displaced homemakers to become emotionally and economically self-sufficient through life skills training, career decision making, education or vocational training and supportive services. Evening divorce and bereavement support groups for men and women. For information call 856-415-2222 (Mon.-Fri.). *E-mail*: peopleintransition@gccnj.edu

HUDSON

Women's Project Groups *Professionally-run.* Education, support, workshops and groups to help women on subjects such as self-esteem, domestic violence, employment and stress management. Meets various days and times, Christ Hospital, 176 Palisade Ave., Jersey City. Call Michele Bernstein 201-795-8375 ext. 8416 (day).

HUNTERDON

Career and Life Planning Center *Professionally-run.* Offers support and assistance to displaced homemakers. Education, mutual sharing, guest speakers, literature and newsletter. Meets various days (both days and evenings) at Educational Services Commission, Sandhill School Campus, 215 Rt. 31, Flemington. Call Denise Brown Kahney 908-788-1453 (day). *Website:* http://www.NORWESCAP.org or www.dhnj.org *E-mail*: dbrownkahney@hcesc.com

MIDDLESEX

"balance" - Women's Support Group *Professionally-run.* An inspiring gathering that focuses on the emotions, thoughts and views of women facing stress and challenging lives. Meets 1st and 3rd Tues., 7pm, Women's Resource Center, Robert Wood Johnson University Hospital, One RWJ Place, New Brunswick. Before attending call Mariggela Kartatos 732-253-3115.

Women Helping Women in Metuchen Offers various self-help support groups for women dealing with such issues as separation and divorce, self-esteem, mid-life, exploring your marriage and co-dependency. Groups meet weekly and run for 10 weeks. Dues $8/wk members; $10/wk non-members. Meets various days and times in Metuchen. Call 732-549-6000 (day). *Website:* http://www.whwnj.com *E-mail*: helpline@whwnj.com

MONMOUTH

Women's Support Group Helps women who are displaced homemakers (facing the loss of their primary source of income due to separation, divorce, disability or death of spouse). Issues addressed include self-sufficiency, career development, assertiveness, self-esteem, divorce, separation, widowhood and other related topics. Groups are set-up as needed in Asbury Park, Long Branch, West Keansburg and Lincroft. Call Robin Vogel 732-495-4496 (day) or Mary Ann O'Brien 732-229-8675.

MORRIS

Familias en Paz *Professionally-run. (BILINGUAL)* Support group for Latino women who want to improve their personal life through education, insight and self-empowerment. Discusses issues such as domestic abuse, relationships and other issues of interest to women. Education, advocacy, guest speakers, literature and buddy system. Meets Mon., 7-9pm, Sister Catherine Health Center, Community Room (in basement), 400 West Blackwell St., Dover. Call Alberto Olarte 973-625-7035 (day), 973-537-3855 or 201-919-4742 (eve - after 9pm). *E-mail*: user9398@optonline.net

Morris County National Organization For Women Goals are to bring women into full participation in the mainstream of American society. Dues $35/yr. Sliding scale $15-34. Meets 1st Tues., 7:30-9pm, Morris Plains. Call 973-285-1200 (day). *Website:* http://www.erights4all.com *E-mail*: morriscountynow@hotmail.com

UNION

Older Women's League (Voice of Mid-Life and Older Women) Education and advocacy focusing on the critical issues facing women as they age. Literature. Dues $35/yr. Meetings vary. Call Teresa 908-862-5454 ext. 124 (day).

WARREN

Transitions Center for Displaced Homemakers *Professionally-run.* Provides support services, vocational counseling and career training for displaced homemakers. For women who have lost their primary source of income due to divorce, separation, death or disability of her spouse. Registration fee $10.

Meets various times, 108 East Washington Ave., Rt. 57, Washington. Call 908-835-2624 (day/eve). *E-mail*: transitions@norwescap.org

NATIONAL

Business and Professional Women/USA *National. 1300 chapters. Founded 1919.* Organization comprised of working women, to promote workplace equity and provide networking opportunities. Lobbying efforts, tri-annual magazine, periodic publications, resource center and grassroots community action projects. Annual national convention. Local group information available online. Write: Business and Professional Women/USA, 1900 M St., NW, Suite 310, Washington, DC 20036. Fax: 202-861-0298; *Website:* http://www.bpwusa.org *E-mail*: memberservices@bpwusa.org

National Organization for Women *National. 500 chapters. Founded 1966.* NOW is an action organization that seeks social, political, economic and legal equity between women and men through grassroots organizing, lobbying, litigation, protests and demonstrations. Educational meetings, national newsletter and chapter development guidelines. Write: NOW, 1100 H Street NW, Suite 300, Washington, DC 20005. Call 202-628-8669; TDD: 202-331-9002; FAX: 202-785-8576. *Website:* http://now.org *E-mail*: now@now.org

Older Women's League *National. 60+ chapters. Founded 1980.* Membership organization that advocates on behalf of various economic and social issues for midlife and older women (social security, pension rights, employment, caregiver support, elder abuse, etc.). Newsletter and chapter development guidelines. Dues $25/yr. Write: OWL, 3300 North Fairfax Dr., Suite 218, Arlington, VA 22201. Call 1-800-825-3695; Fax: 703-812-0687. *Website:* http://www.owl-national.org *E-mail*: owlinfo@owl-national.org

SOWN (Supportive Older Women's Network) *Model. 32 groups in Philadelphia area. Founded 1982.* Helps women (age 60+) cope with their specialized aging concerns. Support groups, leadership training, consultation, telephone support, outreach and networking. Newsletter. Write: SOWN, 2805 N. 47th St., Philadelphia, PA 19131. Call 215-477-6000; Fax: 215-477-6555. *Website:* http://www.sown.org *E-mail*: info@sown.org

Need help finding a specific group? Give us a call – we're here to help! Call 1-800-367-6274

WORKAHOLICS

NATIONAL

Workaholics Anonymous World Service Organization, Inc. *International. 100+ groups. Founded 1983.* 12-Step. Fellowship for men and women who feel their work lives have gotten out of control. Also for affected family members and friends. Provides mutual support in solving problems of compulsive overworking. Available phone and online support and information for those wishing to start a chapter. Offers self-study book, "Workaholics Anonymous Book of Recovery." Write: Workaholics Anonymous, P.O. Box 289, Menlo Park, CA 94026-0289. Call 510-273-9253. *Website:* http://www.workaholics-anonymous.org *E-mail*: wso@workaholics-anonymous.org

YOUTH / STUDENTS

(see also toll-free helplines)

BURLINGTON

Youth Partnership Group Adult supervised activities for youth (ages 13-21) with complex emotional, mental health or behavioral issues to help them express what they have been through and share concerns. Rap sessions. Meets Thurs., 6:30-8:30pm, Family Support Organization of Burlington County, 774 Eayrestown Rd., Lumberton. Call Jamison Gsell 609-265-8838 (day).

CAMDEN

Youth Partnership Group Adult supervised activities for youth (ages 13-21) with complex emotional, mental health or behavioral issues to help them express what they have been through and share concerns. Rap sessions.

Atco Meets Wed., 6:30-8pm, Winslow High School, 10 Coopers Folly Rd. Call 856-662-2600 (day).

Merchantville Meets Thurs., 6:30-8pm, Camden County Family Support Organization, 23 W. Park Ave., Ste. 103-104. Call 856-662-2600 (day).

CUMBERLAND

Pink Roses, Inc. Mutual support for young women (ages 11-19) to make better choices by sharing feelings, thoughts, problems and experiences with rap sessions, guest speakers, literature, phone help and buddy systems. Meets 2nd Wed., 6:30-8pm, The Gateway Family Enrichment Center, 155 Spruce St., Bridgeton. Call Regina 856-451-1133.

ESSEX

Youth Partnership Group Adult supervised activities for youth (ages 13-21) with complex emotional, mental health or behavioral issues to help them express what they have been through and share concerns. Rap sessions, guest speakers, literature, newsletter and phone help. Meets Tues., 6-8pm, Family Support Organization of Essex County, 60 Evergreen Place, East Orange. Call Yvonne Rouse or Hazeline Pilgrim 973-395-1441 (day).

GLOUCESTER

Teen Recovery Group *Professionally-run.* Support for teenagers who need a safe place to discuss problems dealing with drugs, alcohol or any other issues they may face. Meets Thurs., 7-8:30pm, Washington Township Municipal Building, 523 Egg Harbor Rd., Washington Township. Call 856-589-6446 (day).

HUDSON

TMS Support Group *Professionally-run.* Support and education for teenagers, under age 20, who are pregnant or recently gave birth. Guest speakers. Meets Thurs., 4pm, NHCAC, Jersey City Clinic, 324 Palisades Ave., 2nd Floor, Jersey City. Call Beatriz Amador 201-459-8888 ext. 3018 (day) or Rossetty Fernandez 201-876-8900 ext. 226. *E-mail*: BAmador@nhcac.org

HUNTERDON

Youth Partnership Group Adult supervised activities for youth (ages 13-21) with complex emotional, mental health or behavioral issues to help them express what they have been through and share concerns. Rap sessions. Meets every other Fri., 6-8pm, Family Support Organization, 4 Minneakoning Rd., Flemington. For meeting information call Stanley Croughter 908-788-8585 (day). *Website:* http://www.fsohsw.org

MIDDLESEX

Youth Partnership Group Adult supervised activities for youth (ages 13-21) with complex emotional, mental health or behavioral issues to help them express what they have been through and share concerns. Educational series, advocacy, social group, newsletter, phone help and buddy system. Meets Fri., 6-8pm, Family Support Organization of Middlesex County, 1950 Route 27 North, Suite D, North Brunswick. Call Dylys Koney or Sam Hartman 732-940-2837 (day). *E-mail*: dkfsomiddlesex9@msn.com

SOMERSET

Youth Partnership Group Call Stanley Croughter 908-788-8585.

SUSSEX

Teen Support Group *Professionally-run.* Sharing and encouragement for teenagers dealing with everyday stress. Donation $5 towards refreshments, literature and space rental. Meets Mon., 3:30-4:30pm, Partnership for Social Services Family Center, 48 Wyker Rd., Franklin. Call 973-827-4702. *Website:* partnershipforsocialservices.org

UNION

Youth Partnership Group Adult supervised activities for youth (ages 13-21) with complex emotional, mental health or behavioral issues to help them express what they have been through and share concerns. Rap sessions. Meets 2nd and 4th Wed., 6:30-8:30pm, Family Support Organization, 137 Elmer St., 1st Floor, Westfield. Also girls group (ages 13-17) in Elizabeth. Call Kathy Wagner 908-789-7625 (day).

NATIONAL

SADD (Students Against Destructive Decisions) *National. 10,000 groups. Founded 1981.* Provides prevention and intervention tools to eliminate impaired driving, end underage drinking, drug abuse and other destructive decisions. Offers community awareness programs, literature, sponsors SADD chapters and group development guidelines. Write: SADD, 255 Main St., Marlborough, MA 01752. Call 1-877-723-3462 or 508-481-3568; Fax: 508-481-5759. *Website:* http://www.sadd.org *E-mail*: info@sadd.org

ONLINE

Conduct Disorders Parent Message Board *Online.* Support for parents living with a child with one of the many behavior disorders including: attention deficit hyperactivity disorder, oppositional defiance disorder, conduct disorder, depression and substance abuse. Parents with children of all ages welcome. *Website:* http://www.conductdisorders.com

Pregnant Teen Support *Online.* Email list support group for teens (ages 12-20) who are facing an unplanned, unexpected or unwanted pregnancy. *Website:* http://health.groups.yahoo.com/group/Pregnant_Teen_Support

RARE ILLNESSES

49XXXXY SYNDROME

49XXXXY *National network. Founded 1990.* Mutual support and networking for families affected by 49XXXXY disorder. Information, pen pals, phone support and newsletter. Write: 49XXXXY, c/o Elise Watzka, 870 Miranda Green, Palo Alto, CA 94306. Call 650-941-2408. *Website:* http://klinefeltersyndrome.org/49er.htm *E-mail:* epqatzka@iname.com

AARSKOG SYNDROME

Aarskog Syndrome Parents Support Group *International network. Founded 1993.* Mutual support, networking and sharing of ideas for families of children and adults affected with Aarskog syndrome. Pen pal club, email addresses and contact pages with mailing addresses for support via correspondence. Free complimentary packet for individuals in the US and Canada. Write: Aarskog Syndrome Family Support Group, c/o Shannon Caranci, 62 Robin Hill Lane, Levittown, PA 19055-1411. *E-mail:* shannonfaith49@msn.com

ACIDEMIA

Organic Acidemia Association, Inc. *International. Founded 1982.* Support, information and networking for families affected by organic acidemia and related disorders. Dues $25/yr. Internet listserv, family conferences, research information, advocates newborn screening and tri-annual newsletter. Write: Organic Acidemia Association, c/o Kathy Stagni, 13210 35th Ave. North, Plymouth, MN 55441. Call 763-559-1797; Fax: 763-694-0017. *Website:* http://www.oaanews.org or http://www.paresearch.org or http://www.mmaresearch.com or http://www.ivasupport.org *E-mail:* oaanews@aol.com

ACID MALTASE DEFICIENCY (POMPE DISEASE)

Acid Maltase Deficiency Association (AMDA) *International network. Founded 1995.* Support and information for persons affected by Pompe disease (acid maltase deficiency). Newsletter, literature, phone help, information and referrals. Supports research into the cause and cure. Write: AMDA, P.O. Box 700248, San Antonio, TX 78270. Call 210-494-6144; Fax: 210-490-7161. *Website:* http://www.amda-pompe.org *E-mail:* tianrama@aol.com

ACNE SCARS

Acne Scar Support Group *Model. Founded 2001.* Goal is to share results from scar-revision procedures and to offer information about results for those interested in scar-revision. Offers a support group, phone support and email pen pals. Write: Acne Scar Support Group, 5500 Friendship Blvd., Apt. 821, Chevy Chase, MD 20815-7258. Call Greg 301-718-0952 *Website:* http://www.geocities.com/grege20815/washdcacnescarsupportgrp.html *E-mail:* gregestrada@verizon.net

ADDISON'S / ADRENAL DISEASE

CAMDEN

Addison's Support Group Mutual support and information for those with Addison's disease. Rap sessions, literature, phone help and guest speakers. Meets Sat., 4 times/yr., St. Pius Parish Center, Kresson Rd., Cherry Hill. Call Janice Judge 856-354-6029. *E-mail:* JanPT@aol.com

NATIONAL

National Adrenal Diseases Foundation *National. 31 affiliated groups. Founded 1984.* Dedicated to serving the needs of those with adrenal disease and their families, especially through information, education and support. Quarterly newsletters, pamphlets and group development guidelines. Write: NADF, 505 Northern Blvd., Suite 200, Great Neck, NY 11021. Call 516-487-4992. *Website:* http://medhelp.org/nadf *E-mail:* nadfmail@aol.com

AGENESIS OF THE CORPUS CALLOSUM

ACC Network, The *International network. Founded 1989.* Helps individuals with agenesis (or other anomaly) of the corpus callosum, their families and professionals. Helps identify others who are experiencing similar issues to share information and support. Phone support, information, newsletter and referrals. Coordinates listserv, an electronic discussion group on the internet. Write: ACC Network, University of Maine, 5749 Merrill Hall, Room 118, Orono, ME 04469-5749. Call 207-581-3119; Fax: 207-581-3120. *Website:* http://www.umaine.edu/edhd/research/accnetwork.htm *E-mail:* um-acc@maine.edu

AICARDI SYNDROME / INFANTILE SPASMS

(also see epilepsy/seizure disorders)

NATIONAL

Aicardi Syndrome Newsletter, Inc. *International network. Founded 1983. 5 regional chapters.* Support for families with daughters with Aicardi syndrome, a rare seizure disorder that affects primarily females and is characterized by seizures and retinal lesions. Resources, research projects, information and referrals. Biennial conferences, phone support network, research group and newsletters. Dues $25/year. Write: Aicardi Syndrome Newsletter, Inc., c/o Denise Park Parsons, 1510 Polo Fields Ct., Louisville, KY 40245. Call 502-244-9152. *Website:* http://www.aicardisyndrome.org *E-mail:* newsletter@aicardisyndrome.org

ONLINE

Infantile Spasms List *Online. 1300+ members. Founded 1998.* Support and information for parents and caregivers of children with infantile spasms. Opportunity to discuss their children, treatment options and offer support. *Website:* http://health.groups.yahoo.com/group/infantilespasms

ALAGILLE SYNDROME

Alagille Syndrome Alliance *National network. Founded 1993.* Support network for anyone who cares about people with Alagille syndrome, a rare, multi-symptom genetic disorder. Disseminates information. Aims to increase awareness in general public as well as health professionals. Newsletter, phone support, medical advisory board, information and referrals. Write: Alagille Syndrome Alliance, c/o Cindy L. Hahn, President, 10500 S.W. Starr Dr., Tualatin, OR 97062. Call 503-885-0455. *Website:* http://www.alagille.org *E-mail:* alagille@earthlink.net

"Loneliness is the universal comorbidity of illness."
-- Michael Stein, M.D., Professor of Medicine and Community at Brown University Medical School, from his book, The Lonely Patient: How We Experience Illness, 2007.

ALBINISM

NOAH (National Organization for Albinism Hypopigmentation) *National. Local chapters and contact people. Founded 1982.* Support and information for individuals, families and professionals about albinism (a lack of melanin pigment). Encourages research leading to improved diagnosis and treatment. Newsletter, online community and regional gatherings, chapter development guidelines and national conference. Dues $20/individual; $25/family. Write: NOAH, P.O. Box 959, East Hampstead, NH 03826-0959. For information on NJ support group information call 1-800-473-2310 or 603-887-2310; Fax: 800-648-2310. *Website:* http://www.albinism.org/ *E-mail:* info@albinism.org

ALOPECIA AREATA

MIDDLESEX

Alopecia Support Group Mutual support and encouragement for persons with alopecia and their families. Meets 3rd Tues. (Jan., Mar., July, Sept., Nov.), Robert Wood Johnson University Hospital, 1 Robert Wood Johnson Place, BMSCH Conference Room, New Brunswick. For further information call 732-418-8110.

NATIONAL

National Alopecia Areata Foundation *National. Founded 1981.* Support network for people with alopecia areata, totalis and universalis. Goals are to set up support groups around the country, educate the public and fund raise for research. Quarterly newsletter and support group guidelines. Write: National Alopecia Areata Foundation, 14 Mitchell Blvd., San Rafael, CA 94903. Call 415-472-3780; Fax: 415-472-5343. *Website:* http://www.naaf.org *E-mail:* info@naaf.org

ALSTROM SYNDROME

Alstrom Syndrome International *International network. 5 affiliated groups (Canada, France, Brazil, Japan and UK). Founded 1995.* Provides support and networking for families affected by Alstrom syndrome. Supports medical research initiatives to more fully understand the complexities of Alstrom syndrome and develop better therapies for Alstrom patients. Publishes a quarterly newsletter. Provides information resources to families, educators, researchers and physicians. Write: Alstrom Syndrome International, 14 Whitney Farm Rd., Mount Desert, ME 04660. Call 1-800-371-3628 or 207-288-6385; Fax: 207-244-7678. *Website:* http://www.jax.org/alstrom *E-mail:* jdm@jax.org

ALVEOLAR CAPILLARY DYSPLASIA

Alveolar Capillary Dysplasia Association *International network. Founded 1996.* Mutual support for families who have lost a child to alveolar capillary dysplasia (ACD), a congenital lung disorder. Aim is to share information while offering supportive environment to share fears and concerns. Encourages research into cause and cure. Literature, networking, information newsletter and referrals. Write: ACDA, c/o Steve and Donna Hanson, 5902 Marcie Court, Garland, TX 75044-4958. *Website:* http://www.acd-association.com *E-mail:* sdesj@verizon.net

AMYLOIDOSIS

NATIONAL

Amyloidosis Network International *International network.* Information and support for persons affected by amyloidosis, an accumulation of abnormal proteins. Networks individuals together for support. Provides education to the public and professionals about the disease. Write: Amyloidosis Network International, Inc., 7118 Cole Creek Dr., Houston, TX 77092-1421. Call 1-888-269-5643.

Amyloidosis Support Groups *International. 19 regional groups. Founded 2004.* Support for patients, caregivers, families, those who lost loved ones to amyloidosis and friends of amyloidosis patients. Support groups, educational materials, brochures and posters. Write: Amyloidosis Support Groups, 232 Orchard Dr., Wood Dale, IL 60191. Call 1-866-404-7539. *Website:* http://www.amyloidosissupport.com

ANDROGEN INSENSITIVITY

AISSG-USA (Androgen Insensitivity Syndrome Support Group) *Founded 1995.* Provides information and support to people affected by androgen insensitivity syndrome (AIS) and related conditions, including adults with the condition, parents of AIS children and professionals working with AIS. Information and referrals, phone support, regional and national support group meetings, literature, advocacy and newsletters. Write: AISSG-USA, P.O. Box 2148, Duncan, OK 73534-2148. *Website:* http://www.aissgusa.org *E-mail:* aissgusa@hotmail.com

ANENCEPHALY

ONLINE

Anencephaly Support Foundation *Online. Founded 1992.* Provides support for families who have had a baby born with anencephaly or couples who are continuing a pregnancy after being diagnosed with anencephaly. Information and resources for parents and professionals. Phone support, member discussion board, chat room and pregnancy message board. Registration required. Write: Anencephaly Support Foundation, 20311 Sienna Pines Court, Spring, TX 77379. *Website:* http://www.asfhelp.com *E-mail:* info@asfhelp.com

ANGELMAN SYNDROME

Angelman Syndrome Foundation, Inc. *National network. Founded 1992.* Mission is to advance the awareness and treatment of Angelman syndrome through education and information, research and support for individuals with Angelman syndrome, their families and other concerned persons. Write: Angelman Syndrome Foundation, 3015 E. New York St., Suite A2265, Aurora, IL 60504. Call 1-800-432-6435 or 630-978-4245; Fax: 630-978-7408. *Website:* http://www.angelman.org *E-mail:* info@angelman.org

ANKYLOSING SPONDYLITIS

NATIONAL

Spondylitis Association of America *International network. 25 affiliated groups. Founded 1983.* Research, advocacy, support, education for patients, families, friends and health professionals concerned with ankylosing spondylitis and related diseases (reactive arthritis/Reiter's syndrome, psoriatic arthritis and inflammatory bowel disease). Publications, videotapes and newsletter. Guidelines available to start support groups. Write: Spondylitis Association of America, P.O. Box 5872, Sherman Oaks, CA 91413. Call 1-800-777-8189 or 818-981-1616 (in CA); Fax: 818-981-9826. *Website:* http://www.spondylitis.org *E-mail:* info@spondylitis.org

ONLINE

KickAS.org *Online. 4000+ members.* Support and information for persons with ankylosing spondylitis and related disorders. Provides inspiration, friendship and humor. Message board. Separate forums for affected persons, families, friends and affected teens. *Website:* http://www.kickas.org

ANORCHIDISM

STATEWIDE

Anorchidism Support Group - USA Provides information and support for families and persons affected by anorchidism (absence of the testes), whether congenital or acquired. Newsletter, information and referrals, phone support, pen pals and literature. Write: Anorchidism Support Group - USA, c/o Marianne Bittle, 4 Funny Bone Court, Sicklerville, NJ 08081. Call 856-740-1748 (eve). *Website:* http://freespace.virgin.net/asg.uk/ *E-mail:* asg.uk@virgin.net

NATIONAL

Anorchidism Support Group *International network. Founded 1995.* Information and support for families and persons affected by anorchidism (absence of the testes), whether congenital or acquired (aka testicular regression syndrome, anorchia, vanishing testes syndrome or absent testes). Newsletter. Provides information and support via phone, letter or email. An information leaflet available on request. Write: Anorchidism Support Group, P.O. Box 3025, Romford, Essex RM3 8GX, England. Call 44(0)1708 372597 (will return phone calls outside of UK; please allow for time difference when phoning). *Website:* http://freespace.virgin.net/asg.uk *E-mail:* asg.uk@virgin.net

ANORECTAL MALFORMATIONS

Pull-thru Network, The *International. 2 affiliated groups. Founded 1988.* Support and information for the families with children born with anorectal, colorectal or urogenital disorder and any of the associated diagnoses. Disorders include, but are not limited to cloaca, bladder exstrophy, imperforate anus, VACTERL/VATER association, anal stenosis, cloacal exstrophy and Hirschsprung's Disease. Maintains a database for member networking. Quarterly magazine, online discussion group, weekly chat for members, phone support and literature. Dues $30/year - free membership available upon request. Write: The Pull-Thru Network, 2312 Savoy St., Hoover, AL 35226-1528. Call 205-978-2930. *Website:* http://www.pullthrough.org *E-mail:* info@pullthrough.org

"In helping others, we shall help ourselves, for whatever good we give out completes the circle and comes back to us." --- Flora Edwards

ANOSMIA / PAROSMIA

ONLINE

Anosmia *Online. Founded 1999.* Provides mailing list and resources for people with anosmia (lacking the sense of smell). *Website:* http://groups.yahoo.com/group/anosmia

Congenital Anosmia Forums *Online* forum for persons who suffer from congenital anosmia (born without a sense of smell). Provides support and information. *Website:* http://www.anosmia.net/

Parosmia Smelling Disorder *Online.* Provides mutual support and information for persons who have distortions of their smell. *Website:* http://health.groups.yahoo.com/group/parosmia/

ANTIPHOSPHOLIPID ANTIBODY SYNDROME

APS Foundation, Inc. *Founded 2005.* Dedicated to fostering and facilitating joint efforts in the areas of education, public awareness, research and patient services in an effective and ethical manner. Offers support, understanding and education to Antiphospholipid Antibody Syndrome patients, family, friends and caregivers. Write: APS Foundation of America, Inc., P.O. Box 801, La Crosse, WI 54602-0801. Call 608-782-2626; Fax: 608-782-6569. *Website:* http://www.apsfa.org *E-mail:* tina@apsfa.org

APERT SYNDROME

Apert Syndrome Pen Pals *National network. Founded 1992.* Group correspondence program for persons with Apert syndrome to share experiences. Pen pals, phone help, information and referrals. Write: Apert Syndrome Pen Pals, P.O. Box 115, Providence, RI 02901. Call 401-837-3327. *E-mail:* christinebucci2001@yahoo.com

"Feelings of worth can flourish only in an atmosphere where individual differences are appreciated, mistakes are tolerated, communication is open and rules are flexible – the kind of atmosphere that is found in a nurturing family."
-- Virginia Satir

APRAXIA

(see also speech)

BERGEN

Apraxia Network of Bergen County Support for parents and caregivers of children with apraxia. Mutual sharing, socials, guest speakers, literature and education. Suggested donation $10/yr. Meets 4 times/yr., River Edge. Call Jeanne 201-741-4035 (afternoon, evenings and weekends). *Website:* http://www.speechville.com/communication-station/new-jersey-network.html *E-mail:* jbmistletoe@optonline.net

NATIONAL

Apraxia Kids (A program of The Childhood Apraxia of Speech Association) *National. Founded 2000.* Information and support for parents of children with apraxia of speech, a motor speech disorder. Provides encouragement for parents to start support groups. Education, newsletter, literature, conferences, information, listserv, message boards, e-mail and help desk referrals to self-help groups nationwide. Write: Apraxia Kids, 1151 Freeport Rd., Suite 243, Pittsburgh, PA 15238. *Website:* http://www.apraxia-kids.org *E-mail:* helpdesk@apraxia-kids.org

ARACHNOIDITIS

ONLINE

COFWA (Circle of Friends With Arachnoiditis) *Online. Founded 1998.* Support group which communicates primarily through the use of e-mail. Provides avenue for support, caring, sharing of information and friendly conversations with someone who knows what you are going through on a daily basis. *Website:* http://health.groups.yahoo.com/group/cofwa/

ARNOLD CHIARI MALFORMATION

ONLINE

World Arnold Chiari Malformation Association *Online. International. 4400+ members. Founded 1996.* Provides information, support and understanding to persons concerned with Arnold Chiari malformation. Separate adult and children's online support groups. Write: World Arnold Chiari Malformation Association, c/o Bernard Meyer, 31 Newton Woods Rd., Newtown Square, PA 19073. Call

610-353-4737. *Website:* http://www.pressenter.com/~wacma or http://wacma.com *E-mail:* chip@pressenter.com

ARTERIO VENOUS MALFORMATION / BRAIN ANEURYSM

MIDDLESEX

Kathleen McCriskin Brain AVM/Aneurysm Support Group Provides mutual support and encouragement for persons with brain aneurysms, arterio-venous malformations (AVM) or subarachnoid hemorrhage. Rap sessions and guest speakers. Meets 4th Wed. (except July/Aug.), 7pm, JFK Medical Center, Neuroscience Conference Room, 65 James St., Edison. Call Nancy Vassallo 732-321-7000 ext. 68973.

ARTHROGRYPOSIS

ONLINE

Adults with AMC (Arthrogryposis) *Online. 178 Members. Founded 2001.* Offers support for adults with arthrogryposis to come together and communicate with others affected by AMC. *Website:* http://groups.yahoo.com/group/amc_adults/

Arthrogryposis Support Group *Online. 184 Members. Founded 2000.* Offers an online support group for children, adults and family members of people with arthrogryposis. *Website:* http://groups.yahoo.com/group/arthrogryposissupportgroup/

ASHERMAN'S SYNDROME

Asherman's Syndrome Online Community *Online.* Community of women worldwide who have been diagnosed with Asherman's syndrome (aka intrauterine or uterine synechiae). Provides support by sharing of information and knowledge. *Website:* http://www.ashermans.org *E-mail:* ashermansbook@yahoo.com

"We cannot hold a torch to light another's path without brightening our own."
-- Ben Sweetland

ATAXIA

NATIONAL

National Ataxia Foundation *International. 73 groups. Founded 1957.* Assists families with ataxia. Provides education for professionals and the public. Encourages prevention of ataxia through genetic counseling. Promotes research into causes and treatment. Information and referral, newsletter and assistance in starting support groups. Group development guidelines. Write: National Ataxia Foundation, c/o Michael Parent, 2600 Fernbrook Lane, Suite 119, Minneapolis, MN 55447. Call 763-553-0020; Fax: 763-553-0167. *Website:* http://www.ataxia.org *E-mail:* naf@ataxia.org

ONLINE

A-T Children's Project *(BILINGUAL) Online. Founded 1993.* Enables families of children affected by ataxia telangiectasia to seek information and share thoughts with other families. Family online forum, information and workshops. Write: A-T Children's Project, 668 S. Military Trail, Deerfield Beach, FL 33442. Call 954-481-6611 or 1-800-543-5728. *Website:* http://www.atcp.org *E-mail:* info@atcp.org

AUTOIMMUNE DISORDERS

OCEAN

Autoimmune Information Network Mutual support for patients with any one of over 140 autoimmune diseases. Family members welcome. Rap sessions, literature, phone help, advocacy, guest speakers and buddy system. Meets 4th Sun., 1-3pm, Ocean Medical Center, Conference Room C, 425 Jack Martin Blvd., Brick. Call Barbara Yodice 732-262-0450 (day/eve). *Website:* http://www.aininc.org *E-mail:* autoimmunehelp@aol.com

NATIONAL

American Autoimmune Related Diseases Association, Inc. *National. 2 affiliated groups. Founded 1991.* Mutual support and education for patients with any type of autoimmune disease. Advocacy, referrals to support groups, literature, conferences and quarterly newsletter. Supports research, physician symposium and provides assistance in starting groups. Dues/newsletter subscription $24. Write: American Autoimmune Related Diseases Association, 22100 Gratiot Ave., Eastpointe, MI

48021-2227. Call 586-776-3900; Fax: 586-776-3903. *Website:* http://www.aarda.org *E-mail:* aarda@aarda.org

BARTH SYNDROME

The Barth Syndrome Foundation *(MULTILINGUAL) International. Founded 2000.* Offers support to affected individuals and families. Provides information, support awareness, medical database, diagnostic and clinical descriptions, fact sheets, moderated listserv information available on website, research, outreach, newsletter, referrals, pen pals and biennial conference. Peer-to-peer mentoring program. Write: The Barth Syndrome Foundation, P.O. Box 974, Perry, FL 32348. Call 850-223-1128; Fax: 850-223-3991. *Website:* http://www.barthsyndrome.org *E-mail:* bscontact@barthsyndrome.org

BATTEN DISEASE

Batten Disease Support and Research Association *International. 20 affiliated groups. Founded 1987.* Emotional support for persons with Batten disease. Information and referrals, support group meetings, phone support, conferences and newsletter. Assistance provided for starting new groups. Write: Batten Disease Support Research Association, 166 Humphries Dr., Suite 2, Reynoldsburg, OH 43068. Call 1-800-448-4570. *Website:* http://www.bdsra.org *E-mail:* bdsra1@bdsra.org

BECKWITH WIEDEMANN

ONLINE

Beckwith Wiedemann Family Forum *(MULTILINGUAL) Online. 250 members. Founded 2000.* Promotes support and the lively exchange of Beckwith Wiedemann information and support. Membership is open to anyone interested in BWS. *Website:* http://www.geocities.com/beckwith_wiedemann/ or http://groups.yahoo.com/group/bwschat/

BEHCET'S SYNDROME

American Behcet's Disease Association *National network. Founded 1978.* Mutual support and information for Behcet's patients, their families and professionals. Newsletter (transcribed on tape for visually impaired), information and referrals, phone support, pen pals, conferences and medical advisory board. Pamphlets, literature and press kit. Write: American Behcet's Disease Association,

P.O. Box 19952, Amarillo, TX, 79114. Call 1-800-723-4238 (9am-2pm CST). *Website:* http://www.behcets.com *E-mail:* cfornabaio@behcets.com

BELL'S PALSY / FACIAL PARALYSIS

(see also neurological disorders)

Bell's Palsy Research Foundation *National network. Founded 1995.* Provides information, support and referrals for treatment and rehabilitation to persons diagnosed with Bell's Palsy and other forms of facial paralysis due to acoustic neuroma, Ramseys-Hunt syndrome, pregnancy-induced palsy or Lyme disease. Provides referrals, phone support, intensive facial rehabilitation for all types of residual patients and advocacy. Write: Bell's Palsy Research Foundation, 9713 Lookout Pl., Montgomery Village, MD 20886. Call 301-330-3223. *Website:* http://www.bellspalsy.com *E-mail:* DrTargan@erols.com

BENIGN ESSENTIAL BLEPHAROSPASM

MONMOUTH

Benign Essential Blepharospasm (BEB) Support Group Provides information and support to persons with benign essential blepharospasm (BEB). Networks people together with similar symptoms. Guest speakers, literature and phone help. Meets Sat., 2 times/yr. (May and Nov.), Jersey Shore University Medical Center, Highway 33, Neptune. Call Bonnie 732-922-4429 (day).

NATIONAL

Benign Essential Blepharospasm Research Foundation, Inc. *National. 170 groups. Founded 1981.* Provides information and emotional support to persons with benign essential blepharospasm (BEB). Networks people together with similar symptoms. Doctor referrals and education. Supports research. Bimonthly newsletter. Local group development guidelines. Voluntary contributions. Write: B.E.B. Research Foundation, P.O. Box 12468, Beaumont, TX 77726-2468. Call 409-832-0788. Fax: 409-832-0890. *Website:* http://www.blepharospasm.org *E-mail:* bebrf@sbcglobal.net or bebrf@blepharosapsm.org

"No man or woman of the humblest sort can really be strong, gentle and good, without the world being better for it, without somebody being helped and comforted by the very existence of that goodness." -- Alan Alda

BLADDER EXSTROPHY

Association for the Bladder Exstrophy Community *International network. Founded 1991.* Mutual support for persons affected by bladder exstrophy (parents of children with bladder exstrophy, adults, healthcare professionals and others interested in exstrophy). Newsletter, literature, information and referrals, informal pen pal program, conferences, advocacy and directory of members. Informal kids e-mail exchange. Dues $25/yr. Write: Association for the Bladder Exstrophy Community, 3075 First St., La Salle, MI 48145. Call Cindy Buckley 1-866-300-2222. *Website:* http://www.bladderexstrophy.com *E-mail:* admin@bladderexstrophy.com

BRACHIAL PLEXUS INJURY / ERB'S PALS

The Brachial Plexus Palsy Foundation *International. 4 affiliated groups. Founded 1994.* Information, resources, education and support for families and individuals affected by brachial plexus palsy (also known as brachial plexus injury or Erb's palsy). Online support message board, annual family event and annual fundraiser. Write: Brachial Plexus Palsy Foundation, 210 Springhaven Circle, Royersford, PA 19468. Call 610-792-4234; Fax: 610-948-0678. *Website:* http://www.brachialplexuspalsyfoundation.org *E-mail:* contact@brachialplexuspalsyfoundation.org

BRONCHIECTASIS

ONLINE

Bronchiectasis Chat Group *Online.* Email support group for people who have bronchiectasis and their relatives. *Website:* http://health.groups.yahoo.com/group/bronchiectasis/

CANAVAN DISEASE

(see also leukodystrophy)

Canavan Foundation *International. Founded 1992.* Provides information and education for persons affected by Canavan's. Offers literature, phone support, conferences and advocacy. Supports research. Online support available. Write: Canavan Foundation, 450 West End Ave., New York, NY 10024. Call 212-873-4640 or 1-877-422-6282; Fax: 212-873-7892. *Website:* http://www.canavanfoundation.org *E-mail:* info@canavanfoundation.org

CAVERNOUS ANGIOMA

Angioma Alliance *Online. Founded 2002.* Support and information for any person affected by cavernous angioma of the brain and spine. Educational materials, support via a community forum, listserv, chats and contact information for research studies. Maintains tissue/DNA bank and patient registry. Site available in Spanish, and (in a limited way) Portuguese. Hosts annual national family conferences and scientific workshops for researchers. Works to increase physician and public awareness of the illness. Call 1-866-432-5226. *Website:* http://www.angiomaalliance.org *E-mail:* info@angiomaaliance.org

CEREBROCOSTOMANDIBULAR SYNDROME

Cerebrocostomandibular Syndrome Support Group *National network. Founded 1998.* Provides support and guidance to families of children with cerebrocostomandibular syndrome (recessed lower mandible and rib anomalies). Exchange of messages through email. Guidelines and help available for starting new groups. Write: Tara Montague, 7 Primrose Dr., Burlington, NJ 08016. Call 609-239-7831. *E-mail:* tara@marysplacerehab.com

CFC SYNDROME

CFC International *International network. Incorporated in 1999.* Mutual support for parents and healthcare providers of children with cardiofaciocutaneous syndrome. Strives to find and disseminate information on CFC syndrome. Offers newsletter, information, referrals, online listserv and phone support. Medical advisors. Genetic testing is now available to confirm the syndrome. International clinic and family conferences every two years. Write: CFC International, c/o Brenda Conger, 183 Brown Rd., Vestal, NY 13850. Call 607-772-9666 (eve). *Website:* http://www.cfcsyndrome.org *E-mail:* bconger@cfcsyndrome.org

CHARCOT-MARIE-TOOTH DISEASE / PERONEAL MUSCULAR ATROPHY / HEREDITARY MOTOR SENSORY NEUROPATHY

NATIONAL

Charcot-Marie-Tooth Association *National. 25 affiliated groups. Founded 1983.* Information support for patients and families affected by Charcot-Marie-Tooth disorders (also known as peroneal muscular atrophy or hereditary motor sensory neuropathy). Referrals, newsletter, phone help, support groups and conferences. Assistance starting similar groups. Write: Charcot-Marie-Tooth Association, 2700 Chestnut Parkway, Chester, PA 19013. Call Pat Dreibelbis 1-800-606-2682 or 610-499-9264; Fax: 610-499-9267. *Website:* http://www.charcot-marie-tooth.org *E-mail:* cmtassoc@aol.com

Hereditary Neuropathy Foundation *International network. Founded 2001.* Sharing and caring for those with Charcot-Marie-Tooth disease and other hereditary neuropathies. Extensive library of support materials and resources available. Publishes informational brochures and children's book. Write: Hereditary Neuropathy Foundation, 1751 2nd Ave., Suite 103, New York, NY 10128. Call 212-722-8396. *Website:* http://www.hnf-cure.org *E-mail:* info@hnf-cure.org

CHARGE SYNDROME

CHARGE Syndrome Foundation, Inc. *International network. Founded 1993.* Networking of families affected by CHARGE Syndrome (coloboma of the eye, choanal atresia, cranial nerve abnormalities, characteristic ears and other problems). Publications include CHARGE syndrome brochure, New Parent packet (12+ pgs), "CHARGE Syndrome: A Management Manual for Parents" (270 pgs), and conference papers. Membership ($15/families; $20/professionals; $30/organizations) includes quarterly newsletter and parent-to-parent support. Conferences in odd years (e.g. 2005). Write: Marion A. Norbury, c/o CHARGE Syndrome Foundation Inc., 409 Vandiver Dr., Ste. 5-104, Columbia, MO 65202-1563. Call 573-499-4694 (Voice/Fax); Families only call 1-800-442-7604 (day/eve); *Website:* http://www.chargesyndrome.org *E-mail:* marion@chargesyndrome.org

CHEMICAL HYPERSENSITIVITY / ENVIRONMENTAL ILLNESS

NATIONAL

H.E.A.L. (Human Ecology Action League, Inc.) *National. 40+ chapters. Founded 1977.* Education and information for persons concerned about the health effects of environmental exposures. Quarterly newsletter. Other publications include: information sheets, resource list, directories, reading list and book "Fragrance and Health." Referrals to local and regional chapters and support services. Dues $26/yr. (US); $32/yr. (Canada); $38/yr. (Int'l). Write: HEAL, P.O. Box 29629, Atlanta, GA 30359-0629. Call 404-248-1898; Fax: 404-248-0162.

Website: http://members.aol.com/HEALNatnl/index.html *E-mail:* HEALNatnl@aol.com

National Center for Environmental Health Strategies *National network. Founded 1986.* Fosters the development of creative solutions to environmental health problems with a focus on indoor air quality, chemical and electrical sensitivities and environmental disabilities. Clearinghouse and technical services, educational materials, workshops, community outreach, policy development, research, support and advocacy for persons injured by chemical/environment exposures. Special projects on school-related exposures and Gulf War Veterans. Books, publications and newsletter. Focuses on access and accommodation rights. Free information packets. Write: National Center for Environmental Health Strategies, 1100 Rural Ave., Voorhees, NJ 08043. Call Mary Lamielle 856-429-5358 or 856-816-8820 (cell). *Website:* http://www.ncehs.org *E-mail:* marylamielle@ncehs.org

CHROMOSOME 18 DISORDERS

NATIONAL

4P- Support Group *International. Founded 1984.* Provides support and information to families of children with chromosome 4 conditions. Offers phone support and biographies on other children with these conditions. Quarterly newsletter. Write: 4P- Support Group, Attn: Larry Bentley, Executive Director, P.O. Box 1676, Gresham, OR 97030. Call 503-661-1855. *Website:* http://www.4p-supportgroup.org

Chromosome 9P- Network *International network. Founded 1983.* Provides information, parent-to-parent networking and technical support to parents of children with 9P- and other deletions of 9P, ring 9, mosaic, translocations, inverted 9p, etc. Facilitates research to further understand monosomy 9P. Information, referrals, phone support and yearly conferences. Write: Chromosome 9P- Network, P.O. Box 54, Stanley, ID 83278. *Website:* http://www.9pminus.org

Can't find an appropriate group in your area? The Clearinghouse helps people start groups. Give us a call at 1-800-367-6274

Chromosome 18 Registry Research Society *International network. Founded 1990.* Provides support and education concerning disorders of chromosome 18. Encourages and conducts research into areas that impact families. Links affected families and their physicians to the research community. Newsletter, phone support, annual conference, information and referrals. Dues $20/US; $25/Int'l. Write: Chromosome 18 Registry Research Society, c/o Gloria Ellwanger, 7155 Oakridge Dr., San Antonio, TX 78229. Call 210-657-4968 (voice/fax). *Website:* http://www.chromosome18.org *E-mail:* office@chromosome18.org

Chromosome 22 Central *International network. Founded 1996.* Networking and support for parents of children with any chromosome 22 disorder. Supports research. Offers literature, phone support, newsletter and pen pals. Online bulletin boards. Write: Chromosome 22 Central, 237 Kent Ave., Timmins, Ontario, Canada P4N 3C2. Call 705-268-3099; Fax: 705-268-3099. *Website:* http://www.c22c.org *E-mail:* a815@c22c.org or c22c@ntl.sympatico.ca

Chromosome Deletion Outreach *National network. Founded 1992.* Organization providing support and information to families affected by rare chromosome disorders. Membership free. Write: Chromosome Deletion Outreach, P.O. Box 724, Boca Raton, FL 33429-0724. Call 561-395-4252; Fax: 561-395-4252. *Website:* http://www.chromodisorder.org *E-mail:* info@chromodisorder.org

Disorders of Chromosome 16 Foundation *International network. Founded 1998.* Provides support and information to families of children affected by any chromosome 16 disorder, including partial trisomy 16 and unbalanced translocations. Information and referrals, phone support and literature. Write: DOC16, 1321 Marcy St., Iowa City, IA 52240. Call Alex or Dan Schaeffel at 319-354-5478. *Website:* http://www.trisomy16.org *E-mail:* danalex@avalon.net

National Center for Chromosome Inversions *National network. Founded 1992.* Mutual support for families affected by chromosome inversions. Phone support, pen pal program, information and referrals. Write: National Center for Chromosome Inversions, 282 SE Anastasia St., Lake City, FL 32025-1730. Call 386-752-1548 (voice/fax). *E-mail:* ncfci@msn.com

"You can't stay in your corner of the forest waiting for others to come to you. You have to go to them sometimes." -- A. A. Miline (said by Winnie the Pooh)

CLUB FOOT

ONLINE

Clubfoot Mailing List *Online. Founded 1998. 420 members.* Support group for parents of children with clubfoot/feet, persons with clubfoot/feet or anyone needing support on this topic. Goal is to provide support, friendship and encouragement. Operates through an email mailing list. Must subscribe to list to join group. *Website:* http://health.groups.yahoo.com/group/clubfoot/

COBALAMIN

Cobalamin Network, The *International network. 2 chapters. Founded 1985.* Emotional support and information for families of children affected by inborn errors of cobalamin metabolism. Referrals to pediatric metabolic practitioners. Write: Cobalamin Network, P.O. Box 174, Thetford Center, VT 05075 or Cobalamin Network, 207 E. 14th Pl., Cut Off, LA 70345. Call 802-785-4029, 802-785-3112 or 985-798-5631. *E-mail:* SueBee18@valley.net or menta@cajunnet.com

COCKAYNE SYNDROME

Share Care Cockayne Syndrome Network *(BILINGUAL) International network. Founded 1981.* Mutual support and networking for families affected by Cockayne syndrome. Sharing of information between families and professionals. Maintains registry of families. Information, referrals, newsletter and phone support. Website and pamphlet available in Spanish, Japanese, German and Portugese. Write: Share Care Cockayne Syndrome Network, P.O. Box 282, Waterford, VA 20197. Call 703-727-0404. *Website:* http://www.cockayne-syndrome.org *E-mail:* JackieClark@aol.com

COFFIN-LOWRY SYNDROME

Coffin-Lowry Syndrome Foundation, The *International network. Founded 1991.* Serves as a clearinghouse for information on Coffin-Lowry syndrome. Forum for exchanging experiences, advice and information with other CLS families. Seeks to become a visible group in the medical, scientific, educational and professional communities in order to facilitate referrals of newly diagnosed individuals and to encourage medical and behavioral research. Maintains mailing list of families and professionals. Provides newsletter, family support and informational packet. Write: The Coffin-Lowry Syndrome Foundation, c/o Mary

Hoffman, 3045 255th Ave., S.E., Sammamish, WA 98075. Call 425-427-0939 (after 5:30pm PST). *Website:* http://clsf.info or group discussion Website: http://groups.yahoo.com/group/clsfoundation/ *E-mail:* clsfoundation@yahoo.com

COGAN'S SYNDROME

ONLINE

Cogan's Contact Network *Online Network. Founded 1989.* Mutual support and sharing of experiences and strategies for persons with Cogan's Syndrome. Aim is to help people understand Cogan's, a rare disorder that affects hearing, eyes, balance, etc. Networking, pen pals and literature. Online dues $12/yr. Write: YUPPA/Cogan's Contact, P.O. Box 145, Freehold, NJ 07728-0145. Call Anthony 732-761-9809 (TDD). *Website:* http://www.coganssyndrome.info *E-mail:* uscogans@juno.com

CONGENITAL ADRENAL HYPERPLASIA

NATIONAL

CARES Foundation Inc. *International. 48 regional support groups. Founded 2001.* Goal is to educate the public and professionals about all types of congenital adrenal hyperplasia, the symptoms, diagnostic protocol, treatment, genetic frequency and the necessity for early intervention through newborn screening. Offers information and support to affected individuals and their families. Write: CARES Foundation, 2414 Morris Ave., Suite 110, Union, NJ 07083. Call 1-866-227-3737 or 973-912-3895; Fax: 973-912-8890. *Website:* http://www.caresfoundation.org *E-mail:* info@caresfoundation.org

Congenital Adrenal Hyperplasia *National division of MAGIC. Founded 1989.* Offers educational and emotional support to families of children with congenital adrenal hyperplasia. Provides information and referrals, kids program, phone support, annual convention, networking and quarterly newsletter. Assistance in starting new groups. Write: Mary Andrews, CAH Division of MAGIC Foundation, 6645 W. North Ave., Oak Park, IL 60302. Call 1-800-362-4423; Fax: 708-383-0899. *Website:* http://www.magicfoundation.org *E-mail:* mary@magicfoundation.org

CONGENITAL CENTRAL HYPOVENTILATION / ONDINE'S CURSE

WARREN

CCHS Family Network Support for families of children with congenital central hypoventilation syndrome (under 18 welcome). Phone help, advocacy, pen pals and literature. Family conference every 2 years, otherwise communicate via phone, letters and quarterly newsletters. Call Desiree Cougle 908-852-2082 (day/eve); Fax: 908-850-9537. *Website:* http://www.cchs.org

ONLINE

CCHS Network (Congenital Central Hypoventilation) *International network. Founded 1990.* Mutual support for families caring for a child who has congenital central hypoventilation syndrome (aka Ondine's curse). Provides physician directory, family newsletter, chatroom, equipment information, information and referrals. Facilitates and supports CCHS research. Holds family educational conferences every three years. Provides online referrals to local support groups. Write: CCHS Network, c/o Mary Vanderlaan, 71 Maple St., Oneonta, NY 13820. Fax: 607-431-4351. *Website:* http://www.cchsnetwork.org *E-mail:* vanderlaanm@hartwick.edu

CONGENITAL CYTOMEGALOVIRUS DISEASE

National Congenital Cytomegalovirus Disease Registry *National network. Founded 1990.* Parent support network that provides support to families of children with congenital cytomegalovirus disease (CMV). Information, referrals, newsletter and literature. Write: National Congenital Cytomegalovirus Disease Registry, c/o Feigin Center, Suite 1150, MC3-2371, Houston, TX 77030-2399. Call Carol Griesser, RN 832-824-4387; Fax: 832-825-4347. *Website:* http://www.bcm.edu/pedi/infect/cmv *E-mail:* cmv@bcm.edu

CONJOINED TWINS

Conjoined Twins International *International network. Founded 1996.* Support for conjoined twins, their families and professionals. Offers peer support, professional counseling, crisis intervention, telephone helpline, pen pal network, videos, information and referrals. Peer counseling, speakers' bureau, registry of affected families and membership directory. Write: Conjoined Twins International,

P.O. Box 10895, Prescott, AZ 86304-0895. Call 928-445-2777. *Website:* http://www.conjoinedtwinsint.com *E-mail:* dwdegeraty@myexcel.com

CORNELIA DE LANGE

Cornelia de Lange Syndrome Foundation, Inc. *National. 2500+ member families. Founded 1981.* Provides support and education to families affected by Cornelia de Lange syndrome. Supports research. Newsletter. Annual meetings. Professional network. Write: Cornelia de Lange Syndrome Foundation, 302 West Main St., Suite 100, Avon, CT 06001. Call 1-800-223-8355 or 860-676-8166; Fax: 860-676-8337. *Website:* http://cdlsusa.org *E-mail:* info@cdlsusa.org

CORTICOBASAL GANGLIONIC DEGENERATION

ONLINE

CBGD (Corticobasal Ganglionic Degeneration) Support Network *Online. 455 members Founded 1998.* Support for anyone affected by corticobasal ganglionic degeneration (a rare neurological disorder characterized by cell loss in the brain). Offers education, information and newsletter. Networks members together for emotional support. Write: CBGD Support Network, c/o Theresa Roberts, 1941 Stevely Ave., Long Beach, CA 90815. *Website:* http://health.groups.yahoo.com/group/cbgd_support

COSTELLO SYNDROME

International Costello Syndrome Support Group *International network. Founded 1996.* Mutual support for parents of children with Costello syndrome. Information and referrals, literature, phone support, pen pals, online chat room and newsletter. Write Colin and Cath Stone, 90 Parkfield Rd. North, New Moston, M40 3RQ, United Kingdom. Call +44 161 682 2479. *Website:* http://wwwcostellokids.org.uk *E-mail:* c.stone8@ntlworld.com

CREUTZFELDT-JAKOB DISEASE

STATEWIDE

CJD Foundation Information support to family members and friends of victims of Creutzfeldt-Jakob disease. Phone help, speakers bureau, literature. Call Marie Kassai 201-791-8425 (eve). *E-mail:* mariek43@optonline.net

NATIONAL

CJD (Creutzfeldt-Jakob Disease Foundation, Inc.) *National network. Founded 1993.* Provides support to families who have a loved one with, or have lost a loved one to this illness. Seeks to promote research, education and awareness of Creutzfeldt-Jakob disease. Hosts online support chat every 2nd and 4th Tuesday, 7:30 - 9:30 pm (EST). Write: Creutzfeldt-Jakob Disease Foundation, P.O. Box 5312, Akron, OH 44334. Call 1-800-659-1991. *Website:* http://cjdfoundation.org *E-mail:* help@cjdfoundation.org

ONLINE

CJD Voice *Online.* Provides information and emotional support to persons who have lost a loved one to Creutzfeldt-Jakob disease, a fatal brain-deteriorating disorder. Advocacy. Email discussion group, message board and scheduled chatroom sessions. *Website:* http://www.cjdvoice.org *E-mail:* tunket60@sbcglobal.net

CRI DUCHAT (5P) SYNDROME

5P- Society *International network. Founded 1987.* Support organization for families having a child with 5P- syndrome (aka cri du chat), a genetic disorder characterized by a high-pitched cry. Dedicated to facilitating flow of information among affected families and medical professionals. Listing of families in U.S. and Canada. Newsletter. Annual meeting. Write: 5P-Society, P.O. Box 268, Lakewood, CA 90714-0268. Call 1-888-970-0777; Fax: 562-920-5240. *Website:* http://www.fivepminus.org *E-mail:* director@fivepminus.org

CROUZON SYNDROME

ONLINE

Crouzon Support Network *Online.* Support group for individuals and families who are dealing with Crouzon syndrome and other craniofacial anomalies. A place to share experience, mutual support, inspiration and information. *Website:* http://health.groups.yahoo.com/group/crouzons

"Have the courage to act instead of react." -- Earlene Larson Jenks

CUSHING'S DISEASE

NATIONAL

Cushing's Help and Support *International. Founded 2000.* Support and information for persons with Cushing's disease. Offers support to family and friends. Message boards, literature, chat room, guest speakers, annual national conference, pen pals, phone support network and advocacy. Write: Cushing's, 13222 Point Pleasant Dr., Fairfax, VA 22033-3515. Call 1-877-825-0128; Fax: 703-378-8517. *Website:* http://www.cushings-help.com *E-mail:* CushingsSupport@aol.com

Cushing's Support and Research Foundation, Inc. *International. Founded 1995.* Provides information and support to patients with Cushing's. Newsletter and networking so patients can contact others with Cushing's. Write: Cushing's Support Research Foundation, Inc. 65 East India Row, 22B, Boston, MA 02110. *Website:* http://CSRF.net *E-mail:* cushinfo@csrf.net

CUTIS LAXA

Cutis Laxa Internationale International. *Founded 2001.* Support group for those afflicted with any type of cutis laxa, a rare genetic disorder. Networking , promotes research and advocacy. Dues $50/yr or L22/yr. Write: Cutis Laxa Internationale, 35 route des Chaignes, 17740 Sainte Marie de Re, France. Call 33 (0)5 46 55 00 59. *Website:* http://www.orpha.net/nestasso/cutislax *E-mail:* mcjlboiteux@aol.com

CYSTINOSIS

ONLINE

Cystinosis Research Network *Online. Founded 1996.* Dedicated to supporting and advocating for continued research, providing family support and education programs. Professionals and caregivers are welcome to join. Promotes and supports research that will lead to a better understanding, improved treatments and a cure for cystinosis. Dedicated to improving awareness and education of cystinosis and to be utilized as a resource for families and public. Programs include support group, networking, toll-free number, website, newsletter and family conferences. Website to improve awareness and education of cystinosis for patients, families and physicians. Non-moderated but members must be pre-approved by CRN. Write: Cystinosis Research Network, 10 Pine Ave., Burlington, MA 01803. Call

1-866-276-3669 or 781-229-6182; Fax: 781-229-6030. *Website:* http://www.cystinosis.org *E-mail:* CRN@cystinosis.org

DANCING EYE SYNDROME / KINSBOURNE SYNDROME/ OPSOCLONUS / MYOCLONIC ENCEPHALOPATHY

NATIONAL

Dancing Eye Syndrome *International network. Founded 1988.* Support and information for families of children with dancing eye syndrome (aka Kinsbourne syndrome, opsoclonus myoclonus or myoclonic encephalopathy of infants), a disorder consisting of loss of balance, irregular eye movements and muscle jerking. Newsletter and phone help. Write: Dancing Eye Syndrome, c/o J. Stanton-Roberts, 78 Quantock Rd., W. Sussex BN13 2HQ, England. Call 01903-532383 (voice/fax). *E-mail:* support@dancingeyes.org.uk

Opsoclonus-Myoclonus Support Network *National network. Founded 1994.* Networking for parents of children with opsoclonus-myoclonus syndrome through phone and online messages. Doctor referrals, consultation. Literature and current research information. Write: Sandra Greenberg, 2116 Casa Linda Dr., West Covina, CA 91791. Call 626-919-2448. *Website:* http://www.geocities.com/opso-myoclonus *E-mail:* sandragreenberg@hotmail.com

DANDY-WALKER SYNDROME

Dandy-Walker Syndrome Network *International network. Founded 1993.* Provides mutual support, information and networking for families affected by Dandy-Walker Syndrome. Phone support. Write: Dandy-Walker syndrome Network, c/o Desiree Fleming, 5030 142nd Path, Apple Valley, MN 55124. Call 952-423-4008.

DEGOS DISEASE (MALIGNANT ATROPHIC PAPULOSIS)

ONLINE

Degos Patients Support Network *Online.* Support and information for persons with Degos Disease (aka malignant atrophic papulosis or Kohlmeier-Degos disease), an extremely rare thrombotic vasculopathy affecting people of all ages all over the world. Message board for patients, their families and caregivers. Secure section with access to discussion forum and other information for medical professionals only. *Website:* http://www.degosdisease.com *E-mail:* judith@degosdisease.com

DENTATORUBRAL PALLIDOHUYSIAN ATROPHY

DRPLA (Dentatorubral Pallidoluysian Atrophy) Network *International network. Founded 1999.* Support and information for persons affected by dentatorubral pallidoluysian atrophy, a rare genetic disorder that leads to physical and cognitive problems. Phone support, pen pals, online and email discussions. Write: DRPLA, c/o Frank J. Marone, Ph.D., 1426 46th Ave., San Francisco, CA 94122-2903. Call 415-753-5695 or 1-800-499-7803. *E-mail:* bmsca@juno.com

DERCUM'S DISEASE / ADIPOSIS DOLORSA

ONLINE

Dercum's Disease *Online. Founded 1998.* Support for persons with Dercum's disease (aka adiposis dolorsa), characterized by fatty lipomas under the skin that cause pain. Aim is to eradicate the pain and suffering of Dercum's disease through finding the cause and cure. Forum for personal stories, links to support groups and medical articles. *Website:* http://www.dercum.org *E-mail:* dercum@dercum.org

DIABETES INSIPIDUS

Diabetes Insipidus Foundation, Inc. (MULTILINGUAL) *International network. Founded 1996.* Support for families and professionals coping with neurogenic/central, nephrogenic, gestagenic and dipsogenic/polydipsic diabetes insipidus. Provides information and referrals, phone support and advocacy. Website includes articles (English, French and Spanish). Message board and 24 hour chat room. Newsletter. Write: Diabetes Insipidus Foundation, 5203 New Prospect Dr., Ellicott City, MD 21043. Call Mary Evans-Lee 706-323-7576; Fax: 410-247-5584. *Website:* http://www.diabetesinsipidus.org *E-mail:* info@diabetesinsipidus.org

"One person can make a difference, and every person must try."
-- John F. Kennedy

DUANE'S RETRACTION SYNDROME

ONLINE

Duane's Retraction Syndrome *Online. 1061 member. Founded 1999.* A place for those affected by Duane's retraction syndrome (an eye mobility disorder) to share experiences and information with others. *Website:* http://health.groups.yahoo.com/group/duanes/

DUBOWITZ SYNDROME

NE Dubowitz Syndrome Support *National. Founded 1997.* Information, education, support and networking for parents of children with Dubowitz syndrome and concerned professionals. Information on assistive technology and educational issues. Referrals, pen pals, advocacy and information on geneticists. Write: NE Dubowitz Syndrome Support, c/o Sharon Terzian, 106 Verndale St., Warwick, RI 02889. Call 401-737-3138. *Website:* http://www.dubowitzsyndrome.net *E-mail:* dubowitzsyndrome@netzero.net

DYSAUTONOMIA

NATIONAL

Dysautonomia Foundation, Inc., The *International. 13 chapters. Founded 1951.* Provides peer support, information and referrals for families affected by familial dysautonomia. Raises funds for medical and clinic research. Aims to raise public awareness about the disease. Testing for all Ashkenazi Jewish individuals is now available. Newsletter. Write: Dysautonomia Foundation, Inc., 315 West 39th St., Suite 701, New York, NY 10018. Call 212-279-1066; Fax: 212-279-2066. *Website:* http://www.familialdysautonomia.org *E-mail:* info@familialdysautonomia.org

FD Hope *National.* Parent-run foundation that supports cutting-edge research. Provides information, newsletter and FD-Net (email network for families and professionals). Write: Kenneth M. Slaw, PhD, c/o FD Hope, 1170 Green Knolls Dr., Buffalo Grove, IL 60089. Call 847-913-0455.

National Dysautonomia Research Foundation *National network. Founded 1996.* Provides support, educational material and medical referrals for persons who have dysautonomia (a disorder of the autonomic nervous system). Networking, literature, advocacy, phone support and conferences. Encourages research. Online email and discussion support forum, groups and free downloadable online Patient Handbook. Write: National Dysautonomia Research Foundation, P.O. Box 301, Red Wing, MN 55066-2108. Call 651-267-0525 (day); Fax: 651-267-0524. *Website:* http://www.ndrf.org *E-mail:* ndrf@ndrf.org

National Society For MVP Dysautonomia *National. 59 affiliated groups. Founded 1987.* Assists individuals suffering from mitral valve prolapse and dysautonomia to find support and understanding. Education on symptoms and treatment. Newsletter and literature. Write: National Society for MVP Dysautonomia, 880 Montclair Rd., Suite 370, Birmingham, AL 35213. Call 205-592-5765 (day) or 1-800-541-8602 (day); Fax: 205-592-5707. *Website:* http//www.mvprolapse.com *E-mail:* staff@MVProlapse.com

DYSTONIA

MONMOUTH

Central Jersey Dystonia Support Group Support and education for persons with dystonia. Newsletter. Meets Sat., 4 times/yr., Freehold. Call Janice and Len 732-409-1112 (day). *E-mail:* cjdystonia@aol.com

NATIONAL

Dystonia Medical Research Foundation *International. 110 chapters. Founded 1976.* Provides education, awareness and support groups for persons with dystonia. Fundraises for research. Newsletter, information and referrals to local groups. Also offers guidelines for starting similar groups. Write: Dystonia Medical Research Foundation, 1 E. Wacker Dr., Suite 2430, Chicago, IL 60601-1905. Call 312-755-0198 (US), 1-800-361-8061 (Canada); Fax: 312-803-0138. *Website:* http://www.dystonia-foundation.org/ *E-mail:* dystonia@dystonia-foundation.org

DYSTROPHIC EPIDERMOLYSIS BULLOSA

DEBRA of America (Dystrophic Epidermolysis Bullosa Research Association) *National network. 3 chapters. Founded 1980.* Support and information for families affected by epidermolysis bullosa. Promotes research, provides education for patients, families and professionals, emergency financial support, emergency wound care supplies, New Family Advocate program, newsletter, biennial national conference, information and referrals . Write: DEBRA of America, 5 W. 36th St., Room 404, New York, NY 10018-7179. Call

212-868-1573 or 1-866-332-7276; Fax: 212-868-9296. *Website:* http://www.debra.org *E-mail:* staff@debra.org

EAR ANOMALIES

ONLINE

Atresia-Microtia Group *Online. 900+ members.* Forum for people, and parents of children, with aural atresia and/or microtia. Issues addressed include emotional support, hearing aids, ear reconstruction and insurance. *Website:* http://health.groups.yahoo.com/group/AtresiaMicrotia/ *E-mail:* toAtresiaMicrotia-owner@yahoogroups.com

ECTODERMAL DYSPLASIAS

National Foundation for Ectodermal Dysplasias *National network. Founded 1981.* Distributes information on ectodermal dysplasia syndrome and treatments. Provides support programs for families and funds research projects. Quarterly newsletter. Annual family conference and regional conferences, dental implant program and scholarship opportunities. Directory of members for informal contacts among families. Write: National Foundation for Ectodermal Dysplasias, 410 E. Main St., Box 114, Mascoutah, IL 62258-0114. Call 618-566-2020; Fax: 618-566-4718. *Website:* http://www.nfed.org *E-mail:* info@nfed.org

EHLERS-DANLOS SYNDROME

Ehlers-Danlos National Foundation *National. 35 local groups. Founded 1985.* Provides resources for Ehlers-Danlos syndrome patients, families and health care professionals. Mission is to disseminate accurate information, provide a network of support and communication and to foster and support research. Online message boards for EDNF members. Write: Ehlers-Danlos National Foundation, 3200 Wilshire Blvd., Suite 1601, South Tower, Los Angeles, CA 90010. Call 213-368-3800; Fax: 213-427-0057. *Website:* http://www.ednf.org *E-mail:* staff@ednf.org

ELLIS VAN CREVELD SYNDROME / CHRONDROECTODERMAL DYSPLASIA

Ellis Van Creveld Support Group *International network. Founded 1997.* Provides support and information for families affected by Ellis Van Creveld syndrome (aka chondroectodermal dysplasia), an extremely rare form of dwarfism.

Networks families together for support. Literature, advocacy, phone help, information and referrals. Connects with medical community to find ways to save the lives of infants born with this genetic disorder. Write: Ellis Van Creveld Support Group, 17 Bridlewood Trail, Honeoye Falls, NY 14472. Call 585-624-8277 (day/eve). *E-mail:* PattiMO44@aol.com

ENCEPHALITIS

NATIONAL

Encephalitis Information Resource *International network. Founded 1994.* Provides support and information for persons with encephalitis (inflammation of the brain) and their families. Aims to educate public and professionals about the condition. Newsletter, information and referrals. Write: Encephalitis Information Resource, 7b Savile St., Malton, North Yorkshire, Y017 7LL UK. Call +44 (0) 653 699 599 (voice/fax). *Website:* http://www.encephalitis.info *E-mail:* mail@encephalitis.info

ONLINE

Encephalitis Global *Online.* Provides support and information for encephalitis survivors, caregivers, loved ones and for interested persons. Includes a guide for newly diagnosed persons, links, downloadable information pamphlet, group discussions and live chats. *Website:* http://www.encephalitisglobal.com *E-mail:* EncephalitisGlobal@shaw.ca

Encephgroup *Online. 494 members. Founded 2000.* Support group for survivors of all types of encephalitis and their family members, caregivers and friends. *Website:* http://health.groups.yahoo.com/group/encephgroup/

EOSINOPHILIA-MYALGIA SYNDROME

National Eosinophilia Myalgia Syndrome Network *National network. Founded 1993.* Mutual support for persons with eosinophilia myalgia syndrome (EMS), caused by using L-tryptophan. Families welcome. Information and support through online support groups, phone contacts and newsletter. Medical and legal information, advocacy, literature and conferences. Write: National Eosinophilia Myalgia Syndrome Network, Attn: Jann Heston, P.O. Box 3016, 155 Delaware Ave., Lexington, OH 44904-1212. Call 614-583-5720; Fax: 614-737-7384. *Website:* http://www.nemsn.org *E-mail:* NEMSN2005@aol.com or jheston@gmail.com

ERYTHROMELALGIA

The Erythromelalgia Association (TEA) *International network. Founded 1999.* Provides support and information to those diagnosed with erythromelalgia. Offers education to increase awareness of this rare condition within the medical profession and the general public. Fundraises to promote research into the causes, diagnostic methods and treatments. Write: The Erythromelalgia Association, 200 Old Castle Lane, Wallingford, PA 19086. Call 610-566-0797. *Website:* http://www.erythromelalgia.org *E-mail:* membership@erythromelalgia.org

ESSENTIAL TREMOR

(see also neurological disorders)

International Essential Tremor Foundation *International. 77 affiliated groups. Founded 1989.* Provides information and support for persons affected by essential tremor. Information and referrals, literature and research updates. Quarterly newsletter. Dues $30. Write: International Essential Tremor Foundation, P.O. Box 14005, Lenexa, KS 66285. Call 1-888-387-3667 or 913-341-3880; Fax: 913-341-1296. *Website:* http://www.essentialtremor.org/ *E-mail:* STAFF@essentialtremor.org

FABRY DISEASE

Fabry Support Information Group (FSIG) *National network. Founded 1996.* Dedicated to dispensing information and encouraging mutual self help as a means of emotional support to Fabry patients and family members. Newsletters, networking of members, discussion page, information and referrals. Write: Fabry Support Information Group, P.O. Box 510, Concordia, MO 64020. Call 660-463-1355; Fax: 660-463-1356. *Website:* http://www.fabry.org *E-mail:* info@fabry.org

FACIAL DISFIGUREMENT

(see also specific disorders, burn victims, accidents)

NATIONAL

AboutFace USA *National. Founded 1991.* Provides emotional support and information to persons with facial differences and their families. Network database of 900+ families who have similar concerns. Promotes public education and awareness. Also has cleft advocate program which provides online parent-patient support network. Newsletter, information and referrals. Write: AboutFace USA,

P.O. Box 158, South Beloit, IL 61080-0158. Call 1-888-486-1209; Fax: 702-341-5351. *Website:* http://www.aboutfaceusa.org *E-mail:* debbie@aboutfaceusa.org

Forward Face *Model. 1 group in New York. Founded 1978.* Mutual support for people with craniofacial disfigurement and their families. Strongly advocates educating members and the public in the quest for understanding and acceptance. Liaison with medical personnel. Newsletter and videotapes. Dues $30. Teen/young adult support group called The Inner Faces. Write: Forward Face, 317 E. 34th St., 9th Floor, Suite 901A, New York, NY 10016. Call 212-684-5860; Fax: 212-684-5864. *Website:* http://www.forwardface.org *E-mail:* info@forwardface.org

Let's Face It *National. Founded 1987.* Mission is to advance knowledge about, by and for people with facial differences and to promote their full and equal participation in society. Provides information and resources for persons with facial differences, their families, professionals and the public. Write: Let's Face It, c/o University of Michigan, School of Dentistry / Dentistry Library, 1011 N. University, Ann Arbor, MI 48109-1078. *Website:* http://www.dent.umich.edu/faceit/ *E-mail:* faceit@umich.edu

FACIOSCAPULOHUMERAL DISEASE / LANDOUZY-DEJERINE

(see also muscular dystrophy)

FSH Society, Inc. (Facioscapulohumeral Disease) *National network. Founded 1991.* Support, information, education, networking and advocacy for individuals with facioscapulohumeral disease (aka Landouzy-Dejerine muscular dystrophy). Purpose is to increase awareness, understanding and conduct research and education on the second most prevalent muscular dystrophy in adults. Funds research through grants to researchers. Acts as a clearinghouse for information on the FSHD disorder and on potential drugs and devices designed to alleviate the effects of the disease. Newsletter, support group meetings, conferences and literature. Write: FSH Society, 3 Westwood Rd., Lexington, MA 02420. Call Carol Perez, Executive Director 781-860-0501 or Daniel Paul Perez, President CEO, 781-862-8422; Fax: 781-860-0599 or 781-863-0788. *Website:* http://www.fshsociety.org *E-mail:* solvefshd@fshsociety.org

FACTOR V LEIDEN / THROMBOPHILIA

ONLINE

Factor V Leiden Mailing List and Digest *Online.* Mailing list that offers support and information for persons affected by Factor V Leiden (thrombophilia), a hereditary blood coagulation disorder. Daily digest (condensed version of the mailing list) also available. *Website:* http://www.fvleiden.org

FATTY OXIDATION DISORDER

FOD Family Support Group *International network. Founded 1991.* Opportunity for families dealing with fatty oxidation disorders (i.e. MCAD, LCHAD, VLCAD, SCAD, etc.) to network with others dealing with these rare, genetic metabolic disorders. Phone support, email list, information and referrals. Write: FOD Family Support Group, c/o Deb Lee Gould, MEd, Dir., 2041 Tomahawk, Okemos, MI 48864. Call 517-381-1940; Fax: 866-290-5206. *Website:* http://www.fodsupport.org *E-mail:* deb@fodsupport.org

FETAL ALCOHOL SYNDROME / DRUG-AFFECTED

NATIONAL

FEN (Family Empowerment Network) *National network. Founded 1992.* Support, education, advocacy and training for families of children and adults with fetal alcohol spectrum disorders or fetal alcohol effects and interested professionals. Family retreats. Fetal alcohol spectrum disorder (FASD) resources, education and referrals for diagnosis. Networks families together for support. Membership is free. Assistance in starting support groups. Monthly parent teleconferences. Write: Family Empowerment Network, c/o University of Wisconsin Department of Family Medicine, 777 S. Mills St., Madison, WI 53715. Call 1-800-462-5254 or 608-262-6590; Fax: 608-263-5813. *Website:* http://www.fammed.wisc.edu/fen *E-mail:* fen@fammed.wisc.edu

Fetal Alcohol Syndrome Family Resource Institute *International. Founded 1990.* Coalition of families and professionals concerned with fetal alcohol syndrome/effects. Educational programs, brochures and information packets. Regional representatives being identified. Support group meetings, advocacy, information referrals, phone support and conferences. Write: Fetal Alcohol Snydrome Family Resource Institute, P.O. Box 2525, Lynnwood, WA 98036. Call

1-800-999-3429 (in WA) or 253-531-2878 (outside WA); Fax: 425-640-9155. *Website:* http://fetalalcoholsyndrome.org *E-mail:* vicky@fetalalcoholsyndrome.org

FG SYNDROME

ONLINE

FG Syndrome Homepage *Online. Founded 1998.* Support network for persons interested in FG syndrome, a genetic condition resulting in multiple congenital anomalies. Newsletter, listserv, conferences, fundraising and general family support. Write: FG Syndrome Family Alliance, 946 NW Circle Blvd., #290, Corvallis, OR 97330. Call 617-577-9050. *Website:* http://www.fg-syndrome.org *E-mail:* info@fg-syndrome.org

FIBRODYSPLASIA OSSIFICANS PROGRESSIVA

International Fibrodysplasia Ossificans Progressiva Association *International network. Founded 1988.* Serves as a support network for families dealing with fibrodysplasia ossificans progressiva (FOP). Supports education, communication and medical research. Newsletter. Write: International FOP Association, Box 196217, Winter Springs, FL 32719-6217. Call 407-365-4194; Fax: 407-365-3213. *Website:* http:/www.ifopa.org *E-mail:* together@ifopa.org

FRAGILE X SYNDROME

STATEWIDE

Fragile X Association Organization of parents and professionals dedicated to improving the lives of individuals and families affected by Fragile X syndrome. For information call Jennifer Keenan 856-985-3257. *Website:* http://www.fragilexnj.org

NATIONAL

FRAXA Research Foundation *International. 30 affiliated groups. Founded 1994.* Information and support on Fragile X syndrome. Funds medical research, investigator-initiated grants and postdoctoral fellowships. Newsletter, literature. Some chapters have support group meetings. Guidelines available on starting a similar group. Write: FRAXA Research Foundation, 45 Pleasant St., Newburyport, MA 01950. Call 978-462-1866; Fax: 978-463-9985. *Website:* http://www.fraxa.org *E-mail:* kclappFRAXA@comcast.net

National Fragile X Foundation, The *International. 55 groups. Founded 1984.* Mission includes phone and email support, promoting awareness, education, research and legislative advocacy regarding Fragile X syndrome, a hereditary condition which is the most common known cause of inherited mental impairment. Services also include a quarterly journal, research grants, local, national and international conferences and educational resources (books and videotapes for a fee). Write: National Fragile X Foundation, P.O. Box 190488, San Francisco, CA 94119-0488. Call 1-800-688-8765; Fax: 925-938-9315. *Website:* http://www.FragileX.org *E-mail:* NATLFX@FragileX.org

FREEMAN-SHELDON

Freeman-Sheldon Parent Support Group *International network. Founded 1982.* Provides emotional support for parents of children with Freeman-Sheldon syndrome, and for adults with this syndrome. Sharing of helpful medical literature. Provides information on growth and development of individuals affected. Participates in research projects. Members network by phone, mail and through a members-only listserv. Newsletter. Write: Freeman-Sheldon Parent Support Group, 509 E. Northmont Way, Salt Lake City, UT 84103. Call 801-364-7060. *Website:* http://www.fspsg.org *E-mail:* info@fspsg.org

GALACTOSEMIA

Parents of Galactosemic Children, Inc. *National network. Founded 1985.* Information and mutual support for parents of galactosemic children. Publications, pen pals, conferences, phone support and online message board. Write: Parents of Galactosemic Children, c/o Michelle Fowler, P.O. Box 2401 Mandeville, LA. 70470. Call 1-866-900-742. *Website:* http://www.galactosemia.org *E-mail:* president@galactosemia.org

GASTROESOPHAGEAL REFLUX

PAGER (Pediatric/Adolescent Gastroesophageal Reflux Association) *National network. Founded 1992.* Offers support and information for parents whose children suffer from gastroesophageal reflux (GER), an inappropriate backwash of stomach contents into the esophagus that affects seven million children and fifty million adults. Educates the public on this disorder. Newsletter, literature and telephone support network. Helps new chapters start when leaders are identified. Extensive free information is available via website and mail. Write: PAGER, P.O. Box 486, Buckeystown, MD 21717. Call 301-601-9541. *Website:* http://www.reflux.org *E-mail:* gergroup@aol.com

GAUCHER DISEASE

National Gaucher Foundation *National. 2 chapters. Founded 1984.* Provides information and assistance for those affected by Gaucher disease. Provides education and outreach to increase public awareness. Operates the Gaucher Disease Family Support Network. Quarterly newsletter, phone support, medical board and guidelines to help start similar groups. Write: National Gaucher Foundation, 61 General Early Dr., Harpers Ferry, WV 25425. Call 1-800-428-2437; Fax: 304-725-6429. *Website:* http://www.gaucherdisease.org *E-mail:* ngf@gaucherdisease.org

GENETIC DISORDERS

(see also specific disorder)

Genetic Alliance, The *International network. Founded 1986.* Provides technical assistance to genetic support groups and disseminates information to the public on available resources and referrals. Fosters a partnership among consumers and professionals to enhance education and service for the needs of individuals affected by genetic disorders. Supports networking efforts of members of government agencies, professional groups, service providers and organizations. Write: Genetic Alliance, 4301 Connecticut Ave., NW, Suite 404, Washington, DC 20008. Call 202-966-5557; Fax: 202-966-8553. *Website:* http://www.geneticalliance.org *E-mail:* information@geneticalliance.org

GLYCOGEN STORAGE DISEASE

Association For Glycogen Storage Disease *U.S. and Canadian network. 3 affiliated groups. Founded 1979.* Mutual support and information sharing among parents of children with Glycogen Storage disease. Fosters communication between parents and professionals, creates public awareness and encourages research. Newsletter, phone support and conference. Offers GSDnet support group online. Write: Association for Glycogen Storage Disease, P.O. Box 896, Durant, IA 52747. Call 563-785-6038 (voice/fax). *Website:* http://www.agsdus.org *E-mail:* maryc@agsdus.org

"Give what you have. To someone. It may be better than you dare think."
-- Longfellow

GOLDENHAR SYNDROME

Goldenhar Syndrome Support Network *International network. Founded 1998.* Emotional support and information for families affected by Goldenhar Syndrome (aka hemifacial microsomia). Information and referrals, newsletter, literature and advocacy. Online support group. Write: Goldenhar Syndrome Support Network, c/o Barb Miles, 9325 163 Street, Edmonton, AB T5R 2P4, Canada. *Website:* http://www.goldenharsyndrome.org *E-mail:* support@goldenharsyndrome.org

GORLIN SYNDROME / NEVOID BASAL CELL SYNDROME / BASAL CELL CARCINOMA NEVUS SYNDROME

NATIONAL

Basal Cell Carcinoma Nevus Syndrome Life Support Network *National network.* Provides support services to patients, families and medical professionals dealing with the many manifestations of basal cell carcinoma nevus syndrome (aka Gorlin syndrome or nevoid basal cell syndrome). Annual retreat and conference. Offers online forum, quarterly newsletter and periodic regional meetings. Write: Sheila LaRosa, Basal Cell Carcinoma Nevus Syndrome Life Support Network, P.O. Box 321, Burton, OH 44021. Call 1-866-834-1895; Fax: 440-635-0267. *Website:* http://www.bccns.org *E-mail:* info@bccns.org

Gorlin Syndrome Group, The *International network. 3 affiliated groups. Founded 1992.* Provides support and information for individuals with Gorlin (aka nevoid basal cell carcinoma) and their families. Information on coping skills, treatments and current research. Helpline, newsletter, meetings and networking. Write: The Gorlin Syndrome Group, c/o Margaret Costello, 11 Blackberry Way, Penwortham, Preston, Lancashire PR1 9LQ England. Call +440 1772517624. *Website:* http://www.gorlingroup.co.uk *E-mail:* info@gorlingroup.co.uk

GRANULOMATOUS

Chronic Granulomatous Disease Association Inc. *International network. Founded 1982.* Support information for persons with chronic granulomatous disease, their families and physicians. Networks patients with similar CGD-related illnesses. Support through correspondence and phone. Publishes medical research articles semi-annually. International registry of patients. Referrals to physicians. Write: Chronic Granulomatous Disease Association, 2616 Monterey Rd., San

Marino, CA 91108. Call 626-441-4118. *Website:* http://www.cgdassociation.org *E-mail:* cgda@socal.rr.com

GUILLAIN-BARRE SYNDROME

GBS/CIDP Foundation *International 160 chapters. Founded 1980.* Emotional support, hospital visitation and education for people affected by Guillain-Barre syndrome, Chronic Inflammatory Demyelinating Polyneuropathy and its variants. Promotes support, education and research. Newsletter, pen pals, phone network and online chat room. Group development guidelines and international symposium. Write: GBS/CIDP Foundation International, International Office, The Holly Building, 104 1/2 Forrest Ave., Narberth, PA 19072. Call 610-667-0131 (9am-3:30pm EST); Fax: 610-667-7036. *Website:* http://www.gbsfi.com *E-mail:* info@gbsfi.com

HALLERVORDEN-SPATZ

NBIA Disorders Association *International network. Founded 1996.* Provides emotional support to families affected by neurdegeneration with brain iron accumulation (NBIA) - a rare, progressive neurological disorder, resulting in iron deposits in the brain that causes loss of muscle control. Formerly Hallervorden-Spatz syndrome. Educates public on neurodegenerations with brain iron accumulation. Supports and monitors research. Newsletter, literature, phone support network, pen pals and advocacy efforts. Write: NBIA Disorders Association, 2082 Monaco Ct., El Cajon, CA 92019-4235. Call 619-588-2315; Fax: 619-588-4093. *Website:* http://www.NBIAdisorders.org *E-mail:* info@NBIAdisorders.org

HELLP SYNDROME

HELLP Syndrome Society, The *National network. Founded 1996.* Mission is to raise awareness about HELLP syndrome (hemolysis, elevated liver enzymes and low platelet count), to support research and provide support to affected families. This syndrome affects pregnant mothers and is usually in tandem with pre-eclampsia. Brochure, newsletter and online message board. Write: The HELLP Syndrome Society, P.O. Box 44, Bethany, WV 26032. *Website:* http://www.hellpsyndrome.org *E-mail:* HELLP1995@aol.com

HEMANGIOMA

NATIONAL

Hemangioma Support System *National network. Founded 1990.* Provides parent-to-parent support for families with children affected by hemangiomas. Write: Hemangioma Support System, c/o Cynthia Schumerth, 1484 Sand Acres Dr., DePere, WI 54115. Call 920-336-9399 (after 8:30pm CST).

NOVA (National Organization of Vascular Anomalies) *National.* Provides support for patients and their families in the diagnosis of hemangioma and vascular malformations. Networks families together for support. Offers videos, doctor referrals, free medical conferences, educational and support materials. Online newsletter. Holds international conferences. Contact K. Hall at khall@mail.novanews.org for more conference information. Write: NOVA, P.O. Box 0358, Findlay, OH 45840. Call 419-425-1589. *Website:* http://www.novanews.org *E-mail:* admin@mail.novanews.org

HEMIFACIAL SPASM

ONLINE

Hemifacial Spasm Association *Online. Founded 2001.* A support community of individuals who had or are presently suffering from hemifacial spasm (HFS) and are eager to provide information, understanding and support to other individuals and their families when coping with hemifacial spasm. *Website:* http://www.hfs-assn.org *E-mail:* info@hfs-assn.org

HEMIPLEGIA

CHASA (Children's Hemiplegia And Stroke Association) *National network. Founded 1996.* Offers support and information to families of children who have hemiplegia due to stroke or other causes. Local support groups, annual family retreat and medical conference, college scholarships and online resources. Write: CHASA, 4101 W. Green Oaks, Suite 305, PMB 149, Arlington, TX 76016. Call 817-492-4325. *Website:* http://www.chasa.org or http://www.kidshavestrokes.org *E-mail:* info437@chasa.org

HEMOCHROMATOSIS / IRON OVERLOAD

Iron Overload Diseases Assoc., Inc. *International network. Founded 1980.* A clearinghouse of support and information for hemochromatosis and other iron overload disease patients, their families and physicians. Encourages research and public awareness. Bi-monthly newsletter "Ironic Blood." Membership dues $50/yr. Write: Iron Overload Diseases Association, 433 Westwind Dr., N. Palm Beach, FL 33408. Call 561-586-8246. *Website:* http://www.ironoverload.org *E-mail:* iod@ironoverload.org

HEMOPHILIA

STATEWIDE

Hemophilia Association of New Jersey Self-help support for persons with hemophilia their families. Provides information and referrals, advocacy, educational seminars, phone networking, peer counseling, guest speakers, financial assistance and vocational counseling. Dues $20/yr. Write: Hemophilia Association of New Jersey, 197 Route 18 South, Suite 206 North, E. Brunswick, NJ 08816. Call Julie Frenkel 732-249-6000 (day). *Website:* http://www.hanj.org *E-mail:* mailbox@hanj.org

NATIONAL

National Hemophilia Foundation *National. 48 chapters. Founded 1948.* Dedicated to finding better treatments and a cure for bleeding and clotting disorders. Aims to prevent complications of these disorders through education, advocacy and research. Write: National Hemophilia Foundation, 116 W. 32nd St., 11th Floor, New York, NY 10001. Call 1-800-424-2634; Fax: 212-328-3777. *Website:* http://www.hemophilia.org *E-mail:* info@hemophilia.org

HEREDITARY HEMORRHAGIC TELANGIECTASIA / OSLER-WEBER-RENDU SYNDROME

HHT Foundation International, Inc. *International. Founded 1991.* Mutual support and education for persons interested in hereditary hemorrhagic telangiectasia (aka Osler-Weber-Rendu syndrome). Supports clinical and genetic research. Counseling and advice for patients. Referrals to appropriate treatment centers. Annual patient/doctor conference. Tri-annual newsletter "Direct Connection." Aims to protect all members under the Right To Privacy Act. Dues

$45/yr. Write: HHT Foundation International, P.O. Box 329, Monkton, MD 21111. Call 1-800-448-6389 (U.S.) or 410-357-9932 (International); Fax: 410-357-9931. *Website:* http://www.hht.org *E-mail:* hhtinfo@hht.org

HERMANSKY-PUDLAK SYNDROME / CHEDIAK HIGASHI SYNDROME

Hermansky-Pudlak Syndrome Network *International network. 2 affiliated groups. Founded 1992.* Mutual support and education for families affected by Hermansky-Pudlak Syndrome and Chediak Higashi Syndrome. Networks families together for support. Newsletter and annual conference. Supports research. Write: Hermansky-Pudlak Syndrome Network, c/o Donna Jean Appell, 1 South Rd., Oyster Bay, NY 11771-1905. Call 1-800-789-9477 (voice/fax) or 516-922-3440; Fax: 516-922-4022. *Website:* http://www.hpsnetwork.org or http://www.chediak-higashi.org *E-mail:* hpsnet@att.net

HISTIOCYTOSIS-X

Histiocytosis Association of America *International network. Founded 1985.* Mutual support and information for parents and patients with this group of rare disorders. Includes erdheim-chester disease, sinus histiocytosis rosai dorfman, xanthogranuloma, hemophagocytic lymphohistiocytosis, pulmonary eosinophilic granuloma, histiocytosis and familial erythrophagocytic lymphohistiocytosis. Provides parent-patient directory to facilitate networking and communication. Funds research. Literature, pamphlets (some available in Spanish) and newsletter. Write: Histiocytosis Association of America, 332 North Broadway, Pitman, NJ 08071. Call Jeff Toughill, President 856-589-6606; Fax: 856-589-6614. *Website:* http://www.histio.org *E-mail:* histiocyte@aol.com

HOLOPROSENCEPHALY

NATIONAL

Families for HoPE, Inc. Offers support and education to families of infants and children diagnosed with holoprosencephaly (HPE), a congenital brain malformation. Offers support for all stages of the HPE journey. Write: Leslie Harley, President, Families for HoPE, Inc., 1219 N. Wittfield St., Indianapolis, IN 46229. Call 317-898-5556. *Website:* http://www.familiesforhope.com *E-mail:* info@familiesforhope.com

ONLINE

Holoprosencephaly Support Group *Online. 507 members. Founded 1999.* Mutual support for parents and families of children with holoprosencephaly (HPE). HPE is a rare birth disorder caused by the failure of the forebrain of the embryo to properly divide, causing defects in the development of the face and brain structure and function. *Website:* http://health.groups.yahoo.com/group/holoprosencephaly/

HYDROCEPHALUS

NATIONAL

Guardians of Hydrocephalus Research Foundation *National network. Founded 1977.* Information and referral service to persons affected by hydrocephalus. Phone networking for parents of children with hydrocephalus. Referrals to doctors, literature and books for children and adults with hydrocephalus (in English and Spanish). Free newsletter. Membership fee $30/yr. Write: Guardians of Hydrocephalus Research Foundation, 2618 Ave. Z, Brooklyn, NY 11235. Call Marie Fischetti 718-743-4473; Fax: 718-743-1171. *Website:* http://www.ghrforg.org *E-mail:* ghrf2618@aol.com

Hydrocephalus Association *(BILINGUAL) National network. Founded 1984.* Provides support, education and advocacy for people with hydrocephalus and their families. Provides a wealth of resource materials on hydrocephalus for all age groups, quarterly newsletter, directory of neurosurgeons, bi-annual national conference and scholarships for young adults. Support and information available in English and Spanish. Write: Hydrocephalus Association, 870 Market St., Suite 705, San Francisco, CA 94102. Call 1-888-598-3789 or 415-732-7040; Fax: 415-732-7044. *Website:* http://www.hydroassoc.org *E-mail:* info@hydroassoc.org

National Hydrocephalus Foundation (NHF) *National and international network. 2 chapters. Founded 1979.* Mission is to establish and facilitate a communication network, provide informational and educational assistance for individuals and families affected by hydrocephalus, increase public awareness, promote and support research on the cause, prevention and treatment of hydrocephalus. Guidelines to help start support groups available. Help Sheets, brochures, physician referrals, 24-hour contact, quarterly newsletter and more. Write: National Hydrocephalus Foundation, 12413 Centralia Rd., Lakewood, CA 90715-1623. Call 1-888-857-3434 or 562-924-6666 (voice/fax). *Website:* http://nhfonline.org *E-mail:* hydrobrat@Earthlink.net or debbifields@nhfonline.org

HYPERACUSIS / SENSITIVE HEARING

Hyperacusis Network, The *International network. Founded 1991.* Mutual support and sharing of information, education for individuals and their families with hyperacusis recruitment (hypersensitive hearing). Promotes research into cause and cure. Newsletter, phone support, pen pals, information and referrals. Write: The Hyperacusis Network, P.O. Box 8007, Green Bay, WI 54308. Call 920-866-3377 (eve). *Website:* http://www.hyperacusis.net *E-mail:* earhelp@yahoo.com

HYPOPARATHYROIDISM

Hypoparathyroidism Association Inc. *(MULTILINGUAL) International network. 2334 members from 62 countries. Founded 1994.* Dedicated to improving the lives of people with all forms of hypoparathyroidism, a rare medical disorder. Guidelines available for starting a similar group. Association promotes awareness of this disorder through quarterly newsletter and website. Online newsletter, member gallery, a forum, chat room and extensive compilation of links and various articles. Write: Hypoparathyroidism Association Inc., c/o James E. Sanders, P.O. 2258, Idaho Falls, ID 83406. Call 208-524-3857. *Website:* http://www.hpth.org *E-mail:* Hypoparathyroidism@hypoparathyroidism.org or hpth@cableone.net or hpth@hpth.org

ICHTHYOSIS

F.I.R.S.T. (Foundation for Ichthyosis Related Skin Types) *National network. Founded 1981.* Provides support for people with ichthyosis through networking with others. Public and professional education. Supports research on treatment and cure. Advocacy issues. Quarterly newsletter, publications and bi-annual conference. Dues US/$40; Int'l/$50. Write: FIRST, 1364 Welsh Rd., G2, North Wales, PA 19454. Call 1-800-545-3286 or 215-619-0670; Fax: 215-619-0780. *Website:* http://www.scalyskin.org *E-mail:* info@scalyskin.org

IDIOPATHIC THROMBOCYTOPENIC PURPURA

Platelet Disorder Support Association *Founded 1998. 7 chapters.* Provides information and support to persons who have ITP (idiopathic thrombocytopenic purpura) and related blood disorders. Members regularly exchange messages. Support meetings, conferences, advocacy, newsletter and written material. Online and printed information and support for women with ITP who are, or are thinking about, becoming pregnant. Write: Platelet Disorder Support Association, c/o Joan

Young, President, 133 Rollins Ave., Suite 5, Rockville, MD 20852. Call 1-877-528-3538. *Website:* http://www.pdsa.org or http://www.itppeople.com *E-mail:* pdsa@pdsa.org

IMMUNE DEFICIENCY

NATIONAL

Immune Deficiency Foundation *National. Founded 1980.* Provides support and education for families affected by primary immune deficiency diseases. Newsletter, handbook, videotape and educational materials for public and medical professionals. Networks individuals and family members affected by immune deficiency. Scholarships and fellowship program. Group development guidelines. Write: Immune Deficiency Foundation, 40 W. Chesapeake Ave., Suite 308, Towson, MD 21204. Call 1-800-296-4433. *Website:* http://www.primaryimmune.org *E-mail:* idf@primaryimmune.org

ONLINE

SCID Mailing Group *Online network. Founded 1997.* Online self-help group for families afflicted with severe combined immune deficiency or who have lost a child to this very rare genetic disorder which results in severe infections. Provides opportunity for families to share information and resources with one another. *Website:* http://www.scid.net *E-mail:* SCIDemail@scid.net

INCONTINENTIA PIGMENTI

Incontinentia Pigmenti International Foundation *International network. Founded 1995.* Dedicated to research, family support and physician awareness on incontinentia pigmenti. Maintains international database of patients. Write: Incontinentia Pigmenti International Foundation, 30 East 72nd St., 16th Floor, New York, NY 10021. Call 212-452-1231; Fax: 212-452-1406. *Website:* http://imgen.bcm.tmc.edu/IPIF *E-mail:* ipif@ipif.org

INFECTIOUS ILLNESS, GENERAL

PKIDs (Parents of Kids with Infectious Diseases) *National network. Founded 1996.* Provides informational and educational support for parents of children with chronic viral infectious diseases, with an emphasis on Hepatitis B and C. Opportunity for parents, children and teens to share information and experiences. Publications, advocacy, phone support, online email list, support group and other resources. Write: PKIDS, P.O. Box 5666, Vancouver, WA 98668. Call 1-877-557-5437 or 360-695-0293; Fax: 360-695-6941. *Website:* http://www.pkids.org *E-mail:* pkids@pkids.org

INTESTINAL MULTIPLE POLYPOSIS

IMPACC (Intestinal Multiple Polyposis Colorectal Cancer) *National network. Founded 1986.* Support network to help patients families dealing with familial polyposis and hereditary colon cancer. Information and referrals, encourages research, educates professionals and public. Phone support network, correspondence and literature. Write: IMPACC, c/o Ann Fagan, P.O. Box 11, Conyngham, PA 18219. Call Ann Fagan 570-788-1818 (day) or 570-788-3712 (eve); Fax: 570-788-4046. *E-mail:* impacc@epix.net

INVERTED DUPLICATION 15

IDEAS (IsoDicentric 15 Exchange, Advocacy Support) *International network. Founded 1994.* Support, information and advocacy for people affected by isodicentric and chromosome 15q duplication. Information and referrals, phone support, literature, newsletter, international conferences and parent match program. Write: IDEAS, 18 Kings Rd., Canton, MA 02021. Call 503-253-2872. *Website:* http://www.idic15.org *E-mail:* info@idic15.org

KABUKI SYNDROME / NIIKAWAKUROKI SYNDROME

Kabuki Syndrome Network *International network. Founded 1997.* Provides mutual support and information for families affected by Kabuki syndrome (aka Niikawakuroki syndrome). Coordinates family directory. Literature, phone support, pen pals and newsletter. Brochure in English and Spanish available. Write: Kabuki Syndrome Network, c/o Dean and Margot Schmiedge, 8060 Struthers Cr., Regina, Saskatchewan, Canada S4Y 1J3. Call Dean and Margot Schmiedge 306-543-8715. *Website:* http://www.kabukisyndrome.com *E-mail:* margot@kabukisyndrome.com

"We need to give each other the space to grow, to be ourselves, to exercise our diversity. We need to give each other space so that we may both give and receive such beautiful things as ideas, openness, dignity, joy, healing and inclusion."
-- Max De Pree (Leadership is an Art)

KALLMANN'S SYNDROME / HYPOGONADOTROPHIC HYPOGONADISM

ONLINE

HYPOHH (Helping You to be Positive about Hypogonadotrophic Hypogonadism) *Online.* Provides information, support, and encouragement to persons suffering from Kallmann's syndrome and other forms of hypogonadotrophic hypogonadism. Promotes awareness of the causes, symptoms and treatments for these disorders. Open to families and friends. *Website:* http://www.hypohh.net/ *E-mail:* hypohh@fsmail.net or neilsmith38@hotmail.com

KAWASAKI DISEASE

ONLINE

Kawasaki Families' Network *E-mail listserv. Founded 1996.* Provides a means of circulating information and support for families affected by Kawasaki disease, an inflammatory illness which primarily threatens the cardiovascular system. Members can exchange messages online. Write: Kawasaki Families' Network, c/o Vickie Machado, 46-111 Nahewai Place, Kaneohe, HI 96744. Call 808-525-8053. *E-mail:* vicki.machado@verizon.net

KENNEDY'S DISEASE

Kennedy's Disease Association, Inc. *National network. Founded 2000.* Mutual support and information for persons with Kennedy's disease (aka spinal and bulbar muscular atrophy), their families and caregivers. Opportunity to share personal experiences to help alleviate the feeling of aloneness and to engender hope and a positive attitude. Sharing of information regarding diagnosis, treatment and current research. Online chat room every two weeks. Write: Kennedy's Disease Association, Inc., P.O. Box 1105, Coarsegold, CA 93614-1105. Call 559-658-5950. *Website:* http://www.kennedysdisease.org *E-mail:* info@kennedydisease.org

We can also refer callers to over 100 individuals who are seeking others to help start new support groups throughout NJ. Give us a call for more information.
1-800-367-6274

KLINEFELTER SYNDROME

NATIONAL

Klinefelter Syndrome and Associates *National network. 4 affiliated groups. Founded 1990.* Mission is to educate, encourage research and foster treatment and cures for symptoms of sex chromosome variations. These include, but are not limited to: XXY, XXX, XYY, XXXY, XXXXXY, XXYY. Brochures are available that describe basic symptoms, diagnoses and treatments. Newsletter ($25/US; $27/Canada; $30/Int'l - US$). Write: Klinefelter Syndrome and Associates, 11 Keats Court, Coto de Caza, CA 92679. Call 1-888-999-9428; Fax 949-858-3443 *Website:* http://www.genetic.org *Email:* help1@genetic.org

ONLINE

Klinefelter Syndrome Support Group Offers online support group information. Provides email list to chat with others, information on variations of the disorder, conferences and information on local support group meetings. *Website:* http://klinefeltersyndrome.org

KLIPPEL-FEIL SYNDROME

KFS Circle of Friends, The *International network. Founded 1996.* Provides information on Klippel-Feil syndrome, a rare, congenital disorder primarily comprised of cervical-spine fusion, renal abnormalities and scoliosis. Networks families together for emotional support. Support and information provided mainly online, but literature and pen pals are available. Write: The KFS Circle of Friends, 154 Aberdeen St., #11, Fredericton, NB, E3B 1R5, Canada. *Website:* http://members.fortunecity.com/bethc/kfs.html *E-mail:* kfscircle@gmail.com

KLIPPEL-TRENAUNAY

Klippel-Trenaunay Support Group *National network. Founded 1986.* Provides mutual support and sharing of experiences among families of children with KT and adults with KT. Newsletter, phone support and meetings every two years. Online mailing list. Write: KT Support Group, 5404 Dundee Rd., Edina, MN 55436. Call 952-925-2596. *Website:* http://www.k-t.org *E-mail:* ktnewmembers@yahoo.com

LEAD POISONING

United Parents Against Lead *National. 7 chapters and affiliates. Founded 1996.* Organization supporting parents of lead poisoned children and who work to end the continuing threat of lead poisoning through education, advocacy, resource referral and legislative action. Membership $10/individual; $25/family; $100/organization. Write: United Parents Against Lead, P.O. Box 24773, Richmond, VA 23224. Call 804-714-1618; Fax: 804-714-0798. *Website:* http://www.upal.org *E-mail:* info@upal.com

LEUDODYSTROPHY

United Leukodystrophy Foundation, Inc. *National network. Founded 1982.* Provides information and resources for leukodystrophy patients and their families. Communication network among families. Promotes research, public and professional awareness. Quarterly newsletter. National conference. Dues $25/family; $50/professional. Write: United Leukodystrophy Foundation, 2304 Highland Dr., Sycamore, IL 60178. Call 815-895-3211 or 1-800-728-5483; Fax: 815-895-2432. *Website:* http://www.ulf.org *E-mail:* janet@ulf.org

LISSENCEPHALY

Lissencephaly Network, The *International network. Founded 1991.* Support for families affected by lissencephaly or other neuronal migration disorders as well as physicians and therapists. Helps relieve the stress of caring for an ill child. Research updates, newsletter and database of affected children. Networking of parents. Write: Lissencephaly Network, c/o Dianna Fitzgerald, 10408 Bitterroot Ct., Ft. Wayne, IN 46804. Call 260-432-4310; Fax: 260-432-4310. *Website:* http://www.lissencephaly.org *E-mail:* LissencephalyOne@aol.com

LOIN PAIN HEMATURIA SYNDROME

Hearts and Hands *Model. 1 group in NC. Founded 1993.* Emotional, spiritual and educational support for persons with either rare or undiagnosed illnesses and their families. Has a registry for loin pain hematuria syndrome. Write: Hearts and Hands, c/o Winoka Plummer, 1648 Oliver's Crossing Circle, Winston-Salem, NC 27127. Call 336-785-7612. *Website:* http://www.geocities.com/hotsprings/spa/2464/index.html

LOWE SYNDROME

Lowe Syndrome Association *International network. Founded 1983.* For parents, friends, professionals and others who are interested in Lowe Syndrome. Provides medical and educational information and online discussion. Supports medical research. Offers booklet, newsletter. International conference. Dues $15 (can be waived if parents are in need). Write: Lowe Syndrome Association, 18919 Voss Rd., Dallas, TX 75287. Call 612-869-5693; Fax: 612-866-3222. *Website:* http://www.lowesyndrome.org *E-mail:* info@lowesyndrome.org

LYMPHANGIOLEIOMYOMATOSIS

LAM Foundation, The *International network. Founded 1995.* Provides education for doctors, patients and support for women and their families who have LAM (lymphangioleiomyomatosis). LAM is a rare lung disease affecting only women, where smooth muscle cells grow throughout the lungs. A newsletter for general distribution and patient Listserv, Personal Journeys, Lung Transplantation Booklet, advocacy program and newsletter solely for patients. Write: The LAM Foundation, c/o Leslie Sullivan-Stacey, 4015 Executive Park, Cincinnati, OH 45241. Call 513-777-6889; Fax: 513-777-4109. *Website:* http://thelamfoundation.org *E-mail:* info@thelamfoundation.org

MALIGNANT HYPERTHERMIA

Malignant Hyperthermia Association of the U.S. (MHAUS) *National network. Founded 1981.* Information, education and support for malignant hyperthermia-susceptible patients and their physicians. Conducts limited research. Newsletter, literature and regional conferences. Write: MHAUS, 11 E. State St., P.O. Box 1069, Sherburne, NY 13460-1069. Call 1-800-644-9737 or 607-674-7901; Fax: 607-674-7910. *Website:* http://www.mhaus.org *E-mail:* info@mhaus.org

MANNOSIDOSIS / GLYCOPROTEIN STORAGE DISEASE

ISMRD (International Advocate for Glycoprotein Storage Disease) *International network. Founded 1999.* Provides emotional support for families affected by any glycoprotein storage disease. Offers educational resources for medical community. Promotes research to develop treatments. Phone support, literature, pen pals, newsletter, advocacy, information and referrals. Online message boards, chat rooms and email discussions. Write: ISMRD, 2980 East

Pillar Dr., Whitemore Lake, MI, 48189. Call 734-449-9038. *Website:* http://www.ismrd.org

MAPLE SYRUP URINE DISEASE

Maple Syrup Urine Disease Family Support Group *National network. Founded 1982.* Opportunity for support and personal contact for those with maple syrup urine disease and their families. Provides information on MSUD. Aims to strengthen the liaison between families and professionals. Encourages research and newborn screening for MSUD. Newsletter ($10/yr), phone support, conferences and advocacy. Write: MSUD Family Support Group, c/o Sandra Bulcher, 82 Ravine Rd., Powell, OH 43065. Call 740-548-4475. *Website:* http://www.msud-support.org *E-mail:* dbulcher@aol.com

MARFAN SYNDROME

National Marfan Foundation *National network. 100+ chapters, support groups and telephone contact persons. Founded 1981.* Provides information on Marfan syndrome and related connective tissue disorders to patients, families and physicians. Provides a means for patients and relatives to share experiences and support one another. Supports and fosters research. Conference, newsletter and publications. Write: National Marfan Foundation, 22 Manhasset Ave., Port Washington, NY 11050. Call 1-800-862-7326 ext. 10 or 516-883-8712; Fax: 516-883-8040. *Website:* http://www.marfan.org *E-mail:* staff@marfan.org

MARIENSCO-SJOGREN SYNDROME

Mariensco-Sjogren Syndrome Support Group *National network. Founded 2000.* Support for families affected by Marinesco-Sjogren syndrome (MSS), a rare genetic disorder characterized by ataxia, cataracts, small stature and retardation. Encourages research into the cause and cure. Information and referrals. Write: MSS Support Group, 1640 Crystal View Circle, Newbury Park, CA 91320. Call 805-499-7410. *Website:* http://www.marinesco-sjogren.org *E-mail:* mss@marinesco-sjogren.org

MASTOCYTOSIS

Mastocytosis Society, The *International network. Founded 1994.* Mutual support through a newsletter for persons with mastocytosis (a proliferation of mast cells), their families, friends and professionals working with them. Email discussion group for patients and researchers. Fundraising for research and phone support. Write:

TMS, c/o Rita Barlow, P.O. Box 284, Russell, MA 01071. Call 413-862-4556. *Website:* http://www.tmsforacure.org *E-mail:* jbar5@verizon.net

MCCUNE-ALBRIGHT SYNDROME

McCune-Albright Syndrome/Fibrous Dysplasia Division *International network. Founded 1990.* Provides support for families of McCune-Albright syndrome patients. Newsletters, updated medical information, phone support and annual conventions. Dues $30/yr. Write: McCune-Albright Syndrome/Fibruous Dysplasia Division, c/o MAGIC Foundation, 6645 West North Ave., Oak Park, IL 60302. Call 1-800-362-4423; Fax: 708-383-0899. *Website:* http://www.magicfoundation.org *E-mail:* mary@magicfondation.org

MEMBRANOPROLIFERATIVE / GLOMERULONEPHRITIS TYPE II

Kidneeds *National network. Founded 1997.* Grassroots support network for parents of children with membranoproliferative glomerulonephritis (MPGN) type 2 (aka dense deposit disease), a rare kidney disorder. Provides money for research on MPGN type 2. Phone support, newsletter and advocacy. For grant information please see website. Write: Kidneeds, P.O. Box 1324, Iowa City, IA, 52244. Call 319-338-6404 (voice/fax). *Website:* http://www.medicine.uiowa.edu/kidneeds *E-mail:* kidneedsMPGN@yahoo.com

MENKES KINKY HAIR SYNDROME

ONLINE

Menkes Kinky Hair Syndrome *Online. Founded 1999.* Support and information for those affected with Menkes kinky hair syndrome (related to deficient levels of copper in the cells). Also known as Kinky Hair Disease and Steely Hair disease. Message boards and chat rooms. *Website:* http://groups.yahoo.com/group/menkes_kinky_hair/

METABOLIC DISORDERS

NATIONAL

CDG Family Network Foundation *International network. Founded 1996.* Support for parents of children diagnosed with congenital disorders of glycosylation, an inherited metabolic disease affecting all body parts, especially the central and peripheral nervous systems. Support is attained primarily online, but the group also provides information and referrals, bi-annual newsletter, phone support and advocacy. Bulletin board for families to interact with questions, comments and updates. Write: CDG Family Network, c/o Cynthia Wren-Gray, President, P.O. Box 860847, Plano, TX 75074. Call 1-800-250-5273; Fax: 903-640-8254. *Website:* http://www.cdgs.com *E-mail:* cdgaware@aol.com

CLIMB - National Information Advice Centre for Metabolic Disease *International network.* Provides support and information for individuals and their families dealing with over 700 metabolic conditions. Newsletter, phone support, pen pals, annual conference and befriender network. Small administration fee required for posts. Write: Climb Building, 176 Nantwich Rd., Crewe, CW2 6BG UK. Call 0044 870 77 00 326 (day); Fax: 0044 870 77 00 327. *Website:* http://www.climb.org.uk *E-mail:* info@climb.org.uk

Purine Research Society *National. Founded 1986.* Supports DNA research, looking for mutations in DNA, both nuclear and mitochondrial, that might cause autistic/epileptic symptoms in patients. Purine metabolic diseases include gout, purine autism, Lesch-Nyhan syndrome, ADA deficiency and others. Offers publications and reference information including a purine-restricted diet. Write: Purine Research Society, c/o Tahma Metz, 5424 Beech Ave., Bethesda, MD 20814. Call Tahma Metz 301-530-0354; Fax: 301-564-9597. *Website:* http://www.PurineResearchSociety.org *E-mail:* purine@erols.com

METATROPIC DYSPLASIA DWARFISM

(see also growth disorders, short/tall)

Metatropic Dysplasia Dwarf Registry *National network. Founded 1980.* Support and information for persons affected by metatropic dwarfism. Networks families and shares information. Offers phone support, limited literature, information and referrals. Write: Metatropic Dysplasia Dwarf Registry, 3393 Geneva Dr., Santa Clara, CA 95051. Call 408-244-6354; Fax: 408-296-6317. *Website:* http://www.lpbayarea.org/metatrophic *E-mail:* figone@netgate.net

MILLER'S SYNDROME

Foundation for Nager and Miller Syndromes *International. Founded 1989.* Networking for families that are affected by Nager or Miller syndromes. Provides referrals, library of information, phone support, newsletter, brochures and scholarships for Camp About Face. Write: Foundation for Nager and Miller Syndromes, c/o De De Van Quill, 13210 South East 342nd St., Auburn, WA

98092. Call 1-800-507-3667 or 253-333-1483; Fax: 253-288-7679. *Website:* http://www.fnms.net *E-mail:* ddfnms@aol.com

MITOCHONDRIAL DISORDERS

United Mitochondrial Disease Foundation (UMDF) *National network. 10 chapters. 24 affiliated groups. Founded 1995.* Promotes research and education for the diagnosis, treatment and cure of mitochondrial disorders and provides support to affected individuals and families. Chapter and support groups, networking for families affected by mitochondrial disease, a genetic degenerative disease. Quarterly newsletter, information and referrals, library of medical publications, patient registry, phone help and annual symposium. Awards research grants. Write: UMDF, 8085 Saltsburg Rd., Suite 201, Pittsburgh, PA 15239. Call 412-793-8077; Fax: 412-793-6477. *Website:* http://www.umdf.org *E-mail:* info@umdf.org

MOEBIUS SYNDROME

Moebius Syndrome Foundation *International network. Founded 1994.* Communication and support network for persons with Moebius syndrome (a paralysis of the 6th and 7th cranial nerves) and their families. Information, education and fund raising for research. Newsletter, phone support, informal meetings and national conference. Help with starting groups. Write: Moebius Syndrome Foundation, P.O. Box 147, Pilot Grove, MO 65276. Call Vicki McCarrell 660-834-3406 (eve) or 660-882-5576 ext. 120 (day); Fax: 660-834-3407. *Website:* http://www.moebiussyndrome.com *E-mail:* vickimc@iland.net

MOTILITY DISORDERS

(see also specific disorder)

Association of Gastrointestinal Motility Disorders, Inc. *International network. Founded 1991.* Support and education for persons affected by digestive motility disorders. Serves as educational resource and information base for medical professionals. Physician referrals, video tapes, large variety of educational materials, networking support, symposiums and several publications. General membership dues $35/US; 42/Int'l (can be waived). Write: AGMD International Corp. Headquarters, 12 Roberts Dr., Bedford, MA 01730. Call 781-275-1300; Fax: 781-275-1304. *Website:* http://www.agmd-gimotility.org *E-mail:* gimotility@msn.com

MOVEMENT DISORDERS

WE MOVE *Discussion forum.* Support and exchange of information and ideas among various movement disorder communities for patients, families and caregivers. Includes forums for such disorders as essential tremor, myoclonus, dystonia, corticobasal degeneration, Rett syndrome and many more. Write: WE MOVE, 204 West 84th St., New York, NY 10024. *Website:* http://www.wemove.org *E-mail:* wemove@wemove.org

MUCOLIPIDOSES / MUCOPOLYSACCHARIDOSES / MORQUIO'S SYNDROME

NATIONAL

International Morquio Support Group, The *International network. Founded 1999.* Provides support and education for families of children with Morquio Type A. Helps educate health care professionals about this lysosomal storage disease. Funds research. Maintains database of families. Referrals to physicians and medical information. Pen pals, phone support, conferences, newsletter, online guestbook and helpful links. Write: Morquio Support Group, P. O. Box 64184, Tucson, AZ 85728-4184. Call 520-744-2531; Fax: 520-744-2535. *Website:* http://www.morquio.com *E-mail:* mbs85705@yahoo.com

National MPS Society *National. Founded 1974.* Support for families with mucopolysaccharidoses and mucolipidoses. Public education, fund-raising for research and parent referral service for networking. Quarterly newsletter and phone support network. Write: National MPS Society, c/o Barbara Wedehase, P.O. Box 736, Bangor, ME 04402-0736. Call 207-947-1445; Fax: 207-990-3074. *Website:* http://www.mpssociety.org *E-mail:* info@mpssociety.org

MUCOLIPIDOSIS TYPE 4

ML4 Foundation *National network. Founded 1983.* Support network for families of children diagnosed with mucolipidosis type 4, a genetic disorder, characterized by variable psychomotor retardation that primarily affects Ashkenazi Jews. Supports fund-raising for research. Phone support, information and referrals. Write: ML4 Foundation, 719 E. 17th St., Brooklyn, NY 11230. Call 718-434-5067; Fax: 718-859-7371. *Website:* http://www.ml4.org *E-mail:* www@ml4.org

MULLERIAN ANOMALIES

ONLINE

Mullerian Anomalies of the Uterus *Online.* Support and information for those with mullerian anomalies of the uterus such as bicornuate, septate, unicornauate, hypoplastic and didelphys uteria. Weekly chat, email list and message board. *Website:* http://health.groups.yahoo.com/group/MullerianAnomalies/

MULTIPLE ENDOCRINE NEOPLASIA TYPE I

NATIONAL

Multiple Endocrine Neoplasia Society (MENS) *International network. 21 affiliated groups. Founded 1995.* Mutual support to persons afflicted with familial multiple endocrine neoplasia type 1 (aka Wermer syndrome or adenomatosis) and their families. MEN1 affects the endocrine glands. Literature, information and referrals, phone support and pen pals. Access to doctors and current research. Dues $10/yr. Write: MENS, Box 100, Meota, SK, Canada S0M 1X0. Call 306-892-2080; Fax: 306-892-2587. *Website:* http://www.mensociety.net *E-mail:* mensociety@sasktel.net

ONLINE

Pheochromocytoma Information Group *Online.* Offers support through information for persons affected by pheochromocytoma or multiple endocrine neoplasia syndrome. *Website:* http://www.pheochromocytoma.org

MULTIPLE HEREDITY EXOSTOSES

ONLINE

MHE and Me: A Support Group for Kids with MHE *Online. (A member of The MHE Coalition) Founded 1999.* Provides peers and a supportive community to children suffering from multiple hereditary exostoses (a genetic disorder in which benign cartilage-capped bone tumors grow from growth plates of long bones or surface of flat bones). Develops information and literature to assist children and their families in dealing with the disease. Advocacy, information and referrals, phone and email support. Write: MHE and Me, c/o Susan Wynn, 14 Stony Brook Dr., Pine Island, NY 10969. Call 845-258-6058. *Website:* http://www.mheandme.com *E-mail:* mheandme@yahoo.com

MHE Coalition, The *Online. 4 affiliated groups. Founded 2000.* Support and information for persons and their families affected by multiple hereditary exostoses, a skeletal disorder characterized by the formation of abnormal bony growths. Promotes and encourages research to find the cause, treatment and cure. Newsletter, networking, literature, advocacy, online groups, information and referrals, phone support, pen pals. Write: MHE Coalition, 8838 Holly Lane, Olmsted Falls, OH 44138. Call Chele Zelina, President 440-235-6325 (eve). *Website:* http://www.mhecoalition.com *E-mail:* CheleZ1aol.com

MYASTHENIA GRAVIS

STATEWIDE

Myasthenia Gravis Foundation - Garden State Chapter Public and professional education about MG, patient support, fund-raising for research, phone help, peer-counseling, outreach and professional speakers. State newsletter. Monthly board meetings. Area representatives in most counties. Membership dues $20/yr (can be waived). Quarterly meetings in various locations throughout NJ. Write: Myasthenia Gravis Foundation, P.O. Box 4258, Wayne, NJ 07474-4258. Call 1-800-437-4949 (in NJ) or 973-835-4444 (day); Fax: 973-835-4452.

OCEAN

Myasthenia Gravis Support Group Support and education for patients with myasthenia gravis. Families, friends and caregivers welcome. Guest speakers, buddy system and phone help. Meets 4th Sun., 1pm, Ocean Medical Center, 425 Jack Martin Blvd., Brick. Call Barbara Yodice 732-262-0450. *Website:* http://www.aininc.org *E-mail:* autoimmunehelp@aol.com

NATIONAL

Myasthenia Gravis Foundation of America, Inc. *National. 33 chapters. Founded 1952.* Promotes research and education into myasthenia gravis, a chronic neuromuscular disease. Provides supportive services for patients and families. Information and referral. Newsletter, support groups, various web-based services, annual and scientific meetings. Write: Myasthenia Gravis Foundation, 1821 University Ave. W., Suite S256, St. Paul, MN, 55104. Call 1-800-541-5454 or 651-917-6256; Fax: 651-917-1835. *Website:* http://www.myasthenia.org *E-mail:* mgfa@myasthenia.org

ONLINE

Myasthenia Gravis Patient-To-Patient *Online.* Offers email support and chat rooms. Share problems, solutions and support. *Website:* http://pages.prodigy.net/stanley.way/myasthenia/patient.htm *E-mail:* Stan_way@yahoo.com

MYCOSIS FUNGOIDES

ONLINE

Mycosis Fungoides UK *Online.* Support for any person affected by mycosis fungoides. Provides chat room and message board. Offers medical information links and support. *Website:* http://groups.msn.com/MycosisFungoidesUK

MYELOPROLIFERATIVE DISEASE

ONLINE

MPD-Net *Online. Founded 1989.* Support network enabling persons with myeloproliferative disease to share their experiences and problems. Supports research. Publishes materials pertaining to MPD. Professional involvement. Newsletter, phone support, conferences, information and referrals. Online listserv with 1800 members with MPD who exchange emails about their disease. Write: MPD-Net, c/o Joyce Niblack, 115 E. 72nd St., New York, NY 10021. *Website:* http://www.mpdinfo.org *E-mail:* JNiblack@mpdinfo.org

MYOSITIS

Myositis Association, The *International network. 65 groups. Founded 1993.* Dedicated to serving those with polymyositis, dermatomyositis, juvenile myositis and inclusion body myositis. Provides education and support. Also serves as a clearinghouse between patients and scientists. Newsletter, research reviews, literature and phone support. Area meetings available as well as annual conference. Guidelines available for starting similar groups. Fundraising for research. Dues $35. Write: The Myositis Association, 1233 20th St., NW, #402, Washington DC, 20036. Call 202-887-0088 (day); Fax: 202-466-8940. *Website:* http://www.myositis.org *E-mail:* tma@myositis.org

MYOTONIA CONGENITA FORUM

ONLINE

Myotonia Congenita *Online. Founded 2001.* Forum for people with myotonia congenital, their friends and families. Ask questions and share tips for living with myotonia congenita. *Website:* http://www.myotoniacongenita.org (click on forum) *E-mail:* jan@accessfitness.com

MYOTUBULAR MYOPATHY

Myotubular Myopathy Resource Group *International network. Founded 1993.* Information for patients, parents and doctors regarding myotubular myopathy, a family of three rare muscle disorders usually causing low muscle tone and diminished respiratory capacity. Exchanging of successes with other affected families. Phone support, literature, information and referrals. Write: Myotubular Myopathy Resource Group, c/o Pam Scoggin, 2602 Quaker Dr., Texas City, TX 77590. Call 409-945-8569. *Website:* http://www.mtmrg.org *E-mail:* pam@scoggin.com

NAGER SYNDROME

Foundation for Nager and Miller Syndromes *International. Founded 1989.* Networking for families that are affected by Nager or Miller syndromes. Provides referrals, library of information, phone support, newsletter, brochures and scholarships for Camp About Face. Write: Foundation for Nager and Miller Syndrome, c/o DeDe Van Quill, 13210 South East 342nd St., Auburn, WA 98092. Call 1-800-507-3667 or 253-333-1483; Fax: 253-288-7679. *Website:* http://www.fnms.net *E-mail:* ddfnms@aol.com

NAIL PATELLA SYNDROME

Nail Patella Syndrome Networking/Support Group *International network. Founded 1995.* Support network for persons with nail patella syndrome to exchange information. Links to a research study and other NPS-related sites. Provides information and online chat. Write: Nail Patella Syndrome Networking/Support Group, 67 Woodlake Dr., Holland, PA 18966. *Website:* http://hometown.aol.com/PACALI/npspage.html *E-mail:* PACALI@aol.com

NARCOLEPSY

Narcolepsy Network *National. 100 affiliated support groups. Founded 1986.* Support for persons with narcolepsy and other sleep disorders, their families and interested others. Helps with coping skills, family and community problems. Provides advocacy, education and supports research. Newsletter, conferences, phone support and group development guidelines. Dues $35. Write: Narcolepsy Network, 79A Main St., North Kingston, RI 02852. Call 1-888-292-6522 or 401-667-2523; Fax: 401-633-6567. *Website:* http://www.narcolepsynetwork.org *E-mail:* narnet@narcolepsynetwork.org

NECROTIZING FASCIITIS / FLESH EATING BACTERIA

National Necrotizing Fasciitis Foundation *Online.* Provides education and support for persons affected by necrotizing fasciitis (aka flesh-eating bacteria). Aim is to educate public and advocate for research. Provides literature, phone support, newsletter, pen pals, conferences, information and referrals. Publishes "Surviving the Flesh-Eating Bacteria: Understanding, Preventing, Treating And Living With the Effects of Necrotizing Fasciitis." *Website:* http://www.nnff.com

NEMALINE MYOPATHY, CONGENITAL

Nemaline Myopathy Foundation *National network. Founded 1991.* Grassroots group that offers newsletter that networks families affected by pediatric/adult Nemaline Myopathy for support and information. Pen pals, literature, phone support, information and referrals available through several Yahoo e-groups targeting age groups and Spanish speaking families. NM conventions organized to meet researchers and other families. Write: Nemaline Myopathy Foundation, P.O. Box 5937, Round Rock, TX 78683. Call 512-388-7985. *Website:* http://www.nemaline.org *E-mail:* davidmcd@btopenworld.com

NEUROCARDIOGENIC SYNCOPE

Neurocardiogenic Syncope Fainting List *Online. 323 members. Founded 2005.* Support and understanding for those suffering from neurocardiogenic syncope, dysautonomia, orthostatic hypotension, neurally mediated hypotension, low blood pressure and other diseases that can cause fainting, heat sensitivity, nausea or dizziness. Open to families and friends. Sharing of stories, struggles, triumphs and information. Must become a member. *Website:* http://health.groups.yahoo.com/group/NCS_F/

NEUROFIBROMATOSIS

(see also specific disorder)

STATEWIDE

Children's Tumor Foundation NJ Chapter Self-help groups information for persons with neurofibromatosis and their families (under 18 welcome). Support groups meet at Pascack Valley Hospital in Westwood and Muhlenberg Hospital in Plainfield. Newsletter, guest speakers. Annual dues $35 single, $50 family/yr. For information call Donna Oettinger 201-265-3296. *Website:* http://www.ctf.org *E-mail:* donnanf@aol.com

Neurofibromatosis, Inc. Mid-Atlantic Region *Founded 1979.* Serves Virginia, District of Columbia, Delaware, New Jersey, Pennsylvania, West Virginia and North Carolina. Provides support and advocacy for those with neurofibromatosis. Provides free printed materials, conducts meetings with a realtime captionist for the hearing impaired, publishes 5 newsletters a year; videos on NF and Camp New Friends; provides peer-counseling; appropriate medical education, social referrals and speakers. Promotes research and funds some clinical studies. Write: Neurofibromatosis, Inc. Mid-Atlantic, 8855 Annapolis Rd #110, Lanham, MD 20706. Call 1-866-261-1271; Fax: 301-577-0016. *Website:* http://www.nfmidatlantic.org *E-mail:* nfmidatlantic@aol.com

NATIONAL

Children's Tumor Foundation *National. 50 chapters. Founded 1978.* For patients with neurofibromatosis and their families. Promotes and supports research on the causes of and cure for NF. Provides information and assistance education. Dues $40/year. Quarterly newsletter. Professional grants awarded for research. Write: Children's Tumor Foundation, 95 Pine St., 16th Floor, New York, NY 10005. Call 1-800-323-7938 or 212-344-6633; Fax: 212-747-0004. *Website:* http://www.ctf.org *E-mail:* info@ctf.org

Neurofibromatosis, Inc. *National. 8 groups. Founded 1988.* Dedicated to individuals and families affected by the neurofibromatoses (NF-1 NF-2) through education, support, clinical and research programs. Newsletter, networking, video, printed materials, phone support, information and referrals. Assistance in starting groups. Write: Neurofibromatosis, Inc., P.O. Box 18246, Minneapolis, MN 55418.

Call 301-918-4600 or 1-800-942-6825 (patient inquiries); Fax: 301-918-0009. *Website:* http://www.nfinc.org *E-mail:* NFInfo@nfinc.org

NEUROLOGICAL DISORDERS

ONLINE

Picks-Support *Online. Founded 1999.* International support forum group set up by caregivers of people with various types of fronto-temporal dementia (includes Pick's Disease, Frontotemporal Dementia, Primary Progressive Aphasia, Frontotemporal Lobe Degeneration, Dementia with Lewy Bodies and Corticobasal Ganglionic Degeneration). Group is made up of caregivers and anyone who has an interest in this area. Discussion list allows communication in a supportive environment. *Website:* http://health.groups.yahoo.com/group/picks-support/

NEVUS, CONGENITAL / NEUROCUTANEOUS MELANOSIS

NATIONAL

Nevus Network *(MULTILINGUAL) International network. Founded 1983.* Provides a network of support and information for people with a large brown birthmark called a giant congenital nevus and/or an associated condition called neurocutaneous melanosis. Write: Nevus Network, 600 SE Delaware, Suite 200, Bartlesville, OK 74003. Call 419-853-4525 or 405-377-3403. *Website:* http://www.nevusnetwork.org *E-mail:* info@nevusnetwork.org

Nevus Outreach, Inc. *International network. Founded 1997.* Dedicated to improving awareness and providing support for people affected by congenital pigmented nevi and finding a cure. Literature, 24-hour support hotline and international conferences. Write: Nevus Outreach, Inc., 600 SE Delaware, Suite 200, Bartlesville, OK 74003. Call 918-331-0595 or toll-free hotline 1-877-426-3887. *Website:* http://www.nevus.org

NIEMANN-PICK DISEASE

National Niemann-Pick Disease Foundation, Inc. *International network. Founded 1992.* Provides support for families affected by Niemann-Pick disease type A, B and C. Promotes and supports research. Provides newsletter, family directory, networking, family conference, phone support, information and referrals. Guidelines available to help start similar groups. Dues $20. Write: National

Niemann-Pick Disease Foundation, P.O. Box 49, 401B Madison Ave., Fort Atkinson, WI 53538. Call 920-563-0930; Fax: 920-563-0931. *Website:* http://www.nnpdf.org *E-mail:* nnpdf@idcnet.com

NOONAN SYNDROME

Noonan Syndrome Support Group *International network. Founded 1996.* Provides information for persons with Noonan syndrome, their families and interested others. Networks individuals together for peer support. Information and referrals, speakers bureau, phone help. Write: Noonan Syndrome Support Group, P.O. Box 145, Upperco, MD 21155. Call 1-888-686-2224 or 410-374-5245. *Website:* http://www.noonansyndrome.org *E-mail:* info@noonansyndrome.org

NYSTAGMUS

American Nystagmus Network *National. Founded 1999.* Network of persons affected by nystagmus, an involuntary, rapid movement of the eyeball. Open to parents of affected children, adults with nystagmus and interested professionals. Provides general information. Promotes research into cause and cure. Email discussion group, discussion board, biannual newsletter and conferences. Write: American Nystagmus Network, Inc., 303-D Beltline Place #321, Decatur, AL 35603. *Website:* http://www.nystagmus.org *E-mail:* webmaster@nystagmus.org

ODOR (BODY / BREATH)

NARA (Not A Rose Association) / BOSS (Body Odor Support Services) *Model. 1 group in GA. Founded 1998.* Mutual support for persons suffering from "odorous" conditions of the body, breath or unknown sources. Offers coping skills. Write: NARA/BOSS, 1492 Baron Count, Stone Mountain, GA 30087. Call 770-279-0200. *E-mail:* annhenry99@yahoo.com

OPITZ–G/BBB SYNDROME

Opitz-G/BBB Family Network *International. Founded 1994.* Support, encouragement, education and sharing of successes and ideas for families affected by Opitz-G/BBB syndrome. Maintains database of members, literature, information, e-group, phone support and newsletter. Referrals to other families. Family conferences. Write: Opitz Family Network, P.O. Box 515, Grand Lake, CO 80447. Call 970-627-8935; Fax: 970-627-8818. *Website:* http://www.opitznet.org *E-mail:* opitznet@mac.com

ORTHOPEDIC

Totally Hip *Online. Founded 1996.* Support to help relieve the fear of total hip replacement surgery, share experiences and offer moral as well as spiritual support to patients. Helps answer questions on hip replacement. Also forum to discuss other joint problems. Click on bulletin board at website for message exchange. ***Website:*** http://www.totallyhip.org *E-mail:* Linda@totallyhip.org

OSTEOGENESIS IMPERFECTA

ESSEX

NJ Osteogenesis Imperfecta Support Group Purpose is to share information, support and improve the quality of life for people affected by O.I. Rap sessions, guest speakers and phone help. Information and referrals. For meeting information call Rosemarie or JoAnn 201-489-9232 (day).

NATIONAL

Osteogenesis Imperfecta Foundation *National. 30 affiliated support groups. Founded 1970.* Support and resources for families dealing with osteogenesis imperfecta. Provides information for medical professionals. Supports research. Literature, quarterly newsletter and phone support network. Write: Osteogenesis Imperfecta Foundation, 804 W. Diamond Ave., Suite 210, Gaithersburg, MD 20878-3836. Call 1-800-981-2663 or 301-947-0083; Fax: 301-947-0456. ***Website:*** http://www.oif.org *E-mail:* bonelink@oif.org

OSTEONECROSIS / AVASCULAR NECROSIS

ONLINE

ON/AVN Support Group International Association, Inc. *Online.* Support for persons who suffer from ostenecrosis (aka avascular necrosis). Goal is to inform and educate the world about osteonecrosis and offer emotional support to both those with ON/AVN and their families. Provides information and referrals. Also has special section for youth with ON/AVN. Open to those with other chronic bone, joint or muscular conditions and persons with joint replacements. Write: ON/AVN Support Group International Association Inc., 8500 Henry Ave., P. O. Box 118, Philadelphia, PA 19128. ***Website:*** http://www.osteonecrosisavnsupport.org *E-mail:* avinfo@avnsupport.org

Osteonecrosis Self-Help Group *Listserv. 1,200 members. Founded 1998.* Designed as an open forum for those having experience with the chronic bone disorder osteonecrosis (aka avascular necrosis). All are welcome to join in and share successes and frustrations in getting diagnosed and treated. Exchange of coping skills dealing with this "on again off again" chronic disease. *Website:* http://health.groups.yahoo.com/group/osteonecrosis/

OXALOSIS HYPEROXALURIA

Oxalosis and Hyperoxaluria Foundation *National network. Founded 1989.* Provides support and current information for patients, families and medical professionals in the field of primary hyperoxaluria and oxalate stone disease. Educates the public, supports research, newsletter, information and referrals, phone support, pen pals, conferences and funds research. Yearly dues $25/ind.; $50/prof.; $100/business. Write: Oxalosis Hyperoxaluria Foundation, 201 E. 19th St., #12E, New York, NY 10003. Call 1-800-643-8699 or 212-777-0470; Fax: 212-777-0471. *Website:* http://www.ohf.org *E-mail:* info@ohf.org

PAGET'S DISEASE

National Association for the Relief of Paget's Disease *Model. 2500 Member network. 5 regional groups in UK. Founded 1973.* Offers support to persons with Paget's disease. Aims to raise awareness of this disorder through newsletter and publications. Sponsors research. Phone support, literature, information and referrals. Guidelines available for starting similar groups. Write: National Association for the Relief of Paget's Disease, 323 Manchester Rd., Walkden, Worsley, Manchester M28 3HH, UK. Call +44-161-799-4646. *Website:* http:www.paget.org.uk *E-mail:* director@paget.org.uk

PANCREATITIS

ONLINE

Pancreatitis Association International *Online. Founded 1999.* Online internet discussion group which serves as a means of support and information. *Website:* http://health.groups.yahoo.com/group/pancreatitis

PANHYPOPITUITARISM

Panhypopituitarism Division *International network. Founded 1990.* Provides support for families affected by panhypopituitarism. Newsletters, updated medical information, phone support, annual conventions and Kids Program. Online assistance available in finding or forming local support groups. Dues: $30 US, $40 Canada, $45 overseas/year. Write: Panhypopituitarism Division, MAGIC Foundation, 6645 W. North Ave., Oak Park, IL 60302. Call 1-800-362-4423; Fax: 708-383-0899. *Website:* http://www.magicfoundation.org *E-mail:* mary@magicfoundation.org

PANNICULITIS

ONLINE

Erythema Nodosum Support Group *Online. Founded 2003.* Mutual support of erythema nodosum and pyoderma gangreblosum patients and available resources. *Website:* http://health.groups.yahoo.com/group/erythema_nodosum_group/

Panniculitis *Online. 300+ members. Founded 1999.* Support for persons afflicted with any form of panniculitis (Weber Christian, erythema nodosum, mesenteric panniculitis, erythema induratum, lupus panniculitis, subcutaneous sarcoid, etc.) Offers message boards, information and chat rooms. *Website:* http://groups.yahoo.com/group/Panniculitis

PAPILLOMATOSIS

STATEWIDE / NATIONAL

Recurrent Respiratory Papillomatosis Foundation Networking for families affected by recurrent respiratory papillomatosis. Interested professionals are welcome. Newsletter and phone support. Write: Recurrent Respiratory Papillomatosis Foundation, P.O. Box 6643, Lawrenceville, NJ 08648-0643. Call Bill Stern 609-530-1443; Fax: 609-530-1912. *Website:* http://www.rrpf.org *E-mail:* bills@rrpf.org

"Although the world is full of suffering, it is also full of overcoming it."
-- Helen Keller

PARRY-ROMBERG SYNDROME

ONLINE

The Romberg's Connection *Online. Founded 1997.* Offers mutual support for persons affected by Parry-Romberg's syndrome (aka progressive facial hemiatrophy or Romberg's syndrome), their families and friends. Parry-Romberg syndrome is a rare disorder causing atrophy to usually one half of the face. Aim is to locate affected persons and offer strength, hope, courage and friendship. *Website:* http://www.geocities.com/HotSprings/1018/ *E-mail:* rombergs@hotmail.com

PEMPHIGUS

International Pemphigus Foundation *International network. 16 affiliated groups. Founded 1994.* Provides support and information on pemphigus and related autoimmune blistering diseases for patients, families, friends and the medical community. Computer listserv. Literature, newsletter, information and referrals, advocacy and phone support. Computer support group. Write: International Pemphigus Foundation, 1540 River Park Dr., Suite 208, Sacramento, CA 95815. Call 916-922-1298; Fax: 916-922-1458. *Website:* http://www.pemphigus.org *E-mail:* pemphigus@pemhigus.org

PERIODIC PARALYSIS

Periodic Paralysis Association *Online.* Provides information and support to individuals with periodic paralysis and non-dystrophic myotonias (disorders characterized by episodic paralysis and weakness), their families and health care professionals. Offers links to online specialist referrals, private e-mail listserv, Ask-the-experts, online newsletter and patient advocacy. Write: Periodic Paralysis Association, 1101 Douglas Dr., Tracy, CA 95304-5879. Call 626-638-3326; Fax: 626-698-0789. *Website:* http://www.periodicparalysis.org *E-mail:* inquire@periodicparalysis.org

PETER'S ANOMALY

ONLINE

Peter's Anomaly Support Group *Online.* Support for families of children with Peter's anomaly. Offers message board and forum. Also many useful links. *Website:* http://www.petersanomaly.org *E-mail:* rmcginn66@yahoo.com

PEUTZ JEGJERS SYNDROME

ONLINE

Peutz Jeghers Syndrome Online Support Group *Online. 200+ members worldwide. Founded 2000.* Provides information for individuals with Peutz Jeghers syndrome, their families, interested medical professionals and researchers. Provides peer support (matching individuals and their families) and medical referrals. Must subscribe to view the archives. *Website:* http://www.peutz-jeghers.com *E-mail:* pj4steph@aol.com

PHEOCHROMOCYTOMA / MULTIPLE ENDOCRINE NEOPLASIA SYNDROME

Pheochromocytoma Information Group *Online.* Offers support through information for persons affected by pheochromocytoma or multiple endocrine neoplasia syndrome. *Website:* http://www.pheochromocytoma.org

PIERRE ROBIN

Pierre Robin Network *National network. Founded 1999.* Support and education for individuals, parents, caregivers and professionals dealing with Pierre Robin syndrome or sequence. Literature, newsletter, information, advocacy, online email group and bulletin board. Outreach committee comprised of families worldwide available to correspond via mail, phone, in person or email. Write: Pierre Robin Network, 3604 Biscayne, Quincy, IL 62305. Fax: 217-224-6659. *Website:* http://www.pierrerobin.org *E-mail:* info@pierrerobin.org

PINK DISEASE

Pink Disease Support Group *International network. Founded 1989.* Support group for people who had Pink disease (babyhood mercury toxicity) and their relatives. Provides information, support and newsletters by mail and email. Online chat group. Dues $15/yr. (Australia); or $25/yr. (Int'l). Write: Pink Disease Support Group, P.O. Box 134, Gilgandra NSW, Australia 2827. *Website:* http://www.pinkdisease.org *E-mail:* pinkdisease@bigpond.com

PITUITARY DISORDERS

Pituitary Network Association *International network. Founded 1992.* Mutual support for persons with all types of pituitary disorders and diseases. Promotes early diagnosis, medical and public awareness and continued research to find a cure. Newsletter, information and referrals, phone support, resource guide, patient conferences. Write: Pituitary Network Association, P.O. Box 1958, Thousand Oaks, CA 91358. Call 805-499-9973; Fax: 805-480-0633. *Website:* http://www.pituitary.org *E-mail:* PNA@pituitary.org

PITYRIASIS RUBRA PILARIS

ONLINE

Pityriasis Rubra Pilaris (PRP) Support Group *Online. Founded 1997.* An online discussion forum for anyone diagnosed with the rare skin disease pityriasis rubra pilaris (PRP). Discussion forum members include caregivers and interested family members, spouses, children, parents, friends and partners. Registration is required to participate. *Website:* http://www.prp-support.org *E-mail:* jeremyb@pcug.org.au or rgreene@temple.edu

PORPHYRIA

NATIONAL

American Porphyria Foundation *National network. Founded 1981.* Supports research, provides education and information to the public, patients and physicians, networks porphyria patients and support groups. Quarterly newsletter, pen pal program, phone network. Group development guidelines available. Donation $30/yr. Write: America Porphyria Foundation, P.O. Box 22712, Houston, TX 77227. Call 713-266-9617; Fax: 713-840-9552. *Website:* http://www.porphyriafoundation.com *E-mail:* porphyrus@aol.com

Canadian Porphyria Foundation, Inc. *International. Founded 1988.* Dedicated to improving the quality of life for people affected by porphyria, a group of rare genetic disorders characterized by disturbances of porphyria metabolism. Offers programs of awareness, education, service, advocacy and support. Promotes awarenesss of porphyria through educational literature, articles, newsletters, information and referrals. Offers support groups and advocacy. Encourages and supports research. Assistance in starting groups. Write: Canadian Porphyria Foundation, Inc., P.O. Box 1206, Neepawa, Manitoba, Canada R0J 1H0. Call

1-866-476-2801 or 204-476-2800; Fax: 204-476-2800. *Website:* http://www.cpf-inc.ca *E-mail:* porphyria@cpf-inc.ca

PRADER-WILLI SYNDROME

STATEWIDE

NJ Chapter Prader-Willi Syndrome Association This uncommon birth defect affects appetite, growth, metabolism and behavior. Provides educational materials and coordinates research on Prader-Willi syndrome. Parents meet twice a year. Write: NJ Chapter, Prader-Willi Syndrome Association, c/o Douglas Taylor, 16 Gettysburg Way, Lincoln Park, NJ 07035. Call Douglas Taylor 973-628-6945. *Website:* http://www.pwsausa.org/nj *E-mail:* pwsa.nj@gmail.com

NATIONAL

Prader-Willi Syndrome Association *National. 38 chapters. Founded 1975.* Support and education for anyone impacted by Prader-Willi syndrome. Bi-monthly newsletter. Membership dues $35. Many publications available. Chapter development kits available. Write: Prader-Willi Syndrome Association, 5700 Midnight Pass Rd., Suite 6, Sarasota, FL 34242. Call 1-800-926-4797 or 941-312-0400; Fax: 941-312-0142. *Website:* http://www.pwsausa.org *E-mail:* national@pwsausa.org

PRECOCIOUS PUBERTY

Precocious Puberty Support Network *National network. Founded 1989.* Network and exchange of information for children who are experiencing precocious puberty and their families. Information and referrals, phone support, pen pals, annual convention, conferences, literature and newsletter. Membership: $35 US, $40 Canada, $45 overseas/year. Write: Precocious Puberty Support Network, c/o MAGIC Foundation, 6645 W. North Ave, Oak Park, IL 60302. Call 1-800-362-4423 or 708-383-0808; Fax: 708-383-0899. *Website:* http://www.magicfoundation.org *E-mail:* mary@magicfoundation.org

"It is expressly at those times when we feel needy that we will benefit the most from giving." -- Ruth Ross

PRIMARY LATERAL SCLEROSIS / HEREDITARY SPASTIC PARAPLEGIA

NATIONAL

Spastic Paraplegia Foundation, Inc. *National. Founded 2002.* Offers support and information to those affected by primary lateral sclerosis and hereditary spastic paraplegia. Supports research. Offers regional and email support groups, online chat group, newsletter and information. Write: Spastic Paraplegia Foundation, Inc., 375 Julianna Circle, Franklin, TN 37064. Call 703-495-9261. *Website:* http://www.sp-foundation.org

ONLINE

PLS Friends *Online.* Opportunity for persons with primary lateral sclerosis, a progressive neuromuscular disease, to share information and support via an online discussion group. Fosters support and an exchange of ideas among PLS patients, their relatives, caregivers and health care professionals. Must subscribe to join online groups, http://groups.yahoo.com/group/PLS-FRIENDS/join *Website:* http://www.geocities.com/freyerse/ *E-mail:* synapsePLS@comcast.net

PROGRESSIVE OSSEOUS HETEROPLASIA

Progressive Osseous Heteroplasia Association *National network. Founded 1995.* Support network for patients and families affected by progressive osseous heteroplasia. Fundraising for research. Write: Progressive Osseous Heteroplasia Association, 33 Stonehearth Square, Indian Head Park, IL 60525. Call 708-246-9410 (voice/fax). *Website:* http://www.pohdisease.org *E-mail:* POHA@comcast.net

PROGRESSIVE SUPRANUCLEAR PALSY

BURLINGTON

Caregivers Support Group Support for anyone caring for an individual with progressive supranuclear palsy, Alzheimer's or Parkinson's disease. Meets 1st Tues., 6:30-7:30pm, Care One at Evesham, 870 East Route 70, Marlton. Call Carol Solomon 856-985-1180 (day).

NATIONAL

Cure PSP (Society for Progressive Supranuclear Palsy, Inc.) *International network. 75 affiliated groups. Founded 1990.* Provides support for patients with progressive supranuclear palsy and their families. Advocacy. Offers newsletter, information and referrals, phone support, conferences, listserv, educational materials and assistance in starting support groups. Write: Society for Progressive Supranuclear Palsy, Executive Plaza III, 11350 McCormick Rd., St. 906, Hunt Valley, MD, 21031. Call 1-800-457-4777 or 410-785-7004; Fax: 410-785-7009. *Website:* http://www.curepsp.org *E-mail:* info@curepsp.org

PROSTATE PROBLEMS

NATIONAL

Man To Man Program *National. 300 affiliated groups. Founded 1990.* Support and education for men with prostate cancer to enable them to better understand their options and to make informed decisions. Phone support, information and referrals, support group meetings, education and support visitation program. Newsletter. Some chapters invite wives and partners; other chapters have wives and partners meet separately. Assistance available for starting new groups. Call American Cancer Society 1-800-227-2345. *Website:* http://www.cancer.org

Patient Advocates for Advanced Cancer Treatment (PAACT) *International. 150 affiliated groups. Founded 1984.* Provides support and advocacy for prostate cancer patients, their families and the general public at risk. Information relative to the advancements in the detection, diagnosis, evaluation and treatment of prostate cancer. Information, referrals, phone help, conferences, newsletters and group development guidelines. Write: PAACT, P.O. Box 141695, Grand Rapids, MI 49514-1695. Call 616-453-1477; Fax: 616-453-1846. *Website:* http://www.paactusa.org *E-mail:* paact@paactusa.org

US TOO International Prostate Cancer Education Support Network *International. 300 affiliated groups. Founded 1990.* Mutual support, information and education for prostate cancer patients, their families and friends. Provides newsletter, information, phone support and assistance in starting new groups. Write: US TOO International, Inc., 5003 Fairview Ave., Downers Grove, IL 60515-5286. Call 1-800-808-7866 or 630-795-1002 (day); Fax: 630-795-1602; *Website:* http://www.ustoo.org *E-mail:* ustoo@ustoo.org

ONLINE

Male Chronic Pelvic Pain Network *Online.* Support and information for men affected by male chronic pelvic pain syndrome (aka chronic prostatitis, interstitial cystitis and pelvic myoneuropathy). Exchange of information forum. *Website:* http://www.chronicprostatitis.com

PROTEUS SYNDROME

Proteus Syndrome Foundation *International network. Founded 1991.* Provides education and support for families or children with Proteus syndrome. Supports research into cause and cure of this disorder. Newsletter, pen pals, literature and database of families. Fundraising. Write: Proteus Syndrome Foundation, 4915 Dry Stone Dr., Colorado Springs, CO 80918. Call Kim Hoag 719-264-8445 (day) or Barbara King 901-756-9375 (day); *Website:* http://www.proteus-syndrome.org *E-mail:* kimkhoag@adelphia.net or jakebabs@aol.com

PSEUDO-OBSTRUCTION

Association of Gastrointestinal Motility Disorders, Inc. *International network. Founded 1991.* Support and education for persons affected by digestive motility disorders. Serves as educational resource and information base for medical professionals. Physician referrals, video tapes, large variety of educational materials, networking support, symposiums and several publications. Dues $35/US; $42/Int'l (can be waived). Write: AGMD International Corp. Headquarters, 12 Roberts Dr., Bedford, MA 01730. Call 781-275-1300; Fax: 781-275-1304. *Website:* http://www.agmd-gimotility.org *E-mail:* gimotility@msn.com

PSEUDOTUMOR CEREBRI

ONLINE

Pseudotumor Cerebri Support Network *Online. 1,000 members. Founded 1995.* Provides information, discussion forum, newsletter and online book "PTC Primer: Living With Pseudotumor Cerebri." *Website:* http://www.pseudotumorcerebri.com

Need help finding a specific group? Give us a call – we're here to help!
Call 1-800-367-6274

PSEUDOXANTHOMA ELASTICUM

STATEWIDE

NY-NJ Chapter of PXE International Promotes support, education, advocacy research for those with pseudoxanthoma elasticum and their families. Patient tissue registry, listserv and email connection. Guest speakers, pen pals, phone help and literature. Meets quarterly in various locations. Call Judy Roller 732-297-7055. *Website:* http://www.pxe.org *E-mail:* jroller123@aol.com

NATIONAL

National Association for Pseudoxanthoma Elasticum *National network. Founded 1988.* Support, education, research and advocacy for persons with PXE, their families, interested others and professionals. Phone support, newsletter, information and referrals. Donations appreciated and tax deductible. Write: National Association for Pseudoxanthoma Elasticum, 8760 Manchester Rd., St. Louis, MO 63144-2724. Call 314-962-0100 (voice/fax). *Website:* http://www.pxenape.org *E-mail:* napestlouis@sbcglobal.net

PXE International, Inc. *International. 41 affiliated groups. Founded 1995.* Initiates, funds and manages research, supports patients and educates clinicians. Offers support groups, listservs, phone and mail contacts, literature and semi-annual newsletter. Offers assistance in starting similar group. Write: PXE International, Inc., 4301 Connecticut Ave. NW, Suite 404, Washington, DC 20008-2369. Call 202-362-9599; Fax: 202-966-8553. *Website:* http://www.pxe.org *E-mail:* info@pxe.org

PULMONARY HYPERTENSION

Pulmonary Hypertension Association *National network. 130 support groups. Founded 1990.* Support and information for patients with pulmonary hypertension (a cardio-vascular disease), their families and medical professionals. Encourages research, promotes awareness and provides resource referrals. Networking, phone help, pen pals and assistance in starting groups. Membership $15 (includes quarterly newsletter, twice yearly). Write: Pulmonary Hypertension Association, 801 Roeder Rd., Suite 400, Silver Spring, MD 20910. Call 1-800-748-7274 or 301-565-3004; Fax: 301-565-3994. *Website:* http://www.phassociation.org *E-mail:* pha@phassociation.org

RARE DISORDERS, GENERAL

NATIONAL

Hearts and Hands *Model. 1 group in NC. Founded 1993.* Emotional, spiritual and educational support for persons with either rare or undiagnosed illnesses and their families. Also has a registry for loin pain hematuria syndrome. Write: Hearts and Hands, c/o Winoka Plummer, 1648 Oliver's Crossing Circle, Winston-Salem, NC 27127. Call 336-785-7612. *Website:* http://www.geocities.com/hotsprings/spa/2464/index.html

National Organization for Rare Disorders *National network. Founded 1983.* Information and networking for persons with any type of rare disorder. Literature, information and referrals. Advocacy for orphan diseases. Networks persons or families with the same disorder for support. Guidelines available for starting similar groups. Write: NORD, 55 Kenosia Ave., P.O. Box 1968, Danbury, CT 06813-1968. Call 1-800-999-6673 or 203-744-0100; TDD: 203-797-9590; Fax: 203-798-2291. *Website:* http://www.rarediseases.org *E-mail:* orphan@rarediseases.org

RAYNAUD'S DISEASE

Raynaud's Association, Inc. *National. Founded 1992.* Mutual support group to help Raynaud's sufferers cope with day-to-day activities to maintain or improve their quality of life. Aims to increase awareness of the disease among public and medical communities. Assists in supporting treatment research efforts. Newsletter, information and referrals, special event meetings and literature. Dues $20 (optional). Write: Raynaud's Association, 94 Mercer Ave., Hartsdale, NY 10530. Call Lynn Wunderman 1-800-280-8055; Fax: 914-946-4685. *Website:* http://www.raynauds.org *E-mail:* info@raynauds.org

REFLEX ANOXIC SEIZURE DISORDER

STARS (Syncope Trust And Reflex Anoxic Seizures) *International network. Founded 1993.* Network of parents and sufferers of syncope and reflex anoxic seizure (characterized by temporary heart stoppage and a seizure-like response to any unexpected stimuli), also known as Stephenson's seizure, white breath holding or pallid infantile syncope. Information, education, literature, syncope message board and videos. Supports research. Write: STARS, P.O. Box 175, Stratford Upon Avon, Warwickshire, CV37 8YD, UK Call: +44(0)17894 50564 or 0 800

0286362 (24 hr. helpline UK only); Fax: 011-44 01789 4505682 (UK). *Website:* http://www.stars.org.uk *E-mail:* trudie@stars.org.uk

RESTLESS LEG SYNDROME

MIDDLESEX

Central New Jersey Restless Legs Syndrome Support Group A group of RLS patients and medical professionals who help raise awareness of RLS and share in the latest information, research and medical break through regarding RLS. Families welcome. Rap sessions, guest speakers, literature, newsletter and phone help. Meets 3 to 4 times per year, Sat., Neuroscience Institute Conference Room, JFK Medical Center, 65 James St., Edison. Call Elizabeth Visone 973-715-3868 (day). *E-mail:* ElizabethVis@aol.com

NATIONAL

Restless Legs Syndrome Foundation *National network. 100 affiliated groups. Founded 1992.* Promotes awareness and information about restless legs syndrome. Offers network of support and educational groups nationwide. Publishes a free information booklet. Members receive a quarterly newsletter. Write: RLS Foundation, 819 2nd St. SW, Rochester, MN 55902-2985. Call 507-287-6465 or 1-877-463-6757 (to request information); Fax: 507-287-6312. *Website:* http://www.rls.org *E-mail:* rlsfoundation@rls.org

RETT SYNDROME

International Rett Syndrome Association (IRSA) *International. 17 affiliated groups. Founded 1985.* For parents, interested professionals and others concerned with Rett syndrome. Provides information and referral, peer support among parents and funds research. Quarterly newsletter. Dues $30/individual; $35/family; $40/int'l. Write: IRSA, 9121 Piscataway Rd., Suite 2B, Clinton, MD 20735-2561. Call 1-800-818-7388 or 301-856-3334; Fax: 301-856-3336. *Website:* http://www.rettsyndrome.org *E-mail:* admin@rettsyndrome.org

REYE'S SYNDROME

National Reye's Syndrome Foundation *National. 4 affiliated chapters, 189 representatives in 45 states. Founded 1974.* Devoted to spreading the awareness of Reye's syndrome, a disease affecting the liver and brain which affects persons of all ages and races. Provides support, information and referrals. Encourages research.

Representatives are usually a parent, sibling or survivor, but is open to any interested person. Sponsors Halloween Awareness Program which distributes free pamphlets to individuals willing to pass them out to trick or treaters. Write: National Reye's Syndrome Foundation, P.O. Box 829, Bryan, OH 43506. Call 1-800-233-7393; Fax: 419-636-9897. *Website:* http://www.reyessyndrome.org *E-mail:* nrsf@reyessyndrome.org

ROBINOW SYNDROME

Robinow Syndrome Foundation *National network. Founded 1994.* Aim is to locate, educate and support persons affected by Robinow syndrome (also known as fetal face syndrome), a very rare, genetic dwarfing syndrome. Online support and newsletter, bi-annual conventions, family networking. Write: Robinow Syndrome Foundation, c/o Karla Kruger, P.O. Box 1072, Anoka, MN 55303. Call Karla Kruger 763-434-1152 (voice/fax). *Website:* http://www.robinowfoundation@comcast.net *E-mail:* kmkruger@comcast.net

ROSACEA

ONLINE

Rosacea Support Group *Online. 680+ members. Founded 1998.* Email support group for rosacea sufferers, their family and friends. *Website:* http://health.groups.yahoo.com/group/rosacea-support

RUBINSTEIN-TAYBI SYNDROME

Rubinstein-Taybi Parent Group USA *National network. 465 member families. Founded 1984.* Mutual support, information and sharing for parents of children with Rubinstein-Taybi syndrome. Information, phone contact, parent contact list, chat room and listserv. Write: Rubinstein-Taybi Parent Group, c/o Garry and Lorrie Baxter, P.O. Box 146, Smith Center, KS 66967. Call 1-888-447-2989. *Website:* http://www.rubinstein-taybi.org and http://www.rubinsteintaybi.com *E-mail:* lbaxter@ruraltel.net

RUSSELL-SILVER SYNDROME

Russell-Silver Syndrome Support Network *National network. Founded 1989.* Network and exchange of information for parents of children with Russell-Silver syndrome. Information and referrals, phone support, pen pals, conferences, annual convention and literature. Membership: $30/US, $40/Canada, $45/overseas. Write:

Russell-Silver Syndrome Support Network, c/o MAGIC Foundation, 6645 W. North Ave., Oak Park, IL 60302. Call 1-800-362-4423 or 708-383-0808; Fax: 708-383-0899. *Website:* http://www.magicfoundation.org *E-mail:* mary@magicfoundation.org

SARCOIDOSIS

NATIONAL

Foundation for Sarcoidosis Research, The *National network. Founded 2000.* Provides information, resources and research news on Sarcoidosis (a multi-system disease that causes inflammation of the body's tissues) to patients, their families and their physicians. Online support offers patients a safe environment to share their stories and participate in discussion groups. Write: Foundation for Sarcoidosis Research, 2502 North Clark Street, Chicago, IL 60614. Call Debbie Durrer 773-525-2510; Fax: 773-525-2512. *Website:* http://www.stopsarcoidosis.org/ *E-mail:* info@stopsarcoidosis.org

Sarcoid Networking Association *National network. 3 chapters. Founded 1992.* Provides support and education for sarcoidosis patients, their families and friends through newsletter, correspondence, phone and email. Publication "Sarcoidosis Networking" published 4 times a year. Provides information on local groups. Offers seminars, conferences, research, advocacy and meetings. Assistance in starting new groups. Write: Sarcoid Networking Association, 6424 151st Ave. East, Sumner, WA 98390-2601. Call: 253-826-7737 (voice/fax) or 253-891-2106. *Website:* http://www.sarcoidosisnetwork.org *E-mail:* sarcoidosis_network@prodigy.net

SELECTIVE MUTISM

BERGEN

SMG ~ CAN Connections Provides support and education for parents and professionals involved with a selectively mute child. Rap sessions, guest speakers, literature and phone help. Dues $45/yr. Meets 3rd Mon., 12:45-2:30pm, Manito School, 111 Manito Ave., Oakland. Call Gail Kervatt 973-208-1848. *Website:* http://www.selectivemutism.org *E-mail:* kervatt@optonline.net

NATIONAL

Selective Mutism Foundation, Inc *National. Founded 1992.* Pioneering group that offers mutual support for professionals and parents of children with selective mutism or social phobia (a psychiatric anxiety disorder in which children are unable to speak in social situations). Includes social anxiety and shyness. Also open to adults who had or have outgrown the disorder. Provides information and online support. Website contains DSM revisions, research studies, printable brochures, literature and publications. Write: Carolyn Miller, P.O. Box 13133, Sissonville, WV 25360 or Sue Newman Mercado, P.O. Box 936165, Margate, FL 33093. *Website:* http://www.selectivemutismfoundation.org *E-mail:* sue@selectivemutismfoundation.org or carolyn@selectivemutismfoundation.org

ONLINE

Selective Mutism Group, The *Online. Founded 1999.* Devoted to educating and promoting awareness on selective mutism and other related childhood anxiety disorders. Online support group for parents, teachers and professionals dealing with selective mutism. *Website:* http://selectivemutism.org *E-mail:* sminfo@selectivemutism.org

SEMANTIC-PRAGMATIC DISORDER

ONLINE

Semantic-Pragmatic Disorder Forum *Online.* Opportunity for persons affected by semantic-pragmatic disorder, a communication disorder and their families. SPD is characterized by problems in processing the meaning of language. *Website:* http://forums.delphiforums.com/pragma/start

SEPTO OPTIC DYSPLASIA / OPTIC NERVE HYPOPLASIA / DEMORSIER SYNDROME

NATIONAL

Septo Optic Dysplasia Division - MAGIC Foundation *National network. Founded 1989.* Provides public education and networking for families of children with septo optic dysplasia. Information and referrals, phone support, pen pals, annual convention and conferences. Membership is $35/US, $40/Canada, $45/International. Write: Septo Optic Dysplasia Division, c/o The MAGIC Foundation, 6645 W. North Ave., Oak Park, IL 60302. Call 1-800-362-4423; Fax:

708-383-0899. *Website:* http://www.magicfoundation.org *E-mail:* mary@magicfoundation.org

ONLINE

Focus Families *Online.* Email support group for parents of children with septo-optic dysplasia and optic nerve hypoplasia (aka deMorsier syndrome). Opportunity to share experiences. Online newsletter and annual conference. *Website:* http://www.focusfamilies.org/focus/ *Email:* support@focusfamilies.org

SHINGLES

STATEWIDE

Shingles Telephone Support Group Telephone network to provide support encouragement to people suffering with shingles. Contact Laura 732-928-7696 (day/early eve) or Barbara 201-447-5978 (day).

SHWACHMAN-DIAMOND SYNDROME

Shwachman Diamond Syndrome Foundation *National network. Founded 1994.* Patient advocacy organization whose goals are to support research towards a cure and improve medical management of symptoms. Link families for emotional support and provides them with the most current medical information available which is provided through the knowledge and cooperation of a professional medical advisory board. Write: Shwachman Diamond Syndrome Foundation, 710 Brassie Drive, Grand Junction, CO 81506. Call 1-877-737-4685 (day) or 614-939-2324; Fax: 970-255-8293. *Website:* http://www.shwachman-diamond.org

SICKLE CELL DISEASE

NATIONAL

Sickle Cell Disease Association of America, Inc. *National. 60 chapters. Founded 1971.* Education for the public and professionals about sickle cell disease. Support and information for persons affected by the disease. Supports research. Quarterly newsletter, chapter development guidelines, phone network, videos, online network, research updates and forum. Write: Sickle Cell Disease Association of America, 231 E. Baltimore St., Suite 800, Baltimore, MD 21202. Call 1-800-421-8453; Fax: 410-528-1495. *Website:* http://www.sicklecelldisease.org

SJOGREN'S SYNDROME

OCEAN

Sjogren's Syndrome Support Group Support for persons afflicted with Sjogren's syndrome. Dues $15/yr. Meetings vary, Pine Beach. Call Cinde 732-914-1019 (day). *Website:* http://www.sjogrens.org

NATIONAL

Sjogren's Syndrome Foundation, Inc. *National. 78 groups. Founded 1983.* Information and education for Sjogren's syndrome patients, families, health professionals and the public. Opportunities for patients to share ways of coping. Stimulates research for treatments and cures. Newsletter "Moisture Seekers," chapter development assistance, video tapes and annual symposium. Sjogren's handbook. Write: Sjogren's Syndrome Foundation, Inc., 6707 Democracy Blvd., Suite 325, Bethesda, MD 20817. Call 301-530-4420; Fax: 301-530-4415. *Website:* http://www.sjogrens.org

SMITH-LEMLI-OPITZ

Smith-Lemli-Opitz/RSH Foundation *International network. Founded 1988.* Network of families with children with Smith-Lemli-Opitz (RSH) syndrome. Exchange of information, sharing of similar experiences and correspondence between families. Provides education to medical community, new parents and others. Phone support. Newsletter 2x/per yr. Dues $10/yr. Write: Smith-Lemli-Opitz/RSH Foundation, c/o Cynthia Gold, P.O. Box 212, Georgetown, MA 01833. Call 978-352-5885. *Website:* http://www.smithlemliopitz.org *E-mail:* info@smithlemliopitz.org

SMITH-MAGENIS SYNDROME

PRISMS (Parents Researchers Interested in Smith-Magenis) *International network. Founded 1993.* Parent-to-parent program offering support, advocacy and education for families affected by Smith-Magenis syndrome. Information, referrals, literature, phone support and newsletter. Dues $30. Write: PRISMS, Inc,. P.O. Box 741914, Dallas, TX 75374-1914. Call 972-231-0035. *Website:* http://www.prisms.org *E-mail:* info@prisms.org

SOTOS SYNDROME

Sotos Syndrome Support Association *International network. Founded 1984.* Provides information and mutual support for families of children with Sotos syndrome. Newsletter, phone support, pen pals, annual conference, information and referrals. Write: Sotos Syndrome Support Association, P.O. Box 4626, Wheaton, IL 60189. Call 1-888-246-7772. *Website:* http://www.well.com/users/sssa *E-mail:* sssa@well.com

SPASMODIC DYSPHONIA

NATIONAL

National Spasmodic Dysphonia Association *National. 35 affiliated support groups. Founded 1990.* Dedicated to advancing medical research into the causes and treatments for spasmodic dysphonia. Promotes physician and public awareness of the disorder through outreach and sponsoring support activities for people with SD and their families through educational materials, annual symposiums, support groups and on-line resources. The NSDA is the only organization that is entirely dedicated to Spasmodic Dysphonia. Offers assistance in starting similar groups. Newsletter. Write: National Spasmodic Dysphonia Association, 300 Park Blvd., Suite 415, Itasca, IL 60143. Call 1-800-795-6732. *Website:* http://www.dysphonia.org *E-mail:* kkuman@dysphonia.org

Spasmodic Dysphonia Support Group of New York *Model. Founded 1987.* Provides members with the latest information regarding spasmodic dysphonia, as well as emotional and practical support. Offers workshops and discussions. Encourages education for the public and physicians. Guest speakers, information and referrals. Write: Spasmodic Dysphonia Support Group of NY, c/o A. Simons, 67-33 152 St., Flushing, NY 11367. Call 718-793-2442. *Website:* http://www.dystonia.org

SPASMODIC TORTICOLLIS

National Spasmodic Torticollis Association *National. 75 chapters. Founded 1983.* Advocacy group providing information and support to spasmodic torticollis patients and their families. Network of support groups and volunteers on-call to talk with other patients. Quarterly magazine, annual symposium. Educates the public and medical community. Supports research. Email support. Write: National Spasmodic Torticollis Association, 9920 Talbert Ave., Fountain Valley, CA

92708. Call 1-800-487-8385 or 714-378-7837; Fax: 714-378-7830. *Website:* http://www.torticollis.org *E-mail:* NSTAmail@aol.com

SPASTIC PARAPLEGIA / FAMILIAL SPASTIC PARAPLEGIA

Spastic Paraplegia Foundation, Inc. *National. Founded 2002.* Offers support and information to those affected by primary lateral sclerosis and hereditary spastic paraplegia. Supports research. Offers regional and email support groups, online chat group, newsletter and information. Write: Spastic Paraplegia Foundation, Inc., 375 Julianna Circle, Franklin, TN 37064. Call 703-495-9261. *Website:* http://www.sp-foundation.org

SPINAL MUSCULAR ATROPHY

Families of S.M.A. (Spinal Muscular Atrophy) *(MULTILINGUAL) International. 29 chapters. Founded 1984.* Funding of research, support and networking for families affected by spinal muscular atrophy types I, II, III, adult onset and Kennedy's. Educational resources, group development guidelines, quarterly newsletter, pen pals, phone support and videotapes. Online message boards and kids corner support. Write: Families of SMA, P.O. Box 196, Libertyville, IL 60048-0196. Call 1-800-886-1762 or 847-367-7620; Fax: 847-367-7623. *Website:* http://www.fsma.org or http://www.curesma.com *E-mail:* info@fsma.org

STEVENS JOHNSON SYNDROME

Stevens Johnson Syndrome Foundation *International network. Founded 1995.* Provides to the public and medical communities information on adverse allergic drug reactions. Aim is to quicken diagnoses to avoid permanent damage. Literature, phone support, information and referrals. Write: Stevens Johnson Syndrome Foundation, P.O. Box 350333, Westminster, CO 80035. Call 303-635-1241. *Website:* http://www.sjsupport.org *E-mail:* sjsupport@aol.com

STICKLER SYNDROME

Stickler Involved People *International network. Founded 1995.* Network that offers support and education for persons affected by Stickler syndrome. This genetic disorder affects connective tissues, including the joints, eyes, palate, heart and hearing. Phone support, information and referrals, annual conference, literature and newsletter. Online listserv. Write: Stickler Involved People, 15 Angelina Dr., Augusta, KS 67010. Call 316-259-5196. *Website:* http://www.sticklers.org *E-mail:* sip@sticklers.org

STREP, GROUP B

Canadian Strep B Foundation *International network. Founded 2003.* Educates the public about group B streptococcal infections during pregnancy. Information and referrals, advocacy and phone support. Group development guidelines available. Write: Patricia Normand, President, The Canadian Strep B Foundation, 1712 Montee Sauvage, Prevost, Quebec JOR 1TO. Call 1-877-873-7424 or 450-224-7718. *Website:* http://www.strepb.ca *E-mail:* info@strepb.ca

STURGE-WEBER

The Sturge-Weber Foundation *International network. Members in 50 states and internationally. Founded 1987.* Mutual support network for families and professionals involved with Sturge-Weber syndrome, Port Wine Stains, or Klippel Trenaunay syndrome. Disseminates information, funds and facilitates research. Newsletter, E-news monthly, phone support, pen pals, active email support group. Educational materials for schools, parents and clinicians. Biennial conference. Write: Sturge-Weber Foundation, P.O. Box 418, Mt. Freedom, NJ 07970. Call 1-800-627-5482 or 973-895-4445; Fax: 973-895-4846. *Website:* http://www.sturge-weber.com *E-mail:* swf@sturge-weber.com

SYRINGOMYELIA / CHIARI MALFORMATION

American Syringomyelia Alliance Project *International network. Founded 1988.* Support, networking and information for people affected by syringomyelia and chiari malformation, their families and friends. Newsletter, phone support, pen pals, conferences. Also offers online message boards and chat rooms. Write: American Syringomyelia Alliance Project, P.O. Box 1586, Longview, TX 75606-1586. Call 903-236-7079 or 1-800-272-7282; Fax: 903-757-7456. *Website:* http://www.asap.org *E-mail:* info@asap.org

TAKAYASU'S ARTERITIS

Takayasu's Arteritis Association *Model. Founded 1995.* Education and support for persons with Takayasu's arteritis (an inflammation of the large elastic arteries and aorta), their families and health professionals. Network program, information, phone and on-line support, literature, newsletters, research conferences and resources. Write: Takayasu's Arteritis Association, 2030 County Line Rd., Suite 199, Huntingdon Valley, PA 19006. Call 1-800-575-9390 (access code 00). *Website:* http://www.takayasus.org *E-mail:* admin@takayasus.org

TAY-SACHS DISEASE

National Tay-Sachs Allied Diseases Association *(BILINGUAL) International. 5 affiliated groups. Founded 1957.* Dedicated to the treatment and prevention of Tay-Sachs, Canavan and related genetic diseases. Provides information and support services to individuals of all ages and families affected by these disorders as well as caregivers and the public at large. The strategies for achieving these goals include public and professional education, research, genetic screening, support services i.e., peer support group for parents, grandparents, extended family members and advocacy. Translations available in Spanish, Russian, Hebrew and French. Write: National Tay-Sachs Allied Diseases Association, 2001 Beacon St., Suite 204, Boston, MA 02135. Call 1-800-906-8723 or 617-277-4463; Fax: 617-277-0134. *Website:* http://www.ntsad.org *E-mail:* info@ntsad.org

TEMPOROMANDIBULAR JOINT DYSFUNCTION (TMJ)

TMJ Association *International. Founded 1986.* Developed by two patients suffering from TMJ (diseases and disorders that cause pain and dysfunction in and around the temporomandibular or jaw joint). Resource and advocacy organization for TMJ sufferers and their families, as well as a resource for researchers and health professionals. Write: TMJ Association, P.O. Box 26770, Milwaukee, WI 53226-0770. Call 262-432-0350; Fax: 262-432-0375. *Website:* http://www.tmj.org *E-mail:* info@tmj.org

TOURETTE SYNDROME

STATEWIDE

Tourette Syndrome Association of NJ, Inc. Mission is to support the needs of families of persons with Tourette syndrome, as well as adults with TS. Offers advocacy for persons with Tourette. Provides education to the public and professionals. Offers peer-counseling, and a quarterly children's group. Support group meetings in Atlantic, Bergen, Burlington, Mercer, Middlesex, Monmouth, Morris and Somerset Counties. Write: Tourette Syndrome Association of NJ, Inc., 50 Division St., Suite 205, Somerville, NJ 08876. Call 732-972-4459. *Website:* http://www.tsanj.org

MORRIS

Tourette Family Support *Professionally-run.* Provides support network and education for parents of children with Tourette syndrome. Guest speakers and literature. Meets 1st Thurs. (every other month), 7-8:30pm, Saint Clare's Hospital, 25 Pocono Rd., Auditorium, Denville. Pre-registration required. Before attending call Karoline Neumann 973-625-6199 (day).

SOMERSET

Tourette Syndrome Support Group Support for persons with Tourette syndrome. Meets Jan., Mar., June, Sept., Nov., 7-9pm, Somerset Medical Center, 110 Rehill Ave., Conference Room C D, Somerville. Call 908-685-2814 (day).

NATIONAL

Tourette Syndrome Association *National. 35 chapters. Founded 1972.* Dedicated to identifying the cause, finding the cure and controlling the effects of Tourette syndrome through education, research and service. Provides support services to families and professionals to enable patients to achieve optimum development. Chapter development guidelines and newsletter. Dues $45. Write: Tourette Syndrome Association, 42-40 Bell Blvd., Bayside, NY 11361-2820. Call 718-224-2999; Fax: 718-279-9596. *Website:* http://tsa-usa.org *E-mail:* ts@tsa-usa.org

ONLINE

TS Family Support *Online. 485 members. Founded 1999.* Supportive mailing list for parents or family members of children who have Tourette's Syndrome. *Website:* http:/health.groups.yahoo.com/group/TSFamilySupport/ *E-mail:* TSFamilySupport@yahoogroups.com

TRACHEO ESOPHAGEAL FISTULA / ESOPHAGAL ATRESIA

NATIONAL

TEF/VATER Support Network *International. 6 groups. Founded 1990.* Offers support and encouragement for parents of children with tracheo esophageal fistula, esophageal atresia and VATER. Aims to bring current information to parents and the medical community. Newsletter, information referrals and phone support.

Write: TEF/VATER Support Network, c/o Greg Terri Burke, 15301 Grey Fox Rd., Upper Marlboro, MD 20772. Call 301-952-6837; Fax: 301-952-9152. *Website:* http://www.tefvater.org *E-mail:* tefvater@ix.netcom.com

ONLINE

EA/TEF Child and Family Support Connection, Inc. *Online.* Provides information and support for families of children with esophageal atresia and tracheoesophageal fistula. Offers pamphlets, brochures and discussion forum. *Website:* http://eatef.org *E-mail:* info@eatef.org

TRACHEOSTOMY

ONLINE

Aaron's Tracheostomy Page *Online. Founded 1998.* Mutual support and information sharing for persons who have, or anticipate having, a tracheostomy. Open to parents of children, patients, families, caregivers and professionals. Through a listserv, members are given a chance to support each other, ask questions and offer coping tips. Write: Trachties, 102 Morene Ave., Waxahachie, TX 75165. *Website:* http://www.tracheostomy.com

TRANSVERSE MYELITIS

Transverse Myelitis Association *National. Over 6000 members in 80 countries.* Offers support and education to persons with transverse myelitis and other neuroimmunologic diseases of the central nervous system (e.g. acute disseminated encephalomyelitis, optic neuritis and neuromyelitis optica, Devic's disease) and their families. Networks families together for support. Provides research literature, newsletter and membership directory. Investigates, advocates for and supports research and treatment efforts. Provides a support forum for communication. Bulletin board. Assists in the development of local support groups. Fund-raises for research. Conducts symposia and workshops. Write: Tranverse Myelitis Association, c/o Sandy Siegel, 1787 Sutter Parkway, Powell, OH 43065-8806. Call 614-766-1806. *Website:* http://www.myelitis.org *E-mail:* ssiegel@myelitis.org

TREACHER COLLINS SYNDROME

Treacher Collins Connection *National network. Founded 2001.* Provides support, networking and education for individuals who are affected by Treacher Collins syndrome. Write: Treacher Collins, P.O. Box 120416, Boston, MA 02112.

Call Judy 704-545-1921. *Website:* http://www.tcconnection.org *E-mail:* judy@tcconnection.org

TRIGEMINAL NEURALGIA / TIC DOULOUREAUX

Trigeminal Neuralgia Association *National. 65+ groups. Founded 1990.* Provides information, mutual support and encouragement to persons with trigeminal neuralgia and related facial pain disorders. Families are welcome. Helps to reduce the isolation of those affected. Aims to increase awareness, promote research into the cause and cure. Quarterly newsletter, phone support, educational information and patient advocacy. Write: Trigeminal Neuralgia Association, 925 Northwest 56th Terrace, Gainesville, FL 32605. Call 1-800-923-3608 or 352-331-7009; Fax 352-331-7078. *Website:* http://www.endthepain.org *E-mail:* tnanational@tna-support.org

TRIPLE-X SYNDROME

Triple X Support Group *International network. Founded 1997.* Provides support, resources and informational materials to parents of children with triple X syndrome (aka trisomy X or 47, XXX syndrome). Aims to educate professionals and the public on this syndrome. Networks parents together for support. Literature, referrals, phone support. Write: Triple X Support Group, c/o Helen Clements, 32 Francemary Rd., Brockley, London, England SE4 1JS. Call (020)86909445. *Website:* http://www.triplo-x.org *E-mail:* helenclements@hotmail.com

TRISOMY

STATEWIDE

S.O.F.T. (Support Organization For Trisomy) Support for families of children with trisomy 18 or 13 and related disorders. Education about trisomy, implications to families and community. Meets various times and locations. Call Colleen Frazier 609-567-4151, Pat O'Toole 215-663-9652 or Kathleen Johnson 215-489-2678. *E-mail:* kathy.johnson.1sw@verizon.net

NATIONAL

SOFT (Support Organization For Trisomy) *National. 50 chapters. Founded 1979.* Support and education for families of children with trisomy 18 and 13 and related genetic disorders (including trisomy 9). Education for professionals. Quarterly newsletter, pen pal program, phone network, regional gatherings, annual international conference and booklets. Online information on finding a local support group. Dues $25. Write: SOFT, c/o Barbara Van Herreweghe, 2982 S. Union St., Rochester, NY 14624. Call Barbara Van Herreweghe 585-594-4621 or 1-800-716-7638 (for families); Fax: 585-594-1957. *Website:* http://www.trisomy.org *E-mail:* barbsoft@rochester.rr.com

ONLINE

Trisomy 21 Online Community *Online.* Offers support and information those who have been touched by Trisomy 21 (Down's syndrome). Chat group and several forums. *Website:* http://www.trisomy21online.com

TUBE FEEDING

Oley Foundation, Inc. *National. 51 affiliated groups. Founded 1983.* Provides information and psychosocial support for home nutrition support (intravenous or tube-feeding) patients, their families, caregivers and professionals. Programs include bimonthly newsletter, national network of volunteers providing patient support, annual summer conference, regional meetings, patient-to-patient networking and information clearinghouse. Write: Oley Foundation, c/o Albany Medical Center, 214 HUN Memorial, MC-28, Albany, NY 12208. Call 1-800-776-6539 (day) or 518-262-5079; Fax: 518-262-5528. *Website:* http://www.oley.org *E-mail:* BishopJ@mail.amc.edu

TUBEROUS SCLEROSIS

Tuberous Sclerosis Alliance *National. Founded 1974.* Dedicated to finding a cure for tuberous sclerosis while improving the lives of those affected. Provides research, support and education among individuals, families and the helping professions. Newsletter, peer networking programs, conferences and information. Write: Tuberous Sclerosis Alliance, 801 Roeder Rd., Suite 750, Silver Spring, MD 20910-4467. Call 301-562-9890 or 1-800-225-6872; Fax: 301-562-9870. *Website:* http://www.tsalliance.org

TURNER'S SYNDROME

NATIONAL

Turner Syndrome Society of the U.S. *National. 20 chapters. Founded 1987.* Self-help for women, girls and their families affected by Turner syndrome. Increases public awareness about the disorder. Quarterly newsletter, chapter development assistance, advocacy, education and annual conference. Write: Turner Syndrome Society U.S., 14450 TC Jester, Suite 260, Houston, TX 77014. Call 1-800-365-9944 or 832-249-9988; Fax: 832-249-9987. *Website:* http://www.turnersyndrome.org *E-mail:* tssus@turnersyndrome.org

Turner Syndrome Support Network *National network. Founded 1989.* Network and exchange of information for parents of children with Turner's syndrome. Information and referrals, phone support, pen pals, conferences, literature, annual convention and newsletter ($30yr). Write: Turner Syndrome Support Network, c/o MAGIC Foundation, 6645 W. North Ave., Oak Park, IL 60302. Call 1-800-362-4423 or 708-383-0899; Fax: 709-383-0899. *Website:* http://www.magicfoundation.org *E-mail:* mary@magicfoundation.org

Turner's Syndrome Society (Canada) *National. Founded 1981. 5 chapters.* Provides support and education to Turner's syndrome patients and their families. Tapes, publications, referral to U.S. and Canada groups. Newsletter. Pen pal program, chapter development guidelines and annual conference. Write: Turner's Syndrome Society, 323 Chapel St., Ottawa, ON, Canada, K1N 7Z2. Call 1-800-465-6744 or 613-321-22677; Fax: 613-321-2268. *Website:* http://www.turnersyndrome.ca *E-mail:* tssincan@web.net

TWIN TO TWIN TRANSFUSION SYNDROME

Twin to Twin Transfusion Syndrome Foundation *(MULTILINGUAL) International. 12 national coordinators. Founded 1989.* Dedicated to providing immediate and lifesaving educational, emotional and financial support for families, medical professionals and caregivers before, during and after pregnancy with twin to twin transfusion syndrome. Dedicated to saving the babies, improving their future health and care, furthering medical research, providing neonatal intensive care, special needs and bereavement support. Pen pals, newsletter, literature, phone support, visitation and conferences. Guidelines for professionals on multiple birth loss during pregnancy. Help in starting new chapters. International registry. Website in many languages. Write: TTTS, 411 Longbeach Parkway, Bay Village, OH 44140. Call 1-800-815-9211 or 440-899-8887. *Website:* http://www.tttsfoundation.org *E-mail:* info@tttsfoundation.org

"Those who walk together strengthen each other."
-- a thousand-year-old proverb from the Swahili peoples of eastern Africa

UNDIAGNOSED ILLNESS

Hearts and Hands *Model. 1 group in NC. Founded 1993.* Emotional, spiritual and educational support for persons with either rare or undiagnosed illnesses and their families. Also has a registry for loin pain hematuria syndrome. Write: Hearts and Hands, c/o Winoka Plummer, 1648 Oliver's Crossing Circle, Winston-Salem, NC 27127. Call 336-785-7612. *Website:* http://www.geocities.com/hotsprings/spa/2464/index.html

UREA CYCLE DISORDERS

NATIONAL

National Urea Cycle Disorders Foundation *National network. Founded 1989.* Links families, friends and professionals who are dedicated to the identification, treatment and cure of urea cycle disorders, genetic disorders causing an enzyme deficiency in the urea cycle. Networks families together for support, educates professionals/public and supports research. Phone support, literature and newsletter. Dues $35. Write: National Urea Cycle Disorders Foundation, 4841 Hill St., La Canada, CA 91011. Call 1-800-386-8233; Fax: 818-952-2184. *Website:* http://www.nucdf.org *E-mail:* info@nucdf.org

ONLINE

ASA Kids *Online.* Opportunity for parents of children with argininosuccinic aciduria to come together for support and information. Discussion board, stories on affected children and links. *Website:* http://www.geocities.com/oliphint4/index.html

TRUE Kids (Transplanted to Resolve Urea-cycle Enzyme-deficiency) *Online.* Mutual support and information for families of transplanted children with urea cycle disorder. *Website:* http://www.geocities.com/paulajoe123/

Urea Cycle Disorder Discussion Board *Online.* Opportunity for parents caring for a child with a urea cycle disorder to discuss concerns and ideas. Goal is to increase awareness of urea cycle disorders in order to improve diagnosis. *Website:* http://www.2endure.com

VATER ASSOCIATION

NATIONAL

TEF/VATER Support Network *International. 6 groups. Founded 1990.* Offers support and encouragement for parents of children with tracheo esophageal fistula, esophageal atresia and VATER. Aims to bring current information to parents and the medical community. Newsletter, information and referrals, phone support. Write: TEF/VATER Support Network, c/o Greg Terri Burke, 15301 Grey Fox Rd., Upper Marlboro, MD 20772. Call 301-952-6837; Fax: 301-952-9152. *Website:* http://www.tefvater.org *E-mail:* tefvater@ix.netcom.com

VATERS Association Family Network, The Message board that connects VACTERLS/VATER families with those who have been there, done that. Sharing of stories, advice and support to create a network of those who have survived VACTERLS and can help others make it through. Write: VACTRLS Association Family Network (VAFN), 215 Gould St., Plymouth, PA 18651. *Website:* http://groups.msn.com/vaterssyndromevafn/ *E-mail:* mother2zoe@aol.com

VELO-CARDIO-FACIAL SYNDROME / SHPRINTZEN SYNDROME / 22Q11 DELETION SYNDROME

Northeast VCFS Support Group *National network. Founded 1996.* Support and resource network for families coping with velo-cardio-facial syndrome (aka Shprintzen syndrome, 22q11 Deletion syndrome). Provides information and literature, conferences and assistance in starting local groups. Listserv. Write: Northeast VCFS Support Group, c/o Maureen Anderson, 2 Lansing Dr., Salem, NH 03079. Call 603-898-6332 (voice/fax). *Website:* http://www.vcfsef.org *E-mail:* mladja@aol.com

VENTILATOR USERS

NATIONAL

International Ventilator Users Network *International network. Founded 1987.* Information sharing between ventilator users and health care professionals experienced in home mechanical ventilation. Annual directory ($8). Quarterly newsletter (free with membership dues of $25). Write: International Ventilator Users Network, 4207 Lindell Blvd., Suite 110, St. Louis, MO 63108-2030. Call

314-534-0475; Fax: 314-534-5070. *Website:* http://www.post-polio.org/ivun *E-mail:* ventinfo@post-polio.org

ONLINE

Vent-Users-List *Online.* Provides a forum for people who require a ventilator (respirator) to breathe to support and communicate with others who share the same condition. *Website:* http://www.makoa.org/ventuser.htm

VESTIBULAR DISORDERS

(see also deaf, hard-of-hearing)

Vestibular Disorders Association *International. 125 independent groups. Founded 1983.* Information, referrals and support for people affected by disorders caused by inner ear problems. Public education, group development assistance, quarterly newsletter, library of resources and support network. Distributes several videotapes and publishes 70 documents, including full-length books on Meniere's disease and benign paroxysmal positional vertigo (BPPV). Write: Vestibular Disorders Association, P.O. Box 13305, Portland, OR 97213. Call 1-800-837-8428 or 503-229-7705; Fax: 503-229-8064. *Website:* http://www.vestibular.org *E-mail:* info@vestibular.org

VITILIGO

NATIONAL

American Vitiligo Research Foundation *National. 36+ groups and 4 international groups. Founded 1995.* Raise awareness, educate and support not only the patients but family members also. Networking, literature, newsletter, information and referrals, yearly seminars and conferences. Billboards and public services announcements. Write: American Vitiligo Research Foundation, P.O. Box 7540, Clearwater, Fla. 33758. Call 727-461-3899; Fax: 727-461-4796. *Website:* http://www.avrf.org *E-mail:* vitiligo@avrf.org

ONLINE

Vitiligo Support International, Inc. *Online. Founded 2000.* Provides social support, information and resources to persons affected by vitiligo. Active message boards, chats and international physician referral. Includes "just for kids" page. Write: Vitiligo Support International, Inc., P.O. Box 4008, Valley Village, CA 91617. *Website:* http://www.vitiligosupport.org *E-mail:* info@vitiligosupport.org

VON HIPPEL LINDAU

VHL Family Alliance (Von Hippel-Lindau Syndrome) *(MULTILINGUAL) International network. 28 US chapters; 11 foreign affiliates. Founded 1993.* Opportunity for families affected by VHL to share their knowledge and experiences with each other and the medical community. Goal is to improve diagnosis, treatment and quality of life for VHL families. Newsletter, phone support and education, tissue bank and handbook. Literature available in Spanish, German, French, Japanese, Dutch and other languages. Funds research. Assistance in starting local chapters. Write: VHL Family Alliance, 2001 Beacon St., Suite 208, Boston, MA 02135-7787. Call 1-800-767-4845 or 617-277-5667; Fax: 858-712-8712. *Website:* http://www.vhl.org *E-mail:* info@vhl.org

VOMITING, CYCLIC

Cyclic Vomiting Syndrome Association *International. 30+ affiliated groups. Founded 1993.* Mutual support and information for families and professionals dealing with cyclic vomiting syndrome, abdominal migraine and related disorders. Networking, phone support, educational materials and research support. Newsletter. Write: Cyclic Vomiting Syndrome Association, c/o Debra Waites, 3585 Cedar Hill Rd. NW, Canal Winchester, Ohio 43110. Call 614-837-2586; Fax: 614-837-2586. *Website:* http://www.cvsaonline.org *E-mail:* waitesd@cvsaonline.org

VULVAR DISORDERS

National Vulvodynia Association, Inc. *National. 100 affiliated groups. Founded 1994.* Provides information and support to women with vulvodynia. Educates health care professionals and the public about this condition. Newsletter, literature, information and referrals, phone support and advocacy. Write: NVA, P.O. Box 4491, Silver Spring, MD 20914-4491. Call 301-299-0775; Fax: 301-299-3999. *Website:* http://www.nva.org *E-mail:* mate@nva.org

"People who share a common direction and sense of community can get where they are going quicker and easier because they're traveling on the strength of one another." -- Great Northern Geese, Lesson One

WAGR SYNDROME

International WAGR Syndrome Association *International network. 3 affiliated groups. Founded 2000.* Provides information and support to persons with WAGR Syndrome or aniridia, their families, physicians and teachers. Phone support, literature, free bi-annual newsletter, networking, information and referral. Encourages research. Email group. Write: International WAGR Syndrome Association, P.O. Box 1346, Manassas, VA 20108. Call 210-481-9288. *Website:* http://www.wagr.org

WALDENSTROM'S MACROGLOBULINEMIA

International Waldenstrom's Macroglobulinemia Foundation *International. 30 affiliated groups. Founded 1994.* Provides support and information to persons with Waldenstrom macroglobulinemia, their families and caregivers. Information and referrals, phone support, conferences, newsletter and literature. Regular support group meetings. Provides assistance in starting new groups. Write: Int'l Waldenstrom's Macroglobulinemia Foundation, 3932D Swift Rd., Sarasota, FL 34231. Call 941-927-4963; Fax: 941-927-4467. *Website:* http://www.iwmf.com *E-mail:* info@iwmf.com

WEGENER'S GRANULOMATOSIS

Vasculitis Foundation *National. 35 affiliated groups. Founded 1986.* Emotional support and information for patients with life-threatening uncommon Wegener's granulomatosis and related vascular illnesses. Provides information to patients and physicians about this disorder. Educates families, friends and general public about the devastating effects of Vasculitis, the symptoms and treatment. Dues $25/U.S.; $30/Int'l (includes bimonthly newsletter). Write: Vasculitis Foundations, P.O. Box 28660, Kansas City, MO 64188-8660. Call 1-800-277-9474; Fax: 816-436-8211. *Website:* http://www.wgassociaton.org *E-mail:* vf@vasculitisfoundation.org

WILLIAMS SYNDROME

Williams Syndrome Association *National network. 16 chapters. Founded 1982.* Purpose is to encourage research related to Williams syndrome, find and support families with Williams syndrome, and share information among parents and professionals re: educational, medical and behavioral experiences. Newsletter. Write: Williams Syndrome Association, P.O. Box 297, Clawson, MI 48017-0297.

Call 1-800-806-1871 or 248-244-2229; Fax 248-244-2230. *Website:* http://www.williams-syndrome.org *E-mail:* info@williams-syndrome.org

WILSON'S DISEASE

Wilson's Disease Association *International network. Founded 1979.* Provides information and referrals about Wilson's disease, a genetic disorder that causes excessive amounts of copper accumulation in the body, affecting the liver and brain. Provides mutual support and aid for those affected by the disease and their families. Promotes research into treatment and cure. Quarterly newsletter. Provides phone support network. Offers e-mail group. Write: Wilson's Disease Association, 1802 Brookside Dr., Wooster, OH 44691. Call 1-888-264-1450 or 330-264-1450. *Website:* http://www.wilsonsdisease.org *E-mail:* mary.graper@wilsonsdisease.org

WORSTER-DROUGHT

Worster-Drought Syndrome Support Group *Model.* Provides support and information for families, of children with worster-drought, a form of cerebral palsy. Offers phone support in the United Kingdom. Pen pals, networking of families, literature and newsletter. Write: Worster-Drought Syndrome, c/o Contact a Family, 209-211 City Road, London EC1V 1JN, UK. Call 020 7383 3555; Fax: 020 7383 0259. *Website:* http://www.wdssg.org.uk/ *E-mail:* national.contact@wdssg.org.uk

XERODERMA PIGMENTOSUM

Xeroderma Pigmentosum Society *International network. Founded 1995.* Provides sharing of support, information and coping skills for families affected by xeroderma pigmentosum. Quarterly informational newsletter. Promotes research into finding a cure. Information and referrals, phone support, conferences, literature, advocacy in community, education and protection. Free window tinting on homes of patients. Camp Sundown for patients of all ages and their families. Write: XP Society, 437 Snydertown Rd., Craryville, NY 12521. Call 518-851-2612 (voice/fax). *Website:* http://www.xps.org *E-mail:* carn@xps.org

Can't find an appropriate group in your area? The Clearinghouse helps people start groups. Give us a call at 1-800-367-6274

X-LINKED HYPOHOSPHATEMIA / FAMILIAL HYPOPHOSPHATEMIC RICKETS / VITAMIN D RESISTANT RICKETS

ONLINE

XLH Network *Online. Founded 1996.* Volunteer organization offering support and information for individuals and families affected by X-linked hypophosphatemia (aka X-linked hypophosphatemic rickets, familial hypophosphatemic rickets or vitamin D resistant rickets). Also open to those affected by similar disorders including autosomal dominant hypophosphatemic rickets and tumor-induced osteomalacia. Open to interested professionals dedicated to understanding in terms of support, research and developing new treatments. Exchanges and disseminates information. Offers an online brochure and members listserv. Write: The XLH Network, Inc., c/o Joan Reed, 4562 Stoneledge Lane, Manlius, NY 13104. *Website:* http://www.xlhnetwork.org *E-mail:* joan.reed@lhnetwork.org

"You cannot hope to build a better world without improving the individuals. To that end each of us must work for our own improvement, and at the same time share a general responsibility for all humanity, our particular duty being to aid those to whom we think we can be most useful."

-- Marie Curie

MENTAL HEALTH RESOURCES

MENTAL HEALTH ADMINISTRATORS

Offers assistance and advocacy for mental health consumers and families when they are experiencing difficulties with the mental health system. Also provides referrals to mental health providers by county.

ATLANTIC	Sally Williams 609-645-7700 ext. 4307
BERGEN	Susan Boggia 201-634-2753
BURLINGTON	Gary Miller 609-265-5610
CAMDEN	Chuck Steinmetz 856-663-3998
CAPE MAY	Patricia Devaney 609-465-1055
CUMBERLAND	Ethan Aronoff 856-453-7804
ESSEX	Joseph Scarpelli 973-228-8021
GLOUCESTER	Kathleen Spinosi 856-384-6870
HUDSON	Jim Gallagher 201-271-4344
HUNTERDON	Pamela Pontrelli 908-788-1253
MERCER	Marc A. Celentana, Ph.D. 609-989-6574
MIDDLESEX	Lori Dillon 732-745-4518
MONMOUTH	Charles D. Brown 732-431-7200
MORRIS	Laurie Becker 973-285-6852
OCEAN	Jill Perez 732-506-5374
PASSAIC	Francine Vince 973-225-3700
SALEM	Dr. Isaac A. Young 856-339-8618
SOMERSET	Pam Mastro 908-704-6302
SUSSEX	Cindy Armstrong 973-579-0200 ext. 1212
UNION	Tom Graham 908-527-4846
WARREN	Shannon Brennan 908-475-6331

COMMUNITY HEALTH LAW PROJECT

Promotes protecting the rights of persons with any disability. Community Health Law Project represents low income individuals who are disabled physically, have a mental illness and/or elderly and are unable to afford private attorneys. Offers counseling, referrals, advocacy, training, education, etc. *Website:* http://www.chlp.org

CAMDEN	856-858-9500
ESSEX	973-680-5599; TTY/TTD 973-680-1116
MERCER	609-392-5553
MONMOUTH	732-502-0059
UNION	908-355-8282

INTENSIVE FAMILY SUPPORT PROGRAMS

STATEWIDE

Intensive Family Support Services Offers supportive activities to assist families with a relative diagnosed with mental illness. Families are offered a variety of services based on the individual's need. Services are available to any family and are free of charge. Psychoeducation, single family consultations, family support, respite, advocacy and referrals. Call 1-866-626-4437.

MENTAL HEALTH ASSOCIATIONS

STATEWIDE

Mental Health Association in New Jersey Helps mental health consumers and their families explore services available in their community. Also advocates for needed services. Write: MHA in NJ, 88 Pompton Ave., Verona, NJ 07044. Call 973-571-4100; Fax: 973-857-1777. *Website:* http://www.mhanj.org *E-mail*: info@mhanj.org

ATLANTIC	609-272-1700
CAMDEN	856-966-6767
ESSEX	973-509-9777
HUDSON	201-653-4700
MERCER	609-656-0110
MONMOUTH	732-542-6422
MORRIS	973-334-3496
OCEAN	732-905-1132
PASSAIC	973-478-4444
UNION	908-272-0300

MENTAL HEALTH PACT TEAMS

Community based program for adults with a serious and persistent mental illness. There are strict registration criteria, e.g., previous hospitalization is required.

ATLANTIC	609-404-1974
BERGEN	201-398-9110
BURLINGTON	609-261-6627
CAMDEN	856-428-7632
CAPE MAY	609-463-8990
CUMBERLAND	856-691-8579
ESSEX	973-466-1300
GLOUCESTER	856-251-1414
HUDSON	201-653-3980
HUNTERDON	908-835-8660
MERCER	609-394-5285
MIDDLESEX	732-257-6100
MONMOUTH	732-842-2000 ext. 4301 or 4302
MORRIS	1-888-626-2111 or 973-625-7084
OCEAN	732-349-0515
PASSAIC	973-470-3056 (press 9 after connecting)
SALEM	856-691-8579
SOMERSET	908-704-8252
SUSSEX	1-888-626-2111 or 973-625-7084
UNION	908-352-0242
WARREN	908-835-8660

"Community is no longer something that we are born into. It is now something that we must choose."

-- Dr. Robert Wuthnow,
in his book, Sharing the Journey:
Support Groups and America's New Quest for Community, 1994

LOCAL COMMUNITY HELPLINES

These helplines provide information and referrals to local services and agencies. Many also provide crisis intervention and listening services. Some publish directories of local community services.

ATLANTIC

Contact Cape/Atlantic 609-823-1850 (24 hr) Information and referral, active listening, and reassurance calls to elderly and disabled. Serves Atlantic and Cape May Counties. Sponsored in part by United Way. *E-mail:* contact-c-a@excite.com

Intergenerational Services Dial 211 (may not be available from public or cell phones, or from some larger workplace phone systems) or 1-888-426-9243 (24 hr). Provides information and referral services to local services and agencies.

BERGEN

Community Resource Council 201-343-4900 (9am-5pm) Information and referral services, crisis intervention. Youth helpline 1-866-FOR-R-YOUTH.

First Call For Help Dial 211 (211 is not available from public phones, some cell phones and from some larger workplace phone systems), 1-800-435-7555 (24 hr). Provides information and referral for local services and agencies. *Website:* http://www.firstcall.org *E-mail:* help@firstcall.org

BURLINGTON

Contact of Burlington County 856-234-8888 (crisis intervention, rape care and sexual assault services, reassurance "care calls"); Kids Line: 609-261-2220; Teen Line: 609-871-1433; Pet Friends for grieving pet owners: 856-234-4688. Also acts as a 2-1-1 call center. Dial 211 (may not be available from some public, cell phones, or from some larger workplace phone systems) for information and referral regarding social services. All services are free. *Website:* http://www.contactburlco.org *E-mail:* contact333@contactburlco.org

CAMDEN

Contact Community Helplines *(South Jersey only)* 1-877-266-8222 (24 hr crisis); 856-795-4980 (reassurance calls to elderly and hearing impaired shut-ins (Mon.-Fri., 9am-4:30pm). Provides information, referrals and listening service.

Sponsored by United Way. *Website:* http://www.contacthelplines.org *E-mail:* info@contacthelplines.org

First Call For Help *(South Jersey only)* Dial 211 (may not be available from public or cell phones, or from some larger workplace phone systems), 1-800-331-7272 or 856-663-2255 (8am-4:30pm). Will take calls after 4:30pm for emergencies. Information and referrals. Sponsored by UOSS Community Information Systems. *Website:* http://www.infonet.org

CAPE MAY

Contact Cape/Atlantic 609-463-4564 (24 hr) Information and referral, active listening and reassurance calls to elderly and disabled. Serves Atlantic and Cape May Counties. Sponsored in part by United Way. *E-mail:* contact-c-a@excite.com

First Call For Help 609-729-2255 (Mon.-Fri., 8:30am-4:30pm) Information and referrals to local services and agencies. Serves Cape May County. Sponsored by United Way.

CUMBERLAND

Contact Community Helplines *(South Jersey only)* 1-877-266-8222 (24 hr) Listening, information and referrals. Serves Gloucester, Salem and Cumberland Counties. Sponsored by Contact USA. *Website:* www.contacthelplines.org *E-mail:* info@contacthelplines.org

ESSEX

Contact We Care 908-232-2880 (24 hr) Information and referrals, crisis and suicide helpline, listening. Covers Bergen, Union, Essex, Middlesex, Morris, Passaic and Somerset counties.

First Call for Help Dial 211 (may not be available from public or cell phones and from some larger workplace phone systems) or 1-800-435-7555 (24 hr) Information and referrals to local services and agencies. *Website:* http://www.firstcall.org *E-mail:* help@firstcall.org

"You need to be aware of what others are doing, applaud their efforts, acknowledge their successes and encourage them in their pursuits. When we all help one another, everybody wins." -- Jim Stovall

GLOUCESTER

CONTACT Community Helplines *(South Jersey only)* 1-877-266-8222 (24 hr) crisis counseling; reassurance calls 856-795-4980 (Mon.-Fri., 9am-4:30pm) Provides information, referrals, and listening services. Sponsored by United Way. *Website:* http://www.contacthelplines.org *E-mail:* info@contacthelplines.org

First Call For Help-Gloucester County Dial 211 (may not be available from public or cell phones, or from some larger workplace phones) or 1-800-648-0132 (24 hr) Information, referrals, active listening, crisis counseling and referrals for homeless. Serves Gloucester County. Funded by United Way.

HUDSON

First Call for Help of Essex and West Hudson *(BILINGUAL)* Dial 211 (may not be available from public or cell phones and from some larger workplace phone systems) or 1-800-435-7555 (24 hr) Information and referrals to local services and agencies. *Website:* http://www.firstcall.org *E-mail:* help@firstcall.org

HUNTERDON

Hunterdon Helpline Dial 211 (may not be available from public or cell phones, or from some larger workplace phone systems); 1-800-272-4630, 908-735-4357 (24 hr) or TDD 908-782-4357 is also available. Information and referrals, friendly visits and assurance calls offered to the elderly. Suicide prevention hotline. Assistance for the homeless and hungry. Provides information for Hunterdon County Links Transport Service. Professional and volunteer run. Serves Hunterdon, Monmouth and Somerset Counties. Sponsored by United Way. *Website:* http//helplinehc.org

MERCER

Contact of Mercer County 609-896-2120 (24 hr) Crisis counseling, listening, information and referrals. Kids Line: 609-896-4434. *Website:* http://www.contactofmercer.org *E-mail:* contactofmercer@verizon.net

Info Line of Central Jersey Dial 211 (may not be available from public or cell phones, or from some larger workplace phone systems) or 1-888-908-4636 (24 hr) Provides information and referral to local services and agencies. Serves Mercer and Middlesex Counties. Sponsored by United Way of Greater Mercer.

Mercer County Hispanic Association *(SPANISH)* 609-392-2446 (Mon.-Fri., 9am-4:30pm) Information and referrals, assistance with job searches, youth services, women's issues and housing.

MIDDLESEX

Contact We Care 908-232-2880 (24 hr) Information and referrals, listening, crisis and suicidal helpline. Covers Bergen, Union, Essex, Middlesex, Morris, Passaic and Somerset counties.

Info Line of Central Jersey *(BILINGUAL)* Dial 211 (may not be available from public or cell phones, or from some larger workplace phone systems) or 1-888-908-4636 (Voice/TDD) (24 hr) Provides information and referral to local services and agencies. Serves Middlesex and Mercer Counties. *Website:* http://www.info-line.org *E-mail:* help@info-line.org

MONMOUTH

Helpline 732-219-5325 (24 hr) Crisis counseling, psychiatric emergencies, screening and referrals. Serves Eastern Monmouth County. Sponsored by Riverview Medical Center.

Hunterdon Helpline Dial 211 (may not be available from public or cell phones, or from some larger workplace phone systems) or 1-800-272-4630 (24 hr) Provides information and referrals to local services and agencies. Serves Monmouth, Somerset, and Hunterdon.

MORRIS

First Call For Help Dial 211 (may not be available from public phones, some cell phones and from some larger workplace phone systems) or 1-800-435-7555 (24 hr). Provides information and referral for local services and agencies. *Website:* http://www.211firstcall.org *E-mail:* info@211firstcall.org

Peer-to-Peer Support Line 1-877-760-4987 (5-10pm) Non-crisis peer counseling for mental health consumers. Provides support, information and resources.

We can also refer callers to over 100 individuals who are seeking others to help start new support groups throughout NJ. For more information, give us a call: ***1-800-367-6274***

OCEAN

Contact of Ocean County Dial 211 (may not be available from public or cell phones or from some larger workplace phone systems) or 732-240-6100 (24 hr) Provides crisis intervention and listening services. Information and referrals on local services and agencies. *Website:* http://www.contactocean.org *E-mail:* contactofoceanco@aol.com

PASSAIC

First Call For Help Dial 211 (may not be available from public or cell phones and from some larger workplace phone systems) or 1-800-435-7555 (24 hr). Provides information and referral for local services and agencies. *Website:* http://www.firstcall.org *Email:* help@firstcall.org

SALEM

Contact Community Helplines *(South Jersey only)* 1-877-266-8222 (24 hr crisis counseling) or 856-795-4980 Provides nformation, referrals and listening services. *Website:* http://www.contacthelplies.org *E-mail:* info@contacthelplines.org

SOMERSET

Contact We Care 908-232-2880 (24 hr); TDD: 908-232-3333 (7am-11pm) Information and referrals, crisis and suicidal helpline, listening. Covers Bergen, Union, Essex, Middlesex, Morris, Passaic and Somerset counties.

Hunterdon Helpline Dial 211 (may not be available from public or cell phones, from some larger workplace phone systems) or call 1-800-272-4630 (24 hr). Provides information and referrals to local and regional services and agencies. Serves Somerset, Hunterdon, and Monmouth counties. *Website:* http://www.somersetonline.org

SUSSEX

Sussex County Helpline Dial 211 (may not be available from public or cell phones or from some larger workplace phone systems) or 973-209-4357 (24 hr). Confidential listening, information and referrals. Also offers assistance in homeless emergencies and protective services. Funded by United Way.

UNION

Contact We Care 908-232-2880 (24 hr) Information and referrals, crisis and suicidal helpline, listening. Covers Bergen, Union, Essex, Middlesex, Morris, Passaic, and Somerset counties. *Website:* http://wwwcontactwecare.org *E-mail:* contactw@bellatlantic.nex

First Call For Help Dial 211 (may not be available from public or cell phone, also from some larger work place numbers) or 1-800-435-7555 (24 hr). Provides information and referral to local services and agencies. *Website:* http://www.unioncountynj.org

WARREN

First Call for Help Dial 211 (24 hr) (may not be available from public or cell phones, or from some larger workplace phone systems) (24 hr), 1-877-661-4357 or 908-454-4850. Information and referrals. Central Holiday Intake (meals on holidays). Information on housing for persons with AIDS. Serves Warren County. Funded in part by United Way. Fax 908-454-2968. *Website:* http://www.norwescap.org

Warren County Office for the Disabled 1-877-589-2253 Provides information and referral services to people with all types of disabilities. The office also offers community outreach and disability awareness education programs.

"Everybody can be great...because anybody can serve. You don't have to have a college degree to serve. You don't have to make your subject and verb agree to serve. You only need a heart full of grace. A soul generated by love."

-- Martin Luther King, Jr.

PSYCHIATRIC EMERGENCY SERVICES

The psychiatric emergency services listed below provide crisis/suicide intervention with trained professionals. Some counties provide mobile crisis services. All are available 24 hours a day. Hotlines should be contacted only in case of real mental health emergencies.

ATLANTIC
Atlantic City Medical Center 609-344-1118

BERGEN
Psychiatric Emergency Screening Program 201-262-4357

BURLINGTON
Screening Crisis Intervention Program 609-835-6180

CAMDEN
Kennedy Memorial Hospital 856-428-4357
Steininger Center 856-541-2222

CAPE MAY
Burdette Tomlin Hospital 609-465-5999

CUMBERLAND
Cumberland County Guidance Center 856-455-5555

ESSEX
East Orange General Hospital 973-672-9685
Newark Beth Israel Hospital 973-926-7416

GLOUCESTER
CMHC of Gloucester County 856-845-9100

HUDSON
Jersey City Medical Center 201-915-2210
Bayonne Hospital 201-858-5286

HUNTERDON
Hunterdon Medical Crisis Line 908-788-6400

MERCER
Helene Fuld Medical Center 609-394-6086

MIDDLESEX
University of Medicine and Dentistry NJ 732-235-5700

MONMOUTH
CentraState Medical Center 732-780-6023
Monmouth Medical Center 732-923-6999

MORRIS
Chilton Memorial Hospital 973-831-5078
Morristown Memorial Hospital 973-540-0100
Saint Clare's Health Services 973-625-0280

OCEAN
Kimball Medical Center 732-886-4474

PASSAIC
Barnert Hospital 973-977-6996
Chilton Memorial Hospital 973-831-5078
St. Mary's 973-470-3025

SALEM
Salem County Healthcare Common 856-299-3001

SOMERSET
Richard Hall CMHC 908-526-4100

SUSSEX
Newton Memorial Hospital 973-383-0973

UNION
Muhlenberg Hospital Helpline 908-668-2599
Trinitas Hospital 908-994-7131

WARREN
Warren Crisis Line 908-454-5141

TOLL-FREE HELPLINES

The following toll-free numbers may be a helpful, cost-free resource for persons seeking additional information on a particular subject. These non-profit agencies provide information and referrals, literature and other services. If not indicated as a *(New Jersey)* toll-free number, the helpline is a national resource.

ADOPTION / FOSTER CARE

Foster and Adoptive Family Services *(New Jersey)* 1-800-222-0047 (Mon.-Fri., 9am-6pm) Provides training, offers support services and answers questions on becoming a foster or adoptive parent, scholarships to foster and adoptive youth, holiday toy drive, and fostering wishes for children. Sponsored by Division of Youth and Family Services. *Website:* http://www.FAFSonline.org. *E-mail:* mawrachow@FAFSonline.org.

National Adoption Center 1-800-862-3678 (Mon.-Fri., 9am-5pm) Information on adoption agencies and support groups. Network for matching parents and children with special needs. *Website:* http://www.adopt.org/ *E-mail:* NAC@adopt.org

AGING / SENIOR CITIZENS

Alliance for Aging Research 1-800-639-2421 Citizen advocacy organization that strives to improve the health and independence of older Americans through public and private research. Promotes healthy aging among people of all ages. Provides statistics on the health and well-being of older persons. *Website:* http://www.agingresearch.org

Eldercare Locator 1-800-677-1116 (Mon.-Fri., 9am-8pm EST) Provides information for families and friends of the elderly (ages 60+). Referrals to area agencies on aging for information on insurance, medicaid, taxes and respite care. Information for disabled also provided on these subjects. *Website:* http://www.eldercare.gov

Freedom Eldercare *(New Jersey)* 1-866-737-3336 (24 hr) Free information and referral service to assist individuals in navigating the complex healthcare system. Specialists represent the fields of nursing, social work and geriatric care management. *Website:* http://www.freedomeldercare.com

Lifeline Programs *(New Jersey)* 1-800-792-9745 (Mon.-Fri., 8:30am-5pm recording) Information on pharmaceutical and utility benefits for qualified seniors and the disabled.

National Council on Aging 1-800-424-9046 Information to the aged, families and professionals. *Website:* http://www.ncoa.org

National Institute on Aging 1-800-222-2225 (Voice/TTY; Mon.-Fri., 8:30am-5pm) Provides publications on topics of interest to older adults, doctors, nurses, social activities directors, health educators and the public. Sponsored by federal government. *Website:* http://www.nia.nih.gov *E-mail:* niaic@jbs1.com

NJ Ease 1-877-222-3737 (Mon.-Fri., 8:30am-5pm) Provides information to seniors, disabled, veterans and their caregivers on available local benefits and programs. Information on housing options, nursing homes, elder abuse issues, assisted living facilities, transportation, nutrition, caregivers, insurance, healthcare, long-term care, social activities, volunteer opportunities and care management.

Senior Citizen Information and Referral *(New Jersey)* 1-800-792-8820 (Mon.-Fri., 8:30am-5pm) Provides information and referrals to services for senior citizens (ages 60+) and their caregivers. Elder abuse issues. Makes referrals to local county offices on aging. Sponsored by NJ Department of Health and Senior Services. *Website:* http://www.state.nj.us/health/senior

AIDS

AIDS Information *(BILINGUAL)* 1-800-448-0440 (noon-5pm EST); TTY: 1-888-480-3739 Resource information on clinical trials for AIDS and HIV+ patients. Information about current treatments and prevention techniques. Provides live online assistance. *Website:* http://aidsinfo.nih.gov *E-mail:* contactus@aidsinfo.nih.gov

American Social Health Association 1-800-227-8922 (Mon-Fri., 9am-6pm EST) Provides information, materials and referrals concerning all types of sexually transmitted infections. Specialists will answer questions via phone or email on transmission, risk reduction, prevention, testing and treatment. *Website:* http://www.ashastd.org or http://www.iwannaknow.org (for teens)

CDC National Prevention Information Network *(BILINGUAL)* 1-800-458-5231 (Mon.-Fri., 9am-8pm EST); TTY: 1-800-243-7012 Provides information on resources, educational materials, sexually transmitted diseases (including

AIDS/HIV), tuberculosis and communities at risk. Many different services and publications offered. *Website:* http://www.cdcnpin.org *E-mail:* info@cdcnpin.org

CDC National STD/AIDS Hotline *(BILINGUAL)* 1-800-232-4636 (24 hr); TTY: 1-888-232-6342 (24 hr) Education and research about AIDS, HIV and sexually transmitted diseases. *Website:* http://www.cdc.gov *E-mail:* cdcinfo@cdc.gov

Gay Men's Health Crisis *(BILINGUAL)* 1-800-243-7692 Provides information and referrals for persons affected by AIDS (including gay men, lesbians , bisexuals, transgenders, straights and immigrants). *Website:* http://www.gmhc.org *E-mail:* lynns@gmhc.org

New Jersey AIDS/STD Hotline *(New Jersey)* 1-800-624-2377 (24 hr); TTY: 973-926-8008 (24 hr) Information and referral on AIDS/STD. Counseling, treatment information and referrals to testing locations. Sponsored by NJ Department of Health.

Project Inform *(BILINGUAL)* 1-800-822-7422 (Mon.-Fri., 10am-4pm PST) Information about experimental drugs, treatment of AIDS, volunteer training programs, quarterly newsletter and journal. *Website:* http://www.projectinform.org *E-mail:* info@projectinform.org

TEEN AIDSline *(New Jersey)* 1-800-618-8336 (Mon./Wed./Thurs., 4:30-9:30pm) Confidential helpline that provides information and referrals to teens regarding HIV/AIDS and related issues. *Website:* www.TeenAIDSonline.com *E-mail:* TeenAIDSline@acsnj.org

ALCOHOL

Addictions Hotline of NJ *(New Jersey)* 1-800-238-2333 (Voice/TDD) (24 hr) Crisis counseling, information and referrals for all kinds of drug and alcohol related issues (both prescription and illegal drugs). Sponsored by NJ Div. of Narcotics and Drug Abuse, Office on Prevention, Trenton.

Community Recovery *(New Jersey)* 1-800-292-8262 Offers services for veterans who are experiencing problems with drugs or alcohol. The program offers a wide variety of services throughout the state.

National Association for Children of Alcoholics 1-888-554-2627 Advocates for children and families affected by alcoholism and other drug dependencies. Helps children hurt by parental alcohol and drug abuse. Newsletter, advocacy, policy making, literature, videos and educational materials. *Website:* http://www.nacoa.org *E-mail:* nacoa@nacoa.org

National Clearinghouse for Alcohol and Drug Information *(BILINGUAL)* 1-800-729-6686; Spanish: 1-877-767-8432; TTY: 1-800-487-4889 Information on alcohol, tobacco, drug abuse and prevention. Referrals to treatment centers, research, groups, drugs in the work place, community programs, AIDS, addiction and drug abuse. *Website:* http://www.ncadi-samhsa.gov *E-mail:* ncadi-info@samhsa.hhs.gov

National Council on Alcoholism and Drug Dependence 1-800-622-2255 (24 hr) Provides information on counseling and treatment services for alcohol or drug abuse. Prevention, education programs and newsletter. *Website:* http://www.ncadd.org *E-mail:* national@mcadd.org

National Organization on Fetal Alcohol Syndrome 1-800-666-6327 Provides information and referrals on fetal alcohol syndrome. Offers free packet of information. *Website:* http://www.nofas.org

ALOPECIA AREATA

Locks of Love 1-888-896-1588 Provides custom hairpieces to financially disadvantaged children with long-term medical hair loss. Uses donated hair. *Website:* http://www.locksoflove.org/ *E-mail:* info@locksoflove.org

ALZHEIMER'S

Alzheimer's Disease Education and Referral Center *(BILINGUAL)* 1-800-438-4380 Provides information and publications on Alzheimer's disease to health and service professionals, patients, their families, caregivers and public. Sponsored by National Institute on Aging. *Website:* http://www.alzheimers.org *E-mail:* adear@alzheimers.org

Alzheimer's Disease Helpline *(New Jersey)* 1-800-424-2494 Information, counseling, referrals and support for Alzheimer's and related disorders. Also offers assistance for caregivers.

American Health Assistance Foundation 1-800-437-2423 (Mon.-Fri., 9am-5pm) Provides educational information and funds research for Alzheimer's disease, glaucoma, heart disease and macular degeneration. *Website:* http://www.ahaf.org

ATTORNEY

Legal Services of New Jersey *(BILINGUAL)* 1-888-576-5529 (Mon.-Fri., 8am-5:30pm) Provides free legal advice over the phone for low income persons for civil cases (housing, landlord, tenant, public assistance and entitlements, family law and domestic violence, consumer law and bankruptcy, employment law, immigration, etc). *Website:* http://www.lsnj.org

National Organization of Social Security Claimant's Reps 1-800-431-2804 Provides referrals to social security lawyers who assist claimants in getting social security. *Website:* http://www.nosscr.org

BLIND

American Foundation for the Blind 1-800-232-5463; TDD: 212-502-7662 (Mon.-Fri., 8:30am-4:30pm) Clearinghouse of information and referrals for the blind. Catalog of publications available. *Website:* http://www.afb.org *E-mail:* afbinfo@afbnet

American Health Assistance Foundation 1-800-437-2423 (Mon.-Fri., 9am-5pm) Provides educational information and funds research for Alzheimer's disease, glaucoma, heart disease and macular degeneration. *Website:* http://www.ahaf.org

Braille Institute 1-800-272-4553 (Mon.-Fri., 8:30am-5pm PST) Provides publications, cassettes and free books for visually impaired children. Free Braille calendar. Referrals to resources. Tapes on vision loss available to companies and organizations. *Website:* http://www.brailleinstitute.org *E-mail:* info@brailleinstitute.org

DB-Link: National Consortion on Deaf-Blindness 1-800-438-9376 (Voice); TTY: 1-800-854-7013 Information and referral on education, health, employment, technology, newsletter, communication and recreation for children who are deaf/blind. *Website:* http://www.dblink.org *Email:* dblink@tr.wou.edu

Glaucoma Research Foundation 1-800-826-6693 or 415-986-3162 (Mon.-Fri., 8:30am-5pm PST) Non-profit, phone support network for persons with glaucoma, free literature and funds research. *Website:* http://www.glaucoma.org *E-mail:* info@glaucoma.org

Guide Dog Foundation 1-800-548-4337 Provides guide dogs to the blind free of charge. *Website:* http://www.guidedog.org *E-mail:* info@guidedog.org

Guiding Eyes for the Blind 1-800-942-0149 Dedicated to enriching the lives of blind and visually impaired men and women by providing them with guide dogs free of charge. *Website:* http://www.guidingeyes.org *E-mail:* info@guidingeyes.org or student@guidingeyes.org (for students interested in guide dog training).

Hadley School for the Blind 1-800-323-4238; TTY: 847-441-8111 Provides free distance education to blind and visually impaired persons using Braille materials, large print or audio-cassettes. *Website:* http://www.hadley.edu *E-mail:* info@Hadley.edu

Library of Congress National Library Blind and Physically Handicapped 1-800-424-8567; TDD: 202-707-0744 (8:00am-4:30pm EST) Refers callers to libraries that have information on books on tapes and in Braille available for qualified blind or handicapped persons who can't read standard print. *Website:* http://www.loc.gov/nls *E-mail:* nls@loc.gov

New Jersey Library for the Blind and Handicapped English: 1-800-792-8322; Spanish: 1-800-582-5945; TDD: 1-877-882-5593 (Mon.-Fri., 9am-4pm and Sat., 9am-3pm except July/Aug.) Information on provision of recorded materials, large print, Braille and radio reading service. Deaf and hard of hearing awareness program offers over 700 videos, books on hearing loss and deafness. Assistive devices such as: TTYs, baby cry signalers, bed vibrators, closed captioned decoders, and assistive listening devices. Sign language interpreting services for library events. Sponsored by Bureau of State Library, Thomas Edison State College. *Website:* http://www.njlbh.org *E-mail:* njlbh@njstatelib.org

NJ Commission for the Blind and Visually Impaired 1-877-685-8878 (Mon.-Fri., 9am-5pm voice mail) Information and referral for persons with a visual impairment regarding educational, social, occupational and vocational services.

Prevent Blindness America 1-800-331-2020 (Mon.-Fri. 8:30am-5pm EST) Fights vision loss through research, education and direct services. Provides referrals to local services. Offers literature on vision, eye health and safety. *Website:* http://www.preventblindness.org *E-mail:* info@preventblindness.org

Recording For The Blind and Dyslexic 1-866-732-3585 (Mon.-Fri., 8:30am-4:30pm EST) Provides information on recorded textbooks and consumer publications to eligible persons with print and learning disabilities. Information on volunteer programs for recording CDs. Membership $100/1st year; $35/subsequent years. *Website:* http://www.rfbd.org *E-mail:* custserv@rfbd.org

Research to Prevent Blindness 1-800-621-0026 Provides publications and information on various eye diseases including macular degeneration, cataracts, glaucoma, diabetic retinopathy, corneal disease, retinitis pigmentosa, amblyopia/strabismus, uveitis, general information and funds research. *Website:* http://www.rpbusa.org

Retinitis Pigmentosa International 1-800-344-4877 Provides support and information for persons affected by retinitis pigmentosa and their families. Supports research. *Website:* http://www.rpinternational.org *E-mail:* info@rpinternational.org

BRAIN TUMOR

Pediatric Brain Tumor Foundation 1-800-253-6530 Mission is to find the cause and cure of pediatric brain tumors through the support of research; to aid in the early detection of children's brain tumors; to improve the quality of life of children through better and less invasive treatments and to provide hope, emotional support and information to children and their families. *Website:* http://www.pbtfus.org or http://www.ride4kids.org *E-mail:* pbtfus@pbtfus.org

BUSINESS

SCORE (Service Corps of Retired Executives) 1-800-634-0245 Provides counseling for starting or maintaining businesses. Referrals to local chapters. *Website:* http://www.score.org

U.S. Small Business Administration 1-800-827-5722 Provides information, training and literature on starting and financing small businesses. *Website:* http://www.sba.gov

CANCER

AMC Cancer Information and Counseling Line 1-800-525-3777 (Mon.-Fri., 8:30-5pm MST) Provides current medical information and counseling for cancer issues. *Website:* http://ww.amc.org

American Cancer Society *(MULTILINGUAL)* 1-800-227-2345 (24 hr) Information and referral on various issues related to cancer (treatment, services, literature, transportation, equipment, encouragement and support). *Website:* http://www.cancer.org

Anderson Network 1-800-345-6324 (Mon.-Fri., 8am-5pm CST) Matches cancer patients with others with exact diagnosis for support. *Website:* http://www.mdanderson.org

BLOCH Cancer Hotline 1-800-433-0464 Networks persons with cancer and home volunteers with same type of cancer. Free books about cancer. *Website:* http://www.blochcancer.org *E-mail:* hotline@hrblock.com

Cancer Care, Inc. 1-800-813-4673 (Mon.-Thurs., 9am-7pm; Fri., 9am-5pm) Free counseling for cancer patients and their families. Financial assistance, information and referrals, community and professional education. Teleconference programs. On-going telephone and in-person support groups. *Website:* http://www.cancercare.org *Email:* info@cancercare.org

Cancer Hope Network 1-877-467-3638 One-on-one support offered to cancer patients and their families undergoing cancer treatment from trained volunteers who have survived cancer themselves. *Website:* http://www.cancerhopenetwork.org *E-mail:* info@cancerhopenetwork.org

Cancer Information Service *(BILINGUAL)* 1-800-422-6237 Provides information about cancer and cancer-related resources to patients, the public, and health professionals. Offers one-on-one smoking cessation counseling and literature. Free publications. Sponsored by National Cancer Institute. *Website:* http://www.cancer.gov

Cancer Research Institute 1-800-992-2623 (Mon.-Fri., 9am-5pm) Provides general cancer resource information. Supports leading-edge research aimed at developing immunologic methods of preventing, treating and curing cancer. *Website:* http://www.cancerreseaarch.org *E-mail:* info@cancerresearch.org

CureSearch 1-800-458-6223 Active in the search to cure childhood cancer. Involved with research, care, public awareness and fundraising, information and e-newsletter. *Website:* http://www.curesearch.org *Email:* info@curesearch.org

Dana Farber Cancer Institute Family Studies Cancer Risk Line 1-800-828-6622 Information regarding familial cancers. *Website:* http://www.partners.org

Gilda Radner Familial Ovarian Cancer Registry 1-800-682-7426 (Mon.-Fri., 9am-5:30pm EST) Information on the warning signs of cancer, diagnostic tests and family history. Sponsored by Roswell Park Cancer Institute. *Website:* http://www.ovariancancer.com

Gynecologic Cancer Foundation 1-800-444-4441 Makes referrals to physicians who specialize in the treatment of gynecological cancer. Referrals to doctors, brochures, literature and online resources. *Website:* http://www.wcn.org *E-mail:* info@thegcf.org

Hereditary Cancer Institute 1-800-648-8133 (Mon.-Fri., 8am-4:30pm CST) Studies family-linked cancer. Counseling, information on clinical trials, cancer and hereditary factors.

International Myeloma Foundation 1-800-452-2873 Information, seminars, grants and newsletter on myeloma. *Website:* http://www.myeloma.org *E-mail:* info@myeloma.org

Locks of Love 1-888-896-1588 Provides custom hairpieces to financially disadvantaged children with long-term medical hair loss. Uses donated hair. *Website:* http://www.locksoflove.org/ *E-mail:* info@locksoflove.org

Look Good...Feel Better 1-800-227-2345 Helps cancer patients improve their appearance during treatment. Free workshops across the country. *Website:* http://www.cancer.org

Lung Cancer Alliance 1-800-298-2436 Operates a national "phone buddies" program, comprehensive helpline and many other additional services for persons with lung cancer and their families. *Website:* http://www.lungcanceralliance.org *E-mail:* info@lungcancerallicance.org

Ovarian Cancer Research Fund 1-800-873-9569 Dedicated to advancing and supporting laboratory and clinical research that promotes the development of new therapies and techniques for early detection, screening and treatment of ovarian cancer. Educational outreach, public awareness projects, including videos and resource materials available. *Website:* http://www.ocrf.org

Patient Advocate Foundation 1-800-532-5274 Provides education and legal counseling to cancer patients (relative to a diagnosis) concerning managed care, discrimination, insurance and financial issues. *Website:* http://www.patientadvocate.org *E-mail:* help@patientadvocate.org

Skin Cancer Foundation 1-800-754-6490 (Mon.-Fri., 9am-5pm EST) Provides free packets of information on skin cancer and treatment. *Website:* www.skincancer.org *E-mail:* info@skincancer.org

Susan G. Koman Breast Cancer Foundation 1-800-462-9273 (Mon.-Fri., 9am-4:30pm) Information on breast cancer and breast health. *Website:* http://www.komen.org/

CAREERS

Career Information Hotline *(New Jersey)* 1-800-222-1309 (Mon.-Fri., 8:30am-4:30pm) Provides descriptions and outlooks on various careers. Has information on New Jersey vocational schools, national colleges, graduate school programs and New Jersey day care centers. Publishes a sample resume, and information on job interviews. Not a job search agency. Sponsored by NJ Dept. of Labor. *Website:*http://www.wnjpin.net/coei *E-mail:* rmassan@dol.state.nj.us

National Job Corps Information Line *(BILINGUAL)* 1-800-733-5627 (24 hr) Referrals to job corps training for persons age 16-24. Helps persons to earn high school equivalency diplomas. *Website:* http://www.jobcorps.dol.gov

CHILD ABUSE

American Humane Association 1-800-227-4645 MST) Mission is to protect children and animals from abuse, neglect and cruelty. Advocates on behalf of children (capital/corporal punishment, child protective services, medical neglect, etc) and animals. *Website:* http://www.americanhumane.org *E-mail:*info@americanhumane.org

Child Abuse Hotline *(New Jersey)* 1-800-792-8610 (24 hr); TDD: 1-800-835-5510 (24 hr) Accepts reports of child abuse or neglect. Emergency response for children at risk. Anonymous if callers prefer. Sponsored by Division of Youth and Family Services, Trenton.

Child Help Inc. *(BILINGUAL)* 1-800-422-4453 (24 hr) General information on child abuse and related issues. Referrals to local agencies for child abuse reporting. Crisis counseling. *Website:* http://www.childhelp.org

Child Welfare Information Gateway 1-800-394-3366 (Mon.-Fri., 8:30am-5:30pm) Provides information on all aspects of child maltreatment. *Website:* http://www.childwelfare.gov *E-mail:* info@childwelfare.gov

Prevent Child Abuse America *(New Jersey)* 1-800-244-5373 Provides information workshops, literature, and child abuse prevention information. Aim is to prevent child abuse (not for reports of active abuse situations). *Website:* http://www.preventchildabuse.org

Project Child Find *(New Jersey)* 1-800-322-8174; TDD: 609-984-8432 (Mon.-Fri., 8:15am-4:15pm) Information and referrals for children, from birth to 21 years, with any developmental delay. Sponsored by Dept. of Education. *Website:* http://www.state.nj/education

U.S. Customs Service 1-800-232-5378 Will take reports on child pornography on the internet. Aim is to stop this form of child sexual abuse. *E-mail:* c3@customs.treas.gov

CHILD CARE

Healthy Families *(New Jersey)*1-800-244-5373 For any new parent who feels alone, frightened or overwhelmed. Offers support, education, links to health care and assists in helping to meet family needs. Stays with parents as their child grows. Services are free and will work with persons to help them to be the best parent they can be.

National Association for Family Child Care *(BILINGUAL)* 1-800-359-3817 (Mon.-Fri. 8am-5pm MST) Provides information and training for in-home care providers. Newsletter. *Website:* http://www.nafcc.org

National Child Care Information Center 1-800-616-2242 (Mon., Tues., Thurs., Fri. 8:30am-5:30pm; Wed. 8:30am-8pm EST) Provides information to enhance and promote quality child care. *Website:* http://nccic.acs.f.hhs.gov *E-mail:* info@nccic.org

Registered Family Day Care Line *(New Jersey)* 1-800-332-9227 (Mon.-Fri., 9am-5pm) Callers can obtain the telephone number of their local Child Care Resource and Referral System to get information about various child care options and subsidized child care services. Caregivers can also learn how to become a registered family day care provider. Provides information on how to evaluate the child care environment to make an informed decision on the selection process.

CHILD SUPPORT

New Jersey Child Support Information 1-800-621-5437 (for existing cases); 1-877-655-4371 (customer service) Provides information on child support issues and problems. *Website:* http://www.njchildsupport.org

CHOLESTEROL

UAB Eat Right 1-800-231-3438 (Mon.-Fri., 8am-4pm EST) Information on nutrition and related topics (weight loss and cholesterol). Sponsored by Nutrition Information Services.

CHARITY / SERVICE ORGANIZATION

AmVets 1-800-244-6350 Makes referrals to used clothing collection agencies and provides pick-up information.

Goodwill Industries 1-800-741-0186 Provides employment and training services for people with disabilities and other disadvantaging conditions (welfare dependency, illiteracy, criminal history, homeless). *Website:* http://www.goodwill.org

Volunteers of America 1-800-899-0089 Provides local human service programs and opportunities for individual and community involvement in volunteer programs that deal with social problems. Also has Retiree Volunteer Coalition. *Website:* http://www.volunteersofamerica.org *E-mail:* info@voa.org

Volunteers of America of Delaware Valley *(New Jersey)* 1-800-281-4354 Provides local human service programs and opportunities for individual and community involvement in volunteer programs that deal with social problems. Also has Retiree Volunteer Coalition. *Website:* http://www.voadv.org

COMPLAINT

Directors Action Line *(New Jersey)* 1-800-331-3937 (Mon.-Fri., 9am-5pm) Responds to concerns and questions about the Division of Youth and Family Service and its services. Also answers questions regarding DYFS and refers callers to other assistance if needed.

Long Term Care Systems *(New Jersey)* 1-800-792-9770 (Mon.-Fri., 8:45am-4:45pm; answering machine other times) Complaint line for hospitals, nursing homes, residential care facilities and assisted living. Sponsored by State Facilities. *Website:* www.state.nj.us.health

CONSUMER

FDA Consumer Affairs 1-888-463-6332 (Mon.-Fri., 10am-4pm) Information on any FDA-regulated products (food and drugs). Has information on rare illnesses, starting businesses, freedom of information act, health and medical issues. Free literature. Referrals to toll-free numbers. Assists in emergency situations. *Website:* http://www.fda.gov

National Do Not Call Registry 1-888-382-1222 An opportunity to limit the telemarketing calls that are received. The registry was created to offer consumers a choice regarding telemarketing calls. *Website:* http://www.donotcall.gov

New Jersey Division of Consumer Affairs *(New Jersey)* 1-800-242-5846 Takes complaints against businesses, advisory and professional boards, health clubs, home repairs, car dealerships and charities. Information on Lemon Law (automobiles), weights and measures, legalized games of chance, Bureau of Securities, etc. *Website:* http://www.njconsumeraffairs.com *E-mail:* AskConsumerAffairs@lps.state.nj.us

Opt Out 1-888-567-8688 Organization that removes your name and address from all mailing lists offered by the main consumer credit reporting agencies (Trans Union, Experian, Equifax and Innovis) which advertise and send out new charge card offers. When writing include your first, middle and last name (including Jr., Sr., etc), current address, previous address (if you've moved in the last six months), social security number, date of birth and signature.

Toy Safety Hotline 1-877-486-9723 Provides information on toy safety. Brochures. Information on best selling age-appropriate toys. *Website:* http://www.toy-tia.org

U.S. Consumer Product Safety Commission *(BILINGUAL)* 1-800-638-2772; TTY: 1-800-638-8270 Computer operated recorded information on product safety. Takes reports on unsafe products. *Website:* http://www.cpsc.gov *E-mail:* info@cpsc.gov

CREDIT COUNSELING

Consumer Credit Counseling Services 1-800-388-2227 With touch-tone phone, callers can find out about credit counseling services in their local areas. Sponsored by the National Foundation for Consumer Credit. *Website:* http://www.nfcc.org

CRIME VICTIMS

Consumer Response Center 1-877-382-4357 Assistance for people who are victims of fraud. Complaints are shared with law enforcement agencies. Does not resolve individual disputes. Sponsored by Federal Trade Commission. *Website:* http://www.ftc.gov

GAINS Center 1-800-311-4246 option #2 Provides information on services for people with co-occurring mental health and substance abuse disorders who come in contact with the justice system. Provides technical assistance, needs assessment and literature to communities. *Website:* http://gainscenter.samha.gov *E-mail:* gainsebp@prainc.com

Juvenile Justice Clearinghouse 1-800-851-3420 (Mon.-Fri., 8:30am-7pm) Information and referrals regarding juvenile justice programs and Department of Justice.

National Center for Victims of Crime 1-800-394-2255 Provides information, referrals, and advocacy to crime victims nationwide. An affiliate to the National Crime Victim Bar Association which provides referrals to file civil suit against perpetrators and other responsible individuals. Also operates Stalking Resource Center which provides training and technical assistance on the issue of stalking. *Website:* http://www.ncvc.org *E-mail:* gethelp@ncvc.org

National Criminal Justice Referral Service 1-800-851-3420 (Mon.-Fri., 10am-6pm EST) Provides information on all aspects of the criminal justice system and support for victims. *Website:* http://www.ncjrs.org

National Institute of Corrections 1-800-995-6423 ext. 70147 (Mon.-Fri., 8am-5pm) Provides information and technical assistance regarding those diagnosed with mental illness in prison. *Website:* http://www.nicic.org *E-mail:* aault@bob.gov

NJ Bias Crime Victims' Support Service *(New Jersey)* 1-800-277-2427 Makes referrals to law enforcement agencies, advocacy groups and mental health professionals for victims of bias crimes. Sponsored by the NJ Office of Bias Crime and Community Relations. *Website:* http://www.njbiascrime.org

Stalking *(New Jersey)* 1-800-572-7233 (24 hr) Support and information for anyone with a restraining order, who is being stalked in New Jersey. Sponsored by the Prevention of Violence Against Women.

Victims of Crime Compensation Board *(New Jersey)* 1-800-242-0804 Provides counseling, information on compensation and referrals for victims of violent crimes. Can help in emergency situations for qualified persons, otherwise leave message. Sponsored by Victims of Crimes Compensation Board. *Website:* http://www.state.nj.us/victim *E-mail:* njvictims@yahoo.com

We Tip Hotlines *(BILINGUAL)* 1-800-782-7463 *(general)*; 1-800-873-7283 *(felony)* Takes reports on crimes or felonies.

CYSTIC FIBROSIS

Children's Organ Transplant Association 1-800-366-2682 (Mon.-Fri., 8am-5pm EST) Non-profit organization that provides public education on organ transplants. Assists families in fund-raising for transplant and transplant-related expenses. Assistance for all children and adults with cystic fibrosis who are U.S. citizens in need of an organ transplant. *Website:* http://www.cota.org *E-mail:* cota@cota.org

Cystic Fibrosis Foundation 1-800-344-4823 (Mon.-Fri., 8:30am-5:30pm) Provides information, brochures, insurance information, pharmaceutical services and updates on research. *Website:* http://www.cff.org *E-mail:* info@cff.org

DEAF

ASHA Hearing and Speech Helpline *(BILINGUAL)* 1-800-638-8255 (Voice/TDD) (Mon.-Fri., 8:30am-5pm EST) Information on speech, hearing and language disabilities. Referrals to ASHA certified clinics. Database of information on listening devices. Sponsored by American Speech Language and Hearing Assn. *Website:* http://www.asha.org *E-mail:* actioncenter@asha.org

Better Hearing Institute 1-800-327-9355 (Mon.-Fri., 9am-5pm EST) Information and literature on any hearing-related issue. *Website:* http://www.betterhearing.org

Captioned Media Program 1-800-237-6213 (Voice); TTY: 1-800-237-6819 (Mon.-Fri., 8:30am-5pm EST) Provides free loan program for open captioned media for the deaf or hearing-impaired. Also provides captioned materials for family members and professionals who work with hard of hearing. Sponsored by US Dept. of Education. *Website:* http://www.cfv.org *E-mail:* info@cfv.org

DB-Link: National Consortion on Deaf/Blindness 1-800-438-9376 (Voice); TTY: 1-800-854-7013 Information and referral on education, health, employment, technology, communication and recreation for children who are deaf-blind. Newsletter. All services are free of charge. *Website:* http://www.tr.wou.edu/dblink *E-mail:* dblink@tr.wou.edu

Dial-A-Hearing Screening Test 1-800-222-3277 (Mon.-Fri., 9am-5pm EST) Offers over the phone hearing screening for persons (aged 14+). Provides hearing information and referral services. *Website:* http://www.dialatest.com *E-mail:* dahst@aol.com

Division of Deaf and Hard of Hearing *(New Jersey)* 1-800-792-8339 (Voice/TTY) (Mon.-Fri., 8:30-4:30pm) Information and referral for the deaf and hard of hearing. Interpreter referral service. Sensitivity training available for the public. *Website:* http://www.state.nj.us/humanservices/ddhh/index.html *Email:* Brian.shomo@dhs.state.nj

HEAR Now 1-800-648-4327 (Mon.-Fri., 8am-5pm) Helps financially needy individuals obtain hearing aids. Collects used hearing aids for recycling. Newsletter, information and referrals. *E-mail:* nonprofit@starkey.com

Hearing Aid 1-800-521-5247 ext. 3 or 734-522-7200 (Mon.-Fri., 8am-5pm EST) Provides general literature on hearing aids and hearing loss. Referrals to hearing instrument specialists. Leave name and address, information will be mailed. Sponsored by International Hearing Society. *Website:* http://www.ihsinfo.org *Email:* amarkey@ihsinfo.org

Hearing Aid Assistance to the Aged and Disabled (HAAAD) *(New Jersey)* 1-800-792-9745 (24 hr) Provides a $100 reimbursement to eligible persons who purchase a hearing aid. Sponsored by NJ State Dept. of Health, Div. of Senior Affairs.

John Tracy Clinic for Preschool Deaf Children 1-800-522-4582 (Mon.-Fri., 8am-4pm PST) Information and support for parents and preschool deaf children. Free correspondence course for parents. *Website:* http://www.jtc.org

National Cued Speech Association 1-800-459-3529 or 301-915-8009 (Voice/TTY) Encourages and supports the use of cued speech for communication, language development and literacy. Networking, literature, advocacy, information and referrals, phone support, conferences and family camps. *Website:* http://www.cuedspeech.org *E-mail:* info@cuedspeech.org

National Institute on Deafness and Other Communication Disorders 1-800-241-1044; TTY: 1-800-241-1055 Referrals to national agencies on hearing, speech, language, smell, taste, voice and balance disorders. Publishes fact sheets, brochures, information packets and newsletters. *Website:* http://www.nidcd.nih.gov *E-mail:* nidcdinfo@nidcd.nih.gov

New Jersey Library for the Blind and Handicapped *(New Jersey)* English: 1-800-792-8322; Spanish: 1-800-582-5945; TDD: 1-877-882-5593 (Mon.-Fri., 9am-4pm; Sat., 9am-3pm except July/Aug.). Information on provision of recorded materials, large print, Braille and radio reading service. Deaf and hard of hearing awareness program offers over 700 videos, books on hearing loss and deafness. Assistive devices such as: TTYs, baby cry signalers, bed vibrators, closed captioned decoders and assistive listening devices. Sign language interpreting services for library events. Sponsored by Bureau of State Library, Thomas Edison State College. *Website:* http://www.njstatelib.org *E-mail:* njlbh@njstatelib.org

DENTAL

Dental Care for Handicapped 1-888-471-6334 Information on free dental care for qualified elderly, disabled or chronically ill patients. Services include dentures, crowns and other significant dental work. *Website:* http://www.nfdh.org

DEPRESSION

Speak Up When You're Down *(New Jersey)* 1-800-328-3838 (24 hr) Resources for anyone experiencing postpartum depression, their families and friends. *Website:* http://www.njspeakup.gov

National Institute of Mental Health Information Line *(BILINGUAL)* 1-800-421-4211 (publications) Phone system that takes orders for free brochures on depression and anxiety. Sponsored by National Institute of Mental Health. *Website:* http://www.nimh.nih.gov

DIABETES HELPLINE

National Diabetes Education Program *(BILINGUAL)* 1-800-438-5383 or 1-800-860-8747 Provides educational information on diabetes. Publishes "Do Your Level Best" kit and diabetes kit to public and health care professionals. Sponsored by National Institute of Diabetics, Digestive and Kidney Diseases and Center for Diabetes Control and Prevention.

National Institute of Diabetes and Digestive and Kidney Diseases 1-800-891-5390 (kidney); 1-800-860-8747 (diabetes); 1-800-891-5389 (digestive diseases) Provides referrals and literature on a broad range of subjects concerning diabetes, digestive disorders, kidney disease, metabolic and endocrine disorders, hematologic diseases, urologic disorders. *Website:* http://www.niddk.nih.gov *E-mail:* nkudic@info.niddk.nih.gov

DISABILITY

Abledata 1-800-227-0216 Provides information, publications and consumer reviews of all types of assistive technologies for persons with disabilities. Sponsored by National Institute on Disability and Rehab Research and U.S. Dept. of Education. *Website:* http://www.abledata.com/ *E-mail:* abledata@orcmacro.com

Access Board *(BILINGUAL)* 1-800-872-2253 or 202-272-0080 Advocates for accessibility. Provides publications and forms to press charges against agencies that are not accessible. Website: http://www.access-board.gov *E-mail:* info@access-board.gov

ADA Technical Assistance Line *(BILINGUAL)* 1-800-514-0301 (Mon., Tues., Wed., Fri., 10:30am-4:30pm; Thurs., 12:30-5pm); TDD: 1-800-514-0383 Provides free publications on the American Disabilities Act. A new publication will be available each month in a limited supply. *Website:* http://www.ada.gov

Assistive Technology Advocacy Center of NJ *(formerly Back In Action)* Buy or sell equipment 1-800-554-2626; Information and funding assistance: 1-800-342-5832 (Voice) (Mon.-Fri., 9am-5pm) Maintains listing of used equipment available for sale. Information on assistive technology. Catalog of equipment published quarterly ($6).

Canine Companions for Independence 1-800-572-2275 Trains dogs to assist people with physical and developmental disabilities. Also has opportunities for people interested in volunteering to raise puppies. *Website:* http://www.cci.org

Childcare Plus 1-800-235-4122 Information and referrals to families of children with disabilities. Provides training and technical assistance for childcare providers and other early childhood professionals. *Website:* http://www.ccplus.org *E-mail:* ccplus@ruralinstitute.utm.edu

Disabled American Veterans 1-877-426-2838 Provides free, professional assistance to veterans and their families in obtaining benefits and services earned through military service and provided by the department of Veterans Affairs and other agencies of the government. Guidelines for developing chapters. *Website:* http://www.dav.org *E-mail:* feedback@davmail.org

Disabled and Alone 1-800-995-0066 Helps families and caretakers of disabled persons make lifetime plans for the care of their loved one after they are gone. One time membership fee. *Website:* http://www.disabledandalone.org *E-mail:* info@disabledandalone.org

Division of Disability Services *(New Jersey)* 1-888-285-3036; TDD: 609-292-1210 Information and referral services for persons of all ages with disabilities. Serves as the chief link between state government and the county offices on disabilities. Publishes a statewide directory of disability services. *Website:* www.state.nj.us/humanservices/dds

Easter Seals National Headquarters Disability Helpline *(BILINGUAL)* 1-800-221-6827 (Mon.-Fri., 8:30am-5pm CST) Provides disability resource packets for children and adults with disabilities. Online directory available. *Website:* http://www.easterseals.com

Families and Advocates Partnership for Education 1-888-248-0822; TTY: 952-838-0190 (Mon.-Fri., 8am-5:30pm) Support and education for families of children with any disability. Advocates for the Individuals with Disabilities Education Act. Literature, training sessions, information and referrals. *Website:* http://www.fape.org *E-mail:* fape@pacer.org

Family Support Center of New Jersey 1-800-372-6510 (Mon.-Fri., 8am-5pm) Information and referral agency offering services to individuals with a disability or families who live with a family member with special needs. Also works with professionals who service this community. A support network for parents is also available through the center. *Website:* http://www.fscnj.org *Email:* jacqui.moskowitz@fscnj.org

Friends' Health Connection *(New Jersey)* 1-800-483-7436 Communication support network that connects patients and caregivers with any disorder, illness or handicap. Members are networked with each other based on health problem, symptoms, lifestyle, interests, occupation, location and other criteria. Communicate via letters, phone and e-mail. It is intended for emotional support, not for romantic purposes. Also provides educational, therapeutic and recreational programs. Membership $19.95 first year, $9.95 thereafter. *Website:* http://www.friendshealthconnection.org *E-mail:* info@friendshealthconnection.org

HEATH Resource Center 1-800-544-3284 (Voice/TDD) Information and referrals on post-secondary education and adult training programs for people with disabilities. Sponsored by U.S. Dept. of Education. *Website:* http://www.heath.gwu.edu

Job Accommodation Network 1-800-526-7234 or 1-877-781-9403 (Voice/TDD) (Mon.-Fri., 9am-6pm) Information on accommodations for people with disability. Sponsored Office of Disability Employment Policy and Dept. of the Labor. *Website:* http://www.jan.wvu.edu *E-mail:* jan@jan.icdi.wvu.edu

Library of Congress National Library Blind and Physically Handicapped 1-800-424-8567; TDD: 202-707-0744 (Mon.-Fri., 8:30am-5pm EST) Refers callers to libraries that have information on books on tapes and in Braille available for qualified blind or handicapped persons who can't read standard print. *Website:* http://www.loc.gov/nls *E-mail:* nls@loc.gov

Lifeline Programs *(New Jersey)* 1-800-792-9745 (Mon.-Fri., 8:30am-5pm) Recorded information on pharmaceutical and utility benefits for qualified seniors and the disabled.

National Accessible Apartment Clearinghouse 1-800-421-1221 Maintains a database of over 46,000 accessible apartments nationwide. Helps people with disabilities find accessible apartments. Owners and managers may also use this service to register their accessible units. *Website:* http://www.accessibleapartments.org

National Council on Independent Living 1-877-525-3400; TTY: 202-207-0340 Provides information and referrals to independent living centers. *Website:* http://www.ncil.org *E-mail:* ncil@ncil.org

National Institute for Rehab Engineering 1-800-736-2216 (day) Provides information, advice and referrals to people with all types of disabilities about assistive technology equipment. Aim is to help people with disabilities to be more independent and self-sufficient. *Website:* http://www.theofficenet/nire

National Dissemination Center for Children with Disabilities *(BILINGUAL)* 1-800-695-0285 (Voice/TTY) (Mon.-Fri., 9am-5pm) Provides information on disabilities with a special focus on children (birth to age 22). Services include information, referrals, technical assistance to parents, educators, caregivers and advocates. Referrals to support groups. Publications available for a small fee. *E-mail:* nichcy@aed.org

New Jersey Library for the Blind and Handicapped *(BILINGUAL)* English: 1-800-792-8322; Spanish: 1-800-582-5945; TDD: 1-877-882-5593 (Mon.-Fri., 9am-4pm; Sat., 9am-3pm except July/Aug.) Information on provision of recorded materials, large print, Braille and radio reading service. Deaf and hard of hearing awareness program offers over 700 videos, books on hearing loss and deafness. Assistive devices such as: TTYs, baby cry signalers, bed vibrators, closed captioned decoders and assistive listening devices. Sign language interpreting services for library events. Sponsored by Bureau of State Library, Thomas Edison State College. *Website:* http://www.njlbh.org *E-mail:* njlbh@njstatelib.org

NJ Protection and Advocacy, Inc. 1-800-922-7233; TTY: 609-633-7106 (Mon.-Fri., 9am-5pm) Provides legal assistance and advocacy services to citizens of New Jersey with any type of disability (both physical and mental). Information and referral services, educational programs, technical assistance and training. *E-mail:* advocate@njpanda.org *Website:* http://www.njpanda.org

NJ WINS (Work Incentive Programs) 1-877-659-4672 or 1-888-322-1918 Enables social security administration beneficiaries with disabilities to make informed choices about work and assists them in exploring work incentives that are available. *Website:* http://www.njwins.org *E-mail:* njwins@cpof-nj.org

"I'm glad I understand that while language is a gift, listening is a responsibility."
-- Nikki Giovanni

Northeast ADA and IT Center *(BILINGUAL) (New Jersey)* 1-800-949-4232 (Voice, TDD and Spanish) Provides free technical assistance to employers, individuals with disabilities, state and local government agencies and others in the implementation of the Americans with Disabilities Act. They also provide free training workshops and awareness programs. *Website:* http://www.northeastada.org *E-mail:* northeastada@cornell.edu

Project Child Find *(New Jersey)* 1-800-322-8174; TTY: 609-984-8432 (Mon.-Fri., 8:15am-4:15pm) Information and referrals for children, from birth to 21 years, with any developmental delay. Sponsored by Dept. of Education.

Rural Institute on Disabilities 1-800-732-0323 (Mon.-Fri., 8am-5pm MST) Provides assistance for disabled children and adults who live in rural areas. Technological services, early intervention and services for the elderly. Conducts research, rural transportation, employment and health promotion for disabled. *E-mail:* rural@uralinstitute.umt.edu

SNAP (Special Needs Advocate for Parents) 1-888-310-9889 Support for parents of special needs children. Referrals to educational advocates, support groups, attorneys and other resources. Medical insurance problem solving. Assistance with estate planning. Newsletter, speakers' bureau and interactive bulletin boards. *Website:* http://www.snapinfo.org *E-mail:* info@snapinfo.org

Through the Looking Glass 1-800-644-2666 (Mon.-Fri., 8:30am-5pm); TTY: 1-800-804-1616 Information and referrals for disabled parents or parents of disabled children. Newsletter and phone support. *Website:* http://www.lookingglass.org *E-mail:* tlg@lookingglass.org

U.S. Equal Employment Opportunity Commission *(MULTILINGUAL)* 1-800-669-4000; TTY: 1-800-669-6820 Information, speakers, technical assistance, training and referrals regarding enforcing ADA and prohibiting discrimination in employment of disabled persons. *Website:* http://www.eeoc.gov

DISCRIMINATION

Equal Employment Opportunity *(New Jersey)* 1-800-669-4000 (Mon.-Fri., 8am-4:30pm) Investigates allegations of discrimination due to race, creed, age, religion, gender or disabilities. Sponsored by Federal Government.

Office for Civil Rights 1-800-368-1019 (Mon.-Fri., 8:30am-5:30pm) Refers people who feel they have been discriminated against. Sponsored by the Dept. of Health and Human Services. *Website:* http://www.ed.gov/offices/ocr

DOMESTIC VIOLENCE

National Domestic Abuse Helpline for Men and Women 1-888-743-5754 (24 hr) *(Crisis line)* Provides crisis intervention and support services to men and women who are dealing with domestic violence. *Website:* http://www.noexcuse4abuse.org *Email:* help@noexcuse4abuse.org

National Domestic Violence Hotline 1-800-799-7233; TTD: 1-800-787-3224 Information and referrals for victims of domestic violence. *Website:* http://www.ndvh.org

NJ Domestic Violence Hotline *(New Jersey)* 1-800-572-7233 (24 hr) Information and referrals for victims or perpetrators of domestic violence. *Website:* http://www.womanspace.org

DOWN SYNDROME

National Down Syndrome Society 1-800-221-4602 (Mon.-Fri., 9am-5pm EST) Information and referral. Free packets to new parents, information on education, support groups, medical research, newsletter, phone support and conferences. Fax: 212-979-2873. *Website:* http://www.ndss.org *E-mail:* info@ndss.org

DRUG ABUSE

Addictions Hotline of NJ *(New Jersey)* 1-800-238-2333 (Voice/TDD) (24 hr) Crisis counseling, information and referrals for all kinds of drug and alcohol related issues (both prescription and illegal drugs). Sponsored by NJ Div. of Narcotics and Drug Abuse, Office on Prevention, Trenton.

American Council for Drug Education *(BILINGUAL)* 1-800-488-3784 Provides general information on drug abuse and treatment. Brochures and referrals to crisis counseling. Publications. Affiliated with Phoenix House.

Community Recovery *(New Jersey)* 1-800-292-8262 Offers services for veterans who are experiencing problems with drugs or alcohol. The program offers a wide variety of services throughout the state.

Drug Policy Information Clearinghouse 1-800-666-333 (Mon.-Fri. 10am-6pm) Sends out information on drug abuse, and publications on national drug policies. *Website:* http://www.whitehousedrugpolicy.gov *E-mail:* ondcp@ncjrs.org

National Association for Children of Alcoholics 1-888-554-2627 Advocates for children and families affected by alcoholism and other drug dependencies. Helps children hurt by parental alcohol and drug abuse. Newsletter, advocacy, policy making, literature, videos and educational materials. *Website:* http: www.nacoa.org *E-mail:* nacoa@nacoa.org

National Clearinghouse for Alcohol and Drug Information *(BILINGUAL)* 1-800-729-6686; Spanish: 1-877-767-8432; TTY: 1-800-487-4889 Information on alcohol, tobacco and drug abuse. Information on prevention, referrals to treatment centers, research, groups, drugs in the work place, community programs, AIDS and addiction. *Website:* http://www.ncadi-samhsa.gov *E-mail:* ncadi-info@samhsa.hhs.gov

National Council on Alcoholism and Drug Dependence 1-800-622-2255 Provides information on counseling and treatment services for alcohol or drug abuse. Prevention and education programs. Newsletter. *Website:* http://www.ncadd.org *E-mail:* national@mcadd.org

National Inhalant Prevention Center 1-800-269-4237 Provides information and referrals to persons concerned about inhalants. Literature, training, quarterly newsletter and technical assistance. Conducts national inhalant and poisons awareness week. *Website:* http://www.inhalants.org *E-mail:* nipc@io.com

National PRIDE Youth Programs 1-800-668-9277 Trains youth volunteers on how to conduct drug prevention education. *Website:* www.prideyouthprograms.org *E-mail:* info@prideyouthprograms.org

DWARFISM

Little People's Research Fund, Inc. 1-800-232-5773 (Mon.-Fri., 9am-5pm EST) Referrals (primarily research) and literature on dwarfism. Networks parents together. *Website:* http://www.iprf.org

"No man is an island, entire of itself; every man is a piece of continent, a part of the main." -- John Donne

DYSLEXIA / LEARNING DISABLITIES

International Dyslexia Association 1-800-222-3123 (Mon.-Fri., 8:30am-4:30pm) Provides information and referrals for persons with dyslexia. *Website:* http://www.interdys.org *E-mail:* info@interdys.org

National Center for Learning Disabilities 1-888-575-7373 Provides information and referrals for learning disabled adults and children. *Website:* http://www.ld.org

Recording For The Blind and Dyslexic 1-866-732-3585 (Mon.-Fri., 8:30am-4:30pm) Information on recorded textbooks and consumer publications to eligible persons with print or learning disabilities. Information on volunteer programs for recording CDs. Membership dues $100/1st year; $35/subsequent years. *Website:* http://www.rfbd.org *E-mail:* custserv@rfbd.org

EATING DISORDERS

New Jersey Eating Disorders Helpline *Professionally-run.* 1-800-624-2268 (Mon.-Fri., 10am-5pm) Provides information and referrals for dealing with all types of eating disorders. Feel free to leave a message and your call will be returned. *Website:* http://www.edhelp.com *E-mail:* livctr@aol.com

National Eating Disorders Association 1-800-931-2237 Provides information on local professional services and support groups nationwide for persons with eating disorders. Free literature and training conferences. *Website:* http://www.nationaleatingdisorders.org *E-mail:* info@NationalEatingDisorders.org

EDUCATION

Federal Student Aid Information Center 1-800-433-3243 (Mon-Fri, 8am-midnight; Sat. 9am-6pm EST) Information available regarding information on student aid. Sponsored by U.S. Dept. of Education. *Website:* www.fafsa.ed.gov

Goodwill Industries 1-800-741-0186 Provides employment and training services for people with disabilities and other disadvantaging conditions (welfare dependency, illiteracy, criminal history and homeless).

HESAA Hotline, The *(New Jersey)* 1-800-792-8670, TDD: 609-588-2526 (Mon.-Fri., 9am-5pm) Information on colleges and universities, TTY: 609-633-7106 adult evening and Vo-Tech education. financial aid *Website:* http://www.HESAA.org

National Job Corps Information Line *(BILINGUAL)* 1-877-872-5627 (24 hr) Referrals to job corps training for persons age 16-24. Helps persons to earn high school equivalency diplomas. Sponsored by National Job Corps Alumni Assn. *Website:* http://www.doleta.gov

ENERGY / UTILITIES

Energy Efficiency and Renewable Energy Clearinghouse 1-877-337-3463 (Mon.-Fri., 9am-5pm) Free information on energy efficiency and renewable energy. Answers technical questions. Provides referral to other organizations. Sponsored by Dept. of Energy. *Website:* http://www.eere.energy.gov (publications)

Lifeline Utility Assistance Program *(New Jersey)* 1-800-792-9745 (24 hr) Utility assistance to residents of NJ who are 65+ years old or who are 18 and older and receive Social Security Disability and meet the income eligibility guidelines. Recipients may receive up to $150.

NJ Weatherization and Home Energy Assistance Program 1-800-510-3102 Provides home weatherization and insulation. Heating and cooling assistance to eligible New Jersey residents.

ENVIRONMENTAL

American Public Information on Environment 1-800-320-2743 (Mon.-Fri., 8:30am-5pm CST) Information, education and aid to families with environmental concerns. *Website:* http://www.americanpie.org *E-mail:* info@americanpie.org

Center for Disease Control and Prevention Helpline 1-800-232-4636; TTY: 1-888-232-6348 Provides information on emergency preparedness and response including bioterrorism, chemical emergencies, radiation emergencies, mass casualties, natural disasters, severe weather, recent outbreaks and incidence. *Website:* http://bt.cdc.gov/disasters/

Chemical Information Referral Center 1-800-424-9300 Takes reports on emergency chemical or other hazardous spills. *Website:* http://www.chemtrec.org *E-mail:* customerservice@chemtree.com

EPA (Environmental Protection Agency) 1-800-426-4791 Provides information on safe drinking water and policy regulations on a variety of environmental concerns. *Website:* http://www.epa.gov/safewater *E-mail:* sdwa@epa.gov

Indoor Air Quality Info Clearinghouse 1-800-438-4318 (Mon.-Fri., 9am-5pm EST) Provides information and referral on indoor air quality, pollutants and sources, health effects, control methods, commercial building operations and maintenance. Sponsored by the EPA. *Website:* http://www.epa.gov/iaq/ *E-mail:* iaqinfo@aol.com

National Lead Information Center and Clearinghouse *(BILINGUAL)* 1-800-424-5323 (Mon.-Fri., 8am-6pm EST) Provides information on lead-based paint for the home and safe work practices for renovating. Distributes EPA literature. *Website:* http://www.epa.gov/lead *E-mail:* hotline.lead@epamail.epa.gov

EPILEPSY

Epilepsy Information Service 1-800-642-0500 Answers general questions on epilepsy. Free literature, workshops and conferences. *Website:* http://www.WFUBMC.edu

EYE CARE

Eye Care America Seniors: 1-800-222-3937; Diabetes Eye Care: 1-800-272-3937; Children: 1-877-887-6327 Assists financially disadvantaged persons (children and seniors) in obtaining medical eye care. Sponsored by American Academy of Ophthalmology Foundation. *Website:* http://www.aao.org

FACIAL DISFIGUREMENT

Children's Craniofacial Association 1-800-535-3643 (Mon.-Fri., 8:30am-4:30pm CST) Provides information and support for children with craniofacial disfigurement and their families. Makes referrals to doctors and support groups. Disseminates educational booklets. Information on free medical clinics, Cher's Family Retreat and advocacy. *Website:* http://www.ccakids.com

FACES: The National Craniofacial Association 1-800-332-2373 (Mon.-Fri. 9am-5pm EST) Non-profit organization dedicated to assisting children and adults with craniofacial disorders resulting from disease, accident or birth. Financial assistance, referrals to support groups, newsletter, information and referrals to services and medical professionals. *Website:* http://www.faces-cranio.org *E-mail:* faces@mindspring.com

FOOD HANDLING / FOOD CO-OP

America's Second Harvest 1-800-771-2303 Provides hunger relief through a network of over 200 food banks and food-rescue programs. *Website:* http://www.secondharvest.org

Center for Food Safety and Applied Nutrition 1-888-723-3366 (Mon.-Fri., 10am-4pm) Provides information on food safety, cosmetics and colors, seafood and women's nutritional health. Sponsored by FDA. *Website:* http://www.cfsan.fda.gov

Meat and Poultry Hotline 1-800-535-4555 or 1-888-674-6854 (Mon.-Fri., 10am-4pm EST) Answers safe handling questions. Information on food handling. Helps persons understand labels on meat and poultry. Will answer questions about safe handling procedures. Sponsored by US Dept of Agriculture. *Website:* http://www.fsis.usda.gov *E-mail:* mphotline.fsis@usda.gov

S.T.O.P. (Safe Tables Our Priority) 1-800-350-7867 Support, education, and advocacy for victims and families of victims of foodborne infectious diseases (E coli, salmonella listeria, shigella, vibrio and many others). Newsletter, phone and online networking. *Website:* http://www.safetables.org *E-mail:* director@safetables.org

FOOT CARE

Foot Care Information Center 1-800-366-8227 Provides literature and referrals on foot care and podiatric medicine. Referrals to podiatrist. Sponsored by American Podiatric Medical Association. *Website:* http://www.apma.org

GAMBLING

Council on Compulsive Gambling of New Jersey 1-800-426-2537 (24 hr) Information to help compulsive gamblers. Referrals to self-help groups, in-patient treatment programs, counseling services and free evaluations for the compulsive gambler. Speakers' bureau. *Website:* http://www.800gambler.org *E-mail:* ccgnj@800gambler.org

National Council on Problem Gambling 1-800-522-4700 Information, referrals to support groups and counseling for compulsive gamblers. *Website:* http://www.ncpgambling.org *E-mail:* ncpg@ncpggambling.org

GASTROINTESTINAL DISORDERS

National Institute of Diabetes and Digestive and Kidney Diseases 1-800-891-5390 (kidney); 1-800-860-8747 (diabetes); 1-800-891-5389 (digestive diseases) Provides referrals and literature on a broad range of subjects concerning diabetes, digestive disorders, kidney disease, metabolic and endocrine disorders, hematologic diseases, urologic disorders. *Website:* http://www.niddk.nih.gov *E-mail:* nkudic@info.niddk.nih.gov

GRANTS / FUNDING

Foundation Center Customer Service 1-800-424-9836 Provides information on grant providers and funders. Grant writing for non-profit projects. Offers course on proposal writing. Free library. *Website:* http://fdncenter.org

HEALTH

Alliance for Informed Choice on Vaccinations *(New Jersey)* 1-800-613-9925 To address the concerns about the safety of vaccines and the right to informed consent. Literature, advocacy and phone help.

American Board of Medical Specialties 1-866-275-2267 Will tell you if your physician is board certified. *Website:* http://www.abms.org

American Dietetic Association *(BILINGUAL)* 1-800-366-1655 Information on diet. Referrals to dietitians. Brochures sometimes available. Sponsored by National Center for Nutrition and Diatetics. *Website:* http://www.eatright.org

American Health Assistance Foundation 1-800-437-2423 (Mon.-Fri., 9am-5pm) Provides educational information and funds research for Alzheimer's disease, glaucoma, heart disease and macular degeneration. *Website:* http://www.ahaf.org

American Running Association 1-800-776-2732 or 301-913-9517 (Mon.-Fri., 9am-5pm) Information on aerobic sports. Referrals to sports medicine clinics, podiatrists and orthopedists. *Website:* http://www.americanrunning.org/ *E-mail:* run@americanrunning.org

CDC Traveler's Health Helpline 1-877-394-8747 Provides information for persons traveling overseas. Includes vaccinations, diseases, safe food and water, traveling with children, persons with special needs, etc. *Website:* http://www.cdc.gov/travel/

Center for Human Genetics 1-800-283-4316 Provides information on disorders currently under study by the Center for Human Genetics. These include: Alzheimer's, ALS, asthma, autism, Bethlehem myopathy, Chiari malformation, CMT, cardiovascular, facioscapulohumeral muscular dystrophies, focal segmental glomerulosclerosis, spastic paraparesis, glaucoma, benign intraepithelial dyskeratosis, hypophosphatemic rickets, limb-girdle muscular dystrophy, MS, neural tube defects, osteoarthritis, Parkinson's and tuberous sclerosis. See website for complete list. *Website:* http://www.chg.mc.duke.edu

Centers for Disease Control and Prevention *(BILINGUAL)* 1-800-232-4636 Provides information on health related topics, vaccinations, traveler's health, grants, genetics, hoaxes, rumors and emergency responses. Information is available via the phone or online. *Website:* http://www.cdc.gov *E-mail:* inquiry@cdc.gov

DES Action USA 1-800-337-9288 Information for women who were prescribed DES during pregnancy and their children. Referrals and education for the public and health workers. Quarterly newsletter.

FDA Office on Orphan Product Development 1-800-300-7469 Provides referrals for persons who need a rare orphan drug. *Website:* http://www.fda.gov/orphan

Health Information *(New Jersey)* 1-800-367-6543 (Mon.-Fri., 8:30am-6pm) Assistance by professionals who route callers to the appropriate department for information. Information on VA Hospitals, health certificates, shots required for overseas, senior services, public health issues, complaints about health care providers etc. Sponsored by Dept. of Health and Senior Services. *Website:* http://www.state.nj.us/health/commiss/contact.shtml

March of Dimes 1-888-663-4637 Dedicated to decreasing the incidence of birth defects, infant mortality, low birth weight and lack of prenatal care. Provides information, referrals and literature. *Website:* http://www.marchofdimes.com

Medicare + Choice Helpline Assistant *(BILINGUAL)* 1-800-633-4273 Provides information on Medicare, Medigap and health plan options. Publications, and audiotapes. Sponsored by federal government. *Website:* http://www.medicare.gov

Minority Health Resource Center 1-800-444-6472; TTD: 301-251-1432. (Mon.-Fri., 9am-5pm EST) Federally-funded library service that provides information and referral to sources on health problems for minorities. *Website:* http://www.omhrc.gov

National Center on Complementary and Alternative Medicine 1-888-644-6226; TTY: 1-866-464-3615 Provides information on clinical trials and current research projects conducted on alternative medicine. *Website:* http://nccam.nih.gov *E-mail:* info@nccam.nih.gov

National Health Information Center 1-800-336-4797 (Mon.-Fri., 9-5:30pm EST) Helps the public and health professionals locate health information through identification of health and information resources. Information and referral systems. Distributes publications and directories on good health and disease prevention topics. *Website:* http://www.healthfinder.gov *E-mail:* info@nhic.org

National Immunizations Information Hotline *(BILINGUAL)* 1-800-232-4636; TTY: 1-888-232-6348 Information on immunizations for infants and adults, referrals to health care professionals. *Website:* http://www.cdc.gov/nip *E-mail:* nipinfo@cdc.gov

National Institute for Occupational Safety and Health 1-800-356-4674 or 513-533-8326 Information on all aspects of occupational health and safety. *Website:* http://www.cdc.gov/niosh *E-mail:* eidtechinfo@cdc.gov (for publications)

National Library of Medicine 1-888-346-3656 Provides information and referrals to help callers research health questions. *Website:* http://www.nlm.nih.gov *E-mail:* custserv@nlm.nih.gov

National Reference Center for Bioethics Literature 1-800-633-3849 (Mon.-Fri., 9am-5pm) Provides information via e-mail, websites or mail on bioethical topics. Will do limited searches on special topics. *Website:* http://bioethic.georgetown.edu *Email:* bioethics@georgetown.edu

National Women's Health Information Center 1-800-994-9662; TTY: 1-888-220-5446 (English/Spanish) (Mon.-Fri., 9am-6pm EST) Provides information and referrals for all women's health questions and any questions on breast feeding. *Website:* http://www.womenshealth.gov

National Women's Health Resource Center 1-877-986-9472 Provides information on women's health issues. Dedicated to helping women make informed decisions about their health. *Website:* http://www.healthywomen.org *E-mail:* info@healthwomen.org

NJ Family Healthline 1-800-328-3838 (24 hr) Provides information and referral to programs on family planning, pre-natal care, child health, pediatric HIV infection and special child health care. Information on WIC program which provide nutritional assistance for qualified women with children up to age of 5 years. Sponsored by United Way.

NORD (National Organization for Rare Disorders) 1-800-999-6673; TDD: 203-797-9590 (Mon.-Fri., 9am-5pm) Information and networking for persons with rare disorders. Literature. *Website:* http://www.rarediseases.org *E-mail:* orphan@rarediseases.org

"Su Familia" Health Helpline *(BILINGUAL)* 1-866-783-2645 (9am-6pm EST) Provides confidential health information to Hispanic patients and their families. Provides bilingual fact sheets for a wide variety of health topics. Sponsored by the National Alliance for Hispanic Health. *Website:* http://www.hispanichealth.org *E-mail:* alliance@hispanichealth.org

To Your Health *(New Jersey)* 1-888-838-3180 Provides educational materials and information to residents of New Jersey within the managed care system. Helps the consumer understand their rights under commercial and government sponsored managed care programs. *Website:* http://www.chlp.org

UAB Eat Right 1-800-231-3438 (Mon.-Fri., 8am-4pm CST) Information on nutrition and related topics (weight loss and cholesterol). Sponsored by Nutrition Information Services

Visiting Nurse Association of America 1-888-866-8773 Referrals to local Visiting Nurse Associations. *Website:* www.vnaa.org *E-mail:* vnaa@vnaa.org

HEART

American Health Assistance Foundation 1-800-437-2423 (Mon.-Fri., 9am-5pm) Provides educational information and funds research for Alzheimer's disease, glaucoma, heart disease and macular degeneration. *Website:* http://www.ahaf.org

American Heart Association (BILINGUAL) 1-800-242-8721 (Mon.-Fri., 6am-midnight; Sat, 8am-10pm EST) Information on heart health and support groups. *Website:* http://www.americanheart.org

Arrhythmogenic Right Ventricular Dysplasia Registry 1-800-483-2662 Provides information on ARVD. A nurse coordinator will answer questions about ARVD and help with diagnosis. Raises funds for research. Offers referrals to doctors conducting studies. *Website:* http://www.arvd.org

Cardiac Arrhythmias Research and Education Foundation, Inc. 1-800-404-9500 or 425-788-1987 (Mon.-Fri., 9am-5pm) Support, education and registry for individuals and families affected by long QT syndrome and other genetic arrhythmias. Helps to create community forums for mutual support. *Website:* http://www.longqt.org *E-mail:* care@longqt.org

NIH National Heart, Lung and Blood Institute Helpline 1-800-575-9355 Provides recorded information on the prevention and treatment of high blood pressure and high cholesterol.

Texas Heart Institute Heart Information Service 1-800-292-2221 Answers questions on cardiovascular via phone, mail or e-mail. Literature on aneurisms, cholesterol, heart transplants, stroke patients, women and heart disease. Information on support groups. *Website:* http://www.texasheartinstitute.org *E-mail:* his@heart.thi.tmc.edu

HOMOSEXUALITY

Gay and Lesbian National Hotline 1-888-843-4564 (Mon.-Fri., 4pm-midnight; Sat., noon-5pm EST) Provides information and referrals for gays, lesbians, transgendered and persons with questions about their sexuality. Information, referrals and peer counseling. *Website:* http://www.glnh.org *E-mail:* info@glbtnationalhelpcenter.org

HOSPICE

Caring Connections 1-800-658-8898; Spanish 1-877-658-8896 (Mon.-Fri., 9am-5pm EST) Provides free resources and information to help people make decisions about end-of-life care and services before a crisis occurs. *Website:* http://www.caringinfo.org *Email:* caringinfo@nhpco.org

Children's Hospice International 1-800-242-4453 or 703-684-0330 (volunteer info) (Mon.-Fri., 9am-5pm EST) Refers patients to hospices and specialists in their areas. Bibliography, manuals. *Website:* http://www.chionline.org *E-mail:* info@chionline.com

Hospice Education Institute 1-800-331-1620 Provides information and referrals regarding hospice care. *Website:* http://www.hospiceworld.org *E-mail:* hospiceall@aol.com

Hospice Foundation of America 1-800-854-3402 Provides education and information on hospice care. Sponsors research. Offers teleconference series "Living with Grief" for bereaved families. Audiotapes for clergy. Fax: 202-638-5312. *Website:* http://www.hospicefoundation.org *E-mail:* hfaoffice@hospicefoundation.org

National Hospice and Pallative Care Organization *(BILINGUAL)* 1-800-658-8898 (Mon.-Fri., 9am-5pm EST) Information for hospice care for terminally ill persons. Referrals to hospice programs nationwide. *Website:* http://www.nhpco.org *E-mail:* caringino@nhpco.org

HOSPITAL

Hill Burton Hotline 1-800-638-0742 or 301-443-5656 (Mon.-Fri., 9am-5pm) Information about free hospital care for eligible persons (low income). Directories of medical centers that are part of Hill Burton program throughout US. *Website:* http://www.hrsa.gov/hillburton.com *E-mail:* dfcrcomm@hrsa.gov

National Association of Hospital Hospitality Houses 1-800-542-9730 Makes referrals to hospital hospitality housing that provide lodging for families of hospital patients and/or hospital outpatients. *Website:* http://www.nahhh.org

Shriner's Hospital 1-800-237-5055 or 813-281-0300 (Mon.-Fri., 8am-5pm) Information on free hospital care available to children under the age of 18 needing treatment for burns, spinal cord injury, cleft palate or orthopedic care. *Website:* http://www.shrinershq.org

HOUSING

Community Connections 1-800-998-9999; TDD: 1-800-483-2209 Provides information about housing and community development, homeless prevention, first-time home buyer programs, veterans, low income housing and HUD. *Website:* http://www.comcon.org

Housing and Mortgage Finance Agency *(New Jersey)* 1-800-654-6873 (Mon.-Fri., 8am-5pm) Information on mortgages available to first time home buyers and buyers in targeted areas. Offers low down payment and low interest rate mortgages. *Website:* http://www.nj-hmfa.com

National Accessible Apartment Clearinghouse 1-800-421-1221 Maintains a database of over 46,000 accessible apartments nationwide. Helps people with disabilities find accessible apartments. Owners and managers may also use this service to register their accessible units. *Website:* http://www.accessibleapartments.org

NJ Housing Resource Center *(New Jersey)* 609-278-7411 Information on finding and listing affordable housing. Helps people with disabilities find housing options. *Website:* http://www.njhousing.gov/ *E-mail:* mgumpert@njhmfa.state.nj.us

IMMIGRANT

Immigration and Naturalization Services 1-800-375-5283; TTY: 1-800-767-1833 (Mon.-Fri., 8-10am and 4pm-6pm) Comprehensive information for immigrants including naturalization processes, adjustment of status for permanent residency and travel documents. Also has information on international services and border patrols. *Website:* http://www.uscis.gov/graphics/index.htm

IMMUNE DEFICIENCY

Jeffrey Modell Foundation 1-866-463-6474 (24 hr) Provides information on specific primary immune deficiency diseases. Referrals to major medical centers, psychiatric and social support services. Information on insurance reimbursement.

IMPOTENCE

Impotence Information Center 1-800-843-4315 Provides free information about the causes and treatments of impotence. This includes brochures and a list of local physicians. *Website:* http://www.americanmedicalsystems.com

"The greatest good you can do for another is not just share your riches, but reveal to them their own." -- Disraeli

INCONTINENCE

Incontinence Information Center 1-800-843-4315 Provides free information about the causes and treatments of incontinence. This information consists of brochures and a list of physicians who treat incontinence within the caller's geographic area. *Website:* http://www.americanmedicalsystems.com

National Association for Continence *(BILINGUAL)* 1-800-252-3337 (Mon.-Fri., 8am-5pm EST) Clearinghouse of information on incontinence. Physician locater service. *Website:* http://www.nafc.org *E-mail:* memberservices@nafc.org

INSURANCE

Hurricane Insurance Information Center 1-800-942-4242 (24 hr) Provides general information on hurricane insurance. *Website:* http://www.iii.org

Insurance Information Institute 1-800-331-9146 Provides information on home and auto insurance. Also provides hints and literature on preventing theft and accidents. Information on organizations which have information on health and life insurance. *Website:* http://www.iii.org

New Jersey Family Care Hotline *(MULTILINGUAL) (New Jersey)* 1-800-701-0710; TTY: 1-800-701-0720 (Mon. and Thurs. 8am-8pm; Tues., Wed., Fri. 8am-5pm) Provides information on health insurance to uninsured children and teens up to age 18. *Website:* www.njfamilycare.org

KIDNEY DISEASE

American Kidney Fund *(BILINGUAL)* 1-800-638-8299 (Mon.-Fri., 9am-5pm EST) Provides information, referrals and financial assistance to kidney patients. Counselors available to answer questions about kidney disease and transplants. *Website:* http://www.kidneyfund.org

Kidney and Urology Foundation of America *(BILINGUAL)* 1-800-633-6628 Dedicated to helping persons afflicted with any debilitating kidney, urologic or related diseases. Offers education, information, health fairs, grants, patient scholarships, physician referrals, fellowship and Pediatric Enrichment program. *Website:* http://www.kidneyurology.org *E-mail:* info@kidneyurology.org

National Institute of Diabetes and Digestive and Kidney Diseases 1-800-891-5390 (kidney); 1-800-860-8747 (diabetes); 1-800-891-5389 (digestive diseases) Provides referrals and literature on a broad range of subjects concerning diabetes, digestive disorders, hematologic diseases, kidney disease, urologic disorders, metabolic and endocrine disorders. *Website:* http://www.niddk.nih.gov/

National Kidney Foundation *(BILINGUAL)* 1-800-622-9010 (Mon.-Fri., 8:30am-5:30pm EST) Provides education and research information on kidney disease. Referrals to local affiliates. Fax: 212-689-9261. *Website:* http://www.kidney.org

LEGISLATIVE

League of Women Voters *(New Jersey)* 1-800-792-8683 (Mon.-Fri., 9am-4:30pm) Provides information regarding voting, New Jersey government and election information. Membership $50/yr. *Website:* www.lwvnj.org

Legislative Information and Bill Room *(New Jersey)* 1-800-792-8630; TDD: 1-800-257-7490 (Mon.-Fri., 8:30am-5pm) Information on the status of bills, calendar and roster. Referrals. Sponsored by NJ Office of Legislative Services. *Website:* http://www.njleg.state.nj.us *E-mail:* leginfo@njleg.org (legislative matters only).

Project Vote Smart 1-888-868-3762 Non-partisan information about all elected officials and candidates for federal, state and local gubernatorial offices. *Website:* http://www.vote-smart.org

U.S. Government Federal Information Center *(BILINGUAL)* 1-800-688-9889 (voice) (Mon.-Fri., 8am-8pm EST); TTY: 1-800-326-2996 Information about federal government programs and agencies including patents, taxes, jobs, social security, passports, visas, dept. of states, veteran affairs, rules and regulations. *Website:* http://www.firstgov.gov

LEPROSY

American Leprosy Missions 1-800-543-3135 (Mon.-Fri., 8am-5pm EST) Provides information on projects and programs that fight leprosy in 23 countries. *Website:* http://www.leprosy.org *E-mail:* amlep@leprosy.org

LIFE-THREATENING ILLNESS

Caring Connections 1-800-658-8898 (Mon-Fri., 9am-5pm) Provides information and education concerning end-of-life issues. Includes caregiver questions. *Website:* http://www.caringinfo.org *E-mail:* consumers@nhpco.org

Catastrophic Illness in Children Relief Fund *(New Jersey)* 1-800-335-3863 Provides financial assistance to families of children 21 and under who have experienced an illness or condition which is not covered by insurance or any State or Federal program. For medical bills which exceed 10% over the family income.

Friends of Karen *(NJ/ NY/ CT)* 1-800-637-2774 (Mon.-Fri, 9am-5pm) Dedicated to helping families with children affected by life-threatening illnesses. Provides emotional and financial assistance in the NY metropolitan area. Information packets available. *Website:* http://www.friendsofkaren.org

Medical Escrow Society 1-800-422-1314 (24 hr) Provides information on obtaining advance cash from life insurance policies for persons with a life threatening illness or who are over age 65. *Website:* http://www.lifeassets.net

LITERACY

Literacy Volunteers of New Jersey, Inc. *(New Jersey)* 1-800-848-0048 (Mon.-Fri., 9am-4pm) Refers callers who read below 5th grade level and persons for whom English is a second language to LVA programs statewide. Also has information on other adult education programs. Refers potential volunteers to LVA training programs.

National Literacy Hotline 1-800-228-8813 (24 hr) or 202-233-2025 (Mon.-Fri., 9am-5pm) Information and referrals to local literacy programs. Referrals for both volunteers and people needing literacy services. *Website:* http://www.nifl.gov

LUNG DISEASE

Allergy and Asthma Network - Mothers of Asthmatics *(BILINGUAL)* 1-800-878-4403 Provides emotional support and patient education resources for persons with asthma and allergies. Newsletter. *Website:* http://www.aanma.org *E-mail:* info@aanma.org

National Jewish Lung Line 1-800-222-5864 (Mon.-Fri., 10am-6:30pm) Information and referrals. Registered nurses answer questions on all types of lung diseases. Referrals to doctors and free literature. *Website:* http://www.njc.org *E-mail:* lungline@njc.org

Office on Smoking and Health 1-800-232-4636 (Mon.-Fri., 8am-4pm EST) Provides information on the affects of tobacco on health, how to stop smoking, second hand smoke, and other current topics relating to tobacco. Sponsored by Federal Government. *Website:* http://www.cdc.gov/tobacco *E-mail:* tobaccoinfo@cdc.gov

LYME DISEASE

Lyme Disease *(New Jersey)* 1-800-792-8831 (Mon.-Fri., 8am-5pm) Provides NJ residents with information about Lyme disease. Sponsored by the NJ Dept. of Health. *Website:* http://www.state.nj.us/health/ed/f_lyme.htm

National Lyme Disease Foundation 1-800-886-5963 Provides information and referrals for Lyme disease. Education, literature and advocacy. Need touch-tone phone.

MARRIAGE

Retrouvaille 1-800-470-2230 For couples who have a seriously troubled marriage. Retrouvaille (pronounced "retro-vay", is the French word for "rediscovery"). Couples spend one weekend together working to save their relationship. Program is volunteer-run by couples whose marriages were saved by their having participated in a Retrouvaille weekend. The program may have a Catholic priest involved as a resource person for some sessions, it is open to couples of any and no faith. The weekend experience is followed by several weekly support group meetings. Check website for more information, availability and local phone contacts. Those without Internet access, call toll-free number, leave message with your town and state (return call may take several days). *Website:* http://www.retrouvaille.org

MARROW TRANSPLANTS

Caitlin Raymond International Bone Marrow Registry 1-800-726-2824 Comprehensive international resource for patients and physicians conducting a search for unrelated bone marrow or cord blood donor. *Website:* http://www.crir.org *E-mail:* info@CRIR.org

National BMT LINK 1-800-546-5268 Provides information and referral for bone marrow and stem cell transplants for patients, family and professionals. Referrals to support groups. Peer-support, online phone support groups, information on becoming a donor and educational booklets. *Website:* http://www.nbmtlink.org

National Marrow Donor Program 1-800-627-7692, 1-800-654-1247 or 1-800-526-7809 (Mon.-Fri., 8am-5pm CST) Provides information on bone marrow and stem cell transplants and information on becoming a marrow donor. Maintains computerized data bank of available tissue-typed marrow donors nationwide. Provides patient advocacy to assist patients through the donor search and transplant process. *Website:* http://www.marrow.org

MENINGITIS

Meningitis Foundation 1-800-668-1129 (Mon.-Fri., 8am-5pm) Support for persons with spinal meningitis and their families. Provides information, education, supports research and live chat rooms. *Website:* http://www.musa.org *E-mail:* jcallahan@musa.org or support@musa.org

MENTAL HEALTH

Compeer 1-800-836-0475 Provides volunteer "friends" for children and adults who receive mental health treatment. Fax: 585-325-2558 *Website:* http://www.compeer.org *E-mail:* cmpeerp@rochester.rr.com

Family Support Resources *(New Jersey)* 1-866-626-4437 (24 hr) Automated information line provides local NJ contacts for Intensive Family Support Services and National Alliance on Mental Illness groups. Sponsored by NAMI-NJ.

Girl's and Boy's Town National Hotline *(BILINGUAL)* 1-800-448-3000; TDD: 1-800-448-1833 (24 hr) Provides crisis intervention, information and referrals for general population. Free and confidential. Short-term crisis intervention. Works with children and families. *Website:* http://www.girlsandboystown.org

National Alliance for Research on Schizophrenia and Depression 1-800-829-8289 Provides information on schizophrenia, depression and bipolar disorder. Has information on research being conducted on these disorders. Newsletter, literature and brochures. *Website:* http://www.narsad.org

National Institute of Mental Health Information Center 1-866-615-6464 Provides information and literature on anxiety, phobias, obsessive-compulsive and depression. Leave name and mailing address and they will mail literature to you. *Website:* http://www.nimh.nih.gov

National Mental Health Association 1-800-969-6642 (Mon.-Fri., 9am-5pm); TDD: 1-800-433-5959 Provides free information on over 200 mental health topics including bipolar disorder, depression, bereavement, post-traumatic stress disorder and warning signs of mental illness. Referrals to local mental health services. Distributes free national directory of local mental health associations and offers low-cost materials. Advocates to remove stigma of mental illness and for mental health benefits parity. *Website:* http://www.nmha.org *E-mail:* infoctr@nmha.org

National Mental Health Services Information Center *(BILINGUAL)* 1-800-789-2647 Refers callers to mental health organizations nationwide. *Website:* http://www.mentalhealth.samhsa.gov *E-mail:* nmhic-info@samhsa.hhs.gov

NJ Mental Health Cares Helpline 1-866-202-4357; TTY 1-877-294-4356 (Mon.-Fri., 8am-8pm) Provides information and referral to all public mental health services in New Jersey. Answers questions regarding mental health and illness. Staffed by mental health professionals.

NJ Psychological Association 1-800-281-6572 or 973-243-9800 (Mon.-Fri., 8:30am-4:30pm) Provides referrals to psychologists in your area by specialty and language. *Website:* http://www.psychologynj.org *E-mail:* NJPA@psychologynj.org

State Division of Mental Health Helpline *(New Jersey)* 1-800-382-6717 (Mon.-Fri., 8:30am-5pm) Provides information on state mental health services and takes complaints about them. *Website:* http://www.state.nj.us/humanservices/dmhs *E-mail:* dmhsmail@dhs.state.nj.us

Summit Hospital *(New Jersey)* 1-800-753-5223 or 908-522-7000 (24 hr) Information for drug or psychiatric problems. Referrals to community mental health centers. Sponsored by Summit Oaks Hospital.

TARA 1-888-482-7227 or 212-966-6514 Education and advocacy organization. Provides information on borderline personality to families, consumers, and providers. Referrals to clinicians, treatment programs, self-help groups, BPD Journal, speakers' bureau, professional conferences and advocacy. *Website:* http://www.tara4bpd.org *E-mail:* taraapd@aol.com

Value Options *(New Jersey)* 1-877-652-7624; TTD: 866-896-6975 (24 hr) Provides comprehensive information on all emotional, behavioral and mental health services for children up to the age of 18 and their families.

MENTAL RETARDATION

American Association on Mental Retardation 1-800-424-3688 (Mon-Fri, 9am-5pm EST) General information on mental retardation. *Website:* http://www.aamr.org *E-mail:* anam@aamr.org

Clearinghouse on Aging and Developmental Disabilities 1-800-996-8845; TTY: 312-413-0453 Aim is to promote independence, productivity, inclusion and self-determination of older adults with mental retardation. Provides training, technical assistance and materials to patients, families and professionals.

METABOLIC DISORDER

National Institute of Diabetes and Digestive and Kidney Diseases 1-800-891-5390 (kidney); 1-800-860-8747 (diabetes); 1-800-891-5389 (digestive diseases) Provides referrals and literature on a broad range of subjects concerning diabetes, digestive disorders, kidney disease, hematologic diseases, urologic disorders, metabolic and endocrine disorders. *Website:* http://www.niddk.nih.gov *E-mail:* nkudic@info.niddk.nih.gov

NIH Osteoporosis and Related Bone Diseases Resource Center *(MULTILINGUAL)* 1-800-624-2663 or 202-223-0344; TDD: 202-466-4315 Provides written information to patients, professionals and the public. Resources and information on metabolic bone diseases such as osteoporosis, Paget's disease, osteogenesis imperfecta and primary hyperparathyroidism. Annotated bibliography on current research to professionals. *Website:* http://www.osteo.org *E-mail:* niamsboneinfo@mail.nih.gov

World Life Foundation 1-800-289-5433 Provides support, research, information and referrals for persons interested in rare metabolic disorders. Provides air transportation for ambulatory patients who need non-emergency treatment.

MILITARY / VETERANS

Army Community Service/Family Support *(New Jersey)* 1-800-877-2380 Military affiliated only. Family advocacy, parent education, employment readiness, relocation assistance, support groups and a wide variety of resources.

Community Recovery *(New Jersey)* 1-800-292-8262 Offers services for veterans who are experiencing problems with drugs or alcohol. The program offers a wide variety of services throughout the state.

Department of Veterans Affairs 1-800-827-1000 (Mon.-Fri., 8am-4pm) Provides comprehensive information on available programs and services for veterans including pensions, vocational rehab, survivor's benefits, presidential memorial certificates, education programs and home loan programs for dependents. Special programs for disabled, homeless, minority and women veterans. *Website:* http://www.va.gov/ or http://www.va.gov/womenvet

Disabled American Veterans 1-877-426-2838 Provides free, professional assistance to veterans and their families in obtaining benefits and services earned through military service and provided by the department of Veteran Affairs and other agencies of the government. Guidelines for developing chapters. *Website:* http://www.dav.org *E-mail:* feedback@davmail.org

Disabled Veterans Assistance Line 1-800-378-4559 (24 hr) Provides assistance and referrals for returning disabled service members, recently medically retired service members and spouses of disabled service members. Supports veterans of Operation Iraqi Freedom, Operation Enduring Freedom, as well as all disabled veterans of other conflicts and campaigns or wars.

National Veterans Service Fund, Inc. 1-800-521-0198 (9am-4pm, Mon.-Fri. EST) Provides social services for Vietnam and Persian Gulf War veterans, and their families. Focus is on those with disabled children. Publications. Also offers online bulletin board. *Website:* http://www.vvnw.org

Paralyzed Vets of America 1-800-424-8200; TTY/TTD: 202-872-1300 (Mon.-Fri., 8:30am-5pm EST) Information, referral and advocacy for disabilities and paralyzed vets. *Website:* http://www.pva.org

VA Special Issues Helpline 1-800-749-8387 Refers Gulf war veterans and veterans affected by agent orange with medical problems to local Gulf war and Agent Orange coordinators at local VA medical centers. Other special issues addressed.

Veterans Counseling Hotline *(New Jersey)* 1-866-838-7654 (24 hr) Provides peer support, clinical assessment and case management, family resources, and referral to a comprehensive mental health network of providers if necessary. Developed by the NJ Department of Military and Veterans Affairs.

Veterans of the Vietnam War, Inc. 1-800-843-8626 (Mon.-Fri., 8am-4pm) Membership organization open to all veterans and their supporters. Educates public about post-traumatic stress disorder, veteran health issues, Agent Orange and POW/MIA issues. Maintains a Find-a-Vet locator service, publishes newsletter, works with homeless veterans and incarcerated vets. *Website:* http://www.vvnw.org *E-mail:* vvnwnatl@epix.net

MISSING CHILDREN/ADULTS

Child Find of America Hotline 1-800-426-5678 (Mon.-Fri., 9am-5pm EST) Helps parents to locate children. Helps lost children who need assistance. Also offers support services. All services are free. *Website:* http://www.childfindofamerica.org *E-mail:* information@childfindofamerica.org

National Center for Missing Adults (NCMA) 1-800-690-3463 Operates as the national clearinghouse for missing adults, providing services and coordination between various government agencies, law enforcement, media and most importantly the families of missing adults. *Website:* http://www.missingadults.org

National Center for Missing and Exploited Children 1-800-843-5678 (24 hr) Information regarding missing and exploited youth. Helps parents locate missing children. *Website:* http://www.missingkids.com

Vanished Children Alliance 1-800-826-4743 (24 hr) Provides emotional support and technical assistance to families of missing children. Case management, search assistance, family reunification program, information and referral. *Website:* http://www.vca.org *E-mail:* info@vca.org

MULTIPLE SCLEROSIS

Multiple Sclerosis Foundation 1-800-441-7055 or 1-888-673-6287 (Mon.-Fri., 9am-7pm EST) Support services for those diagnosed with multiple sclerosis. Grants for research, information and referrals on traditional and alternative treatments. Online doctors forum, newsletter and phone support. *Website:* http://www.msfocus.org *Email:* support@msfocus.org

MUSCULAR DYSTROPHY

Muscular Dystrophy Family Foundation, Inc. 1-800-544-1213 (Mon.- Fri., 8:30am-3:30pm) Provides services, resources, home medical equipment and adaptive devices to help people with muscular dystrophy and their families. Provides comprehensive direct services. *Website:* http://www.mdff.org *Email:*mdff@mdff.org

NEPHROGENIC DIABETES INSIPIDUS

Nephrogenic Diabetes Insipidus Foundation 1-888-376-6343 Provides information and support to persons affected by nephrogenic diabetes insipidus. *Website:* http://www.ndif.org *E-mail:* info@ndif.org

NEUROLOGICAL IMPAIRMENT

National Institute of Neurological Disorders 1-800-352-9424 (Mon.-Fri., 8:30am-5pm) Provides information on neurological disorders and stroke. Sponsored by N IH. *Website:* http://www.ninds.nih.gov

NICOTINE

NJ Quitline 1-866-657-8677; TDD: 1-866-257-2971 (Mon.-Fri. 8am-8pm; Sat., 11am-5pm) Information and counseling for anyone who has a nicotine addiction. Serves all of New Jersey. Sponsored by NJ State 1998 Master Settlement. *Website:* http://www.nj.quitline.com

Office on Smoking and Health 1-800-232-4636 or Info specialists 770-488-5705 (Mon.-Fri., 8am-4pm EST) Provides information on the affects of tobacco on health, how to stop smoking, second hand smoke, and other current topics relating to tobacco. Sponsored by Federal Government. *Website:* http://www.cdc.gov/tobacco *E-mail:* tobaccoinfo@cdc.gov

ORGAN DONATION

Children's Organ Transplant Association 1-800-366-2682 (Mon.-Fri., 8am-5pm EST) Non-profit organization that provides public education on organ transplants. Assists families in fund-raising for transplant and transplant-related expenses. Assistance for all children and adults with cystic fibrosis who are U.S. citizens in need of an organ transplant. *Website:* http://www.cota.org *E-mail:* cota@cota.org

Living Bank - National Organ and Transplant Registry, The *(BILINGUAL)* 1-800-528-2971 Provides donor cards, educational materials and referrals to medical schools for persons wishing to donate their bodies after death. *Website:* http://www.livingbank.org *E-mail:* info@livingbank.org

National Foundation for Transplants 1-800-489-3863 or 901-684-1697 (Mon.-Fri., 8:30am-4:30pm CST) Provides support services, financial assistance and advocacy to adult and child organ and bone marrow transplant candidates and recipients. Assists in fund-raising activities. *Website:* http://www.transplants.org *E-mail:* jhill@transplants.org

National Minority Organ Tissue Transplant Education Program 1-800-393-2839 Provides educational information on preventative measures and organ transplants. Referrals to physicians. *Website:* http://www.nationalmottep.org

New Jersey Organ and Tissue Sharing Network 1-800-742-7365, 1-800-541-0075 (24 hr donor referral line) or 973-379-4535 (Mon.-Fri., 8:30am-5pm) Federally designated, state-certified procurement organization responsible for recovering organs and tissues for NJ residents in need of transplants. Issues donors cards. *Website:* http://www.sharenj.org *E-mail:* tsn@sharenj.org

OSTEOPOROSIS

NIH Osteoporosis and Related Bone Diseases Resource Center *(MULTILINGUAL)* 1-800-624-2663 or 202-223-0344; TDD: 202-466-4315 Provides written information to patients, professionals and the public with resources and information on metabolic bone diseases such as osteoporosis, Paget's disease, osteogenesis imperfecta, and primary hyperparathyroidism. Annotated bibliography on current research to professionals. *Website:* http://www.osteo.org *E-mail:* niamsboneinfo@mail.nih.gov

Osteoporosis Helpline 1-888-934-2663 (Mon.-Fri., 9am-5pm EST) Provides general information and fact sheets on the symptoms, causes and treatment of osteoporosis. Offers referrals to osteoporosis specialists. *E-mail:* toneyourbones@uab.edu

"True charity is the desire to be useful to others with no thought of recompense."
-- Emanuel Swedenborg

PAGET'S

NIH Osteoporosis and Related Bone Diseases Resource Center *(MULTILINGUAL)* 1-800-624-2663; TDD: 202-466-4315 Provides written information to patients, professionals and the public with resources and information on metabolic bone diseases such as osteoporosis, Paget's disease, osteogenesis imperfecta and primary hyperparathyroidism. Annotated bibliography on current research to professionals. *Website:* http://www.osteo.org *E-mail:* niamsboneinfo@mail.nih.gov

Paget's Foundation 1-800-237-2438 (Mon.-Fri., 9am-5pm) Information, brochures, patient's guide, doctor referrals, professional packets and newsletter on Paget's disease of the bone, as well as primary hyperparathyroidism. *Website:* http://www.paget.org *E-mail:* pagetfdn@aol.com

PARKINSON'S

National Parkinson's Foundation 1-800-327-4545 (Mon.-Fri., 8:30am-5pm) Professional will answer any question on Parkinson's disease. *Website:* http://www.parkinson.org *E-mail:* mailbox@parkinson.org

Parkinson's Disease Foundation, Inc. 1-800-457-6676 *International. Founded 1957.* A leading national presence in Parkinson's disease research, education and public advocacy. Provides educational materials and support service through toll-free helpline, web service and print/video materials. *Website:* http://www.pdf.org *E-mail:* info@pdf.org

PARENTING

Healthy Families *(New Jersey)* 1-800-244-5373 For any new parent who feels alone, frightened or overwhelmed. Offers support, education, links to health care and assistance in helping to meet the family needs. Stays with person as child grows. Services are free and will work with person to be the best parent they can be.

Kinship Navigator Program *(BILINGUAL)* *(New Jersey)* 1-877-816-3211 Information and referrals for a wide range of services designed for caregivers of sisters, brothers or grandchildren. Support group referrals, child care resources, respite, educational issues, custody, medical resources and other legal issues.

PEDICULOSIS ASSOCIATION

National Pediculosis Association 1-800-446-4672 Provides information and materials concerning head lice. Books, videos and literature. *Website:* http://www.headlice.org *Email:* npa@headlice.org

PESTICIDE

National Pesticide Information Center 1-800-858-7378 (6:30am-4:30pm PST) Information on most aspects of pesticides. (No information related to antimicrobials ie. water purifiers and disinfectants. Brochures available by calling or going to website. Sponsored by EPA. *Website:* http://npic.orst.edu *E-mail:* npic@ace.orst.edu

PET LOSS SUPPORT

PetFriends *(New Jersey)* 1-800-404-7387 (24 hr) Compassionate phone support, information and referrals to people who have lost, or anticipate losing, a pet through death or other separation.

Pet Loss Support Hotline 1-800-565-1526 Offers a non-judgmental outlet for people to express their feelings and concerns when faced with difficult times regarding their pets. Staffed by veterinary students with grief training.

POISON HELPLINE

New Jersey Poison Control Centers 1-800-222-1222 (24 hr) Emergency helpline that provides information on medication errors, drug overdoses, food poisoning, food safety, etc.

POLICE OFFICERS HELPLINE

Cop-to-Cop *(New Jersey)* 1-866-267-2267 (24 hr) Serves active and retired policemen and their families. Retired officers and mental health professionals offer callers support. Provides support and referrals for counseling, mental health, substance abuse, partial care and inpatient treatment.

"There is no greater loan than a sympathetic ear." -- Frank Tyger

PREGNANCY / CHILDBIRTH HELPLINE

Antiepileptic Drug Pregnancy Registry *(MULTILINGUAL)* 1-888-233-2334 (8:30am-5:00pm EST) Registry of women who are taking antiepileptic drugs and who are pregnant. Helps to determine which medications are associated with increased risks. Physicians are encouraged to refer women. *Website:* www.aedpregnancyregistry.org

Family Helpline, The *(MULTILINGUAL) (New Jersey)* 1-800-843-5437 (24 hr) Confidential and untraceable help for teens to talk about all the options available. Refers caller to a local confidential assistance. *Website:* www.pa-of-nj.org

National Abortion Federation 1-800-772-9100 (Mon.-Fri., 8am-9pm; Sat.-Sun., 9am-5pm) Information and referrals regarding abortions. Financial aid. *Website:* http://www.prochoice.org

National Hispanic PreNatal Helpline *(BILINGUAL)* 1-866-783-2645 (9am-6pm) Provides health information on pregnancy, referral to healthcare centers and doctors. Sponsored by the National Alliance for Hispanic Health. *Website:* http://www.hispanichealth.org *E-mail:* alliance@hispanichealth.org

National Life Center, Inc. 1-800-848-5683 Provides counseling and information for pregnant women. Referrals to testing sites, baby clothes and formula. *Website:* http://www.nationallifecenter.com *E-mail:* nlc1stway@snip.net

New Jersey Safe Haven Infant Protection Act *(New Jersey)* 1-877-839-2339 Offers a safe haven for a person voluntarily relinguishing their infant under 30 days old. Completely confidential. Also answers questions from the public and offers support to those considering giving up or the abandonment of their infant.

OTIS (Organization of Teratology Information Services) *(MULTILINGUAL)* 1-866-626-6847 (Mon.-Fri., 8:30am-4pm PST) Provides local referrals to agencies that provide information concerning prenatal drug, medication, chemical, and other potentially harmful exposures. *Website:* http://www.otispregnancy.org/ *E-mail:* OTISPregnancy@pharmacy.arizona.edu

Planned Parenthood 1-800-230-7526 *(BILINGUAL)* (Mon.-Fri., 8:30am-5pm) Referrals to neighborhood planned parenthood clinics nationwide. *Website:* http://www.plannedparenthood.org/

Pregnancy Hotline *(New Jersey)* 1-800-848-5683 (24 hr) Free, confidential information for pregnant women regarding pregnancy testing, adoption information, legal assistance, baby clothes, formula, adoption referrals, shelters for women and girls. *Website:* http://www.nationallifecenter.com *E-mail:* nlc1stway@snip.net

Pregnancy Hotline 1-800-238-4269 (24 hr) Information and counseling to pregnant women. Referrals to free pregnancy test facilities, foster and adoption centers. Sponsored by Bethany Christian Services. *Website:* http://www.bethany.org

Safe Place for Newborns/Newborn Lifeline Network 1-877-440-2229 (24 hr) Provides referrals to locations where mothers can safely/anonymously take their babies to be placed for adoption. *Website:* http://www.safeplacefornewsborns.com *Email:* safeplace@safeplacefornewborns.com

PRESCRIPTION, LOW COST HELPLINE

PAAD (Pharmaceutical Assistance) *(New Jersey)* 1-800-792-9745 (8am-5pm) Financial assistance to the aged (65 or older) or disabled to help pay for medications. Hearing aid assistance also offered. Sponsored by NJ State Pharmaceutical Assistance Program.

Pharmaceutical Patient Assistance Directory Line 1-800-762-4636 Mails a directory of various pharmaceutial assistance programs for persons who cannot afford prescriptions on their own. Leave name and address on answering machine. *Website:* http://www.phrma.org

Rx4NJ (A Partnership for Prescription Assistance) *(New Jersey)* 1-888-793-6765 Information on specific types of discounted or free prescription medications. A no-cost service of NJ pharmaceutical companies. Call or visit their website to answer questions. *Website:* http://www.rx4nj.org

Senior Gold Prescription Discount Program *(New Jersey)* 1-800-792-9745 (Mon.-Fri., 8:30am-5pm) Pharmaceutical assistance to residents of NJ, (age 65+) years old, or who are 18 and older and receive social security disability and meet the income eligibility guidelines.

PROSTATE HELPLINE

Prostatitis Foundation 1-888-891-4200 Provides support and education to men with prostatitis. Encourages research funding. Information and referrals. Newsletter $1. *Website:* http://www.prostatitis.org

EX-PROSTITUTE HELPLINE

HIPS Hotline 1-800-676-4477 Provides crisis peer counseling and support for persons involved in, or affected by, the sex industry. Counseling and information provided for sex workers and their families in a non-judgmental, supportive atmosphere. *Website:* http://www.hips.org

PSYCHIATRIST/PSYCHOLOGIST HELPLINE

New Jersey Psychiatric Association 1-800-345-0143 (Mon.-Thurs., 9am-1pm) Provides referrals to psychiatrists. Lists by language, geographical areas and problems. Information packets available. *Website:* http://www.psychnj.org *E-mail:* psychnjoptonline.net

NJ Psychological Association 1-800-281-6572 (Mon.-Fri., 8:30am-4:30pm) Provides referrals to psychologists in your area by specialty and language. *Website:* http://www.psychologynj.org *E-mail:* NJPA@psychologynj.org

Therapist Network *(New Jersey)* 1-800-843-7274 Makes referrals to local mental health associations, mental health professionals and other resources.

RADIATION HELPLINE

CDC Emergency Preparedness and Response Helpline 1-800-232-4636; TTY: 1-888-232-6348 Provides information on emergency preparedness and response including bioterrorism, chemical emergencies, radiation emergencies, mass casualties, natural disasters, severe weather, recent outbreaks and incidence. *Website:* http://bt.cdc.gov/disasters/

National Association of Radiation Survivors 1-800-798-5102 Provides general information for persons exposed to ionizing radiation from the development, production, testing, use or storage of nuclear weapons and nuclear waste. Advocacy, research and public education. *Website:* http://www.radiationsurvivors.org/ *E-mail:* nars@radiationsurvivors.org

RAPE / INCEST / SEXUAL ABUSE HOTLINE

National Sexual Violence Resource Center 1-877-739-3895 Provides information and referrals relating to all aspects of sexual violence to persons and agencies. Resources includes statistics, research, legal, statutes, and prevention. Not for crisis situations.

New Jersey Coalition Against Sexual Assault 1-800-601-7200 (24 hr) Information and referral. Provides information on services for sexual assault victims and their families. Also crisis intervention and accompaniment services to hospital, police, court and short-term counseling. Calls are automatically routed to the caller's local county information services. *Website:* http://www.njcasa.org

RAINN (Rape, Abuse and Incest National Network) 1-800-656-4673 (24 hr) Provides support and confidential crisis counseling for victims of sexual assault. Callers are automatically routed to the crisis center nearest to them. *Website:* http://www.rainn.org *E-mail:* info@rainn.org

REHABILITATION HELPLINE

American Medical Rehabilitation Providers Association 1-800-368-3513 or 1-888-346-4624 Refers callers to rehabilitation hospitals or centers. *Website:* http://www.amrpa.org

Center for Rehab Technologies 1-800-726-9119 (voice/TTY) Provides information on products, technology, resources, and services for persons with disabilities. *Website:* http://www.assistivetech.net or http://techconnections.org/ *E-mail:* catea@coa.gatech.edu

National Rehabilitation Information Center 1-800-346-2742; TTY: 301-459-5984 (Mon.-Fri., 9am-5pm EST) Library and information center on disability and rehabilitation of all types. Sponsored by U.S. Dept of Education. *Website:* http://www.naric.com *E-mail:* naricinfo@heitechservices.com

REYE'S SYNDROME HELPLINE

National Reye's Syndrome 1-800-233-7393 (Mon.-Fri., 8am-5pm EST) Guidance to families affected by Reye's Syndrome. Helps increase public awareness. Fund-raising. *Website:* http://www.reyessyndrome.org *E-mail:* nrsf@reyessyndrome.org

ROSACEA HELPLINE

National Rosacea Society 1-888-662-5874 Information and educational materials on rosacea (a chronic, acne-like condition of the facial skin). *Website:* http://www.rosacea.org *E-mail:* rosacea@aol.com

RUNAWAY HOTLINE

National Runaway Switchboard 1-800-621-4000 (24 hr) Provides crisis intervention, information, and referrals for runaways regarding shelter, counseling, food pantries, and transportation. Suicide and crisis counseling. Greyhound bus tickets available for qualifying kids. Parents are welcome to call for assistance. *Website:* http://www.nrscrisisline.org *E-mail:* info@nrscrisisline.org

RURAL ISSUES HELPLINE

Rural Information Center 1-800-633-7701 Information on rural issues. Provides brief database searches for free. *Website:* http://www.nalusda.gov/ric *E-mail:* ric@nal.usda.gov

SCLERODERMA HELPLINE

Scleroderma Research Foundation 1-800-441-2873 Provides referrals to doctors and clinics nationwide that treat scleroderma. Conducts research into the cause and cure of scleroderma. *Website:* http://www.srfcure.org

SELF-ABUSE HOTLINE

SAFE (Self-Abuse Finally Ends) Alternative Info Line 1-800-366-8288 Provides recorded information on dealing with self-abuse and self-mutilation and treatment options. *Website:* http://www.selfinjury.com

SEPTEMBER 11TH HELPLINE

NJ Disaster Mental Health Helpline 1-877-294-4357 (Mon.-Fri., 8am-8pm) Offers assistance to those affected by 9/11 with counseling services. *Website:* http://www.njmentalhealthcares.org

SEXUALLY TRANSMITTED DISEASE HELPLINE

American Social Health Association 1-800-227-8922 (Mon-Fri., 9am-6pm EST) Provides information, materials and referrals concerning sexually transmitted infections. Specialists will answer questions via phone or email on transmission, risk reduction, prevention, testing and treatment. *Website:* http://www.ashastd.org or http://www.iwannaknow.org (for teens)

CDC National Prevention Information Network *(BILINGUAL)* 1-800-458-5231 (Mon.-Fri., 9am-8pm EST); TTY: 1-800-243-7012 Provides information on resources, educational materials, sexually transmitted diseases (including AIDS/HIV), tuberculosis and communities at risk via touch tone phone or online. Many different services, publications offered. *Website:* http://www.cdcnpin.org *E-mail:* info@cdcnpin.org

CDC National STD/AIDS Hotline *(BILINGUAL)* 1-800-232-4636 (24 hr); TTY: 1-888-232-6342 (24 hr) Education and research about AIDS, HIV and sexually transmitted diseases. *Website:* http://www.cdc.gov *E-mail:* cdcinfo@cdc.gov

SOCIAL SECURITY HELPLINE

National Organization of Social Security Claimant's Reps 1-800-431-2804 (voice mail) Provides referrals to social security lawyers who assist claimants in getting social security.

NJ WINS (Work Incentive Programs) 1-877-659-4672 or 1-888-322-1918 Enables social security administration beneficiaries with disabilities to make informed choices about work and assist them in exploring work incentives that are available. *Website:* http://www.njwins.org *E-mail:* njwins@cpof-nj.org

Social Security 1-800-772-1213 (Mon.-Fri., 7am-7pm); TTY: 1-800-325-0778 Provides information on all aspects of social security, supplemental security income and Medicare. Can speak with a person or use touch-tone phone to hear messages. *Website:* http://www.socialsecurity.gov

SPINAL CORD INJURY HELPLINE

Christopher and Dana Reeve Paralysis Resource Center 1-800-539-7309 Information and referrals. Publishes a free book "Paralysis Resource" for consumers. Book is available in English and Spanish. *Website:* http://www.paralysis.org *E-mail:* info@paralysis.org

Foundation for Spinal Cord Injury Prevention, Care and Cure 1-800-342-0330 Dedicated to the prevention, care and cure of spinal cord injuries through public awareness, education, and funding research. Free counseling for victims and their families. Networking of patients and families. *Website:* http://www.fscip.org/ *E-mail:* info@fscip.org

National Spinal Cord Injury Hotline *(BILINGUAL)* 1-800-962-9629 (Mon.-Fri., 9am-5pm EST) (24 hr for new injuries) Information, referral and peer support for spinal cord injured persons and their families. *Website:* http://www.spinalcord.org *E-mail:* info@spinalcord.org

Paralyzed Vets of America 1-800-424-8200 (Mon.-Fri., 8:30am-5pm EST) TTY/TTD: 202-872-1300 Information, referral and advocacy for paralyzed vets. *Website:* http://www.pva.org

STUTTERING HELPLINE

Stuttering Foundation of America 1-800-992-9392 or 1-800-967-7700 (24 hr) Information and referrals for stutterers and those who treat stutterers. Phone support and conferences. Maintains a nationwide referral list of speech pathologist that specialize in stuttering. *Website:* http://www.stutteringhelp.org *E-mail:*info@stutteringhelp.org

SUDDEN INFANT DEATH HELPLINE

American SIDS Institute 1-800-232-7437 (24 hr) Dedicated to the prevention of sudden infant death syndrome. Promotes infant health through research. Education and support for families. *Website:* http://www.sids.org *E-mail:* prevent@sids.org

First Candle/SIDS Alliance 1-800-221-7437 (24 hr) Information on medical research, referrals to local support groups, referrals to community services and education. *Website:* http://www.firstcandle.org *E-mail:* sidshq@charm.net

SUICIDE PREVENTION HELPLINE

Suicide Prevention Helpline *(BILINGUAL)* 1-800-784-2433 National suicide prevention line that routes callers to a local or regional suicide crisis hotline.

SURGERY HELPLINE

American Society of Plastic Surgeons 1-800-635-0635 Referrals to plastic surgeons. Information on particular plastic surgeons as to their particular qualifications. *Website:* http://www.plasticsurgery.org

Facial Plastic Surgery Information Service 1-800-332-3223 Makes referrals to board certified plastic surgeons. *Website:* http://www.plasticsurgery.org

TAX INFO HELPLINE

IRS Federal Tax Information 1-800-829-1040 (24 hr) Information regarding federal tax questions, problems and refund information (30 day waiting period for written requests.) *Website:* http://www.irs.gov

NJ Tax Talk 1-800-323-4400 Provides status of refunds and (at certain times of the year) Homestead Rebate applications. Order forms and publications or listen to recorded tax topics. To contact customer service call 609-292-6400 (Mon-Fri, 8:30am-4:30pm). *Website:* http://www.state.nj.us/treasury/taxation

TRANSPORTATION HELPLINE

ACCESS LINK *(New Jersey)* 1-800-955-2321; TTY: 1-800-955-6765 Provides people with disabilities paratransit service comparable to the local bus service. Specifically for people whose disability prevents them from using existing local bus service.

Air Ambulance Central 1-800-843-8418 Will fly patients from anywhere for needed medical services. *E-mail:* airmedusa@aol.com

American Red Cross 1-800-733-2767 (Mon.-Fri., 8am-5pm EST) Provides disaster relief, emergency, health, safety and community services. *Website:* http://www.redcross.org

Angel Flight 1-877-247-5433 (24 hr) Provides referrals to 1,200 volunteer pilots who will fly needy patients for medical care. *Website:* http://www.angelflightne.org

Miracle Flights for Kids 1-800-359-1711 (Mon.-Thurs., 7:30am-6pm PST). Arranges airplane travel for children and adults with healthcare problems. Need doctors note and 16 days notice. *Website:* http://www.miracleflights.org

National Patient Travel Center 1-800-296-1217 (Mon.-Fri., 10:30am-12:30pm) Information and referral for persons who need cost effective transportation for specialized treatment after an illness or accident. *Website:* http://www.patienttravel.org

NJ Transit Accessible Services 1-800-772-2222; TTY: 1-800-772-2287 Provides accessible public transportation including rail, light rail and bus service in New Jersey and into parts of New York and Philadelphia. Services include accessible rail and light rail vehicles and stations, lift-equipped and kneeling buses. Also operates the ADA paratransit service, Access Link. Sponsored by NJ Transit. *Website:* http://www.njtransit.com

World Life Foundation 1-800-289-5433 Provides support, research, information and referrals for persons interested in rare metabolic disorders. Provides air transportation for ambulatory patients who need non-emergency treatment.

TRAUMA HELPLINE

American Red Cross 1-866-438-4636 (Mon.-Fri., 7am-11pm EST) Provides disaster relief, emergency, health, safety and community services. *Website:* http://www.redcross.org

American Trauma Society 1-800-556-7890 or 301-420-4189 (Mon.-Fri., 8:30am-4:30pm EST) Provides referrals and educational materials on the prevention of physical traumas. *Website:* http://www.amtrauma.org *E-mail:* info@amtrauma.org

CDC Emergency Preparedness and Response Helpline 1-800-232-4636; TTY: 1-888-232-6348 Provides information on emergency preparedness and response including bioterrorism, chemical emergencies, radiation emergencies, mass casualties, natural disasters and severe weather, recent outbreaks and incidence. *Website:* http://bt.cdc.gov/disasters/

Think First Foundation/National Injury Prevention 1-800-844-6556 (Mon.-Fri., 9am-5pm) Aims to prevent brain, spinal cord and other traumatic injuries through education and training. Information for children and teens. *Website:* http://www.thinkfirst.org *E-mail:* thinkfirst@thinkfirst.org

UROLOGIC DISEASE HELPLINE

American Urological Association Foundation 1-800-828-7866 or 1-866-746-4282 (Mon.-Fri., 8:30am-5pm) Educational information for patients and others interested about urological diseases. *Website:* http://www.auafoundation.org/

Kidney and Urology Foundation of America *(BILINGUAL)* 1-800-633-6628 Dedication to helping persons afflicted with any debilitating kidney, urologic or related diseases. Offers education, information, health fairs, grants, patient scholarships, physician referrals, fellowship and Pediatric Enrichment program. *Website:* http://www.kidneyurology.org *E-mail:* info@kidneyurology.org

National Institute of Diabetes and Digestive and Kidney Diseases 1-800-891-5390 (kidney); 1-800-860-8747 (diabetes); 1-800-891-5389 (digestive diseases) Provides referrals and literature on a broad range of subjects concerning diabetes, digestive disorders, kidney disease, hematologic diseases, urologic disorders, metabolic and endocrine disorders. *Website:* http://www.niddk.nih.gov *E-mail:* nkudic@info.niddk.nih.gov

VACCINATIONS

Alliance for Informed Choice on Vaccinations 1-800-613-9925 Addresses the concerns about the safety of vaccines and the right to informed consent. Literature, advocacy and phone help.

Centers for Disease Control and Prevention *(BILINGUAL)* 1-800-232-4636 Provides information on health related topics, vaccinations, traveler's health, grants, genetics, hoaxes, rumors and emergency responses. Information is available via the phone or online. *Website:* http://www.cdc.gov *E-mail:* inquiry@cdc.gov

VARICELLA ZOSTER VIRUS

VZV Info Line (Varicella Zoster Virus) 1-800-472-8478 Provides recorded information on varicello zoster virus. Free packets of information available for chicken pox, shingles and post-herpetic neuralgia. *Website:* http://www.vzvfoundation.org

"Shared pain decreases; shared joy increases." -- Author Unknown

WELFARE HELPLINE

Division of Family Development *(New Jersey)* 1-800-792-9773 (Mon.-Fri., 8am-4:30pm) Information on welfare and food stamps. Sponsored by Dept. of Human Services.

Goodwill Industries 1-800-741-0186 Provides employment and training services for people with disabilities and other disadvantaging conditions (welfare dependency, illiteracy, criminal history and homeless). *Website:* http://www.goodwill.org

WISH GRANTING FOR ILL CHILDREN HELPLINE

A Special Wish Foundation 1-800-486-9474 (Mon.-Fri., 9am-4:30pm EST) Grants wishes to children with terminal illnesses or life threatening disorders. *Website:* http://www.spwish.org *E-mail:* jallen@spwish.org

Believe in Tomorrow Foundation 1-800-933-5470 Provides programs and services for children with life threatening illnesses. *Website:* http://www.believeintomorrow.org

Children's Wish Foundation International 1-800-323-9474 (Mon.-Fri., 8:50am-5pm EST) Grants wishes to terminally ill children up to age of 18. *Website:* http://www.childrenswish.org *E-mail:* wish@childrenswish.org

Dream Factory 1-800-456-7556 Grants dreams for children with a life threatening or critical chronic illness. *Website:* http://www.dreamfactoryinc.com *E-mail:* info@dreamfactoryinc.com

Give Kids the World Foundation 1-800-995-5437 Offers a 51-acre, non-profit resort for use by children with life-threatening illnesses whose one wish is to visit Central Florida's best-loved attractions. *Website:* http://www.gktw.org

Make-A-Wish Foundation 1-800-722-9474 Grants wishes to children with serious illnesses or life threatening medical conditions. *Website:* http://www.wish.org

Starlight Children's Foundation 1-800-274-7827 (9am-5pm, Mon.-Fri. PST) Grants wishes for seriously ill children. Also provides a variety of in-hospital services that focus on distraction entertainment. *Website:* www.starlight.org *Email:* info@starlight.org

WOMEN'S HELPLINE

Endometriosis Helpline *(BILINGUAL)* 1-800-370-2943 Offers information on endometriosis, the cause, treatment options and clinical trials. Also, conducts research and offers referrals. *Website:* http://www.nichd.nih.gov *E-mail:* informationresourcecenter@mailnih.gov

National Women's Health Information Center *(BILINGUAL)* 1-800-994-9662; TTY: 1-888-220-5546 (Mon.-Fri., 9am-6pm EST) Provides information and referrals for all women's health questions and any questions on breast feeding. *Website:* http://www.womenshealth.gov

National Women's Health Resource Center *(New Jersey)* 1-877-986-9472 (Mon.-Fri., 9am-5pm) Information and resources about health concerns. By talking with staff, consumers will learn the key questions and issues to discuss with their physicians/health care professionals.

North American Menopause Society 1-800-774-5342 Provides free packets of information on menopause. Referrals to clinicians and discussions groups. *Website:* http://www.menopause.org

Women's Referral Central *(New Jersey)* 1-800-322-8092 (24 hr) Information and referrals on any issues concerning women. Education, homelessness, child support, custody, personal growth and domestic violence.

YOUTH HELPLINE

Action, Parent and Teen Support 1-800-367-8336 (24 hr) Provides referrals to all types of agencies and services for troubled teens and their parents. *E-mail:* actionprogram@aol.com

Children's Defense Fund 1-800-233-1200 (Mon.-Fri., 9am-5pm CST) Advocacy for children who cannot speak for themselves. Emphasis on low income and disabled children. Develops prevention programs to help children. Training seminars to develop Confident Kids Support Groups. *Website:* http://www.childrensdefense.org *E-mail:* dcfinfo@childrensdefense.org

FACES (For All Children Experiencing Stress) *(New Jersey)* 1-877-653-2237 Information for teens coping with anxiety, stress, peer pressure and other issues that can be overwhelming. Monitored bulletin boards and chat rooms for kids, teens and parents. *Website:* http://www.NJFACES.org

Girl's and Boy's Town National Hotline *(BILINGUAL)* 1-800-448-3000; TDD: 1-800-448-1833 (24 hr) Provides crisis intervention, information and referrals for general population. Free and confidential. Short-term crisis intervention. Works with children and families. *Website:* http://www.girlsandboystown.org

NineLine 1-800-999-9999 (24 hr) Nationwide crisis/suicide hotline. Referrals for youth or parents regarding drugs, domestic violence, homelessness, runaways, etc. Message relays, reports of abuse. Helps parents with problems with their kids. If all counselors are busy, stay on line and one will be with you as soon as possible. Sponsored by Nine Line/Covenant House. *Website:* http://www.covenanthouse.org/

Safe Sitter 1-800-255-4089 Trains adolescents (ages 11-13) on how to be effective baby sitters. *Website:* http://www.safesitter.org *E-mail:* safesitter@safesitter.org

"The majority of us lead quiet, unheralded lives as we pass through this world. There will most likely be no ticker-tape parades for us, no monuments created in our honor.

But that does not lessen our possible impact, for there are scores of people waiting for someone just like us to come along; people who will appreciate our compassion, our unique talents.

Someone who will live a happier life merely because we took the time to share what we had to give.

Too often we underestimate the power of a touch, a smile, a kind word, a listening ear, an honest compliment, or the smallest act of caring, all of which have a potential to turn a life around.

It's overwhelming to consider the continuous opportunities there are to make our love felt."

--Leo Buscaglia

<u>GREAT NORTHERN GEESE, LESSON V</u>

At a distance, a flock of Great Northern Geese appears to be guide by a single lead bird winging courageously through the oncoming elements. When the lead bird tires, however, it rotates back into the formation and another bird flies at the point position.

Lesson Learned:

Shared burdens are diminished. Rain shine, it pays to take turns doing the hard tasks in life and sharing both the leadership and the load.

NATIONAL / LOCAL CLEARINGHOUSES

SELF-HELP CLEARINGHOUSES

To locate a support group for your concern, review the list below of Self-Help Clearinghouses to see if there is one that serves your community. Our clearinghouse can provide information on other clearinghouse services, both nationally and internationally. Give us a call 1-800-367-6274 (NJ only) or 973-326-6789. Self-help clearinghouses assist in the finding and forming of local groups. Some clearinghouses also provide training workshops, distribute "how-to" materials, publish directories and offer newsletters.

NATIONAL

American Self-Help Clearinghouse Maintains database of national self-help headquarters and model one-of-a-kind groups. Referrals to self-help clearinghouses nationwide. Offers assistance to persons interested in starting new groups. Director: Ed Madara. Write: American Self-Help Clearinghouse, 100 E. Hanover Ave., Suite 202, Cedar Knolls, NJ 07927-2020. Call 973-326-6789; Fax: 973-326-9467. *Website:* http://selfhelpgroups.org *E-mail*: ashc@cybernex.net

National Self-Help Clearinghouse Provides information and referrals to self-help groups and regional self-help clearinghouses. Encourages and conducts training of professionals about self-help. Carries out research activities. Publishes manuals and training materials. Write: National Self-Help Clearinghouse, c/o CUNY, Graduate School and University Center, 365 Fifth Ave., Suite 3300, New York, NY 10016. Call 212-817-1822. *Website:* http://www.selfhelpweb.org *E-mail*: info@selfhelpweb.org

CONNECTICUT

Connecticut Self-Help Support Network *Founded 1981.* Information and referrals to support groups. Provides technical assistance in starting and maintaining groups. Group leadership training, educational workshops and conferences. Publishes directory of self-help groups, newsletter and other publications. Write: Connecticut Self-Help Support Network, c/o Joanne Richardson, The Consultation Center, 389 Whitney Ave., New Haven, CT 06511. Call 203-624-6982; Fax: 203-562-6355. *Website:* http://www.theconsultationcenter.org *E-mail*: info@theconsultationcenter.org (attention: self-help)

NEW YORK

Institute for Human Services/HELPLINE *(Steuben, Allegany and Chemung Counties) Founded 1984.* Information and referrals to local services and agencies, as well as local support groups. Provides assistance to new and existing self-help groups. Also acts as a 24-hour crisis and referral line. Newsletter, information and referral. Write: Institute for Human Services/Helpline, 6666 County Rd. 11, Bath, NY 14810. Call 1-800-346-2211 (in NY); Admin: 607-776-9467. *Website:* http://www.ihsnet.org *E-mail*: helpline@ihsnet.org

Mental Health Association of Monroe County Provides information and referrals to local support groups. Assistance in starting new groups, training workshops and how-to materials. Directory of local groups published online. Write: MHA, 320 North Goodman St., Rochester, NY 14607. Call Cindi Licata 585-325-3145 ext. 113; Fax: 585-325-3188. *Website:* http://www.mharochester.org

National Self-Help Clearinghouse *Founded 1976.* Provides information and referrals to self-help groups and regional self-help clearinghouses. Encourages and conducts training of professionals about self-help. Carries out research activities. Publishes manuals and training materials. Write: National Self-Help Clearinghouse, Graduate Center of CUNY, 365 Fifth Ave., Suite 3300, New York, NY 10016. Call 212-817-1822. *Website:* http://www.selfhelpweb.org *E-mail*: info@selfhelpweb.org

New York City Self Help Center Information and referrals to support groups in the five boroughs (Manhattan, Bronx, Staten Island, Queens and Brooklyn). Assistance to new and developing groups. Write: NYC Self-Help Center, 120 W. 57th St., Suite 608, New York, NY 10019. Call 212-586-5770 (Mon.-Thurs.); Admin: 212-399-2685 ext. 209; Fax: 212-399-2475.

Niagara Self-Help Clearinghouse *(Niagara County) Founded 1985.* Information and referrals to local support groups. Provides technical assistance to new groups. Networks with other community resources. Helps with new group development and holds group leader training. Directory of self-help groups and mental health video/book library. Write: Niagara Self-Help Clearinghouse, c/o MHA in Niagara County, 36 Pine St., Lockport, NY 14094. Call 716-433-3780; Fax: 716-433-3847. *Website:* http://www.mhanc.com

Self-Help Clearinghouse *(Rockland County) Founded 1951.* Information and referrals concerning self-help groups. Provides consultation and assistance to new groups that are forming. Publishes newsletter and self-help group directory ($3). Offers assistance starting support groups. Write: Self-Help Clearinghouse, c/o MHA of Rockland County Inc., 706 Executive Blvd., Suite F, Valley Cottage, NY 10989. Call 845-267-2172 ext. 422; Fax: 845-267-2169. *Website:* http://www.mharockland.org *E-mail*: hyattm@mharockland.org

Self-Help Resource Center *(Broome County) Founded 1998.* Information and referrals to local self-help groups. Maintains an updated database and publishes a directory of local self-help groups. Presents free consumer conferences designed to educate public about psychiatric diagnoses and self-help methods for symptom management. Presents ongoing workshop series which offers a variety of topics including artistic expression, community involvement, leadership and wellness. Assistance provided to start support groups. Write: Self-Help Resource Center, 153 Court St., Binghamton, NY 13901. Call 607-771-8888; Fax: 607-771-8892. *Website:* http://www.yourmha.com *E-mail*: mha@stny.rr.com

Westchester Self-Help Clearinghouse *Founded 1979.* A central resource for mutual-aid support groups. Provides information and referrals to mutual-aid support groups in Westchester County. Assists in the formation of new groups. Provides community education and publishes a directory of self-help groups every other year. Phone networks for newly separated women and newly widowed men and women. Director: Lenore Rosenbaum, MS. Write: Westchester Self-Help Clearinghouse, 845 N. Broadway, White Plains, NY 10603. Call 914-761-0600 ext. 308; Fax: 914-761-5859. *E-mail*: lrosenbaum@wjcs.com

PENNSYLVANIA

Self-Help Information Network Exchange (SHINE) *(Lackawanna County)* Provides information and referral to support groups in northeastern Pennsylvania. Sponsors workshops and special events for self-help advocates. Brochure. Community resource library. Write: SHINE, 538 Spruce St., Suite 420, Scranton, PA 18503. Call 570-961-1234 (24 hr); Admin: 570-347-5616; Fax: 570-341-5816. *Website:* http://www.vacnepa.org *E-mail*: shine@vacnepa.org

"To teach in a self-help group is to learn twice." -- Ed Madara

"The majority of us lead quiet,
unheralded lives as we pass through this world.
There will most likely be no ticker-tape parades for us,
no monuments created in our honor.

But that does not lessen our possible impact, for there are
scores of people waiting for someone just like us to come along;
people who will appreciate our compassion, our unique talents.

Someone who will live a happier life merely because we
took the time to share what we had to give.

Too often we underestimate the power of a touch, a smile,
a kind word, a listening ear, an honest compliment, or the
smallest act of caring, all of which have a potential to turn a
life around.

It's overwhelming to consider the continuous opportunities
there are to make our love felt."

--Leo Buscaglia

INDEX

B

E

F

O

P

S

V

W